# THEOLOGY AND THE RELIGIONS

# THEOLOGY AND THE RELIGIONS

## A Dialogue

*Edited by*

VIGGO MORTENSEN

WILLIAM B. EERDMANS PUBLISHING COMPANY
GRAND RAPIDS, MICHIGAN / CAMBRIDGE, U.K.

Wm. B. Eerdmans Publishing Co.
255 Jefferson Ave. S.E., Grand Rapids, Michigan 49503 /
P.O. Box 163, Cambridge CB3 9PU U.K.

Printed in the United States of America

08  07  06  05  04  03      7  6  5  4  3  2  1


**Library of Congress Cataloging-in-Publication Data**

Theology and the religions: a dialogue / edited by Viggo Mortensen
        p.    cm.
    Proceedings of a conference held in May 2002 at the University of Aarhus, Denmark.
    Includes bibliographical references.
    ISBN 0-8028-2674-1 (pbk.: alk. paper)
1. Religious pluralism.    2. Religions — Relations.    3. Christianity and other
religions.    4. Theology of religions (Christian theology)    I. Mortensen, Viggo.
BL85.T45    2003
201'.5 — dc21

                                                    2003060522

www.eerdmans.com

# Contents

*Contents*

*Contents*

## III. THEOLOGY OF RELIGIONS

## IV. EPILOGUE

# Acknowledgments

Our thanks go to all who have contributed to this book. Coming from different traditions and corners of the world, the contributors push the discussion on multiculturality, interreligious dialogue, and theology of religions to a new level.

The study project "Theology Meets Multireligiosity" received support from the University of Aarhus, the Danish Research Council for the Humanities, the Areopagos Foundation, Aarhus Stiftstidendes Fond. Their support has made this whole endeavour possible and indeed enjoyable.

For competent assistance with the conference and very able work on the manuscript, we give thanks to Bente Stær, Helle Meldgaard, Lene Suh Nicolaisen, and the highly professional members of the editorial team of William B. Eerdmans Publishing Compagny.

Finally, our thanks go to William B. Eerdmans Publishing Company and Bill Eerdmans, Jr., personally for accepting this voluminous book for publication.

Viggo Mortensen

# Theology Meets the Religions

VIGGO MORTENSEN

The academic study of religion and Christian theological reflection are undergoing great changes as a response to the present situation characterized by globalization and multireligiosity. The religious encounter has become globalized and happens everywhere. This affects all religions, and Christianity, being a global religion, is affected in a special way.

Globalization and the mobility that comes with modern mass communication and travel further a development toward multiethnic and multicultural societies. With the multicultural comes the multireligious. A growing body of multicultural studies offers insight into various aspects of the emerging multicultural situation. But the religious side is often forgotten. Within the emerging multireligious societies the whole question of the relationship between culture and religion is raised in a new manner. Sometimes we see two opposing trends develop, a harmonization of cultural and religious difference and at the same time a stress upon what makes the individual and the different groups special. The consequence is a growth in plurality in religions and worldviews. This situation calls for a thorough analysis drawing upon the resources of cultural analysis, religious studies, and theology.

This book will contribute to this analysis. The different contributions go back to a conference, "Theology Meets Multireligiosity," held at the University of Aarhus, Denmark, in May 2002. The conference — the first international conference hosted by the newly created Center for Multireligious Studies — addressed important issues and questions concerning the new religious development. Studies were presented documenting how the religious traditions are changing and developing in new contexts. Other papers explored how a Christian theology can react to these changes. In a multireligious society, interreligious dialogue becomes mandatory and there is a need for a systematic reflection on the issues inherent in dialogue, especially in relation to a newly formulated theology of religions. Thus this book is organized under the following three headings:

- Multiculturality and Multireligiosity
- Interreligious Dialogue
- Theology of Religions

Why do we need multireligious studies? The brief answer is, because it is necessary in order to understand what happens and to become wiser. But the field is wide-open and, in order to be covered fully, needs the cooperation of several disciplines. What characterizes this volume is an extensive collaboration between the disciplines of religious studies and theology. More theoretical papers on multiculturality and multireligiosity are supplemented with case studies drawn from situations in various parts of the world.

Globalization furthers a development toward multiethnicity and multiculturality. Demographic changes are happening because of well-known factors such as population growth, unequal distribution of resources, and war. As long as these factors persist, people will be on the move, because with globalization they have the means to do so. An attempt is made to regulate this development through national and international legislation. Because of this and because of history, multicultural societies look different in different parts of the globe. But the underlying problem is always the same: how to negotiate differences. People with different ethnic backgrounds come with a certain culture. This culture should of course at all times be respected. But then people with a certain culture live in the midst of another culture or in a mix of cultures. The immediate result is that diversity is growing and pluralism is reigning. How, then, to deal with this diversity? This is the center of the discussion on multiculturality: negotiating differences.

The debate is oscillating between assimilation and segregation, and a host of different metaphors has been employed to illustrate different models for a well-functioning multicultural society: melting pot, rainbow, symphony, salad bowl. Each tries to capture a specific trait within a given development in society. The more assimilationist models are often criticized for not fully respecting the diversity of different indigenous cultures. Therefore, often more segregationist models are preferred. People should not be given culture; culture is integrated in their very being, but they need to be given rights. Thus one envisages a society where different groups live side by side guarded by group rights and given privileges according to their needs. This "pillarization" of society allows for a "parallel development" for the different groups. "Parallel development" was the phrase used in South Africa for apartheid. Thus it is not sustainable to follow this road. It will lead to the segmentation and ghettoization of society; sooner or later it will explode, often in violence.

It is therefore very urgent that new models are invented for a future multicultural society. Let me propose two new metaphors: the artichoke and Lego blocks.

The artichoke produces a beautiful flower, but before it flowers it can be consumed. The very tasty artichoke bottom surrounded by the different leaves can symbolize the fertile ground for the common values that need to be nurtured in a healthy society. The leaves can symbolize the diversity in cultural expressions and forms. This diversity is nourished from the common. If the common ground is not developed, then the plant will wither away. Diversity should be celebrated, but it can only come to full fruition if it is nourished from and contributes to the common good.

Another "Danish" metaphor is Lego. The different building blocks come in a variety of forms and colors, but they are all constructed in a way that allows them to be put together to form functional units. And if one is going to construct a house, it must be placed on a plate that can form the solid foundation for the intended building.

This book contains contributions from all over the world, but there is a focus on Europe. At the moment in Europe there is a certain amount of perplexity concerning how to organize multicultural societies. Integration has in many places not been successful, and a European *Leitkultur* has not manifested itself convincingly. At the same time, there is a growing opposition to what is perceived as a governing elite's manipulation in order to achieve specific political goals.

If a violent "clash of civilizations" is to be avoided, it is mandatory that the resources that might be inherent in the reigning diversity are put to work for the common good. When talking about the cohesion of late modern societies, it is obviously necessary to concentrate on the common, the common goals, the common values. Religion then enters the scene, because religion plays a major part when it comes to individual identity formation and the cohesion of society. Thus it is difficult to reflect on possible models for a multicultural society without taking religion into account.

But with multiethnicity and multiculturality religiosity comes in multiple forms. Multireligiosity becomes the order of the day. Many strategies can be observed as response to the cultural and religious diversity: from pluralism and relativism over syncretism to fundamentalism. One of the more scary factors in the changing religious scene is the growth of fundamentalism within several of the world's religions. If we do not think relativism, syncretism, or fundamentalism is the right foundation for society, we need to find a new basis. This is the most urgent topic for conversation. It has to be generated through dialogue, dialogue between cultures and between religions. We cannot have multiple religions living side by side — peacefully — without interreligious dialogue.

In the section of this book covering interreligious dialogue, this viewpoint is substantiated and several papers offer constructive examples of what could be the contribution of formal and informal interreligious dialogue. And by way of selected case studies, it is also pointed out how difficult a task it is. In addition, several aspects of the tense relationship between mission and dialogue are analyzed. Christianity is born out of interreligious dialogue, so it is difficult to imagine a Christianity that is not somehow engaged in interreligious dialogue.

And you cannot — from a Christian point of view — seriously engage in interreligious dialogue without a sound theology of religions. That is why the third part of the book deals with theology of religions as a challenge to the churches. The traditional models of exclusivism, inclusivism, and pluralism are scrutinized, and new avenues moving beyond the traditional models are explored.

Finally, at the end the editor draws together what he has learned from the journey toward multireligious studies and points a way forward in evaluating the reigning religious pluralism.

A specific trait that characterizes this volume is that in addition to building on more than one discipline, it also brings together different traditions. In theology and religious studies it is possible to identify specific traits that are prevalent within the Anglo-American, the Continental (German), and the Nordic traditions. Meeting in Denmark, in many ways the crossroads and the intersection of these different traditions, the conference entitled "Theology Meets Multireligiosity" offered a unique possibility of bringing these traditions into fruitful cooperation. In the following pages you can see how.

PART I

# MULTICULTURALITY AND MULTIRELIGIOSITY

# Multiculturalism, Postcolonialism, and the Apocalyptic

VÍTOR WESTHELLE

What is multiculturalism? How is it related to our age? And what are its implications for theology and religion? The task of this essay is to address these questions. Initially I propose to examine the interface between the age in which we live, the time in which these questions emerge, and what Antônio Govea Mendonça, a Brazilian sociologist of religion, has called "the return of the sacred savage,"[1] i.e., the vigorous and plural forms of religious manifestations when global modernization was suggesting that secularization would progressively spread itself throughout the world. Such unexpected presumed religious "resurgence," not only in what used to be called backward or primitive parts of the world but indeed in the very centers of some of the most industrialized and technologically advanced nations, has led so many to propose that we have entered a new era, an era that no longer shares the basic traits of modernity, i.e., a postmodern age, an age of multicultural and multireligious awareness (as if there had been only one religion and one culture before).

There is some irony in the fact that we are asking ourselves about multiculturalism and multireligiosity almost as if it were a new phenomenon, as if to suggest that we come from an epoch in which cultures and religions were unified or at least moving toward a common goal. The irony lies in the fact that we ask this question in societies that have worked with the assumption that Western modern scientific reason, moral discernment, and aesthetic values (the three basic spheres of knowledge and power in the modern West) would finally triumph and the world would become secular. The so-thought-of irresistible force of modernity and the process of modernization as it was and is spreading throughout the world would inevitably lead to secularization, to a global civili-

---

1. Antônio Govea Mendonça, "A Inserção do Protestantismo e a 'Questão Religiosa' no Brasil," *Estudos Teológicos* 27, no. 3 (1987): 219.

zation, and to an interconnected web of cultural expressions. But the "multi-" prefix in the title of these discussions suggests that what we are experiencing is far from what a unified project would or could conceive.

## A Misreading

The first argument I would like to propose here is that the very question of the relationship between this "new" multireligious consciousness and our age has to do with a superficial perception that we had about religion and our time in the West since the Enlightenment. In suggesting this, I am saying that the very temptation to rename our age, or to claim that we are in a new phase of world history, is a way of masking that the West (which postulated the connection between modernization and the idea of a unified universal history, the global village, and so forth) has ignored or overlooked the fact that its rules and norms were never really universal. It is like saying — in the face of the mounting evidence for the vigorous persistence of the religious phenomenon — that we in the West were not wrong, only the times have changed, a new age has dawned, and so no one needs to be accountable for or explain a possible misreading of the recent past. My argument here is that such a rationale is embedded in a sociological misreading of the last centuries, since the Enlightenment in the West. Some of its peculiar trademarks, particularly the yoking of modernity and secularism, were inappropriately taken as a universal rule.

I will begin this discussion with a confession the North American sociologist of religion Peter Berger made not long ago in an article published in the *Christian Century:* "In the course of my career as a sociologist of religion I made one big mistake . . . which I shared with almost everyone who worked in this area in the 1950s and '60s; [it] was to believe that modernity necessarily leads to a decline in religion."[2]

Berger's argument is that modern pluralism erodes values and beliefs that once were taken for granted as being self-validated. However, this does not necessarily lead to secularization and the elimination of all values and beliefs. On the contrary, by introducing incredulity, doubt, and uncertainty, modernity has even multiplied these values and beliefs in the search for certainties, generating on the one hand fundamentalism and totalitarian beliefs and ideologies and, on the other hand, a radical relativism that easily slides into nihilism. Between these two extremes is a pendulum movement characteristic of modernity itself.

2. Peter Berger, "Protestantism and the Quest for Certainty," *Christian Century,* August 26–September 2, 1998, p. 782.

The religious phenomenon, however, does not pertain only to either of these extreme options, absolutism or nihilism; it is also situated in the middle of this spectrum where certainties are weak and coexist with doubts in institutions that are fragile and malleable. This is the case with most of the mainstream Protestant churches characterized by some liberal persuasions within stable and affluent societies.

By focusing on the experience of these "weak" churches (to use Berger's expression), analysts were inclined to establish a strict correlation between modern reflexivity and the malleable or "weak" character of these churches. In other words, the more modern reflexivity expressed itself, the weaker the institutions became. And if the process continues — so goes the argument — it will reach a point in which these institutions will simply dwindle into extinction.

However, here is where we find a surprise. These weak institutions can survive and will, as Berger has shown,[3] not as a matter of course but out of a renewed commitment from those who are part of them. It was the dissolution of the taken-for-granted certainties and the "weakening" of modern institutions, particularly the churches, which led social scientists to the impression that modern pluralism would inevitably lead to the decline of religion. Pluralism, as the "coexistence and social interaction of people with different beliefs, values and lifestyles,"[4] does not necessarily lead to an increasing secularism, not even to secularization, though this has occurred in northern Europe, for example (and thus became the paradigm for the rest of the world).

This is to me the crux of the problem in addressing the present awareness of multiculturalism. We are bewildered in the face of an issue that we have falsely diagnosed, and often, in order to avoid recognizing it, we evade it. What needs to be recognized is that pluralism, which accompanied incredulity and doubt in the systems of belief and values, does not eliminate beliefs and values; it only makes them more diverse with very different levels of commitment depending on where one is situated in the spectrum of the pendulum.

However — and this is the issue I want to examine further — it was exactly this modernity which launched, in the midst of corroding former certainties, the search for new ones, or else it surrendered to nihilism. And among the new certainties — the sciences, political economy, psychoanalysis, self-help techniques, etc. — there was inserted this one: that secularization and the decline of religion would inevitably be yoked together. The renaming of the present (as in "postmodernity") is often an evasion of a problem caused by the misreading of the characteristic features of modernity itself.

3. Berger, p. 794. Berger here relies on the work of Helmut Schelsky.
4. Berger, p. 782.

## The Enlightenment

The situation is always more complex than it seems. If on the one hand modernity did away with taken-for-granted verities and values, on the other hand it evoked new certainties, or maintained the old ones on other bases. The fate of religion was in no way different.

To illustrate this, let us take Christianity, the religion of the very context in which the Enlightenment — as the modern project par excellence — took place. The taken-for-granted or self-validating evidences that sustained Christianity were its so-called historical proofs: the narratives of the biblical miracles and Jesus' fulfillment of the Old Testament prophecies. From Celsus in the second century until the eighteenth century, not even the great critics of Christianity based their criticism on the supernatural character of these proofs; they only questioned the interpretation given to them and the claims of exclusivity and uniqueness attached to them.[5]

By the middle of the nineteenth century David Friedrich Strauss summarized the impasse many of his generation were feeling, and proposed for theology to embark in a new venture. The new task he devised for theology would take place in an age that could no longer afford to be indifferent to the attacks on positive religion, which included the likes of Spinoza, the British Deists, Reimarus, Edelmann, Voltaire, Diderot, Lessing, Fichte, the skeptics, the advocates of natural religion, or plain atheists. Thus Strauss describes the task of theology in the face of what he regarded as the hopeless future of the old religion, and thus also of theology as it was being practiced until then: "Theology is productive only insofar as it is destructive. Its task in the present consists in demolishing a building that is no longer grounded on the foundations of the modern world. But to prevent that it falls upon the head of its inhabitants, this task should be carried out with care, step by step, but without losing any time."[6]

Stone by stone the edifice of positive religion, adorned by an assortment of theological dogmas, was to be demolished. From its foundations little was of use. "Monks of atheism," in the expression of Heinrich Heine, were decoding the signs of the times in the palimpsest of European history and prophesying the "process of putrescence of the absolute" (K. Marx). The age of reason, argued Strauss, could no longer tolerate the "science of idiots of the ignorant consciousness,"[7] as he called the conservative theologies of his day (and would

---

5. Origen, *Contra Celsum* 1.28, 38; 2.28, 48-51.

6. David Friedrich Strauss, *Die christliche Glaubenslehre in ihrer geschichtlichen Entwicklung und im Kampf mit der modernen Wissenschaft dargestellt*, 2 vols. (Tübingen and Stuttgart: C. F. Osiander, F. H. Köhler, 1840-41), 2:624.

7. Strauss, 2:625.

certainly include thinkers of other religions that would not adhere to the Enlightenment ideas).

However, the persistence of the religious phenomenon, even within the context of the Christian faith, proved to be grounded in foundations deeper than the venerable "historical proofs." Its survival was not accomplished by the metamorphoses in the inventory of doctrines, metaphysicians, Deists, or the proponents of natural religion put forward. What became clear as early as the first half of the nineteenth century was that the "proofs" were really "proofs of faith" not contingent upon a historical foundation. Faith indeed makes the miracle (R. Bultmann). In an ironic way, when Lessing summarizes the basic claim the Enlightenment makes upon religious consciousness ("Accidental truths of history can never become the proofs of necessary truths of reason"),[8] he is already suggesting the symmetrical counterpart of his thesis: the proofs of necessary truths of reason are not the criteria to validate or invalidate accidental truths of history, such as miracles or the fulfillment of Old Testament prophecies.

In other words, an imaginary cathedral sustained by faith can be the *depositum fidei* better than a real one. Bruno Bauer, with his characteristic sarcasm, describes this in a text from 1841 called "Theological Shamelessness": "The era before the Enlightenment and the [French] Revolution is called the good time of faith, as if faith had lost its power or even no longer existed. Totally false! Now the true age of faith irrupted and the religious consciousness reached its fullness."[9] If the contemporary interpreters of the religious phenomenon in modern times had listened to Bauer, they might have avoided the error that Berger confessed he shared with his generation.

This is then my first point, namely, that religious pluralism in modern times is not a new phenomenon. It was only masked under the assumption that history was universal and was moving along secularizing tracks. Religious pluralism as much as multiculturalism has always existed and continues to exist alongside what the West calls modernity, even to the point of being sustained and furthered by the very relativism regarding certainties that modernity introduced.

---

8. Gotthold Ephraim Lessing, *Lessings Werke,* 6 vols. (Leipzig: Philipp Reclam, n.d.), 6:223.

9. Bruno Bauer, *Feldzüge der reinen Kritik* (Frankfurt: Suhrkamp, 1968), p. 44.

Vítor Westhelle

## Postcolonialism

However, if it is the case that we have not diagnosed our time well enough, it is also true that something has changed. But this has to do more with geography than with history, more with places than with eras, more with location than with epochs, more with attitudes than with ages. Neither religion nor pluralism was absent from a world the West believed was becoming one (the "global village," remember?). What we are observing is precisely the emergence of voices and faces that before were caricatured, imposed, and invented. What has happened is that the Eurocentric worldview — the patterns of science and rationality, morality, religion, aesthetics, and politics, which were defined out of Europe and are the marks of what is called the West and its colonial project — is now becoming decentered, postcolonial. If colonialism is the domination of the other by political, economic, cultural, scientific, or moral means, multiculturalism is the awareness that not only are there other players that work with frames different from the ones that established the hegemony of the West, but also that this awareness has brought upon the West the consciousness of its own particularity, its own contextuality, its own epistemic location.

Such an indicator of a postcolonial consciousness, however, is only a cipher that announces a departure, a departure from a condition until then not yet articulated. What it does, on the one hand, is shift the gaze from the Eurocentric colonial project; on the other hand, it entertains other sociocommunitarian paradigms, other forms of knowledge, arts, morality, as well as spirituality that still survive, albeit in disguise, in places that have been colonized and are still being globalized. Multiculturalism in this postcolonial perspective is then the announcement of a departure from a particular way of seeing the world that thought of itself as being universally defined. It is a departure from the West as the gravitational center of the world.[10]

Nonetheless, the announcement of a departure is still not the same thing as being in the other's locale; the criticism to one's own discourse is still not the discourse of the other — it is still not heteroglossy.[11] This "other" of the West-

---

10. And in this it shares, ironically, the same spirit of the Enlightenment, which was defined by Kant as a "departure." Immanuel Kant, "Beantwortung der Frage: Was ist Aufkärung?" in *Ausgewählte kleine Schriften* (Hamburg: Felix Meiner, 1965), p. 1: "Aufklärung is der Ausgang des Menschen aus seiner selbsverschuldeten Unmündigkeit."

11. See Mikhail M. Bakhtin, *The Dialogic Imagination* (Austin, 1982), p. 428. "Thus at any given moment of its historical existence, language is heteroglot from top to bottom: it represents the co-existence of socio-ideological contradictions between the present and the past, between differing epochs of the past, between different socio-ideological groups in the present, between tendencies, schools, circles and so forth" (p. 291).

ern colonialism, in its form of reasoning, making moral judgments, theologizing, or establishing aesthetic values, is the colonized whose voices, as dissonant, and explosive, as they may sound, are now being heard. Multiculturalism indicates an intention that is not yet fully realized. And this intention is precisely the one of leaving the very project that defines the West since the 1500s as the axis of the world: the scientific revolution with Copernicus, the Reformation with Luther, the conquest of the Americas with Columbus, and the communication breakthrough with Gutenberg.

In this context the question is whether Christianity can be dissociated or clearly distinguished from the colonial project and from the missionary vocation of the churches of the West. It is this incapability to recognize the irreducible plurality of the world that has foddered most of modern Christian theology. In the monumental document that opens the history of modern Protestant theology, Schleiermacher's *Glaubenslehre,* this Western arrogance and blindness find their most drastic expression when he discusses the impossibility of new heresies appearing in Christianity. For him, "new heresies no longer arise, now that the church recruits itself out of its own resources; and the influence of alien faiths on the frontier and in the mission-field of the Church must be reckoned at zero." And then the great Berliner adds condescendingly: "[T]here may long remain in the piety of the new converts a great deal which has crept in from their religious affections of former times, and which, if it came to clear consciousness and were expressed as doctrine, would be recognized as heretical."[12] But this obviously will not happen. If the rest of the world and all the other faiths cannot make a difference for Christianity, it is quite logical to assume that either Christianity has isolated itself in a confined sectarian and esoteric position or, which is the case, it understands itself to be the religious conqueror of the world. The very word *hairesis* in Greek also means to conquer, to plunder, and to colonize. Hence for a heretic there cannot be any other. Straight logic: for the colonizer, the colonized cannot be a colonizer; therefore he cannot be a heretic. A supreme "heresy" will not allow others to challenge its dominance.

It is indeed something else to look at all of this from a postcolonial perspective in and by which the limits of the Western *epistemes,* its equation of knowledge and power, are recognized. In the words of Homi Bhabha, it is this "heretical" renaming of the world from another location that allows us to realize that the West, with its science, politics, morality, aesthetics, and religion, is but one cultural context among many others, dominant though it is — a claim

---

12. Friedrich Schleiermacher, *The Christian Faith* (Edinburgh: T. & T. Clark, 1989), p. 96 (*Der christliche Glaube,* 2 vols. [Berlin: de Gruyter, 1960], 1:128).

that poststructuralism in the West itself has already made. Bhabha recognizes this when he acknowledges his indebtedness to this Western school: "My use of poststructuralist theory emerges from this postcolonial contramodernity. I attempt to represent a certain defeat, or even an impossibility, of the 'West' in its authorization of the 'idea' of colonization. Driven by the subaltern history of the margins of modernity — rather than by the failures of logocentrism — I have tried, in some small measure, to revise the known, to rename the postmodern from the position of the postcolonial."[13]

It is in this sense that multiculturalism (as well as postmodernity) receives a distinctive and definable character. The following question in an essay by Lyotard should be taken seriously in its rhetorical intention: "Can we continue to organize the events around us regarding the human and the non-human world with the help of the idea of a universal history of humanity?"[14] The very idea of a universal history appears to be a Western idea and not a universal one. But how did the West develop this blindness as to its own particularity (Kant and Herder)? Why did it see its history as the universal destiny of the world (Hegel)? Why does the West announce the end of history when other histories are happening? The answer to these questions must be sought in the very logic of colonialism and some of its hidden mechanisms.

## Dissimulation

While one should not deny the power of the globalization project, which is the extension of colonialism by other means, one should not underestimate the fact that doubts about its viability are already parasites of its very process of domination. And they reveal themselves by the very existence of the other and his or her capacity to preserve individuality. There are two mechanisms by which resistance is practiced. The first one is dissimulation, or what Homi Bhabha and Octavio Paz also call mimicry.

Under the conditions of Western hegemony (hegemony meaning being able to rule and dominate without overt use of force), the subaltern (subaltern being those who externally submit to the power of hegemony without overt resistance) people could only express themselves by dissimulating their own cultural uniqueness and their beliefs. This is a commonly observed phenomenon among subaltern peoples who hide their own identity behind the mask the col-

---

13. Homi K. Bhabha, *The Location of Culture* (London: Routledge, 1994), p. 175.

14. Jean-François Lyotard, "Historie universelle et differences culturelles," *Critique* 41 (May 1985): 559.

onizer expects to see or imposes. Native religions in many places survive under the formal canopy of Christian liturgy, for example. But dissimulation is a much broader phenomenon hardly perceived by those who have had no experience with subaltern groups (like those who think communication can be open and neutral, as in the "force of the better argument" in Habermas, or the "veil of ignorance" in Rawls). But dissimulation is not a lie; it is an act of self-protection while still resisting and preserving an identity, albeit hidden in the face of being confronted by an overwhelming supremacy. Dissimulation, Paz reminds us, "is an activity very much like that of actors in the theater, but the true actor surrenders himself to the role he is playing . . . the dissembler never surrenders or forgets himself, because he would no longer be dissembling if he became one with his image . . . [he] shuts himself away to protect himself."[15] Building on Jacques Lacan's interpretation of mimicry, Bhabha reiterates the same point: "[M]imicry is like camouflage, not a harmonization of repression of difference, but a form of resemblance that differs from or defends presence by displacing it in part, metonymically."[16]

The unrecognized process of dissimulation or mimicry, which is now much better understood and recognized, is largely responsible for the very misreading of the supposed concomitance between modernization and secularization. The success of dissimulation lies in the fact that it makes the colonizers blindly believe that their project of making the colonized like them is working. They often do not realize that they are spectators of the mimicry of their own projections and expectations.

## The Apocalyptic

The end of a given hegemony is signaled when the dissembler removes the mask and risks presenting her or his own identity, risks confrontation. But the end of hegemony is always the beginning of an overt violence. This is what seems to me much more pressing at this particular juncture, not so much the long history of dissimulation that has been described by many anthropological studies. What is now being experienced is what happens when dissimulation is suspended, when the mimicry stops and the person steps into the arena to establish his or her history. The reverse and corresponding side of the recently proclaimed United States "war against terrorism" is the recognition that hege-

15. Octavio Paz, *The Labyrinth of Solitude* (New York: Grove Weidenfeld, 1985), pp. 29 and 42.

16. Bhabha, p. 90.

mony is no longer working and that force, repression, and violence have to be applied because the other is revealing his or her face. Indeed, it is a revelation in two senses: it is a showing but also an apocalyptic. The term "apocalyptic" as I am using it does not refer only to a literary genre, such as we have in the book of Daniel or in Revelation. I am using the term in a broader sense to describe the situation in which for several reasons dissimulation no longer works as a strategy for survival, and any negotiation is canceled.

If we go back to what I suggested to be the basic characteristics of recent times, i.e., that we find ourselves often polarized between a radical commitment to certainty (be it in a faith, in scriptures, in a political system, or even in science, and so forth), on the one hand, and the eroding sense of any foundation that leads to nihilism on the other, the apocalyptic is the impossibility to hold the middle. The result is polarization on either side or simultaneously on both sides, namely, nihilism and unassailable certainty at once. The two extremes are often interchangeable. And this polarization is normally not an option but an attitude in response to the incapability to find a negotiated solution.

This agonistic consciousness of lack of mediations, the evanescence of compromise solutions, and also a fast alternation between the extremes of nihilism and fundamental certainties characterize the apocalyptic. The apocalyptic is an ethos shared by those who no longer have or feel that they have means or mediating instances to negotiate their existence. Apocalyptic is a tactic without strategy. There is no calculation. The act of resistance to and defiance of the dominant power becomes an end in itself; it is not a way of repositioning oneself; it is not a regrouping to seek another end. (The only other possible end is Armageddon itself.)

The apocalyptic views history as a fragmented reality, not as a totality to be built, a universal epic to be composed, a metaphysics to be envisioned, or a systematic theology to be written. The apocalyptic attitude or ethos is that of responding to such a fragmented situation. This ethos can be defined by the polarization that characterizes this age, as if any action would be final, any meaning being either vacant, absent *(apousia)* or there being an imminent, immediate sense of presence *(parousia)*, or indeed both at the same time. How best to describe this but with Luther's own apocalyptic verve: *revelatio sub contraria specie.* The apocalyptic is, therefore, signaled by the disappearance of commerce ("And the merchants of the earth weep and mourn . . . since no one buys their cargo any more," Rev. 18:11) and of the means for commerce (". . . and the sea was no more," Rev. 21:1). Even religious institutions, as demarcated spaces for transaction with the *tremendum et fascinans,* lose their mediating character, becoming either empty or the other extreme where religion becomes practically everything, permeating every aspect of existence (the new Jerusalem has no temple, Rev. 21:22). The apocalyptic is the religious language of subaltern groups, societies, and peoples when the awareness of their condition is raised. The apocalyptic is "the heart of a heartless world" (Marx). This is its tragedy but also its consoling promise.

## Conclusion

In my reading, what we are experiencing as the result of a long colonial process is that the Western powers — above all now the USA — are gradually losing not yet their domination, but their hegemony. And what earlier could remain hidden in dissimulation is now being openly contested in an apocalyptic attitude. It is here that religions have evaded subjection to the three fundamental spheres of knowing that have been maintained in the West since the Enlightenment: science, morality, and art with their corresponding criteria, truth, justice, and taste.[17] And some of these religious expressions and affections are indeed harboring apocalyptic sentiments. Hence I surmise that the task of theology is now precisely that of gathering these fragments of a plural history, of a multicultural reality, and of a religious pluralism, and building a mosaic, knowing that we do not have the whole panorama encompassed within the cultural frame we have adopted — or which possesses us. Every other is and remains ultimately irreducibly the other.

---

17. Jürgen Habermas, *The Philosophical Discourse of Modernity* (Cambridge: MIT Press, 1993), pp. 16-19.

13

# Cultivating Corporate Identity: Transformation Processes in Postmodern Religious Markets

FRIEDRICH WILHELM GRAF

## Religion from the Economic Perspective

In 1963 Peter L. Berger published "A Market Model for the Analysis of Ecumenicity." Here the prominent sociologist of religion described two seemingly contradictory developments in the religious markets of the USA. On the one hand, one could observe various new cooperations between the different denominations, the formation of new churches resulting from the amalgamation of diverse smaller religious groups and an intensive reception of the ecumenical movement, originating in Europe. On the other hand, one found an increase in the tendency of all denominations and churches in the United States to reformulate old denominational identities. According to Berger, these processes of "re-denominationalization" could not be interpreted as a "reaffirmation" of old denominational or confessional identities.[1] Even before the influential work of Eric Hobsbawm, Berger maintained that in order to adequately interpret the processes of this new reflection on one's own denominational identity, one should not speak of a "rediscovery" but rather of an "invention."[2] Berger's message was that denominational identity is not simply given, but created and constructed in certain social, cultural, and religious environments — according to demand. Following on from this, it would be false, he argued, to then assume an antithesis or contradiction between the ecumenical departures of the twentieth century, on the one hand, and the processes of "inventing" denominational identities on the other. Berger combined microsociological analyses of the processes of identity construction in the individual "mainline Protestant churches"

---

1. Peter L. Berger, "A Market Model for the Analysis of Ecumenicity," *Social Research: An International Quarterly of Political and Social Science* 30 (1963): 77-93, here 77.
2. Berger, p. 79.

with a macrosociological model which was intended to shed light on the apparently paradoxical simultaneity of ecumenism and new inventions of denominational identities. For his macrosociological model he referred to modern economic concepts. The interpretative or analytical potential of Berger's model depends on the extent to which one is (experimentally) willing or able to view the denominations and churches as economic actors on the religious markets of modern pluralistic societies: "the denominations involved in the paradoxical situation are perceived as economic units which are engaging in competition within a free market."[3]

Berger's article is probably one of the first sociological studies which tries to interpret religious developments in economic terms. Referring to the religious market in America, Berger was able to show that the practical ecumenical movement organized by the bureaucracies of the individual denominations or churches — that is to say, the concrete cooperation with other religious groups — frequently follows the economic imperatives of lowering costs and optimizing services. The theological legitimation of such ecumenicity is, in contrast, both historically and practically of secondary importance, he claimed: the primary concern is to rationalize the cutthroat competition between rival suppliers of religious services. The aim is to restrain an unregulated laissez-faire capitalism by forming cartels so as to reduce the number of competitors and divide up the religious market between the remaining larger units. Berger spoke explicitly of "ecclesiastical mergers,"[4] i.e., church amalgamations with a cumulative effect. According to this theory, the new "inventions" of denominational identity are not to be seen as a countervailing movement, but rather as an effective strategy of optimization developed by religious actors facing a market that is shaped by growing cartelization. And it is precisely here, within this framework of economic model, Berger proposes, that the specific power of the invention of denominational identity discloses itself: if the products of small-scale suppliers disappear from the market as a result of cartelization, the remaining products are in danger of being exposed to the constraints of standardization and de-specification. How then, we might ask, can a consumer be convinced of the superiority of a specific religious product? Berger speaks of "quality through competition." In the complex games of supply and demand, which are characteristic of modern consumer societies, it is crucial to the market success of a product that its special quality be recognizable. Irrespective of the material quality of their products (or services), all actors on the religious market are forced to consider the autonomy of consumers and "package" their products in

3. Berger, p. 79.
4. Berger, p. 86.

the best possible way. Religious providers, in particular, rely on a specific image and promotion to secure the sale of their goods or services, Berger claims. The new "denominationalism" can therefore be conceived as an economically rational reaction to market conditions: the more standardized the products of different suppliers become, the more important "marginal differentiation" becomes, that is to say, the greater the need to emphasize specific differences between products and to underline the distinctive features of one's own product. In short, the theological or ecclesiastico-political consequences of Berger's analysis of religious markets in the age of ecumenical cartelization can be reduced to the simple formula: the greater the supply of ecumenicity, the higher the demand for a specific promotion of denominational identity.

In 1963 Berger expressly emphasized the limits of his economic model, stressing that it had been developed for the USA, the classic country of a strong religious pluralism. Nonetheless, the religio-theoretical effects of his short essay were far-reaching: together with his other writings on modern religious pluralism and works on constructivist epistemology and the sociology of knowledge (which are now seen as classics),[5] Berger's "Market Model for the Analysis of Ecumenicity" helped motivate not only sociologists of religion but also social scientists of other disciplines and economists to investigate the possible heuristic power of economic concepts and models for observing and interpreting religious change in the modern age. Above all, the neoliberal Chicago School of Economics supported the development of "religious economy theory," which has, meanwhile, been institutionalized in the English-speaking world as a relatively independent socioscientific discipline. With respect to religious beliefs and practices, i.e., mentalities that are often regarded as irrational, the classic "rational choice theory" has proved extremely productive. This theory has furnished innovative insights into the operations of religious markets and the behavior of consumers under the conditions of a relatively open, non- (or only minimally) regulated market. Applying it to religious processes implies a premise of great import: it assumes, namely, that individuals or consumers behave in exactly the same way in religious matters as they do when choosing other products. They act upon a choice between goods arrived at by comparing the costs and benefits, in search of the maximal gain. Demand also steers supply on the free religious markets. In addition, the rational choice theory makes it possible to follow the trends of religious behavior more precisely than before and to raise the question of why one religion or denomination is more successful than its competitors. Since the 1980s, leading economists of religion in the United

---

5. Cf. Peter L. Berger and Thomas Luckmann, *The Social Construction of Reality* (New York, 1967).

States, such as Laurence R. Iannaccone, Roger Finke, and Rodney Stark, have worked and elaborated on a theorem of pluralism that has been verified by several large-scale empirical studies:[6] on the whole, religious participation is far greater on open markets with a relatively high number of competitive religions or denominations than in conditions where religion is not geared to market principles, i.e., not pluralistic, owing to a close, traditional proximity to the state, for instance. Thus one central insight of modern religious economy theory is: when religious pluralism increases, consumers' willingness to participate in religion grows accordingly. Under the conditions of consumer autonomy, a diverse range of goods stimulates a surge in demand.

To my knowledge, the questions and concepts of the more recent economics of religion have, as yet, been only partly received by continental Europe. This failing is unfortunate inasmuch as the perspective of modern religious economy theory affords a far subtler and more differentiated perception of the numerous processes of religious change than that offered by the concepts and interpretative models of the classic sociology of religion. This is particularly well evidenced by the difficulties that arise when using the terms "secularization" or "de-Christianization." As with other termini from the modernization theory of the classical sociology of religion, the concept of secularization can only provide an extremely distorted picture of the religious transformation processes within the complex societies of the modern age.[7] Above all, the concepts of secularization developed within the context of the sociotechnological modernization theories of the 1950s assume that social modernization is more or less tantamount to a decline in religion. Seen from a different angle, however, one finds that the opposite is the case, especially since the 1970s. In view of the various religious renaissances, it would seem reasonable to suppose that we are, at present, witnessing an expansion of the "religious field" (Pierre Bourdieu).[8] In modern societies, religion remains a valuable and highly contested resource of symbolic capital for many individuals and collective actors. Negotiations

---

6. As an introduction compare Laurence R. Iannaccone, "Religious Markets and the Economics of Religion," *Social Compass* 39 (1992): 123-31. For the analytical frame of reference see Gary S. Becker, *Human Capital*, 2nd ed. (New York, 1975); Becker, *The Economic Approach to Human Behaviour* (Chicago, 1976).

7. Cf. Friedrich Wilhelm Graf, "Dechristianisierung. Zur Problemgeschichte eines kulturpolitischen Topos," in *Säkularisierung, Dechristianisierung und Rechristianisierung im neuzeitlichen Europa, Bilanz und Perspektiven der Forschung*, ed. Hartmut Lehmann, Veröffentlichungen des Max-Planck-Instituts für Geschichte, vol. 130 (Göttingen, 1997), pp. 32-66.

8. Pierre Bourdieu, *Das religiöse Feld. Texte zur Ökonomie des Heilsgeschehens* (Constance, 2000).

over the borders between the religious field and other areas, such as the political field, continue unabated. Also, the religious markets of the past thirty years have seen fierce fights for new religious bids. Esotericism is booming, and the diverse forms of "body religion" have won over many younger, achievement-oriented people who are prepared to invest a great deal of time, energy, and money in their bodies. In this new service industry, there is a growing awareness that "a meaning in life" is a resource which is in short supply and in need of tender care and attention. Even within the traditional, large-scale religious organizations of the churches we find seemingly contradictory developments: while the number of people leaving the main churches continues to grow, studies testify to a new upward trend of ecclesiastic activity among those who have distanced themselves from the church in the past. Certain "hard-line," strongly binding forms of Christian religiousness, which outsiders readily describe and dismiss as "fundamentalist," have gained new appeal in diverse Roman Catholic milieus. Conversions are on the increase.

## Christian Churches as Actors on Pluralistic Religious Markets

Religious economy theory, as developed above all in Chicago, offers concepts for observing the behavior of collective actors (such as ecclesiastical organizations) in the religious field. Following the overarching outlines of the classical modern period around 1900, the German-speaking sociology of religion had drawn on the distinctions between church, sects, and mysticism developed by Georg Simmel, Max Weber, Ernst Troeltsch, and other cultural scientists. Even then both Roman Catholic and Protestant theologians found it very difficult to translate the conceptual offers of this sociology of religion into their theological language games on the essence of the church, their role in modern societies, and their relations to other religious organizations. The antiliberal theologies of the 1920s, which attempted, by way of dogmatic language games, to formulate a theological identity of the church in distinct disassociation from its social environments, only added to the difficulties in mediating between the internal theological understanding of the church and the external cultural and socioscientific perception of the churches as religious organizations. Only a few theologians warmed to the idea of taking up an external, viz., detached, perspective and trying to review themselves and their conduct in relative terms. This was especially true of the history of the ecumenical movement and the new ecumenical theologies which were of significance to the history of theology in the twentieth century. Ecumenical processes of rapprochement — that is to say, the quest for consensus — were institutionalized mostly as an exchange between theological experts, who tried to come to an understanding on theological disputes via exegetical reflection and work on dogmatic terminology. In these dogmatic language games one discussed the controversial questions of doctrine which have been handed down since the time of the Reformation and the ensuing epoch of denominationalization. Yet the self-descriptions of those involved in these negotiations remained dominated, as a rule, by traditional theological interpretative patterns. Often the self-perception of ecumenical functionaries or theologians committed to ecumenical dialogue reveals a lack of detachment vis-à-vis their own role. At all events, the willingness here to embark on critical self-reflection and self-examination is significantly less developed than in other academic cultures. It is possible that a more or less naive belief in progress has also contributed to this state of affairs: one likes to see oneself as an agent driving on the advance of an "ecumenical age" of Christianity, where divisions, rifts, and denominational provincialism supposedly no longer exist.

The hermeneutic models and concepts of religious economy theory allow us to explore our perception of the behavior of ecumenical actors on pluralistic religious markets and experiment with other, external perspectives that are possibly more effective in furthering our cognition. For the language of modern economic theory possesses a specific rationality: the economic approach makes it possible to describe aims accurately, to assess costs and benefits, to calculate profits and losses with greater precision, and to record the fluctuations in prices on the virtual stock exchange of religious markets. Also, as regards individual religious services — from christenings to funerals, from Sunday services to pastoral counseling — this framework enables a precise recording of the market shares of the competing suppliers, whether they be Christian churches or non-Christian religious organizations of whatever kind. In short, the economics of religion presents us with analytical instruments which are particularly attractive for investigating the new religious pluralism in societies which were once shaped traditionally by a more or less clear monopoly of the Christian churches (or one Christian church).

Focusing, first of all, on ecumenical discourse, we raise the following questions: What, in economic terms, do ecumenical actors do when they negotiate about doctrinal questions? Are they conducting talks on a takeover, i.e., discussing the acquisition of a religious competitor by a rival firm in the interest of strengthening its market position? Or are they negotiating a merger in the hope of being able to utilize a synergy effect? Is the objective to generate a joint monopoly or, by means of classical cartelization, to increase the sales prospects of specific products? Is the primary concern to strengthen the corporate identity of the churches on the fiercely competitive religious markets? Or is one looking for ways of stabilizing the sales markets of the individual churches in these discussions on the age-old contentious issues of dogma? Which products are being negotiated exactly? And which religious services are possibly ignored by ecumenical dialogue?

The spectrum of possible answers to these questions is relatively broad. While some actors dream of setting up a large-scale monopoly, others hope ecumenical talks will facilitate a takeover (friendly or no) of smaller churches and/ or "religious groups" by the Roman Catholic Church. Other actors seek, through ecumenical agreement and concrete cooperation, to forge cartels against a social environment that is seen to be hostile and structurally a-Christian; they see ecumenicity primarily as an antidote to the so-called secularism of the modern man. At all events, ecumenism here is conceived as a reaction to the — in their eyes, abhorrent — decline in traditional, ecclesiastical religiousness, the so-called de-Christianization. Several Protestant functionaries of the ecumenical movement represent yet another model and seek to interpret the popular phrase "reconciled difference" in the sense of a viability of the given institutional variety of Christian churches, expecting that one's "partners" no longer behave like rivals on the religious markets. On the whole, it can be said that the ecumenical approach to the search for consensus is shaped by a striking lack of realistic and clearly defined goals. Many actors cannot give clear answers to the elementary yet essential questions of what they want exactly and what they are actually doing when they communicate with one another on the doctrinal questions of the past. This lack of clarity about their own actions has, in the meantime, become the issue of a separate theological discourse: in the debates on the so-called "reception" of ecumenical consensus. Ecumenical functionaries like to lament that they have reached an agreement on the most important doctrinal questions, but that this has not "caught on" "in the churches" or "at grassroots level." Does this complaint mirror an unacknowledged recognition that their negotiations lack relevance? Is there no demand for these products of dogmatic consensus? Is one manufacturing unmarketable products?

## Protestant Identity

A realistic theological self-perception requires the ability to accept hard facts. Under the conditions of the modern age, even the "religious system" (Niklas Luhmann)[9] of a society answers to a capitalistically shaped logic of exchange. There is no less competition on the modern markets of religious goods and ser-

9. Niklas Luhmann, *Funktion der Religion* (Frankfurt am Main, 1977).

vices than in other markets. This elementary situation of competitive markets forces all rival actors to examine their own strengths and weaknesses, and to critically compare these marketing opportunities with those of the other suppliers. As a result, the various denominational churches and academic theology face two tasks: Firstly, they must develop strategies which facilitate a subtly differentiated perception of their competitors. Secondly, they must acquire and cultivate skills in self-observation to a far greater extent than they have done in the past. In the following I shall concentrate on this second task: the self-observation of Protestantism in comparison with other Christian actors or providers, above all vis-à-vis the Roman Catholic Church.

In the ecumenical debates of Lutheranism — in view of Viggo Mortensen's life history; above all the theological work in the Lutheran World Federation (Lutherischer Weltbund) comes to mind — there is still very little willingness to explore such a realistic self-perception. Here the tendency is to sketch a picture of ecumenical dialogue with vague theological concepts in which hard elements such as power, influence, consumer loyalty, product quality, marketing, corporate identity, globalization competence, and internal management play only a secondary role. Many positions on the current ecumenical developments held by Lutheran church officials and university theologians engaged in the ecumenical business reflect a tendency to repress unpleasant realities. However, it makes sense to speak of the ecumenical movement within Christianity — and indeed, of self-assertion in conditions of heightened multireligiosity — only if the potential of the different kinds of relevant capital at one's disposal is taken into consideration. Ecumenical actors have highly different market positions; abstracting from this fact can only lead to a distorted evaluation of reality.

How can we briefly outline this ecumenical asymmetry? On the one hand we find global players who have plentiful stocks of symbolic capital at their disposal. Such actors have a great deal of cultural capital at hand owing to their intensive cultivation of tradition, their strong orientation toward unchanging rituals of remembrance, and the emphasis they place on the ecclesiastical institution and religious office. The Roman Catholic Church is financially the most powerful nongovernmental organization in the world. In signs and symbols, ritual self-enactments and theological self-interpretations, it reveals a decisive will to power. Only rarely are Protestant ecumenical functionaries aware of the fact that the Catholic Church still sees itself as a political unit analogous to the state. The Vatican, de facto the last predemocratic state on the European continent, has never relinquished the legal privileges granted to it by international law. On the inside, the Catholic Church places great demands of commitment on the individuals socialized (in Roman Catholic terminology: communalized!) within its religious institutions. From the sociopolitical perspective, the Catholic Church sees itself as an overarching cultural and ethical watchtower: it seeks to bind the lifestyle of the faithful to the norms of its church teachings and stands up against other protagonists in the public sphere by laying claim to ethical hegemony. This is asserted using a moral theology based on time-honored theories of its natural right and spiritual welfare work that combines prophetic rhetoric with pastoral guidance. What is decisive in all this is that in its doctrines, rites, canon law, and other public self-portrayals, the Roman Catholic Church defines itself primarily by way of its demonstrative institutionalism or, rather, clear visibility. It sees itself as a strong institution which, in the sense of the modern "inventing of traditions," offers its services as an indispensable institutional basis for successful human sociality. Its distinct visibility is asserted theologically primarily by its understanding of the church as a sacrament, and also by giving the so-called ecclesiastical offices a sacramental character.

Protestant pictures of the Roman Catholic Church are, from time to time, shaped by the interpretative models of the liberals during the Kulturkampf of the nineteenth century. Rome is then regarded as the medieval fortress of an ultramontane reaction, forever pitting itself against the achievements of the modern age. This latent identification of Roman Catholicism with that which is backward and regressive prevents one from recognizing the conservative modernity that shapes the church politics of the Catholic authorities. Neither is Rome dogmatically petrified nor are the authorities impervious to the particular contextual conditions of their actions. On the contrary, the politics and theology of the Roman Catholic Church reveal a high degree of flexibility and a strategically functional way of dealing with its own symbolic assets. It also has access to a rich inventory of semantics which enables it to modify earlier positions and to present revisions as the consequence of deeper theological insight. It is therefore not tenable to contend that Catholicism resists modernity on principle. The history of the Second Vatican Council is a pertinent example of how the Catholic Church can combine faithfulness toward the specific tradition of its institution, above all to the doctrinal decisions of the First Vatican Council, with the cautious adoption of new concepts.[10] The reaction of the Roman Catholic Church to the processes of functional differentiation is efficient inasmuch as it recognizes the *relative* autonomous laws of other cultural

---

10. Cf. Friedrich Wilhelm Graf, "Die nachholende Selbstmodernisierung des Katholizismus?" in *Das II. Vatikanum. Christlicher Glaube im Horizont globaler Modernisierung*, ed. Peter Hünermann, Programm und Wirkungsgeschichte des II. Vatikanums, vol. 1 (Paderborn, Munich, Vienna, and Zürich, 1998), pp. 49-66.

spheres and trenchantly emphasizes the autonomy of religion. Here it lays an avant-garde claim to be the exclusive institution of true Christianity and human religion, and achieves a great deal by fostering its specific corporate identity.

It is far more difficult, by contrast, to describe the specific marketing opportunities of the other, Protestant actor. Indeed, from the economically informed perspective, the question is whether (or to what extent) it is at all possible to describe the Protestant interlocutor in the singular as *a* participant. Are there not de facto several vying protagonists at work here? Do these Protestant actors not have highly different capital investments and products at their disposal? Irrespective of how we answer these questions, it would seem that we are facing the concrete situation where, even if one can fictitiously conceive the Protestant churches or Protestant world associations as a (relatively) unified acting subject, in comparison with the Roman Catholic Church this unit reveals great weaknesses on the current religious markets. To be sure, this Protestant unit possesses a rich reservoir of cultural capital; Protestant traditions play a formative part in many cultural spheres. Nonetheless, the specific nature of church Protestantism is such that there is little commitment to reflecting on the cultural presence of Protestantism and only minimal effort made to regenerate and strengthen its own particular cultural capital. The cultivation of traditional religious symbols has become increasingly less important for Protestant religious culture, and "the word," once so central, no longer plays such a relevant role in the self-identification of Protestantism as a whole. For many, forming a canon is considered "un-Protestant," and cultivating a consciousness of tradition rarely a concern. Naturally this can be seen as a consequence of Protestant individualism and the diffusion of its cultural traditions into general sociocultural discourses interpreted as a welcome expression of the universalization of Protestantism. Yet this situation presents the organization of the church with a significant problem: the lack of willingness within Protestantism to take up a constructive position on the history of one's own denominational origins and cultivate its specific symbolic potential promotes a weakening of the cultural memory of the ecclesiastical organization. This, in turn, impedes the shaping of identity and impairs future perspectives. Protestant churches are in danger of becoming social actors who are only capable of developing relatively weak binding forces and, in the absence of clear goals, of giving contradictory public signals. Also, they show very little readiness to activate their symbolic capital.

We can describe this structural weakness of Protestant actors on the modern, pluralistic religious markets in economic terms: as a marketing problem. The Roman Catholic Church claims to be the best and, indeed, only convincing supplier of quality products on the religious market. This facilitates a strong corporate identity and self-confident marketing strategies. Its Protestant counterparts, however, are barred from marketing their products along similar lines. Thanks to their theological understanding, neither can they declare the given plurality of Christian units illegitimate, nor can they lay claim to a monopoly within Christianity. For Protestants there will always be an unbridgeable ecclesiological asymmetry vis-à-vis the self-understanding of the Roman Catholic Church. This ecclesiological asymmetry is inexorable: in the sense of Confessio Augustana 7, Protestants are necessitated to differentiate between the church in general and a particular denominational church. Never can they directly identify a particular, empirical church with the true church of Jesus Christ. In this respect they are denied the possibility of laying claim to exclusiveness. In a market with a multiplicity of religious suppliers, they are forced into the difficult role of having to pronounce explicitly that the given plurality of Christian actors and the great variety of their products be legitimate.

This is not the place for developing a Protestant corporate identity *materialiter,* in the language games of dogmatics, for instance. Rather, my concern here is a structural problem: from the Protestant perspective of a legitimate plurality of the Christian religion, denominational diversity can be rendered comprehensible as an expression of the wealth of Christianity. Such a hermeneutic of legitimate plurality recognizes that the truth of Christianity is known in different ways, because it is at no one's direct command. Competition in the field of Christianity is not a disadvantage but, theologically, a gain, in that Christian truth is always truth "for me," referring to the distinctive life history and self-interpretation of an individual. This has far-reaching consequences for the self-portrayal of Protestantism on the religious markets of the present day, and for its product management. One central insight of Protestantism is that the truth of Christianity is known in a variety of ways, because it can be communicated pluralistically as truth for individuals. Against such a reflective acceptance of plurality one can raise the question of whether this approach does not dissolve the concept of Christianity into a great variety of Christianities. In fact, Ludwig Marcuse, one of Ernst Troeltsch's Jewish students, proposed abandoning the phrase "the essence of Christianity" in favor of "the essence of Christianities."[11] This, too, can be shown to be perfectly justifiable in economic terms: all competing ecclesiastical actors offer Christian products. Nonetheless, it would be incorrect to describe the differences between their

11. Cf. Ludwig Marcuse, "Das Wesen der Christentümer," in *Was halten Sie vom Christentum? 18 Antworten auf eine Umfrage,* ed. Karlheinz Deschner (Munich, 1957), pp. 110-15.

products by referring solely to external "packaging": the historically handed-down difference between the churches also embraces elementary divergences in their understanding of religion, Christianity, and devoutness.

Compared with Roman Catholicism, Protestantism is a form of Christianity that is shaped by a paradoxical unity of ecclesiasticism and that which goes beyond ecclesiasticism. The reformational protest lived on the knowledge of an immediacy between God and the individual, which can be fulfilled in a religious culture only if the old symbolic capital of the individual is activated in his or her daily lifestyle and conduct. As a result, it is not the fate of the church as an institution that deserves attention, but the transfer of religio-symbolic capital into the reflectively lived lives of individuals, who try to confirm their individuality within the medium of religious language and symbolism. Put economically: Protestantism will not be able to gain larger shares of the market by offering itself as a light variant on Roman Catholic clericalism, or by directly competing with the beautifully and colorfully packaged products of Roman heteronomy. Protestantism can only gear itself successfully to the rationale of market economy by attending to and fostering its own specific symbolic capital: its cultures of religiously reflective individuality. And it is the very conditions of the pluralistic modern age that make its religious products and services highly attractive: for Protestantism offers symbolic interpretations for a fundamental absoluteness of the individual, who otherwise, in all social contexts, can only experience himself or herself as conditioned. Protestantism is able to recognize the fragility of the individual because it has symbolic resources to transcend such fragility and point beyond to a supraempirical ideal whole. That is no inferior religious product by any means, even when measured against the great number of partly old and partly new non-Christian religious products of the present day.

At all events, the fiercely competitive conditions of the religious markets of the early twenty-first century require that one protects the corporate identity of one's own products. In multicultural societies and on multireligious markets, the decisive task of theology is to pursue mnemonic work on its particular denominational identity. The other popular approach of pointing out the correspondence between one's own products and those of other suppliers defeats the object: for when multireligiosity increases, the demand for the specific presentation of denominational identity increases accordingly. For the diverse forms of Protestantism this means the following: more multireligiosity demands an intensified and specifically denominational defense of the religious rights of the individual.

# Multiculturality and Multireligiosity: Introducing the Theme

## THEODOR AHRENS

The spelling program of my computer, installed by Microsoft, has not yet registered the words "multireligiosity" and "multiculturality." Should we conclude then that both terms have not yet arrived at the level of small coinage as far as the common sense of the Anglo-Saxon middle class is concerned? Perhaps!

1. *Multicultural and multireligious.* Not long ago we discussed Christianity and cultures. Among theologians it was quite common to discuss the polarity of Christianity and cultures, speaking of Christianity as a matter of course in the singular, thus emphasizing the ecumenicity/catholicity of the gospel, while speaking of cultures in the plural, thus emphasizing their particularities and different configurations. Put theologically, there is only one gospel transmitted in four canonical and countless noncanonical versions. The gospel, being the living word of the Good Shepherd, invites all people to live their lives in the spirit of Christ. This way the Word affirms its competency to interpret human existence wherever and however it may have been shaped by the particularity of local languages and cultures, and transform it into an experience of faith.

2. Today we have ceased to conceive of cultures as if they were clearly separated milieus, set apart from each other by clearly recognizable borderlines and identity markers.[1] We find it more difficult to interpret a certain people's lifestyles and worlds of religious imagination, as if these were shaped by *one* particular cultural pattern we could lift out from a set of lifestyles, structures, worlds of imaginations, etc.

---

1. As previous generations of ecumenists and missiologists may have done under the impact of Ed. B. Tylor's book *Primitive Culture* (1871).

Of course, we recognize and discuss the homogenizing effects that worldwide processes of exchange of commodities and of ideas have on the lifestyles of people. These processes are not all that new, but have gained enormous momentum in recent times,[2] a development generally considered to be *politically incorrect.* Some sort of trivial world culture is being globalized along with these processes; boundaries, if there are any, seem ineffective and irrelevant.

Concurrently one may observe many countermovements which, in the name of cultural and/or religious identity, claim their *right to be different.* The importance of boundaries and identity markers is being reemphasized by groups and people's movements whose aspirations are usually considered *politically correct.*

Whether such political labels are good or bad, it may be safe to claim that today we, ecumenists, missiologists, and scholars of religion, are more inclined to consider cultures as *relatively open systems usually built up from a number of subsystems resulting in an interaction of different milieus* which, notwithstanding their separateness, form large *civilizations* covering fairly large areas on the globe. Such civilizations would be identifiable because they nourish their particular *mentalities.* To keep such a civilization together, it would need a shared literary canon from which expectations of human behavior flow, and along with that, an elite which formulates and propagates such expectations. It would further need a network of communicative processes upholding a continual flow of news and meanings, moving between regions and cities, groups and classes, large populations and different subcultures, in order to make up a social body shaped by particular mentalities. So far, so good. Our modern societies fall into different milieus, and at times one may get the impression that, in many a case, there is hardly any communicative link between them. The arrival of large groups of migrants, who settle here permanently, does not simply add to this problem, but changes our situation in that many migrant groups represent different civilizations, are shaped by different values systems and religions, and want to maintain these, at least to a certain degree. Hence new religious and cultural subsystems are established. To what degree do, should, or actually could they interact with other cultural/religious subsystems? Is the problem of migrants a problem of those migrants?

Christian churches and their intellectuals cannot escape the necessity to reflect on what this question entails. Whatever viewpoints we may have to share with each other on religions, their commonalities and their differences, the fact is that Christian leaders and intellectuals have to come forward with sugges-

---

2. Cf. William McNeill, *The Rise of the West: A History of the Human Community with a Retrospective Essay* (Chicago and London, 1990).

tions on how to interact with other religions within the framework of a civil society. The nativity church in Bethlehem has become a symbol for that challenge. Where, and why, do attempts to understand the alien and to live with each other peacefully continue to break down? Why does multiculturality not work? Could it be that the boom of dialogue, rhetoric, and serious academic work about interreligious relations has been caused by the collapse of the U.S. concept of *civil religion?*

3. Our second buzzword, "multireligiosity," brings to the fore a particular dimension of multiculturality. We used to talk about *pluralism.* Religious pluralism is, of course, a social fact. The word "pluralism" also stands for a political imperative or necessity. In a modern, democratic society no religion may translate its truth, or its moral claims, into a blueprint for societal order. In fact, to acknowledge this as a ground rule is a precondition for interreligious peace in any society. Thirdly, the term "pluralism" refers to a basic condition of the human self, of our psyche, of the constitution of the individual. No identity is built of one single thread of tradition; convictions, values, fantasies foreign to faith in Christ confront us not from outside, not only in society at large, but they arise from within our inner self. As we strive for a life which is in accord with the gospel, we clarify our own hearts and minds in regard to convictions that lack that accord. We are "aliens" to ourselves, a fact we have known for some time (Rom. 7:19). As Peter Berger has pointed out, part of our modern condition is that as individuals we are more than ever confronted with moral and cognitive choice. The individual is held responsible to chart out his or her draft for a life(style) — even if only a small, privileged people seem to have the opportunity to do so.

4. *Interculturality of Christianity.* From its earliest beginnings, Christianity placed its notion of God in his relationship with mankind in an intercultural and also an interreligious perspective. The intercultural dynamics of Christianity continue to unfold. Christianity falls into an ever greater number of Christian dialects. Unity and diversity both lie at the roots of Christianity. The identity of Christianity remains a contested concept. The question, in a missiological perspective, is how to interpret *what is going on* as Christianity unfolds its intercultural dynamics. What *transformations on the level of essential Christianity* take place, and how do these affect ecumenical relationships between North and South, East and West? How much difference is acceptable, and who is going to decide that question? Further: How do we account for the fact that churches in the North and churches in the South deal quite differently with the word "mission"?

What do we consider an appropriate representation of the gospel in our own situation? Churches in Europe reel under the effects of secularization, particularly where church-state relationships were, or still are, close. Membership is crumbling. While churches in Europe may have neither the personnel nor the vision, nor the money needed, to overcome their crisis, they are forced to reposition themselves within the European context. And they are busy doing this. Bilateral church dialogues, such as those at Leuenberg or Porvoo, may be looked at on two levels: on one level they may be seen as exercises in consensus building among religious elites; on another level they appear as signals from churches repositioning themselves on the religious market, forming something like intercontinental *religious trusts*. Ecumenism seen in that perspective is not so much a matter of good will as of survival interests. Fair enough! Should churches trying to improve their prospect adjust to what appear to be the demands of the religious market? The wisdom of such pragmatism is doubtful (Rom. 12:2). Anything and everything can be made compatible if one takes the heart out of the matter. At a deeper level lies the question of how churches could make good for the enormous loss of credibility and relevancy in a pluralistic society. Question: Mindful of good and bad past experiences, what does Christianity have to offer in a dialogue of cultures and religions?

5. *Religion and violence.* Counterstory to the globalization story: After the East-West conflict ended in 1989, there is no longer any strategic interest in development aid. The belief that societies falling to pieces in the South did not affect the safety of societies in the North has been discredited, as we all know by now. Violence is linking these societies now in a new way: new forms of war[3] emerging from the periphery threaten the safety of people and places in the North.

Some people claim that the heart of the matter lies in the fact that religion is the currency of violence. Even if that notion is too simplistic, the question remains: How should we deal with the dark side of religions and of religion? For a start, one must acknowledge that there have been and continue to be shortcuts from violence back to religion and from religion straight to violence. Therefore the link between *religion and violence* should concern us, not only on the level of action (What should Christians, religious people, any people do or cease to do?) but, more deeply, on a level of religious imagination (What kind of god do

---

3. Cf. Mary Kaldor, *Neue und alte Kriege. Organisierte Gewalt im Zeitalter der Globalisierung* (Frankfurt, 2000), and Wolfgang Sofsky, *Zeiten des Schreckens. Amok, Terror, Krieg* (Frankfurt, 2002), pp. 147ff.

Christians believe or not believe in?).[4] Some people contend that religions in general, and monotheistic religions in particular — because they raise the issue of *truth* — carry a special potential for violence. Others claim that the *truth of any and every religion* is to tame violence by transforming foundational social violence into violence acted out ritualistically on a symbolic level of action (R. Girard).

If that were so, then we must note that the capacity of religions to contain violence on a symbolic level of action seems to be fading. Whatever *frontier of religious fundamentalism* we observe, be it violence against medical doctors in the United States, or Hindu-Muslim antagonism over Ayodhya, or Christian-Muslim antagonism in Indonesia, or so-called interreligious violence elsewhere, most of these and other similar conflicts were not originally about religion but about questions concerning social and political participation. Later, during the course of events, religions were made a factor in those conflicts. *It seems to have been rather easy to tap the worlds of religious imagination* in order to promote violence and to plant in people a consciousness of serving a godly purpose in a cosmic war between good and evil. If, in fact, every and any particular religious tradition may be tapped to fire the hearts and minds of warriors and would-be martyrs in order to force a better world by *sacrificing* their lives, then we may have to discuss either how to get the religions out of the picture of such conflicts or to place the issue of violence at center court in any interreligious dialogue.

4. Cf. my paper: "Das Kreuz mit der Gewalt. Religiöse Dimensionen der Gewaltproblematik," in *Mission nachdenken* (Frankfurt, 2002), pp. 199-232.

# Multicultural Society: Dilemmas and Prospects

ELISABETH GERLE

In the early twentieth century children in schools were taught to become Christians in our part of the world. In the fifties and sixties children were taught about different religions. In the eighties they were taught to learn from religions. Today nobody dares to teach or to talk about religion at all.

This was the broad picture given by the British sociologist Paul Heelas from Lancaster when he recently gave a lecture entitled "Spiritual Revolution: From Religion to Spirituality" at Lund University. What does such a picture have to do with multicultural communities? Quite a bit, I think. The Scandinavian countries have experienced a period where the monolithic Lutheran society went through a secularization process that to various degrees opened up for plurality.[1]

In Sweden the school system went in the fifties from a confessional Lutheran school to a de-confessionalized school that emphasized neutrality, objectivity, and technical knowledge. Schools were supposed to be similar all over the country and seen as a democratic project to bring children from different social backgrounds together. Equality was a key value. During that period religions were thought to gradually disappear from the public sphere. Hence religions were taught about, not learned from. They were seen as part of a cultural heritage and as a way to understand foreign cultures, less as resources in a continuing interpretation of life to find meaning and direction. Occasionally some schools in the nineties have developed teachings from religions in an attempt at multicultural coexistence, also in public schools. In the rapid development of

---

1. That the Scandinavian countries are different from one another is obvious. In Sweden the formal relationship between the state and the Lutheran church ended at the turn of the millennium. In Denmark the Parliament is the decisive body making decisions also about books and hymnals in the church.

independent, so-called free schools, there is a spectrum from confessional Christian or Muslim schools to other ideological or philosophical expressions. Some of these have been accused of having a too-narrow curriculum. Creationist Christian schools, for instance, tend to omit all information about Darwinism and the development of species. Many Muslim schools do not teach about Hinduism and Buddhism as religions, and treat girls and boys as genetically and socially quite different, something that might be difficult in societies that expect women and men to fulfill similar roles as citizens.[2]

In Denmark independent schools with various philosophical emphases have a history going back to Grundtvig and the people high school movement. Being a big admirer of Grundtvig for his attempts to bring nature, culture, and Christianity together, I have to admit that I find the national sentiment in his project difficult to handle in a multicultural society with ambitions toward pluralism and religious coexistence. Especially as I here want to emphasize that there is no power-indifferent truth.

This conference wants to address society and multiculturalism. Community rather than society is, however, more frequently referred to in relation to pluralism and cultural exchange or encounter. It is a sign of postmodernity or late modernity to emphasize community. We talk about things that are not given, that are no longer self-evident. Hence community and identity are important contemporary notions. This may be due to an influence from the United States, which is built upon group identities, while belonging in Europe tended to be given in the past. Grace Davie has pointed out that western Europe and the United States have basically different histories. The United States is held together by the principle of competing institutions. Consequently religious presence in society is related to engagement by groups. Europe, on the other hand, has had a historical principle of belonging which gives religion an integrative role.[3] This principle may however be one of the factors making it difficult for migrants within Europe or from other parts of the world. Migrants do not, per definition, belong. Thus have Europeans become more interested in community discourses.

It could also be that theologians tend to be more interested in analyzing small communities than the broader society. They seem closer to religion. So much of religious life is relegated to private arenas in late modernity. Religious institutions are not at the center of society anymore.

2. See further Elisabeth Gerle, *Mångkulturalism för vem?* (Multiculturalism for whom?) (Nya Doxa, 1999).

3. Grace Davie, *Religion in Modern Europe: A Memory Mutate* (Oxford: Oxford University Press, 2000).

Yet, I think that if multicultural communities with any respect for the notion of community are to emerge, it will relate to the broader society and the
conditions under which communities exist in society. I would therefore here
address some of those conditions as well. As ethics is my academic field, I will
particularly focus on values. It has to do with relationships between the individual and the group and to which values the broader society gives priority.

## Late Modernity

At the beginning I also want to mention that I prefer the term "late modern" to
"postmodern." In accordance with Ulrich Beck and Anthony Giddens, I claim
that there are many values and discoveries of modernity that we want to hold
on to, yet with another openness. While postmodernity emphasizes the abrupt
shift from modernity, late modernity emphasizes the need to sort out good and
bad sides and to continue to develop some of the valuable sides of modernity.
Radical postmodern thought may, in my view, too easily give a philosophical,
ethical rationale for the new grand narrative, the global market, where communities are created out of consuming markets and every moment is a situation
for individual performance. Here belonging is related to consuming capacity.
Or it may open the door for what postcolonial thinkers describe as the nostalgia
for a distant, idealized past without contemporary challenges. Here radical
postmodern thought easily lends support to petrification or reintroduction of
conservative customs labeled as cultural respect. Hence I would argue in favor
of using the term "late modernity," where one of the dominant features is individualism. Whether such individualism becomes atomistic or related to other
persons has a lot to do with how we handle the relationship between the individual and the collective, but also between community and society. I would like
to show in this paper that the interpretation of what is good and what is bad has
a lot to do with from which perspective the story is being told. There is no
power-indifferent truth. Ambiguity is part of our late modern challenge that
constantly forces us to ask: Good life for whom?

Ronald Ingelhart shows in his comparative study of forty-three countries
with different cultural backgrounds and levels of modernization that the authority and legitimacy of institutions are crumbling. This most likely has to do
with growth in active, self-determined engagement.[4] It is easy for leaders of established religious institutions to see this as a threat where people do not re-

---

4. Ronald Ingelhart, *Modernization and Post-modernization — Cultural, Economic, and
Political Change in Forty-Three Societies* (Princeton, 1997), pp. 78ff.

spect their authority. Nevertheless, it could just as easily be seen as a positive factor in the ongoing reinterpretation of traditions as well as in the search for new politics. But it is different from the past. Top-down models are being challenged, and many search for renewal from below.

Actually, this may be congenial in a worldview affirming that the good life is always being created in new ways in new contexts by the Creator, Redeemer, and Holy Spirit in a revolutionary trinitarianism. Inspired by Irenaeus's ideas about incarnation where human growth, fulfillment, and salvation go beyond a creational origin, i.e., they are something to come, I would like to explore some conditions for respectful multiculturalism in European late modernity.

Our time, as all times, needs to ask the questions Aristotle raised about how we can materialize or implement the hidden opportunities *(energeia)* in our context. How could it be? The question of how it was always implicitly contains the question about how it is and even more the third question: how could it be *(enteleki)*.[5]

While there are many contemporary tendencies to idealize multicultural communities of the past, such as the millet system in the Ottoman Empire, I think we need to find new ways where crucial values of modernity, such as democracy, human rights, equality, and respect for the person, are integrated in our vision.

Neither modernity nor the resistance to modernity and the idealized past provide a full vision for the future. Hence we need to use the strength of late modernity, the freedom to sort out good and bad features of the past in order to explore the values we want to emphasize in our vision for the future. *Openness* is one of those values that need to be acknowledged. *Epistemological openness* has flourished in several places and during many periods of humanity since ancient times. Many premodern societies may on the other hand be characterized as closed and suspicious toward new information and knowledge. They have not been particularly open. Modernity, as well, has been criticized for its absolute convictions and certainty of its own values by sociologists such as Zygmunt Baumann and others. Such a modern lack of openness is visible when Europe is becoming an immigrant continent rather than an exodus world.

Cosmopolitan people from, e.g., Lebanon and Teheran as well as premodern people from Anatolia or Pakistan meet with people in Scandinavia who just recently left farming and fishing and therefore think of themselves as very modern. As so many people in Western modernity, they are epistemologically convinced that they are right and know the whole truth, especially

---

5. Anders Ehnmark uses this distinction in his essay "Erik Gustaf Geijer som modernist," in *Alla tiders Geijer* (Geijersamfundet, 2001), p. 43.

if they adhere to a secularist vision of society rather than a secular. In that sense premodern and modern worldviews reinforce each other's polarized understanding of "we and them" as completely different. This is even truer in what I call antimodern groups, who hold resistance to modernity as a formative identity and where revelation is set up against reason, divine against human, past against the present and the future. Many contemporary fundamentalist groups on the Christian Right in the United States or in Islamist networks could be identified as antimodern movements who organize themselves out of resistance to basic values of modernity such as democracy, human rights, and women's emancipation. Yet these groups and networks are themselves an outcome of modernity and would not be able to exist without modern technology.

I would here like to distinguish between secularization and secularism. Secularization may be interpreted in accordance with secularization theology as a divine process creating an awareness of divine presence in all spheres of society against attempts to confine God's work to the church. It may also be seen as liberating from a monolithic authority of the church that throughout history has been used oppressively. A secularist society, on the other hand, is a replacement of a religious world horizon with a worldview where science, technology, and especially economy are given a divine role to define what life is about and where epistemology and ethics are limited to these three areas, i.e., there is no truth or important values to be found outside of them. I would like to argue that a truly multicultural society needs some of the basic elements of secularization opening up for pluralism. Such pluralism may, however, be swallowed by secularist attitudes reintroducing another type of fundamentalism. It may, however, be as difficult for religious people to adjust to a secularist society that has relegated God to privacy and given economy the defining chair as it is to relate to a monolithic, religious society with another dominant religion. This is one of the areas where many Jews, Christians, and Muslims have more in common than what is dividing them.

I would therefore argue in favor of a late modern approach that is less polarized. Rather than abandoning the search for truth and the good life, this would be a shared pursuit where many groups and perspectives are invited to participate. It is to give up certainty but not the search for truth. While the antimodern think the truth and the good life is something we have left or are leaving, and that we ought to hold on to it or rediscover it, the highly modern think they already have found the truth and the good life, something others ought to discover. A late modern approach, on the other hand, perceives the future as open with an insight that there is no power-independent truth. Such a perspective has realized that what used to be labeled truth sometimes was a certainty built upon ignorance or resistance to disturbing information. While it is human to strive for certainties, it is wise to realize that the modern tendency to equalize truth and certainty is the opposite of openness.

Traditions from the past have many features that ought to be nurtured, other sides that are oppressive and need to be challenged. The good life is possible in new ways in the future when we search for truth together. An epistemological openness, a willingness to learn and listen also to others, to discover new facts, experiences, and perspectives is also connected to *ethical openness*. This is, however, not the same as ethical relativism. But it is an insight that especially the West too often has universalized their particular truth and ethics and launched their way as the universal way for the world, just the way we now do with the global economy. An ethical openness is to challenge the old triumphalist universalism, as well as relativism claiming that "anything goes" and that we cannot communicate across cultures. Rather, openness to explore ethics in multiple ways is to take the pursuit of the good life and a good society seriously. With Gayatri Spivak, we on the other side need to steer ourselves through "the Scylla of cultural relativism and the Charybdis of nativist culturalism."[6]

My question is whether we in late modernity are mature enough today for a new kind of spirituality built on mysticism with greater humility in relation to the inner core, God, where interpretations are left more open and where democracy and human rights are central values. In the postindustrial society where information is replacing industrial production, we are facing a new fundamental transformation that Marc Luyckx describes.

> In the present crisis, indeed, one of the main developments has been the questioning of the radical separation between religion and politics. Distinctions are still made but there is no longer any opposition between the religious and secular worlds, between ethics and political life or between male and female. Diversity is accepted as a dynamic state rather than as a transitional phase. Analytic logic, which is linear and "modern," has been called into question by the new complexity and non-linearity and by the possibilities of horizontal communication and networking. Although reason is not being discarded, its hegemony (and, in the words of Max Weber, its "disenchanting" function) are on the way out. The quest for meaning is being extended into areas until now reserved for reason. One might therefore be heading towards the "re-enchantment" of the world. The epistemology is actively tolerant. Nobody owns the Truth, but it does exist. Post-

---

6. Gayatri Chakravorty Spivak, *A Critique of Postcolonial Reason: Toward a History of the Vanishing Present* (Cambridge: Harvard University Press, 1999), p. 6.

industrial cosmology envisages thus a "post-secularised world" in the sense that it is open to the transcendental but opposed to any authoritarian or vertical imposition of religious authority. It acknowledges that it is important for all civilisations to be receptive to that which is alien, whatever form this may take.[7]

## Defining the Term "Multicultural": Toleration for Whom?

The term "community" is ambivalent. It sounds inviting but is also excluding. It is often used in a way that implicitly accepts or reinforces lack of openness. This influences also the notion of multiculturalism, especially in the public debate. The lack of clarity about what one means by multicultural societies is a dilemma. Liberal or progressive politics has been unclear about how to define multiculturalism. There is a big difference between an insightful understanding that cultural, religious, and ethnic roots are important for people and creating a society with ethnic groups living in different parts of a city. While the first version of multiculturalism accepts as a fact that we all carry many cultural, religious, ethnic, class, gender, and other layers of identity, the second version reinforces an understanding of culture, religion, and ethnicity as something static that does not change and develop over time. This second version tends to turn a blind eye if ethnic or religious communities are turned into captive communities for their members, especially for young women who are supposed to accept that the human rights the surrounding society takes for granted are not for them. This has to do with a tension that Will Kymlicka has pointed out in various writings, namely, how to promote toleration of difference for the group while protecting the right of individuals to dissent from the group or to be influenced by other values on how to live.[8] Yet, in the public as well as in the academic debate, multiculturalism or cultural pluralism, identity politics or the politics of difference often means ethnic diversity where the focus is on the group level.

A mixture of cultural relativism, civilizational critique against the West, and solidarity with the Third World shaped political rhetoric and integration policies in many countries in the West. The fact that immigrants may enrich societies was transformed into a view that immigrants could not but enrich

7. Marc Luyckx, "Paths Toward a Dialogue between Religions" (paper presented at the second Euro-Islam conference in Mafraq, Jordan, June 10-13, 1996, inititated by the Swedish Ministry for Foreign Affairs).

8. See, e.g., Will Kymlicka, *Multicultural Citizenship* (New York: Oxford University Press, 1995).

them.[9] Those who questioned were accused of being xenophobic or racist. The choice to keep one's original cultural identity, with societal support, became the goal for Swedish immigration politics from the 1970s onward. The goal was the possibility for the ethnic group to stay together as a group. This goal was said to be in the interest of both individuals and the whole society.[10] An idealized understanding of community as something static, given, and good became an implicit part of this rhetoric on cultures as something to protect. In this rhetoric it was "the other" as clients to be taken care of that needed protection. As the rhetoric of le Pen and Pia Kjørsgaard has shown, it is easy to turn this kind of argumentation into a need to protect the majority culture, understood in static terms.

There are, however, good reasons to be skeptical about group rights when they turn a blind eye to respect for the human being. As we all know, there are situations when the ethnic or religious group is not a valuable support but rather a prison within monolithic cultures. In most occasions, however, a group belonging may be what helps the individual to flourish. This is especially important for minorities in hostile surroundings. Some suggestions floating around in Europe and emerging as new legislation in Denmark, e.g., to provide lesser support for immigrants during their first years, can be seen as a way to even further make individuals completely dependent on the ethnic group, increasing distrust toward the majority society. However, we need to search "means of addressing cultural diversity that simultaneously protect groups and empower individuals to escape the dictates of the group and/or to mobilize resources to change the group."[11]

A society where people from different traditions and religions very rarely meet to exchange experiences is likely to do the opposite. It may easily reinforce tendencies in modern, plural, secular societies to compare the best in contemporary times with the worst of the history of the other. Many immigrant communities do the reverse. They feel threatened by a secularist society with a commercialized view of women that they want to distance themselves from. A portrayal of decadent Western women is then a useful tool to

9. This thesis has been argued by Thomas Gür, author and journalist originally from Turkey. He has argued in many articles and books for the right of the individual to dissent from the ethnic group. See, e.g., Gür, "Integrationspolitikens kollaps," *Sydsvenska Dagbladet,* April 14, 2002, p. B2.

10. See, e.g., Kjell Östberg, in the first study of discrimination, 1984 (*diskriminering-sutredningen,* 1984).

11. Avigail Eisenberg, "Cultural Pluralism Today," in *Understanding Contemporary Society: Theories of the Present,* ed. Browning, Halcli, and Webster (Beverly Hills, Calif.: Sage, 2000), p. 387.

dismantle everything in the dominant society. That the rejection of modern things and values is selective is obvious. There are many sides of modern societies that are accepted and desired. What is rejected and what is accepted has to do with power. To paraphrase the moderate Muslim feminist Riffat Hassan: When there is something men want, such as computers, cellular phones, etc., it is called modernization. When women want emancipation, it is called Westernization.[12]

Hence the emergence of ethnic enclaves in Scandinavia and in Europe is problematic when they tend to be the only existing community for people living there. If they never meet with other ethnic groups or with the dominant society around work or education or leisure activities, how would cultures develop in interaction with others?

Furthermore, injustice may easily be disguised as multiculturalism. Praxis with segregated housing, schools and economy and emerging ghettoization are often rationalized in the name of multiculturalism. Avigail Eisenberg points out that more often than not have social and cultural pluralism coexisted and reinforced social inequality. Plural societies often contain a division of labor that follows cultural lines and allows some cultures to dominate others. Individuals then live side by side but separately. As we have seen in South Africa during apartheid, "differentiation of people on the basis of culture is not a guarantee that social equality will be enhanced."[13] The ambitions and politics for society, therefore, ought to be to create mixed living areas, work, education, and leisure activities where people from different cultures and religions are able to meet.

Yet neglect of ethnicity or cultural/religious belonging is not the solution. We need to continue to ask how cultural and religious membership, but also identities such as class and gender, affect the distribution of power and resources and make a difference to one's opportunities and well-being. Liberal politics failed because it did not make the connection between class, gender, and the distribution of power. As religion in Europe has often had an integrative role, the division of power is not equally distributed among people with Christian identity and people with Muslim or Jewish identity.

12. This was something Riffat Hassan pointed out at the UN Women's Conference on Women and Development, Beijing, 1995.
13. Eisenberg, p. 388.

## The Dilemma of Trust

1. A crucial dilemma in multicultural societies that I want to raise has to do with trust. First, from a stranger's perspective: Is it possible for anybody from outside to trust a society with strong, historic, monolithic Lutheran roots, such as, e.g., the Scandinavian countries? Is it, on the other hand, possible to trust a secular society? This, in my view, is one of the basic questions for migrants who live as minority communities.

Most premodern societies have tribal features. Family, relatives, and the tribe are the basis for survival. The Hebrew Scriptures tell the stories about Abraham and Sarah, Ishmael, Rebekah and Isaac, Leah, Rachel and Jacob, Lot and the journey to the country of Canaan where trust among the members of the tribe was crucial. To expect people from premodern countries, often with weak or corrupt states, to start trusting the surrounding society and a welfare state may be expecting a lot.[14] What if this modern society does not appear trustworthy? What if the values of the dominant society seem alien and questionable? Then it is hard to abandon the values of the family or tribe. For most tribes this solidarity is essential. It is more important than freedom for the individual. To keep control and loyalty, male members *accept* the position of controllers of female sexuality. Women's sexuality is namely considered a threat, as it invites outside aggression and is tempting to inner disobedience and treason. Hence a woman may not be allowed to make her own choices. Such freedom is in itself a threat against the tribe. This interpretation of female confinement is not uncommon even among philosophers.[15] Theologians argue along the lines of a static interpretation of creation with given roles in society. The same story told from women's perspectives usually points to other factors such as double standards and interests in upholding male superiority. They point out that the "liberal" rhetoric about multiculturalism meaning ethnic enclaves is reinforcing or reintroducing male, authoritarian, ethnic leadership where the values of democracy and human rights are remote.[16]

For many women the issue of trust, therefore, is even more complicated. Who is there to trust in a new society if they are to claim individual freedom and

14. The Swedish Islamologist Jan Hjärpe is often pointing to the concept of the strong state as a reason for Muslim immigrants to accept new values and norms. The welfare state is for them often considered in analogy to the ideal Muslim community, *umma*.

15. See the discussion on this in an article by Göran Rosenberg, "Mannen som inte trodde på Sverige" (The man that did not believe in Sweden), *Dagens Nyheter,* February 16, 2002, p. A2.

16. See, e.g., Susan Moller Okin, *Is Multiculturalism Bad for Women?* (Princeton: Princeton University Press, 1999).

respect for themselves as persons? Their family may adhere to traditional value systems that comply with male superiority, while the state and the surrounding society in the new country may hide behind a veil of cultural pluralism and respect that in reality pushes women and children back to the dominance of patriarchal ethnic leaders. Male hegemony is often given divine sanction drawing on certain stories and mainstream traditions. The very same male dominance is on the other hand challenged by other stories in the very same scriptures, stories that women often refer to. Such countertraditions within religions as well as modern values are often used as emancipatory by women.[17] This intra- as well as interreligious conflict may be quite intense. Anthony Giddens (2000) states that democracy within the family is a feature of modernity. Hence the voices of young women refusing to merely adjust to patriarchal traditions with arranged marriages and double standards in relation to sexuality can be seen as signs of modernization within premodern communities that are taking place all over the world and within all religious and cultural traditions. In these struggles women are often invoking Holy Scriptures, Jesus, the prophet Muhammad, or other religious leaders. Yet there is a risk that women in such periods of transition may be abandoned from two sides. If they want to make independent choices about how to live their lives, they cannot expect support either from the family whose hierarchy is challenged from within or from the state that too often has labeled respect for patriarchy as cultural respect.[18]

Liberal philosophers used to argue that modernity has led us to exchange strong commitment toward a few (the family, the tribe) for weaker commitment toward everybody (the state). It is often pointed out that the positive side of this is that it has become possible to combine our need for collective protection and social dignity with individual freedom. The negative side is that such solidarity with everybody in a society might become or be seen as so weak as no commitment at all. This is particularly dangerous for people with a stronger need for protection than their aim for freedom. Masoud Kamali from the Centre of Multiethnic Research in Uppsala points out that those who lack a national state such as the Kurdish or the Palestinian people may be particularly vulnerable.[19] For them it might be especially dangerous to exchange commitment toward family, tribe, or the ethnic community for the vague commitments of modern society.

17. Fatima Mernissi in a Muslim context and Rosemary Radford Ruether in a Christian context are two good examples.

18. Catherine A. MacKinnon, *Towards a Feminist Theory of the State* (Cambridge: Harvard University Press, 1989).

19. Staffan Kihlström, "Regeringen anklagas för ökad segregation," *Dagens Nyheter,* April 5, 2002, p. A2.

These liberal thoughts have, however, developed out of the notion that the human being is a man, not a woman. Yet many of these principles are applicable also to women, but in a more complicated way. Therefore one always needs to mention women and men and situate people as gendered.

Bringing this dilemma of trust even further, in my view, is the dismantling of welfare politics in connection with open markets and corporate competition. A corporate hunt for low taxes, weak employment protection, and lax environmental standards has elsewhere been described as a contemporary "race toward the bottom." Trusting the modern state as an alternative community in this context may be a crucial dilemma for people of premodern heritage, and may explain some of the reemergence of strong ethnic, religious, sometimes antimodern, fundamentalist communities in the West. This, of course, is adding even more pressure on women who may be more confined to the family. While immigrants just a few decades ago arrived as industrial workers, most of them today come as refugees or asylum seekers who have great difficulty entering the workplace. This is hard, almost impossible, even for privileged and sophisticated immigrants. Simultaneously work ethics is connected to being a good worker. You are supposed to be employed or at least to be unemployed with an openness to start working at any time.[20] Only a good worker is seen as a good citizen.

Another issue related to welfare politics is that late modern societies engage their members mainly as consumers, only partially as producers. What makes people belong and be seen as normal today is if they can consume rather than if they are employed. This makes it almost impossible for poor people to become accepted as citizens. People without decent income, credit cards, or good prospects for the future perform poorly as consumers. While modern industrial societies needed the poor as a reserve army to be employed, they are not needed at all in late modern consumerism. This, of course, makes mutual trust difficult. For ordinary taxpayers and good consumers, the poor become bad investments. They will not pay back or give any profit. Rather they are like a black hole that gives nothing back, except possibly problems.[21] Rich immigrants, on the other hand, are often seen through the eyes of puritan work ethics, being judged if they are able to consume and travel without being employed with good salaries.

---

20. This is often said to be due to Martin Luther, even if it probably has more to do with John Calvin and even more with the puritan ethics of early industrial societies that has shaped much of our work ethic in modernity. See Max Weber, *Die protestantische Ethik und der Geist der Kapitalismus* (Tübingen: Mohr, 1934).

21. See further Zygmunt Bauman, *Work, Consumerism, and the New Poor* (Buckingham, Philadelphia, Open University Press, 1998), for this discussion.

2. A dilemma for dominant societies may be memory or anamnesis. It is important to remember their own indigenous history. Established cultures and established churches have a tendency to compare their best with the worst of the other. The nonestablished do the same, but with less power over a common discourse.

Not everything in historic cultures is valuable or good. Roman Catholic countries have their history of repression and the Orthodox theirs. Similarly, the Lutheran monolithic states have had many oppressive features. Some of them have been criticized and gradually overcome. Freedom of expression and the right to choose have not been achieved without struggles in relation to religious and political authorities. Another difficult value system to overcome in all these various traditions has been a gender hierarchy where women's subordination often has been given religious and biblical legitimacy. However, one rarely hears anybody address a traditional Lutheran or Roman Catholic view on women, while it is common to hear references to the view on women in Islam. Yet many features are similar. In all these traditions complementarity has been and is being used as a disguise for demanding submission of women. Struggles that now are being fought among Muslim and Jewish communities have parallels in the Christian traditions.[22]

## Prospects for Respectful Cohabitation

In light of the arguments above, a first step toward respectful coexistence may be to realize that people from all regions live in various relationships to modernity, but also that there are various relationships between religion and modernity.

As a summary I once again ask the questions of power and situatedness: What kind of multiculturalism are we aiming for? A society with ethnic enclaves living next to one another but not with one another? Or an understanding of multicultural societies emphasizing the individual, realizing that we all live with overlapping identities? While the first seems to presuppose a strong group that is self-sufficient, the other seems to presuppose a very strong individual that is self-sufficient. While the first may reinforce patriarchy and various forms of ethnic or religious essentialism, the second may lead to atomistic

22. See, e.g., Anne Sofie Roald, "Feminist Reinterpretation of Islamic Sources: Muslim Feminist Theology in the Light of the Christian Tradition of Feminist Thought," in *Women and Islamization: Contemporary Discourse on Gender Relations,* ed. Karin Ask and Marit Tjomsland (Oxford: Berg, 1998), and Gerle, *Mångkulturalism för vem?*

individualism and assimilation where cultures and religions are considered obsolete and where, therefore, a secularist vision of society is being pursued. The first may be described as a multicommunitarian vision, and the other as the well-known liberal vision. Neither vision provides any power analysis; neither analyzes relations between various groups where citizenship, ethnicity, religion, and class/consuming capacity are important variables; neither delves within the group where class, age, gender, and other factors are crucial for the well-being and life capabilities of the individual.[23]

I would therefore like to argue in favor of a third view steering between the liberal Scylla and the communitarian Charybdis. This third view is a society that facilitates overlapping communities. In such multitudes of spaces power relations between groups and within groups are made visible and sometimes challenged.

This third vision is a society where people meet to work and to search for a good life together. They meet with different people in different groups, something that enhances strong individuals as well as strong groups. Such groups could allow vulnerability and weakness, something that the liberal, atomistic vision does not. Yet the communities are not as static, traditional, and closed as many of the communitarian visions for community are. In this pursuit of a good life there are some elements of living together, side by side. Yet many arenas are there to be shared where people of various ethnic and religious origins live with one another, not only next to one another. In these various spaces there is a constant renegotiating of what is good or bad, right or wrong, not only within groups or intraculturally, but also between groups, interculturally or interreligiously. Just as truth cannot be absolutized as in secularist modernity and in fundamentalist antimodernity, the search for truth may not be abandoned as in radical postmodernism. Yet power analyses must always be part of this pursuit. Ethnicity, gender, geographical origin, and many other factors affect which truths are being formulated as the common truths.

These arguments are relevant also for religions! Ecumenical people, therefore, ought to resist the liberal divide where religious thought and praxis are relegated to the private sphere. They also need to resist an idealized understanding of closed communities. Religious thought and praxis need to be part of the public arena where many voices can be heard. In such open societies reli-

23. See further Martha C. Nussbaum, *Women and Human Development* (Cambridge: Cambridge University Press, 2000). Nussbaum argues that women in much of the world today are less well nourished than men, less healthy, and more vulnerable to physical violence and sexual abuse. She argues that international politics and economic thought must be sensitive to gender difference as a problem of justice. I am arguing along similar lines.

gious thought and praxis can be criticized. Various religious sources may also be inspirational to interreligious cohabitation with democracy, human dignity, and openness for the divine mystery at the center.

# Multiculturalism between Cosmopolitanism and Communitarian Nationalism

## ULF HEDETOFT

Let me open this brief presentation by giving you some central aspects of current debates on multiculturalism while referring to arguments presented in two recent publications.

The first: In a book called *Citizenship and Migration: Globalization and the Politics of Belonging,* Stephen Castles and Alistair Davidson argue that we are witnessing the beginnings of the "end of national belonging." What they argue is that "The context for a citizenship based on belonging to a single nation is being eroded," though the process of erosion and redefinition of citizenship "in response to globalization" is uneven.[1] However, even nation-states that until recently were seen as extremely homogeneous have been forced into realizing that they are now on the fast track toward becoming multiethnic societies, in turn engendering the creation of a "new layer of citizenship above that of the nation — the citizen who does not belong."[2]

The second reference is from Bhikhu Parekh's book, *Rethinking Multiculturalism.* At the beginning of a central chapter he argues that "A multicultural society faces two conflicting demands and needs to devise a political structure that enables it to reconcile them in a just and collectively acceptable manner. It should foster a strong sense of unity and common belonging among its citizens. . . . Paradoxical as it may seem, the greater and deeper the diversity in a society, the greater the unity and cohesion it requires to hold itself together and nurture its diversity."[3]

These two positions outline the contours of a contested field of para-

---

1. Stephen Castles and Alistair Davidson, *Citizenship and Migration: Globalization and the Politics of Belonging* (New York: Macmillan, 2000), p. 156.

2. Castles and Davidson, p. 157.

3. Bhikhu Parekh, *Rethinking Multiculturalism* (New York: Macmillan, 2000), p. 196.

doxes, contradictions, conflicting demands: a kind of continuum between ethnic communitarianism, more or less radical forms of multiculturalism, and the global erosion of national forms of belonging and loyalty. But they also indicate that a multiethnic society is not to be taken, a priori, as one having a multicultural political program or ideology. Where multiethnicity is a mere question of societal and cultural composition, multiculturalism refers to a politically ordered interactive dynamics between society and culture, public and private, civil and political society, homogeneity and diversity.

It seems fair to say that there exist two fundamental positions, a "liberal" and an "assimilationist," though both come in different variants.

Champions of the liberal position either defensively contend that polities based on multiculturalism are feasible and necessary in a globalized world and can be achieved through intergroup tolerance, or more optimistically see them as humane and future-oriented, as strategies proactively guaranteeing the loyalty of diverse groups to the same overarching polity.

Adherents to the assimilationist position counter that the most stable political regime is one based on a oneness of culture and ethnicity, that this is the only way to safeguard civic responsibility toward the state, and that minorities must be taught to assimilate to the dominant cultural premises. On this view, belonging is basically indivisible, and national allegiance is incompatible with a politically condoned diversity of cultural practices.

Liberal positions refute this objection by claiming for instance that belonging consists of several layers, where some, as long as they remain cultural and private, may well be directed toward a "foreign/minority cultural/religious setting" and others, more public and political, toward the political culture and practices of the "host country"/core ethnicity. Integration is possible without full-blown assimilation. Assimilationists, on the other hand, insist that democracy and solidarity can only come to fruition on the basis of ethnically close-knit societies.

Both positions are fraught with serious internal problems. Multiculturalists have difficulties defining the cultural *limits* and *preconditions* of political entities, i.e., how much diversity and what kinds of diversity a nation-state can abide without falling apart, and how its constitutional basis and administrative practices may be orchestrated to safeguard a feeling of solidarity and commitment to shared values. And assimilationists are hard put to define what "cultural homogeneity" actually implies and how much difference this homogeneity can absorb — i.e., its *degree of closure* around itself, in light of the fact that its protagonists normally subscribe to ideals of freedom and individualism too.

Three salient elements should be emphasized. First, that "multiculturalism" has little if anything to do with the cultural properties of each component entity, nor with the "encounter" and "assimilability" of these cultures measured on the prima facie evidence of their cultural characteristics per se — rather the question is one of the *functional benefits or drawbacks* of multicultural societies for the political order and stability of a country.

This is why multiculturalism is a method of both inclusion and exclusion: minority cultures that do not conform to the recipe of "unity in diversity" and differentiation between civic-political and ethno-cultural forms of identity and belonging are not part and parcel of the multicultural compact (cf. certain black and Muslim organizations in the USA, aboriginal organizations in Australia).

Second, that the terms on which this process of political identity contention is being carried imply that core national "indigenousness" and its territorial basis and circumferences are being squeezed from multiple sides: from liberal, outward-looking globalizers as well as from xenophobic, anti-immigrant political factions and movements; from nongovernmental organizations (NGOs) protesting globalization as well as from national political leaderships who increasingly tend to compromise national sovereignty and devise new ways of protecting the national borders from unwanted intrusions; from immigrant and refugee organizations who not only seem to embody the "global threat" to traditional ways of life but insist on their right to their own cultural-political preferences; and from international human-rights institutions which tend to support such particularistic claims-making processes.

Third, that there are "unintended consequences" of the overriding paradox. In one sense "ethnic identity" has been estranged by the conflictual processes through which the nation-state has attempted to adapt to and incorporate globalization. The immediate results are both multiculturalist strategies and popular and political reactions intent on maintaining the stability and identity of the "old order."

But in another sense this is also an ethnic emancipation process, since it gives a multiplicity of politico-cultural actors far more latitude to (re)define and (re)configure their identity-as-interests and interests-as-identities. This is what is usually referred to as the politics of identity. This process goes upward toward the creation of transnational interest/identity patterns (transnational NGOs, the European Union, migrant organizations), but also downward in a particularistic process of national or regional separatism; of local "subculturalization" (back to authentic culture!); of regionally based transborder identity constructions, like the Danish/Swedish Øresund-project; or of social collectivities using or constructing their own special identity for reasons of cultural fortification, political protest, or socioeconomic claims making.

Though internationalization and globalization are evident in all this, the national context seems to be far from defunct. Rather the opposite is true — and partly due to transnational processes no doubt: multiculturalism, at least in Europe, seems to be in a state of crisis, where its limits as a method of integration are being exposed almost on a daily basis and the assimilationist paradigm, most obviously in the form of "right-wing populism" but also rather widespread perceptions of global civilizational clashes, is reasserting itself. Briefly: liberal multiculturalism currently finds itself squeezed between cosmopolitanism and different forms of "communitarian" nationalism.

## Could We Possibly Find Any Help or Solution in the American Model?

As we all know, the United States is an "immigrant country" of liberalism and entrepreneurship. Historically, assimilationist "melting pot" strategies of political identity have given way to multicultural, "hyphenated" strategies. Further, identity based on civic values and citizenship on *ius soli* principles has one of its main origins in the USA. And finally, the USA represents a "postmodern" blend of mobility, individualism, bottom-up identity politics/claims-making strategies, acceptance of multiculturalism, and instrumentalist approaches to belonging. Whether we see contemporary developments in the light of a possible diffusion of the American model to the rest of the world, or just as a possible learning experience in comparative perspective, the similarities with developments in other parts of the world are there and might contain a lesson.

Possibly. But it would be wrong to reduce all the processes reviewed to a copycat version of American multiculturalism. First, some instances constitute reaffirmations of the homogeneous model in modernized forms (like the recuperation of central European sovereignties). Second, other instances of novel identity formations come about as reactions to and not emulations of American cultural influences. Third, European models of multiculturalism are/were often very differently configured (like Dutch pillarization) and prioritize an interventionist state far more strongly.

And fourth, there is also a more fundamental distinction. The immigrant case may serve as illustration: The USA requires newly arrived (would-be) citizens to pledge a solemn and highly "assimilationist" oath of allegiance to the American Constitution and the U.S. flag, while upholding an official discourse of multicultural liberalism and societal diversity. Thereafter the former Mexican can refer to himself as a "Hispanic American" (i.e., he came from a Spanish-speaking country but is now fully American — and can in future tick off the appropriate ethnic box on the census forms). He can keep his religion, as long as it stays private and particular: religious pluralism, rather than a problem, is a sine qua non for Americans, for whom the notion of an official state religion is anathema. Many European states, conversely, require no public pledge or similar display of allegiance (though the idea is making inroads in some countries — e.g., the United Kingdom and Denmark), but instead set up all manner of integration programs, monitor the progress of their reluctantly accepted newcomers, uphold a discourse of national homogeneity, make it very (for the time being: increasingly) hard for immigrants to acquire national citizenship at all, and never really get round to a full-fledged separation between church and state.

In this light, multiculturalism and the politics of multiple belonging in Europe are often seen as either emergency strategies of toleration for the maintenance of continued loyalty to a state or as a process of impending identity fragmentation. In the USA the multiplicity of cultures and the vehemence of identity politics form the backdrop for the maintenance of the hegemony of national identity — the pride in America — since this process of contention and negotiation is an integral, proactive part of what it means to be American.[4] Other states/confederations/groups trying to adopt or imitate American forms of social identity are faced with the difficulty that in their settings and given their historical backgrounds, ethno-cultural multiplicity is either foreign to the national political culture and the founding myths of the nation (say, in Germany, France, or Japan) or is very differently and often much more reactively configured (say, in the United Kingdom, Australia, and China).[5] There may well be a lesson to be learned, but there's no model directly to be copied.

One of the most conspicuous differences between Europe and the States — apart from the historical legacies — is that cultural diversity in Europe has never managed to divest itself of its political casing and implications. Whether by endogenous design or ascriptive consequence (reaction to host society treatment), minority cultures clamoring for recognition have tended to overstep (or been interpreted as overstepping) the line between private and public, culture and politics, heterogeneity and homogeneity, on which the viability of multicultural societies depends. This is linked to the question of the essentialism of these new cultures — identity politics officially bases itself on cultural relativism, but this relativism is often neutralized as far as these subnational group

---

4. Cf. John Hall and Charles Lindholm, *Is America Breaking Apart?* (Princeton: Princeton University Press, 1999).

5. See Flemming Christiansen and Ulf Hedetoft, eds., *The Politics of Multiple Belonging* (forthcoming).

identities and their internal organization are concerned. Where national collectivities are frequently trapped in a kind of hypocritical argumentative loop, between subscribing to both enlightened rationality and *ius sanguinis* organicism, "ethnic" spokespersons for multiculturalism in Europe find themselves confronted by their own contradictory rationale, caught between public relativism and internal absolutism.

The balance between the two forms of political identity configuration is bound to be precarious, liminal, risky. The threats are obvious, the opportunities more limited. If we are to get out of the grips of the current crisis of multiculturalism, the resurgence of communitarian populism, and transcend beyond both traditional nationalism and the potential anomie of "the citizen who does not belong," then we probably have to recognize that standard forms of multiculturalism are passé and that we have to find new ways of organizing — and politically recognizing — social interactions between individuals and cultures, ways that are sensitive both to a global world and to more local forms of identification and belonging. The first prerequisite is to overcome essentialism, the second to acknowledge that it is possible to agree politically but not necessarily culturally (and then do it), and the third to break down antagonistic separations between self and other. I don't have the answer to how to do this in precise terms, and even if I did, I'm not sure a drawing-board model is really the way out — solutions have to be found at the level of hands-on practical, social experiment, and cannot depend on formalized theorems or flowcharts — though debates such as these can hopefully provide some valuable inspiration.

# Beyond the Multireligious — Transculturation and Religious Differentiation: In Search of a New Paradigm in the Academic Study of Religious Change and Interreligious Encounter

## KLAUS HOCK

Before getting into the matter of theoretical reflection, I would like to start with two stories that may help to highlight my point of departure as well as to shed some light on the effects brought about by introducing the category of "transculturation" in the field of religious studies.[1]

## Christianizing Africa or Africanizing Christianity?

### The Case of Andreas Riis: The Ambiguous Result of Religious Change

The first story takes us back to nineteenth-century West Africa. The Basel Mission — at that time quite a new foundation — had embarked on mission projects in the region of the so-called Gold Coast in present-day Ghana. These projects were far from successful: out of nine missionaries sent out between 1828 and 1840, only one survived the onslaught of tropical diseases — Andreas Riis. In his renowned four-volume study on the planting of Christianity in Africa, C. P. Groves gives us just a minor hint as to why Riis may have survived: "Riis' life was despaired of, but thanks to a Negro doctor, he was given treatment that pulled him through."[2] Yet Groves doesn't go into any detail of this successful healing, and he also refrains from any comments on this event. However, this event is not without theological significance: properly speaking, it was an Afri-

1. This paper draws its inspiration from the discussions of a research group of scholars from the universities of Berlin (Humboldt University), Leipzig, and Rostock, especially from a paper that is part of a major research project on "Transculturation — Mission and Modernity in Africa." I am especially indebted to my colleagues, Prof. A. Feldtkeller, Prof. A. Jones, and Prof. A. Wirz.

2. C. P. Groves, *The Planting of Christianity in Africa*, vol. 1 (London/Redhill, 1948), p. 300.

can healer who laid the foundation of Christianity in that region — by practicing not just any sort of healing, but a healing that is deeply rooted in African traditional religion. Therefore we could say that Riis survived by in a way converting to an African religion — he left "his" world of European Christianity for "the other" world — the world of spirits and demons, of herbal medicine and African powers of healing.

I suppose I would meet with heavy opposition in talking about "conversion," being confronted with arguments like: this was not a conversion, healing is just *one* aspect of African religion, and the whole issue is too complex to draw any far-reaching conclusions of theological relevance. However, the last-mentioned argument could open a different perspective — namely, it is just because this issue is so complex that it must not be neglected. Rather, this event shows that in the context of early missionary contact there were variegated processes of communication and interaction between missionaries and locals, and that the faith of those involved wasn't left unaffected by this interaction. This holds true of both locals and missionaries. Therefore, it would be totally misleading to interpret the encounter between Christianity and African religions as a unilateral relationship between an active and powerful religion here and a passive and weak religion there. At the very heart of the issue remains the old question: Are we dealing with the Christianization of African religious traditions or, vice versa, the Africanization of Christianity? Well, maybe this question is neither very new nor very intriguing. But the important issue is that time and again we observe interreligious encounters bringing about religious change without unambiguous results.

## The Christianization of Islam and the Islamization of Christianity

### The Case of Pfander and al-Kairanawi: The Usefulness of the Rival's Weapon

My second story illustrates the fact that in processes of clear, even radical differentiation between religious traditions, important features of the "other" tradition may be used for consolidating and positioning the "own" tradition against the other. Occasionally the rival religion is criticized and attacked with the rival's weapon.[3] A striking example of this is the nineteenth-century controversy be-

3. This is the title of a German study analyzing the Kairanawi-Pfander controversy by Christine Schirrmacher, *Mit den Waffen des Gegners. Christlich-muslimische Kontroversen im 19. und 20. Jahrhundert* (Berlin, 1992).

tween the Christian missionary Karl Gottlieb Pfander and the Muslim scholar al-Kairanawi. While Pfander held to a conservative biblicistic view of the Bible, his opponent was very much acquainted with the contemporary debate on historical-critical exegesis in European academic theology. There al-Kairanawi found all the arguments he needed to challenge Pfander's view: on the basis of traditional Muslim understanding of scripture, he used the findings of modern historical research to corroborate the charge of *tahrîf* (that is, the accidental or deliberate alteration of the Scriptures in the Christian tradition) and to question the legitimacy of the biblical Scriptures generally. Pfander had to surrender — he had nothing to set against al-Kairanawi's arguments. Consequently, for Pfander the controversy ended in a disaster — which he was eager to gloss over in the public reports he sent back to Europe. Despite the fact that this controversy had deepened the alienation between Christianity and Islam, it had nevertheless taken place in a tense field of religious encounter providing the necessary tools for al-Kairanawi's apologetics: al-Kairanawi had adapted the methods of modern Christian theology in order to use them against Christianity. Ironically enough, al-Kairanawi's "Christianized" apologetics encountered a traditional-biblicistic, nearly "Islamic" understanding of Scripture on the part of Pfander.

## The Study of Religious Chance and the "Cultural Turn"

Dealing with questions of religious change and interreligious encounter is part and parcel of religious studies. In "classical" history of religions, Günter Lanczkowski had developed a "typology of religious chance" in order to categorize various forms of religious change.[4] Likewise, Michael Pye had suggested a model of typical processes in interreligious intercourse by distinguishing between contact, ambiguity, and recoupment.[5] But then the discourse in religious studies didn't focus anymore so much on types of religious contacts; rather, the question of religious change was dealt with under the category of syncretisms.[6] So far, however, the debate about syncretisms has not proved very fruitful — at least as far as religious studies is concerned. Consequently, some scholars of religion suggested that syncretisms as an analytical category be dropped and its usage restricted to theological discourses.[7]

4. G. Lanczkowski, *Begegnung und Wandel der Religionen* (Düsseldorf and Cologne, 1971).
5. M. Pye, "The Transplantation of Religion," *Numen* 16 (1969): 234-39.
6. For example, see M. Pye, "Syncretism and Ambiguity," *Numen* 18 (1971): 83-93; Pye, "Syncretism versus Synthesis," *Method and Theory in the Study of Religion* 6 (1994): 217-29.
7. R. D. Baird, "Syncretism and the History of Religions," *Journal of Religious Thought* 24 (1967/68): 42-53.

In fact, theology seems to be more flexible in this respect — at least at first glance. Time and again theology had to deal with questions of religious chance in the context of the missionary expansion of Christianity, thereby developing a broad variety of concepts, like adaptation, accommodation, indigenization, inculturation, contextualization, incarnation, or communication. But time and again, all these concepts had to face harsh criticism. Maybe this has to do with the problem of developing a conclusive concept that could provide plain and unequivocal categories for the study of religious chance. For example, theological discourses talking about inculturation occasionally distinguish between successful and abortive inculturation. However, this distinction discloses more information on the position of the one making use of it than on the issue itself.

The debate about religious change and interreligious relations has recently been affected by the dynamics of another debate — the discussion on the understanding of "religion," generally.[8] This debate has to be seen against the background of major changes in the academic landscape, namely, the so-called cultural turn:[9] since the early 1990s, the focus of academic research has shifted to culture and cultural dimensions. Consequently, once-peripheral topics have now moved into the very center of academic interest. This is especially the case with religions and religious studies.[10] All of a sudden the focal point is on religions — religions as alleged or real agencies of regional tensions and global conflicts, religions in the shape of so-called new religious movements, or religions in relation to questions of immigration and cultural integration of Muslim, Hindu, or Buddhist immigrants into Europe. Furthermore, the cultural turn in the humanities has had its impact on the academic study of religions, inasmuch as religious studies are now more and more understood as a "social/cultural anthropological discipline" dealing with religions as cultural phenomena.

The cultural turn in the humanities (and consequently in religious studies) isn't just a fashionable trend but rather a reaction to political and social challenges arising from processes of religious pluralization in the context of

8. See, for example, the introductory remarks in W. Braun and R. T. McCutcheon, eds., *Guide to the Study of Religion* (London and New York, 1999).

9. For the German context, cf. M. Lackner and M. Werner, *Der* cultural turn *in den Humanwissenschaften, Area Studies im Auf- oder Abwind des Kulturalismus?* (Bad Homburg, 1999).

10. Again, for the German context cf. H. G. Kippenberg and B. Gladigow, "Herausforderung Religion," in *Religionswissenschaft. Forschung und Lehre an den Hochschulen in Deutschland. Eine Dokumentation,* ed. Deutsche Gesellschaft für Religionsgeschichte (Marburg, 2001), pp. 7-21.

cultural interaction. Consequently, phenomena like the encounter between religions, religious change, inventions and ruptures of religious traditions, etc., have developed enormous dynamics. In order to keep pace with these dynamics, we have to think of new concepts and paradigms for analysis and interpretation. Both the causes and the effects of processes of religious interaction have to be analyzed as specific modes of intercultural interaction. For this purpose, it is suggested that the category of transculturation be introduced.

## Religion and Transculturation

### *The Phenomenon of Transculturation:*
### *Processes of "Othering" in the Colonial Context*

Transculturation is not a new phenomenon. It can be found throughout the history of mankind. Nevertheless, transcultural processes were a salient feature in the colonial period. Consequently, transculturation was at the very heart of the encounter between Christianity and other cultures and religions. Despite its universal claim, Christianity — being deeply marked by European and North American history — was part and parcel of the "twin project" of colonialism and modernization.

In this historical context, missionaries were important agents of transculturation: as critics or even losers of modernization, they were suspicious of it. But in the so-called mission field in Africa and elsewhere, they acted as agents of it.[11] The significance of mission for colonialism and modernization is evident in the missionaries' close communication with the indigenous population which made them the most important agents of "Western" modernity.

On the other hand, the missionaries were dependent on "local" expertise and support, thereby being more and more tied into indigenous networks. Consequently they became agents of both the European impact *and* local interests, thereby imparting European knowledge to the indigenous population and communicating local knowledge to the outside world.[12] Conversely the indigenous population made use of the missionaries for its own purposes, and more often than not, indigenous people acted as agents of chance — think of the

11. For case studies see P. Jenkins, "Villagers as Missionaries: Wurtemberg Pietism as a 19th Century Missionary Movement," *Missiology* 8, no. 4 (1980): 425-32, or W. Ustorf, ed., *Mission im Kontext* (Bremen, 1986).

12. See P. Jenkins, ed., *The Recovery of the West African Past: African Pastors and African History in the Nineteenth Century* (Basel, 1988).

mission activities of indigenous evangelists, think of "Western" education used by the indigenous population as a means of political mobilization, or think of congregations being used as a means of enhancing new forms of solidarity.[13]

The transculturation paradigm has far-reaching consequences for the analysis of religious change and interreligious relations in the context of modern (Christian) mission history: the modern missionary movement is a prominent example of multifaceted processes perpetually transforming cultural and religious identities by destruction, change, and new formation. This transformation takes place in a situation where both missionaries and locals are crossing boundaries, thereby prompting dynamic exchange *and* differentiation. In the course of colonial and mission history, the production of cultural/religious difference coupled with processes of "othering" has created discourses focusing on the radical "otherness" of non-Western cultures as opposed to Western modernity. In recent years some of these discourses have been critically reexamined and dismantled by critical investigation — think of the "invention of traditions."[14] Others still have to be analyzed — like those discourses that talk about "Western modernity," thereby denying any share of the non-Occidental world in the emergence of modernity. Instead of dealing with categories of otherness or stressing the difference between Western modernity and non-Western cultures, the concept of transculturation tries to rediscover the interrelationship of European and indigenous agencies and discourses, thereby highlighting the emergence not of "Western modernity," but of entangled modernities.

## *The Concept of Transculturation: Social Constructs and Open Processes*

Transculturation is not a new concept. As a technical term, it was introduced in the 1940s by the Cuban sociologist Fernando Ortiz, the pioneering scholar of Afro-Cuban studies.[15] However, the origins of the concept can be traced back to the nineteenth century, namely, to Frederick Jackson Turner. According to his so-called *frontier* theory, the American national character originated at the frontier: that is, in the context of confrontation between white settlers on the

13. For case studies see P. Harries, "Exclusion, Classification and Internal Colonialism: The Emergence of Ethnicity among the Tsona-Speakers of South Africa," in *The Creation of Tribalism in Southern Africa,* ed. L. Vail (London, 1989), pp. 82-117.

14. E. Hobsbawm and T. O. Ranger, eds., *The Invention of Tradition* (Cambridge, 1983).

15. F. Ortiz, *Cuban Counterpoint: Tobacco and Sugar* (Durham, 1995). For extensive bibliographical references, see http://www.afrocubaweb.com/ortiz.htm.

one hand and Red Indians and the wilderness on the other.[16] Evidently this was a rather colonialist theory. But it moved the focus from the metropolitan centers of the East Coast to the peripheries of the settlements in the far, "wild" West. By rejecting the approach of Melville Herskovits and his concept of acculturation,[17] Ortiz had in a similar way moved from a metropolitan perspective to one that focused on processes of cultural change and intercultural transformation in peripheral contexts: here he observed what he referred to as transculturation which included both processes of reciprocal acculturation and processes of deprivation (de-culturation) as well as processes of creation (neoculturation) of cultural phenomena. Along this line the concept of transculturation was picked up by Mary Louise Pratt in her study *Imperial Eyes*.[18] According to her analysis, the emergence of central values of "Western" modernity is due to processes of transculturation in "contact zones" at the very periphery of the colonial empires.

The concept of transculturation radically renounces any approaches that consider culture as a clearly definable unit and that tend to identify "culture" and "society" by attributing to each society a specific inherent culture. These approaches run the danger of transforming culture into an essentialistic, static "something" of immutable substance beyond time and space, thereby qualifying cultural difference as something "given." From the perspective of transculturation, however, culture is understood as a social construct and a result of multiple exchanges. Consequently, cultural difference is not something "given." It is rather a discursive creation with a history that can be researched as it is created by processes of "othering." These processes are taking place in the context of a complex communication between various agents — and therefore, the outcome of these processes is quite open and may result in syncretisms and synthesis or in demarcation and isolation. Encounter engenders change, though this change may bring about conflict as well as concurrence. This is due to the fact that transculturation is an open, multidirectional process.

Needless to say, transculturation transcends concepts of cross-culturality as well as multiculturality that cling to an understanding of cultures as homogeneous units. In a way this is even the case with approaches dealing with intercultural processes: intercultural perspectives still take their point of departure from cultures as open and changing entities, but nevertheless as entities. Furthermore, intercultural perspectives focus on processes "between" cultures

16. F. J. Turner, *The Significance of the Frontier in American History* (Ann Arbor, 1966; microfilm reprint of 1893 edition).

17. M. I. Herskovits, *Acculturation: The Study of Cultural Contact* (New York, 1938).

18. M. L. Pratt, *Imperial Eyes: Travel Writing and Transculturation* (London, 1992).

whereas transculturation deals with the dynamics between cultural processes, starting from the observation that "culture" is a social construct created by the concurrence of multiple discourses.

## Transculturation and Religious Studies: Analyzing Religious Change and Interreligious Encounters

So far, transcultural approaches have primarily been put to the test on the level of microstudies, focusing on individual biographies of missionaries and/or indigenous evangelists as loci where processes of cultural transformation can be traced.[19] Nevertheless, transculturation may likewise provide a paradigm relevant to the analysis of religious change on a macro level: the encounter between religions, interreligious relations, religious change and religious pluralism can be referred to as nodal points of "thick" — that is, tense and complex — processes of transculturation.[20] By analyzing these processes, we may gain deeper insights into the dynamics of religious phenomena. Furthermore, the concept of transculturation as an analytical instrument in the study of religious change implies a criticism of the traditional understanding of "religion": in transcultural perspective, religion is not seen as a static unit, as something "given" that can be approached by analyzing its supposed "substance" or "essence." Rather, religion is understood as a product of manifold, multidirectional processes of exchange and interaction. Likewise, as with cultural difference, religious difference is seen as a creation of discourses, the history of which can be researched as it presupposes processes of "othering." This "othering," however, is not a unilateral process but must be seen as a process of complementary discourses: the other's religion — like one's own — is part and parcel of a polycontextual world, and the manifold processes of interaction and exchange bring about changes for *all* involved. Consequently, the results of this cultural/religious differentiation are multifaceted and multifarious. This is due to the

---

19. See the studies in R. Alsheimer and G. Rohdenburg, eds., *LebensProzesse. Biografisches aus der Geschichte der Bremer Westafrika-Mission* (Bremen, 2001), or R. Alsheimer, ed., *Körperlichkeit und Kultur* (Bremen, 2001).

20. For more details and bibliographical information, see K. Hock, "Religion als transkulturelles Phänomen. Implikationen eines kulturwissenschaftlichen Paradigmas in der Religionsforschung," *Berliner Theologische Zeitschrift* 19, no. 1 (2001): 64-82, and as to the interrelation between transculturation and "migration" as an analytical category: Hock, "Catching the Wind: Some Remarks on the Growing Interface of Migration Studies and Studies on African Religions," in *European Traditions of the Study of Religion in Africa*, ed. A. Adogame and F. Ludwig (forthcoming).

fact that transculturation takes its course in processes, which are open and multidirectional, bringing about correlations with a homogenizing or intensifying effect as well as correlations characterized by contradictory, tense, or even mutually annihilating relations.

Transculturation is neither restricted to the historical period of colonialism nor to interreligious encounters in the context of the modern missionary movement. Firstly, in its history of twenty centuries Christianity as a missionary religion has repeatedly experienced the "crossing of boundaries" between cultures and religions, and during this enormous span of time has "produced" a variety of centers and peripheries. In this respect Christianity experienced processes of transculturation long before the modern missionary movement. Secondly, phenomena like the crossing of boundaries or the generation of centers and peripheries can just as well be observed in other religions. Though we should be cautious to transfer notions like "mission" into other religious contexts, the phenomenon of "missionary expansion" is not restricted to the history of Christianity. Consequently we have to deal with a complex interaction in the shape of mutual crossing of cultural and religious boundaries in the context of Jewish, Christian, Muslim, Buddhist, Hindu, etc., expansion.[21] In this perspective we could even understand transculturation as a basic pattern of the history of religions.

## Transculturation as a Normative and Analytical Category

So far we have dealt with "transculturation" as a category facilitating the investigation into the interactions and transfers between cultures. In this respect it does not refer to something like the smallest common denominator beyond the specifics of different cultures. Such a concept could be — and indeed, is — a legitimate category in search of "transcultural" values and principles which are shared beyond boundaries: by providing procedures of identifying intercultural processes of a dynamic concurrence in the area of moral values and ethics, transculturation would function as a means of establishing common grounds in interreligious dialogue. This seems to be one of the objectives of a major interdisciplinary research project at the University of Tübingen, which started just this year — a so-called postgraduate college *(Graduiertencolleg)* entitled "Global Challenges — Transnational and Transcultural Approaches." Here "transculturation" would not serve as an analytical-

---

21. A. Feldtkeller, "Mission aus der Perspektive der Religionswissenschaft," *Zeitschrift für Missionswissenschaft und Religionswissenschaft* 85 (2001): 83-98.

descriptive category but as a synthetic-normative category: as a creative concept, transculturation is supposed to generate shared values by mobilizing cultural resources that are in line with the purpose of working toward the formation of a "global ethos."

Transculturation as a normative concept starts with the observation that the global challenges by far surpass the capacities of political transnational institutions to appropriately deal with these challenges. Consequently there is a demand for tapping the resources of philosophy, ethics, and religions in order to get support for the task of establishing values, principles, and guidelines to promote understanding and cooperation on a global level. Transculturation in this context refers to an approach where (1) global problems are analyzed from different perspectives, taking into account the ethical dimension (preferably from a multidisciplinary perspective), and where (2) analysis and description of global problems find "solutions" on the basis of norms rooted in a global ethics (preferably from an interdisciplinary perspective). The major frame of reference for this concept of transculturation is the globalization paradigm. In this context transculturation serves as a means of integrating the ethical contributions of different cultural traditions into the design of a global ethics, thereby providing orientation beyond cultural peculiarities.

This understanding of transculturation is different from understanding it as an analytical category. This is not to say that we could or should clearly *separate* the descriptive-analytical usage of transculturation from a synthetic-normative usage. But I would suggest that we *distinguish* between both approaches, usages, and implications of "transculturation" in these two contexts and the discourses involved. Again, this is not to say that the descriptive-analytical usage lacks any normative dimensions or that the synthetic-normative usage lacks any analytical qualities. But the two concepts focus on different aspects, and they serve different aims and objectives.

Transculturation as a synthetic-normative category takes effect in the framework of the globalization paradigm. It aims at integrating varied traditions of heterogeneous origin into a model of universal moral orientation. *Cum grano salis,* we could refer to this kind of transculturation as a "deductive" model, brought into alignment with the concept of global ethics and focusing on convergences.

Transculturation as an analytical-descriptive category sets its own framework by referring to synthesizing or concurring as well as pluralizing or contradicting, even mutually neutralizing processes of translation, adaptation, redefinition, and appropriation engendered by the encounter between people coming from different cultural and religious backgrounds. It aims at dissecting both heterogeneous and homogenizing transformations, specifically taking into account aspects of diversity and particularity. *Cum grano salis,* we could refer to this kind of transculturation as an "inductive" model, which is oriented toward the dialectics of globalization versus particularization and focusing on divergences.

Considering the manifold challenges of religious change and pluralization as well as the unprecedented dynamics of interreligious encounter, both concepts of transculturation are of crucial significance for developing new means of analysis and interpretation on the one hand, and of dialogue and orientation on the other. Nevertheless, as mentioned above, I would suggest that we do not have to separate, but to distinguish between, the usages and implications of "transculturation" in these two contexts. Only then may it provide a paradigm that could link different discourses — without merging them — by examining the potential reciprocity of category formation and value orientation.

## Conclusion: Beyond Multireligiosity

In the context of international migration and accelerated globalization in the second half of the twentieth century, the unprecedented dynamics of religious change has brought about new challenges to the academic study of religions. In order to keep pace with these dynamics, I introduced the category of transculturation.

As outlined above, the concept of transculturation transcends discourses dealing with cross-cultural, multicultural, or intercultural dimensions by understanding culture as a social construct and result of multiple exchanges. Consequently transculturation as an open and multidirectional process addresses correspondences as well as divergences, synthesis as well as contrasts, hybridization as well as closure — including what a colleague of mine referred to as "the virtues of mutual misunderstandings."[22] The same holds true if the concept of transculturation is applied to religions. The dynamics of the history of religions has brought forth a situation beyond multireligiosity: religion(s) — both one's own and the "religion of the other" — can no longer be studied as clearly identifiable entities — but as something that is part of a "polycontextual world." Religions are to be seen as (trans)cultural phenomena that are in ceaseless flux and permanent change, with their alleged "substance" de-

22. A. Wirz in his "Transculturation or the Art of Misunderstanding" (paper read at the Seventeenth International Biennial Conference of the African Studies Association, on "Africa's Diversity: Ending the Monologues?" University of Hamburg, May 23-26, 2002).

riving from processes of transcultural communication. Therefore we will have to abandon static concepts and "essentialistic" categories in favor of dynamic categorizing qualifications. "Transculturation" may provide such a category. So far it has not been strangled by theoretical debates. Its parameters and criteria still have to be worked out. But it's worthwhile trying, if we want to accept the challenge of coming to grips with the dynamics of a phenomenon that is characterized by tremendous transitory qualities transcending conventional categories, namely, religious change and interreligious relations in a pluralistic context. For this purpose we need fresh insights from cooperative research in the field of the academic study of religions. Maybe this cooperation will have to go beyond interdisciplinary research, unfolding perspectives and programs of transdisciplinary approaches. This, however, is beyond the scope of this paper.

# Cases

# The Multireligious Multicultural Society: A Case Study of Birmingham, England

CHRIS HEWER

This paper will look at issues in the multireligious situation of Birmingham, one of a growing number of cities in Europe that must rank amongst the most cosmopolitan that have ever existed in world history. It will describe the multireligious nature of the city and seek to present trends within social, cultural, economic, and religious paradigms. The hitherto unique situation of British citizenship that was enjoyed by immigrants to the United Kingdom is now being extended through the acquisition of citizenship of many other European countries and thus citizenship of the European Union.

In England the concepts of multicultural and multireligious society are not necessarily the same thing. Because of Britain's long history as a worldwide imperial power and through her ongoing links to the British Commonwealth and the European Union as well as being a favored place for refugees and asylum seekers, it is common to have many different cultural groups within a single religious community. For example, there are Christian communities in Birmingham from Italy, Ireland, Germany, Poland, Serbia, Greece, Cyprus, Russia, Pakistan, India, Vietnam, various countries in Africa, and the Caribbean islands. Christian services are conducted weekly in at least ten different languages. Thus we can speak of multicultural Christianity in Birmingham. A similar pattern would emerge for the other diffused world religions such as Buddhism and Islam. There are more than five thousand Buddhists in Birmingham drawn from fourteen different schools of Buddhism, with discrete ethnic groups from Burma, India, Sri Lanka, Tibet, Vietnam, Japan, Korea, and Cambodia. The largest communities of Muslims are from Pakistan, Bangladesh, and India, but the oldest is from Yemen, as well as smaller communities from Afghanistan, Albania, Algeria, Bosnia, Palestine, Iraq, Iran, Nigeria, Somalia, the Sudan, Malaysia, Turkey, and so on. In addition, there are groups who have migrated from other European countries where they first settled and gained European citizenship after being originally refugees from a non-European country; for example, a number of Somalis have moved to Birmingham from Belgium and Holland. Also, white and black British converts to Buddhism and Islam bring another dimension to the multicultural multireligious equation. The situation is further diversified by the presence of Asians who spent some generations in East Africa before moving to Britain and a growing number of multi-ethnic marriages producing such combinations as Irish-German-American Buddhists and Irish-Egyptian-Pakistani Muslims.

To give a focus to this paper, I want to concentrate on the multireligious society of Birmingham. This city has about a million inhabitants and is set in the industrial region of the West Midlands, which has a total population of around three million. In the city itself there are reckoned to be about 120,000 Muslims, 45,000 Sikhs, 40,000 Hindus, 5,000 plus Buddhists, 2,600 Jews, about 200 Jain families, as well as smaller communities of Baha'is and Zoroastrians. The 60,000 African and African-Caribbean people have predominantly Christian heritage, but many are Muslim and some are Rastafarian and followers of African traditional religions. Due to the unique relationship between Britain and the Commonwealth, many immigrants came with or were able to apply for full British citizenship. Direct immigration to Britain was halted nearly forty years ago, so we are now well into the second and third generations to be born in Britain; as such, these people have automatic British citizenship. The vast majority of such people in Birmingham today enjoy the full rights of British citizenship and thus have a permanent stake in our British society. This can be seen, by way of example, in the religious buildings of these minority religions. Birmingham has some 115 mosques, 10 of which are purpose-built as such with Islamic architecture, plus 3 more currently under construction. We have the largest Sikh *gurdwara* anywhere outside India, with a total capacity approaching 20,000 people. We have a Burmese-style Buddhist pagoda with an attached purpose-built Theravadian monastery.

The Muslim community makes up about 12 percent of the total city population, but Muslim children constitute 24 percent of the school population. We estimate that over 50 percent of the Muslim population of Britain are under twenty-five years, and that it will at least double in size before it achieves demographic stability, that is, the same number being born as die each year. This means for the future a stable Muslim population in Birmingham of perhaps 250,000 people. The City Council already accepts that Birmingham will become a black and Asian majority city before the year 2020.

One of the issues this raises is the concentration of this black and Asian population in the inner city, the region within a three-kilometer radius of the city center. By way of example, Birmingham is divided into thirty-nine electoral districts. Taking the number of Muslim children (five to eleven years old) in state primary schools in each district, we get an indication of concentration, given that people tend to send their young children to a neighborhood primary school. Muslim children are concentrated in seven districts, in which they make up more than 50 percent of the children. These are all concentrated in the inner-city area. In the highest concentration, 83 percent of the primary school-children are Muslim. It is therefore not surprising that several schools have 100 percent Muslim pupils, and many have 70-plus percent. A child growing up in an Asian Muslim family in such an area will live within, for example, a Pakistani-heritage cultural world up to the age of five, then go to a 100 percent Asian Muslim primary school before transferring to a predominantly Asian Muslim secondary school. Such a child could reach sixteen years of age without having friends from any other community. There is a real question here of education as a preparation for making one's way in wider British society.

When thinking of inner-city areas, we cannot separate religious identity from various forms of social and economic deprivation. The inner city of Birmingham consists largely of nineteenth-century housing with water and sewage systems from the same era, and a street pattern that predates the motor car. Small houses often contain large families, with the demands this places on public services such as health, education, and recreation. Many of the first generation of migrants came as manual workers, but the unskilled jobs for which they were brought have largely disappeared, leading to high levels of unemployment, thus depriving the young people of the role models of working elders within their immediate society. Because of post–Second World War housing clearance and redevelopment, many of the poor white families from the inner city were moved out to new housing estates on the outer fringes of the city in the 1960s. This can lead to perhaps more deprived social conditions in these outer estates than in the nineteenth-century inner city. It is in these predominantly white outer estates that Britain's neo-Fascist and racist groups tend to flower and recruit members. The potential for a lack of social integration and thus possible racist tension is obvious.

When thinking of interreligious relations, we cannot think only of Christian relations with the minority faiths. The current situation in Israel-Palestine has an impact on Jewish-Muslim relations in the city. The tensions in the Indian state of Gujarat remind us that Muslims, Sikhs, and Hindus on the Indian subcontinent have a long history of living together and sometimes erupting into communal violence. Given global communications, it is not unusual that tensions in the subcontinent have their ramifications on the streets of Birmingham.

We must be concerned with not only interreligious relations but also intrareligious relations. It is only in the diaspora that fourteen different schools of Buddhism could interact, reflecting the huge variety that has developed within that religion from the same original teacher and scriptures. Muslims from Pakistan must come to terms with Muslims from Bosnia, Albania, and Kosovo, who have developed quite different Muslim cultural norms. Hindus from quite different schools are forced to set up "ecumenical temples" in a way that would not happen in India. Incidentally, Christians are faced with questions about what to do with church buildings made redundant because of the shift of population; could these, for example, be sold to other religious traditions as places of worship?

Turning to economic, cultural, and political questions, we are faced with yet another dimension of interreligious relations. Many descendants of immigrants have set up substantial commercial enterprises; the Institute of Asian Businesses in Birmingham represents a significant economic force in our society. Should such businesses continue to employ and serve largely their own communities, or should they play a part in the integration of the workforce and consumer base? Birmingham is a world center for the Asian music industry; Asian-language cinemas abound; and there is a growing presence of Asian people in the arts and literature. In some parts of the city it is entirely possible to live a life in a cultural context that is far from traditionally British; for example, one can do all one's shopping and visit a doctor, dentist, optician, lawyer, accountant, post office, or bank all within an Urdu-language Pakistani cultural context. Muslims have for more than a decade been proportionally represented by councilors on the City Council, but these have all traditionally served the Labour Party. In recent years a new phenomenon has arisen with Kashmiri councilors being elected on a single-issue Kashmiri political basis. This can lead to communalism in politics: Muslim councilors aiming to represent only their own community and seeking to advance their causes in city political life.

The channels of communication between British resident communities and those in the countries of origin operate in both directions. Not only are people in Britain affected by events in the countries of origin, but successful patterns of cooperation and living together developed in Britain can have their effect back in the traditional homelands as well. With successive generations being born in Britain, the links with the countries of their grandparents weaken year on year. New ways of living are being developed by which many people have multiple identities, being, for example, British, citizens of the European Union, of Pakistani heritage, and Muslims belonging to the worldwide Muslim community. However this develops, it is clear that there is no going back, and these minority communities are part of the British landscape of the future.

Our European religious history of the last five hundred years is one in which we have dealt with religious difference by segregation and thus ignoring "the other." This can be seen in Germany, Switzerland, France, and Ireland as well as the English religious settlement and the Scandinavian experience. Clearly this will not work in cities like Birmingham in the future. We are embarked on the greatest unplanned sociological experiment in Europe in the last five hundred years, and have no ground plan to see how such diverse communities should develop. We are breaking new ground and learning as we go along.

To end with, I would like to draw attention to a growing paradigm shift in Birmingham society. Until now the minority communities have largely been concerned with their own establishment and setting up their own cultural, social, economic, and religious institutions. The churches, especially the Church of England, have seen themselves as the sole custodians of the spiritual and religious heritage of society. Given the rapidly changing religious landscape of the city, we are now on the threshold of a paradigm shift that will require members of other faith communities to take a share in the responsibility for the social, cultural, spiritual, and moral welfare of the whole of our society. We will have to ask what these religious traditions have to contribute to the common good of British society. What do they have to offer to the development of a truly human life in Britain, not just for their own members but for everyone, including the growing number of people who would describe themselves as secular and nonreligious?

# Confession, Tradition, and Perspectives: Response and Reflection of Afro-Americans to the Age of Religious Pluralism

CALEB OLADIPO

During the second half of the twentieth century, two schools of thought emerged in the study of people of African origin and their beliefs. (1) The first school is the Afrocentric school championed by cultural anthropologists.[1] This school sees Africa as the ancestral home of black people in the diaspora.[2] One of the most celebrated leaders of this Afrocentric school, also known as Africanism,[3] was Melville J. Herskovits. The contention of this school is that the experiences, religions, worldviews, and values of Afro-Americans may best be seen in light of clearly defined traditions and lifestyles that have defined them over time and migrated with them to every part of the world, beginning in the era of enslavement. (2) The second school of thought is simply termed "Atlanticism."[4] The chief proponents of this school are predominantly sociologists of religion. These scholars agree with the Afrocentric school that Africa is the ancestral home of black people in the world. They believe, however, that the currents of a dynamic world have altered the religious beliefs and cultures of Afro-Americans. In his book *The Negro Church in America,* published in 1963,

1. See Isidore Okpewho, Carole Boyce Davies, and Ali A. Mazrui, eds., *The African Diaspora: African Origins and New World Identities* (Indianapolis: Indiana University Press, 1999). Many entries in this work suggested that the first school of thought is Afrocentric.

2. In this paper I am using this term "diaspora" to denote black people in the United States, in Cuba, and in Brazil. This is because people of African descent in these parts of the world exhibit unique religious identities that are different from the black people of the parent continent of Africa as well as those in Europe or Asia.

3. Africanism is the study of those elements of culture found in the New World that are traceable to an African origin. This area of cultural anthropology has been a neglected but not uncontroversial area of academic inquiry in the United States. It was resurrected in 1941 when Melville J. Herskovits published a pioneering work, *The Myth of the Negro Past* (Boston: Beacon Press, 1958; originally published in 1941).

4. Herskovits, *The Myth of the Negro Past.*

E. Franklin Frazier articulated the view that during slavery Afro-Americans lost one identity — their African heritage or the quality of their "Africanness" — and acquired another, being Americans. He postulated in this hypothesis of de-culturization, therefore, that Afro-American worldviews evolved independently of an African influence because slavery was so devastating in America that it destroyed all African elements among Afro-Americans: it destroyed the African family institution and the indigenous African social and religious structure. It also put blacks in close contact with whites, from whom Afro-Americans learned new patterns of thought and behavior that they subsequently adapted to their own cultural and religious idioms.[5]

In the past decade or so a new school of thought called the "Atlanticist school" has taken Frazier's view to a new level of scholarship. It is too simplistic, the Atlanticists claimed, to say that the dynamic culture and religious currents of the Western civilization have not influenced people of African descent as they have influenced all other people in the Western Hemisphere. They contend that there has been a cross-fertilization of religious and cultural ideas. As Isidore Okpewho states, "It seems only reasonable to expect that, after so many centuries of expatriation from Africa, the New World Black sensibility would find it increasingly difficult to keep faith with its ancestral sources (which, we must add, have scarcely remained the same), given the urgency of contingent forces. After a while it becomes hard to draw lines, with any degree of calibrative accuracy, between what is *truly* African and what is not, despite our most cherished ideological convictions."[6]

Like all others in the Western Hemisphere, Afro-Americans have been influenced by modernity and the pluralistic age of the Western societies in a way that has implications on the essence of Afro-American religious life and identity. Thus, in the several centuries that black people have been living in the Western societies, their belief systems have not remained intact and pure. There is a further complication that would be of interest to both Atlanticists and Afrocentric advocates alike. It is of theoretical relevance to religious historians that African cultural and religious history is not solely dependent on indigenous roots. Societies in Africa have long been shaped by major external forces and have been subjected to nonindigenous factors stemming from the neighboring continents of Asia and Europe even before the enslavement years.[7] Thus African civilization itself has been shaped by great migrations of

---

5. E. Franklin Frazier, *The Negro Church in America* (Boston, 1963).

6. Isidore Okpewho, introduction to *The African Diaspora*, p. xviii.

7. See J. D. Fage, with William Tordoff, *A History of Africa*, 4th ed. (London: Routledge, 2002). Chap. 1 is especially helpful because the authors discuss the origins of African society.

people across waters and from distant lands, from other continents and cultures.

The argument of this paper is that Afro-Americans, in their coexistence with a broad spectrum of different peoples, religions, and the currents of multiculturalism, with cultural and religious cross-fertilization from various parts of the world, have themselves been able to fashion a new religious culture in response to what they have encountered in an age of religious pluralism. Their response does not merely depend on the religious categories of their ancestral home or on the hybrid religious climate that has inevitably become their "home" away from home, but on a cross-fertilization and creative mingling of both.

Afro-Americans have responded to the age of religious pluralism by looking into their religious roots in Africa and culling a new religious identity that owes its creation to the multiplicity associated with the age of religious pluralism itself. It seems that the issue of extracting an African religious identity, however, is beclouded by at least two forces of Euro-American intellectual property. (1) The first is the very habit of Afro-Americans to search for their identity within the Atlanticist tradition in a nebulous air of postmodern doubt. When African Americans do this, they restrict their religious identity to a category that only theorizes blackness and excludes Afro-Americans from all but the periphery of a true embrace of their African religious roots. This means that one cannot claim that Afro-Americans are no longer "Africans" because they read the works of Jacques Derrida, shop at Prada, drink Coca-Cola, and watch David Letterman's late night show.[8] The Western historical conditions that have shaped the Afro-American religious experience have not obliterated or negated the energy of the past in Afro-American religious expression. The Afro-Americans, the Afro-Europeans, the Afro-Asians, and all Africans abroad everywhere do not stop being "Africans" because they are various and live in different locations.

(2) The second intellectual force forming the response of Afro-Americans is the tradition that celebrates the dissolution of the walls between various religious identities in our pluralistic age. Religions have scent and sound of permanent "essentials" in their particularity and identifiable language, although the word "religion" itself is a bad noun, whereas the word "religious" is a good adjective. There is something fixed and eternal in the particulars within the mixture of multireligiosity and multiculturalism.

In responding to the age of religious pluralism, Afro-Americans belong as

---

8. Michael J. C. Echeruo, "An African Diaspora: The Ontological Project," in *The African Diaspora*, pp. 3-18.

perfectly to this new age as to the religious world of the African peoples. They call themselves Christian, Muslim, and Jew. Yet they accept gladly their link with the people they believe are their kin in a distant land of Africa.

As one looks closely at the response of Afro-Americans to the age of religious pluralism and draws insights into the sources of periodic conflicts between Christianity and Islam in black religious consciousness, for example, one must ask the following questions: (a) What does it mean to say that one has African ancestry in a religiously pluralistic culture? (b) Is one's ancestry enough to account for certain psychic factors associated with one's encounter with the divine in a different religious tradition? In other words, does one have to be of African birth to be religious in a certain way? (c) How did Africans manage to create a viable religious life for themselves after they were enslaved in the Americas? (d) How were they able to negotiate the social, political, cultural, and spiritual encounter in the world of multireligiosity? (e) What criteria are we to use to measure their success, as they coexisted with other peoples that unkind forces of history and social circumstances have forced them to live with since 1619? (f) How successful have they actually been? These questions and our responses to them could not possibly be exhaustive, even though enormous attention has been paid to this subject in academic circles, symposia, and international academic conferences such as this one.

All in all, it is rather clear that Afro-Americans and their progeny confronted a host of religious environments and built a dynamic religious life for themselves. A more practical question beneath the threshold of intellectual awareness suggests a bigger and more fundamental issue: How did Afro-Americans build a religious life on ideologies of selfhood that have guided their efforts to adjust to the world in which they find themselves? In other words, what ideology of selfhood guided their efforts? How did they respond to the age of religious pluralism in a spiritual way? Isidore Okpewho gave one answer when he stated that "the slaves held on stubbornly to their ancestral mores not only as a political statement but [also] as a psychological necessity, and found ways of masking their African customs with superficial veneer of European icons when their owners sought to erase their African memories. Long after emancipation, and during reconstruction, the old sense of roots continued to express itself even when time had steadily taken a toll on memories of Africa."[9]

African-descended Americans found an outlet for reassuring themselves of indigenous values they found lacking both in the culture of those who controlled their lives and in freedom. Therefore the cliché that "it was easier to get the Israelites out of Egypt than for Moses to get Egypt out of the Israelites" is

---

9. Okpewho, p. xv.

not only applicable to the nonreligious life of Afro-Americans. The religious energy of the past was not destroyed by geographical boundaries. But one could say, as some scholars have said, that Afro-Americans have been practicing "anti-racist racism"[10] in their religious and political beliefs. What is clear is that Afro-Americans have responded to the age of religious pluralism in at least three ways: (1) in their confession and profession of the essential categories of the Christian faith, the Islamic faith, and Judaism; (2) in rearticulating the religious traditions traceable to their ancestral home in Africa, and cross-fertilizing the old with the new traditions; and (3) in ideological, political, and social perspectives.

## Confession and Profession of Christianity

The profession of an African-centered interpretation of the Christian faith in the Western world by Afro-Americans is more an act of confession and reaffirmation of the Christian faith in the age of religious pluralism than an assimilation of European cultures and Protestant Christianity. If we would move beyond the actual historical circumstances that have called "the black interpretation" of Christianity into play, we would find ourselves in the zone of basic human responses to which Africa as a place of ancestry of Afro-Americans holds no special claims. Thus far a good deal of energy has been employed in arguing for African origins of Afro-American religious expression, dress, music, dance, speech, literature, food, culture, sports, and the performing arts. There is justification to continue to invoke a sense of African origin at crucial points of creativity in Afro-American life, and scholars are quite justified in turning "essentialist" lights on those aspects and categories of Afro-Americans that mirror continental African traditions. Yet one can channel scholarship and energy into highlighting and celebrating the sheer creativity with which the

---

10. Jean-Paul Sartre considered the legitimate aspirations of early Afro-Americans of his days as practicing "anti-racist racism." Almost all the major philosophers in the West shared his view — David Hume (1711-76), Immanuel Kant (1724-1804), Jean-Jacques Rousseau (1712-78), and François-Marie Arouet, known to us as Voltaire (1694-1778). But all did not hide their racism, suggesting that Africans were naturally inferior to Europeans in mental ability. David Hume even argues that there never was a civilized nation of any other complexion than white, nor even any individual eminent either in action or speculation. No ingenious manufacturers amongst them, no arts, no science. He further claimed that a uniform and constant difference could not happen, in so many countries and ages, if nature had not made an original distinction between breeds of men. For details, see Philip D. Curtin, *The Image of Africa: British Ideas and Actions, 1780-1850* (Madison: University of Wisconsin Press, 1964).

blacks of the New World (without African antecedent) have triumphed over determined efforts to erase their racial memories and have created a viable religious existence for themselves. John S. Mbiti's argument on the inseparability of the religious from the secular in continental African daily life and outlook has its basic character and roots in Afro-American social and historical realities that are peculiarly African in origin. But we must explore new factors created by the climate of religious pluralism surrounding the paths blacks have had to cut for themselves beyond the encumbering mists of ancestral antecedents. We need to shake religious pluralism from an obsession with intercontinental burden brought by the new world order and the process of globalization, and devote attention to some of the humble dimensions of black religious experiences. Some of the steps include the way blacks have made Christianity, Islam, and Judaism viable, and the social context in which religion is embedded in the diaspora.[11] Religious continuities between Africa and Afro-Americans will be fully grasped neither by sociologists of religion who do not see that African spirituality belongs to the rich gestalt of human spiritual quest and collective spiritual consciousness as a way the universe is trying to discover itself, nor by cultural anthropologists who do not ask questions about the social and economic environment leading Africans in the diaspora to examine and question the theology behind their conditions of hopelessness. The Afro-American congregations are strong. At the end of the twentieth century, 80 percent of the black congregations in the United States claimed to be Protestant.[12] There is a conscious effort, one would assume, of Afro-Americans in an age of religious pluralism to want to find spiritual and ethical meaning in their history and to want to do so within the context of Christianity, Islam, or Judaism. As C. Eric Lincoln states, "The Black Church evolved not as a formal, black 'denomination,' with a structured doctrine, but as an attitude, or a movement."[13] Reaf-

11. An example of this (from a linguistic point of view) is the success of the French and English languages on the African continent. Today it is estimated that over 360 million Africans speak English as their second language, and more Africans speak French than Frenchmen. Therefore the preservation of the French culture partly depends on the viability of that language by Africans if we assume that language and cultures cannot be separated effectively.

12. In *Black Man's Religion: Can Christianity Be Afrocentric?* (Downers Grove, Ill.: InterVarsity, 1996), Glenn Usry and Craig S. Keener claim that the Christian faith should not be said to be a "white man's" religion and that "The Black church remains the most prominent social institution in the Afro-American community today" (p. 11). C. Eric Lincoln and Lawrence H. Mamiya say 80 percent of all black Christians are in the seven major black denominations. See their book, *The Black Church in the African American Experience* (Durham and London: Duke University Press, 1990), p. 1.

13. See C. Eric Lincoln, ed., *The Black Experience in Religion: A Book of Readings* (Garden City, N.Y.: Anchor Books, 1974), p. 3.

firming the Christian faith, Afro-American churches are a part of the black sacred cosmos in a religiously pluralistic society. In a sense their Christian understanding and confession are a moral alternative to European Christianity and North American mainline denominations. Their Christian response is not, however, to exhibit an aberrational attempt to mimic mainstream white culture, but to see it as a point of departure in their authentic African Christian response to the age. There are, for example, exceptional elements that distinguish Afro-American Christian identity from European Christianity and culture. There is also a historical divergence.

In his pioneering work, *Major Black Religious Leaders: 1755-1940*, Henry J. Young gave a detailed account of how Richard Allen (1760-1831) began the African Methodist Episcopal (AME) Church. Allen and a small group of blacks usually attended Saint George Methodist Episcopal Church in Philadelphia without any serious resentment from the white members of that church. When the number of blacks attending Saint George grew significantly, Allen recollected: "they moved us from the seats we usually sat on, and placed us around the wall." The area reserved for blacks during worship was referred to as "the Negro pew."[14] Absalom Jones, William White, and Dorus Ginnings, also members of Saint George, supported Allen. These men did not want to detach themselves from Saint George. They knew, however, that an independent black congregation would offer them a sense of dignity they did not receive there. Although the white members of the congregation threatened to disown Allen and his friends if they formed a separate church, they left Saint George. This action gave rise to the beginning of the AME Church in the United States in 1794, and Allen subsequently purchased an old frame building and officially opened it for worship in the same year.[15] In 1799 Bishop Asbury ordained Allen as a deacon. Absalom Jones, who originally started with Allen, organized a separate congregation called the African Protestant Episcopal Church (APEC), following a disagreement on ecclesiastical matters. In 1816 all the AME churches gathered in Philadelphia to elect their first bishop. Daniel Coker was elected, but resigned the next day to support Allen, who was consecrated by ordained ministers at the same meeting.[16]

As a response to the age of religious pluralism, almost all African-initiated churches in the United States tend to be evangelical. Perhaps Afro-Americans did not so much convert to Christianity as they converted the God

14. Henry J. Young, *Major Black Religious Leaders: 1755-1940* (Nashville: Abingdon, 1977), p. 28.

15. Young, p. 29. See also Richard Allen, *Life Experience and Gospel Labors* (Nashville: Abingdon, 1983), p. 12.

16. Young, p. 30.

of Christianity to their own spiritual awareness and existential condition.[17] Preaching is based, for example, on biblical stories from the Hebrew Scriptures and the Christian gospel. This, however, is not without practical applications. Holiness and sanctification are emphasized in their charismatic preaching, and sermons are directed to converting the unchurched people to Christianity. A prominent part of their sermons is the social teaching that often emphasizes an egalitarian way of life. The response of the Afro-American Protestant movement to the age of religious pluralism perhaps created a broad civil-rights-movement Christian activism for which the 1960s was only a small segment. This response also influenced Afro-American culture internally. Young observed: "The A.M.E. Church was officially organized in 1816 in Philadelphia, with Richard Allen as the first bishop; the first annual Negro Convention met in 1830 in Philadelphia with Richard Allen as president. The black Church became the vanguard of social activism."[18]

It is important here to mention that although religions in the parent continent of Africa are as varied and diverse as African cultures, there have been unifying influences as well. Africa itself is a large collection of societies shaped by an unusually large variety of influences, and Christians from different regions of Africa are often shaped by the particularities of their cultures. One of the unifying factors in the Afro-American faith community was, however, the social activism championed by Afro-American Christians during the civil rights years. In the 1940s and 1950s, Christians in Africa and Afro-American Christians fought for political freedom simultaneously in ways that one can say were mutually influential. It is important to note, for example, that the day in 1957 that Kwame Nkrumah[19] was sworn in as president of the newly independent Ghana, seven African American students were admitted to a public school in Arkansas for the first time in U.S. history without a protest. Hence, most of the early Christian leaders who fought for political independence in African nation-states were Christians who had received missionary education but later converted churches to political plat-

---

17. Paul Radin insightfully wrote that the Christian God provided the African American slaves with a "fixed point," and rather than being converted to God they converted God to themselves. For the details see Paul Radin, "Status, Phantasy, and the Christian Dogma," in *God Struck Me Dead: Religious Conversion Experience and Autobiographies of Negro Ex-Slaves* (Nashville: Fisk University, Social Science Institute, 1945), pp. i-ix. See also Margaret Washington Creel, "Gullah Attitudes toward Life and Death," in *Africanisms in American Culture* (Bloomington: Indiana University Press, 1990), p. 74.

18. Young, p. 39.

19. Kwame Nkrumah was the father of African nationalism and the first president of Ghana when the country gained political independence from Great Britain in 1957.

forms similar to Afro-American churches in the 1940s and 1950s in the United States.[20]

It is in the style of worship and social activism that Afro-Americans transported their Africanness to the United States most forcefully, not in the substance or essence of their faith. This does not mean, however, that they did not respond in substance to the traditions of the parent continent of Africa.

## Affirmation of the African Religious Traditions

In the religious world of Afro-Americans, much of the Africanness mirrored in the African pantheon of divinities has been appropriated secondhand from other places across the Atlantic. Thus Afro-Americans have to redesign, almost on a clean slate, a new spiritual identity without a direct connection with Africa. More than that, Afro-Americans have to redesign new roles for those old divinities and their manifestation because the African religious antecedent has been partly broken and needed to be refashioned and then welded.

In *Flash of the Spirit,* Robert Farris Thompson sees "ancient African organizing principles of soap and dance as a key element in the evolution of cultural forms in the New World Societies."[21] Yet this idea is not shared universally. Paul Gilroy has voiced the resistance to African origins one can trace to E. Franklin Frazier in the 1940s, whose debates with Melville Herskovits provided fuel and much energy for the studies of Africans in the diaspora. The religious fervor of the black people comes from many corners to the New World, and many factors other than just the transatlantic slave trade are responsible for its continuity. For instance, language plays an important role in the creation of rhetoric in black American pulpits and the new Atlantic culture, and for the writer-activists in the emergence of a type of proto-Pan-Africanism rather than a pure African ancestry.

But certain flaws would be in its internal logic and further weaken one's argument if we must consider Afro-American religious expression as an offshoot of African spirituality, and judge the source of inspiration of Afro-American religious expression primitive, while the product one must judge to

20. For a good study of how Danish missionaries trained Christian leaders to fight for political independence through social activism, see Niels Kastfelt's work, *Religion and Politics in Nigeria: A Study in Middle Belt Christianity* (London: British Academic Press, 1994). The author establishes the fact that one of the most significant political functions of the missionaries was their contribution to the making of new political elites by training them in mission schools.

21. Quoted in Okpewho, Davies, and Mazrui, p. xxii.

be modern, elegant, and robust. A flight from "home" is always a curious paradox since nothing could be more particular than the recognition that a geo-cultural and geo-religious site, however unsuitable or unstable, always has inherent psychological authority over one's spiritual destiny even when it does not enjoy the authority of participation in the journey that leads to an anticipated spiritual destiny fashioned by geo-religiosity. One does not deny the home, yet one must not hold on to it if one wants to participate in the journey fully. When searching for a place to relocate Afro-American religious identity, one will both find it and miss it at the same time.

The relationship of black cultures to multireligious society must deal with both positional and spiritual identity. There is no doubt that the black world has grown to the point that it hardly makes sense to take a unidirectional view that will give privilege to any geographical region above all others. The ideological boundaries between Afro-Americans and Africans must be dissolved. The ideological boundaries that geography has erected between Africa and the New World are now reduced to artificial borders because more than 15 percent of the U.S. population are people of African descent, and the new wave of immigrants to both Europe and America suggests that over a million people of African birth now classify Europe and America as their first home.[22]

But in the final analysis this positionality, in a fundamental sense, is also a statement of identity. Religious dialogue is now more open than ever before, but this is not unrelated to the open dialogue about race and race relations and the impending recognition of the classification "mixed race" for some categories of Americans that do not fit into any of the existing racial categories in the official documents.

The way to understand the religious awareness of the African in the diaspora is not to see it as a critical ontology or a theory or a doctrine, not even as a permanent icon that is accumulating. It has to be considered as an attitude, an ethos, a philosophical life brought by necessity that we can subject to historical and theological analysis of the limits that are imposed on us and experiment with the possibility of going beyond them. Africans in the diaspora are bringing their own bricks to the construction of a universal religious civilization in the current movement of plurality of religions. In a comprehensive study, *The Black Church in the African American Experience* (1990), C. Eric Lincoln and Lawrence Mamiya identified important aspects of Afro-American religious experience. There is no doubt that a strong correlation exists between traditional African religions and Afro-American religious identity. The stimulus for Afro-

22. See Echeruo, "An African Diaspora," and Maureen Warner-Lewis, "Cultural Reconfiguration in the African Caribbean," in *The African Diaspora*.

American religious practice is, however, beyond traditional categories of Christianity or Islam. The religious practice of the Afro-American is tied to the specific cultural ascendancy of African American Protestantism rather than to Roman Catholicism. It was American Protestantism that legitimized the institution of slavery in the United States. Therefore it was Protestantism, not Roman Catholicism, that the early slaves were exposed to. But Afro-American interpretation of Christianity within the broad domain of Protestant tradition is not without the mirror of traditional African religions.

God in black religious experience continues to be tied to the Yoruba concept of Olodumare in West Africa[23] — the ancestral home of most slaves in the United States, particularly those who settled in New Orleans and South Carolina. But the black churches in America are related to West African traditional religions also in a conceptual and moral way. Sociologists of religion call this "a black sacred cosmos."[24] That is to say that a parallel universe of spirituality similar to European Christianity is now emerging among Afro-Americans. One interpretation is that Afro-American churches are not an aberrational attempt that copies mainstream white Christian culture, but rather a response to the age of religious pluralism with a focus that exhibits exceptional elements that distinguish Afro-American religious expressions from European Christianity and culture.

Afro-American churches are new religious and moral alternatives to North American mainline denominations, and they are an important response to the age of religious pluralism. We can identify at least three stages that have led to the birth and rebirth of Afro-American response: (1) the uncritical acceptance of Protestantism in North America, (2) the intellectual stage or the stage of intense examination of Afro-American religious heritage, and (3) the stage of participation and rebirth of African Christian heritage. During the first stage, which corresponded to the enslavement years, African Americans had to assume European Protestantism. Thus they accepted the Protestant Christianity because it was the only denomination they were exposed to. Protestantism also exploited the Afro-Americans by asking them to accept their position as slaves with meekness and humility.[25] In a catechism, the following questions and answers were recorded:

Question: Who gave you a Master and a Mistress?
　Answer: God gave them to me.

---

23. For a comprehensive study of Olodumare, see E. Bolaji Idowu, *Olodumare: God in Yoruba Beliefs* (London: Oxford University Press, 1969).

24. Lincoln and Mamiya, *The Black Church in the African American Experience.*

25. See Young, *Major Black Religious Leaders.*

Question: Who says that you must obey them?
Answer: God says that I must.[26]

This does not mean, however, that the slaves were not practicing traditional African religions on the ground and in secrecy. The second stage coincided with the era of emancipation and produced many articulate Afro-Americans, who were emboldened to interpret Protestantism in a way that fostered cross-fertilization between African traditional religions and Protestant Christianity in the United States. The third stage only began during the last half of the twentieth century when Afro-Americans started to reclaim their African heritage as a legitimate medium of God's revelation. Perhaps what is radically unique about the third stage is that it has become a birth process where traditional African religions are no longer regarded as paganism, but have come to be practiced in public. This is a stage of Afro-Americans becoming players and participating in interreligious dialogue. There is an element of indirectness in this participation because traditional African religions have also survived in North America by blending with Protestantism. Even then, it is in the style of worship, not in substance, that Afro-American religious experience mirrors African traditional religions. Its survival in South America, however, is quite different.

## Afro-American Christianity in South America: Perspectives in a Pluralistic Age

While Afro-American religious experiences have transformed Protestantism in North America, Afro-Brazilian, Haitian, Cuban, and Caribbean religious experiences have transformed Roman Catholicism in South America. Perhaps we can draw from a language example to see the way Afro-Americans have responded to the age of religious pluralism. Maureen Warner-Lewis notes: "The significance of the recovery of African language texts in this century emphasizes the dialectics of change and evolution, in that African languages have coalesced with European languages to create new languages indigenous to the Caribbean — the Dutch, French, English, and Spanish Creoles, yet African languages, in out-surviving that fusion have themselves been reshaped in phonology and syntax by European language forms."[27] The acquisition of indige-

26. See Benjamin Quarles, *The Negro in the Making of America* (New York: Collier Books, 1969), p. 71.
27. Warner-Lewis, p. 20.

nous African languages involved a dynamic process of performance. Subsequent generations of Afro-Americans preserved the phrases in songs, legend, and prayers. An analysis of Yoruba songs recorded in Trinidad indicates an effective and informational range of themes that restored personality to their original singers, and also reflected their traumas and religious beliefs.[28] The co-existence of African-derived liturgical liveliness and European religious resourcefulness on American soil gave birth to the layering and creative response of African Americans to the age of religious pluralism.

It is now a commonplace to say that myths construct the world of African Americans, especially in their association with elements of African religious traditions. Elements of traditional African religions were first exported from West Africa to Brazil in the sixteenth century, but they did not flourish until the nineteenth century. Afro-Brazilian religions mirror African traditional religions substantially and contextually by strongly emphasizing performances. Speeches, drumming, dances, and sacrifices are common in Afro-Brazilian religious expression. Ceremonies that embody traditional African religious substance are often colorful and dramatic and even ecstatic. They evoke the age-old power of divinities and saints.

There is no doubt that in Brazil the old divinities of West Africa have been transformed into the Roman Catholic saints so that devotees can become legitimate worshipers in local and national assemblies. In Brazil divination remains vitally connected with comparable functions in West Africa. Divination invokes the help of the spiritual world for those who are suffering misfortune in the world of the living. Afro-Brazilian religions, like the traditional religions in West Africa, strongly emphasize performance. *Orishas* of the Yoruba people in West Africa and Roman Catholic saints have been given pluralistic-age legitimacy, and there is cross-fertilization between the two among the Roman Catholics in Brazil. Although Afro-Brazilian religious experience and its connection to West Africa have not been supported or encouraged openly and the religious practices that one can trace to West Africa are often forbidden and sometimes prosecuted, it must be pointed out that the association of *orishas* with the Christian saints has given Afro-Brazilians certain legitimacy among the predominantly Roman Catholic populace of Brazil. Even voodoo in Haiti is not unconnected to the traditional religions of the people in West Africa. Among the Caribbean religions, none has gained the attention of religious historians as the Haitian voodoos. This means that many Afro-American practices take roots in West Africa, but the substance of Afro-American religious activities in North America cannot be traced to West Africa alone. Afro-American religious life

---

28. Warner-Lewis, p. 21.

has undergone certain refinement, and the age of religious pluralism has facilitated the cross-fertilization of traditional African religions and Christianity.

## Conclusion

The paradoxical effect of African American religious history is this: while Europeans sailed to Africa in the nineteenth century to teach Africans how to worship like Europeans, African Americans are in both Europe and the Americas today teaching the people of European descent how to worship like Africans.

There are areas of challenge that African Americans will face in the future as they continue to enlarge the boundaries of Christian proclamation in African idioms. These include, but are not limited to, the following: (1) a decay of the role of extended families, (2) mobility of labor and social fragmentation, (3) poverty and demographic shifts from rural to urban areas, and (4) distraction from traditional agrarian concerns and demands in an age of information and technology.

These challenges will alter the transformation process of traditional African religions by Afro-Americans. This is also an indication that their response to the age of religious pluralism has not been completely cemented with the religious beliefs associated with the ancestral home of Africa.

To be sure, traditional African religions are greatly misunderstood. Nevertheless, the beliefs of West Africans continue to be seen as reminiscent of ancient African traditional religions as they linger and take new forms within Christianity as practiced by Afro-Americans.

One can draw three conclusions from the response of Afro-Americans to the age of religious pluralism. First, the age has assisted Afro-Americans to make profound contributions to religious civilization. Second, Afro-Americans have used religion as a catalyst for self-rediscovery. Third, religious awareness is complex, and it is a particular human effort by which Afro-Americans have shaped civilization in the Western world.

# The Centre for Christianity
# in the Non-Western World

GEOMON K. GEORGE

In 1974 there was an important consortium on examining the relationship between the Christian Scripture and non-Christian scriptures held in Bangalore, India. This was the first consultation that brought together Roman Catholic, Orthodox, and Protestant scholars to consider the relationship of the Bible to the scriptures of other religious traditions. This conference was a landmark in the history of the church in India because it was seen as a new phase in the relationship between the church and other religions. From this conference emerged a theological and pastoral ground for applying the Bible interreligiously.

This paper analyzes this conference. In particular it deals with the following questions. Can we use the scriptures of other religions in our worship? In the emerging pattern of a religious pluralism in the economy of salvation, what is the place of Christ? Are the scriptures of other religions inspired? Do all religious scriptures have salvific value? The issues arising from this conference highlighted the theological problems of the Christian community in India regarding this issue.

## An Indigenization of the Bible

In this attempt to make Christian worship in India relevant, Indian Christian theologians could not overlook the religious scriptures of other religions. Paul Puthanangady remarks, "we cannot think of adapting Christian worship to India without taking seriously into account the Indian Scriptures which are a very important source of religious inspirations in India."[1] The Catholic bishops'

1. Paul Puthanangady, "Inculturation of the Liturgy in India Since Vatican II," in *Liturgy: A Creative Tradition*, ed. Mary Collins and David Power (Edinburgh: T. & T. Clark, 1983), p. 72.

conference of India held in New Delhi in 1966 had already developed a program to implement the Vatican II decision for liturgical renewal. The Vatican II liturgical constitution *Sacrosanctum concilium* dealt with the norms for adapting the liturgy to the temperament and traditions of peoples and to "respect and foster" the tradition of other people. The article goes on to suggest that at certain places new adaptations of liturgy are necessary. Thus incorporation of traditional elements of other cultures "might appropriately be admitted into divine worship." Consequently an Episcopal commission for liturgy and a national center were set up in Bangalore, India, to implement inculturation of the liturgy. In this "new" situation the church felt the need and responsibility to provide spiritual leadership "by giving meaning and orientation, inspiration, and guidance and by unifying and discerning — together with the whole Christian community in India."[2]

Consequently the national liturgical center in Bangalore published *pro manuscripto*, a collection in which, along with the biblical and patristic readings from the "Liturgy of the Hours," additional optional, devotional readings are selected from different religious traditions. Furthermore, this was "not a theoretical problem but a practical one" because it was based on the contextual or experiential liturgy found among many Indian Christians. These Christian believers were reading another faith community's sacred texts "for prayer, meditation or contemplation and/or inspiration."[3] According to Amalorpavadass, this practice is occurring in many parts of India and in a few other countries.[4] From this he concludes that non-Christian scriptures are a "source of spiritual nourishment, inspiring, object of meditation and are helpful to prayer." Furthermore, there is the recognition that they are not only inspiring texts but also are "given more or less the value and authority of the Word of God." However, many Indian Christian theologians felt there was a need for deeper study and reflection on the use of non-Christian scriptures.

It is in this context of inculturation of liturgy that a research seminar on nonbiblical scriptures was held December 11-17, 1974, under the auspices of the National Biblical, Catechetical and Liturgical Centre in Bangalore, India. The seminar facilitated discussion on the following areas of interest: Bible, patrology, history of liturgy, theology, comparative study of religions — Hinduism and Islam — and philosophy of language. The goal of the seminar was to un-

---

2. D. S. Amalorpavadass, *Statement on Non-Biblical Scriptures* (Bangalore: National Biblical, Catechetical and Liturgical Centre, 1976), p. 14.

3. D. S. Amalorpavadass, "Introductory Speech," in *Research Seminar on Non-Biblical Scriptures* (Bangalore: National Biblical, Catechetical and Liturgical Centre, 1974), p. 40.

4. Amalorpavadass does not provide the location of these churches.

derstand "the place and role of non-Biblical scriptures outside and inside the official worship of the Church, the Liturgy."[5]

The starting point of the seminar was the understanding of God as actively present in the whole world. The variety of religious experiences "spring from the action of the Spirit," despite their inadequacies.[6] The Holy Spirit is active within these scriptures, manifesting in different ways the mystery of God. The task therefore is this: "we Christians in India, sharing in a common life and heritage of our people, must relate ourselves to the religious experience embodied in these scriptures, and we must seek to express their relationship to the Christian community."[7]

## The Mystery of Christ in Other Scriptures

In the emerging pattern of a religious pluralism in the economy of salvation, what is the place of Christ? Fr. Ignatius Puthiadam, in his article "Reflections on Hindu Religious Texts," comments on his personal interreligious reading journey. In this spiritual journey he has discovered a "deeper mystery" in Hindu scriptures. This mystery has led him to discover "the unknown Christ and Christianity of Hinduism, Buddhism and Jainism but also the unknown Hinduism, Buddhism, and Jainism of Christianity."[8] So for Puthiadam, the goal is to "see God who first came to me in Christ and who in other ways has manifested himself to me in the depth and variety of my forefathers' 'anubhava.'"[9]

Sister Vandana from Acharya, Christa Prema Seva Ashram, argues that Christian reading of other scriptures provides new ways of understanding the "mystery of Christ." In her article "Reflections of a Christian on the Upanishads," she starts from biblical passages that illustrate that God is active in all history. "Then surely we can be justified in trying to discover the Hidden Christ of Upanishads and to 'discern the seeds of the Word' as Vatican II calls them, in listening to the Spirit of Christ speaking to us through other scriptures." Thus Christ can truly say, "all scriptures (not only the Old Testament) speak of me" (Luke 24:27).[10]

Fr. Ignatius Hirudayam, in his article "Canonical Books of Saivism and

---

5. D. S. Amalorpavadass, foreword to *Research Seminar on Non-Biblical Scriptures*, p. 3.
6. Amalorpavadass, *Statement on Non-Biblical Scriptures*, p. 39.
7. Amalorpavadass, *Statement on Non-Biblical Scriptures*, p. 40.
8. Ignatius Puthiadam, "Reflections on Hindu Religious Texts," in *Research Seminar on Non-Biblical Scriptures*, pp. 300-314, here 313.
9. Puthiadam, p. 311.
10. Sister Vandana, "Reflections of a Christian on the Upanishads," in *Research Seminar on Non-Biblical Scriptures*, pp. 237-59, here 238.

Vaishnavism in Tamil," makes a similar argument based on his own personal readings of sacred texts from Tamil Hinduism. From his interfaith dialogue experience he concludes that "when Christian texts are read or heard meditatively along with sacred texts from Tamil Hinduism, they spring to life in an unprecedented manner." Reflecting on this, he asks whether or not it is possible "that the same Author of human salvation revealed himself at sundry times to sages of other cultures and inspired them to record their experiences so that these records in their own time may help express the unfathomable mystery of Christ in an even richer manner till the eschaton."[11]

The above views can be theologically traced to *praeparatio evangelica*. These thinkers recognize certain elements of truth found in other religions and argue that Christ came not "to destroy but to fulfil." Those who take this position explain the elements of truth in other religions as the work of Christ as the eternal Logos. Thus Christ can be seen as fulfilling their deepest spiritual desires, which are corrected and completed by the gospel. In this view Hindu scripture, for example, "gives us many openings into the mystery of Christ,"[12] or the mystical understanding in the Gita foreshadowing the love of Christ. This view retains "the Bible as normative Scripture to justify its supremacy or co-opts them into its own structure in a patronising way."[13] Furthermore, even if similar expressions are found in more than one religious tradition, "the metaphor does not need to spring for the same ideas."[14]

## Revelation and Inspiration

Since the attitude of the church toward other religions shifted to a more positive appreciation, the question of the role of non-Christian scriptures within the economy of salvation needed to be reconsidered. The conference reflected on the relationship between Christian understanding of revelation and inspiration in relation to non-Christian scriptures. The question was: Is inspiration and revelation the same in every religion? And if different, "can we understand them in a broad sense or analogically"?

In the article "Insight as Inspiration and 'Anubhava' as Revelation in the Hindu Scriptures," T. M. Manickam attempts to use indigenous terms for the

11. Ignatius Hirudayam, "Canonical Books of Saivism and Vaishnavism in Tamil," in *Research Seminar on Non-Biblical Scriptures*, pp. 431-44, here 444.

12. Stanley J. Samartha, *One Christ, Many Religions* (New York: Orbis, 1991), p. 73.

13. Samartha, p. 73.

14. R. Panikkar, "Research Seminar on Non-Biblical Scriptures: Review," *Religion and Society* (Bangalore) 23 (June 1976): 110-11.

concepts of inspiration and revelation. He says, "inspiration in the Hindu scriptural tradition is understood as 'insight' of the *rshi;* insight is a gift of the Divine who manifests himself in the *Cit* (consciousness) of the *rshi* as 'Anubhava' (experience). Anubhava is revelation communicable to the extent of the intelligibility of the insight which the *rshi* has, and to the extent of the descriptive function of symbols, myths, languages and poetry."

Manickam makes two levels of distinction in revelation. The first seems to be interpersonal, in that the divine execution of "infusing" "the rays of divine mysteries" in human beings is part of revelation, and insight is the human response to the act of revelation. However, God initiates this act of human response. The second part of revelation is "the transmission of revelation" experience received through *anubhava*. This transmission can be identified as "revelation in so far as it is faithful communication of the original insight of the *rshi*."[15] However, the imposition of Christian terms such as "revelation" and "inspiration" in relation to non-Christian scriptures may be foreign to Hindu thought. S. Arulsamy observes, "Hindu scholars do not value their scriptures because they are 'revealed' or 'inspired.' Their approach to their (Hindu) scriptures is in terms of their 'eternal,' 'impersonal' and 'valid' characters."[16] In reviewing the book *Research Seminar on Non-Biblical Scriptures,* R. Panikkar observes that "it is clear that the very expression of 'scripture' is a rather inadequate formulation in many cases. Quran and Adhi Grant can certainly be called 'sacred scriptures' but with the sruti it is an altogether different problem."[17]

The conference concluded that "inspiration" couldn't be used as a term of "descriptive-object language." Inspiration "is meaningful only in the context of faith-experience of the one who is speaking." In other words, it is the community that provides "inspiration" to a text. Scriptures, therefore, are the "objectification" of the faith experience of a community. Michael Amaladoss, in his article "Text and Context: The Place of Non-Biblical Readings in the Liturgy,"[18] provides a framework for this position. Examining the authority of scriptures from a sociological perspective, he argues that the criteria for the authority of a particular scripture is not inherent within a text but rather the

15. T. M. Manickam, "Insight as Inspiration and 'Anubhava' as Revelation in the Hindu Scriptures," in *Research Seminar on Non-Biblical Scriptures,* pp. 325-39, here 325.

16. S. Arulsamy, "Can Hindu Scriptures Take the Place of the Old Testament," *Indian Theological Studies* 21, no. 3-4 (1984): 319.

17. Panikkar, p. 110.

18. Michael Amaladoss, "Text and Context: The Place of Non-Biblical Readings in the Liturgy," in *Research Seminar on Non-Biblical Scriptures,* pp. 210-20. The quotations in this and the next four paragraphs are from this article.

community in which that particular text becomes sacred affirms it. The scriptures become the word of God in the context of the faith community. "The scriptures do not become the Word of God because this character is conferred on them by faith. They do not function and act as the Word of God outside the context of faith. To think otherwise would be to confer a magical efficacy on the scriptures."

Amaladoss criticizes a certain kind of "encounter theology" that tends to overlook the relation between faith and theology, which can only become alive in the context of the believing community. He believes that in liturgy one can see how liturgy becomes a basic character of symbols. He attempts to articulate "the communicational operational structure of the liturgy" out of which he attempts to understand the relation between text and context. This would then be able "to lead us to formulate certain conclusions regarding the use of non-Christian scripture in the liturgy."

Amaladoss defines liturgy as "the symbolic action of a community." The liturgy has no spectators but only participants. Liturgy "is a collective self-expression of the community; an affirmation of its faith; a celebration of its life; a creative re-living of an experience." This self-expression takes on an action — a symbolic action. Amaladoss wants to convey to the reader that the encounter between God and humanity is always through symbol. It conveys a meaning, and this affirmation is immanent only to the community.

He goes on to see the relation between symbolic action and context. He argues that the function of liturgy is related directly to the context of the community of faith; its main purpose is the renewal of the faith community. Amaladoss recognizes the use of nonscriptural elements like the homily or nonscriptural readings like the acts of the martyrs or letters of saints or bishops. This event, for Amaladoss, has a double awareness. The first is that through the use of these elements there can be a powerful "call of God and [provocation of] a creative response and commitment." The second factor is the acknowledgment that while God has manifested his power, glory, and love and has called us to respond in the events recorded in the Bible, it is not exclusive. In other words, in sacred scriptures other than the Christian Scripture, there may be events and stories that will challenge us to respond to the call of God. He admits that "the Spirit continues to be active and speak to the Church in the life of the martyrs and holy men, in the events of history and in the signs of the times which need to be interpreted."

This awareness for Amaladoss does not mean that the Bible is given less importance. The Bible will always remain central for Amaladoss. However, he qualifies this by saying "centrality does not mean totality. Hence the use of the elements to provide a resonance to the message of the inspired word, provided it is done in the context of faith which discerns and interprets, seems entirely justifiable."

It is therefore possible that a "wider" community can recognize inspiration of all sacred narratives. As Albert Nambiaparambil, secretary of CBCI Dialogue Commission, points out, in order for interscriptural reading to be "valid," participants must feel they are part of the community of the faith experience.[19] For him, in the context of dialogue with people of other faiths, this can take place. In light of these observations, the conference concluded that inspiration of non-Christian scriptures can take place "only in so far as its experience of itself is no longer that of a closed group but of a community that is open and moving towards the formation of a new, wider community that would be as wide as God's economy of salvation."[20]

George Soares-Prabhu, a New Testament scholar, endeavors to illustrate how it is possible to relate the Old Testament and New Testament through "analogical inspiration" and extend this definition to nonbiblical scriptures so that one can read the Bible along with nonbiblical scriptures. In the article "The Inspiration of the Old Testament as Seen by the New and Its Implication for the Possible Inspiration of Non-Christian Scriptures," he argues for the inclusion of nonbiblical scriptures in the liturgy of the church. He illustrates this by showing the absorption of non-Jewish narrative materials in the Old Testament.

To understand inspiration in non-Christian scriptures, Soares-Prabhu turns to the Old Testament, "a non-Christian scripture that has been made Christian." Taking the status of the Old Testament in the church, he argues that the inspiration of the Old Testament is not self-evident. Observing that many quotations from the Old Testament are found in the New Testament, he suggests that New Testament authors attempted to "Christologize" the Old Testament by making it a book that speaks about Christ. Consequently biblical Scripture assumes/receives inspiration when read in light of Christ. Consequently inspiration is something added to them.

Using the three models, the law-gospel model, the salvation history model, and the traditio-historical model, he asks, just as the Old Testament is an inspired text when read in the light of the New Testament, can the non-Christian scriptures, when read in the light of the Christ, be an inspired word of God?[21] He believes the answer will depend on how one understands the Old

19. Albert Nambiaparambil, "Religious Language in a Dialogic Context: A Linguistic Approach," in *Research Seminar on Non-Biblical Scriptures,* pp. 569-79.

20. Amalorpavadass, *Statement on Non-Biblical Scriptures,* p. 24.

21. George M. Soares-Prabhu, "The Inspiration of the Old Testament as Seen by the New and Its Implication for the Possible Inspiration of Non-Christian Scriptures," in *Research Seminar on Non-Biblical Scriptures,* pp. 99-112, here 106.

Testament being "fulfilled." He asks, "is its inspired meaning an arbitrary imposition on the original meaning of the text . . . or is it organically related to its original meaning? Is the Old Testament, that is, intrinsically related to the New, and can this relation be parallel in other, non-Christian Scriptures?"[22]

He rejects both the law-gospel model and the salvation history model as insufficient in favor of the tradition history model. The law-gospel model seeks to present the Old Testament as the preparation of the New Testament, and the salvation history model suggests that Old Testament and New Testament are part of one history of salvation. The tradition history model seeks to present the Old and New Testament as part of a single, living, and continuing tradition because other scriptures are "premonitions of the Word of God." The law-gospel model "exaggerates" the difference between the Old Testament and New Testament, and the salvation history model "glosses" over the differences and "overemphasizes" the similarities. The tradition history model recognizes other scriptures as part of this continuing tradition. In this process he is able to incorporate scriptures of other religious traditions. However, Panikkar observes that "the assumption which make the concept of 'inspiration' relevant are far from being general assumptions of many an Indian tradition and even when the problem is taken 'analogically' the *primum analogatum* is far from being clear."[23]

## Conclusions of the Conference

The final statement given by the participants at the seminar affirmed using the nonbiblical scriptures in Christian prayer and worship. The conclusion states, "in light of this analysis, we consider that non-Biblical readings can find a place in the liturgy of the Word." The purpose of this enterprise is:

1. The texts should be such as to help the community.
2. To celebrate a particular aspect of the mystery of Christ in a special way.
3. Positively promote the community's devotion.
4. Facilitate the community to open-up a new dimension and expression in its Christ-faith experience and even help accelerate the community's movement to the Father in order to realise itself.[24]

22. Soares-Prabhu, pp. 106-7.
23. Panikkar, p. 111.
24. "Inter-disciplinary Workshop on Theological Basis with Special Concerns," in *Research Seminar on Non-Biblical Scriptures*, p. 652.

*Geomon K. George*

The criteria for selecting nonbiblical scriptures are:

1. To the extent that they actualise the faith experience of a particular community as a community.
2. To the extent that the selected texts by themselves tend to open out the celebrating community to the community from which it has borrowed the texts.
3. To the extent that they preserve the historical continuity of the celebrating community with its own religio-cultural heritage.
4. To the extent that they maintain the specific and unique role that the Bible necessarily must have in our Christian liturgy.[25]

The conclusion of the conference highlights the tension between recognizing non-Christian scriptures as revealing the mystery of God on one hand and viewing them as having the role of *praeparatio evangelica* on the other.


## Evaluation

In light of the directives for liturgical renewal provided by the liturgical constitution *Sacrosanctum concilium,* Indian Catholic bishops along with Orthodox and Protestant theologians began to reflect on fostering an indigenous liturgy. S. Arulsamy, reflecting on the research seminar ten years later in the journal *Indian Theological Studies,* remarks, "the whole document of the research Seminar is certainly a significant contribution of the Indian Church to the theology of World religions and to the theology of non-Biblical scriptures."[26]

While the Bible is seen as a collection of various texts and is part of a tradition, these theologians have attempted to widen the concept of inspiration to include nonbiblical texts. The participants considered the gospel to be at the center of God's revelation and viewed non-Christian scriptures as God's continuing witness of God's love and care. The participants recognized that the early Christians inherited the Torah and subsequently never questioned its position.

The methodology of the seminar needs to be examined closely. The research questions beg the conclusion. Arulsamy asks, "was not the whole meeting programmed to legitimate the use of non-Biblical scriptures in Christian life and worship?"[27] Instead of an open-ended inquiry, the conference was jus-

25. "Inter-disciplinary Workshop," p. 652.
26. Arulsamy, p. 318.
27. Arulsamy, p. 318.

tification of an a priori — the need to use other religious narratives in Christian liturgy. R. Panikkar's verdict on the seminar is that "except for a few exceptions it all looks as a superimposition of a ready-made Christian concept, problematic as it is sometimes felt by the contributors themselves, on an alien culture and religion."[28]

The interscriptural reading does not begin with the biblical texts but with the social reality. There is an assumption that in a pluralistic society such as India, the goal is building a "community," and the use of scriptures of other faith traditions will enable this. Theologically there is the recognition that the Holy Spirit is at work in the faith community of other religious traditions. Revelation is not exclusive to biblical texts. Other texts also contain the revelation of God. One gets the feeling that scriptures are used selectively according to what is considered useful to the contemporary context.

The majority of Indian Christians are converts from lower castes for whom the Hindu religious system and their sacred scriptures have been a tool to legitimate their oppression. Therefore, one of the primary questions that needs to be addressed is, how are Dalit Christians to interpret the Hindu scriptures in light of their experience?

In the intertextual reading the concept of hegemony — of ideological domination — merits fundamental examination. While the goal of the 1974 conference varied from pastoral, liturgical, and theological, the aim of the conference was to reflect Indian Christian engagement with nonbiblical scriptures. Methodologically they were attempting to develop a theological understanding of Christianity and other faiths. The method of application, however, was to treat nonbiblical scriptures as their own property and to interpret in their own delights. In this process the conference confirmed the Christian understanding of Christ. Consequently it was a privileged reading of nonbiblical scriptures and a power choice. Sathianathan Clarke, from the United Theological College and a presbyter in the Madras Diocese of the Church of South India, says an exclusive text-oriented discipline does not reflect the issues the majority of Indian Christians face: "Theologising in the Indian context was thought to be an interpretation of Christian faith and doctrine within the framework of Indian scriptural themes, images, symbols and myths. So theology was concerned with Indian religious texts rather than the experience of local Christian people who were Dalits. Rarely do these religious texts reflect the Indian Christian religious world-view and so theology can become so alien as even to become anti-people."[29]

---

28. Panikkar, p. 111.

29. Sathianathan Clarke, "Redoing Indian Theology," *Bangalore Theological Forum* 18, nos. 2-3 (April-September 1986): 129.

Since the vast majority of Indian Christians are Dalits, the question needs to be asked: For whom is Indian Christian theology based on interscriptural reading? It is for a minority of people who are literate in both Hinduism and Christianity and who are concerned with the contextual reality of Hinduism itself. These Indian Christian theologians see in the engagement with Hinduism an opportunity for Christian contextualization for national "Indian" identity. A contextual theology based on the Hindu traditions may have served as a symbolic challenge by Christians of higher-caste origins against the Western representation of Christianity and identified with Sanskritization. However, for Christians of lower-caste origins, interscriptural reading would be viewed as just another expression of power. Therefore, the nature of the religious problem faced by the Dalits needs to be addressed and must become an important criterion if interscriptural reading is to be taken seriously.

## Conclusion

The research seminar took up the challenge of the development of a theological understanding of the use of nonbiblical scriptures in the life and community of the Indian church. Living next to other living faith communities has challenged Indian Christian theologians to ask if there is a place for non-Christian scriptures in the life and worship of the Indian Christian community. The conclusion of the seminar positively affirmed this question by suggesting that nonbiblical scriptures are authentic channels of God's revelation because Christ, who "enlightens all men," is active in every religious scripture.

In effect, interscriptural reading is for a minority of Indian Christians of higher-caste origins and those who are concerned about the contextual nature of "Hinduism" itself. For the majority of Indian Christians who are from lower-caste origins, Hindu scriptures were used to legitimize their oppression. Thus, for them it is another form of power choice controlled by the Christians of higher-caste origin. What we have been able to witness in this conference is that Indian Christian theologians are using Indian religious and philosophical resources in developing a contextual expression of Christianity.

# Inculturated Protestant Theology in Guatemala

VIRGINIA GARRARD-BURNETT

*Christian self-understanding must form [theology] that stops coinciding with the historically determined Western traditions that represent merely the background against which traditions take note of their limitations and Eurocentric specificity.[1]*

This paper will explore theological innovation and issues of identity and resurgence among the indigenous Maya population of the Central American nation of Guatemala. Specifically, this work will examine the efforts of Mayan Protestants to "inculturate" Christian theology, that is, to de-contextualize Christian narratives from their Western cultural references and reposition them within a Mayan telos, or *cosmovisión*. The parameters of this paper are specific, in that it will discuss an evolving theology that is intentional in its creation and Protestant in its perspective. Although there is also a Catholic analogue to this theology, known as "inculturation theology," both the Catholic version and the Protestant theology to be discussed here are distinct in both form, intent, and practice from the older blends of Mayan and Christian beliefs that are generally thought of (with some imprecision) as "religious syncretism"[2] or "folk Catholicism."

1. Jürgen Habermas, "Israel or Athens, or to Whom Does Anamnestic Reason Belong?" in *Liberation Theologies, Postmodernity, and the Americas,* ed. David Batstone et al. (London: Routledge, 1997), p. 251.

2. The literature on the nature of "religious syncretism" is of course extensive, and the term itself is problematic, suggesting a religious form that derives from indigenous people's misunderstandings and misappropriation of religious forms. Hans Seibers has recently suggested that a better explanation of indigenous religious forms is "religious creolization," a term which suggests a purposeful blending of religious cultures that results from the intentional integration of means and symbols from two or more religious traditions (Hans Seibers, "Globaliza-

Protestant Mayanized theology is a direct and conscious response to the historic repression of Guatemala's native indigenous population and of the recent efforts by Mayan intellectuals to create a coherent political movement to represent pan-Mayan political, social, and economic interests. Because of the theology's overtly political genesis, some historical and ethnographic background is necessary to understand the context for its development. Guatemala is the only nation in Latin America with an Indian majority (upwards of 60 percent of Guatemalans are indigenous); but its indigenous population has historically been the object of a virulent racism that has left them with some of the lowest social indicators in the hemisphere. In terms of religious identity, the majority (60 percent) of Guatemalans are Catholic (both orthodox and practitioners of a Mayanized folk Catholicism), although the influence of U.S. missionaries and the rapid growth of independent, local Protestant churches have also resulted in a sizable and expanding Protestant population that accounts for approximately 35 percent of the population, a figure that is higher in Mayan, as opposed to non-Mayan, parts of the country.

Power in the country is vested in a small elite of primarily European origin and in the ladinos, a term which applies both to persons of mixed Indian-European descent and to acculturated indigenous people. Guatemala has historically been the richest nation in Central America in economic and natural resources, but decades of political struggle severely retarded its economic advancement during the second half of the twentieth century. The nation suffered through an unevenly matched and bloody civil war between Marxist guerrillas (the URNG)[3] and the military-controlled government from 1961 to 1996. Although the struggle lasted thirty-six years, the most concentrated period of violence took place between 1981 and 1983, when state repression and violence accelerated sharply, corresponding to the scorched earth campaign in the largely indigenous highlands. During this period alone, at least twenty thousand Guatemalans died violently, upwards of 80 percent of whom were Mayan.[4]

This grim period of genocide of the early 1980s still leaves a strong imprint of terror and its repercussion in the country, but it also elicited a wide va-

---

tion and Religious Creolization among the Q'eqchi'es of Guatemala," in *Latin American Religion in Motion*, ed. Christian Smith and Joshua Prokopy [London: Routledge, 1999], pp. 261-73). A good discussion of the issues surrounding religious pluralism and community identity can be found in Robert S. Carlsen, *The War for the Heart and Soul of a Highland Maya Town* (Austin: University of Texas Press, 1997).

3. Unidad Nacional Guatemalteca Revolucionaria.

4. Patrick Bell, Patrick, Paul Kobrak, and Herbert F. Spirer, *State Violence in Guatemala, 1960-1996: A Quantitative Reflection* (Washington, D.C.: AAAS Science and Human Rights Program, 1999), fig. 4.1, http://hrdata.aaas.org/ciidh/qr/english/.

riety of political and social responses. For our purposes, the most significant of these are the development of (1) the Mayan movement, a political movement by and for Mayan people to assert their own cultural and political rights, and (2) the peace accords of 1996, which conceded to and protected for the Mayan peoples, for the first time in Guatemala's history, specific cultural and political rights.[5]

The Protestant *teología maya* (which I will call here, in a somewhat facile shorthand, Mayanized theology), which is the topic of this paper, is a direct project of this history of political subordination, genocide, and cultural resurgence. By some measures Mayanized theology is as much a political gesture as a theology, for its authors are fully aware of the ways Mayan people have, over time, been able to appropriate a powerful means of domination and subordination (Christianity) and inverted both the means and the message for their own strategies. In this sense the decolonialized theology is much like other types of "liberating" religious discourses such as liberation theology or other theologies tied directly to the political and cultural agendas of subordinate groups, such as the black theology promoted by such figures as James H. Cone in the United States during the 1960s or the feminist theology within the Catholic Church today. This convergence brings to mind David Batstone's suggestion that "political discourse [naturally] has its theological counterpart. The coincidence of the political and the theological should come as no surprise; after all, theological discourse is responding to the same material culture that finds expression in political discourse."[6]

Of central significance to this project is an examination of the ways local innovators adapt and reorganize imported religious "systems" for their own ends.[7] It begs the obvious to state that Christian missionary enterprises in Latin America have been, from the first colonial contacts, grounded in asymmetrical power relations and in the desire to reconstruct not only people's identities but

5. See Edward F. Fischer and R. McKenna Brown, eds., *Maya Cultural Activism in Guatemala* (Austin: University of Texas Press, 1996).

6. David Batstone, "Charting (Dis)Courses of Liberation," in *Liberation Theologies, Postmodernity, and the Americas*, p. 159.

7. I use the phrase "religious systems" here with some caution, and with a caveat offered by David Lehmann, who writes, "[T]here are not grounds for taking the fixed integrity of a religious system for granted or even for believing that religious ensembles, sub-cultures or institutions can be thought of as systems at all. However, the self-image of a religious institution or subculture as possessing its own integrity, or the images it produces of the other as a distinct system, are interesting and important because religion in the modern world is evidently a marker of identity and a mechanism for the production of group/identarian boundaries" ("Charisma and Possession in Africa and Brazil" [unpublished paper, Cambridge University, 2000], p. 2).

also their very consciousnesses. In their work on colonial Christianity in South Africa, John and Jean Comaroff describe religious cultural encounters as "a complex dialectic of invasion and ropost, of challenge and resistance . . . a politics of consciousness in which the very nature of consciousness [is] itself the object of struggle."[8] Given these high stakes and deep asymmetries, religion has remained a contested venue in Guatemala, and the struggle has never been completely one-sided. The object of Mayan theology is to invert and reinterpret the power relations and identity issues implicit in the Christian "project" for their own purposes.

Yet it would be a mistake to think of Mayan theology as nothing more than political rhetoric. Because Christianity has such a long and contested history in Guatemala, religion has often been used as a measure and metaphor for the deeply rooted contradictions and tensions that underlie so much of Guatemala's past and present, and in fact religion — and militant Christianity in particular — sometimes lies at the very heart of these contradictions. Obviously the colonial, imperialist origins of Christianity, both Catholic (Spanish) and Protestant (North American), in a place like Guatemala carry enormous historical weight that cannot be overlooked. Yet Christianity in Guatemala long ago lost its foreign accent and acquired what R. S. Sugirtharajah calls a "vernacular hermeneutics," a local system of value, understanding, and interpretation.[9]

This brings us at last to the particulars of Mayanized Protestant theology. At present, theological innovation is being produced by the Conferencia de Iglesias Evangélicas de Guatemala (CIEDEG), a "liberal" Protestant organization dominated by Mayan Presbyterians. CIEDEG is headed by Vitalino Similox, a Kak'chiquel Maya Presbyterian pastor who was an important intermediary for ecumenical church people associated with the URNG and a pivotal negotiator during the Oslo peace talks, which ended the long war. Similox has been involved as an activist in the Mayan movement, and he ran for vice president of the republic for the Alianza Nueva Nación (ANN), a left-of-center party, during the 1999 presidential elections.

The Presbyterians' prominence in the movement to Mayanize theology is due not only to Similox's influence, but also to historical factors that underscored long-standing concerns within the denomination as to the cultural implications of religious conversion. The Presbyterian church has a long historical presence in Guatemala, and it was the first missionary group to cede full con-

8. John Comaroff and Jean Comaroff, *Of Revelation and Revolution: Christianity, Colonialism, and Consciousness in South Africa*, vol. 1 (Chicago: University of Chicago Press, 1991), p. 250.

9. Rasiah S. Sugirtharajah, *The Bible and the Third World: Precolonial, Colonial, and Postcolonial Encounters* (Cambridge: Cambridge University Press, 2001), p. 175.

trol of the denomination to local leadership (1961). In the mid-1960s the church carved out two Mayan (Kak'chiquel and Mam) synods (administrative districts) to reflect its respect for indigenous *cosmovisión* and theological autonomy.[10] Discursive analysis reveals that Guatemalan Mayans who are Presbyterians often express a highly heterodox body of belief that incorporates conventional Protestant theology; Mayan ideas of sacred geography; culturally encoded, polymorphic notions of the nature of God(s); and a worldview that is consciously grounded in Mayan *cosmovisión,* alongside Protestant emancipation narratives.[11] Although the Presbyterians are a relatively small group in Guatemala and are greatly outnumbered by Pentecostal Protestants, they have a political and social presence in the country that belies their actual numbers. Moreover, the majority of Presbyterians in Guatemala are now Maya.

Although CIEDEG is dominated by the Presbyterians, its membership also includes congregations from many other denominations, including Pentecostals (who make up the vast majority of Guatemala's Protestants, both Mayan and non-Mayan), non-Pentecostal fundamentalists, and independent Protestant denominations. The common denominators of membership are ethnicity — virtually all congregations that belong to CIEDEG are Mayan — and a shared geography of terror, in that the participating congregations are all located near or in areas where military reprisals and massacres of civilians during the civil violence of the early 1980s took place and therefore loom large on the landscape of local memory.[12] While the founding mandate of CIEDEG was to help in the implementation of peace and reconciliation in the region (*camino de Shalom,* or "Shalom road"), its leaders recognized a need to confront the implications of Guatemala's recent history in theological terms.[13]

The notion of creating a new, de-Westernized theology thus grew out of the 1996 peace accords, specifically the Acuerdo sobre Identidad y Derechos de los Pueblos, which specifically offers protection of indigenous religious practices as a cultural right. As a political strategy, the primary purpose of the new theology is to encourage a religious system that supports indigenous cultural rights within the larger context of Mayan resurgence.[14] At the symbolic level

10. See Virginia Garrard-Burnett, *Protestantism in Guatemala: Living in the New Jerusalem* (Austin: University of Texas Press, 1998), p. 114.

11. See David Scotchmer, "Symbols of Salvation: Interpreting Highland Maya Protestantism in Context" (Ph.D. diss., State University of New York at Albany, 1991).

12. See CIEDEG, *La Misión de la Iglesia Evangélica de Guatemala en la Etapa Post-Conflict* (Guatemala City: Ediciones Alternativas, 1998), p. 5.

13. CIEDEG, *La Misión de la Iglesia Evangélica de Guatemala en la Etapa Post-Conflict,* chap. 1.

14. CIEDEG, *La justicia se siembra la Paz, y da su fruto a los artesanos de la Paz,* pamphlet

the Protestant Mayanized theology is an attempt to create an alternative theological paradigm for Mayan Protestants who reject the popular conflation of Protestant religion with Westernization (a process known in Latin America as *mestizaje*) and with conservative politics.

Since the late 1990s, CIEDEG has generated workshops, study groups, literature for use by church groups, political documents, and other means to engender a Mayan-based Christology that seeks to contextualize basic Christian beliefs within a larger system of Mayan cosmology, cultural values, and worldview. At the most basic level, Mayanized theology attempts to reconcile Protestant Christianity with the three central elements of Mayan spirituality: peace with the natural world that sustains life, peace with other people (including the dead), and peace with the deity/ies.[15] But the theology also demands a reexamination of fundamental Christian images, symbols, and archetypes through the lens of "traditional" Mayan *cosmovisión(e)*. This means, at the most basic level, that theology should be expressed in a language that can be easily understood — literally, in the most widely spoken Mayan languages (Kak'chiquel, Mam, and Ki'ché), but also figuratively, through the utilization of symbols, myths, and iconography that are locally understood, valued, and interpreted.

The reasons for embedding Protestant theology within Mayan culture are partially strategic: "How can a Maya accept the Good News of the Gospel," a Mayan theologian asks rhetorically, "if the person who is evangelizing practically requires him to give up what is essential to the profundity of his life, and annul the spiritual and cultural heritage of his ancestors?" But it is also a postmodern reinterpretation of Christianity's claims to unique revelation through the person of Christ. Instead of a conversion narrative based on a traditional Protestant/fundamentalist salvation narrative (before and after salvation through Jesus Christ), Mayanized theology insists upon recognition of the "persistent historic presence of God in our cultures: in the myths, the rituals, the customs, in the community, the services, organizations, in the families, in the humanistic conception of the human being, and in the Earth, as a point of reference in the Universe."[16]

Yet Mayanized theology is by no means universalistic. It embraces a tradi-

---

(2001); Vitalino Similox Salazar, E*vangelismo protestante y espiritualidad maya en el Marco de los Acuerdos de Paz* (Guatemala City: CIEDEG, 1997).

15. See David Scotchmer, "Life in the Heart: A Maya Protestant Spirituality," in *South and Mesoamerican Native Spirituality*, ed. Garry H. Gossens and León Portilla (New York: Crossroad, 1993), p. 507.

16. Vitalino Similox Salazar, *Religión Maya: Fuente de Resistencia Milenaria* (Guatemala City: CIEDEG, 1998), pp. 146-47.

tional Christology which affirms Jesus Christ as "the Savior; without Him there is no hope . . . without him there is no eternal salvation, there is no human face of God outside of Christ." However, within this understanding is that caveat that "the event of Jesus, the Christ is not the exclusive possession or the private property of any culture . . . the Gospel transcends whatever [human] forces attempt to contain it in . . . whether it be cultural or religious."[17]

In a pamphlet published in Guatemala's most widely read daily newspaper, CIEDEG's Similox argued that Christianity not only transcends but actually valorizes indigenous cultures. "God loves all cultures and his salvation does not signify the denigration or renunciation of cultural and historic identity. Evangelization does not signify the announcement of the 'absence of God' in a culture, but [rather] it is an announcement of the good news of 'his presence.'"[18] An evangelical pastor stated the equation more simply: "God was already here," he explained, "when Columbus arrived."[19] Yet some take a more cautious view: "Christ is present in all cultures," writes Mónica Ramírez de López, "but [he] participates actively to transform them. We must rescue our culture, values, customs, and social actions that do not go against the Word of God. But we must reject those that openly or covertly go against Biblical absolutes. From there all culture must always be tested, tried, and judged by the Scripture."[20]

Even this more conservative vantage point, however, provides a point of departure for understanding Mayanized theology. In his 1998 treatise entitled *Maya Religion: Source of Millenarian Resistance,* Similox outlined areas for cultural recovery within Mayan Christianity, so that, in his words, "the Maya may drink from his *own* well."[21] Specifically, the theology demands the reconstruction of theology within the framework of five Mayan cultural paradigms. These include:

- *The recovery of Mayan cultural values, particularly the emphasis on the community over the individual.* This would be expressed in a different em-

---

17. Vitalino Similox Salazar, *Algunos propuestas de la religiosidad Maya hacia un pluralismo religioso, en el marco de los Acuerdos de Paz* (Guatemala City: CIEDEG, 1997), pamphlet.

18. Vitalino Similox Salazar, *Evangelismo protestante y espiritualidad Maya en el Marco de los Acuerdos de Paz* (CIEDEG, published in *Prensa Libre,* May 8, 1997).

19. C. Matthew Samson, "Interpretando la Identidad Religiosa: La Cultura Maya y La Religión Evangélica Bajo Una Perspectiva Etnográfica" (paper presented at the Segundo Conferencia Sobre El Pop Wuj, Quetzaltenango, Guatemala, 30 May–4 June, 1999), p. 9.

20. Mónica Ramírez de López, statement on behalf of the Fraternidad Teológica Latinoamericana, to the Primera Consulta Nacional de CIEDEG, February 1998.

21. Similox, *Religión Maya,* p. 128.

phasis on corporate over individual sins: "The pastor condemns certain sins, for example, laziness, alcoholism . . . witchcraft, idolatry, but never [things like] poor payment for labor, exploitation, or other social sins."[22] Even more to the point, Mayan religious expression is based upon communitarian expression. Within the Protestant context, the emphasis is placed upon the new community of *hermanos/hermanas* (brothers and sisters) in the faith.

- *Reintegrating religion into everyday life, not just relegating it to the Sabbath.* Traditional Mayan spirituality is not so much a system of dogma, but more a systemic spirituality that touches every aspect of life; more a "way of being" than a religion per se.[23] "Protestantism has tended to compartmentalize the practice of religion, which is not the Maya way — we pray before we cut the soil to plant; we pray before we shoot an animal to eat," writes Similox.[24] Mayanized theology, by contrast, calls for a fuller integration of faith into the quotidian details of life (p. 119).

- *The abandonment of the most obviously foreign cultural elements in worship.* This refers to such practices as women and men sitting on different sides of the church rather than as families (a Spanish Catholic custom) and the use of culturally inappropriate hymns translated into Spanish for use in worship services. "Evangelization has been [tantamount to] acculturation," writes Similox. "We received hymns, not only in a different language, but also in another mentality" (pp. 124-25).

- *The creation of a "Mayan hermeneutics."* This includes the utilization of symbols, rites, myths of ancient Mayan culture, whenever possible, to convey Christian allegory. This exposes a double hermeneutic puzzle, because ancient Mayan religious symbols and imagery are buried so deeply beneath the symbols and myths of the dominant culture. The task, then, is to "decode from Mayan sources, such as the ancient chronicles, to decipher the true meanings of the ancient messages" (p. 139).

Within this Mayan hermeneutic the theology calls for recognition of "the sacred duality, that God is both Father and Mother" (pp. 143-44). While this notion runs parallel to what are now standard Western understandings of God's dual-gendered "personhood," it also, within Mayanized theology, carries fundamental ecological implications. In the Mayan context, "The motherness of God is in the form of the Earth *(tierra)*. The

22. Similox, *Religión Maya*, p. 118.

23. Samson, p. 10. See also Guillermo Cook, ed., *Crosscurrents in Indigenous Spirituality: Interface of Maya, Catholic, and Protestant Worldviews* (New York: Brill, 1997).

24. Similox, *Religión Maya*, p. 119. The parenthetical page numbers in the following text are to this work.

earth is a divine gift and the mother of the community . . . [but it is also an embodiment] of the divine pact with Abraham." Conversely, the earth is not only a material symbol of God's covenant, but is also considered sacred as a physical entity.

• *The theology also prescribes the incorporation of other integral material elements of Mayan culture as utensils of worship;* these might include the pine-resin incense, votive candles, pine branches, and grain alcohol to libate holy spaces that are normally utilized in syncretic rituals or in the ancient healing practices now known by many Maya as *brujeria* (witchcraft or magic). Because conventional Protestant practice eschews these material elements, their explicit inclusion marks a clear departure from "noninculturated" Mayan Protestantism (pp. 142-43).

Finally, the inclusion of a third material aspect of worship clearly sets Mayanized theology apart from "orthodox" Protestantism, and this is corn. In both ancient and contemporary Mayan life corn is considered not merely a staff of life, but also the veritable source of life itself, and the planting, harvesting, and consumption of corn is considered a sacramental act. (It is an interesting parallel that colonial Spaniards refused to eat corn, and insisted instead upon planting wheat, so that it could be made into bread and for the host for the Mass.) In a creation myth described in the ancient Mayan holy book the *Popul Vuh*, the Lords of Xabalba created mankind from ears of corn (*hombres de maiz,* or men of corn); in ancient but also in contemporary times, the reproductive cycle of corn forms the nexus of Mayan public celebration and ritual, and corn, in all its varieties of preparation, still makes up the foundation of the Mayan diet.

Thus it should come as no surprise that Mayanized theology reasserts the centrality of corn as a spiritual element, and the identity of Mayan Christians, too, as *hombres de maiz.* "The indigenous person who stops planting corn," exhorts Similox, "leaves behind so many cultural elements that she puts herself at serious risk" (pp. 142-43). The centrality of corn in Mayanized theology is highly symbolic, but it is also strategic, because in both Guatemala and Mexico Protestants have been widely reviled for their refusal to participate in community fiestas and public celebrations. Similox's insistence that Maya Protestants participate in both community celebrations and in the sacred duty of planting corn signals a clear affirmation of ethnic valorization in a Protestant context.

Despite this valorization, it is the reaffirmation of the material aspects of Mayan religious culture that proves a sticking point for many Mayan Protestants regarding inculturated theology. Mayan Protestants assiduously avoid the use of such material "gifts and creatures" as incense, candles, corn veneration, and alcohol. They repudiate these elements as "idolatrous" practices associated with syncretism and, worse still — in their way of thinking — Catholicism, which many Mayan converts, justifiably or not, negatively associate with spiritual domination and a repudiated pagan past. As another Mayan theologian, Antonio Otzoy, explained, "It was not long ago when Protestantism came; we were all Catholics then, and they would tell us, 'you are all pagans because you are Catholics.' . . . The Protestant Church in Guatemala is an anti-Catholic Church."[25] Otzoy has suggested that the sublimation of Mayan religious forms within Catholicism has produced a fierce Protestant bias against what he calls the "double paganization" *(doble paganización)* of Mayan spiritual imagery.[26] Thus the task remains for Protestant Mayanized theology to reclaim the patrimony of Mayan religious language, rituals, and symbolism not so much from the pre-Christian past, but from its strong association with Catholicism.

This issue illustrates as well as any the disconnect that exists between the discourse of Mayanized theology, articulated as it is by well-educated Mayan pastors and intellectuals, and everyday Maya believers, who as yet have been reticent in their acceptance of inculturated Protestant theology. This is most apparent among the Pentecostals, who recoil at any formal reconciliation between a type of spirituality they now consider idolatrous and the "Christian way" *(camino)*. Yet there is growing evidence that at the grassroots level, even Pentecostals are beginning to accommodate their indigenous worldview with Protestant beliefs. This is evinced by Pentecostal *acciones de gracias,* prayer services held at the planting and harvest of corn, and in informal discourse, as Mayan Protestants contemplate their unique place in the Christian *koinonia*. The questions they raise and the answers they devise suggest a reconciliation of Mayan beliefs within a Christian cosmology, rather than the other way around. This is well illustrated in the explanation a rural Mayan evangelical pastor gave of his understanding of the relationship between the holy scriptures of Christianity and ancient Mayan religion, the Bible and the *Popul Vuh*.

> I found that in the Bible, it says you have to have respect, right? In the Bible, it also says to honor the father and the mother, no? And there is one God, God the father, etc. In Mam [the pastor's Mayan language group], that is "elder," right? But the concept is the same. . . . So I think that it is possible to see that the people before [pre-Christian Mayans] had the concept; it's much clearer that there was religion and there was faith in God [in the New

25. Antonio Otzoy, "Hermandad de Presbiterios Maya," in *Primera Consulta, La Misión de la Iglesia Evangélica de Guatemala en la Etapa Post-Conflict* (Guatemala City: Ediciones Alternativas, 1998), pp. 38-39.

26. Otzoy, p. 38.

World] maybe in the time of Abraham — we don't know, right? Because unfortunately, we don't have the dates. Our ancestors had a great book (the *Popul Vuh*), but our enemies [the Spanish friars] burned [it], right? . . . what I want to say is that in reading the Bible, I arrived at the conclusion that they [the ancient Mayan ancestors] had it, when they were here on the earth, carrying a faith in the kingdom of God.[27]

The rural pastor's exegesis suggests that although Mayanized Protestant theology has been created around the political project of Mayan cultural revitalization in the aftermath of the civil war, the larger object of "decolonializing" and reconciling long-held beliefs with their new religion is quite compelling to many Mayan Protestants for reasons that reach well beyond political expediency. As anthropologist Matt Samson has noted, "If the Bible is seen as a source of primordial authority and as a point of religious identity for Mayan Protestants, there also exists among them a strong impulse to include the ancestors of the family with them now that are on what they feel is the right path, through their conversion."[28] It is perhaps in this fashion that Mayanized theology is making the transition from its genesis as the theological counterpart to a political discourse, to a vernacular hermeneutics in which is embedded a culturally meaningful narrative of salvation.

27. Samson, pp. 11-12. This is a paraphrase and translation of a much longer text that is printed in full in Samson's article.
28. Samson, p. 12.

# Multireligiosity Meets Theology:
## The Sri Lankan Tamils in Denmark

MARIANNE C. QVORTRUP FIBIGER

I have done fieldwork among Sri Lankan Tamil Hindus in Denmark since 1994, and wrote a Ph.D. dissertation about the meaning or function and adaption of religion in a cultural encounter, focusing on this particular group. In this article I will take as my starting point my research among the Tamils, where I see the Tamils as one example of the refugee and immigrant groups coming to Denmark, making the country not as religiously homogeneous as earlier — even though more than 80 percent of the citizens are still members of the Danish national church and more than 100,000 of the approximately 400,000 refugees and immigrants in Denmark are Christians.

I will stress how the Sri Lankan Tamil Hindu religious tradition has gone through what can be called a theologization process in its adaption to the modern Danish society and as a consequence has become institutionalized.

Theologization mainly means two things:

1. A consensus making of many local traditions into an overall, mutually accepted common religion, meaning that the local traditions become reduced into and encompassed in an overall theology. For the Sri Lankan Tamil Hindus this means a special Danish Tamil Hindu religion. This is important because newcomers have to deal with this situation. In other words, they find a new expression of their tradition, which in some aspects differs from the tradition they know from home.

2. An awareness of the specific religious elements of life. Commonly a lot of the refugee and immigrant groups coming to the West have never reflected on different layers of life as different categories or systems; and what we will categorize as religion just has been a part of their overall worldview and common behavior. Or as the Tamil Hindus often stress: "In Sri Lanka we just saw Hinduism as a way of life. Here in Denmark we have become more aware of its particularities as a religious faith."

These two aspects made me choose for this conference what may be a somewhat controversial title, where I try to turn the theme of the conference a bit upside down. But it is very important for me to emphasize that all religions are dynamic and in a state of flux when they have to be adapted to new environments and new needs for their members. Otherwise they will disappear, because religion is in my view nothing in itself, but only what people make it to be. Or, as Clifford Geertz puts it: "[A] French ethic in a Navaho world, or a Hindu one in a French world would seem only quixotic, for it would lack the air of naturalness and simple factuality which it has in its own context."[1] Aspects of tradition have to change. Otherwise tradition will stop contributing with focal points explaining what makes people a specific entity, different from others. As a result, a cultural encounter may often strengthen the central focal points in the tradition, which gives a religious and ethnic awareness.[2] At the same time, though, tradition is adapted to the demands of the new society so that it can constitute a new system which is relevant to its members.

The outcome of this is a tension between an awareness of tradition and the adaptation of this tradition. It also leads to a reassessment of the foundation of the tradition, allowing it to communicate internally within the specific community and externally with the community at large, and in so doing, leading to a specific tradition that is Danish, local Hindu/Muslim/Buddhist, and so forth, which people in some aspects find nowhere else. In this process religion will take over the role as a common denominator instead of the local traditions. In that way religion loses its local character and instead gets a new character, which suits the Danish society and the new demands of its members. For the second or at least third generation of refugees and immigrants, it means a change of focus from behavior rules to confession, where you are Muslim/Hindu/Buddhist because of faith, not because of social conformism.

---

1. Clifford Geertz, *The Interpretation of Cultures* (New York: Basic Books, 1973), p. 130.

2. It is important to notice that the Tamils in Denmark represent both an ethnic group and an ethnic category. Glazer and Moynihan have introduced this differentiation. Where the term "ethnic group" is referring to an internal self-understanding, being a special ethnic group from the beginning of history (a static point of view), the term "ethnic category" is dealing with the fact that ethnic affiliation is changing due to time, history, and surroundings, and is caused by the circumstances (the dynamic aspect). Rohit Barot, ed., *Religion and Ethnicity: Minorities and Social Change in the Metropolis* (The Netherlands: Kok Pharos, 1993), p. 4.

*Marianne C. Qvortrup Fibiger*

## The Sri Lankan Tamils as an Example

In Denmark we have around nine thousand Sri Lankan Tamils, more than eight thousand of whom are Hindus. The rest are mainly Catholic Christians, and only a few are Muslims.[3] The first Tamils came to Denmark in 1983 because of the escalating conflict in Sri Lanka. They were mostly men, and they were categorized as ipso facto refugees. Today they have married or have been reunited in Denmark with the family they had to leave. More than half the Tamils have become Danish citizens — a hallmark of their sincere intention to stay in Denmark and be a part of society. This open statement, which gives the Tamils not only a new nationality but also a new geographic point of contact, creates a need to show that being a part of society does not necessarily mean being an invisible part of society as an assimilation strategy stresses.

One of the most open manifestations of the Tamils being a part of the Danish society is the existence of the two Tamil Hindu temples or *kôyils*, Śree Sithy Vināyakar[4] and Śree Abirāmi Amman,[5] in two small towns in the middle of Jutland, where most of the Tamils are concentrated. This is in accordance with an old Hindu Tamil saying: "Do not live in a village where there is no temple,"[6] which means you have to stay at a place where the communication with and the manifestation of God is made possible. In that way the Sri Lankan Tamil Hindus who are true to the Hindu faith cannot find any religious obstacle to prevent them from being a part of society.

Compared to most other refugee and immigrant groups in Denmark, the Sri Lankan Tamils are already very integrated in the Danish society. Most of them have work, their children are doing well in the Danish schools, they often choose to speak Danish to each other, and they have adopted many of the Danish traditions but do it in a way that makes the tradition their own or gives it a symbolic meaning that does not clash with what they consider core matters of their tradition. "In kindergarten and in school our children make Easter and Christmas decorations and even though we are Hindus, we decorate our house with them as we do not want to disappoint our children. At Christmas we give

---

3. Because Statistic Denmark, who register all newcomers to Denmark, do not take religious but only geographic affiliation into account, it is difficult to give an exact figure for religious groupings.

4. Vināyakar is another name for Pilliayar or Ganeśa, the elephant-headed son of Śiva.

5. This temple is dedicated to a mother goddess named Abirāmi representing the dynamic creative power *śakti*. She is a manifestation of Pārvatī, the wife of Śiva.

6. In Tamil: *kôyil illāta ūril kutiyirāte* (S. Suseendirarajah, "Religiousness in the 'Aiva Village,'" in *Religiousness in Sri Lanka*, ed. John Ross Carter [Colombo, Sri Lanka: Marga Institute, 1979], p. 183).

each other presents, we eat Christmas duck, like our children's Danish friends do, and we wrap up an extra present telling our children it is from their grandparents in Sri Lanka. They can then say at school that they have got a present from them as well. But we do not sing Christmas carols or go to church."[7]

This example shows that the Sri Lankan Tamils adapt to the new environment and the modern Danish society, but without embracing all aspects of it. Or, in other words, the Sri Lankan Tamils both want to retain a specific Tamil integrity and to have an open cultural communication with the Danish society at large with changes, but also with an increasing awareness of focal elements of their tradition as a consequence. It is important to emphasize this "double movement" because it leads to a more or less deliberate compartmentalization strategy related to both internal representations (inside the specific Sri Lankan Tamil Hindu group) and external representations (the Tamil group as such), and these two in some way overlapping compartmentalization relations to the public sphere inter alia the Danish society at large. I will follow this dialectic in this article.

The analytical use of compartmentalization that I apply in the distinction between internal and external representation and how it is changing due to the new circumstances in the public sphere is inspired by Milton Singer and his elaboration on how Madrasi Hindu industrial leaders were mentally categorizing the industrial public sphere and the private domestic sphere as two distinct areas not only socially and culturally but also in relation to behavior, norms, and conduct precepts. Singer concludes: "In this compartmentalization, the work sphere is 'ritually neutralized,' that is, relatively freed from customary norms and ritual restrictions. This makes it easier to experiment with and learn about new products, processes, and social relations."[8] In my point of departure this distinction gives a hint on how it is possible to try new and possibly threatening things in the neutral public area, before integrating them as part of tradition. A clue is that in spite of this mental compartmentalization, the two spheres are in permanent interrelated communication, where parts of the elements which are accepted in the public sphere will slowly become an accepted part of the private sphere in a natural innovative process.

One outcome of this compartmentalization strategy for the Sri Lankan Tamil Hindus in Denmark is an institutionalization of Hinduism. The temple as an internal representation has become the religious bearer per se, because

7. This quote is from a Tamil Hindu male in his forties.

8. Milton Singer, *When a Great Tradition Modernizes: An Anthropological Approach to Indian Civilisation* (London: Pall Mall Press, 1972), p. 349. See also Singer, "Beyond Tradition and Modernity in Madras," in *Comparative Studies in Society and in History,* vol. 13 (Cambridge: Cambridge University Press, 1971).

Hinduism as a way of life does not go hand in hand with modern Danish society characterized as functionally differentiated as, for example, Anthony Giddens characterizes it. He uses the term "disembedding" to refer to this process of differentiating, i.e., the process resulting in a society divided in expert systems.[9]

At the same time, this division means that new claims and new demands are put on the expert system or internal representation, as *the* representation of Tamil Hinduism in Denmark. This makes the believing Tamil Hindus emphasize the right ritual conduct, or orthopraxis, when it comes to temple worship, especially in relation to the *pūjā* (sermon). At the same time, however, they want it to suit the new public demands, which means they adjust the time for the temple worship so it fits the working hours. As a consequence they only conduct one smaller public *pūjā* a day, at evening, in the Śree Sithy Vināyakar temple.[10] But on Friday evening they do a longer *pūjā,* and they put much effort into it because they want to keep up all the religious precepts. The worshipers who eat meat during the week only eat vegetarian food on Fridays before going in the temple, and they clean their houses Thursdays because Friday is the day during the week they must be purified. This also influences especially the behavior of the women, who often fast that day as a representative for the whole family, and they do not go in the temple when they are having their period. And when it comes to the *pūjā* in the temple, the involved are very aware of following the right conduct scheme, which makes them more aware of that part of religion. Or, as one well-esteemed priest from Munneswaram in Sri Lanka told me during a visit there: "The *pūjā* you see in the Śree Sithy Vināyakar temple here in Denmark is in many ways closer to the tradition if you compare it with *pūjā* conducted in smaller temples in Sri Lanka."[11]

This compartmentalization strategy, which in some respects leads to a demand for closeness, in others to an openness, gives us a clue to how the Tamil Hindus deal with the integration process, so they become a visible part of the Danish society without erasing what they feel are the focal points of tradition. Due to this fact the tradition has to change in some respects so that it can fit to the new demands both inside the group and outside in relation to society.

9. Anthony Giddens, *Modernity and Self-Identity: Self and Society in the Late Modern Age* (Cambridge: Polity Press, 1991), pp. 17-18.

10. This concept is beginning to change, because they have just begun to conduct public *pūjās* every evening — but in a minor form but including *abhisekam* (bathing of the gods). Only a few worshipers are coming to the temple on these days.

11. I did fieldwork in Sri Lanka in 1997 and compared the temple conduct as it takes place in the Śree Sithy Vināyakar temple with temples in Negombo, Sri Lanka, and can only agree with his point of view.

This relation between the Sri Lankan Tamil Hindus and their temple, in which they can be together cultivating their religious self-awareness, makes it thus easier for them to communicate out of the system or open themselves in other aspects. Because of this common fundament, which they can lean on and turn back to, they feel more encouraged to face challenges in other situations in society. In other words, the collective memory will always be there.[12]

According to the point of view of this paper, the collective memory is the same as the religious tradition that takes place in the temple. Paul Connerton stresses the importance of this collective memory when trying to understand how a memory within a group is sustained.[13] He argues in comparison with myth, that ritual has significantly less potential for variance:

> All rituals, it is true, have to be invented at some point and the details of their articulation may develop or vary in content and significance over the course of time. None the less, there remains a potential for invariance that is built into rites, but not into myths, by virtue of the fact that it is intrinsic to the nature of rituals — but not of myths — that they specify the relationship that obtains between the performance of ritual and what it is that the participants are performing. It follows that if considerable precautions are to be taken to assure the identity of a culture's symbolic material, it will be advisable to direct those precautions to ensuring the identity of its ritual.[14]

This fits in with the observation made in the Śree Sithy Vināyakar temple. As mentioned before, the worshipers stress the right ritual conduct, and in doing so they are able to preserve the collective memory and at the same time to sustain the temple as a self-referential room, being a visible symbol in the modern Danish society characterized by being functionally differentiated.

## Conclusion

In Denmark the Hindu Tamil tradition has to adapt to a society which it has not been a part of in a long historical and dialectical process. This means that the tradition has to adapt to the new demands to be able to continue being relevant for its members. At the same time, it cannot change what are seen as its fo-

---

12. Paul Connerton, *How Societies Remember* (Cambridge: Cambridge University Press, 1989).

13. Connerton, p. 1.

14. Connerton, p. 57.

cal points. Otherwise it will stop being a central meaning giver in a sensitive integration process. In the adaption to the modern Danish society characterized by being functionally differentiated, the tradition's adaption process makes it an exclusive religious expert system including all the Sri Lankan Tamil Hindus. This process can be called a theologization process, where the overall common elements founded by the Śaiva Siddhanta theology and the work of the Sri Lankan Tamil reformist Arumugar Navalar are emphasized and the local behavior patterns are erased and called "superstition." This is an example of what Giddens calls strategic conduct.[15]

As I hope will be clear from the examples given in this article, the relation between tradition and modernity does not necessarily lead to a break or an either-or selection. The tradition is adapted to fit the demands of modernity, which for the Sri Lankan Tamil Hinduism in Denmark leads to an institutionalization of the religious tradition, whereas on the other hand the keeping up of the, let's say, "cultivated" religious tradition is emphasized. So what the national church in Denmark faces in relation to refugee and immigrant groups is not multireligiosity but different interpretations of theology or different confessions, which at least in the third or fourth generation more or less have the same point of departure for all, being a part of the Danish modern society, which in some ways can be called a Protestant or modern viewpoint, focusing on the individual choice and a personal relation to faith. In that perspective it is a point that tradition and modernity have to be treated as congruous, not as departing entities. It is the relationship between the two that gives a special awareness of what constitutes the focal points of the tradition-based system, and in what way it can communicate with the modern society at large, and the individual needs being a part of both the modern Danish society and a religious community. The outcome is a special Danish Hindu/Muslim/Buddhist tradition, which in some aspects in the adaption process will slowly get more in common with the society it has become a part of than the society it left. It means less multireligiosity because the local, maybe national traditions slowly disappear.

15. Anthony Giddens, *The Consequences of Modernity* (Cambridge: Polity Press, 1990).

# The Danish Church Responds to Multireligiosity

HANS HAUGE

## The One and the Many

The world was ever multicultural, multiethnic, multireligious, and multilingual. "Multi" is old and real. Unity is more like a dream. Or it used to be a dream. The world was never one, but sometimes people dreamed of one world. Philosophy and theology always posited the precedence of the one over the many. Empires had as a motto "Unity in variety."[1] This was in fact the British Empire's Platonic ideal and the European Union's.[2] Or think of the ideals *e pluribus unum* or *ut unum sint*. The first — American dream — is now being changed into *e pluribus plures*. *Unum* is disappearing, or so it seems.

Today — *and this is new* — the ideal or nightmare of one world, unity, is perhaps being realized before our very eyes as globalization and individualization. The precedence of one over many is being realized technologically and juridically in terms of money, Internet, and human rights. This is an ideal situation for the Catholic Church, but a problem for particularist Protestant ones. Therefore, it seems, philosophy, theology, culture, radical politics, and the human sciences have begun positing the many — the manifold — over the one, difference over sameness, heterogeneity over homogeneity. There is only the multitude. We love difference today. That's what makes us rather similar. Oneness is parasitic transcendence.

Modern warfare, for instance, is essentially a police action undertaken with reference to universal human rights against some unruly groups in the periphery. "Make law, not war" is the new motto. No one wants to conquer new

---

1. Or "Variety in unity"; see J. Williamson, *The Story of the British Empire in Pictures* (London, n.d.).
2. EU's purpose: "to build unity through diversity."

land, so in that sense the world is definitely postcolonial and postnational. Nobody wants Afghanistan, Palestine, or Kosovo; that is to say, the Americans or NATO do not want them even though local nationalists do. Some refer to this as the return of empires; others see a new empire as the only solution to problems in premodern, Third World states; some claim empire has already materialized before our very eyes;[3] most commentators just refer to all this as globalization.

Empires do not fear variety or the manifold, only nation-states do, and they are declining. The various multiplicities or difference may in fact be disappearing, and therefore we see groups trying to resurrect, i.e., invent, it. Multiculturalism may be the ideology of the waning of the nation-state. At least the nation-state is an appearance being globalized from the inside.[4] Globalization is its essence, its inside. Nationality is a false front.

What's new is when the nation-state is being described or imagined[5] as *multicultural*. It is a contradiction in terms to operate with such an entity, because the nation's ideal is and was one people, one church, one religion, one ethnic group, *ein Volk,* "we the people," meaning: many is or as one.[6] This was of course never realized anywhere, but the unity and homogeneity were imagined by many to be real and even worth dying for. The nation-state was made by war and makes war.

Thomas Hobbes's ideal state, the Leviathan, the mortal god, was one composed of many. Its purpose was to put an end to religious wars. It was successful. The result of the Thirty Years' War was, as is well known, the now-so-much-discussed Westphalian state, that is to say, the territorial state, which then, in its turn, produced first dynastic and after that endless national wars. This led to the dream of the unification of Europe.

Rousseau's *volonté generale* was many as one or the submergence of the individual in the community. The nation-state was the disappearance of the individual in the *Volksgemeinschaft.* The multicultural nation-state is the end of the nation-state and a threat to any national or *established* church such as the Danish one, or the Russian or the Greek one. The church is not threatened in secular liberal states like the United States or Turkey, if one is permitted to call the mosque a church.

Multicultural, multiethnic, multireligious — the three words are slogans

---

3. These are the opening words of Michael Hardt and Antonio Negri's "new communist manifesto": *Empire* (Cambridge, Mass., 2000).

4. Says German sociologist Ulrich Beck.

5. I am all the time referring to Benedict Anderson's indispensable *Imagined Communities* (London: Verso, 1983).

6. Similarly it was a contradiction when Lionel Jospin said he wanted Europe to be a federation of nation-states.

heard on CNN in a commercial for Malaysia. Multiplicity attracts tourists. If Malaysia and Denmark can both be characterized with the same three words, something has definitely changed. Or are the two countries really comparable? Well, yes, in the sense that both can be described as states; but Malaysia was never a nation-state — a map of the country is proof enough. Can Malaysia cope with globalization better than Denmark? Perhaps so.

Multicultural, multiethnic, and multireligious: the trinity's function is to symbolize the postmodernity of Malaysia — and Denmark. There is another reason why I mention Malaysia: its prime minister, Mohammed Mahatir, once said Asian values are universal, European values are just European. Denmark is presently — like most other states, including Malaysia — being characterized by the trinity of "multi-" words.

I introduce Mahatir's dictum since universality is also at stake. Behind the church's evangelism has always been a belief in the universality of its message. There have always been many religions, and the Christian church was ever surrounded by multireligiosity. The primitive church had no power, but it had the truth. Therefore it evangelized. The Constantine and post-Constantine church had power and truth. Therefore it evangelized. And thus it continued, roughly speaking, until decolonization in the 1960s. Imperial missionaries could find signs of the one and true religion in the religions of most primitive tribes. Today's anthropologists may find universal structures beneath all religions, but these structures are not Christian. The postmodern church in a globalizing world may have power, but it has no truth — not officially. At least it hides the truth under a humanitarian cloak.

It is as if Christianity has become particularized or simply smaller. A Danish theologian once claimed that Jesus — the Truth — was the particular and only the creator God was the universal — i.e., only God transcended Christianity.[7] A Christianity without incarnation may be its future version, or else we shall have to be looking for the "hidden Christ of Islam," to slightly change Raimundo Panikkar's phrase.[8]

We have our religion; they have their religion; and the two can dialogue and interact and respect each other but should be left intact and *the same size.* They should not be permitted to grow. This particularizing of churches was a result of the church's integration in the nation-state. Today's so-called progressive church leaders — as opposed to conservative evangelizing ones — in fact

---

7. K. E. Løgstrup was his name. His book on ethics, *The Ethical Demand,* exists in an English translation (Notre Dame: University of Notre Dame Press, 1997).
8. I am thinking of Panikkar's book, *The Hidden Christ of Hinduism* (Maryknoll, N.Y.: Orbis, 1981).

try to freeze the situation as it is. The progressive strategy is pretty much like world politics during the Cold War, when the world was divided between West and East. We promise not to evangelize if the Muslims do, too. Islam has taken over the role of communism. The Left loves it; the Right fights it.

And as is always the case, one[9] forgets the Hindus, and we have difficulty visualizing the conflicts in India that are much more dangerous than the much less complex postcolonial civil war in the Middle East.

## Multiculturalism

Multiculturalism is not a word that describes anything. It is a discourse that constitutes its object, just like nationalism did or does. The unity or multiplicity is in the description, not in any societal reality described. Just as the unity or national identity was imagined — because it did not exist — multiculturalism is imagined. In order for it to be imagined, it first has to be taught. This is what schools do. Canada was, I believe, the first country to adopt multiculturalism as official policy. Toronto prides itself for being the world's most multicultural city.

Nineteenth-century Canada used to be "His Dominion" and Protestant, although most people living there were Catholics. In Protestant America south of the border the Catholic Church was the single largest religious body around 1850. To say a nation is Protestant — as it was also once said about both Sweden and England — is again not a description. It is to create a difference.[10]

By going multicultural Canada solved a problem. It was an impossible state with two nations, and that means trouble; however, this did not cause serious problems for a great many years because Canada was not meant to be a nation-state but a dominion. A dominion was intended as an alternative to the nation-state, but an unsuccessful one. Successful was the unification of churches into the United Church of Canada. And of course, there never was a state church like in the Scandinavian countries, nor an established one like in England.

Canada was forced to become a nation-state like the rest, which led to unrest in Quebec. Multiculturalism was Pierre Trudeau's liberal solution. It made majority Anglophone culture one out of many and a smaller one, and the Francophone minority was made one out of many but a bigger one. Quebec, however, was not too happy about multiculturality. It wanted to maintain its

9. "One" is us in Europe or the media.
10. England was Protestant because Spain was Catholic.

distinct society and came up with a new idea: interculturalism or the *contrat social* from 1990. And no one liked the idea of a multilingual society, so the compromise became many cultures but two languages (and only one in Quebec). In practice this meant severing the bond between language and culture, a bond we believe in in Denmark.

It is easier to govern a multicultural society because then one cannot count cultures. One, two, many. One culture, two cultures — multicultural.

Bosnia, the Dayton agreement ordered, should become multi — everyone feared a Muslim Bosnia. One culture is dangerous. Many hate American culture because it is the only one.

## Four Phases of Danish History

They say Denmark is being transformed from a mono-religious into a multireligious society. We go from one to many: many cultures, ethnic groups, and languages. But it is not true. That's a good example of getting one's history wrong, and hence the basis for national identity. Monoculture is multiculturalism's other. Multiculturalism has had to construct a monoculture as not only boring but dangerous and as something prior. A multicultural culture is often advertised as more colorful and entertaining than a national homogeneous one. Certainly the monocultural nation-state was not a *Spassgesellschaft*. I know, I grew up in its school system.

I did not, however, grow up in a country with one religion, although I was told so and although the multicultural rewriting of national history tells me so. Denmark was always multireligious, but it had one church. What is happening is an unchurching in this country as in Germany and Britain.

The church had to deal with as many religions and diverse readings of the same text — the Bible — in the old days as it has to now. What's new? At least not the existence of many religions. Every Danish village was divided between various religious sects and groups — in many places just two, very much like in England in the old days with Evangelicals versus Low Church or church and chapel.[11]

Let me divide Danish history, the history of its state and its church and territory, into four periods. First, ancien régime or absolutism from 1660 to 1849. Denmark-Norway was a fair-sized imperial state. Second, nation-state from 1849 with the introduction of democracy. Losing wars and territory to

---

11. See Jeremy Paxman, *The English: A Portrait of a People* (New York: Overlook Press, 2000), where he describes the religious violence in England.

Prussia (called Germany). A Dane is a non-German. Third, the labor-party state or the welfare state from 1945 to 1989. The welfare state is Lutheranism secularized and called a "universalist" one because all got money gratis without having done anything to deserve it. Faith alone is enough. The church loved it. It no longer had to do good deeds. Fourth, Denmark becomes a postmodern, multicultural European network state from 1989 onward. The conglomerate state Denmark-Norway and the duchies (Schleswig and Holstein) were in the first period, as few Danes realize because we are never told the true story in our history books, an imperial state with a flourishing slave trade, which explains why Copenhagen looks the way it does. The realm had colonies in India and on the Gold Coast, and sugar plantations in the West Indies. There was a cold Nordic empire: Iceland, the Faeroe Islands, and Greenland. In northern Norway there were the Sami people.

It was a multilingual empire, and people in power spoke German. It was multiethnic but mono-religious, although there was religious freedom in the Danish West Indies from 1700 onward. There simply were too many different religious groups. Famous Danish hymn writer and nationalist churchman N. F. S. Grundtvig had two older brothers who died as missionaries in Danish Guinea. Kierkegaard financed his life from money made by slave trade. His fiancée, Regine Olsen, spent her life in the colonies. Denmark established a university in "Frederiknagore" in India.[12] Denmark was a large country in terms of territory, and it still is. It is a united kingdom consisting of three nations, of which only one is a member of the European Union. The imperial nature of the Danish national church can still be seen when the Danish bishops visit Greenland and the Faeroe Islands with the queen on certain ecclesiastical occasions. Denmark is never experienced in this way but imagined as a small homogeneous ideal labor-party state.

As in many other European ancien régime states, the Danish church responded to multireligiosity with force and persuasion. State and church were one, and in a sense there was no church. Everything — at least in theory — was state, and there were no civil society and no market. But society and a market developed alongside the state and hence made religious awakenings and revivals — the beginning of free churches — possible. In a state with a weak state, like the United States, they saw countless awakenings, and some of them reached this country toward the end of the nineteenth century. Awakenings were in fact modernizing forces. As time passed the Danish church had to respond to growing multireligiosity in a new and more democratic way. Inner

---

12. Today's Serampore. There are still contacts between the Danish church and the Tranquebar Mission.

Mission, evangelicals, Grundtvig's followers, Baptists, and later Mormons were still harassed, ridiculed, or ignored but not jailed. With the Constitution of 1849 the peculiar institution — the *Folkekirke* — that is, the people's church — was invented. The constitution had the state support of the Evangelical-Lutheran church, whatever "support" meant. Money? That's what the church thinks.

The constitution was partly an imitation of the Belgian one, and its author was a clergyman, D. G. Monrad, a Hegelian who believed in a strong state and feared the populace.[13] Clergymen had much influence on politics, and many are still members of parliament. Politics and religion were never separated in this country.

The free churches were criticized, but they could not be stopped. Chapels — "mission houses," as they were called — were built in the capital and all over the country and given biblical names like Tabor or Bethesda,[14] but the official culture and the church construed the pietistic evangelicals as the other which every society has to construct in order to get an identity.

In Denmark, by the middle of the nineteenth century, and after the introduction of democracy (1849), integration was no longer religious but had become national. The church and the state could disregard the religious differences because even if people had different religions, they belonged to the same nation — *cuius regio eius natio* replaced absolutism's *eius religio*. Religion was no longer needed to integrate.

The church had become so thoroughly nationalized that to be a Christian and a Dane were in effect the same. Christianity had become nationalized, and so it still is for many Danes. It is a civil religion.

By the 1960s the many religions and all awakenings had almost disappeared; there could come no more revivals. We had big government or the labor-party state. The welfare state was almost total, the market controlled, and civil society nearly nonexistent. There were many other "foreign" religions, such as Islam and Buddhism, but outside the territory; for inside the borders there was no religion, or if there was religion it was belief in the state, in the work ethic, or in some form of nonutopian Marxism. The welfare state took over most of the church's social tasks and thus tried to make the church superfluous. The state was the caring father. Philanthropy was low rent. The church was left with one task: to preach every Sunday and keep silent and out of politics. It did, and nobody paid much attention to it. Religion was disappearing

13. He immigrated to New Zealand.

14. Many are ruins today. No one wants to preserve them; most find their presence slightly embarrassing.

anyway. So most sophisticated theologians responded to the situation by becoming demythologizing existentialist Bultmannians or "Tillichic"[15] preachers.

There were not many religions but only one: state as religion. People relied on the social-democratic state, which made them feel secure, and they never went to church. They feared the Kierkegaardian God-is-dead gospel preached there, which deprived them of the solace and comfort of religion. A church historian abolished eternal life in the fifties, and we had a scandal about it pretty similar to the Bishop Robinson "honest to God" one in England. The situation was like in the good old absolutist days: the state had full control of the church and its theologians. The church never protested. The theologians could say whatever they wished. And they did. The people — *das Volk* — loved the church. Its message imploded in the big black hole of the silent majority who used baptism as another commodity provided by the nanny welfare state.

This was all before 1989, or 1972 when immigration began and Denmark entered the European Union. Both civil society and free markets returned in people's imaginations. Many churchmen resisted the new tides. Nationality was threatened, and thereby their brand of Danish Christianity, they felt, and they were right.

The church had to face up to modernity, and modernity meant *secularism*. That is no longer the case. Many believed the rise of industrial societies would mean a shift from traditional value systems to modern or postmodern value systems: Ronald Inglehart calls these systems rational, tolerant, trusting, and postmodern self-expressiveness.[16] Inglehart is *the* theorist of postmaterialist values.

The church developed skills for dealing with modernity, secularism, postmaterialism, and rationality, and came to quite like it all. There were the so-called new religions, but they could be dismissed offhand as countermodern — but then suddenly, unexpectedly, the church and the theologians had to face up to — not modernity — but religion, return of religion, "revenge of God," many religions, multireligiosity. Samuel Huntington had foreseen this, and therefore all took him to task.[17] Religious traditions were still powerful despite forces of modernization, and Inglehart had to revise his theory.

The church or its theologians were unprepared for this new situation and at first tried to live on as if there were no religion and even defended secularism. Theology and the church had not been used to defending Christianity against

15. To use John Updike's happy phrase.

16. See Ronald Inglehart, "Culture and Democracy," in *Culture Matters: How Values Shape Human Progress*, ed. Lawrence E. Harrison and Samuel P. Huntington (New York, 2000).

17. See Samuel P. Huntington, *The Clash of Civilizations and the Remaking of World Order* (New York, 1997).

other religions but against its detractors — the secular intellectuals and areligious people. They had come to believe in metaphor instead of the letter. They simply did not know what to say to a Muslim, let alone someone who believed in a life hereafter or eternal damnation. Everyone had forgotten Schleiermacher and felt that evangelizing was bad taste. Mission was replaced by "dialogue." The art of converting other people was forgotten.

In 1970 — more than thirty years ago — 7,000 Muslims in Copenhagen sent a petition to 150 clergymen and received not a single answer. The church ignored them even if they were empirically present. They were not seen even if they were there. The pastors passed by as in the parable of the Good Samaritan. The Muslims asked if they could be given one of the many empty Copenhagen churches. No answer. Today the same clergymen support the Muslims' wish to build mosques and want dialogue with them. Why now and not then? And why no dialogue with Mormons? Now or then? The reason seems not to be religious but for the sake of national integration.

In 1973 a sociologist said the Danes should decide whether they wanted to be a multicultural or a monocultural society. No one reacted. Most left-wing politicians and labor union leaders were against the foreign workers because they had been invited by the evil capitalists to steal honest Danish workers' jobs. To be favorable toward immigration was right-wing. And that perhaps explains the church's silence back in the politicized 1970s.

In one of Denmark's leading anti-Christian and antichurch newspapers, *Politiken,* one political commentator wrote: At present, there are 170,000 Muslims in Denmark, therefore the country is *multiethnic.* He said this is a fact. There is nothing to discuss. It is nonpolitical. Therefore, he went on, church and state must separate. Two things: How on earth can 170,000 Muslims make the country multi-anything? And is ethnic and religious the same? When did immigration cease to be something political and become a depoliticized fact? When there were 100,000? Seven thousand wasn't enough. The issue could be discussed in 1973, but not in 2002. Can Muslims be counted? Can Christians? No.

How many Christians are there in Denmark? One hundred thousand. That's the average number regularly attending services, in which case the Christians are a minority. Or many more. All the baptized ones? Then the number is 83 percent. Or a few converted ones or no one? Majorities mean nothing in religion, said Montesquieu. And he was right. Neither do numbers. Similarly cultures are uncountable if there are more than two. The "multi-" prefix is often used to cover up something. When used in this country, it more often than not means not many *but two.* No one is, as I said, concerned with Jehovah's Witnesses or Hindus. Multireligiosity was not a problem when there were many religions and many religious people; it was invented when there were two religions, one of which people actually believed in.

Some modernist theologians cling to modernization theories and Enlightenment values and declare Islam premodern or traditional. But they — the modernists — are considered reactionaries instead of the Muslims.

There are Muslims and Christians — *two* religions — in this country, like many other places. Two cultures and not many. And when there are two, there is a clash. We used to — or the socialists did — divide people into classes, and after the disappearance of the aristocracy there were in late capitalism only two classes left to fight each other. Classes clashed. Then classes disappeared and were replaced by races as analytical categories.[18] With two religions the situation is "Canadian" and invites a Canadian solution — multiculturalism. Let two be many.[19]

Rousseau, one of the fathers of the nation-state, said there were four things every citizen had to accept: the existence of god, life in the hereafter, happiness for the just and punishment for the unjust after death, and the most important: the sanctity of the social contract. One had to subscribe to that contract or go into exile.

Why did different religions matter in the old days? Because it was a serious matter which religion you belonged to. *It all had to do with life in the hereafter.* If you did not belong to the true church, the result was eternal damnation. Most people today do not subscribe to the first three tenets — and the state functions without such a subscription. A group of Danish socialist politicians are now beginning to take up Rousseau's last principle: the sanctity of the social contract. They want new citizens to sign such a contract in an attempt to exclude too-religious people. That's worship of the state.

We have now entered the fourth phase. (1) Absolutism, (2) nation-state, (3) welfare state, (4) postmodern condition. In the first phase the state took over the church and the multireligious was either ignored or suppressed. It was found especially in the colonies. In the second, the church married itself to the nation; the many new religions were no threat to the integrity of the nation-state. Nationalism was the one new religion and differences were wiped out. All spoke the same religious language, namely, the mother tongue.

In the third phase the church acquiesced and claimed it shared the values of the labor-party state. It did not have to respond to many religions because

18. I am not interested in classes and races as empirical categories.
19. I am inspired by Werner Link's critique of Huntington in *Die Neuordnung der Weltpolitik* (Munich, 1998). Link claims Huntington's seven or eight civilizations are really only two: the West versus the rest.

apparently there were not many religions. The only one was a kind of market religion, consumerism, which the state, the school, the social democrats, and the church detested.

How is the church to respond to postmodern multireligiosity? By becoming a part of the marketplace and civil society. The state is shrinking, so any future alliance with the state is impossible in any case. The church married the state after 1849. It had no choice because it had no other means of subsistence. Now the churches are leaving their husband states because these states no longer have power nor (tax) money. The modern state is just one institution or system amongst many others. The church is already becoming an actor on the market and in the media. It is becoming visible. It will in the future take back many of the tasks that were taken over by the welfare state. It will again have to run hospitals, schools, banks, newspapers, labor unions, and so forth. It is a question of getting rid of the state and of letting the church organize itself. It has already begun. The avant-garde churches are to be found in South Korea, the United States, China, or in sub-Saharan African states. The dechurching of Europe is also its provincialization.

PART II

INTERRELIGIOUS DIALOGUE

# Interreligious Dialogue: Theory and Experience

NOTTO R. THELLE

With this introduction I do not attempt to answer the numerous questions or moderate the many challenges we encounter in interreligious dialogue. My only intention is to invite you to reflection and sharing in an atmosphere of trust, mental hospitality, and willingness to learn. Interreligious dialogue is a demanding exercise, but dialogue about dialogue also requires our full attention, and is sometimes even more challenging than the direct encounter face-to-face with representatives of other religions.

I will first share a few remarks about interreligious dialogue, and then conclude with a fictitious account of an encounter that could never have happened — that between Buddha and Jesus.

## The Purpose of Dialogue

Some time ago I was asked to give a lecture about the purpose of dialogue. My first response was to protest and say that dialogue has no purpose. It is a way of life, like sleeping and breathing, eating and working, playing and loving. You don't have to explain why you breathe or work or love. You just do it. To be a human being is to be in dialogue. You don't explain why. It has no purpose. That also applies to interreligious dialogue.

When that is said, I have to admit that of course dialogue has a purpose and a direction. There are ways of eating and working and playing and loving that are meaningless or destructive. In the same way there are ways of talking together that destroy our humanity. When relationships break down and are re-

---

This essay served as the introduction to the workshop on interreligious dialogue at the Aarhus symposium "Theology Meets Multireligiosity," May 13-15, 2002.

placed by suspicion and animosity, dialogue becomes a method of restoring the broken relations. When I use the word "dialogue" here, I want to reserve it for the meaningful dialogue, the way of relating that aims at establishing trust, mutual respect, tolerance, or — one might hope — love. To put it paradoxically, one might say that the purpose of dialogue is to establish a situation in which dialogue has no other purpose than being in a trusting relationship.

Dialogue is people who meet and talk together about their concerns. They knock at each other's doors, are invited into the houses of the others, cross borders, find themselves at the boundary where they listen, observe, and speak. And something happens.

## Theory and Practice

There is nothing as practical as a good theory. But many theories are out of touch with practice, and are therefore misleading. Things look different when they appear not as themes in a book, but as persons, faces, bodies, mouths, and eyes that claim to be taken into consideration. Dialogical experience makes us accountable. So we are in need of theories about interreligious dialogue that are rooted in experience and hence can help us understand the implications of dialogical practice.

It happens, on the other hand, that interreligious dialogue goes on without theoretical reflection. One is satisfied with the experience and not interested in theoretical reflection. In fact, it may even disturb the mutual trust and openness. At least that may be the case in certain situations and for some people, particularly at the level of everyday encounters where people of different faiths live side by side as neighbors. Such seemingly unreflecting interfaith relations may actually express deep understanding of the processes, even though no words are used for theoretical explanations.

In the long run, however, both individuals and religious communities will feel the need for deeper reflection. Sooner or later we need to take a step back and ask ourselves what is happening, which processes the dialogue stimulates, and what our involvement implies for our life of faith. That is important not only for the sake of the identity of the religious tradition, but also for the dialogical process. There is nothing as practical as a good theory.

## Levels of Dialogue

I have already indicated that there are levels of dialogue. My own experiences from Japan and Norway suggest at least four levels, even though the various levels cannot be clearly distinguished and are often interrelated. They may be characterized in different ways, but let me suggest the following:

- dialogue at the level of theology and philosophy, often conducted by scholars of religion;
- various types of spirituality dialogue, often less interested in theoretical exchange than in sharing of spiritual practice such as prayer and meditation;
- dialogue aiming at cooperation about common concerns, such as poverty, discrimination, injustice, conflicts, militarism, the environment, etc.; and
- the everyday dialogue between neighbors of diverse faiths.

Some people tend to rank the different types of dialogue, regarding for example the sharing of spirituality as more meaningful than cooperation about common concerns, or the philosophical academic dialogue as far more important and challenging than the everyday dialogue on the level of common people. I think we should abandon that type of ranking. People's everyday interactions may sometimes be carried on with more wisdom than that of the philosophers in their academic exercises. The various types of dialogue belong to different contexts; they are expressions of different concerns and cannot easily be compared. But they may all lead to experiences and insights that are relevant for the other levels of dialogue.

## Hospitality

In my encounter with Buddhism in Japan I have often been struck by the hospitality and generosity with which I have been received. I have often experienced a deeper spiritual fellowship with Buddhist friends than with Christian colleagues. This has been a reminder to me that hospitality is a basic biblical virtue, and an inspiration to understand that interfaith dialogue must be developed in a spirit of hospitality. Dialogue needs an open space of freedom in order to function, a mutual trust which does not use the encounter as an opportunity for manipulating apologetics, a generosity of the mind which lets the other be the other without trying to define him or her according to one's own categories.

*Notto R. Thelle*

## Identity and Change

The experience of dialogue leads to change. One may be committed to one's own tradition, faithful to the precious insights of the creed, eager also to share one's faith with the other. Things look different when one meets at the boundary, or when one is invited into the spiritual realm of the other. The other is different from the way he or she was described in the books, and one has to integrate that into a new understanding of the other. One's own spiritual home looks different when experienced and shared in dialogue with persons from other faiths, and that has to be integrated in a new self-understanding.

We tend to regard identity as something essentially unchanging in one's personality or in one's tradition. I know I am the same person as the little boy fifty years ago, or as the adolescent, the proud father of the first daughter, the young missionary who came to Japan to convert people, the university professor. . . . But I also know that these persons existed many personalities ago. There is continuity, of course. I recognize the same bodily movements, the same freckles, the same irritating habits, and the same strong points. But fortunately I am not the same. Things have changed, sometimes radically — thoughts, emotions, relationships, the body — innumerable changes which indicate that identity is nothing static, but is maintained in a continuous process of change and integration.

We often tend to forget that religions also change in similar ways. Christianity has changed in the encounter with new cultures and religious traditions. The early church is different from the medieval church, which is different from modern church life. We search for Christian identity in the Bible and the wisdom of the church, and see a continuing but ever changing identity. There are in fact many Christianities, and in a similar way there are many Islams and Buddhisms and Judaisms. And it would be strange to expect that the experiences from interreligious dialogue should not contribute to changes in the understanding of one's faith. A Christian who has met the Buddha is not the same as before. A Buddhist who has met the Christ is not the same.

## A Dialogue That Never Took Place:
## A Fiction about Buddha and Jesus

Instead of continuing my reflections on dialogue experiences, I would like to conclude by describing a dialogue which never took place and never could happen, but certainly has taken place in many people's minds: the encounter between Jesus and Buddha.

One lived in tropical India, with humid heat and abundant fertility, but also floods and drought and destruction. The other came from Palestine in west Asia, where fertile fields and villages were scattered among barren mountains and dry wilderness. They were also separated by four or five centuries, which — measured in geographical distance — might be even further apart than distant continents.

So they never met, but the question remains: What would have happened if they had met? What would they have said if they had the opportunity to meet?

I have invited them. If Buddha really had the supernatural ability to break the limits of time and space, it might be possible. If Christ is really sitting at the right hand of the Father, he is endowed with divine omnipresence.

But where should they meet? The meeting place would be decisive for the content of their talk.

Most dialogues between their disciples take place in books. A book is usually a no-place where the teachings of the two masters are purified and reduced to philosophical propositions and arguments. Good enough, but something is missing. The words are abstracted from the concrete life. There is no accent or dialect, apart from the intellectual dialects of scholars. There is no smell from slums and back streets, or fragrance from the houses of the rich. There is no skin touching skin, no bodies, no eyes that meet, no hands stretching out to greet the other, no fists clenched. In scholarly books it is seldom possible to discern the cries of pain and joy.

So we have to search for other places. Should it be streets crowded by people or a distant desert? Are they surrounded by rich or poor? Do they speak the language of aristocrats and intellectuals, or that of peasants and workers? Do they speak Indian dialects, or Greek and Aramaic? The place is decisive, the context is a mold for the text. What is more natural than to let them visit each other in their own homelands.

Let us go by seniority. India is the first meeting place. Jesus has heard the rumors of Buddha. The stories have spread westward. And now — above the limits of time and space — he moves eastward, and is approaching his goal. On the way he has met people who are touched by the Master. He registers hope in their eyes. There is a new energy in their words. A seed is sown, a new expectation that something will grow, that the mind some day will open like a brilliant lotus.

There he is, sitting in lotus position in the shade of the trees outside a village, surrounded by his disciples and a multitude of people from the neighboring villages. He seems to be somewhat withdrawn, his eyes half closed as if he were looking inward. But he is certainly present, responding to their questions. When he once in a while looks up, people realize that his eyes penetrate them, revealing their inner ugly desires and pure yearnings. But it is a compassionate look, a clear light that gives them new aspirations about a way out of pain and agony.

Jesus is watching Buddha for some time from the shadows, waiting for the right moment. Now it has come. Buddha looks up. "I have been waiting for you," he says. "Where did you get the light in your eyes? What is your secret?"

Jesus does not answer immediately, but follows the local custom, circling around the Buddha, and then blessing him: "Shalom! Peace be with you! You are not far from the kingdom."

"What do you mean?"

"I see a pure heart, and blessed are the pure in heart, for they shall see God."

"How do you know me?"

"I saw you when you were sitting under the bodhi tree. You are a true Aryan in whom there is no guile."

After a while Buddha speaks: "Come and join my company. Today we shall sit quietly in meditation. Tomorrow we will talk. I will hear more about the kingdom and your God. I have seen the flame of light and love in your eyes, and I want to know where that flame comes from. Perhaps you could speak to the multitudes."

The two masters stay together for some days, perhaps even weeks. In the daytime they meet people, or travel. In the evenings they speak quietly with each other.

Would they enjoy the mutual company? Would Buddha be impressed by the Jewish God Jesus said he represented, the creator of heaven and earth, the father of all life? Would he want to be part of the kingdom Jesus proclaimed? Did it make sense at all? Would Jesus adapt his preaching to new circumstances, different expectations, different needs and passions and pains?

Who knows? In the beginning Jesus would just listen and watch. But I am sure the dialogue would lead to a deep friendship. Jesus would certainly be puzzled by Buddha's detachment, his emphasis on karma and self-power, the endless cycle of rebirth. He would see the compassion behind his cool detachment, and nod in admiration of his penetrating analysis of impermanence, pain, and greed. But he would perhaps comment that among all the people he had met, many of them were victimized less by their own karma than by the actions of other people. He would say that the primary reason for moral action is not one's own edification and inner peace, but the well-being of the neighbor. Morality is for the sake of others, not oneself. Buddha would perhaps hesitate for ·
some moments, but finally comment that in his experience a truly awakened mind was also a compassionate mind.

We don't have time for details, and it is up to our imagination to describe their experiences. But before Jesus returned, they agreed to meet again, next time in Galilee. Then they bade farewell.

"I love you, Buddha," Jesus said and kissed the other.

Buddha bowed in deep reverence and said, "Jesus, you are my friend."

Some time after that Buddha really came to Galilee. Jesus was surrounded by people, mostly unlearned and poor, with some skeptical scholars of religion in the periphery. Again Jesus was proclaiming that the kingdom of God was coming, the signs were obvious for anyone who had eyes to see. People were excited and said, "We have never seen things like this. God is visiting his people." They sensed that the finger of God was touching them. "If the finger of God is at work, it is a sign that the creator is restoring his creation. His loving rule is here among us."

Sick people were healed, restored to the life God had originally designed for them. To people who had sunk deeply into despair and guilt he said, "Your sins are forgiven!" Outcasts were invited into the fellowship. The downtrodden straightened their backs and looked around with a new dignity.

Buddha stood waiting with his disciples, watching. Ananda registered the tears in Buddha's eyes. He was puzzled, for that had never happened before. "Are your tears an auspicious sign of something?" he asked. His gentle face could not conceal his own emotions.

"Oh, Ananda," Buddha said. "I am really moved. I have never seen anything like that. They call him a prophet, but I have never liked prophets. To me he seems more like an awakened one, but so different. I have spoken against passion because it enslaves people. But his passion liberates. I have described anger as a poisonous snake in our minds. But his anger is pure, and I don't understand that prophetic rage. His words about the heavenly Father are beautiful, but they make no sense, for I know there is no eternal God in all the ten thousand worlds."

Again they spent days and weeks together. Buddha spoke to the masses, talked with people under four eyes. His quiet compassion and penetrating mind helped people to quiet down and watch their own hearts. The kingdom was not only out there, but something within as well. Some of them began to see how their lives were perverted and painful because they were trapped in their own passions. Buddha registered that Jesus also knew a lot about the kingdom within, that his simple words about faith in God's eternal and unchanging love went along with a keen awareness of impermanence and the ever changing uncertainties of the world. But he had problems with the burning passion in his preaching. He did not believe in that type of prophetic emotionalism. But on the other hand he was attracted to it, because it touched his own heart, and challenged the unbearable injustices in society.

What happened to them? Did they change? Did they drift apart again? Were they too different to work together?

We don't know. But something had certainly happened between them, for when they bade farewell, their expressions had changed.

Buddha said, "I love you, Jesus!" Then he embraced the other and kissed him.

And Jesus bowed in deep reverence and said, "Buddha, you shall always be my friend!"

# Secular Values in the Midst of Faith:
# A Critical Discourse on Dialogue and Difference

LAMIN SANNEH

## Introducing the Argument

Few things divide people more than what they have in common. There is a similarity syndrome that says the more someone is like you, the more familiarity will breed contempt. Ogden Nash (1902-71) makes a related point when he declared in one of his poems that "one would be in less danger from the wiles of a stranger if one's own kith and kin were more fun to be with." One need only reflect for a moment on family feuds or intracommunal strife to realize how adjacency or proximity does not guarantee harmony. People fight often because they want the same thing, or make peace because they embrace difference. As G. K. Chesterton put it as long ago as 1908: "Modern hostility is a base thing, and arises, not out of a generous difference, but out of a sort of bitter and sneering similarity. It is because we are all copying each other that we are all cursing each other."[1]

As religions, Christianity and Islam are united, perhaps, less by the things they have in common than by what divides them. The misunderstandings between them arise in matters of similarity, not in those of difference. Christians are likely to charge Islam with falsehood from what is familiar to them, say, about prophecy, and Muslims likewise to judge Christianity to be heretical from the monotheist bond they share with Christians. A common faith in God thus aggravates the temper of mutual jealousy. This is true also for nontheistic religions, like Hinduism and Buddhism. Anthropologists have observed a parallel phenomenon in polygamous societies: the children by a common father will nurse a jealous mutual hatred sheltered by their mothers. In these circumstances difference on the distaff side is like a balm from Gilead, like glue for our common solidarity.

1. G. K. Chesterton, "On the World Getting Smaller."

The current conflict between a radical Muslim ideology and the West reflects this similarity syndrome. America is admired for the same reason it is envied, and some of the same people who claim to know it from a distance go on to attack it. American schools are attractive to the children of radicals who call America the Jáhiliyáh and God's enemy. America is accused of being antireligious when religion flourishes there like nowhere else. The separation of church and state that distinguishes America, for example, is not what radical Muslims and others say it is, namely, the public repudiation of religion, but an admission of the irrepressible mutual appeal of church and state. Separation is a safeguard that tries to distinguish between the meat and the sandwich. Religion is too important for government to co-opt, and the state too expedient to be able to sustain faith — a classic Puritan idea, later developed into a pillar of the new nation. America's religious profile makes it accessible without making it compatible with radicalism.

The roots of mutual recrimination, however, go back to our medieval Christian forebears who, emboldened by what was familiar to them in Islam from Christianity, were persuaded they had found evidence of forgery, while their Muslim opponents, armed with a single scripture, viewed the four Gospels, for example, as proof of padding the truth. The "people of the book," *ahl al-kitáb*, as Christians are called, had become the people with false books. It was fodder to the cannon of theologians like al-Ghazālī and Ibn Taymīyah. Similarity can be a deadly trap for mutual recrimination. You scarcely listen to someone if you think you know what he or she is going to say.

Some historians have advanced the argument that the idea of Christianity as "Christendom," that is to say, of faith as territoriality, was copied from the example of the caliphate where the caliph is "the shadow of God on earth." Charlemagne, the Holy Roman Emperor, was the Christian "caliph" for Europeans, an incongruous notion given the fact that the true vicar of Christ was the pope, as Charlemagne knew. At any rate, Christendom became the machinery for armed confrontation with Dár al-Islám. The crusader campaigns to wrest control of Bethlehem and Jerusalem from the Muslims belonged with the view of territoriality as a sacrament of Christian faith. Islam had its Mecca and Medina; the church should have its Bethlehem and Jerusalem. But the Crusades then or now are a completely implausible idea even though writers still talk as if the notion is a secret Western plot. After Antioch, Bethlehem was irretrievable. To become like each other, Christians and Muslims have caused innumerable injuries, and the burden of them, in the language of the English prayer book, is intolerable.

## The Front Line

In their missionary expansion, too, Islam and Christianity share a common vocation, with conversion a commonly recognized response of faith. Thus the vitality of Islam as a historical movement and as personal faith is demonstrated by its having inspired hundreds of millions of men and women down the centuries and across the world. Western engagement with Islam is taking place on this missionary frontier where, as Muslims see it, commitment to truth cannot be postponed indefinitely. The reason is clear. The world is not an alibi for faith commitment. In the commandment to submit and bear witness to the truth, the canon of faith stipulates joining the name of God to that of Muhammad, his superlative messenger. Such submission also taps the world for inescapable religious duty, a world that in the last four or five centuries has been controlled by the West to mundane ends, painful as that is for religious radicals to admit. It is their common global ambition that has complicated relations between Islam and the West.

Muslims recollect in their devotion the successful outcome of the battle of Badr (624 C.E.) as a providential sign of God's favor on Mecca and on the Prophet (Quran 3:120-124). Today, however, battles no longer resound with similar divine approval. Desert Storm of 1991, for instance, left liberated Kuwait a divided camp concerning the West's standing in the Muslim world. The War on Terror and Operation Iraqi Freedom, whatever their merits, have similarly ignited growing resentment among Muslims, filling them with anger that infidels now call the tune. Important disagreements still divide Muslims among themselves, as, for example, those that led to the Iraq/Iran war, but none is more fateful than the theological divide between the Muslim world and the West. Muslim pride in the Prophet's accomplishment has been reawakened by the power and success of an assertive secular West. Merely for Muslims to exempt the Prophet's accomplishment, as many are inclined to do, by assigning the blame for their weakness to something other than Islam, seems a halfhearted repair job, because exempting religion there necessitates exempting it also as remedy for weakness. If religion is not responsible for what we have failed to achieve — and no one says it should be — then it cannot be responsible in helping us to overcome our failure. That makes religion moot though, a scarcely satisfactory outcome.

In mitigation I turn to a different approach by calling our attention to a volume of essays printed several decades ago in Karachi, Pakistan. The book is called *Islam — Our Choice: Impressions of Prominent Converts to Islam*.[2] The

---

2. *Islam — Our Choice: Impressions of Prominent Converts to Islam* (Karachi: Ashraf Publications, 1961; reprint, 1977).

converts in question are Western converts to Islam. In the epilogue the editors pause to take stock of the theme of conversion. They clearly had the West in their sights. But what most struck me was the devout sentiment sincerely expressed for the conversion of the West to Islam. The Mongol invaders, the editors said, descended upon Islam in hordes of destruction and rampage, sweeping the caliphate before them, more than the Crusaders were able to do. Yet the Mongols' power and their success in overcoming the Muslims availed them for nothing, because in the end they converted to Islam and went on to produce some of the greatest art and architecture Islam has known. Maybe a similar end is in store for the West, the editors speculated, so that the very might of the West that has been used to defy and humiliate Muslims will be expended from a long and costly confrontation with the Muslim world, and then the West, too, jaded with materialism and success like the Mongols before them, will convert to Islam, a religion that is better placed to use the great gifts of the West for the glory and service of God.

That sentiment, coming several decades before 9/11, as I said, struck me as unusual. The hope may be delusory — as it certainly is in the eyes of secularists — but the idea that you can take everything away from Muslims, including their towns, cities, countries, and political structures, but as long as they have Islam they will triumph — that confidence I found remarkable. Can it contend against the secular West? I wondered. Can Western materialism inspire and sustain clarity of faith and vision, hope and commitment to God, strength to endure trial and tribulation; can it find the largeness of heart required to tolerate difference and disagreement, and the sense of community necessary to nurture the sacred and the holy that Islam represents? The editors of *Islam — Our Choice* don't think so. Or, to put it less starkly, they don't think materialism has the capacity to bear privation and pressure without crumbling into subjective retreat, and that a spiritual force like Islam knows how to transform materialism by offering it as a gift to God and thus as fruit for ethical use. The West offers no gratitude to God for what God has given it, and so its material power will one day choke it, is the implicit claim. *Kufr* will flood the void from which *shukr* has been banished.[3]

Alfred Guillaume, a scholar of Islam and the translator of the earliest biography of the Prophet, describes in his *Islam* (Penguin Books) how much of the Lord's Prayer Muslims share with Christians — a great deal, it turns out. Yet there is a crucial difference. The prayer, "Thy will be done, on earth as in heaven," with its hints of a redeemed future, becomes for Islam, "as on earth so

3. See my article on *shukr* and *kufr*, in *Encyclopedia of the Qur'an*, 2 vols. (Leiden: Brill, 2001-2), vol. 2.

in heaven," with strains of theocratic vindication here and now, as Isma'il Faruqi has argued. The city of the Prophet, Medina, with Mecca astride it, is a norm in heaven. Religion as realized truth, however, conflicts with Western secular thought that has twice dethroned God: once in the primacy of the people, in the sovereignty of the ballot box, and again in the veneration of the national state. That is why political parties as free associations and nationalism as popular or territorial dogma *(qawmiyah, wataniyah)* continue to be problematic in the Muslim world. The problem really is this: the West cannot, either on those two grounds of peoplehood and nationhood, or on others, be entirely ignored, nor can it be allowed to succeed unchallenged. How then do Muslims, on their own entirely valid grounds, deal with the West?

## The Secular Imperative

There are many issues on which the West will not yield, but the notion of religion as dispensable, or as a differentiated private option, is one of the most stubborn. Churches still exist, it is true, but their meaning has changed drastically. We do not go to church because of a summons from inside the church; we come to church for a reason of our own, which may explain why a visitor is challenged typically in a Protestant church to say why he or she is there. By contrast, the mosque is instituted by divine mandate; you go there, alone or with others, to worship and to reclaim the world rather than, as in a church, to congregate and to celebrate community. You go to the mosque because you are summoned, to the church because you are motivated. Similarly, we speak of rights — human rights, minority rights, the rights of children, of women, of the disabled, of the sick and elderly, etc. — and radical Islamists rub their eyes in disbelief. Rights against one another, maybe, but against God? Impossible. If "right" is a legal cause with claim or restitution as remedy, then it is inapplicable to God. God is not a defendant. Similarly for freedom of expression, even when it insults God and his messenger. Over our dead bodies, says a rising chorus of outraged Muslims. What is freedom against God, and what is success without truth? they ask rhetorically.

Why don't they go back to where they came from? If they don't like our ways, they don't have to stay here. So says a provocative West. But geography cannot solve the dilemmas of theology. The secular West rejects truth in favor of values, and reduces God to opinions about God. It proclaims victory over religion and prospers on account of that. What the West does, however, is not hidden from others, and accordingly, across the boundaries of a converging world, Muslims take note. Even when we in the West act alone and say we have no designs on the values of others, we engage in moral judgment nevertheless. Our way of looking at the world is better than anybody else's. Our values are superior to their dogmas. We tolerate, they exclude; we give, they take; we discuss, they impose; we persuade, they threaten; we help, they harm; we affirm, they reject; we include, they exclude; and so on. In several public statements since 9/11, for example, former President Clinton has expressed himself in those terms. We claim a human source for our values; they claim a divine source, and ask: Can the human contend with the divine? Can the creature defy the Creator? For us diversity is charter of our common values; for them difference is justification for fatwas of condemnation. We celebrate diversity; they peddle difference. It does not occur to us when we offer diversity as a remedy for difference that it is really a dogma of intolerance.

Such polarities are too simplistic, as everyone recognizes. The two societies are now inextricably intertwined. The West is a living reality in Muslim lands, and Muslims are a growing presence in the West. Placed in each other's way at that useful level, they have not avoided being entangled also at the intellectual, spiritual level. The matter is closer than that: the West has its own images of Islam and Muslims, and beyond the obligatory cultural politeness, those images are not flattering, perhaps understandably, while the Muslim world produces for popular consumption its own often garbled stereotypes of the West. The political cartoon becomes effigy in an adversarial milieu, with Muslim youths burning images of Western leaders and Western tabloids parading caricatures of bearded Muslim fanatics.

What confuses Muslims, nevertheless, is how Christians as religious people seem content to maintain churches but defer to reason what it means to bear witness to God. Muslims are uncomprehending as to how Christians can come to such a position and still remain religiously serious. How can the edifice of faith maintain itself if it establishes itself on the shifting dunes of rational approval? It is much simpler for Muslims to assume that Christianity has long abandoned its truth claims than for them to enter into a complicated debate about how Christianity has modernized its theology to accommodate itself to the world. Many theologians, with one part of their mouth, speak lucidly of a transcendent God while, with the other part, they urge that religion be made to fit within the bounds of reason alone. Theology, as al-Farabi pointed out, originally meant just that for the Greeks, to make God accountable to reason. Muslims, however, remain unpersuaded of the worth of religion once rational sovereignty takes it over.

## Bridge as Detour

In the deep gulf between the Muslim world and the secular West, Muslims have not been reassured even by professed Western interest in the Sufi Muslim tradition, since the West takes the Sufis as conceding the distinction between spirituality and worldly concerns. In other words, the West recruits the Sufis in the battle to isolate religion and to remove it from public life. Muslims suspect the West of using the Sufi reputation to promote a denial of Islam's claim about the necessary integration of ethics and politics. In the way the West has set up a solid wall of separation between church and state, Sufism is captured on one side of the wall and then emptied of its Islamic vitality. Sufism as religion without creed and sacrament, as spirituality without obligation, appeals to the West's emancipated ideal. Hence the draw of figures, for instance, like Rūmī and Omar Khayyám in the Muslim tradition, and in Christianity, of Albert Schweitzer and Dag Hammarskjöld.

The Western penchant for spirituality has allowed raiding other religions for their common subjective residue. In the hands of the accomplished, such as Joseph Campbell and Matthew Fox, say, the forays into spirituality can indeed look like much overdue cutting down of dead wood and an uncaging of the soul. Spirituality, defensible on the theory that man does not live by bread alone, seems like an innocuous way of filling the gap that has opened up in the process of separating church and state, a theme Robert Bellah and his colleagues have expounded in *Habits of the Heart*. Not infrequently, however, spirituality takes a downturn to become a device for stripping or suspending difference. Popular mysticism often is a stratagem of mass distraction, say the religious masters. As the Quran declares, God will not be outstripped or superseded by our stratagems (Quran 70:60). (Al-Hujwiri, an eleventh-century Sufi, recounts an anecdote about a fellow Sufi who declined the company of a renowned saintly figure, not from an inflated sense of his own worth but from a concern about being distracted from obligations laid down in the canon, including turning up for prayers.) Muslims in the main do not accept that religion as creed is secondary or derivative, and so they have reined in Sufi mystics, however useful mystics may be for getting the West's attention.

## Closeness without Encounter

The Muslim instinct here is self-consistent, the instinct that says articulating and implementing ideals, practical as well as religious, depends on a premise that itself is not at the same time open to doubt. The same is true for secularists. You cannot call into question the basis on which you are doing the questioning. It seems Muslims are right that truth is unavoidable: you have to be committed even to be open-minded, and especially committed to question religion! The Western attitude of discounting religion rests on committed faith in the secular alternative, in the primacy of individual autonomy. So Muslims press: How can the West claim there are no absolutes when such a statement is itself an absolute, explaining why the West promotes liberal secularism as universally normative? Has the West not thus absolutized what it acknowledges as a relative claim, and by so doing relativized the absolute? By rejecting religion the West has invested itself in its own absolutes. So, for example, the Western practice of going to war to defend economic and military interests, and stockpiling weapons of mass destruction for that purpose, shows what sacrifices the West is willing to make for what it believes. Such a position raises issues for religious people generally. However, when the West goes further and claims that religion is a matter of individual choice and personal opinion, and is not worth defending or dying for, then it evokes an appropriate Muslim rejoinder demanding religion as public truth.

The secular idiom is a form of religion in which the doctrines of individual rights, the right to privacy, and free speech are enshrined (to use appropriate religious figures) into law. In two world wars this century, for example, the West has sacrificed over 65 million lives in the name of national and international security. In pursuit of that ideal the state has moved to appropriate the vocabulary of martyrdom and to grant indulgences by way of medals and other civic public awards to veterans, living and dead. Muslims look askance at all these acts of civic moralization. National heroism is a residue public piety bequeathed by a privatized faith. But notice the limited territorial range and currency of national heroes, in contrast to the saints of religion.

The secular national state as the fundamental building block of the present world system, and as the legal basis of national and international jurisdiction, seems unassailable, at least as a root idea. There is no alternative way for anyone, including the Muslim world, to participate in the world without embracing national jurisdiction and the international obligations it recognizes. Yet what seems a logical development of national experience in the West is far from the case in the Muslim world. Necessity rather than principle has led to the entrenchment of the idea of national legality in the worldwide Muslim community *(umma)*, and that necessity has caused Muslim leaders to cultivate the principle of prudence in paying lip service to the separation of church and state against Islamic teaching about truth being one and inseparable from political affairs.

But when they look for the role of Christians in secular society, Muslims are astonished to find the Christian church rather marginal in public; except as a lobby or spectator, it matters not. And so they wonder whether this religious absence in the territorial sphere of the sovereign national state is due to the inhospitable nature of secularism, causing Christians to walk out before Christianity could be emasculated, or whether Christians, flirting with their fate, have colluded with secularism and relinquished all claims to absolute truth, leaving an orphaned Christianity to seek shelter in private benevolence. In any case, the secular order is where the action is, and so Muslims must come to it without religion. Western diplomacy, constructed on the foundations of a politically pacified Christianity, has now found itself face-to-face with an unamenable Muslim world.

In spite of Dár al-Islám and the West being divided by a common heritage of public ethics, the Muslim presence in the West suggests at least two fundamental facts about our age: first, that the world is indeed becoming smaller and becoming one, as Wendell Willkie (1892-1944) so eloquently argued a few generations ago;[4] and second, that our civilization is on trial for its moral life, as Arnold Toynbee (1889-1975) tried to tell us a long time ago.[5] We have tried to respond to these changes, but so far with a divided mind. One vain response has been to dwell in a nostalgic way on our similarities with Islam, putting our assurance in the overspill of those doctrines and rituals that resemble our own. That approach has led to a dead end. As Chesterton quipped, there are two ways of getting home: one is to stay there, and the other is to travel in a straight line until you come back to where you started. Common ground means simply staying put. In the drive for common values we throw out distinctions. So the West opted for a second approach by designating a comparative intercultural formula in which similarities, religious and cultural, get mainframe attention while differences, religious or otherwise, get deleted. Whatever its limitations, that view of religion is a change from the Enlightenment position that all we need in order to live are facts, not norms and values. Still, the present stress on common values has its own shortcomings; it leaves us with the irony of diversity as a remedy, if not an enemy, of difference.

A qualification to the issue of religious differences being intractable is an echo of the Enlightenment view that religion is itself intractable. As Albert Camus asks provocatively, would it not be better for God if we refuse to believe in him? — and perhaps, too, in Camus, one wonders.

4. Wendell Willkie, *One World* (Urbana: University of Illinois Press, 1966).
5. Arnold J. Toynbee, *Civilization on Trial* (New York: Oxford University Press, 1948).

Lamin Sanneh

## Difference and Dialogue

When Bernard Lewis first propounded the thesis of a "clash of civilization" in an *Atlantic Monthly* article,[6] he was giving voice to a reality implicit in the order of things. As a lifelong student of Islam and the Muslim world, Lewis was keenly aware that the logic of the secular imperative confronted with the logic of Muslim truth claims makes a clash all too likely, if not necessary.

One response to this dispiriting account of relations is containment, though that cannot be a long-term solution. Spatial separation is impractical as well as undesirable. Although Lewis did not say that, dialogue is the alternative to the civilizational clash he describes, yet for dialogue to work the terms have to be commensurate, so that we can have dialogue, for example, not between public reason and subjective truth, but between contrasting views of revelation and the public good. Dialogue cannot go back to medieval theological presuppositions about common ground or to modern ideas of universal values.

Our medieval heritage is not reassuring for us. When Pope Boniface issued the bull *Unam Sanctam* in 1302, declaring the church as the only institution with authority to grant salvation, he was giving voice to the culmination of what started with Emperor Theodosius's decrees of 380 and 391, the first requiring all citizens of the empire to become Christians, and the second proscribing all non-Christian religions. The Council of Florence in 1442 and the Roman catechism of 1566 pushed the process further by condemning nonbelievers and, with the catechism, by declaring the infallibility of the church. All these actions had in common the idea of territoriality as a sacrament of faith, with the church complementing in the religious sphere what the state had become in the political sphere. Uniformity of rule and doctrine had its validation in state and church autonomy in their respective domains. A common rule of church and state, however, sowed the seeds of future conflict.

In spite of that, we misunderstand the historical nature of this joining of powers by attacking the church as blind and bigoted, not realizing how successive developments in church doctrine reflected increasing differentiation in the role and function of the state vis-à-vis the church. Consequently, when the notion of sovereignty underwent structural shifts from changes in the idea of political obligation, as described, for example, in Saint Thomas More's *Utopia*, the problem of religious plurality asserted itself with new force. Nicholas of Cusa, a fifteenth-century German cardinal, for example, recognizing that the destruc-

6. Bernard Lewis, "The Roots of Muslim Rage," *Atlantic Monthly*, September 1990, pp. 47-60. The idea has since been developed into a larger statement by Samuel Huntington, *The Clash of Civilizations and the Remaking of World Order* (New York: Simon and Schuster, 1997).

tive wars between Christians and Muslims were a challenge theology could not ignore, proposed "one religion in the plurality of religious rites" *(religio una in rituum varietate)*. Nicholas was astute in his view that it was similarity and common ground that explained why Muslims and Christians felt so intolerant of each other, rather than the affirmation of difference and variety. It is sobering to think that in that crucial sense Nicholas has not been superseded even today. *Nostra Aetate* of Vatican II (1962-65) may be seen as a vindication of Nicholas. His novel approach drew attention to the issue of the one and the many, of one God and the many practices by which religious people seek a path to God. Truth is one, and Muslims and Christians demonstrate that by the practices they observe separately. Acknowledgment of difference, in Nicholas's formulation, should be by virtue of the truth that God is one, not by virtue of evading that truth or denying that we have diverse practices. To put it in our language, difference is not a denial of our oneness but an asset in our diversity. This position affirms Christianity or the West without denying other religions and cultures.

Many people continue to feel the need to repudiate Christianity or the West as a prerequisite for affirming diversity and supporting tolerance in the world. As well as rejecting one culture, people are asked to embrace other cultures as a show of equality and pluralism. The provocative idea that criticism of the West will assure an appreciative view of other cultures has predictably produced a backlash with the positive and negative changing hands: repudiating other cultures is for the religious right a condition for affirming Christianity. That explains why dialogue has fallen as a casualty of both the left and the right. The left reduces religion to a matter of common values, to an upbeat opinion that offends no one, while the right restricts religion to chauvinism, infused with rousing jingoism. And so dissidents on the left, for example, accuse the United States of promoting a pax Americana that is an arrogant violation of other cultures, while their counterparts on the right salute the flag as a sign of God's favor. The left romanticizes other cultures and the right demonizes them, a hint here that the two sides are cross cousins.

## The Ethic of Difference

A statement attributed to Dr. Robert Edgar, the head of the National Council of Churches in the United States, an association of mainline Protestant churches, understands religion as a flag of cultural convenience, useful as a fraternity handshake, as has been said, but otherwise secondary, if not an impediment, in building trust and understanding. The reasoning he reportedly advances for tolerance is somewhat circular: religions must not, for the sake of dialogue, dilute their own distinctions, their own truth claims, but dialogue should take place nevertheless, without regard to distinctions, without acknowledgment of truth claims. "Dialogue," says Dr. Edgar, "is best built on relationships. People have to get to know each other, to trust each other, to like each other, and in some cases to even love each other before real learning and listening takes place."[7] On the grounds that truth should be a cultural quorum, that statement takes off with the dialogue cart without the religious horse. But if you could achieve that much trust and understanding up front, why would you need to drag in religious truth claims? Not only have you thereby diluted religious distinctions, you have made dilution itself into a religion, into a truth claim. An appropriate institutional expression of it would be, say, "The National Council of Mutual Approbation." That is the circularity, with a hint of solipsism.

## Commitment and Criticism

Prophetic religion turns our attention in another direction. Accordingly, Islam's truth claim that God is never overtaken or outmatched by events and stratagems, never jostled by human cunning (*wa má nahnu bimasbúqína*, Quran 70:41), places God at close range of our personal insecurities and historical perplexities, with a call to make sovereign truth count in the conflict of mundane passions. It is Abraham in the Quran, no less, where he is called the man of pure faith, who asked the people, "What think you then of the Lord of all Being?" (37:85; the word translated "think" is *zann*, meaning to surmise or to suppose on a whim). Abraham persisted, pressing the people whether they would settle for a falsehood, for idols in place of God (37:93). Faith, according to the Quran, is about unyielding personal scrutiny, not about soothing slogans. In the final analysis, the Quran insists, God will not be outwitted (*fa'arádú bihi kaidan*, 37:96). A similar note is sounded in ancient Hebrew Scripture (Isa. 43; 44; 46).

Offering a gloss on the ancient prophet, a wizened, agonized rabbi reflected on the travail of his people by reminding them that Zion is holy only if the law of God does go forth from it, which is not at all the same as saying that

7. "Top Evangelicals Critical of Colleagues over Islam: Negative Remarks Are Called Dangerous," *New York Times*, May 8, 2003, p. A22. The negative remarks in question were statements by Rev. Franklin Graham that Islam was "a very evil and wicked religion," and those by Rev. Jerry Vines of the Southern Baptist Convention that Muhammad was "a demon-possessed pedophile," and Islam inherently evil and violent. The *Times* returned to the subject in a front-page report, "Seeing Islam as 'Evil' Faith, Evangelicals Seek Converts," May 27, 2003.

any law which goes forth from Zion is holy (Mic. 3:9-10, 12). The ancient prophet calls his community to trust in God rather than in worldly security.

> Woe to those who go down to Egypt for help
>     and rely on horses,
> who trust in chariots because they are many
>     and in horsemen because they are very strong,
> but they look not to the Holy One of Israel. (Isa. 31:1)[8]

Jeremiah was equally forthright with his people when he told them they faced a life-and-death choice: "Behold, I set before you the way of life and the way of death. . . . O house of David! Thus says the LORD: 'Execute justice in the morning, and deliver from the hand of the oppressor him who has been robbed.' . . . 'And do no wrong or violence to the alien, the fatherless, and the widow, nor shed innocent blood in this place'" (Jer. 21:8, 12; 22:3).

War was not far from the mind of the great prophets of Scripture, and against it they brought to bear the truth claim about the omnipotent power of God. God is the arbiter of history who

> shall judge between the nations,
>     and shall decide for many peoples;
> and they shall beat their swords into plowshares,
>     and their spears into pruning hooks;
> nation shall not lift up sword against nation,
>     neither shall they learn war any more. (Isa. 2:4)

It is God's desire that the people

> shall not labor in vain,
>     or bear children for calamity;
> for they shall be the offspring of the blessed of the LORD,
>     and their children with them. . . .
> They shall not hurt or destroy
>     in all my holy mountain. (Isa. 65:23, 25)

The NT for its part bears witness to Jesus of Nazareth, and one image of him depicts him as the Lamb of God (John 1:29; 1 Pet. 1:19) whom the inspired sages long ago knew after a fashion and called the Suffering Servant (Isa. 53). He became the peace offering, dwelling among his people, "full of grace and truth" (John 1:14; 14:6). "For he is our peace, who has made us both one, and has bro-

8. Biblical quotes are from the Revised Standard Version.

ken down the dividing wall of hostility" (Eph. 2:14). His followers staggered no longer from the weight of their own unbelief but instead felt quickened by a lively hope in the promises of God to Abraham. They formed a new family in the moral life, a family based not on blood, race, and nation, but on personal faith in God's gift (Rom. 4 and 5). The followers of Jesus discovered a new way to serve the world, not for material reward or from self-interest, but by virtue of the example Jesus set (Mark 10:42-45; 1 Cor. 9:15-27). The moral life was thus freed of the recurring self-entanglement that the Sufis also know so well: "I, being self-confined, / Self did not merit, / Till, leaving self behind, / Did self inherit."

It is as such that the message of new life in Christ went on to penetrate the very fiber of Western culture, as the music of Bach and Beethoven, for example, shows. In Rembrandt's famous etching, *The Hundred Guilder Print,* to take an example from the visual arts that was based on the healing miracles in Mark 1:32-34, Christ as healer and teacher "stands at the apex of a wedge of light thrust through the surrounding dark at the center of a motley crowd. Around him are the sick, the lame, the well, the rich and the poor. . . . Everyone there has the chance to receive the look or the touch of grace."[9]

## New World Paradigm

Underlying much of what I have said here is an implicit claim that I should now make explicit. In spite of claims by its radical opponents, America is not hostile to religion but in fact is very hospitable to it — witness the proliferation not only of churches but of mosques, temples, synagogues, pagodas, shrines, meeting houses, chapels, and halls of prayer and meditation, often in close proximity to one another. This situation is not fortuitous. It was conceived as such by the Founding Fathers. Thomas Jefferson, the third president of the United States (1801-9), is usually the one credited with the law on freedom of religion, being responsible, among other things, for the Virginia Act Establishing Religious Freedom of 1786. Yet another person equally important in this sphere was James Madison, Jefferson's successor as president (1809-17) who, for instance, affirmed in 1784 that the establishment of religion as an engine of civil policy would destroy the free exercise of religion according to the dictates of conscience, adding that the infringement of religious freedom is not just an offense

9. Cited in Kenneth Cragg, *Grace Cup* (a quarterly study paper published by the General Synod of the Episcopal Church in Jerusalem and the Middle East), no. 16 (All Saints' Tide 1982), p. 12.

to the state, it is an offense against God. In other words, there are sound religious reasons for tolerance as a political good, Madison argues, saying that in its early years Christianity flourished against every opposition from the state rather than from dependence on the state. Religion exists from the free, unfettered response of faith; a liberal democracy flourishes by the same principle of freedom. Coercion is not a fountain of grace nor of the virtues of democracy. Madison said all

> are to be considered as retaining an equal right to the free exercise of religion, according to the dictates of conscience. While we assert for ourselves a freedom to embrace the religion which we believe to be of divine origin, we cannot deny an equal freedom to those whose minds have not yet yielded to the evidence which has convinced us. If this freedom be abused, it is an offence against God, *not against man.* The Christian religion both existed and flourished, not only without the support of human laws, but in spite of every opposition from them.[10]

Religion is not invented by human policy; so it cannot depend for its truth claims on human enforcement. Truth claims are not a dividend of democracy, with Scripture a manual of constituency leverage. That, says Madison, is the basis for separation, and it demonstrates the innate excellence of religion, making religion worthy of the unfettered assent of men and women. Persuasion, rather than compulsion, is the motive power of moral truth as it is the driving spirit of democracy. Reassuringly, this tolerant view is anticipated in the injunction of the Quran to the effect that "there is no compulsion in religion" (2:256). All this is by way of saying that the Founding Fathers were prescient in intending neither to establish religion nor to suppress it. Their brand of liberalism was auspicious for religion, not hostile to it, and there is no earthly reason why today a pragmatic liberalism should be combative toward religion or in conflict with our freedoms and with the values of dynamic difference.

## Reveille

We should take seriously the moral insight about separation to the effect that the things of God and those of Caesar belong to distinct domains and are entitled to radically different conceptions of truth and values (Mark 12:17). The bidding of Caesar holds us to temporal obligations for our mutual safety and secu-

10. James Madison, "A Memorial and Remonstrance on the Religious Rights of Man," in *Letters and Other Writings of James Madison* (Philadelphia, 1867), 1:162ff., emphasis Madison's.

rity, while the injunction of God calls us, albeit also here and now, to the holy and transcendent for our eternal good. Obedience to Caesar draws on obedience to God like the shadow on the sunlight: the connection between the two is of outward temporal necessity, not intrinsic moral equivalence. Faith has fruits for the public good, but its roots lie in another realm. That means the fruits of religion have untainted public use while the roots of religion have unreserved divine safeguard. Usefulness, accordingly, is not a truth claim, just as faith is not just a public convenience. The uses of religion should not be confused with the sources of religion. The costs of postponing open public discussion of how in that light religion may impinge on politics to tame doctrinaire secularism, and to thwart its radical religious nemesis, are high. The modern cultural project of acceptance of difference and tolerance of diversity is at stake.

# Christian Mission in Multifaith Situations

ANDREW J. KIRK

## Setting the Scene

My focus in this presentation will be on the situation in western Europe, as I understand it. Undoubtedly this part of the continent of Europe is multifaith from an empirical point of view: there are many people who practice the rites, rituals, and ethical values of what John Hick (following Karl Jaspers) has called the "postaxial" religions. It is an interesting and important new phenomenon of the last fifty years. It is a new factor for Christian mission to wrestle with. However, I wish to argue, perhaps controversially, that in the context of west European history, culture, and society, it is a relatively minor feature of every-day reality.[1] The decisive datum, I believe, is the tacit acceptance of a secular worldview and life-form by the overwhelming majority of the inhabitants of this part of the world. If this is the case, the main challenge to Christian mission in this situation has to be contemporary secularity and secularism, not multireligiosity.

My second thesis is that within this context, interreligious dialogue, conceived as a conversation about beliefs and actions from a consciously religious point of view, easily becomes a distraction. I am not wishing to suggest that interreligious dialogue is irrelevant per se. There will be times and places where it will be important. However, in the context of the secularizing process as the major characteristic of recent Western history, it has to be a discussion that *follows* a thorough debate with a basically irreligious culture.

I am arguing that in the Western world there is a missiological presumption in favor of engaging first with a reality shaped by secular assumptions. In

---

1. Notwithstanding the efforts of some Christians, and some parts of the media, to erect it into a major factor within Western social and political life.

part this is due to one of the paradoxes of a secular worldview, namely, that it is quite compatible with religious experimentation. Indeed, it is quite possible that while religious interest is expanding, secular values are also increasing. It is precisely a unique characteristic of the way Western societies have developed that secularity and spirituality can coexist within the same person, so that the embracing of some "spiritual" practices does not indicate necessarily a rejection of fundamental secular values.[2] From a missiological point of view, therefore, in the West the dialogue between Christian discourse and secular assumptions and lifestyles seems, prima facie, more important than interreligious dialogue.

## Defining Mission

By mission I mean the imperative laid upon the Christian community to communicate, through life and words, the transforming good news of Jesus Christ as set forth in the apostolic testimony of the New Testament.[3] I assume that such a task is fundamental to the community's self-definition. For Christian faith the story of Jesus, the Messiah, together with the interpretation of it given by specially appointed messengers (apostles), forms the basis for both explaining and transforming the world. It claims to give an accurate account of ultimate reality, seen and unseen, and thus a true explanation of human life in the universe.

Given that an interpreted story is at the heart of the Christian faith and given that the message implied within it makes a claim to ultimate truth, it has to be related to all other stories. As those engaged in conversation with people of different faith traditions have correctly concluded, this entails debate[4] with the many stories of religious belief systems. However, in the West, during the last half-millennium, the major enduring story has been the gradual emancipation of human thought and life from any religious sphere. The major missiological task of Christianity in this context, therefore, has to be to engage with

2. This is a phenomenon, I believe, not sufficiently recognized by those Christians who proclaim postmodernity to be a new kind of environment that permits a rebirth of spiritual consciousness in the place of a homogenizing materialist culture.

3. For further reflection on the meaning of mission in the contemporary world, cf. J. Andrew Kirk, *What Is Mission? Theological Explorations* (London: Darton, Longman and Todd, 1999).

4. A better translation than "dialogue" of the etymological original, *dialogizomai*. The word also reflects much more accurately what is required when two or more faiths make exclusive and incompatible claims to know the truth. Such claims are, as a matter of fact, an essential part of each religious tradition, when it is true to itself. Dialogue suggests a conversation only about commonly held convictions, while debate engages faith systems at a deeper level.

this particular story. Otherwise, its mission will be fundamentally de-contextualized and, consequently, flawed.

## Interpreting the Meaning of Secular

This leads us to make an attempt to understand the secular nature of the contemporary environment of the West (and many other parts of the world increasingly influenced by Western secular assumptions and ways of living). This is, of course, a mammoth task that can only be undertaken here in a very preliminary way. I will try to lay out the main features of the secular map. It will inevitably be small scale in the sense that many of the details will not be visible, as would be possible in a major survey. I will start from the premise that the secular experience has, at least, the following dimensions: religious, philosophical, social, economic, and psychological.

### *The Secular and Religion*

One of the favorite ways of describing secularity has been by use of the word "loss." A secular world is one in which the unifying force of religious symbols and rituals (as in the Christian year) has disappeared. This symbolism has been called the "sacred canopy," an overarching structure that gives fundamental significance to life. A kind of de-conversion experience has taken place by which, over several centuries, religious beliefs have become marginal to life, where to be irreligious is to be normal, where religious beliefs, where they do exist, have been relocated from the public world to the private, inner experience of the divine or sacred. Holy days, when the sacred (and "secular") reality of the Savior of the world has been celebrated, have become holidays (celebrations of the secular values of rest and relaxation). Opportunities for the healing of the spirit have been transmuted into the recuperation of body, mind, and emotions.

In place of the transcendent, people are focused on the mundane, empirical, and functional. Existence is experienced as one-dimensional. Religious belief is explained by one or another projection theory, i.e., that the divine has been created as a remedy for fear of the unknown, as compensation for an alienated existence, or as a way of coping with loss of childhood.[5] Meanwhile,

---

5. Although these explanations belong respectively to Durkheim, Marx, and Freud, writing 100 to 150 years ago, they still have force as accounts of the reasons for the growth of what is vaguely called "spirituality" in recent years.

*Andrew J. Kirk*

moral ideas of good and evil, right and wrong, are disconnected from the demands of a personal God and seen to rest on the foundation either of natural rights, evolutionary advantage, or utility. Above all, quality of life is understood not to depend any longer on meeting one's presumed spiritual needs through institutionalized religious means.

## The Secular and Philosophy

Human beings have become self-contained in the universe. They no longer accept any reality beyond their own experience. They no longer need to gain knowledge from outside their own reason to understand the origin, meaning, and purpose of life. They are the measure of all things, the only beings in the universe with a mind. They are independent earthly beings, no longer exiled from Paradise (i.e., fallen humanity is normal humanity).[6]

Nevertheless, secular people are driven by a radical skepticism about the possibility of knowing anything. The beginning of wisdom is systematic doubt. Skepticism can only be limited by an appeal to empirical evidence. Knowledge is that which remains when claims about reality can be upheld against refutation by universally valid criteria. Moreover, against medieval asceticism, they have discovered pleasure as the goal of existence. The desires of the body may and should be satiated, as they belong wholly to the individual, have no sacred significance, and one day will disintegrate into oblivion.[7]

Secular, humanist people are protean;[8] they are confined by no bounds. There is no given form to life, no divine agency, no cosmic laws. They do not possess, therefore, any inherent being. They are entirely what they become through their own transforming action, particularly on nature as an object to be used and molded to satisfy their desires. Humans are "species being" (Marx), defined in terms of economic relationships within the collective whole of humanity. They are the result of an impersonal process of selection (Darwin), a chance occurrence that just happened to happen during the evolution of matter. They have killed off God and obliterated all horizons (Nietz-

6. Cf. Seyyed Hossein Nasr, *Religion and the Order of Nature* (Oxford: Oxford University Press, 1996), chap. 5, "The Tragic Consequences of Humanism in the West," pp. 163-90.

7. A professor of theology at the Charles University in Prague recently (January 2002) told me that over 50 percent of deaths in the Czech Republic are no longer marked by a formal funeral — evidence, he concluded, of the belief among a large section of the population that nothing survives the end of physical existence.

8. From the mythical Greek god, Proteus, said to be able to change himself into any number of different forms.

sche), and henceforth there are no limits set from above to what is permitted them.

## The Secular and the Social Environment

Perhaps the most important characteristic of all is the claim to an inviolate right to freedom. There is a revolt against hierarchy, elitism, and the dead hand of the past, against all self-styled guardians of the truth and moral rectitude who determine what is in my best interests and force me to comply. A secular consciousness is one which is experienced as enlightenment, as the discovery (*my* discovery) of the destiny of being — briefly summed up in the immortal words "the right to life, liberty and the pursuit of happiness."

Given that the individual is autonomous and inviolate, he or she has the right (but also the awesome responsibility) to decide what worldview and life-style are worth choosing. Hence political life is founded on the basic idea of the contract in which individual rights are respected and upheld. The legal system is designed to regulate potential and actual conflict between sovereign and equal individuals. The ideal is a minimalist set of laws,[9] in order to allow for a maximum amount of toleration of the views and practices of others, as long as there is a consensus in society that they do no harm to third parties.

## The Secular and Economic Life

The role of government is to allow and encourage the greatest possible amount of space for people to make their own economic decisions. This means, inter alia, enabling an entrepreneurial spirit and refraining from interference in the natural workings of the market which are, by means of an "invisible hand," able to work for the mutual benefit of all.[10] Redistribution of wealth is always coercive. It is only legitimate when the population as a whole freely agrees to forgo one liberty (i.e., the right to enjoy the fruit of one's own labor) for the sake of another (i.e., the right to be protected in times of adversity).

9. As, for example, in the proabortion slogan "Get the law off my body," and in the increasing pressure to decriminalize "soft" drugs and to legalize euthanasia. These three issues manifest clearly a fundamental divide between a secular and Christian view of reality.

10. This argument is now being used as a weapon in the dispute about the effects of global capitalism. Spokespeople for the G8 nations extol the potential of globalization for resolving the situations of extreme poverty in Africa, Asia, and Latin America.

*Andrew J. Kirk*

## The Secular and the Psyche

In one sense the contemporary Western individual is an existentialist at heart: the freedom to choose what one wants to be in the face of the threat of meaninglessness is the only valid end for human beings. To be is to choose to create one's life in a particular way. Where the meaning of life is concerned, all ontologies, claiming any absolute validity through time, are dead. Because truth itself is socially produced, plural, historically contingent, and changing, we no longer choose within a fixed reality, we choose to construct our own reality.

At least two major consequences flow from these beliefs. First, human community dissolves into fragmented bits and pieces. As has "colorfully" been said, an abandonment of common beliefs leads to a situation akin to the blind describing a sunset to the deaf. Secondly, it cannot matter what we choose, as long as our choice is serious and pursued with full conviction and commitment (as in sexual preferences). It is not important whether we choose something without any particular reason or purpose, as long as it feels good to us and doesn't appear to have any harmful consequences for other people.

It is a curious paradox, however, that far from creating a sense of exhilaration, freedom often produces a sense of dread. It may be the dread of loneliness through the inability of sustaining solid, long-lasting relationships, or the terror of taking final responsibility for far-reaching decisions in one's own life. If freedom in a secular perspective necessarily entails freedom from signing up to any values which I have not decided myself, I have to opt for those which I find attractive. But because they are entirely my choice, they have no real value, for they cannot be shared with others on the basis of commonly inherited convictions. Both the logical and existential conclusion of secular independence from a God-given reality is that I (and my species) am alone in the world. And if a neo-Darwinian theory of natural selection through survival is believed as an explanation of human origins, this world is both impersonal and hostile.

The variety of beliefs with their practical consequences that have been enumerated under these five headings go some way to providing a map of the secular consciousness so dominant in the self-assured culture of the West. It would be illusory to think that there could be any prospect of returning to a presecular society, where a commonly accepted religious view of reality again shaped fundamental beliefs, moral sentiments, and social customs. Some Christians and leaders of religious traditions give the impression that the combined forces of the world religions could perhaps turn back the relentless tide of secularism. Even if such an eventuality were possible, would it be desirable? I wish to give reasons why I think this would be a wholly mistaken strategy for Christian mission in a Western context.

## The Secular Challenge to Interreligious Dialogue

Given that interreligious dialogue is now seen in some Christian quarters as the main component of mission, it is necessary to spell out the reasons why it is largely irrelevant to mission in a secular society. There are a number of interlocking arguments.

### *The History of Europe*

Secular society, being a peculiarly Western phenomenon, has come about largely as a set of responses to the previous Christian domination of Europe. In a paradoxical way secularity is partly the consequence of the success of Christian inculturation. The danger of ignoring a peculiar historical process in favor of interreligious dialogue with much more recently arrived immigrants to the European continent is that it diminishes the missiological task by giving undue importance to a marginal reality within the European consciousness. Though the existence of people adhering to different religious traditions has greatly increased in Europe within the last fifty years, they still represent a small minority of the population. Moreover, the particular beliefs, practices, and even clothing of Muslims, Hindus, and Buddhists seem to most Europeans exotic and alien. By and large, normal relations between indigenous Europeans and immigrants become possible insofar as the latter integrate into the secular culture of the former, i.e., that their beliefs and practices are kept firmly to the private world of their own communities, and that they do not violate generally accepted liberal values.

Secular society has to be understood largely by placing it in juxtaposition with the development of Christendom. It is this particularity that alone can make sense of Western history and society as it has evolved in the last half-millennium. Given the missiological challenge posed by secularity, concern with interreligious relationships may well mask a failure of nerve and imagination to come to terms with a specific flow of history.

It seems self-evident, in any case, that dialogue cannot be fruitful unless each side has a firm sense of self-identity. One aspect of this for Christian faith will be its ability to evaluate self-critically and respond positively to the secular onslaught on its beliefs. In other words, it has to engage in a very serious dialogue with secular beliefs before it can meaningfully dialogue with other religions. Unless this prior dialogue substantially fashions the Christian encounter with the religious traditions of the world, the latter will take place in an unreal world. It will be de-contextualized mission.

## The Secular as Religious Critique

Any understanding of interreligious dialogue that takes it to imply a uniting of forces against a secularist worldview would be a grave mistake. There are a number of aspects of the secular that rightly challenge religious people to reflect seriously on their ways of thinking and acting and, where necessary, change them. For example, there is no longer any place in any part of the world where the state should be upholding any particular religion, or requiring people to opt for a religion or interfering in cases of religious conversion. The exercise of political power under the dictates of a privileged religion is a corruption of both religion and politics.[11]

The secular interpretation of religion needs to be listened to, not dismissed, just because some parts of it are true.

## The Secularizing Tendencies of Christian Faith

Part of the recovery of Christian identity, in its rediscovery of its missionary task in the West, is the acknowledgment that a proper understanding of a secular society is not incompatible with Christian faith. Insofar as the chief characteristic of a secular society is the separation of political power from religious tests and ecclesiastical sanctions, the dissenting tradition within European churches eventually won the right of total nondiscrimination. Professor Owen Chadwick in the Gifford Lectures bears this out: "In Western Europe the ultimate claim of the liberal was religious. Liberal faith rested in origin upon the religious dissenter.... Dissenters won a free right to express a religious opinion which was not the accepted or prevailing opinion."[12]

11. Hence the notion of an Islamic republic or Buddhist nation is a dangerous error. Christians, with their memory of the abuse of privilege and power in medieval times and the conjunction of throne and altar in post-Reformation absolutist regimes, should be the first to proclaim that the move from theocracy to democracy in modern times marks an irreversible historical development to be welcomed.

12. Owen Chadwick, *The Secularisation of the European Mind in the Nineteenth Century* (Cambridge: Cambridge University Press, 1985), pp. 26-27.

In due time the logic of dissent was extended to those who did not wish to confess any religious faith.

Within the last two hundred years many European Christians have come to acknowledge that the dissenting tradition is the one most faithful to the apostolic tradition. Conversely, few seek to defend the model of Christendom, in which the church was accorded special powers and privileges.[13] Religious faith has to be a matter of individual conscience; the state has no place in the coercion of belief. The long Christendom phase of European history followed the "Christ of culture" model, identified by Richard Niebuhr,[14] i.e., the identification of Christian faith with a particular political arrangement. Today many Christians have rediscovered a more dialectical relationship between the gospel and culture: Christ in paradoxical relationship to and transforming culture.

Christians in the West are only able to recover a proper "prophetic" distance from society and its political governance because the community of faith (the church) is called to serve first the eschatological kingdom of God and, therefore, only critically the kingdoms of this world. It is well known that other faiths (particularly Islam) find it difficult to make such a sharp distinction between the people of faith and the political community. From its earliest years there has been a theocratic tendency within Islam. It is true that the majority of Muslims now live in nations without a Muslim majority, so they have had to come to terms with living within a system not ruled by Islamic principles. However, it may be said that the Islamic ideal is still a Muslim republic ruled according to shari'ah (the faultlessly revealed law of Allah), a notion too close for comfort to former Christian notions of the identity of the "Christian" kingdoms of this world with the kingdom of God: "One interpretation of Islam's modern predicament is that throughout its history it has been more a civilisation and an empire than a religion. But now that the empire has long since gone and the civilisation is in a state of turmoil, only the religious part is left. However, for Islam religion without a republic is like a body without clothes; it is exposed and vulnerable."[15]

---

13. Nevertheless, there are Christian leaders who continue mistakenly to confuse defense of political privilege in the state with Christian influence in society as a mission strategy.

14. Richard Niebuhr, *Christ and Culture* (New York: Harper, 1951).

15. Andrew J. Kirk, *Loosing the Chains: Religion as Opium and Liberation* (London: Hodder and Stoughton, 1992), p. 83. Cf. also Ali Mazrui, *Cultural Forces in World Politics* (London: James Currey, 1990), pp. 15, 218; Bassam Tibi, *The Crisis of Modern Islam: A Pre-industrial Culture in the Scientific-Technological Age* (Salt Lake City: University of Utah Press, 1988), pp. 45ff., 138-39; Hichem Djait, *Europe and Islam* (Berkeley: University of California Press, 1985), pp. 58-60; Shabbir Akhtar, *A Faith for All Seasons* (London: Bellew Publishing, 1990), pp. 15ff.

Until and unless people of other faith traditions come to accept without reservations the necessity of a fully secular state, Christian participation in interreligious dialogue is severely compromised.

## The Missionary Challenge to Interreligious Dialogue

There is one final element in the argument. This concerns the ability of any faith tradition to undertake a meaningful dialogue with the secular humanist tradition. Here I wish to argue that the Christian faith is in the best position to undertake such a task, even though it has struggled to adjust itself to the radical nature of the challenge. I also wish to argue that a defense of general religious sentiments is a hindrance to the task.

Such assertions may seem counterintuitive. It would seem more plausible to argue that Christianity has manifestly failed to engage fruitfully with secular culture, and therefore it is at least likely that other faith traditions could have more success. This line of reasoning is sometimes supported by the observation that a postmodern perspective has made possible the rebirth of interest in the spiritual dimension of life. A serious exploration of a reality beyond the material is now permitted as an intellectual option in the momentous critique of the positivist tradition in philosophy. Insofar as postmodernity is willing to sanction only a pluralist approach to belief and values, those religious traditions which seem to favor an all-embracing approach to religious experience, namely, those favoring a monistic philosophical explanation of life, would seem to be the most advantaged.[16]

The argument, then, that actual secular society is most conducive to those religious beliefs that have no difficulty finding a way of including all beliefs within their understanding of the universe appears to be irresistible. It is not uncommon, therefore, to find even some Christians embracing the pluralist thesis that all religious experience, including that associated with "New Age" sentiments and with "implicit religion," is an expression of one ultimate "Reality."[17]

16. The other side of this argument is the accusation that the Judeo-Christian tradition (now extended to the so-called Abrahamic faiths) with its tenacious and principled belief in only one God, is the main cause of all kinds of intolerance toward a diversity of beliefs and life-forms. Monotheism, it is argued, excludes (often violently) what is different.

17. Due to the inherent difficulties in coming up with a precise understanding of what is encompassed by religious experience, it is not wholly implausible to argue also that even atheists may experience a sense of deep awe and wonder, akin to religious belief, at the transcendent nature of the universe (or, according to latest hypotheses, universes) as ultimately "Real."

## The Way Forward for Mission?

So far we have argued that the most critical context in which the contemporary mission of the Christian community has to be conceived is secular society. Although the secularizing process is most obvious in the nations most influenced by European history, it is an increasingly global reality. In many ways it poses the most intractable problem for Christian witness globally. We have also argued that concentration on building relations of understanding with people of religious orientation, though important, may nevertheless be a dangerous distraction from the most pressing mission challenge of our times.

We may begin with the working hypothesis that secular belief comprises an identifiable set of convictions which more or less forms the everyday horizon of many people — those we may describe objectively as being irreligious, i.e., not being involved in any kind of regular cultic practices nor appealing to religious beliefs as reasons for their ambitions or behavior. The missionary challenge is to bridge the apparently immense gap between the apostolic message of Jesus Christ — a metanarrative Christians cannot compromise, for it is the defining reality by which they live — and secular consciousness, and to learn how to live as a (missionary) minority in an irreligious age.

We have to take into account the assumption that, superficially, there seems to be less of a gap between Christian faith and the world religions than between the religions and secular beliefs. Added to the fact that secular culture itself seems to be an adversary the religions have in common, it is not surprising that some Christians turn to interreligious dialogue as the mainstay of their missionary outlook. The gathering criticism of globalization, seen as one of the children of a secular consciousness, and the move to find a religiously inspired "global ethic" as a response add fuel to this approach. Nevertheless, I remain convinced that mission with regard to secular consciousness has both a historical and methodological priority over mission as interreligious encounter.

# Toward a Paradigm Shift in Christian Mission: South Asia and North Europe

KAJSA AHLSTRAND

South Asia has a long history as a multifaith society, and reflection on Christian mission in that context is readily available. In northern Europe experiences of the presence of religions other than Christianity are of a more recent date. What can northern Europe learn from South Asia?

In order to point out some possible approaches to the issue, I take as my starting point the Ishvani-Kendra Research Seminar 2000: "A Vision of Mission for the New Millennium" (April 10, 2000), to be found at the Sedos website, www.sedos.org/english/ishvani.htm (viewed October 14, 2002). This Roman Catholic seminar gathered forty-four concerned Christians in Pune from March 9 through 12, 2000. The stated objective was "to sketch out a vision of mission that is adequately responsive to the challenges posed by the contemporary realities of life in our country." "Mission" is here squarely placed in the local context ("our country") and seen as a response to contemporary challenges. The mission theology expressed in the document is related to concrete situations in a context that is partly characterized by the presence of venerable religious traditions, but also by widespread poverty, devastating effects of globalized economy, and religious chauvinist politics.

The participants in the seminar can be described as "reflective practitioners," committed to work for change in their own context. The research was not done with interacademic discussions in mind, but as academic and practical knowledge put to use in a specific context. In a European academic setting it is difficult to find room for the kind of material produced by the seminar. It is not sufficiently "grass-rooted" to be used as a source for what Asian Christians believe about mission, and it is not sufficiently academic to be taken seriously as a scientific paper on mission theology. But I think theologians from the North can benefit from what our colleagues elsewhere have produced in situations where "a vision of mission" is a question that affects politics as well as theology.

Here follows a summary of the paper:

## Preamble

In India it is impossible to reflect on Christian mission without being reminded of the painful experiences of colonization. The Christian message has often been presented in a language and tone smacking of imperialism. Against this background it is important to point out that Indian Christians today have no aggressive designs on the followers of other faith traditions. The participants in the seminar commit themselves to work toward enhanced life for all.

## The Challenge of the Indian Context

There are many valuable aspects of the Indian context: a tradition of harmony, of spiritual values, and of democracy. But there are also disturbing signs such as division, fundamentalism, communalism, social inequality (e.g., the caste system), and economic inequality.

Popular (subaltern) movements of, e.g., Dalits, tribals, and women threaten the stability of India's socioeconomic structures. The inherent social and economic inequalities, if left unrepaired, may lead to the destabilization of democracy. Significant political changes are currently taking place: from centrist to rightist, from the center to the regions, and toward the activism of the popular (sometimes populist) movements.

Globalization is widening the gap between the rich and the poor; ecological disaster threatens; increasing importance of media and communication leads to rapid changes in traditional value systems.

The celebrated Indian religious pluralism and religious tolerance is now at risk. Religion is being seen as a source of identity (linked to culture and ethnicity) excluding "the other." Fundamentalist tendencies are found in every faith tradition. Communalism uses religion as a political tool branding the other as enemy. Every religious group can nurture hurtful memories of the domination of others.

The church is more often seen as an institution than as a witnessing community. It is identified with the Western world. Its leadership sees orthodoxy as more important than authentic Christian life; there is a gap between (male) clergy and the laity, and women are excluded from leadership.

These factors taken together call for a new paradigm for mission.

## Toward a Paradigm Shift

Missiology is often either presented as a history of missions or, based on Matthew 28, interpreted as the command to administer baptism to everyone. The goal of Christian mission is then understood as the salvation of souls. Against this the seminar proposes that the goal of mission is the welfare of the whole creation. The church is not meant to dominate but to serve as leaven in order to facilitate the transformation of the world.

Experiences of the Spirit's action in the world not only set the agenda for the mission of the church, but also enable us to understand mission itself in a fresh way; there is a clear emphasis on newness.

A quotation from #14:

> According to the new paradigm, creation itself is a self-communication of God, who is reaching out to all peoples through the Word and the Spirit in varied ways, at various times, and through the different religions. This ongoing divine-human encounter is salvific. However, God's plan is not merely to save individual souls, but to gather together all things in heaven and on earth. God is working out this plan in history through various sages and prophets. Jesus, the Word incarnate, has a specific role in this history of salvation. But Jesus' mission is at the service of God's mission. It does not replace it. Taking a kenotic form, it collaborates with other divine self-manifestations in other religions as God's mission is moving towards its eschatological fulfilment. As disciples of Jesus we must witness to the Abba and his kingdom of freedom and fellowship, love and justice.

The consequences of this missiology would be for the church in India to be an agent of an ongoing universal reconciliation. The church finds its allies among followers of other religious traditions and persons of good will. Mission is not only to give but also to discover and recognize God's presence and receive God's multiform revelations in others.

The church is the light of the world. This self-understanding should lead to a more authentic community, the redefinition of ecclesial boundaries, and the recognition of a variety of ways of being Christian in the world.

## Characteristics of Mission

Dialogue understands believers from other faith traditions as partners in mission. Dialogue is both the method and the message, supported by common action and shared commitment to the cause of justice.

Mission needs to be prophetic: it confronts personal and structural forces that hamper human growth and frustrate the fulfillment of God's plan for all, which is life in abundance. Individualism, egoism, and insensibility to the common good must be overcome. There is a special commitment to the weak and oppressed, which in patriarchal society often means women.

Mission should oppose all tendencies of cultural nationalism. Intolerance of pluralism, that is, monoculturalism, is inadmissible. Instead we should strive to build a just and egalitarian society.

Christians should be messengers of peace. In practice this means that education in conflict resolution is a prioritized area of missionary involvement. This is especially important in areas prone to religious and ethnic violence.

Christian mission is marked by eschatological openness: fullness of life to all individuals and peoples. We are called to infuse hope in every person for richer relationships between persons and communities.

It is the living memory of Jesus who inspires us, and we are happy to share this memory with others. Jesus is a source of inspiration for a commitment to the good of others in a spirit of humility.

A quotation from #25: "At the same time we do not want to impose on others our way of following Jesus. We are aware that there are many forms of discipleship and that God invites each person to respond to God's call within the concrete circumstances and possibilities of his or her life. We are open to the possibility that others are inspired by and feel called to follow Jesus in their own way different from ours, while we welcome those who wish to join our community of his disciples, namely, the Church."

## Some Pointers for Action

Christianity needs to collaborate with other religions in the promotion of genuine human and cosmic liberation. God is present in every religion and in every human heart.

Dialogue is sharing religious experiences centered on fundamental values of truth and justice. Dialogue groups could be fora for discussing socioeconomic and political issues of relevance, environmental work, and identification with marginalized peoples. Christian education should be in the direction of human community leadership rather than clerical ritualistic ministries.

The Christian mission should encourage political involvement aimed at the protection of the poor and the weak and support of the democratic system and education for democracy. The fostering of a democratic ethos respectful of diversity of cultures and communities is an important task. Democracy is to be understood as protection of minorities, not despotic rule by the majority.

Missionaries need to be reminded that methods are the message. They/we are called to negotiating boundaries, communing across borders; the perspective is that of kenotic universality as opposed to hegemonic universality. We are called to be agents of transformation in society in the manner of light, salt, and leaven.

## Mission in a Northern Multifaith Context

If this sketch is a relevant missiology for India (and there are of course different opinions about that), is it also applicable to another context such as northern Europe?

If it is truly contextual, it cannot be transferred to a different context, but the structure of the document might help us analyze our societies and the parts the churches may play. If we, too, begin our search from our context, what will we find, and what consequences will this lead to in our understanding of mission in our part of the world?

Politically the countries in northern Europe can be described as stable democracies and welfare states, where values such as equality and solidarity are prominent. The population is well educated, the standard of living is relatively high, and people can expect to live longer than in most countries.

The countersignals to this rosy picture are increasingly coming to the fore: the welfare society as we have known it is crumbling. One-third of the population is left behind. More people are on long-term sick leave from their jobs. Xenophobia, national chauvinist movements, and populist political parties are gaining ground. Large segments of the population (first, second, and third generations of immigrants) are not fully accepted by the dominant society and thus suffer from unemployment, relative poverty, bad health, and high crime rate (both as victims and as perpetrators). There are movements that threaten the democratic framework: right-wing, nationalist groups; violent antiglobalization groups; and to a lesser extent, religious (Christian and Muslim) fundamentalist groups. These movements and groups signal that there is no unanimous opinion about where our societies should be going. Various groups of people do not experience our present societies as beneficial to them. We cannot take democratic values for granted. Recently we have seen how vulnerable all of us are to the globalized economy. Pension funds, research grant institutions, even the churches have played the stock market and lost. When the economic situation in general is deteriorating, the most vulnerable are left behind: people with disabilities, immigrants and refugees, the elderly, people with rudimentary education.

Where is the church in this society? There are many examples of how the churches through their diaconal work try to counter the negative trends in society and work with and for the marginalized. But we can also note that the churches are caught up in their own power struggles and to a large extent are considered irrelevant in today's society, except when they can provide space for comfort and nostalgia. The prophetic element is more often than not absent.

The last thing associated with the life of the national Lutheran churches is probably mission in the Nordic countries. When the word is used, it is usually associated with concepts such as proselytism and conversion. It is understood as that activity of the church which aims at gaining more members, preferably from other faith communities. Given that these other faith communities are relative newcomers on the Nordic scene, mission is seldom seen in relation to the daily life of the churches.

The threatening, hostile aspect of the word "mission" must be taken seriously. Can we detect a paradigm shift in the churches' understanding of mission? When theological discussions take place about the meaning of mission in today's world, the tone is often bitter and accusing. The divide seems to be between those who understand mission as "obeying our Lord's command in Matthew 28" and those who would like to replace aggressive mission with friendly dialogue. The Indian document shows that these are not the only two options. For one thing, the biblical understanding of mission cannot be limited to the last sentences in Saint Matthew's Gospel. The Johannine understanding of mission as the giving of life in abundance is central in the Indian document. On the other hand, a peaceful relationship to other faith communities is a prerequisite for the pressing tasks that lie ahead, not a goal in itself. The goal is the transformation of the world. It is incredibly bold of a religious community that gathers less than 3 percent of the population to see "the transformation of the world" as its goal. For centuries it has been believed that this transformation will take place when people from other religions convert to Christianity. The Indian theologians, reflecting on their practice, dare to question this belief. They suggest that the "minority images" of the church as salt and leaven might mean that God intends this transformation to take place through the church as an agent, but not that every human being is called to belong to the church. There is a place for other faith communities. The church is an open communion; no one is born into it; every member has entered from outside. Some enter when they are very young, and are assisted by their families; others enter when they are older, and carry with them a history of faith.

The Nordic national churches have sometimes forgotten that it is abnormal for the church to be a majority religion. To some "folk church" theologians it seems as if the ideal is that 100 percent of the population be church members, and anything short of that is a failure. The presence of other faith communities, "multifaith situations," is then seen as a problem to be overcome. Some would suggest that the solution of the problem lies in the conversion of the other faith communities to Christianity. Others talk of the expulsion of Muslim refugees and immigrants from the Nordic countries as a desirable policy. In both cases the goal is the eradication of the multifaith situation. It is in this situation that the Indian theologians remind us that the missiological problem is not the presence of other faith communities, but the absence of justice and life for all. The multifaith situation is a situation that God has willed. Believers from faith communities and people who would not call themselves religious are not to be regarded as objects for Christian conversion activities, but as friends and allies in the same mission, which is the restoration of creation. The presence of other faith communities can then become an opportunity to praise God for God's wisdom and abundant gifts: how manifold are your works! In wisdom you have made them all (Ps. 104:24).

# Toward an Intercultural Theology:
# Paradigm Shifts in Missiology, Ecumenics,
# and Comparative Religion

VOLKER KÜSTER

The three disciplines missiology, ecumenics, and comparative religion (when taught at a theological faculty) are the sources of what we have started calling intercultural theology. Missiology is nowadays dealing to a large extent with the ways Christianity is taking form in different cultures. Mission is always also culture contact. If ecumenics does not limit itself to the Protestant-Catholic relationship but turns to the pluralism of confessions, denominations, and groups, the cultural dimension will come to the fore as well. Under the premise that religion is a cultural system,[1] all three subdivisions of the pluri-discipline missiology, ecumenics, and comparative religion[2] are then equally concerned with questions of culture contact, which can be qualified more closely as first contact, conflict, and exchange.[3] Culture and religion are related dialectically to one another and penetrate each other. Cultures are man-made complex weaves of meaning and symbol systems, always already

---

1. Cf. Clifford Geertz, "Religion as a Cultural System," in Geertz, *The Interpretation of Cultures: Selected Essays* (New York, 1973), pp. 87-125.

2. Cf. Volker Küster, "Religionsgeschichte, Missionswissenschaft, Ökumenik. Thesen zu einer bedrohten Pluridisziplin," *Deutsches Pfarrerblatt* 97, no. 7 (1997): 342-43.

3. Cf. Urs Bitterli, *Alte Welt — neue Welt. Formen des europäisch-überseeischen Kulturkontaktes vom 15. bis zum 18. Jahrhundert* (Munich, 1992).

This essay was presented on different occasions and in varying forms at the Universities of Birmingham, Aarhus, Utrecht, a gathering of the Ecumenical Association of Third World Theologians (EATWOT) with theological partners in Chateau du Bossey, Switzerland, and the joint assembly of the boards of the Deutsche und Schweizerische Ost-Asien Mission (DOAM/SOAM) in Rheinwiel, Switzerland. Earlier versions are published in *Interkulturelle Hermeneutik und lectura popular. Neuere Konzepte in Theorie und Praxis*, Beiheft zur Ökumenischen Rundschau 72 (Frankfurt am Main, 2002), pp. 219-27; *Voices from the Third World* 25 (2002): 112-19.

open to transcendence. Religions are cultural expressions of an experience of resonance.[4] "Intercultural theology" is therefore an adequate umbrella term for interconfessional, intercultural, and interreligious issues.[5]

## The Situation of the Pluri-discipline Missiology, Ecumenics, and Comparative Religion at the Protestant Faculties

The general trend to favor religious studies over against theology strengthens the position of comparative religion. Where the theological frame is preserved, there is a tendency to find a new name for missiology and ecumenics in reaction to the paradigm shifts these disciplines are undergoing.

1. In Germany the chairs for missiology are in combination with ecumenics and/or comparative religion. While missiology is frequently declared superfluous, ecumenics is nearly absorbed by dogmatics. As a consequence, comparative religion becomes the lead discipline.

2. In the Netherlands most of the chairs for mission and ecumenics will not be reopened. Only at the IIMO in Utrecht and the Theological University Kampen (Thuk) will some kind of follow-up with different labels remain. Comparative religion or history of religions is in the Netherlands a discipline in its own right.

3. With about ten chairs, Germany still claims the most. Besides the two remaining in the Netherlands, the numbers in Great Britain and the Nordic countries Denmark, Sweden, Norway, and Finland vary between one and two chairs.

4. In the United States missiology is established as a practical discipline at the seminaries, while the large schools such as Harvard, Princeton, Yale, Union, and Chicago have chairs for ecumenics and world Christianity. They also hired a number of Third World theologians such as C. S. Song (Berkeley), Kosuke Koyama (Union), Lamin Sanneh (Yale), Chung Hyun-Kyung (Union), Kwok Pui-lan (Cambridge), and Thomas Thangaraj (Candler).

5. Eastern Europe and the Third World are about the only places where new chairs are opened.

---

4. Cf. Gerd Theißen, *On Having a Critical Faith* (London, 1979).

5. Cf. Volker Küster, "Interkulturelle Theologie," in *Religion in Geschichte und Gegenwart*, vol. 4, 4th ed. (2001), pp. 197-99.

## The Emergence of an Intercultural Theology

In the wake of secular emancipation movements in the Third World in the period of decolonization and the building of a new world order after World War II, the then-called younger churches cut the umbilical cord between them and the former mission churches, and contextual theologies developed. The Western mission project and theology of mission underwent a crisis and tried to cope theologically with the new situation. In the 1970s a demographic shift of Christianity from the North to the South, especially Latin America and Africa, became evident. With the fall of the Berlin Wall (1989) and the implosion of the communist bloc, this epoch came to an end. Theology has just begun to reflect on the new developments which became known as globalization.

1. From the late 1960s–early 1970s onward, contextual theologies emerged all over the Third World. As early as 1976 contextual theologians from Africa, Asia, Latin America, and their diasporas in the West organized themselves in Dar es Salaam as the Ecumenical Association of Third World Theologians (EATWOT).[6] Their debates about commonalities, differences, and cross-fertilization are a success story of an intercultural discourse. The representatives of the two great schools of contextual theology, liberation theology and inculturation and dialogue theology, learned from each other and broadened their perception of their particular contexts.

Latin American liberation theologians have been accused of not taking into consideration folk Catholicism as well as the cultural-religious traditions of the indigenous peoples and the African minorities. During the 1980s they changed their attitude considerably. While Latin America was regarded as the most Westernized part of the Third World, liberation theologies in Africa and Asia were more aware of cultural-religious issues from the beginning due to their contexts. African theologians challenged South African black theology for its preoccupation with the race issue. Inculturation and dialogue theologians from Africa and Asia on the other hand were criticized for lacking awareness of socioeconomic and political factors. It was the Asian theologian Aloysius Pieris who pleaded for a merging of the two schools within EATWOT. In the 1990s some sprouting Asian liberation theologies such as Dalit theology in India and Burakumin theology in Japan criticized the traditional dialogue theologies for not paying enough attention to the social implications in the cultural-religious systems of their respective contexts. Further, ecology and gender issues became new items on the theological agenda.

---

6. Cf. Volker Küster, "Aufbruch der Dritten Welt. Der Weg der Ökumenischen Vereinigung von Dritte-Welt-Theologen [EATWOT]," in *Verkündigung und Forschung* 37 (1992): 45-67.

With her plea for an "irruption within the irruption," Ghanaian theologian Mercy Amba Oduyoye signaled the coming of age of Third World women's theology.[7] The women within EATWOT gave Third World theology a fresh impulse. They are in a way the second generation. While some of them are still in their fifties, the grand old men are slowly disappearing. It has to remain at present an open question how contextual theology in the Third World will continue. But the reconstitution of human dignity before God and men contrary to the facts of individual life situations and the right of cultural difference are irrefutable contributions by contextual theologies.[8]

2. The ecclesiological and theological awakening in the Third World is paralleled by a crisis in mission and mission theology in the West. As a matter of fact, many of the chairs for missiology and ecumenics were instituted to observe these developments in the former mission countries. The term "intercultural theology," which indicates a growing awareness of Christian pluralism, is closely connected to the names of Hans Jochen Margull, Richard Friedli, and Walter Hollenweger, the founding editors of the Studies into the Intercultural History of Christianity. Margull and Friedli reacted immediately to the new developments in churches and theologies of the Third World in the late 1960s and early 1970s. They were also pioneers in the debate about interreligious dialogue.[9] Hollenweger has written a three-volume intercultural theology which is an enormous reservoir of material but still lacks some systematic reflection.[10]

3. Here the second generation of postwar missiologists came to the fore. Communication theories, which were applied in mission theology as a helpful tool, were critically reflected on from the perspective of the receiver. Hermeneutics were introduced as a means to understand the other. In Germany Theo Sundermeier tried to reestablish missiology as a hermeneutic discipline encountering the "cultural stranger."[11] Mission is being with the people, living to-

7. Cf. Doris Strahm, *Vom Rand in die Mitte. Christologie aus der Sicht von Frauen in Asien, Afrika und Lateinamerika* (Lucerne, 1997).

8. Cf. Volker Küster, *The Many Faces of Jesus Christ: Intercultural Christology* (London, 2001).

9. Cf. Hans Jochen Margull, *Zeugnis und Dialog. Ausgewählte Schriften* (Ammersbek bei Hamburg, 1992); Richard Friedli, *Fremdheit als Heimat. Auf der Suche nach einem Kriterium für den Dialog zwischen den Religionen* (Zürich, 1974).

10. Cf. Walter J. Hollenweger, *Erfahrungen der Leibhaftigkeit. Interkulturelle Theologie* (Munich, 1979); *Umgang mit Mythen. Interkulturelle Theologie II* (Munich, 1982); *Geist und Materie. Interkulturelle Theologie III* (Munich, 1988).

11. Cf. Theo Sundermeier, *Konvivenz und Differenz. Studien zu einer verstehenden Missionswissenschaft* (Erlangen, 1995); Sundermeier, *Den Fremden verstehen. Eine praktische Hermeneutik* (Göttingen, 1996).

gether, or *"convivence"* as Sundermeier puts it with a term found in Latin America. *Convivence* constitutes a community of helping as well as learning from each other and feasting together. The feast creates space to meet the other, also the cultural-religious stranger. The tension between *convivence* and difference is not neglected but accepted in mutual respect.[12] Another milestone on the theoretical level was Bob Schreiter's analysis of local contextualization processes with the help of communication theories and semiotics.[13] The Christian tradition as such is for him a series of local theologies. With his concept of a "new Catholicity," he now opts for a theology that operates between the local and the global.[14]

Intercultural theology is a necessary tool to link the divergent contextual theologies and to analyze globalized cultural systems in their interaction with Christianity. Its central features are the change of perspective expressed by the recognition of the different identity of the cultural-religious other and the attempt to understand that other in a way that the other can discern himself or herself in my perception. Intercultural theology is creating new space for theological thinking in an age of pluralism.[15]

4. The discourse among contextual theologians in EATWOT as well as the Western discourse on contextual theologies in the pluri-discipline missiology, ecumenics, and comparative religion were focusing on three themes: *liberation, inculturation,* and *dialogue.*[16] Both discourses led to the conclusion that there is a necessity for an intercultural theology.

5. Liberation, inculturation, and dialogue were also the recurring themes in the official documents of the Catholic Church after Vatican II on the topics of mission and the relation to other religions, such as "Redemptoris Missio" (1990) and "Dialogue and Proclamation" (1991). The same is true for the World Council of Churches on the Protestant and Orthodox side, with documents like "Guidelines on Dialogue" (1979) and "Mission and Evangelisation" (1982).

---

12. Cf. Werner Simpfendörfer, "Auf der Suche nach einer interkulturellen Theologie. Herausforderungen — Aspekte — Bausteine," *Junge Kirche* 48 (1987): 266-73; Simpfendörfer, "Interkulturelle Theologie. Wie kann man Ende und Anfang verknüpfen?" in *Evangelische Kommentare* 6 (1989): 37-40. While Sundermeier tries to bear the tension between *convivence* and difference, Simpfendörfer concentrates on the cultural conflicts. Both regard the feast as the exemplary opportunity to experience the cultural stranger. But while Simpfendörfer wants to overcome the strangeness in the feast, Sundermeier wants to give it space.

13. Cf. Robert J. Schreiter, *Constructing Local Theologies* (Maryknoll, N.Y., 1985).

14. Cf. Robert J. Schreiter, *The New Catholicity: Theology between the Global and the Local* (Maryknoll, N.Y., 1997).

15. Postcolonial theory speaks of creating a "third space." Cf. Homi K. Bhabha, *The Location of Culture* (London and New York, 1994).

16. Cf. Schreiter, *The New Catholicity,* p. 126.

But the discussion within and between the churches has not been without tension and conflict. There has been a rather critical stance toward liberation and dialogue theologians on the Catholic side, as indicated by the cases of Leonardo Boff and Tissa Balasuria. In official Vatican documents inculturation is restricted again to mere accommodation. In the ecumenical movement there was a split between the so-called ecumenicals and evangelicals about the question of liberation and interreligious dialogue, which led to the foundation of the evangelical Lausanne movement.[17] Even within this group, however, there is still a certain pluralism regarding the issue of contextualization. Especially evangelicals coming from the Third World feel the need to respond theologically to their contexts of poverty, oppression, and religious pluralism.[18] Evangelicals have always had a missiological interest in the gospel and culture issue.[19] There they meet with Catholicism. The performance of the young Korean woman theologian Chung Hyun-Kyung at the Seventh Assembly of the World Council of Churches in Canberra in 1991 led to a severe conflict with the Orthodox churches on the gospel and culture issue.[20]

6. "Globalization" has become the catchword for the recent changes in the world order.[21] It is signified by the global extension of neoliberal capitalism after the fall of communism and the compression of the world through communication technologies. This change of contexts could not be without consequences for contextual theologies, as can be clearly shown with regard to our three generative themes:

- *Liberation:* The political situation in the Third World has changed. In

17. *Let the Earth Hear His Voice: International Congress on World Evangelization, Lausanne, Switzerland,* ed. James Dixon Douglas (Minneapolis, 1975).

18. Cf. Vinay Samuel and Chris Sugden, *Sharing Jesus in the Two Thirds World: Evangelical Christologies from the Contexts of Poverty, Powerlessness, and Religious Pluralism: The Papers of the First Conference of Evangelical Mission Theologians from the Two Thirds World, Bangkok, Thailand, March 22-25, 1982* (Grand Rapids, 1984).

19. Cf. "The Willowbank Report: Report of a Consultation on Gospel and Culture, Held at Willowbank, Somerset Bridge, Bermuda from 6th to 13th January 1978," Lausanne Occasional Papers 2 (Wheaton, Ill., 1978); Charles H. Kraft, *Christianity and Culture: A Study in Dynamic Biblical Theologizing in Cross-Cultural Perspectives* (Maryknoll, N.Y., 1979).

20. Cf. Chung Hyun-Kyung, "Come Holy Spirit — Renew the Whole Creation," in *Signs of the Spirit: World Council of Churches Official Report Seventh Assembly, Canberra, Australia, 7-20 February 1991,* ed. Michael Kinnamon (Geneva, 1991), pp. 37-47; "Reflections of Orthodox Participants Addressed to the Seventh General Assembly," in *Signs of the Spirit,* pp. 279-82; Athanasios Basdekis, "Canberra und die Orthodoxen. Anfragen und Forderungen an den ÖRK im Anschluss an die 7. Vollversammlung," *Ökumenische Rundschau* 40 (1991): 356-74.

21. Cf. Ulrich Beck, *Was ist Globalisierung?* (Frankfurt am Main, 1997); Malcolm Waters, *Globalization* (New York, 1995).

Latin America, e.g., the military dictatorships were replaced by populist regimes and young democracies. In South Korea the lifelong opposition leader Kim Dae-Jung finally became president, and in South Africa Nelson Mandela managed a peaceful change. *Reconciliation, reparation,* and *reconstruction* are thus the new themes on the theological agenda. But at the same time, the gap between rich and poor increase in the global system. And many Third World countries are shaken by cruel ethnic and religious conflicts. The classic themes of liberation theology thus still remain current.

- *Inculturation:* As far as culture is concerned, globalization theories speak of *localization.* The hyper-culture of consumerism — some have spoken of a McDonaldization or Coca-Colonization of the world — is counteracted by a resurgence of local cultures. But the myth of cultural uniqueness has faded. Cultures are mixed and consist of numerous subcultures. Postcolonial theory speaks in this regard of *hybridization* or *creolization.*[22]

- *Dialogue:* The theological reflection on interreligious dialogue remains ambivalent. At the same time, we are confronted with ethnicity as well as bloody cultural-religious conflicts driven by an ever growing fundamentalism within the different religions. New, nonpatronizing strategies of interreligious solidarity with those who are able to confront the fundamentalists from within their own religious traditions have to be explored.

## Mission and Dialogue: The Paradigm Shift in Mission Theology

What are the implications of the aforementioned developments for a theology of mission? Does it still make sense to talk about Christian mission at all? The answer to this question is yes, but it is impossible today to talk about mission without referring to dialogue.

### Defining the Concepts

In Christian terms mission is being with the people, living the faith in an exemplary way (Matt. 5), telling the biblical stories and relating them to the particular context and individual life situations, helping the needy by healing and feed-

---

22. Cf. Robert J. C. Young, *Colonial Desire: Hybridity in Theory, Culture, and Race* (London, 1995); Ulrich Hannerz, "The World in Creolization," *Africa* 57 (1987): 546-59.

ing them, and inviting everybody to the table of communion. While in the Eucharist Christians should share their religion in a ritual manner with everybody who feels invited and wants to participate, baptism is the rite that incorporates the convert into the Christian community. It presupposes knowledge about the Christian religion, commitment of faith, and testimony to the God triune. Baptism should therefore take place only after a period of living together and learning from each other.[23]

But missionary expansion is a central feature of Christianity, Islam, and Buddhism alike. Nevertheless, there is a lack of a kind of comparative missiology. To name just a few points of comparison: All three rely on religious scripts and teaching for their missionary endeavors. Islam shares with Christianity also the social engagement, which was lacking in Buddhism until recently. Each has a rite of conversion: baptism in Christianity, reciting the *shahada* in Islam, and the triple refuge in Buddhism. Primary religions are not missionary. That is true for Judaism as well, despite proselytism, and partly also for Hinduism, which is in fact a mixture of various kinds of religions. New religious movements stemming from Hinduism such as Hare Krishna and Osho (Bhagwan Shree Rajneesh) are missionizing in the West.

Interreligious dialogue developed out of the necessity to live together in multifaith situations. It has therefore often a concrete occasion and an ethical impetus. In its institutionalized forms it is mainly based on Christian initiative. The so-called dialogue in community or living dialogue of the people who experience the faiths of their neighbors in their daily life, however, has been practiced ever since different religions existed in the same place. But there have also been forms of intellectual, refined dialogue between the learned of different religious traditions in antiquity and the Middle Ages. Modern interreligious dialogue which goes beyond mere ethical questions of overcoming poverty, violence, etc., can be understood as a common search for truth which is always only discernible in a contextual way. In analogy to this dialogue of minds and the dialogue of life, one could speak of a spiritual dialogue or dialogue of hearts regarding the third form of dialogue between the mystics of different religious traditions.[24] Again the initiative is mainly on the Christian side: Christian re-

23. Child baptism is then a matter from second-generation Christians onward. In the first generation it should only take place together with the parents. In some strands of Western Christianity, however, baptism has nowadays become more a family rite than a rite of incorporation into the particular church community.

24. Similar ideas were uttered by Dominic Moghal in his paper presented at the Aarhus Conference. Cf. also Leonard Swidler, "The Dialogue Decalogue: Ground Rules for Interreligious Dialogue," *Current Dialogue*, no. 5 (1983): 6-9, here 9; Diana L. Eck, "What Do We Mean by 'Dialogue'?" *Current Dialogue*, no. 11 (1986): 5-15.

treat centers offering Zen meditation or Sufi dance and Christian ashrams in India are well-known examples. But there are also Zen masters reading Eckhart and Hindu sages who respect Jesus as one of their kind. Recent discussions about sharing spiritual experiences and the possibility of interreligious prayer also belong to this strand of interreligious dialogue.

Mission and dialogue can both only be successful if the local context and the experiences of the people are taken as a starting point and are continuously referred to in the process.

## How to Relate Mission and Dialogue

Basically there are four ways of relating mission and dialogue. The two extreme positions are that dialogue substitutes for mission or that mission instrumentalizes dialogue as a means of converting adherents of other religious communities. While the first stance is advocated by representatives of a pluralist theology of religions, the second is put into practice by evangelical mission circles.

A middle path is taken for instance by the mainline churches in their attempt to keep mission and dialogue apart. The World Council of Churches has separate subunits for mission and evangelization and interreligious dialogue. The Vatican has a separate Congregation for the Evangelization of Peoples and a Pontifical Council for Interreligious Dialogue.

Finally there is the possibility of relating mission and dialogue dialectically. As a matter of fact, there can be no real dialogue without witness. Only someone who has a religious conviction and is willing to share it not only by questioning the other but also by allowing himself to be questioned gives due respect to the religious conviction of the other and can be taken seriously. Hans Jochen Margull, in speaking of vulnerability *(Verwundbarkeit)*, has given this approach a christological foundation.[25]

The double commandment of interreligious dialogue is therefore: (1) to try to understand the religious other in a way that the other can recognize himself or herself in my perception; (2) to give witness and to share the best of one's own faith with each other. Interreligious communication and hermeneutics are interwoven. To communicate one has to understand, and vice versa. With *translation, questioning,* and *exchange,* every interreligious encounter can take on at least three different forms. Translation happens necessarily at the beginning of every dialogue. One tries to understand the thought patterns of the reli-

---

25. Cf. Hans Jochen Margull, "Verwundbarkeit. Bemerkungen zum Dialog," *Evangelische Theologie* 34 (1974): 410-20 (= Margull, *Zeugnis und Dialog,* pp. 330-42).

gious other in one's own frame of reference. In the course of the dialogue, however, the partners might reach a point were one cannot but question the alien faith system. But it may also come to exchange and mutual enrichment. The interreligious encounter not only challenges but also changes the partners in dialogue.[26]

Interreligious dialogue is however not a "discourse without domination." This is probably an ideal that reality cannot meet in any case. Therefore the question of power has to be addressed. In the worst case, long-endured suppression by a dominant religious tradition can escalate into interreligious conflicts.

## Mission and Dialogue in the Context of Interreligious Conflicts

Not only under communism but also in many Islamic countries as well as in Hindu India, Christian mission is forbidden or at least under severe pressure. There are new persecutions of Christians caused by Islamic and Hindu fundamentalism. But there is also Hindu aggression against Muslims and mosques in India, and Muslim aggression against Buddhist monuments in Afghanistan. At the same time, aggressive fundamentalist Christian missions cause religious upheavals in former peaceful multireligious communities. Mission without dialogue is doomed to failure and can cause severe interreligious conflicts. But how to deal with growing religious fundamentalism? Traditional concepts of interreligious dialogue presuppose openness toward the religious other and willingness to communicate. These strategies do not work in a fundamentalist framework. Those who are capable of challenging fundamentalists from within their own religious traditions in a kind of intrareligious dialogue have to be supported in interreligious solidarity. Further strategies of preventing conflict and violence have to be applied to interreligious conflicts.

26. Cf. Volker Küster, "Ein Dialog in Bildern. Reformbuddhismus und Christentum im Werk von Hattigamana Uttarananda," in *Mit dem Fremden Leben,* pt. 2, ed. Dieter Becker and Andreas Feldtkeller (Erlangen, 2000), pp. 17-32; Küster, "Dialog VII: Mission und Dialog," in *Religion in Geschichte und Gegenwart,* vol. 2, 4th ed. (1999), p. 821.

## Mission and Dialogue between Exclusivism, Inclusivism, and Pluralism

Claims to its uniqueness are inherent to every religion. Exclusivism and inclusivism are the two antagonistic strategies to deal with the religious other. Even the so-called pluralist theology of religion is in the end a sublime form of inclusivism. In its move from Christocentrism to theocentrism and finally to a position beyond theism/nontheism, it constructs a metareligion that no longer takes seriously the identity of the religious other nor its own Christian identity.[27]

The Abrahamic religions, Judaism, Christianity, and Islam, all have strong exclusivist tendencies due to their monotheism. That is also true among themselves. But even in blaming one another for being heretical in central patterns of their particular traditions, they still give evidence to their kinship. Jews regard Christianity as heresy because it venerates Jesus Christ as the Messiah. Muslims honor Jesus as one of the prophets but do not regard him as the Son of God, which is from a Christian point of view heretical. The Trinity is for Islam tritheism and therefore heresy. According to Islam, the Jews have falsified the Torah. Judaism and Christianity on the other hand do not accept Muhammad as a prophet.[28]

In Judaism and Christianity the biblical teaching about God creating the world and pneumatology make an inclusivist position possible. Christian teaching about the *logos spermatikos* that works in other religions dating back to Justin found its modern variant in Karl Rahner's "anonymous Christians."[29] For Islam everybody is a born Muslim but does not necessarily follow the right path. The people of the book, Jews and Christians, enjoy protection under Islam. In liberal law schools Buddhism and Hinduism are subsumed here. Only primal religions are in any case subject to mission.

The Asiatic religions Hinduism and Buddhism differ considerably from the strong exclusivism of the Abrahamic religions. The most inclusivist religion is probably Hinduism, which has been capable of absorbing all kinds of religions and religious influences. Shankara's Advaita Vedanta is a philosophical reflection of this phenomenon. The least-exclusivist religion is perhaps Mahayana Buddhism, which presupposes that everybody is a potential Buddha but has to awaken to it to let this become factual. But there arise exclusivist tendencies in some strands of these religions nevertheless.

---

27. Cf., among others, Stanley J. Samartha, *One Christ — Many Religions: Toward a Revised Christology* (Maryknoll, N.Y., 1991).

28. Cf. Volker Küster, "Verwandtschaft verpflichtet. Erwägungen zum Projekt einer 'Abrahamitischen Ökumene,'" *Evangelische Theologie* 62 (2002): 384-99.

29. Cf. Karl Rahner, "Christianity and the Non-Christian Religions," in *Theological Investigations* 5 (New York and London, 1966), pp. 115-34.

Accepting deliberately that other tribes have other gods, tribal religions are in a way the most pluralist type of religion. At the same time, they are strictly exclusivist to the inside. Every member of the tribe is supposed to share the same religion.

Obviously there is no easy way to overcome this *exclusivist-inclusivist dilemma* without giving up considerable parts of one's own religious identity. But it might well be an important step to mutual understanding if one recognizes that all religions have claims toward their uniqueness in common. The ethos of respect and mutual recognition that is central in interreligious encounter can then lead to an approach that does not give up the uniqueness of one's tradition but recognizes the right of the other to have a similar conviction.[30] From a Christian point of view this gives way to a dialogical pluralism that operates in two directions: we reflect internally in a theology of religions over the place of the different religions within the Christian thought system and at the same time develop a theology of dialogue that takes into consideration the positions of the others. Without coming to terms with the existence of other religions in one's own thought system, one will not be able to dialogue. This is probably true for all religious traditions.

As shown by the most controversial issue of *Theology of Mission*, the three disciplines missiology, ecumenics, and comparative religion are undergoing deep changes that are asking for an intercultural approach. Crossing the Rubicon of traditional Western missionary thinking can however not mean neglecting or leaving behind the memories and experiences we have made on the way. To the contrary, reflection on the missionary dimension of Christian faith in the encounter with cultures and religions remains an integral part of intercultural theology.

## The Functions of Intercultural Theology

Intercultural theology has at least four functions:

1. The *heuristic* function, which can be differentiated into hermeneutics, comparative theology, and dialogics:

- *Hermeneutics:* intercultural hermeneutics do not look at the stranger to discover similarities first but accept the stranger in his or her difference.

---

30. Cf. Hans Jochen Margull, "Der 'Absolutheitsanspruch' des Christentums im Zeitalter des Dialogs. Einsichten in der Dialog-Erfahrung," *Theologia Practica* 15 (1980): 67-75 (= Margull, *Zeugnis und Dialog*, pp. 297-308).

The hermeneutic criterion is that the others must be able to recognize themselves in the description of their counterpart.

- *Comparative theology:* intercultural theology, then, also compares and asks for *transcultural constants* without trying to deny the differences. What do men have in common beyond culture?
- *Dialogics:* intercultural dialogue is a common search for truth that is only available contextually. At the same time, truth will always be more than the sum of the contextual truths. The rules of dialogue for the inter-confessional, intercultural, and interreligious encounters have to be negotiated in the process.

2. The *anamnetic* function: intercultural theology collects and preserves the contextual knowledge.

3. The function of *foundational theology:* intercultural theology deals with issues like gospel and culture or clarifies categories such as inculturation, syncretism, and fundamentalism. In order to communicate, a terminological and theoretical framework must be developed out of the contextual debates, which must be constantly tested on its transcultural feasibility.

4. The *ethical* function: intercultural theology develops strategies for dealing with globalization and the new nationalisms and ethnicity as well as the resulting cultural conflicts. Dialogue and conflict are the two interconnected issues for future discussions.

## Intercultural Theology as a New Paradigm

Intercultural theology might well be a paradigm shift that has consequences for theology in toto.

1. The new paradigm intercultural theology is not only formally a new heuristic framework for the whole of theology but is also connected to all its branches in a material way. Intercultural exegesis then deals with the cultural-religious contexts of the biblical literature or the history of the effects of these Scriptures in different cultures. Intercultural church history looks at the cultural factors in the mission history of Christianity. Practical theology searches for orientation in the multicultural society. The web of generative themes[31] of systematic theology such as Trinity, Christology, and ecclesiology, etc., has to be reconsidered interculturally. Then one has to ask what new perspectives are

---

31. Cf. Paulo Freire, *Pedagogy of the Oppressed* (New York, 1970); Volker Küster, *The Many Faces of Jesus Christ* (London, 2001), pp. 33-35.

opened up through the combination of the generative themes of the text with those of the diverse contexts, for instance, liberation, cultural identity, ecology, or gender issues.

2. Besides interdisciplinarity, intercultural theology necessitates also a pluralism of methods and multimediality. Narrativity and aesthetics become equal to the traditional academic theology. Art in all its variations is taken seriously as a theological medium.

3. But if everything is intercultural theology, nothing is intercultural theology. According to its emergence from the pluri-discipline missiology, ecumenics, and comparative religion, intercultural theology should be established in the field of systematic theology and integrate its source disciplines. At the same time, there will always remain a historical and empirical dimension.

4. Intercultural theology is a pluralistic concept. Its theological foundation is in the inner pluralism of the Christian faith as it is expressed in the canon of biblical literature, the doctrine of God triune, and the multitude of confessions, denominations, and groups. This inner state as an open system makes it possible to link Christianity to the pluralism of late modernity, which then is not considered as a threat but as a chance.

# From Communal to Communitarian
# Vision among Religions in India: A Proposal

H. S. WILSON

## I

A small spark can trigger a forest fire if other conditions are conducive. That is what happened in Gujarat. Apparently a fabricated squabble between a Hindu and a Muslim over a petty transaction on the railway platform led to an alleged premeditated attack on a Sabarmati Express train carrying pilgrims and the *Kar Sevaks* from Ayodhya back home to Gujarat on February 27, 2002, at Godhara. The result was the death of fifty-eight Hindu pilgrims/*Kar Sevaks*, burned and charred from a fire caused by pouring gasoline on the train and setting it on fire. The retaliation was equally gruesome, with more than nine hundred Muslims dead (unofficial estimate is two thousand) as a result of Hindu attacks which continued as long as two months after the incident. The methods followed to accomplish this were horrifyingly medieval, if not ancient. Houses were set on fire; children, women, and men were butchered with sharp instruments, iron rods, chains, knives, and swords. Women, young and old, were raped and killed or burned.[1] It was reported that state law enforcement personnel, police and security forces, either connived, collaborated, or showed indifference to such atrocities carried out on their own people only because they belonged to an unacceptable alien/foreign religion! It is also observed that the ongoing conflict in Kashmir and the December 13, 2001, attack on the Indian Parliament building also gave Hindu militants both momentum and respectability in spite of the lawless nature of their acts.

Concerned Indians within the country and abroad were alarmed. "Is sec-

---

1. Syeda Hameed et al., "How Has the Gujarat Massacre Affected Minority Women?: The Survivors Speak," *Ahmedabad: Citizen's Initiative*, April 16, 2002 (www.paknews.com, April 26, 2002).

ularism dead? The soul of India is threatened by the growing acceptability of militant religious fundamentalism" was the caption on the cover page of *India Today* (April 8, 2002), a weekly magazine. The magazine in fact is echoing the sentiments of the concerned Indian citizens about the aftermath of the February 27 attack.

The Indian prime minister, Atal Behari Vajpayee, who visited Gujarat to witness the result of the communal riots, stated in his address to the Muslim victims of the riots at the Shah Alam refugee camp in Ahmedabad, that he was ashamed that so many people had become refugees in their own country. It was estimated that about 97,000 women, men, and children who lost their homes and businesses in riots were moved to temporary settlement camps to give them some protection. Even the world community reacted to these occurrences in India. A European fact-finding team traveled to Gujarat and raised concerns with the political authorities in New Delhi even though the ruling political leadership of the government of India is sensitive to the internationalization of this issue.

Amidst the series of issues between Hindus and Muslims, the mosque and temple controversy at Ayodhya is at the backdrop of the Gujarat incident. The Ayodhya controversy has created a deadlock between supporters of the Babri mosque (built in 1528 by a general of Babar, founder of the Mughal dynasty) and the Rama Temple (claimed to be in that spot from the eleventh century C.E.). The controversy in fact goes back to 1949, when an image of Rama was installed in the mosque by a group of young Hindus. The Hindus who are involved in this controversy continue to claim that Muslim invaders from outside India destroyed temples and built mosques in their places. The fear of the Muslims is that the destruction of the mosque at Ayodhya on December 6, 1992, is only a prelude to the destruction of thousands of other mosques by Hindu extremists.

The bitterness between these religious communities is so intense that in all my years in India I have not come across any persons openly wanting to send out pamphlets persuading members of their community to disassociate with the adversary community. The weekly magazine *The Week* reproduced in its April 7, 2002, edition a pamphlet addressed to Hindus against the Muslims in Gujarat, which reads as follows:

> Jai Shri Ram. Wake up! Arise! Think! Enforce! Save the country! Save the religion! Economic boycott is the only solution! The anti-national elements use the money earned from the Hindus to destroy us! They buy arms! They molest our sisters and daughters! The way to break the backbone of these elements is: An economic non-cooperation movement. Let us resolve: . . .

Friends, begin this economic boycott from today! Then no Muslim will raise his head before us! Did you read this leaflet? Then make ten photocopies of it, and distribute it to our brothers. The curse of Hanumanji be on him who does not implement this, and distribute it to others! The curse of Ramchandraji also be on him! Jai Shiram! [Signed] A true Hindu patriot.

Is such an approach a help or hindrance to the Indian nation? I will argue that such communal parochialism is definitely a hurdle for the total progress of the nation. In an increasingly communally steeped Indian society, one way forward is a determined commitment for a "communitarian" vision of quest for common good for all, regardless of one's religion or ethnicity. Communal tensions and clashes are not uncommon to the Indian society. But what are these communal riots? I am referring to the Hindu-Muslim clashes. It has been observed that the horror of such clashes between these religions during Partition was so overriding "that Indian intellectuals refuse to use the word 'religion' and instead use the word 'communal' as a code for Hindu-Muslim clashes."[2] It is also stated that in fact these are clashes between "religious nationalisms" within a nation-state.[3]

The Indian public response to these riots has been overwhelming. Analysts on television and radio and in national and local newspapers made several suggestions to resolve the issue amicably. In polls and surveys carried out by a number of independent agencies, two out of three opted for a secular solution to the matter while being sensitive to the religious sentiments of the people. Concerned citizens vociferously denounced the politicization of religions and the political use of the incident. The demand by the opposition parties and their sympathizers for the resignation of Narender Modi, the chief minister of Gujarat, which was clear and loud, was skirted by the central government.

In the midst of all these brutalities, the examples of a number of Hindus protecting/caring for Muslim neighbors and vice versa, including some paying dearly for it with severe losses for themselves and their families, were a sign of victory for truth and love, and a witness to the democratic values held by Indians. Mass media made a point to report such acts of bravery, sacrifice, and compassion regularly.

Indians have dealt with religious differences for the past fifty-five years of being an independent nation, and those in leadership now should give priority to promoting programs and projects to move the Indian society toward a holistic interreligious society. The socially constructed differences need to be chal-

2. Akbar S. Ahmed, *Islam Today* (London: I. B. Tauris, 2001), p. 126.
3. Peter van der Veer, *Religious Nationalism: Hindus and Muslims in India* (Berkeley: University of California Press, 1994).

lenged/dismantled, because "social environments, like natural environments, cannot be taken for granted."[4] There has to be a concerted effort to deal with them. To that effect I will make some proposals in this paper.

## II

The bold commitment of the Indian national leaders in 1947 for a new nation built on secular democratic principles should have brought about a better result in unifying people and helping them transcend their religious communalism, ugly manifestations of which have been showing at regular intervals. Even though the democratic ways of societal life have come to stay, the communal riots in India in February/March 2002 raised again the question of appropriate interreligious direction that needs to be pursued so that the secular democratic principles are not tarnished by religious parochialism. The schizophrenic existence of secular democracy and religious parochialism will hamper the progress of the community if that is allowed to continue without a proper remedy.

During their formation stage, almost all world religions faced some opposition, both internal and external. Their sheer survival required some claim for superiority and uniqueness. Such circumstances also gave rise to occasional clashes with surrounding faith communities and with others. But those clashes growing into intolerance, resistance, and threats to other religions and traditions are historical developments and are not core faith affirmations of any of these religions. It is dwelling on the exclusive and resistant attitudes that have mainly contributed to the communalized status of religions.

Almost all major religions have become global communities today and are being accepted globally as important human heritages. That reality demands that religious communities develop a new attitude toward each other and resolve to sort out points of clashes through other social means than exaggerating religious sentiments by clubbing them with historical occurrences/memories real and legendary.

Religions are not only spiritual but also social communities. As such, at times they can benefit from social reforms and transformations that are going on in the larger society. Human community is going through a new sense of consciousness of interconnectedness. The globe as a common home is becoming an increased reality through modern means of transport and communication. The

---

4. Amitai Etzioni, ed., *The Essential Communitarian Reader* (Lanham, Md.: Rowman and Littlefield, 1998), p. xxxvi.

arena of the neighborhood is constantly shrinking. To tackle global issues we need greater solidarity among people, both religious and secular. We need supportive practices to concretize the vision of human interconnectedness.

Religious communities may benefit from some of the secular insights to rejuvenate their own heritage. Drawing on some of the insights coming from the social sciences, I would like to argue that religious communities could benefit from them, especially by paying attention to their social/community life in the contemporary world. These insights can help religious communities to theologically reengage with the inclusive, universal, and positive aspects found in each of their core faith affirmations.

In this paper I am especially paying attention to the proposals from communitarianism,[5] visions from "A Universal Declaration of Human Responsibility,"[6] and insights from a journal article dealing with cultivating positive emotions[7] as a possible way forward. The first gives serious thought to societal organization; the second emphasizes community responsibilities; and the third points out the benefits an individual and community can derive from facilitating the development of positive attitudes. The reason for turning to these insights coming from different disciplines of social sciences is to create a society where religions can exist in greater harmony. It is not an attempt to reduce religions to simple social entities. As Peter Berger has observed, "society is a dialectic phenomenon." Since society is something human beings build, from time to time they need to take steps toward its proper sustenance and preservation with the least destruction and damage. This is crucial, because it is the society humans create/build that in turn shapes humans in their community life. I see a number of overlapping concerns among these three visionary proposals, and as such they can be used to strengthen each other as communities venture out and experiment with them.

To select a few insights and values on communitarianism, I will be drawing from *The Responsive Communitarian Platform*.[8] This document was prepared and signed by a host of academics in the USA in the 1990s. Within a democratic and liberal framework, the communitarians emphasize giving importance to the well-being of communities. Their plea is to recognize and value the importance of interdependence of communities in any given society. The

5. Amitai Etzioni, *The Responsive Communitarian Platform: Rights and Responsibilities,* at www.gwu.edu/~ccps/platformtext.html.

6. "A Universal Declaration of Human Responsibility," September 1, 1997, proposed by the InterAction Council; see www.interactioncouncil.org.

7. Barbara L. Fredrickson, "Cultivating Positive Emotions to Optimize Health and Well-Being," *American Psychological Association Journal,* March 7, 2002, at www.journals.apa.org.

8. Etzioni, *The Responsive Communitarian Platform,* pp. xxv-xxxix.

strength of a society depends on carefully nurturing it with a sense of community responsibility, balancing it with individual rights often overwhelmingly stressed in a liberal-democratic setup. The communitarian proponents vary in their own definitions and emphasis of communitarianism. However, the above-cited document highlights some of the following goals as the common vision:

- Promote shared values and goals with a moral base that originates from the community and reflects the basic human needs of all its members.
- Encourage participation in the social and political life to ensure and preserve the individual liberty and social cohesion.
- Facilitate upholding and preserving moral values mainly through education (in family and school) and not through coercion.
- Ensure that families and schools inculcate a positive orientation to social life and promote values to build a holistic society.
- Ensure that the institutions of state, market, and civil society maintain a balance in promoting the well-being of individuals and groups.
- Guard that democracy is exercised free from undue influence from private money, special interest groups, and corruption in government.
- Foster a spirit of reconciliation. When conflicts arise, people should be motivated to seek a way of resolving them amicably rather than resorting to destructive methods.
- Exercise political responsibilities with a long-term vision and not be constrained by short-term gains.
- Uphold political transparency for the sake of accountability and its authentic involvement in the political affairs.
- Commit to social justice with a goal of reciprocity, that is, each member of the community exercises responsibility to the rest of the members and the community fulfills its responsibility toward each of its members.

If the above goals are to be realized, there has to be a sense of solidarity which needs to be inculcated so that "most of the members most of the time . . . discharge their responsibilities because they are committed to do so" and not because of any exterior compulsions.[9] Further, it is envisaged that such a commitment to a communitarian vision must begin with oneself and one's family, and move from there to the total community of humankind.

The communitarian proposal is not free from criticism. It is observed that "Communitarians have failed to provide a political theory of their own.

9. Etzioni, *The Responsive Communitarian Platform*, p. xxxvi.

There is, for example, no communitarian view on how a community can be created and sustained. Thus they have avoided the key issues of political theory such as the nature of the relationship between the individual and the community, and how to ensure that the power that results from human associations serves the well-being of the whole community."[10] Most humanly constructed theories and proposals will not be foolproof. The issue is whether such theories have the built-in possibilities to engage in creative dialogue for amending, recasting, and renewing their theories and practices for the sake of the greater good and for effectiveness.

The Indian society has been going through a communal totalitarianism; that is, a particular community has been getting too focused on the welfare and gain of its members at the exclusion of its neighboring communities. Religions and their various groupings, denominations and sects, have been equally guilty of such behavior and operation. Politically this functions as a "bloc vote" or "vote bank." To overcome such strangulations, the Indian society needs to reorient itself and benefit from some of the key proposals of communitarianism in balancing between the well-being of a particular community and that of the communities at large. This task will require tailoring to the Indian situation, and that could best be done with the involvement of every segment of the diverse Indian society. Some of the insights and values upheld by the communitarian perspective, if promoted in the Indian multireligious and multicommunity situation, will significantly contribute to the holistic living of the masses of people. The thrust of the communitarians is to maintain a healthy balance between the individual and community rights/privileges and their social responsibilities.

The communitarian core vision and values, mentioned above, in essence appear in "A Universal Declaration of Human Responsibility." The names of those who worked on and were signatories to this declaration constitute an impressive list of former heads of state — presidents, chancellors, prime ministers — as well as heads of a number of international nongovernmental and religious organizations. It is an achievement by itself that such a diverse group from around the world can speak in one voice for the betterment of the human community. Their long-term local and global engagement in sociopolitical affairs of the people gives them special credibility in promoting a sense of holistic community in currently conflicting situations like India.

The declaration recognizes that global interdependence makes it an imperative that humans live in harmony with each other. For such harmonious

---

10. Michael J. R. Cross, *Communities of Individuals: Liberalism, Communitarianism, and Sartre's Anarchism* (Aldershot, U.K.: Ashgate, 2001), p. 210.

living, humanity needs an ethical base which can hold rights and responsibilities in balance. It is interesting that as the group was working on this visionary proposal, one set of ethical guidelines that inspired them among the teachings of other ethical leaders was Mahatma Gandhi's categorization of seven social sins. They are: "1. Politics without principles; 2. Commerce without morality; 3. Wealth without work; 4. Education without character; 5. Science without humanity; 6. Pleasure without conscience; and 7. Worship without sacrifice."[11] It is a shame that the Indian leadership could not seriously consider the ethical principles of its own father of the nation. The issue is, beyond lip service to the wisdom and ethical teaching of Gandhi, that Indians are not unanimous in their following of Gandhi.

Let me capture here some of the salient features of this document. The declaration begins with the firm affirmation of the dignity and equality of all humans. This reality demands that people treat each other in a human way, being fair and honest in relationship. When humans are exclusively insistent on their rights, the apparent result is conflict, division, and endless dispute. Human history is full of examples of such occurrences leading to chaos and destruction. To overcome this, rights/freedom have to be balanced with responsibilities, which is the core emphasis of the document. Global problems demand global solutions. These solutions have to emerge out of ideas and values and norms respected by all cultures and societies, and be carried out in solidarity between one another. Humans, while exercising their rights fairly, should also be motivated to exercise their responsibilities with a commitment to speak and act truthfully, and to avoid all types of violence in resolving disputes. The declaration calls for a guarantee of religious freedom and at the same time expects those who practice religions to behave responsibly, avoiding any act of prejudice and discrimination toward people of other beliefs.

A select group of Hindu and Muslim scholars and accomplished political/community leaders have associated themselves with this declaration, as drafters and/or as signatories. So a collaborative and inclusive global visionary document like this should help Indian religious leaders rise above the current impasse, if there is a commitment to do so. At least concerned citizens can insist on giving due consideration to such global voices.

Will these challenging visions remain wild dreams and utopia, or is there any possibility of accomplishing them? Here I turn to another discipline in the social sciences, psychology. Barbara L. Fredrickson, in her research article "Cultivating Positive Emotions to Optimize Health and Well-Being," argues that by cultivating positive attitudes it is possible to prevent and treat individual and

11. "Universal Declaration," p. 7.

societal problems that have emerged from negative emotions. That message of optimism is a welcome sign in a contemporary society filled with a lot of negativity.

According to Fredrickson, negative emotions (e.g., fear, anger, and sadness) narrow an individual's momentary thought-action repertoire. By contrast, the positive emotions (e.g., joy, interest, and contentment) broaden the thought-action repertoire. The cultivation of positive emotions even has an undoing effect on negative emotions by releasing their hold on an individual's mind and body with an "upward spiral effect."[12] She does recognize that negative emotions at times have useful functions. But when prolonged and used inappropriately, they can create problems both for individuals and the society.

In the last few years, in India, certain religious groups/organizations, through the use of mass media, especially some of the television serial programs, have projected their religion as the most authentic and local. I am here referring to some of the programs based on Hindu religious traditions, which have been presented in such a grandiose way as to entice and even indirectly misguide the religious sentiments of their faithful. They have used myths, symbols, segments of history, traditional stories and teachings to glorify Hinduism and thereby indirectly undermine other religions and their role in the Indian society. Thus negative emotions toward other faiths have been created, contributing to the atmosphere of hatred and suspicion that in some cases has even led to physical destruction of people and their possessions. This in turn has triggered fear, reaction, and negative attitudes among other minority religions like Islam, Christianity, and Sikhism. The incident of February/March in a way is a cumulative effect of such cultivated negative emotions. Is positive emotion going to help in such cases as dealing with the past?

The proponents of positive emotions believe cultivating them not only helps promote thoughts (cognitive activity) but also facilitates the actions needed for social change and mobility. According to Fredrickson, positive emotions have relational repercussions and impact interpersonal relations (p. 6). The promotion of feelings of connectedness and of being cared for is capable of creating strong human bonds. The conducive interpersonal relationship, no doubt, will prevent emergence and escalation of negative emotions. In fulfilling such a role, the positive emotions in fact act as a social resource to deal with the past negative effects and foster a better relational attitude for the future. Positive attitude also serves as an effective antidote for the lingering effects of negative emotions (p. 18). Undoing/rectifying some of the past negative results

12. Fredrickson, p. 16. The parenthetical page numbers in the following text are to Fredrickson's article.

opens a new way forward. Fredrickson also observes that human civilizations have been built through the experience of positive emotions (p. 7). If that claim is universally true, any promotion of positive emotion will only be a boon to human society.

In the past several decades around the globe, a number of interfaith meetings and conferences have suggested, and even facilitated, programs to enhance positive attitudes in practical terms among the followers of different faiths and between groups/sects/denominations within each faith tradition. A number of leaders have also worked very diligently toward a "global ethic" for promoting ecumenical cooperation and action among religious followers of the world.[13] However, the input from the discipline of psychology cited above is an added asset. It demonstrates that the human community has always been wrestling with the issue of positive and negative emotions, and it is essential that societies embark on the promotion of positive emotions because they are possible.

The political parties and bodies of modern India deserve appreciation for maintaining a secular nature of the state ethos since independence and incorporating some of the key values and goals mentioned above (most probably not being aware of the three proposals I am referring to), drawing them from local and global resources and traditions. Their task has been very challenging in the face of the widely diverse and pluralistic society of India, which, as per a recent survey, consists of about "4,599 separate communities . . . with as many as 325 languages and dialects in 12 distinct language families and nearly 24 scripts."[14] Religious affiliations, broad-based and narrowly defined, further add to the complexity of the plurality. However, in their quest to capture the seats of power locally, regionally, and nationally, political parties have often used caste, community, ethnic, linguistic, and religious affiliations for their short-term gains, creating long-term problems. This in turn has contributed to the gradual weakening of secular nationalism and replaced it with various notions of communalisms.

The Bharatiya Janata Party's (BJP) ascendance to power in 1998, and its close alliance with the Vishva Hindu Parishad (VHP), an organization of religious leaders; the Rashtriya Swayamsevak Sevak (RSS), a militant youth organization; and the Bajrang Dal (a youth wing of the VHP), who call themselves "warriors of the Hindutva Revolution"[15] — along with a programmatic emphasis on *Hindutva,* that is, "nativism" of Hinduism, equating an Indian as a

---

13. Hans Kung and Kar-Josef Kuschel, eds., *A Global Ethic* (New York: Continuum, 1993).
14. *India Today,* April 8, 2002, p. 34.
15. See www.HinduUnity.com/bajrangdal.html.

Hindu (stressing religious identity apart from other identities that make an Indian citizen) — is a clear case of such a communalized political phenomenon in India. One of the strong allegations is that the current escalation of the religious tension, with militant Hindus attacking Muslims as well as Christians, was possible because of the sympathy it gets from the BJP and its core leadership, which of course is vehemently denied both by the prime minister (A. B. Vajpayee) and the home minister (L. K. Advani).

## III

India is a birthplace of Hinduism, Buddhism, Jainism, and Sikhism. It has also been a home for two other world religions, Christianity and Islam, soon after their origin in west Asia. These religions are there to stay in spite of major and minor tensions that exist among them. Therefore the only way forward is to develop mutual respect and solidarity among them and not by continuously indulging in claiming superiority for one's religious teachings, community, and sense of patriotism as against the neighbors' faith tradition.

One of the key concerns to the followers of the religions in India is their sense of identity and place in the Indian nation. But when that sense of identity is expressed in terms of inferior and superior groups/communities, in culture, history, tradition, and even loyalty to the Indian nation, it leads to conflicts and suspicion among communities, and leads to communal mentalities. When proper solutions are not found, the result is communities living in perpetual contempt and hatred and trying to undermine and eliminate, if possible, the other. Untested and uncontrolled prejudice/anger causes an unfair reduction of the other person or community as an object of contempt and ridicule, and contributes to further dehumanizing and demonizing. In such a process, the persons and community perpetuating it are themselves reduced to that status. India is experiencing this phenomenon as the confrontation between a section of Hindus and Muslims continues.

In India the Muslims are faced with identity issues because of historical developments that have adversely affected them. These include the sense of the loss of (the Mughal) empire and the capital Delhi (the symbol/center of power) and being brought under the British colonial power, and then being reduced to a minority religion in India. The Hindus feel marginalized by historical developments as well, in spite of being a dominant majority in India. They reckoned with Muslim rule from the twelfth century, including the Mughal Empire from the sixteenth to the eighteenth century, followed by the British colonial rule. When British rule was replaced by a democratic nation-state in 1947, they once again had to be satisfied with a status as a community that is on par with other minority religious communities as per the constitution of the country. These historical and political realities have created a feeling of being besieged among Hindus in spite of their absolute majority in India.

For some of them the matter has become further complicated by Pakistan becoming an Islamic republic, Sri Lanka and Bhutan Buddhist nations, Nepal a Hindu kingdom, and neighboring Bangladesh expressing a strong Muslim identity. Therefore the obvious question for some of them is, Why not a Hindu India? This they substantiate by arguing that at one time Indian Muslims and Christians were Hindus, and it is the conversation practice of these religions which created the problem. Reconvert them and the issue is solved. There is some historical legitimacy in that argument, but does it offer a viable solution for the issue at hand? Is *shudi*, or purification ceremonies to reconvert Muslims to Hinduism, going to do miracles and wonder in the midst of several discriminatory issues that exist within the Indian society? Is the goal to crave a purified Hindu India, a myth par excellence, or to strive toward the betterment of the human community by upholding positive values enshrined in Hinduism and other religions in India?

It is observed that the notion of a Hindu India has a strong Orientalist's influence. According to Van der Veer,

> The orientalists saw India as an ancient Hindu civilization, in which Brahmanical authority was paramount. On the one hand, they stressed that Western and Hindu civilization had the same Indo-European roots. . . . On the other hand, they emphasized the decline of Hindu civilization under Muslim rule and saw themselves as protectors of their Hindu "brethren" against the oriental despotism of Muslims. . . . Indian Islam was simply regarded as part of the great Islamic civilization centering on the Middle East, while Hindus were the true natives of India, whose ancient, pre-Islamic civilization was worth attention but whose present condition was deplorable.[16]

Such an analytical projection naturally contributed to the call of revitalization and assertion of the ancient Hindu religion. When that assertion goes to an extreme, it ends up as a quest to create a Hindu kingdom — *Ram Raj* in India. Such a circumstance also, in some ways, forces Muslims to revitalize their community by trying to recapture the spirit of the glorious era of Muslim rule in India. It is such a clamor for the past and the search for contemporary identity

16. Van der Veer, p. 20; cf. Thomas Blom Hansen, *The Saffron Wave: Democracy and Hindu Nationalism in Modern India* (Princeton: Princeton University Press, 1999), p. 65.

that have created a situation of tension, which needs to be defused with a realistic vision of the common shared future.

It is not difficult to identify the true enemies of the majority of the population of India. They are poverty,[17] illiteracy, easily preventable disease, caste discrimination, oppression of women, unemployment and/or underemployment of youth, etc. These contribute to the manipulation of a number of victims of these negative forces into intolerance, hatred, and communalism of different types. Until those enemies of the Indian population are eradicated, the aim of solving the problems by getting rid of the minority communities or suppressing them is not going to help; rather it will further add to the problem of the nation.

In this conflicting context, once again, the minority and majority privilege issue has become a judicial matter. As I write this paper, the Supreme Court of India is holding a marathon hearing into the rights of minority communities (Muslims, Christians, and others) to administer schools and other educational institutions. The hearing began on April 2, 2002, before a special eleven-member bench of the Supreme Court. The decision is still awaited. Knowing the judicial integrity and independent functioning of the court, and the situation of the country riddled with religious differences, I am hopeful they will come up with a visionary and just solution.

Meanwhile concerned people cannot rest and wait for a miracle to happen. Some of the insights and tools mentioned above, under the proposals of a communitarian societal norm, promotion of community responsibility enshrined in the declaration proposal, and the promotion of programs toward the cultivation of positive emotions, may be put to use or at least experimented with, in whatever appropriate adaptation is needed, so that the Indian society may be able to rise from the conflict of religions to organize itself as a "Community of communities"[18] within the framework of the Republic of India. This does not mean that attempts are not already being made within the country with its own vision and resources. Rather, the proposal here is meant to boost and multiply such efforts for greater and quicker results.

Am I an apostate in proposing that secular insights be used for reconciliation among religious communities? After all, religions are there to give greater meaning to human life, transcending its various real or perceived limitations. There is no doubt that such possibilities are still there within Hinduism, Islam,

---

17. As per the report of the World Food Program (WFP), nearly half the world's hungry people reside in India.

18. Amitai Etzioni, "The Communitarian Model," in *Building a Healthy Culture*, ed. Don Eberly (Grand Rapids: Eerdmans, 2001), p. 247.

and other religions in conflict. These religions can revitalize in the direction of the holistic and life-affirming communities by turning to their own internal resources. However, as it is at present, what we are witnessing is a parochialized phenomenon among considerable sections of Hindus and Muslims in India. This is due to the communities dwelling more on their social entities than on the theological and spiritual resources. Therefore my contention is that such a social captivity of these religious communities can be overcome by using insights from the social sciences, which may hopefully free them to return to their authentic nature of promoting harmony and solidarity between faith communities.

# Multifaith Dialogue in Diverse Settings: The Social Impact, with Special Attention to Indonesia and Germany

OLAF SCHUMANN

In this article[1] I shall limit myself to some remarks about the interreligious relations in Indonesia, and then I shall try to draw some lines of convergence to our situation in Germany.

## Indonesia

Traditionally Islam has been seen as the religion of the suppressed peoples in Southeast Asia because most of them were ruled by sultans who were the natural enemies of the Western colonial powers who started to penetrate into Southeast Asia, first the Portuguese (1512), followed by the Spaniards, and finally Dutch and British rule in most of the region, while Christianity naturally was seen as the religion of the foreign imperial forces. This impression of conflict between indigenous Muslims on one side and foreign Christians together with their local Christian allies on the other side still prevailed in the beginning of the Indonesian nationalist movement early in the twentieth century, when the independence movement started as the *Serikat Islam*, or Islamic Society.

After World War I, however, the situation changed considerably. In their struggle for independence, the Muslims were joined by Marxists, socialists, and also Christians and others, and therefore a religious dimension of the movement was excluded from the national formula which emerged in 1928 and aimed at maintaining the unity of the former Dutch colonial territory and the people living there. It ran: one territory (i.e., the territory of the then Netherlands Indies Colony), one nation (consisting of all tribes, ethnic, racial, social,

---

1. Originally presented at the symposium "Theology Meets Multireligiosity," at Århus University, on May 14, 2002; revised and enlarged for print.

religious groups and other communities and individuals who supported the independence movement), and one language, the *bahasa* Indonesia as the widespread lingua franca of the indigenous merchants who used Malay instead of
the Dutch, Portuguese, or English used by the European merchants. No word
was said about one religion.

Let me say a word about the term "nation" or "nationalism." When used
in Indonesia, it may not at all be confused with the European notion of that
term which was developed in the nineteenth century and became a decisive
motivating factor in the wars at the end of that century and particularly in the
twentieth century. The term used in Indonesia and Malaysia is *bangsa,* or
*kebangsaan,* and that originally means the primordial unity between a ruler and
his subjects, rooted in a common cosmic relationship which was explained in
the myths of origin. Thus the term *bangsa* had to be redefined, because independent Indonesia should become a modern state. Nor did the existing ruler at
that time, the colonial government, fit in this notion of oneness because he was
of foreign origin. And the people who should form the one nation also originated from hundreds of different tribes, races, and ethnic groups, in addition to
numerous individuals from various backgrounds, united only in one aim: to
achieve independence from the colonial government. Thus the bipolarity of the
original *bangsa* between ruler and people had to be abandoned, and as ruler, or
representative of the one *bangsa,* a government would have to be elected by the
*bangsa* itself; this paved the way for a republican state in which the national sovereignty was in the hands of the people and not in those of a personal ruler, and
so it was stated later in the constitution.

There was, however, a problem inherent in the traditional, cosmic-
orientated world conception of most of the Asian peoples and their cultures,
including the Indonesian ones: What is the relationship between unity, or oneness, and diversity? The problem in Indonesia became apparent in the motto
which later was included in the state symbol and was taken from a Hindu poet
from late medieval Indonesia: *Bhinneka tunggal ika*. Does this mean we are different but simultaneously we are one, or we are (or: we seem to be) different but
(in fact) are one? Are difference and oneness two aspects standing on equal
terms, or is difference, or plurality, subordinated to oneness or unity?

It is this ambiguity of the expression *bhinneka tunggal ika* which led to
the ideological struggles which determined Indonesian history since its independence in 1945.

The independent republic Indonesia started its course in history as a parliamentarian democracy. The basic ideology was the *Pancasila,* five principles,
with its famous first one: *Ketuhanan Yang Maha Esa,* or the principle of an all-
one-divinity. But here again the interpretations differ considerably. Islamic pol-

iticians supported by some Christians like to understand it as an obligation to believe in one God, and this would exclude all polytheists like the adherents of the indigenous tribal religions, of Chinese religions and atheists. Therefore this principle often is translated as "Belief in One God."

But this interpretation is refuted by most of the nationalists, and it also contradicts its wording. *Ketuhanan* is an abstraction, rooted in *Tuhan,* the Lord. Therefore, if the belief in one God (or: Lord) would have been intended, it should read *Tuhan yang Maha Esa.* But that clearly is not the case. And further-more, the *Pancasila,* including the first principle, inspires the constitution of the state; it is a constitutional principle, not a theological one. By it the state is obliged to protect the religions and their communities living on its territory. But the state itself is not allowed to promote its own theology. This has to be done by the religious communities themselves. They have to define their reli-gious self-understanding and how they understand their belief in God, and the state may not interfere in this. The state has to be neutral and evenhanded to all its citizens; it may not have a special relationship or obligation to a certain group among them. All citizens have to be treated on equal terms, regardless of their ethnic or religious affiliations. Thus terms like "majority" or "minority" with regard to religious or ethnic affiliations were excluded from the political dictionary. Freedom of religion should be guaranteed in every aspect, including the freedom to choose a religion and to practice it according to the respective belief of its adherents.

From two sides this understanding was challenged or questioned. One was the politically orientated Muslims, or Islamists, who tried to interpret the oneness of the nation also in religious terms pointing to the fact that the big majority of Indonesians were Muslims and therefore, they concluded, had also the right to demand their religion be the dominating one in the state. Their aim actually was to establish Indonesia as an "Islamic state," its constitution being based on the *shari'ah* (whatever that might mean). The non-Muslim minorities should be protected. But here mention was made of a primordial majority and also primordial minorities, and that would have contradicted the basic equality, the égalité, of all citizens, and with it the unity of the nation. Therefore this op-tion was rejected.

But the struggle for the Islamic state challenged the nationalists to come to more precise definitions of their own understanding of the oneness, or unity, of the nation. Already Sukarno in his speech on June 1, 1945, when he for the first time publicly spoke about the *Pancasila* (as it later was called), stressed that the Five Principles reflected the "Weltanschauung" (he used this German term) of all Indonesians. He explained it as an ancient universal worldview of all In-donesians rooted deeply in their primordial cultural and ideological self-understanding, or their Weltanschauung. This reference to the mythological past, however, had a side effect which only later came into the open. That happened definitely when Sukarno, in July 1959, put an end to all discussions about the ideological, or religious, basis of the state and by a presidential decree declared the *Pancasila* to be the only and unchangeable ideology. At the same time, he disclosed his antipathy against the parliamentarian, or "liberal," democratic system which he defined as an import from the West. Already in 1945 ideas were voiced to understand the "unity of the nation" in pure Asian terms, the nation representing something like a huge family. But a family needs a paterfamilias, or a head like the traditional *bangsa*. In early 1945 this point actually was raised already by the Japanese, who at that time occupied Indonesia, and who pointed to the *Tenno* in the Japanese state system and to the role of the former rulers in a traditional *bangsa* as Asian examples. At that time this idea was refused, even by Sukarno himself, who was mentioned by the Japanese as a possible holder of such a position, because most of the nationalist leaders were in favor of a republic. But in 1959 Sukarno complemented his decree about the *Pancasila* by declaring at the same time the establishment of the "Guided Democracy" with himself as the "Great Leader" or guide. To some extent, *bangsa* returned to its original meaning, only in bigger proportion, containing now the whole Indonesian nation.

Thus Indonesia became an integralistic, or totalitarian, state.[2] All plurality in society was to be seen on the way to a final unity. *Bhinneka,* diversity, became subordinate to the oneness.

In this matter, there was no substantial change in General Suharto's domestic policy after he came to power in 1966. For the first principle of the *Pancasila,* the different religions were mainly seen as a moral force, and despite their doctrinal differences their main target should be to motivate their respective adherents to support without any questioning the political and economic plans of the government. Communists and atheists and those accused of sympathizing with them were now, according to the advice of the CIA and Western economic "experts," treated as "infidels" *(kâfirûn)* and therefore killed or confined to prison camps, and thus the Indonesian nation had become a truly religious one, a "nation of believers," in accordance with the *Ketuhanan Yang Maha*

---

2. I discussed this problem in more detail in my contribution: "Adat und Moderne — ein Widerspruch?" in *Injil dan Tata Hidup/The Gospel and Life Order/Evangelium und Lebensordnung. Festschrift Lothar Schreiner,* ed. Adelbert A. Sitompul and Karl H. Federschmidt (Pematangsiantar, Jakarta, and Waltrop, 2001), pp. 303-27; cf. also my article "Zur politischen Dimension von Konvivenz. Die Debatte um das Verhältnis von Staat und Gesellschaft in Indonesien," in *Mit dem Fremden leben,* pt. 1, *Religionen — Regionen,* ed. Dieter Becker (Erlangen, 2000), pp. 193-210.

*Esa.* Suharto and his government did not much care for the differences between the various religious communities. But the introduction of a religious term, "infidels," into the political terminology and as a measure for the treatment of certain citizens proved to be disastrous. "Infidels" are always the others, and it is a subjective matter how one's own relationship with them is defined. Any opponent or "enemy" of the official policy and its interpretation of religion could be styled an "infidel" and thus be deprived of his or her human dignity, and accordingly opponents were not treated as human beings. Thus "infidel" is not a religious term anymore but gets an ideological, or political, connotation.[3] Torture and illegal killing became legitimate. It was difficult for the religious communities, if ever they wanted to do so, to protest such maltreatment, because a sense of religion to defend human dignity did not necessarily include infidels as being the enemies of God.

In the beginning of Suharto's rule the religions were treated as one entity or collectively, representing one aspect of the "unity" with subordinate expressions of diversity. Important for him was their unanimous support for his policy. But at this point he was even less successful than Sukarno, because of the unlimited corruption of his bureaucracy and the unrestrained attempts of his family and allies to control Indonesia's economy, which led to an increasing estrangement between him and the religious communities, who in one or another way had to stand in solidarity with their suffering members. Thus opposition grew also among certain religious groups.

Then the Suharto regime tried to tighten the ideological grip on the religions. The government imposed certain definitions on understanding the *Pancasila* and especially its transcendental dimension as a quasi-religious legitimization of Suharto's power and policy, and therefore the support given to him was a religious obligation which might not be questioned by anyone. Support for the *Pancasila* consequently decreased and people started to question the

3. This politicizing of religious terms during the Suharto era was initiated and inspired by the CIA, who supported the killings for ideological and political, and naturally also economic, considerations. It is alarming to observe that the same pattern of ideologizing religious terms for political and economic purposes is practiced now in full scale by the new Bush, Jr., administration, dividing again the world into righteous believers ("I know how good we are," thus Bush, Jr., after Sept. 11, 2001) and the others styled as the "axis of evil." This division now becomes a part of the "era of globalization"! And again the "enemies" are deprived of their human dignity and treated accordingly, without any legal consequences for the "righteous" killers and torturers. In Indonesia, as well, none of the more than one million murder cases ever has been brought to court. No wonder this pattern is now safely followed by the new "righteous believers" in that country, namely, the Islamic extremist gangs supported by parts of the military which, again, has been brought to power with the help of the U.S. government by ousting the democratically elected president Abdurrahman Wahid in July 2001.

whole concept of unity. Is it only a means to equally exploit the people for the exclusive benefit of those in power? By disseminating issues like social envy ("poor Muslims" are facing "rich Chinese" and "rich Christians") or tribal and social discrimination, distrust and hatred spread. Thus the feeling of togetherness and social solidarity began to erode, and it fell to pieces when Suharto started to support the integralistic understanding of the Islamic politicians and intellectuals at the beginning of the 1990s. He was careful not to recall the option for an Islamic state, but the concept of a "proportional democracy" propagated since that time and implemented by Dr. B. J. Habibie, then minister for technology and research and chairman of the Indonesian Muslim Intellectuals' Association (ICMI), put the (politically oriented) Muslims or "Islamists" in the position of an overall dominating majority, arguing that every religious community should be presented in the political and other official bodies of the state according to the percentage of its members. What had been avoided since the beginning now became a political doctrine: "democracy" was now the rule of a majority based on a primordial community (i.e., a religious one) which would be unchangeable or permanent, as opposed to political majorities or minorities organized in political parties and open to shift into or from power as a result of regular elections. Two areas of potential conflict came thus to the fore: (1) the always present problem of mission or *da'wa* obtained definitely a political dimension in that both were only understood as efforts to increase the members of one's own community and thus strengthen, or weaken, its political role; and (2) the implementation of the "proportional democracy" did not take into account the fact that the Islamic political parties who supported that concept did not represent even the majority among the Muslims themselves: in the relatively free elections of 1955, all Islamic parties together obtained 43.5 percent of the votes (even a minority in the Muslim community if the official statistics at that time which claimed the Muslims to constitute about 90 percent of the Indonesian population were true), and in 1999 they obtained much less: only about 13 percent altogether. This means that the majority of the Islamic community votes against any combination of religious and political goals and power. This means also that the "aspirations of 87% of the Indonesian people" (this is the official proportion of Muslims during the Suharto regime) to dominate the political rule is a mere fiction or unsound pretension of Islamist politicians who have not the support of any majority, and who implement their aspirations only by using the power of the state.

The bloody intercommunal conflicts which increased remarkably at that time and took on civil war–like characteristics after Suharto's fall in May 1998 are a direct consequence of that policy which neglected the diversity of cultures, religions, and ethnic identities and tried to press them into a unitarian or totalitarian system the ideology of which was designed by the government using the symbols of Islam. At the same time, all opponents were treated as subversive elements standing outside the unified body of the nation. If that analysis is true, then of course the following question demands an answer: Why did the people start fighting and killing each other? What were the real motivations or acts which caused that outbreak of violence? Were they motivated by religious convictions? Or by ethnic pride? Or by social envy? Or by what? Since I tried to give a more elaborate explanation at another place, I shall confine myself here to hint only at some aspects.[4]

One of the most fatal decisions was the use, or misuse, of the transmigration programs to change the ethnic and religious composition in various regions, particularly those with a dominant Christian population in eastern parts of Indonesia. The transmigration program itself never has been disputed, principally since it made sense to give farmers from overpopulated areas mainly in Java and Bali a livelihood in other, less densely populated regions. Under the original conception of "One Nation," or *Wawasan Nusantara,* each part of Indonesia being the homeland of every Indonesian, the mixture of people from different backgrounds seemed to be a convincing way to implement a civil, democratic society with equal rights to every citizen, regardless from where he or she comes or where he or she lives. The implementation of the "proportional democracy" proved this presumption to be a political intrigue, aimed to pursue other goals under its cover. At that point it became clear that the religious proportions had changed. The new proportions were taken to legitimize a shift of power from the original inhabitants and their own representatives to government-appointed officials. Regional and local power in the state administration as well as in the army and police and in the judiciary was preferably given to such Muslim newcomers who were willing to serve the goals of the central government, and thus they usually helped deepen the feeling of injustice and of being deprived of personal dignity in cases of legal conflict by their discriminatory judgments and decisions. They acted in the name of the government, and therefore the treatment of the original inhabitants — Christians and sometimes even Muslims — as second-class citizens brought these necessarily into conflict with the ruling power. Only the fear of maltreatment experienced in the past prevented an earlier breakout of self-defense and physical violence. The growing pressure and humiliation, however, prepared the ground for the

---

4. "Problems in Attitudes and Communication between Religious and Ethnic Groups in Indonesia: A Socio-religious Analysis," in *Communal Conflicts in Contemporary Indonesia,* ed. Chaider S. Bamualim and Amelia Fauzia et al. (Jakarta: Pusat Bahasa dan Budaya IAIN, 2002), pp. 157-83.

ferocious violence during the conflicts which started immediately in greater scale the moment Suharto lost his grip on power and the army lost its authority because of its past involvement in those politics and economic exploitation of the people. It should be kept in mind that the only wars the Indonesian army had fought since 1950 were against its own people, with some small exceptions in the early 1960s during the actions against the Dutch in West Irian and some guerrilla actions against Malaysia, both still in the time of Sukarno's "Guided Democracy." It was the fear of the army that kept most of the civilians silent, while some others turned to guerrilla warfare. The newcomers, like the Madurese in West and Central Kalimantan; the Makassarese, Bugis, or Butonese in the central Moluccas and Irian (Papua); the Gorontalese, Tidorese, and Makianese in the northern Moluccas, were accustomed to a combined cultural, tribal, and religious identity, thus viewing outsiders to some extent as inferiors or/and infidels *(kâfirûn)*. They were also suspicious of Muslims from other backgrounds who, because of cultural and genealogical relations, still communicated with their kinship despite their different religious adherence. Remembering the political use of the religious term "infidels" during the regime of Suharto, we can imagine how easy it was again to let it function as an ideological-religious tool. In areas where the local population resented the goals of the government, these newcomers were used to execute the government's policy and, in turn, were protected in their own enterprises. This explains why in various instances the conflicts were not at all among different religious groups but more often between the (Muslim) newcomers, supported by the government and military, and the original inhabitants, Muslims, Christians, and others, who had lived side by side and who defended their common traditional rights and culture together, at least as long as they were not infiltrated by agents from outside who took the religious difference as an issue to disseminate distrust and fear and to legitimize warfare against each other on religious terms.

Concluding, we may say that the intercommunal harmony in the Indonesian state and society was safeguarded as long as the government equally respected the fact that the nation was *bhinneka* (diverse) and *tunggal* (one) alike, or, in other words, as long as the different identities, communal and individual, were not streamlined into a unitarian, or integralistic, system which was designed by the leadership of the state and not based on a common social understanding and agreement of the people. The achievement of such an agreement and understanding was prevented by the later Sukarno and Suharto in that they did not allow the growth of a mature civil society but imposed the idea of an integralistic state where the social values and norms and the political goals were defined by the leadership, pretending of course to act in the name and interest of the people but never consulting them. In cases of dissent the people were accused of subversion and "infidelity," or enmity against the state.

I will now add only very few remarks about what these experiences in Indonesia could mean for our situation in Germany, or in Europe.

## Germany

Many people near us are still enjoying the dream of a basically monocultural society, religious differences being restricted to the traditional denominational ones, but all of them sharing more or less a common culture. I called that a dream because it even was not true in the past where there was a minority living in the midst of a huge majority, namely, the Jewish community. Some of them maintained their exclusive otherness, but others "assimilated" themselves to the culture of the majority and thus contributed considerably to it, but they also were the first victims when the fiction of a German monoculture was to be implemented by force and indoctrination, and the assimilated Jews were excluded from the state administration, and later were economically isolated as well. The *Endlösung* was intended to be the last step in their exclusion. Besides the many other impacts of that ideology, it clearly revealed an option, or a dream, of a monocultural society. I am afraid that this dream has not yet completely disappeared but still is present in the minds of people who not only ridicule the discourse of a multicultural society, but who combine their rejection with warnings of a "racial mixture" of the German people (as if the present Germans were not already a mixture). Dreams usually are not of much help to tackle real problems of actual life. I think we have to realize, at least in Germany, that our societies are not *"multi-culti,"* but are multicultural and multiethnic, and of course, multireligious. There is no use or sense in enforcing the impression of a coherent cultural setting, as was again expressed in Germany during the last year (2001) when discussions about a *Leitkultur,* or a determining and guiding cultural denominator, flared up. Our society is a plural one, and it is no use to deny that fact. Since on other occasions the complaint is voiced that our Western, or German, society has lost most of the ethical and moral norms and values it cultivated in the past, there would be a good chance now to develop a new social dialogue in which the many newcomers participate as cooperative and constructive members to design new and relevant social norms and values for the future which give a comfortable feeling to all members of society. Such dialogue must be motivated by a feeling of togetherness and an awareness of common responsibility for the welfare of the society of which all are members. It is not a matter of winning or losing. Whenever a numerical majority, or a majority based only on power, tries to impose its will and its ideas about values and norms on others, then democracy runs in troubled waters. This has been the experience in Indonesia, where the numerical majority of the Muslims never tried to impose its conception of the state and its ideological basis on the minorities. Whenever there was such an attempt by political groups using religious symbols and untruly claiming to represent the aspirations of a majority, and when they were combined with the "force of order" of the state (military and police), then severe conflict was impending. But what really matters is the capability to transfer values and norms which have been developed in one's own community as exclusive guidelines for communal behavior to become values and norms which are communicable, inclusive, and therefore of social relevance also for others. Both Muslims and Christians and other groups in our societies must be aware that they face the problem of credibility. All face a history in which their moral claims have been distorted. All of them, and particularly also Muslims and Christians, claim to strive for peace; all stress the need to respect human dignity as something given by God and therefore not negotiable. But whenever an occasion occurs, these high values are not applied to other people (just to mention the inhuman and, in fact, unconstitutional treatment of refused asylum seekers in our society or by the administration, or the treatment of those who are considered *kâfirûn* [unbelievers] or outsiders [other examples are many]). Also in our "secular" societies we witness again the introduction of religious terms as political tools, e.g., whenever we hear of an "axis of evil" which has to be combated. "Evil" is a religious term, not a political one. But it is used by both Christian and Muslim politicians who intend to strip "the other" of his or her humanity, and thus legitimize any action taken against them and, simultaneously, disdain anyone who would hesitate or object to such purposes. If Christians and Muslims expect other people to take their religious convictions seriously, they have to start to take them seriously themselves.

Islam and Christianity, both in their respective and special ways, make statements about the liberation of humankind from any kind of slavery, be it slavery imposed by other human beings or slavery of an immature mind, which suppresses or perverts human dignity. But besides this individual message, both religions also emphasize the social responsibility of the liberated individual. Thus involvement in social matters is inherent in the Christian and Muslim messages. In Islam this dimension has been narrowed in the one and a half or two centuries since the conception of Islam as "religion and state" came up. This conception, to make that quite clear, has no roots in the Quran and no support in the biography of prophet Muhammad. It is a modern conception, and it became a political and apologetic tool as an alternative model against the Western concept of a modern, plural, and civilized state which they at first experienced as anything else than what it pretended to be. Western statehood was experienced in the framework of imperialism and colonialism in which all ethical and moral principles which at the same time were promulgated in the West were disregarded. The impression of hypocrisy, mendacity, and unlimited misuse of power was prevalent (and to some extent still is). In that situation Muslim thinkers started to design their own alternative model of a modern state which they tried to root in their own tradition, picking up some elements and events from the history of Islam but often not being able to systematize them. The very controversial discussion among Muslims about the nature of the state, or even an "Islamic state," cannot be described here. But it is very clear that the Western concepts as such were not criticized. It was more the lack of a strong and consequent will to implement their ideals in all aspects which was inviting criticism. As soon as Muslims enter into discussion about a modern, plural, and civil society and a democratic state — and for that they will find plenty of attempts and designs in the history of Islamic social thought — this petrifying model of Islam as religion and state will lose its relevance and thus fall to pieces. The emphases on righteousness and justice, on responsibility and accountability, etc., stressed in the Islamic past are important contributions Muslims may make in a social dialogue on values and norms in a plural society. It is up to us Westerners to make our models of society and state attractive and acceptable. A first step could be to arrange social relations and communication with others on equal terms in accordance with the basic principles of modern statehood and of our modern civilization of which we are proud, but which could not prevent us from terrible wars and crimes.

A final question: Will a social dialogue on ethical values and moral norms and standards in which people on the basis of their religious convictions participate not contradict the separation of religion and state which is one of the famed merits of modern social developments?

I think that in such a question there is a confusion of different things. First, the separation of church and state means an organizational separation. Second, no member of any society is prevented or even prohibited from belonging to a primordial community, be it based on ethnic, religious, or other facts. A person's character is usually formed there, and he or she is educated to respect values and behave according to norms and standards which are accepted there. When taking up positions in society, one cannot become a split person. And therefore no one may be prohibited from bringing values and norms to the fore of a social dialogue which are rooted in the religious or cultural tradition of that community, provided — and I stated this earlier — they can be transformed from exclusive and communal into inclusive and societal norms and values, valuable and suitable to the whole of society. A continuous social dialogue in which all members of different backgrounds meet on equal terms and review the common basis on which they stand and live is of course a condition for the welfare of any plural society. Whenever there are preconditions, like, e.g., in Germany in 2001 when it was demanded that values and norms of the *Leitkultur* remain dominant although no one really could define them or was convinced about their actual strength, then the danger of moving into an impasse is evident. But when, on the other side, one group tries to safeguard its dominance by demonizing another one, as happens at present to the Islamic community and its members and their convictions, then conflict will be invited, and it is a general experience that conflicts which are motivated by defending the honor of transcendental values and beliefs are very grim ones. It remains therefore the responsibility of all mature and responsible members of society to encourage others and participate themselves in social dialogue, and by doing this to pave the way for a peaceful and prosperous living together. There are at present too many examples in the world of terrifying consequences whenever that responsibility of mature members of society is not taken seriously, or when it is prevented by those in power.

There is, of course, another aspect of multifaith dialogue concerned with more religious or doctrinal questions. I personally think such dialogue is also possible, and may even be fruitful provided the partners have enough knowledge about the other religion and are able to explain their own beliefs in such language that not only they themselves but also their partners know and understand what they are talking about. A Christian starting a dialogue with a Muslim by, e.g., stating that for him the Christian teaching about the divine Trinity has no meaning, will soon realize that he is not a very interesting partner for the Muslim with whom he talks. A partner in dialogue expects concern, not indifference. Such multifaith dialogue cannot result in harmonizing statements on doctrinal matters, because the partners have no authorization to make such statements. I state this at the end of my paper to avoid misunderstandings which, however, often occur, as if dialogue is attempting to result in compromising and "syncretistic" statements. Such understanding would be a complete misunderstanding of what dialogue means and aims at. Dialogue means, according to the original meaning of *dialogos*, a common wrestling with problems which are felt to be common and urgent to all partners in dialogue, and which therefore need a common effort to clear them up. Only in social matters, compromises may — and probably should — be the result. In doctrinal matters dialogue may help indicate and destroy misunderstandings and lead to insights and a more comprehensive appreciation of another religion, and at the same time may allow one to come to clearer understandings of such items in one's own religion which became so "familiar" that they were not thought of sufficiently and therefore became nebulous and lost some of their meaning. In a dialogue with Muslims, e.g., Christians get a unique chance to reconsider and reflect on the meaning of the divine Trinity and its relevance for a relational understanding of the basic notions of faith. In discussing different anthropological conceptions, the meaning of justice and redemption may lead to deeper insights of the dimensions of the humane disposition. Thus dialogue on matters of faith may help everyone as well to come to a deeper perception of their own belief.

# Muslim-Christian Dialogue — Global Ethics and Moral Disagreement: A Scandinavian Perspective

## ODDBJØRN LEIRVIK

In this contribution I shall focus on two points which should be of general relevance when speaking about multifaith dialogue: (1) the importance of power relations and minority concerns in dialogue, and (2) the reality of moral disagreement across religious divides. My contextual point of reference will be interreligious relations in Norway.[1]

Multireligiosity is a recent phenomenon in Norway. Until the late 1970s, religious pluralism was largely confined to intra-Christian diversity, a very small Jewish community, and a growing movement of secular humanism. (By secular humanism I mean the Humanist Association, which in Norway functions much like a faith community.) Interfaith dialogue of an organized kind is also a very recent phenomenon in Norway. But during the 1990s it gained considerable momentum and even reached out for global challenges.

The first partners to set up a regular structure for interreligious dialogue in Norway were the Christians and the Muslims. A national Contact Group was established in 1993 and provides a forum for regular dialogue between the Church of Norway, a state church that comprises 86 percent of the population, and the Islamic Council of Norway, which represents important sections of Norway's some hundred thousand Muslims (2 percent of the population).

In interfaith enterprises one should always be wary of asymmetrical power relations, and of who takes the initiative and lays the premises for dialogue work. For the Contact Group the initiative was taken by the national *majority* church. The background of Norway's interfaith council, which was set up in 1996 and given the cumbersome name of Council for Religious and Life Stance Commu-

---

1. For a fuller discussion on moral disagreement in interreligious perspective, see Oddbjørn Leirvik, "Global Ethics and Moral Disagreement after September 11, 2001: A Christian-Muslim Perspective," *Studies in Interreligious Dialogue* 2 (2002).

nities in Norway, is different. It grew out of a *minority* alliance between secular humanists, Muslims, Jews, Buddhists, and the nonconfessional Alternative Network. The minority alliance was formed in 1995 as a protest against the proposal of a new and compulsory subject of religious education in Norwegian primary schools; the minorities felt the new subject was overly self-affirmative by Christianity as the national religion. On the initiative of this minority alliance, the churches were eventually invited to take part in the construction of a nongovernmental interfaith council in Norway. The council works on a consensus basis, which means that the vote of the Church of Norway with its 3.8 million members has no more weight than that of the 800 members of the Baha'i community. The Norwegian Association of Free Churches, which has long experience being a religious minority in a state church situation, constitutes an important part of the interfaith council. The first president of the interfaith council was actually the general secretary of the Association of Free Churches, a Pentecostalist. He was followed by a Buddhist in the next term. And the first secretary of the council is a secular humanist woman who has an office in the headquarters of the state church.

Because of its background and mode of operation, the interfaith council provides a good framework for minority sensitivities, in which the Church of Norway can learn to be a vulnerable faith community rather than a powerful state church. It may be indicative of the last decades' learning process that the church committee which recently proposed the abolishment of the present state church system used the principle of equality and nondiscrimination as their main argument.

In financial terms, the principle of equality has been working for some time. During the last three decades, every faith or life stance community which registers itself has been entitled to exactly the same amount of money in state support per member as the state church receives through public budgets. But many challenges remain, not least the question of how to deal with religion in school in such a way that both the majority and minority communities feel their concerns are met. The interfaith council provides a nongovernmental forum for such discussions in which the minorities in practice are given a veto. But that is still not the case with the Norwegian state politics of religion.

In modern interfaith dialogues, which for a great part reflect the realities of migration and globalization, national and international issues are often interrelated. The Council for Religious and Life Stance Communities in Norway mainly addresses questions of interfaith attitudes and government policies in Norway. But it has also become a springboard for global involvement. In 1998 the interfaith council initiated the so-called Oslo Coalition on Freedom of Religion or Belief, which joins Christians, Muslims, Jews, Buddhists, and secular humanists on a human rights basis. Its plan for 2002 includes interreligious co-operation with relevant partners in countries such as Russia, China, Indonesia, Iran, and Bosnia. Focal points are religion and human rights, gender equality, and interfaith dialogue in areas of communal strife.

The formation of the Oslo Coalition indicates that the well-known Norwegian ambition of international peacemaking has already become an *interfaith* vision. In the case of the Oslo Coalition, Norway's face to the world is a Muslim woman wearing the head scarf. Her name is Lena Larsen, coordinator of the coalition. In 2000 she was also elected president of the Islamic Council — an event of almost historic dimensions. It should be no surprise, then, that women's issues constitute a main focus of the work of the coalition. But it may surprise some that it is headed by a veiled Muslim woman.

Summing up the first part of my contribution, I will once again stress the importance of being sensitive to power relations and minority concerns in interfaith enterprises. In Norway it is mainly the Church of Norway that is challenged to be more sensitive to the minorities and thus more evangelical in the true sense. Conversely, through interfaith relations Muslims in Norway may be challenged to take the situation of Christian minorities in Muslim-majority societies more seriously.

Another lesson to be drawn from interfaith dialogue in such a small country as Norway is the importance of personal, face-to-face relations. Here lie both the strength and the vulnerability of the initiatives in question: they depend — at least in this initial phase — on the mutual commitment and organizational influence of a not too large number of key persons.

In the second part of my contribution I will share some reflections on the relation between (1) affirming general values and (2) taking concrete moral action in dialogue work. I will take responses from Norwegian Christians and Muslims to September 11 and the ensuing bombing of Afghanistan as an example. Five days after September 11 the bishop of Oslo, the general secretary of the Humanist Association, the Jewish rabbi, and the vice president of the Islamic Council stood side by side at an interfaith event which affirmed their joint rejection of religiously motivated violence. Hand in hand, they sang "We shall overcome." In other Norwegian cities, too, there were similar symbolic events, staged by Christians and Muslims together. The events reflect the importance of building personal, interfaith networks which can be activated in times of crisis. Alluding to one of the four main points in the World Parliament of Religions' "Declaration toward a Global Ethic," one might also say that the swift and joint reactions to September 11 reflect an interfaith obligation on "a culture of non-violence and respect for life."

In Norway, official reactions to September 11 were nearly unison among Muslims and Christian leaders. When two weeks after September 11 the Contact Group between the Church of Norway and the Islamic Council had its regular meeting, a press release was formulated in which Christians and Muslims were encouraged to take part in each other's grief and concern. But what happened after the U.S.-led "war on terrorism" was launched, with the bombing of Afghanistan as its first dramatic expression? In Norway the Islamic Council soon voiced their apprehension that the bombing campaign would only inflict more innocent civilian suffering. Perhaps more surprisingly — in view of the fact that the Norwegian government unreservedly supported the bombing — several bishops reacted similarly. On October 12 the Church of Norway's Committee on International Issues went so far as to proclaim that the bombing campaign was both "ethically doubtful and strategically unwise." The committee stated that in the struggle against terrorism, the call of the churches is always to side with the victims — either in the United States or in Afghanistan — and from the perspective of the victims, to call for reconciliation. The next day the church committee's resolution was the top news at the website of the Islamic Council. A few weeks later, converging Muslim and Christian views materialized also in a joint letter from the imam of the largest Pakistani mosque in Oslo and a major official of the Church of Norway to Kjell Magne Bondevik, the Christian Democrat prime minister of Norway. In it Muslim and Christian leaders jointly criticized the government's unreserved support for the American policy, demanded a halt to the bombing for humanitarian reasons, and called for international reactions to terrorism that do not inflict suffering on innocent civilians. The focus was on vulnerability, and the greater responsibility of the more powerful. It is interesting to note that two days before, the mosque in question had expressed its abhorrence of the massacre of Christian worshipers perpetrated in the Pakistani city of Bahawalpur. Their imminent protest may indicate a *Muslim* concern for the vulnerable other.

But the basic attitude of shared concern for the vulnerable other does not necessarily mean agreement on the level of applied ethics. Returning to Norwegian church leaders' reactions to the bombing campaign, I must add that their reactions were not unanimous. When the Church Synod met in mid-November, it had to recognize different moral judgments as to the legitimacy of the bombing campaign. Some church leaders supported it, as a lesser evil. So did probably a good number of Muslims, although their support was not as vociferous as the opponents' protest.

With the exception of Osama bin Laden and his likes, I suppose most of those who voiced their view on the bombing campaign would declare their commitment to a culture of nonviolence and a concern for the most vulnerable ones in conflicts. What we were facing was in fact a moral disagreement on the basis of commonly affirmed values, a disagreement which probably also involved different evaluations on the factual level. In the light of the eventual fall of the Taliban, many would contest the initial evaluation of the church committee that the bombing campaign was "strategically unwise." Apart from divergent views at the factual level, there was also the normative controversy between just war approaches of a more or less restrictive kind and more pacifist stands.

The interesting thing for us was that the moral disagreement did not in any way coincide with cultural and religious divides. *Some* Muslims and *some* Christians joined hands against *other* Muslims and *other* Christians, who held different moral and political views on how terrorism should be combated. This was the case in Norway, and even more so internationally. The World Council of Churches sided with several interfaith and Muslim bodies in criticizing the American bombing campaign. But the bombing campaign itself was based on an interfaith alliance between the increasingly religious leadership of the United States, some important Muslim regimes in the region, and the internal opposition in Afghanistan, which was no less Muslim than the Taliban.

One challenge which arises from my example is how to live with moral disagreement in interreligious dialogue. Globalization implies that disagreements on the level of applied ethics will increasingly be *interfaith* in nature — not in the sense of Christian versus Muslim views, but in terms of controversial Muslim-Christian alliances that converge with corresponding *intra*-Muslim and *intra*-Christian controversies.

The question of religion and violence is not one of Christian versus Muslim views. It has never been and will probably never be. On the level of taking concrete moral action (not only against violence, but also against intolerance, for gender equality, for economic justice, etc.), ethical disagreement cuts right across religious divides. This means that in the future, both the question of well-grounded moral disagreement and the challenge of putting up limits to nonacceptable actions must be tackled on an interreligious basis. On the one hand, Christians and Muslims should learn to be more generous in accepting the fact that affirmation of common values may entail different opinions on how those values should be safeguarded in concrete circumstances. On the other hand, Christians and Muslims (together with other believers and nonbelievers) must also tackle together the task of refuting views and blocking actions that do not respect the integrity and vulnerability of the other.

We have shared some examples from a Norwegian context. The common challenge is to set up structures for interfaith dialogue that are based on face-to-face relations, focused on minority concerns, and aimed at protecting the vulnerability of the other. Those are general values, which can only be lived in the confusing landscape of concrete action and moral disagreement — across religious divides.

# God and Interfaith Relations:
# Some Attitudes among British Christians

MICHAEL IPGRAVE

## Posing the Question

"Do people of other faiths worship the same God Christians worship?" This is a topic rarely discussed explicitly by those engaged in interfaith relations, and some would deny it was either a meaningful or an appropriate point to raise. Yet the question of the identity of the objects of worship in different religions — which for brevity's sake I shall refer to as the issue of (transreligious) divine identity — seems on the face of it a natural area for discussion in a context of religious plurality.

This can be demonstrated by the way the question features in the following dialogue among primary age schoolchildren in the English city of Leicester.[1] The group consists of eight children — four Christians and four Hindus — in a school where the overwhelming majority of students are Muslims. Leading on from a discussion of non-Christians celebrating Christmas, the teacher asks directly: "How many Gods do you think there are?" The Christian and Hindu children, by no means disconcerted by this question, launch into a discussion of the one God and the many gods.

Sharon (Chr.)  I think there's one and he's called all different things.
Sushila (Hi.)  I was going to say that.
Sharon  Same!
Laxmi (Hi.)  Miss, we can't actually say that because we've got so many gods.

---

1. I am indebted to my wife, Julia Ipgrave, for this material, which is drawn from a large corpus of Leicester schoolchildren's interreligious dialogues, gathered as part of her doctoral research (for the University of Warwick) into children's religious understanding.

Sharon  Yeah — but they could be called — um . . .

Meri (Hi.)  You have to believe in all of them, because all of them have got something different, like, special.

Noah (Chr.)  Yeah, because — look, they can all — they can all be the same God, because God can — God can . . .

Sharon  Do lots of things.

Noah  Change into different — like, different features — like he can be in you.

Thomas (Chr.)  He can come to anybody.

Sushila  He can change into anything.

A few minutes later the discussion broadens to include also the God of the majority of their classmates, with reference being made to the "beautiful names" of Allah.

Noah  What I think — what I've been brought up to believe is, there's one God and there's all kinds of names.

Sharon  Yeah, like, there's about ninety-nine names.

Noah  So I don't, like, say all the things that you're calling Shiva. I know, like, Allah as Jesus, because I believe Jesus is just one God, or you call Allah just one God.

Sharon  Yeah, he's got lots of names.

Laxmi  Because, like, some people just go around saying, like, our God made your God, and all that, but . . .

Sharon  We say that only one God created the world.

Teacher  Who says "My God created your God"?

Laxmi  Some people go round — the Muslims go round, saying: "Oh, Allah made this world."

Sharon  I know: "Your God" — Jesus, or something — "didn't make this world."

I find this dialogue fascinating for a number of reasons. The children are exploring the complex issues of transreligious divine identity with an openness and confidence that are refreshing. As they do so, they are touching on questions about the relation between the particular ways in which they recognize that God is apprehended in different religions — what I shall call divine character — and the belief (of the Christians at least) that there is only one God — which I shall refer to as the theme of divine identity. The evidence they bring to support their views in discussion includes teachings from their own traditions, knowledge they have of the views of others, and direct religious experience; all this forms the subject matter of some deeply theological reflections conducted in a setting of dialogue. Lastly, it is evident that this discussion is important for the children because it arises out of the everyday interfaith encounters which mark their school life, particularly with the majority Muslim population. The question of divine identity is, for them, unavoidable.

My impression is that the issues discussed by the children are of equal importance to British Christians of all ages engaging in a context of increasing religious plurality, but the adult discussion rarely reaches a corresponding degree of transparency. In what follows I shall seek to identify and evaluate three major kinds of answers which Christians in Britain are likely to give to the question: "Do people of other faiths worship the same God Christians worship?" I shall refer to these as "radical pluralism," "liberal pluralism," and "trinitarian monotheism." They are summarized respectively by the statements that "the God of Christians is different from the gods of others"; that "the God of Christians is equivalent to the gods of others"; and that "the gods of others are apprehensions of the God of Christians." It will be apparent from my comments that my own sympathies are with the third of these positions. The wider point I wish to make, though, is about the importance of initiating and sustaining a dialogue between Christians who hold to these different positions. This, I believe, can only be for the health of Christians' engagement in interfaith encounter, from whatever standpoint they approach the question.

## Radical Pluralism: God and the Gods as Different

The identity of "other gods" with the God worshiped by Christians could be questioned or denied from a number of different standpoints. A philosophical or theological emphasis on the separate integrities and mutual incommensurability of religious systems would imply that any assertion of divine identity across traditions was simply a category mistake, a failure to appreciate the impossibility of translation across different religious contexts.[2] However, more immediately relevant to many British Christians than such general considerations would be an actual denial of the identity of the Christian God with the gods worshiped in other faiths. Strongly developed examples of this kind of approach can be found in conservative evangelical literature addressing the ques-

2. For example, if the distinctive understanding of God in a given religion is thought of as operating more like a syntactic rule than a lexical item, then these questions of identity would seem to be misplaced. The idea of the Trinity as the "grammar" of Christian discourse (George Lindbeck, *The Nature of Doctrine: Religion and Theology in a Postliberal Age* [Philadelphia: Westminster, 1984], p. 106) could be developed to lend some support to this kind of approach.

tion with particular reference to Islam. While publications of this kind are often ignored in academic theology, they are widely circulated within some parts of the British churches, and can be very influential in forming Christian attitudes toward Muslims. A carefully written pamphlet by Peter Back — entitled simply *Is God Allah?* — can be considered both as a representative of this literature and also as a summary referring to other publications of this type.[3] Back's argument against the equation of Allah with "the God and Father of Jesus Christ" acknowledges that the Quran presents Allah as the unique divine creator of the world.[4] However, he points out, such a claim may be mistaken; and in fact the nonidentity of the two figures is for Back demonstrated by the contradictions between the character of Allah as presented in the Quran and the character of God as presented in the Bible. In general there is the Quranic denial of the Trinity, and in particular its inspirer's failure to meet scriptural tests such as 1 John 4:1-6 ("Every spirit that confesses that Jesus Christ has come in the flesh is from God, and every spirit that does not confess Jesus is not from God"). If one accepts the Quran's testimony to itself as an authentic and accurate revelation from Allah, it follows that Allah is not God but rather a "lying spirit," the spirit of Antichrist.[5]

I wish to point to three significant features of this line of argument — features also to be found in the reasoning of those who follow a similar line. Firstly, the difference in character between Allah and God is held to indicate an actual difference in their identity. Back does consider the alternative view — which he attributes to Cragg and Zwemer[6] — that "Muslims and Christians generally think that they are worshipping the same God and one or the other of the two faith communities holds heretical views about God," i.e., that they differ in their understanding of divine character while referring to the same actual identity. However, he insists that the integrity of the scriptural witness to the (trinitarian) character of God is so strong, and the divergence from this of the

3. Back describes himself as writing against the background of "a certain counter culture which would prevail upon us to take certain things for granted" — i.e., the identity of God and Allah (Peter Back, *Is God Allah?* [Stoke-on-Trent: Tentmaker, 1999], p. 4).

4. He in fact sets out an analysis of a developing sense of Allah's identity, from pre-Islamic times and through successive stages of Muhammad's life, following a theory of Alfred Welch. However, his argument refers primarily to the final stage of this development, summarized in the description of Allah as "the King, the Holy One, the Perfect, the Faithful, the Preserver, the Almighty Ruler, the Majestic" (Alfred T. Welch, "Allah and Other Supernatural Beings: The Emergence of the Qur'anic Doctrine of Tawhid," in *JAAR Thematic Studies* [Atlanta: Journal of the American Academy of Religion, 1976], p. 743 — cf. Surah 59.24).

5. Back, p. 29.

6. Kenneth Cragg, *The Call of the Minaret*, 2nd ed. (Maryknoll, N.Y.: Orbis, 1985), p. 30; Samuel Zwemer, *The Moslem Doctrine of God* (London: Darf, 1987), p. 108, cited by Back, p. 17.

Quranic testimony to the (unitarian) character of Allah is so wide, that the two characters must actually belong to different spiritual entities. Such a prioritization of character as the determinant of identity differs from the mainstream of historic Christian tradition. Medieval theology in the West, for example, affirmed the "material" identity of the God worshiped by Muslims as the true God, while holding their faith to be "formally" in error in rejecting his trinitarian character.[7] Similarly, more moderate voices within evangelical Anglicanism such as Colin Chapman also wish to admit that there is "enough in common between the Christian's idea of God and the Muslim's idea of God for us to be able to use the same word for 'God.'"[8] For Back and those who think like him, however, the fact that the "self-disclosures" of God and Allah are not consistent in their content means that the spiritual selves who are disclosing must be numerically different entities.

Secondly, in establishing this point Back relies heavily on a particular understanding of the nature of scripturally given truth, which relegates any consideration of religious experience to a peripheral place. Thus he emphasizes that his view is not based on "what certain Christians understand about theology, as if their beliefs are just as valid as different beliefs by other Christians," but rather "is true by reason of propositional revelation."[9] It is instructive to contrast his approach with that of Chapman, for example, who while certainly expounding a theology shaped by scriptural assumptions and categories, appeals to three significant nonbiblical facts to validate the identity of God and Allah: first, the use of the word "Allah" by Arabic Christians to speak of God; second, the evidence of the Quran that Muhammad believed Allah was the same God as that worshiped by Christians (and Jews); and third, the attestation of "real continuity" in their knowledge of Allah-God by converts from Islam to Christianity.[10] Back questions the wholeheartedness of the first, denies the relevance of the second, and does not mention the third.[11] He presents his position

---

7. E.g., Norman Daniel, *Islam and the West: The Making of an Image* (Edinburgh: Edinburgh University Press, 1966), p. 64: "It was usual . . . to assume that even what was said in error was said of the same God." The distinction of the material and formal objects of faith, *credere in Deum* and *credere Deo* respectively, is set out by Saint Thomas Aquinas in *Summa theologiae* 2a 2ae 2, 2.

8. Colin Chapman, *Cross and Crescent* (Leicester: InterVarsity, 1994), p. 228.

9. Back, p. 27.

10. Chapman, pp. 229f.

11. In relation to the first, he says, rather curiously: "I am personally aware that not all Christians whose mother tongue is Arabic are comfortable in the use of the term Allah for God" (Back, p. 27). Chapman, however, remarks: "Fourteen million Arabic-speaking Christians in the Middle East speak of God as Allah, and would never think of using a different word" (Chapman, p. 230).

as that of "a Christian who accepts the Bible as the trustworthy Word of God," presenting truth claims conflicting with those of Islam which must be adjudicated on the basis of the Aristotelian logic of the excluded middle.[12]

Thirdly, Back displays a rather complex attitude toward Islam's own account of its beliefs, and specifically toward the Quran's own testimony to itself as revelation. On one hand he thoroughly repudiates Allah's claim to be the true God. Rather, biblical evidence establishes that he is a lying and deceiving spirit, indeed the spirit of Antichrist. At this level he insists that "belief and reality are not the same thing."[13] Muslims who accept the truth of the Quran are therefore subject to delusion. On the other hand, however, precisely in order to establish such a case, it is important for Back to insist that the Quran is in one sense exactly what it claims to be, viz., a disclosure given by Allah to Muhammad: "One would not deny that Muhammad conversed with a spirit being. What is in question . . . is who that spirit being actually is."[14] In this double approach to Islamic authenticity, denying its ultimate theological claims while respecting the authenticity of its internal self-narration, Back represents a common stance among conservative evangelicals. To give just one other example, the widely read book *Who Is This Allah?* by the Nigerian Christian writer G. J. O. Moshay strongly implies that Allah is a demonic spirit masquerading as God, yet also asserts that "One should believe that Muhammad was a prophet, even a prophet of Allah."[15] Of course, it is not difficult to trace a connection between this interpretative approach to the Quran and the same writers' "propositional" view of Christian revelation. Thus both Bible and Quran are accepted as disclosures of truth claims by spiritual entities; their differences lie firstly in the identity of the spiritual entities making the disclosures, and consequently also in the actual validity of the truth claims being made.

There are considerable difficulties in the approach of Back and others like him who deny any identity between the God known to Christians and the object of worship of Muslims or people of other faiths. Most obviously there are the practical problems of initiating or sustaining any kind of interfaith relationship from such a position. If Christians believe the religious life of Muslims

---

12. "God cannot both be 'in Christ' and not 'in Christ' for the straightforward logical reason that 'a' and 'not-a' cannot both be true descriptions of the way things are" (Back, p. 29).

13. Back, p. 21 — cf. also p. 25: "The name in itself is not the reality which it claims to represent."

14. Back, p. 19. He later explains that the alternative is "that Muhammad was self-deceived and that his revelations were the product of his own imagination, and in view of the evidence to hand this is not a suitable conclusion to come to" (p. 30).

15. G. J. O. Moshay, *Who Is This Allah?* (Gerrards Cross, Bucks: Dorchester House, 1994), p. 165.

is founded on a deception and oriented toward a deceiver, it is difficult to see how any positive interaction can occur at the level of faith. Theology here functions not merely on a cerebral level, but also as a powerful emotional barrier: by insisting that Muslims' claimed religious experiences are in fact being systematically misreported, it is inhibitive of basic trust. Of course, an immediate answer to such objections would be to insist that relationships must always be grounded on truth. If the truth is that God and Allah are not the same, then any honest relationships must take that difference as a starting point. Nevertheless, the immense distrust and hostility which such a claim is capable of engendering should at least give pause for very careful examination as to whether it is a necessary, or even a possible, Christian position.

In addition to these pragmatic relational issues, Back's theory can also be challenged on internal grounds of Christian theology. An initial objection would be on the grounds of monotheistic uniqueness. Thus, to propose the real existence of an object (or objects) of worship other than the true God, it could be said, is not an option for Christians, since their faith simply does not provide space in its conceptual universe for more than one "god."[16] Back's answer to this, of course, would be to say that Allah is not a "god" as such, but a false spirit. Yet this suggestion in turn seems difficult to reconcile with any serious recognition of God's providential universality. Why should we suppose that God has allowed "a demonic, misleading spirit . . . [to place] . . . one-sixth of mankind under its spell" for such a prolonged period of human history?[17] Indeed, such a gloomy approach sits uncomfortably with elements of the biblical proclamation, such as Paul's assertion of the identity of the "unknown God" of an Athenian cult, the universally acknowledged "God who is not far from every one of us," and the God who raised Jesus from the dead.[18]

The relegation of experience to such a secondary role in Back's argument is also hard to justify. The Christian Scriptures, after all, include no direct references to any contemporary major non-Christian world faiths apart from Juda-

16. This theme can be traced back to the apostolic church, in Paul's discussion of the status of food sacrificed to idols. It is surprising that Back does not refer in this context to Paul's comment in 1 Cor. 8:5-6: "Indeed, even though there be many so-called gods in heaven or on earth — as in fact there are many gods and lords — yet for us there is one God, the Father, from whom are all things and for whom we exist." These verses are admittedly ambiguous in relation to our present discussion, but they are at least susceptible of interpretation along the lines I am outlining.

17. The words quoted to illustrate the conservative evangelical position are from Abd al-Masih, *Who Is Allah in Islam?* (Villach, Austria: Light of Life, n.d.), p. 78, but they accurately reflect Back's views also (he quotes Abd al-Masih extensively).

18. Acts 17:22-28. This is another NT text which Back ignores. By contrast Chapman, p. 229, lays considerable weight on it.

ism — which is why Back and others like him are forced to interpret future-oriented passages relating to the Antichrist as references to Islam.[19] Yet the absence of specific and unambiguous biblical reference to Islam and to other faiths underlines the importance of an actual experience of those faiths as indispensable for forming a theological response to the question of the identity of their object of worship. This is a point implicit in Chapman's reference to the significance of "continuity" in the experience of God reported by Christian converts from Islam. More broadly, two other categories of religious experience also need to be taken into account in the formulation of a Christian theological answer to the question of divine identity: first, the testimonies of faithful Muslims and other believers when they speak of God as they apprehend him, and second, the renewed or deepened awareness of the divine which many Christians experience in contexts of interfaith encounter.

Thus, assertion of an antithetical distinction in reality, between the true God on the one hand and other objects of worship on the other, seems to raise major problems both for a Christian understanding of God and also for interfaith relations. I have suggested that one root of this distinction can be traced to the prioritization of divine character as the effective determinant of divine identity: the absolutizing of the former leads to unacceptable consequences in relation to the latter. Nevertheless, the conservative evangelical witness can be valuable in holding before Christians the need to recognize and evaluate differences in divine character if an equation of identity is to be made between, say, God and Allah. This, it seems to me, is a weakness with the very different approach of the so-called liberal pluralist theology primarily associated with John Hick.

## Liberal Pluralism: God as Equivalent to the Gods

It could be argued that the word "pluralist" is in fact slightly odd in this context. Whereas the views of Back and others who assert a real distinction between the objects of worship in different religions might fairly be described as "radical pluralism" in that they propose a multiplicity of spiritual beings to explain the multiplicity of religions, the theology of John Hick is the polar opposite of this:

19. It is incidentally interesting to note that, in so doing, they are in one sense engaged in the same task — though from opposite presuppositions — as Muslims who also seek to interpret some New Testament passages as (positive) predictions of the coming of Muhammad — e.g., Muhammad Ali, *The Holy Qur'an: Arabic Text, English Translation and Commentary,* 7th ed. (Lahore: Ahmadiyyah Anjuman Isha'at Islam, 1991), p. 1056 (n. 2496), on the Muhammadan reference of the "Paraclete" passages of John 14–16.

he seeks to identify one common spiritual reality at the center of the world's faiths. "Pluralism" in Hick's usage therefore means something like "accounting for the phenomena of religious plurality" rather than "recognising any reality to spiritual plurality." A number of critics, however, have argued that his systematic denial of the possibility of the latter in fact militates against his ability to deliver the former, and have therefore questioned his use of the word "pluralism."[20] For clarity I shall refer to Hick's position as "liberal pluralism."

Liberal pluralism began with Hick's celebrated "Copernican revolution," the move he believes Christians must make in their understanding of religions: "A shift from the dogma that Christianity is at the centre to the realisation that it is God who is at the centre, and that all religions serve and revolve around him."[21] Later, in response to criticisms that his system did not adequately accommodate nontheistic religions such as Buddhism, Hick modified this theocentrism to speak of "Reality-centredness": "The great world faiths embody different perceptions and conceptions of, and correspondingly different responses to, the Real."[22] Various versions of this kind of liberal pluralism are widely influential among British Christians engaged in interfaith relations today — needless to say, in rather different circles from those who would follow Back's approach. However, it is important to ask of liberal pluralism also the question of divine identity, as follows: Who is the god, or "reality," at the center of this system, and in what relationship does that god stand to the God of Christians? This might seem a strange question to pose, since liberal pluralism is not proposed as a religion but rather as a philosophical (or a "metatheological") way of explaining and reconciling religious plurality. Moreover, divine identity is not the theme around which liberal pluralism was originally constructed. For Hick and for others thinking like him, the primary question was that of salvific scope and instrumentality: Who may be saved, and how? However, liberal pluralism, whatever its metatheological pretensions, makes definite religious claims which are reliant on a particular theology of the identity of its god. The theological evidence for identifying liberal pluralism as something like a distinctive religious tradition has been vigorously presented

20. E.g., J. A. DiNoia, O.P., "Pluralist Theology of Religions: Pluralistic or Non-Pluralistic," in *Christian Uniqueness Reconsidered: The Myth of a Pluralistic Theology of Religions,* ed. Gavin D'Costa (Maryknoll, N.Y.: Orbis, 1990), p. 133: "Pluralist proposals . . . advance a nonpluralistic account." Gavin D'Costa, *The Meeting of Religions and the Trinity* (Maryknoll, N.Y.: Orbis, 2000), p. 20, develops this kind of position to argue that "pluralism" should really be understood as another variety of "exclusivism," though this time based on liberal assumptions.

21. John Hick, *God and the Universe of Faiths* (London: Collins, 1977), p. 131.

22. John Hick, *An Interpretation of Religion: Human Responses to the Transcendent* (London: Macmillan, 1989), p. 240.

by Gavin D'Costa in *The Meeting of Religions and the Trinity*. D'Costa maintains that the liberal pluralism of modern Western writers implicitly relies on commitment to three key claims:

- all religions (with qualifications) lead to the same divine reality;
- there is no privileged self-manifestation of the divine; and
- religious harmony will follow if tradition-specific (exclusivist) claims which claim monopoly over truth are abandoned in favor of pluralist approaches which recognize that all religions display truth in differing ways.

In response to this, D'Costa's contention is that, in honest reality, the attempt to position oneself in a "neutral disembodied location" is impossible, as a "non-tradition-specific-approach" cannot exist. The pluralists, though presenting themselves as "honest brokers to disputing parties," are in fact inviting people to leave their existing religious traditions to "join a common and new one: liberal modernity." This in turn implies espousal of "one of the 'gods' of modernity: unitarian, deistic or agnostic."[23] Hick's espousal of a Copernican revolution involves an insistence that his own Christian religious viewpoint should not and cannot be at the center. His initial move from a christocentric to a theocentric account of religions, and still more his later modification of "theocentric" to "Reality-centred," shows the extent to which he is prepared to detect and root out surviving elements of what he sees as his own self-opinion at the heart of his system. D'Costa, however, argues that the conscious removal of these explicitly Christian elements in fact perversely opens the way for the unrecognized enthronement of implicit elements uncritically drawn from Hick's cultural milieu. In particular, he claims that one of the hidden motivations toward pluralism is a desire not to acknowledge or take seriously the irreducible facts of difference. The real divergences and disagreements that exist between different religions are, he suggests, an embarrassment to the viewpoint of contemporary Western consumerism, which therefore seeks to downplay their significance. Liberal pluralism thus involves a de-prioritization of the specific character of "Absolute Reality" as acknowledged in any given faith, in favor of an undifferentiated assertion of a generalized transreligious unity. Although this project historically has its origins in soteriology, the implications are also clear for our question of the relation between the objects of worship of different faiths. With respect to the identity of the God known to Christians, D'Costa's contention is that the transformation Hick proposes is so drastic that the "interfaith god" who results is different in character from God the Holy

23. D'Costa, pp. 19-20.

Trinity. He asserts that "Hick's 'pluralism' masks the advocation of liberal modernity's 'god,' in this case a form of ethical agnosticism."[24] This may be rather too trenchant a claim, yet there are three related problems in Hick's approach which do raise problems in an identification of the liberal pluralist "reality" with the Trinity. The first concerns the inner structure of Christian faith, and thus the very nature of the God in whom Christians believe. If the Trinity is merely a Christian "apprehension" of the nature of ultimate reality on the same level of validity as other apprehensions, then trinitarianism cannot express the ultimate nature of God. Stanley Samartha, for example, comparing Trinity with the Hindu analysis of the divine as *sat-cit-ananda*,[25] asserts that "Neither . . . could, in linguistic terms, adequately describe the inner ontological working of the Mystery." From this he goes on to conclude that "At best, the two formulations can only be symbolic, pointing to the Mystery, affirming the meaning disclosed, but retaining the residual depth."[26] However, this postulation of a trans-tripersonal primal level of divinity in itself affects the pattern of Christian belief in ways which have been highlighted by Joe DiNoia: "Pluralist accounts of religious predications are reminiscent of modalistic explanations of the doctrine of the Trinity. . . . For modalism, Father, Son, and Holy Spirit finally constitute a practised concealment rather than, as the Gospel was understood to proclaim, a full disclosure of God's identity and purposes."[27] In other words, the constitutive structure of Christian faith is distorted through proposing a "god beyond God" who is ultimately inaccessible and uncommunicated, and the authenticity of God's personal self-disclosure is effectively impugned.

A second problem flows from another way of looking at trinitarianism — as an issue of God's continuing faithfulness in maintaining his personal identity through time. A parallel can be drawn here with the transformation of the early Christian community from a group of entirely Jewish believers into a predominantly Gentile church. Despite pressures to the contrary, notably in the Marcionite crisis, the early church insisted on professing the continuity in identity of its God with the God of Abraham, Isaac, and Jacob. It did so because that was an implication of God's continuing faithfulness: he did not and could not simply change his identity. In the same way and for the same reason, the trini-

---

24. D'Costa, p. 26.

25. "Truth, consciousness, bliss." This Vedantic formula has in fact been adapted extensively by Indian Christians as a way of expressing trinitarian thinking in Indian categories, but Samartha does not allude to this in his discussion.

26. Stanley J. Samartha, "The Cross and the Rainbow: Christ in a Multireligious Culture," in *The Myth of Christian Uniqueness*, ed. John Hick and Paul F. Knitter (London: SCM Press, 1987), p. 76.

27. DiNoia, p. 130.

tarian identity of God cannot simply be explained away as an expendable way in which Christians have in the past chosen to speak of God. As the Western church negotiates its way into a world of religious plurality in a process which may prove almost as traumatic as the apostolic entry into the Gentile world, the same trust in divine faithfulness can give Christians assurance that God must continue really subsistent in his triune identity.

Finally, with reference especially to the second level of Hick's shift, from "theocentric" to "Reality-centred," it has to be asked how much identity of any kind is left for the god or reality at the center of the liberal pluralist system. As D'Costa points out, ultimate reality for Hick, in order to fulfill its central integrating role in his system, has to be beyond all particular distinctions. In particular, it has to transcend the distinction between the personal and the impersonal, which is identified with the boundary between theistic and nontheistic patterns of faith. The danger in this process of generalizing abstraction is that it can lead to a negative theology so severe as to be practically indistinguishable from agnosticism: "The colour, diversity, difference, and detail are bleached of their meaning, for the Real apparently resists all description and is incapable of self-utterance."[28] Against this it could be argued that there is in Christianity (as in other faiths) a long and distinguished practice of apophatic theology, which seeks to express the transcendence of God by successively denying the adequacy of all positive predications applied to him. Within the Christian tradition this has certainly provided a valuable corrective to any tendency to absolutize particular and limited conceptions of God. However, in Christian history apophasis has always been held in balance or tension with the affirmation of positive statements drawn from the core tradition of the faith, and these are accepted through analogical predication to express substantially true insights into the actuality of the divine identity. In the liberal pluralist situation, by contrast, it becomes impossible to use affirmation in this way, since statements drawn from any one religious tradition in principle cannot be privileged over those from any other. In practice, this will mean that differing predications will frequently cancel one another out, so that none of them are available to balance the overall processes of generalizing abstraction which are at the core of the entire system. In short, it becomes very difficult to identify any significant content in the "absolute reality" at the heart of Hick's theology.

In comparing this liberal pluralist approach with what I called the "radical pluralist" approach of Back and other conservative evangelicals, it is interesting to see that again a rather complex attitude is taken to the authenticity of the self-reported experience of people of other faiths. Back closely followed the

28. D'Costa, p. 28.

account of its inspiration by Allah attested by the Quran, yet at the same time refused the ultimate theological claims made by Muslims on the basis of that inspiration. Conversely Hick, to affirm in broad terms the theological validity of every major faith, drastically reinterprets the distinctive self-interpretation of each, so as to provide reductive explanations for the specificities which prevent the various religions' claims from fitting comfortably into the liberal pluralist mold. In particular, the distinctive trinitarian character of God as known to Christians appears to be sacrificed in liberal pluralism to the need to affirm the equal validity of all perceptions of the self-identical divine reality across the various religions.

## Trinitarian Monotheism: The Gods as Apprehensions of God

Given the considerable problems associated with both the above approaches, it is natural to ask whether there are coherent options for Christians lying somewhere between the two poles of what I have called radical pluralism and liberal pluralism. In fact, it does seem plausible to suggest that a "mainstream" view among British Christians would, on the one hand, affirm that people of different faiths in their worship are generally engaging with the true God, while on the other hand insisting that the identity of this God is most fully known as the trinitarian character revealed in the event of Jesus Christ.

With regard to Islam, for example, this is clearly the official teaching of the Roman Catholic Church. Vatican II's declaration *Nostra Aetate* affirms of "the Muslims," that "They worship God, who is one, living and subsistent, merciful and almighty, the Creator of heaven and earth, who has also spoken to men."[29] In support of this confident assertion, it refers to the remarkably frank letter of 1076 from Gregory VII to the Muslim king Anzir, where the pope declared: "We believe and confess one God, although in different ways, and praise and worship Him daily as the creator of all ages and the ruler of this world."[30] Gregory's phrase "in different ways," though, points discreetly to the recognition that Muslims do not share belief in the Trinity, and therefore — from a Christian point of view — do not have access to a full awareness of the character of God.

As compared to the definite statements of Vatican II on the identity of the

---

29. *Nostra Aetate*, cap. 3, in Austin Flannery, O.P., ed., *Vatican Council II: The Conciliar and Post-Conciliar Documents* (Dublin: Dominican Publications, 1975), p. 739.

30. J. Neuner and J. Dupuis, eds., *The Christian Faith: Doctrinal Documents of the Catholic Church*, 5th ed. (London: Harper Collins, 1992), p. 302, no. 1002.

God of Christians and Muslims, the official attitudes of other British churches are notoriously more difficult to identify precisely. It seems to me, though, that the general view of British Anglicans, for example, would be broadly in line with the conciliar position. This can certainly be seen in the 1988 Lambeth Conference's commendation of a document entitled "Jews, Christians and Muslims: The Way of Dialogue," which stated that followers of these three faiths "share a mission to the world that God's name may be hallowed. . . . Each will recall the other to God, to trust him more fully and obey him more profoundly."[31] As a representative and widely respected theologian, Kenneth Cragg sums up the consensus of Anglican thought: "Those who say that Allah is not 'the God and Father of our Lord Jesus Christ' are right if they mean that God is not so described by Muslims. They are wrong if they mean that Allah is other than the God of Christian faith."[32]

Opinions tend to be rather more reserved on the identity of objects of worship in other faiths (apart, of course, from Judaism, where the biblical evidence naturally constrains Christians to affirm the identity of the God of Israel with the Father of Jesus). *Nostra Aetate*, for example, guardedly states that "There is found among different peoples a certain awareness of a hidden power, which lies behind the course of nature and the events of human life. At times there is present even a recognition of a supreme being, or still more of a Father."[33] Complications of course arise for some Christians in some religions from factors such as apparent polytheism, imputations of idolatry, or acceptance of an impersonal conception of the Absolute. Insofar as a single divinity can be discerned as an object of worship within non-Abrahamic faiths, however, Christians in this broad tradition seem generally content to affirm that this is an apprehension of the true God acknowledged by Christians as the Trinity.

What are the features of this inclusively trinitarian approach as compared with either the antithetical discontinuity advocated by conservative evangelicals like Back or the generalizing unitarianism proposed by Hick and the liberal pluralists? Once again three points may be noted. In the first place, there is an attempt to maintain a balanced relation between what I have termed the character of God and the identity of God — that is, between confession of the dis-

31. Anglican Consultative Council, *The Truth Shall Make You Free: The Lambeth Conference, 1988: The Reports, Resolutions, and Pastoral Letters from the Bishops* (London: Church House, 1988), p. 305, para. 27. This reads rather more enthusiastically than an earlier passage in the same document which had cautiously remarked: "Many Christians would also want to affirm Islamic monotheism" (p. 303, para. 18).

32. Cragg, p. 30.

33. *Nostra Aetate*, cap. 2, in Flannery, p. 379.

tinctive trinitarian pattern of God's life as known to Christians and recognition of the universal reality of this God as the sole God. Back's propositionally couched emphasis on the specificity of the former seems to imperil the latter, whereas Hick's indiscriminate promotion of the latter tends to evacuate the former of any meaning. On the possibility of establishing a dialogue with people of other faiths, the assertion of a common divine identity must be primary, as without this no shared spiritual space becomes available for a conversation at the level of faith. Once a relationship is established on the basis of this assertion, though, the specific character of God can become a principal theme of dialogue. The trinitarian pattern of God's life can acquire a primary saliency for Christians, as it provides a coherent witness to the specific way in which they understand the God who is revealed through Jesus Christ: "The distinctive understanding of God as Trinity should be at the centre of any inter faith reflection."[34]

In this connection there seems to be a growing interest among British Christians in exploring how trinitarian belief can itself enable interfaith dialogue.[35] Trinity in this perspective involves the specific character of God not only as apprehended by Christians but also as a way to ground generous and inclusive engagement with other ways of understanding God. Central to such an approach is the recognition of a dynamic interaction between the two "economies" of the Son (or Word) and the Spirit. Explicitly appealing to Orthodox tradition, for example, an influential Anglican document on interfaith relations suggests that a "vision of tension and complementarity between the historically visible, 'named,' determinate presence and memory of God the Son and the more unpredictable, culturally and historically indeterminate witness of the Spirit provides a possibly fruitful vehicle for a 'theology of religions.'"[36]

Secondly, a trinitarian approach of this kind has to take seriously the experiential dimension, in terms both of the accounts of their religion given by people of other faiths and also of the experiences of Christians involved in in-

34. Doctrine Commission of the Church of England, *The Mystery of Salvation: The Story of God's Gift* (London: Church House, 1995), p. 176.

35. This interest is, of course, not restricted to Britain, and recently has been further stimulated by the groundbreaking and fascinating study by S. Mark Heim, *The Depth of the Riches: A Trinitarian Theology of Religious Ends* (Grand Rapids: Eerdmans, 2001).

36. Inter Faith Consultative Group of the Church of England, *Towards a Theology for Inter-Faith Dialogue. Republished with Additional Material for the Anglican Consultative Council* (London: Church House, 1986), p. 20, para. 45. This kind of approach, though, has been strongly criticized from an evangelical viewpoint by Michael Nazir-Ali, who goes so far as to say of the report's pneumatology: "This is not the Holy Spirit of the Bible" (Michael J. Nazir-Ali, "That Which Is Not to Be Found but Which Finds Us," in *Towards a Theology for Inter-Faith Dialogue*, p. 48).

terfaith encounter. I pointed out above that this is an aspect relegated to a secondary position by the conservative evangelical position, which on grounds of propositional revelation denies an identity between God and the gods. To some extent, though from a very different standpoint, a similar downplaying of experience can be detected in the liberal pluralist assertion of a transreligious divine identity which disregards the specific character of the divine as acknowledged in different faiths. Religious experience which relates primarily to the specificity of these characters — for example, devotion to a particular divine manifestation, or obedience to a particular divine ethic — will be relativized by an emphasis on generalizing abstraction designed to construct an overarching commonalty. In contrast to such a diminution of contextual experience compared to universal principles, Rowan Williams speaks of the Logos-Spirit relationship in the Trinity as "taking shape in a particular historical process and social practice," and having to make "reference to the importance of the material and temporal differences among persons."[37] In a trinitarian readiness to engage seriously with difference, he suggests, there may be a more appropriate, because more experientially honest, way of engaging with plurality than either the biblical or the "metatheological" apriorities of radical and liberal pluralism respectively.

Thirdly, though, it would be disingenuous to suggest that this approach is free of theological problems. Indeed, to adherents of either the first or second positions, a claim to hold on to both a universal identity of God and a specific trinitarian character may seem either, at best, simply a restatement of the problem rather than a solution, or at worst, a characteristically dishonest muddle of the type beloved by those who wish to have their cake and eat it. I do not in fact believe that such criticisms are justified, but further careful formulations are certainly necessary to express the relation between the universal affirmation and the specific confession which this approach doubly proposes. In particular, as for the other two positions, the attitude adopted by Christians to the self-narration of other faith communities will be complex in this interpretation. On one hand, the affirmation of transreligious divine identity implies that the religious experiences of non-Christians must in principle be recognized as at least potentially genuine experiences of the true God, and as such they will need to be received by Christians in a respectful and open way. On the other hand, the confession of the Trinity as the true character of God will imply that the inter-

---

37. Rowan Williams, "Trinity and Pluralism," in *Christian Uniqueness Reconsidered*, p. 8. His article is a fine but dense meditation on the implications for dialogue of Raimundo Panikkar's distinctive trinitarian "pluralism," which Williams sees as quite different from the liberal pluralism of Hick, Knitter, et al.

pretation of such experiences must remain subject in Christian theological analysis to a trinitarian understanding, and this will necessarily involve some revision in the others' self-narration. D'Costa suggests that there needs to be in this sense both what he calls auto-interpretation, "a serious engagement with another religion on its own terms," and hetero-interpretation, "a theological evaluation of the meaning of that religion that may not necessarily be in keeping with the sense of those within that tradition." Importantly, though, he insists that "the latter is always reliant on auto-interpretation."[38] That is to say, establishment of the dialogical context is the presupposition for Christian reflection on the dialogical content.

## Continuing the Intra-Christian Discussion

The three positions I have outlined do not, of course, exhaust the actual or possible range of views held among British Christians over the question of transreligious divine identity. However, even from this brief survey several points are clear. Disagreements on this issue among Christians are deep-seated, and involve substantial assumptions about theological method, the evaluation of religious experience, and the importance of divine character vis-à-vis divine identity. The differing positions are likely to give rise to very different approaches to particular interfaith problems — for example, the possibility of acts of shared prayer or worship; the meaning and pattern of interreligious dialogue; the purpose and method of Christian mission. All three positions require a complex handling of the Christian interpretation of the religious experiences reported by people of other faiths. In important ways, the different standpoints each individually highlight theological insights which are important for all Christians. While a consensus over this question seems unlikely within the British churches in the foreseeable future, it is important for all that there should be a vigorous intra-Christian discussion over the issues involved.

38. D'Costa, p. 100.

# The Dialogue Party: Dialogue, Hybridity, and the Reluctant Other

TINU RUPARELL

The practice of interreligious dialogue at the institutional or formal level can — despite the best intentions of institute directors, organizers, church and temple leaders, and other interested groups — often result in rather bad parties. Consider the following caricature of interreligious dialogue:

> After centuries of Western domination and Orientalist subjugation, not to mention the even longer history of mission — arguably one of the most successful forms of covert Westernization in history — good "liberal" leaders from many of the major Christian congregations realize that they must at least begin the task of conversation with their fellow religionists from other faiths. They duly organize conferences and meetings, write monographs, encourage theologians and philosophers to do the same, and invite the religious others, whom they once ruled, to the friendly "table of dialogue" in order better to understand one another in the hopes that centuries of religiously inspired or abetted strife might come to an end.
>
> But all does not go according to plan. Many invited participants refuse to come, or if they come, they refuse to engage in the kind of open, honest dialogue for which the organizers hoped. Other attendees arrive with plans to argue the others into agreeing with them, and raising the emotional, economic, and political stakes so to do. Awkward silences ensue around the putatively friendly table of dialogue as the forthright and evangelical proponents of various traditions argue strongly and vociferously — and it appears, monologically — for their view of the world. Reasoning with these apologists can only go so far, for there are many areas of belief and practice they will not broach.
>
> And this is not the end of the troubles, for many attendees find various details of the conferences not to their liking. The food available for conference-goers is not what they are used to, and in some cases, altogether

inedible by them. The accommodations and meeting rooms are stifling and formalized and do not allow for sitting on the floor as many are accustomed to. Some participants even use presentation software for their talks and publish their materials on the Web for wider dissemination — technologies to which others have no access. This only exacerbates the gulf between the participants. Finally, with no common language, the de facto English-only proceedings need to be translated into many tongues and many feel the translations are not quite hitting their mark.

The meetings acquire the stigma of a liberal dialogian's nightmare and soon run out of steam. Fewer such conferences are organized; academics relegate interreligious dialogue to the margins of "real" scholarly theological discourse, and the ordinary encounters between people of different faiths are neither well understood nor adequately described. No matter how well-meaning the efforts to organize it, formalized and sophisticated interreligious dialogue at the "institutional" level becomes a nonstarter.

As I stated above, this is a somewhat fanciful scenario, but it does raise some pointed questions and highlights some salient difficulties with interreligious dialogue as it is often practiced and theorized in the academy. The various problems encountered in the fictional gatherings just described are writ large in the philosophical and practical aporia faced by those who think and write about the conversation of religions. In what follows I wish to consider some of these problems — particularly the problem of the reluctant conversant — to ascertain whether and to what extent interreligious dialogue is sick, before proposing a rather different vision of dialogue which, I shall argue, responds to at least some of the problems we face.

Firstly, the impetus for dialogue might be questioned. Undoubtedly the centuries of colonial subjugation and the sometimes insensitive or even immoral attitudes and actions by Orientalist missionaries of old are an understandable reason for their heirs to try to right the wrongs of the past. But as Kenneth Surin suggests, to do so is, if not purely patronizing, to peddle a profound illusion — the myth of human unity which proclaims the sheer equality of all people, of which Adorno writes:

> The familiar argument . . . that all people and all races are equal, is a boomerang. . . . Abstract utopia is all too compatible with the insidious tendencies of society. That all men [*sic*] are alike is exactly what society would like to hear. It considers actual or imagined differences as stigmas indicating that not enough has yet been done; that something has still been left outside its machinery, not quite determined by its totality. . . . An emancipated society, on the other hand, would not be a unitary state, but the realization

of universality in the recognition of differences. Politics that are still concerned with such a society ought not, therefore, to propound the abstract equality of men even as an idea. Instead, they should point to the bad equality today . . . and conceive the better state as one in which people could be different without fear. To assure the black that he is exactly like the white man, while he obviously is not, is secretly to wrong him still further. He is benevolently humiliated by the application of a standard by which, under the pressure of the system, he must necessarily be found wanting, and to satisfy which would in any case be a doubtful achievement. . . . The melting-pot was introduced by unbridled industrial capitalism. The thought of being cast into it conjures up martyrdom, not democracy.[1]

Adorno and Surin are here arguing that one of the reasons we try to do interreligious dialogue in the first place is to assuage our guilt for having treated the followers of other religions so poorly in the past. We justify dialogue by relying on a purely mythical ideology of human equality, but this equality is actually only another form of totalizing narrative, one which systematically flattens out real difference under the weight of our shared "human nature" — whatever that is. By saying that we need to talk together as equals because we are, in the end, all the same under the skin, is simply to ignore the real differences between people, to discount the other's irreducible alterity.[2] Thus interreligious dialogue done in the name of common humanity unwittingly homogenizes common humans. Just consider the real villains in Hick's Copernican universe of religions — exclusivist claims to religious truth are nothing less than blasphemies against the Real in Hick's world — to see how totalizing and homogenizing this discourse is. Moreover, supposedly egalitarian interreligious dialogue masks the facts of real human injustice and supports the status quo whereby the wealthy London banker can rest easy at night knowing that both she and the Filipino migrant worker or the Kenyan tea picker, or even the unemployed English shipbuilder, are all in the "same human condition." Their abstract equality allows the banker to conveniently leave unquestioned her possible maleficent role in their lives. It also allows pluralism to be truly global in scope and therefore compatible with the new world order or global gaze which has taken shape over the last part of the twentieth century. It is no coincidence, Surin notes, that the growth of pluralism has paralleled the rise of multinational

---

1. T. W. Adorno, *Negative Dialectics*, trans. E. B. Ashton (London: Routledge and Kegan Paul, 1973), p. 8; as in Kenneth Surin, "A Materialist Critique of Religious Pluralism: An Examination of John Hick and Wilfred Cantwell Smith," in *Religious Belief and Unbelief: Studies Critical and Comparative*, ed. Ian Hammett (London: Routledge, 1990), p. 120.

2. Surin, "A Materialist Critique," pp. 120-21.

companies.³ This globalized religious pluralism depends on and is thus a part of the economy of power which makes the McDonald's hamburger the world food and Coca-Cola the global drink.⁴ People consuming these products, suggests Surin, are tied into Western globalized material culture and implicitly accept the way of life to which it is tied. It is a measure of the amazing success of the globalizing project that the cultural encroachment which inevitably follows the multinationals is, far from being combated, actually a selling point for the products being marketed. "American style" and "world fashion" are strong advertising cues for companies such as Coca-Cola and Benetton respectively. Surin's argument is that the ideology of religious pluralism and the mode of interreligious dialogue it entails are no less globalizing, no less covertly monological, no less modern, and no less capitalist.

So at least one major impetus for interreligious dialogue is suspect. Our colonialist guilt brings with it a form of dialogue built on false, ideological egalitarianism which homogenizes people and ironically further supports the inequalities and injustices wrought by the history of colonialism in the first place. But what about the form and structures of dialogue? These are no less problematic. Firstly, the language in which much interreligious dialogue takes place reflects the history and politics of Orientalist scholarship. Talal Asad's analysis of the translation of unequal languages shows that in interreligious dialogue the language of the weaker (usually Two-Thirds) world will give way to the language of the stronger (Western industrialized) nations:

> To put it crudely: because the languages of Third World societies . . . are weaker in relation to Western languages (and today, especially to English), they are more likely to submit to forcible transformation in the translation process than the other way around. The reason for this is, first, that in their politico-economic relations with Third World countries, Western nations have a greater ability to manipulate the latter. And, second, Western languages produce and deploy desired knowledge more readily than third-world languages do. (The knowledge that Third World languages deploy most easily is not sought by Western societies in the same way, or for the same reasons.)⁵

3. Surin, "A Materialist Critique," p. 121.

4. Kenneth Surin, "The Politics of Speech: Religious Pluralism in the Age of the McDonald's Hamburger," in *Christian Uniqueness Reconsidered: The Myth of a Pluralistic Theology of Religions,* ed. Gavin D'Costa (Maryknoll, N.Y.: Orbis, 1990), 206.

5. Talal Asad, "The Concept of Cultural Transformation in British Social Anthropology," in *Writing Culture: The Poetics and Politics of Ethnography,* ed. James Clifford and George E. Marcus (Berkeley: University of California Press, 1986), pp. 157-58.

This is not merely an issue of language but rationality. As Donald Davidson, among others, has argued, the language in which beliefs and practices are communicated embodies the rationality of the faith community.[6] When the language of discourse belongs to those in positions of socioeconomic advantage, dialogue must favor that language and that rationality. Asad thus highlights another problem with interreligious dialogue as now practiced, and nowhere is this seen more clearly than when we habitually use tired terms and categories such as inclusivism, exclusivism, and pluralism. Quite apart from questions of their rational context and origins, these terms fail (and have always failed) to comprehend the dynamic and fluid nature of religious traditions. To classify views of religious truth in this way may serve the purposes of those with Hickian agendas (for which the terms were, if not originally created, most successfully deployed), but they do not reflect the porous nature of religious boundaries, nor the syncretic history of religious traditions. Religions are not homogenizable entities neatly slotting into such categories as inclusive or exclusive, but families of local belief and practice which themselves have histories of borrowing and contending, differing and expanding with their changing contexts. We have, I argue, been hamstrung through the habitual use of these categories, and it is time to jettison them for other metaphors.

Now let us consider those participants at the dialogue parties who had difficulties with the infrastructure of the event. Not being happy with one's room or food betrays the fact that the venue for meeting and the table of dialogue each must be set by someone or other. These are inevitable choices, for the practicalities of interreligious dialogue necessitate that some issues cannot remain indeterminate, and determining them is neither neutral nor insignificant. This is a rather different point than the question of differing rationalities discussed above, but no less important, for questions of propriety, relevance, decorum, respect, custom, and aesthetics form the horizon within which the conversation of religions takes place. One cannot separate these from more conceptual or formalized aspects of dialogue, and again the tone of interreligious meetings is decided by the numerous smaller and larger details which create it.

So we have considered difficulties surrounding the motivation, language, form, and structure of interreligious dialogue, but I have left the most difficult issue to the end.

One of the most intractable problems which face theorists and practitio-

---

6. This is by now a standard point, and I shall not devote much space here to defending it. See Donald Davidson, "On the Very Idea of a Conceptual Scheme," in his *Truth and Interpretation* (Oxford: Clarendon, 1984).

ners of interreligious dialogue is attempting to talk with an unwilling conversation partner. How does interreligious dialogue proceed when one or more partners in a putative dialogue refuse or are unwilling to participate? Clearly interreligious dialogue requires a certain amount of goodwill by its participants, and those who do not possess this goodwill either do not show up for the conversation and are therefore neglected, or perhaps sit "at the table" of dialogue (so to speak) but fail or refuse to engage in truly open, honest dialogue. In either case, it seems, the would-be dialogian is faced with a serious problem, and this is what I want to consider below.

There are, I think, at least two different kinds of unwilling participants, and I have alluded to these silent attendees in my earlier illustration. The first simply does not show up — either out of contempt for the notion of dialogue between adherents of different faiths or for sheer lack of interest. Neither of these attitudes should be discounted since, for many, the thought of subjecting revealed theological beliefs and practices to the scrutiny of sinful and ignorant humans is folly. It is simply not our place, so they contend, to interrogate divine commands, and even if we did, our limited understandings could only lead to frustration. Better simply to ignore such games and get on with living the life God gives us. So there will be people for whom interreligious dialogue is pointless or possibly pernicious.

Another nonparticipant may actually sit down at the table of dialogue but fail to truly engage in open conversations which are the hallmark of real dialogue.[7] These are the ersatz "dialogians" who do attend the congresses, who do speak to their heathen neighbors, who are willing to share their own faiths and (at least) *seem* interested in learning about other traditions. But they are also the people who will never allow the other to really influence their own religious beliefs and practices. I am sure most people interested in interreligious dialogue have encountered such counterfeit conversation partners — and even if one argues that they do not really exist, my arguments stand, as these attitudes are to greater or lesser degrees evident in a variety of positions on interreligious dialogue. There is the appearance of being willing to listen to the beliefs and practices of another's religion, and this kind of nonparticipant is usually only too willing to share her or his own views, but there is always a reluctance to engage with the other in a way that might interrogate or undermine his or her own cherished beliefs. This group approaches interreligious encounter as apologists

7. These are discussions where each participant is willing to expose his or her beliefs and practices to the full glare of the other's interrogation and investigation. Nothing is held back in such ideal and lamentably rare conversations: one exposes — perhaps to defend, perhaps to learn — all of one's commitments, doubts, strengths, and weaknesses to the other in the faith that she or he will do the same.

or even mercenaries but not as seekers after truth — indeed, they scarcely admit there can be religious truth outside the language of their own tribe. Such a view is seen in most religious traditions: evangelical or fundamentalist Hindus, Jews, Christians, Muslims — all can be seen to hold some form of this attitude. It is what I call "firewall incommensurability" — an admission that there are other religious views in the world, and that it might be important to know about them and perhaps understand something of the way they "work" (that is, how they might affect oneself), just as long as there always stands a clear barrier against allowing any of the other's views to infect one's own religious operating systems. A firewall of exclusivism or incommensurability is erected between the outside and one's own tradition such that any interaction is always essentially one way — from the inside out.

Now before I go further, let me stress the need to respond to this problem. One might assume that the silence of many believers in the interreligious discourse is a mark of their abstention, but we ignore them at our peril, as the events of September 11, 2001, show. I am not for one minute suggesting that a robust program of interreligious dialogue would have kept those planes from their fateful ends, but I do want to argue that the willful neglect, by the West, of (in this case) a small but vocal minority within the Muslim world, and more precisely their view of the world, raised the probability of such terrorist attacks occurring. Surely greater interreligious communication and understanding — even with those who turn their backs on such programs — can only reduce the possibilities of such violence.

But again, how do you talk to the terrorist? If they have, as I stated above, turned their backs on the notion of interreligious (or any other) dialogue, how is conversation possible?

I do in fact think there is a way to continue the conversation of religions even in the face of such intractable reluctance. It requires a new model of dialogue — one which ironically requires real alterity and exploits the dialectic at the heart of all metaphor in order to create hybrid, liminal, or *interstitial* positions between religious tradition — and I will briefly sketch this hermeneutic before applying it to the problem of the terrorist.

Of course, I cannot here delineate this method adequately, but only give you an indicative map of its main features. What I have elsewhere called "interstitial theology"[8] is a hermeneutic for continuing the conversation of religions. It is based on two pillars: a mitigated form of incommensurability and the interactionist view of metaphor afforded by Paul Ricoeur.

8. See my forthcoming monograph, *Dialogue and Hybridity* (Albany: SUNY Press, 2004), for a fuller delineation of this hermeneutic.

If, following George Lindbeck, we view religion on the model of language, we get to the mitigated form of incommensurability I believe best represents the otherness inherent in dialogue.[9] As languages, religions can be mutually translated, but in any kind of translation there is always an open-endedness in the process of semiosis. One can never get a perfect translation, as Umberto Eco has shown,[10] but one can still, through a process of semiotic accretion, communicate a version of the text's meaning to the reader. This kind of incommensurability, where communication is enabled but never closed, where the correspondence between texts is always metaphorically based, is, I would argue, reflective of the porous boundaries of religion. When religions are compared, we do not amalgamate them all under a mythical genus called "religion,"[11] but neither do we throw up our hands in mute defeat in the face of radical alterity. Religious traditions can be usefully compared and contrasted. They do have similar forms and functions, but crucially they are not all "essentially the same." Moreover, if they were as incommensurable as some commentators seem to suggest,[12] we would have no understanding of other faiths as religions (notwithstanding the various genealogies and arguments against the notion of "religion" as a category), nor would the faithful of other traditions understand us and our faiths as such. Religions as languages show a mitigated incommensurability which favors difference but does not disallow similarity. It is this admission, that religious traditions are significantly other, which is the beginning of interstitial theology.

What mitigated incommensurability forces apart, metaphor seeks to bring together, but in a nuanced and dynamic way. Ricoeur's interactionist view of metaphor sees it as a figure of speech whereby one thing is referred to in terms which evince another.[13] In Ricoeur's highly influential account, metaphor is a semantic generator whereby the terms of the metaphor — importantly understood as statements rather than individual words — work to redescribe each other in a hermeneutic spiral. Furthermore, as these metaphor-

9. George Lindbeck, *The Nature of Doctrine: Theology in a Postliberal Age* (London: SPCK, 1984), pp. 33-34.

10. Umberto Eco, "The Semantics of Metaphor," in his *The Role of the Reader: Explorations in the Semiotics of Texts* (Bloomington: Indiana University Press, 1979).

11. John Milbank argues this point in his "The End of Dialogue," in *Christian Uniqueness Reconsidered*.

12. Heim seems to argue this when, relying on Rescher, he advocates different ultimate realities to which different religions refer. See his *Salvations: Truth and Difference in Religion* (Maryknoll, N.Y.: Orbis, 1997), esp. chaps. 4 and 5.

13. This is Janet Soskice's definition, but it is wholly in line with Ricoeur's. See Soskice, *Metaphor and Religious Language* (Oxford: Clarendon, 1984), and Ricoeur's *The Rule of Metaphor: Multi-disciplinary Studies in the Creation of Meaning in Language*, trans. R. Czerny with K. Mcloughlin and J. Costello, S.J. (Toronto: University of Toronto Press, 1977).

ical poles are each connected by a web of reference to both their horizons of language and their corresponding aspects of lived experience, what metaphor brings together are not individual elements of language — semantic sound bites, so to speak — but connected aspects of life. It is in this way that metaphor engages the imagination so that a metaphorical statement evinces a "semantic twist" (in Monroe Beardsley's words) such that a novel interpretation is created. This aspect of metaphor is important for our purposes because it guards against the de-contextualization which traditional interreligious comparisons often effect. By utilizing the structure of metaphor in the ways I shall shortly describe, interstitial theology succeeds in bringing into conversation fuller and more detailed areas of religious life, rather than simply corresponding views of heavenly realms, for example, or analogous doctrines of God. What metaphor creates, rather, is much more important.

As mentioned above, metaphor works by redescribing each pole of the metaphor in terms of the other. While metaphor is not limited to this dyadic structure, it is useful here to explain it in these terms. The dialectic of metaphor must begin with difference (this is why it requires the mitigated incommensurability I alluded to above), for only with this difference is the necessary logical or semantic incoherence, which is the spur to the metaphorical imagination, present. In meeting a metaphorical statement there is a disjunction which the interpreter sees as logically incoherent. The pressure of this disjunction imaginatively calls forth a term's associated commonplaces — what Gadamer calls a horizon of meaning and Voloshinov[14] the apperceptive context — and from this horizon new descriptions are associated with the other term in the metaphor. The process is bi- or multidirectional so that each term in the metaphor is redescribed in terms of the others. In this way the semantic field of a metaphor is effectively stretched to include these new connections. Ricoeur thus calls metaphors semantic generators, as these new connotations, this new metaphorical interpretation, exists between the parent terms of the metaphor, owing allegiance, as it were, to its sources while differing from each. The metaphor is a semantic hybrid which loses not its foundation in its sources but neither can be contained by them. It is the result of an imaginative mutual redescription of its constituent terms and succeeds through its dialectical "both-and" in respecting the alterity of its terms while creating new shared references between them.

So how does interstitial theology build on these twin pillars? If the conversation of religions is understood through the metaphorical model, religious traditions can be usefully compared and contrasted without homogenizing

14. There is some debate in the literature as to whether Voloshinov is a pen name for Mikhail Bakhtin.

them. It will do this through the construction of interreligious, or rather interstitial, metaphors which will create liminal hybrid references between the compared traditions' accepted horizons. What interstitial theology does is hybridize religions through the redescriptive power of metaphor. A simple example might be the notion of a "jesukatha," which brings together the Hindu tradition of scriptural recitation *(katha)* with a Christian worship service. The effect is not only to compare and contrast Christian views of what it is to worship with Hindu notions of the salvific efficacy of sound, but also to create a new hybrid reference which both reflects and creates a novel religious experience. Such experiences speak to the growing number of people in multireligious societies who find themselves between religious traditions, with feet firmly in two or more traditions. Importantly, it also creates new options for its parent traditions, and this is where we finally come back to the problem of the reluctant participant in dialogue.

What I propose is that in the face of silence or hostility, when the only options seem to be reversion to monologue or self-imposed silence, one other possibility is for willing participants of dialogue to consciously hybridize their religious positions or even themselves. Through the use of interstitial theology one can consciously and carefully seek to hybridize one's own religious commitments, practices, and beliefs with those of the reluctant other. In so doing one creates a novel religious location liminal to oneself and the other as well as redescribing the other's and one's own positions in order to contribute new options in the service of religious conversation.

This is, I believe, a fairly radical proposal. What I am arguing for is that when the terrorist refuses to engage in open, honest conversation, due either to contrary ideological commitments or mere disinterest, it may be one's responsibility to carry on the conversation oneself. This is not simply to play the other part in some perverse religious pantomime, but something much more significant — it is nothing less than allowing the other's tradition to interrogate, supplement, edit, magnify, or even significantly change one's own tradition in a hybridizing redescription. It becomes the job of the dialogians to create an intermediary position between themselves and the reluctant other. And this would not be a mere intellectual exercise but would need to create new options for living.[15] It is therefore not a simple, onetime affair, but entering into a pro-

15. This is an important point, though one I cannot develop fully here. Interstitial metaphors refer, most correctly, to the metaphor's poet or reader, for that is the locus of the metaphorical twist in its dialectic. If metaphor did not, in this way, have the possibility of self-transformation, it would not reach beyond the logos into *bios*.

Metaphors are the basis of symbols, and symbols are where metaphors connect language to the world of lived experience. Because the unit of metaphor, and hence interstitial theology, is

cess whereby one risks comfortable certainties for the sake of the other, and this brings forth several questions, not least the problem of motivation.

Returning to the question of impetus, why would anyone seek to do this? Surely to let go of one's own religious commitments for the indeterminacies of a strange hybrid would negate the very reasons one sought dialogue in the first place — and for what? — a mutant hybrid of one's own deeply felt religious commitments with those of a silent or reluctant other? How would one know that what one is hybridizing with is even remotely close to the tradition of one's silent partner? Is this not simply a muddled way of creating even more confusion?

There are, I suggest, religious and nonreligious reasons why one would wish to lay oneself open to hybridization. One religious example of such hybridization might be found in the kenotic incarnation of Jesus, to take a Christian example (though the example of a bodhisattva also comes to mind). The self-emptying required in interstitial hybridization such as I have described has a close analogue, I would argue, in Jesus' kenotic descent into human nature. As I understand the doctrine, *kenosis* is not a self-denial in the sense of complete eradication, but rather a conscious opening up to the other in order to partially become the other. The God-man is precisely the kind of interstitial hybrid required when one party is trying to communicate a new option for living to an obstinate partner. In self-emptying in this way, the divine condescension both changes its own nature and creates a new option for its partner — God becomes human in order that humans may discover their divine likeness. Interstitial theology can thus create the possibility of a redemptive option for the other — one which may be freely accepted or refused, but one which is required if any progress is to be made.

But what about the problem of religious syncretism, or the possibility that one loses oneself altogether? I suggest that the dialectic of metaphor ensures that neither becomes a significant problem. As metaphor always begins in otherness, and for its redescription to work requires this otherness to be conserved, the worry that one loses the self in an interstitial hybrid is groundless. It is only through metaphor that the possibilities of hybridization are created and thus, as with any metaphor, one's own starting point must be conserved in its full alterity. What happens to the self is that it is redescribed, not annihilated, so there is little worry that one becomes something else altogether. Identity is con-

---

the statement rather than the word, interreligious comparisons, under the model I am proposing, avoid abstraction into a mere intellectual exercise. Using interstitial theological metaphors ensures that interreligious comparisons are not plucked, threadlike, from the fabric of life, but rather as if a whole corner of the fabric were grasped by its edge.

served so that the self grows rather than being replaced. The problem of syncretism is also a nonstarter since, apart from legitimate analyses of syncretism as primarily a political rather than an ontological issue,[16] metaphorical redescription may also be understood to stretch the semantic horizon of one's tradition but not to supplant it. Interstitial theology is not a method of grafting and absorbing the other onto oneself, but a form of reorganization, a re-creation of oneself in a fundamentally artistic or imaginative act. This is wholly appropriate and in keeping with contemporary discussions of identity as "oneself as another." Worries about syncretism ignore the accretions necessary in one's own development and owe more to eighteenth-century fear than anything else.

There is legitimate worry, however, in whether or not what one is hybridizing with bears any resemblance to the tradition of one's partner. Of course, without the other's direct participation one may find that one's own attempts caricature the other's tradition. To some extent this is inevitable, but absolute fidelity to the other's tradition is not necessarily needed, nor, it must be said, is it possible even with the full cooperation of the other. In any conversation one will always only grasp a similitude of the positions represented — even one's own. Certainly great care and much time is required when one seeks to represent the other, but this is the same kind of care and respect shown to one's own tradition, not different. To repeat, interstitial theology as a hermeneutic of dialogue is neither easy nor quick, and what it produces cannot be predicted, but its potential for creating novel, liminal theological positions makes the risk acceptable.

Before moving to secular reasons for embarking on the process of kenotic hybridization, I will briefly consider the question of truth with respect to interstitial theology. One might ask what, if anything, of religious truth is got by interstitial theology? That is, if it redescribes religious traditions through metaphorical hybridization with extrinsic faiths, what status do any novel insights bear? There are at least two possibilities here. The more careful response is that the religious truth of interstitial insights must ultimately be tested on pragmatic grounds. I avoid discussion of correspondence with reality as well as coherence with given traditions because, as these insights will be novel, they will likely not cohere simply with received wisdom, nor, as interstitial references are liminal to each tradition, will such truths correspond in any straightforward way to one or another religion's horizon. Rather, interstitial hybrids must be seen to bear fruit for those who encounter or become them. I have not the space

16. Rosalind Shaw and Charles Stuart, ed., *Syncretism/Antisyncretism: The Politics of Religious Synthesis* (London: Routledge, 1994).

to pursue this point here, but this view of the truth of interstitial theology has many affinities to what Rorty calls edifying philosophy.[17] But there is one other, more speculative response. Interstitial theology results in greater pluralization, as more hybrids are formed and found successful. By the principle of plenitude,[18] the greater number of redescriptions created for a given religious tradition is a good per se. If God loves variety, then the truths of interstitial theology may also lie in its ability to provide further instances of acceptable and authentic religious lives.

So, having considered, however briefly, the question of religious truth and interstitial theology, let us move, finally, to the secular basis for such dialogue.

Having a nonreligious motivation for interreligious dialogue may seem strange to some, but it is important to have a nonexplicitly religious basis for hybridizing with the other. My example of *kenosis* above, or even one based on bodhisattvas, would obviously speak most eloquently to Christians and Buddhists respectively, so we need a more "generic" motive, so to speak, if my proposal is to have greater usefulness.

For this I turn to the work of Emmanuel Levinas, whose ethics based on the face of the other give a clarion call for an ethics which makes supererogatory *kenosis* a first responsibility for all morality. While I have too little space to fully develop his thought here, we can focus on the fact that Levinas seeks to ground subjectivity in the other. Our very being as a subject is construed by others, and thus we have at the very core of who we are an ethical relationship — nay, an ethical duty.[19] Indeed, this relationship with the "otherness" of the other — what Levinas calls *the face* — brings me as a subject into being and demands my ethical regard. Levinas writes: "I am responsible for the Other without waiting for reciprocity. . . . It is precisely insofar as the relationship between the Other and me is not reciprocal that I am in subjection to the Other; and I am subject essentially in this sense."[20]

Levinas argues that the creation of our subjectivity relies on the other, and this constitution entails and demands responsibility to and for the other in a nonreciprocal way. This is particularly apropos for interstitial theology as it is precisely in the redescription of our own religious subjectivity that the ethical call

---

17. See Richard Rorty, *Philosophy and the Mirror of Nature* (Princeton: Princeton University Press, 1979), pp. 365-78.

18. See Heim's useful discussion of this principle with respect to interreligious dialogue in his *Salvations,* pp. 164-71.

19. Emmanuel Levinas, *Ethics and Infinity: Conversations with Phillipe Nemo,* trans. R. A. Cohen (Pittsburgh: Duquesne University Press, 1985), pp. 95-101.

20. Levinas, p. 98.

of the face beckons. Levinas claims more than that we are duty-bound to take on aspects of the others' selves. He suggests that in ethics we have already done so.

So let me recap where I have taken this argument. I began by considering some of the difficulties faced by contemporary dialogians through the use of a fanciful scenario. We need to create a new method of interreligious dialogue if we are to respond to arguments that our current models are merely expurgating colonialist sin but repeating it in doing so, that they systematically flatten difference and cling to frail and outmoded conceptual and linguistic categories. I then suggested a mode of dialogue which, I argued, succeeds in maintaining difference while creating new liminal references through which to continue the conversation of religions. Interstitial theology was then put to work to respond to one of the most difficult and now pressing problems faced by dialogians — how to speak to the reluctant neighbor. My proposal is to use interstitial theology to construct liminal, redescriptive hybrids of oneself to both create options for the other's religious *experience* as well as, possibly, to further the pluralization of religious forms of life. I then gave two motives for such supererogatory *kenosis,* one derived from the example of God's condescension in the incarnation and the other based on Levinas's highly nuanced view of subjectivity and ethics. While I have raced through these ideas far too quickly, I trust my readers will not respond through silence.

# Dialogue for Life: Feminist Approaches to Interfaith Dialogue

HELENE EGNELL

Feminism is, according to Ursula King, "the missing dimension in the dialogue of religions."[1] Interfaith dialogue is mostly, at least on the official level, carried out by men, and gender issues have rarely been on the agenda.

Likewise, interfaith dialogue has not played a great part in the development of feminist theology, as Rita M. Gross has lamented.[2] Feminist theology has not dealt explicitly with interfaith issues to a great extent, and there has been a surprising lack of awareness of the importance of dialogue between Christian feminists and those of other faiths.

During the last decade, however, Christian feminist theology has increasingly taken account of the reality of other religions. There is an awareness of the demands of a pluralist society in the literature; interfaith conferences are arranged; and networks for women in theological research and pastoral work are consciously set up as interreligious enterprises. Examples are the African Circle of Concerned Women Theologians, the European Society for Women in Theological Research, and the Initiative Conference of European Women Theologians.

In this paper I will argue that to a certain extent, feminist theology and theology of religions deal with the same issues, and pose similar challenges to the churches. They also pose challenges to each other, which could enrich theological creativity in both fields if taken seriously.

---

1. Ursula King, "Feminism: The Missing Dimension in the Dialogue of Religions" (Faculty of Theology, University of Oslo, Digital Archive, http://www.tf.uio.no/lo/king0198.html).

2. Rita M. Gross, "Feminist Theology as Theology of Religions," *Feminist Theology*, no. 26 (January 2001).

*Helene Egnell*

## Common Challenges to Theology
## from Feminism and Interfaith Dialogue

There are parallels in feminism and interfaith dialogue, regarding issues dealt with as well as in methodology. Marjorie Hewitt Suchocki has pointed out that there is a correlation between religious imperialism and sexism. "Absolutizing one religion, such that it becomes normative for all others, is a dynamic with clear parallels to sexism, whereby one gender is established as the norm for human existence. Therefore the critique of sexism can be extended as a critique of religious imperialism."[3]

This implies that feminist theology and a theology of religions has a common task to criticize absolutism, and would gain much in discovering the common mechanisms behind religious absolutism and sexism.

Diane M. Brewster has argued that the importance of contextuality, the demand that people must be free to define themselves, and the stress on relationships are three principles that interfaith dialogue and feminism have in common.[4] She further argues that both feminism and interfaith dialogue challenge theology on two central points: our understanding of the life and work of Jesus of Nazareth, and the limits of our "God-language."

Christology is apparently a major issue in these areas, though from different viewpoints. In feminist theology the question put by Rosemary Radford Ruether, "Can a male savior save women?" still has not got a definite answer. Not only has the maleness of Jesus, when used as an argument against the ordination of women, been a problem, but other ingredients of traditional Christology have been questioned by feminists, for instance, the idea of a father sacrificing his son (divine child abuse, as someone has put it) and the concept of redemptive suffering that has been used to keep women in abusive relationships.

Consequently a lot of energy has been spent on defining and formulating why Jesus Christ in spite of everything is central to the faith of Christian feminists. Solutions include the rediscovery of the Wisdom tradition, where Jesus is seen as the prophet/incarnation of the female Wisdom principle rather than the male Word. Kwok Pui Lan has highlighted the "hybrid" nature of the Christ concept, claiming that every generation must answer Jesus' question, "Who do you say that I am?"[5]

3. Marjorie Hewitt Suchocki, "In Search of Justice: Religious Pluralism from a Feminist Perspective," in *The Myth of Christian Uniqueness*, ed. Hick and Knitter (Maryknoll, N.Y.: Orbis, 1987), p. 150.

4. Diane M. Brewster, "Feminism and Interfaith Dialogue: Some Parallels and Challenges," *Month* 24, no. 9/10 (1991): 400-404.

5. Kwok Pui Lan, "Feminist Theology at the Dawn of the Millennium: Remembering the Past, Dreaming the Future," *Feminist Theology*, no. 27 (May 2001): 6-20.

These solutions could have significance also for interfaith dialogue, where the problem is how to express the uniqueness of Jesus in terms neither of confrontation nor of fulfillment.[6] The Wisdom concept opens up for a pluralistic approach to other religions in general, as well as provides a point of departure for a common search for wisdom.[7] Kwok Pui Lan gives examples of answers to the question "Who do you say that I am" that are inspired by indigenous Asian religious traditions, like "the feminine principle of Shakti" or "a priest of Han."[8]

The limits of God-language is another area that has engaged feminist theologians. If God is neither male nor female, it is tantamount to idolatry to make male images of God the norm, it has been claimed. Sallie McFague has made us aware of the metaphorical nature of God-language in *Models of God* and *Metaphorical Theology*. Thus feminist theologians explore which metaphors can be used for the divine within the limits of a Christian context. Likewise, interfaith dialogue forces the question of the nature of religious language and symbols, their contextuality and ultimate inadequacy. Brewster puts the question as follows: "many of us involved in interfaith dialogue find much to be treasured in other religious traditions that we encounter. What can we use and still remain Christians?"[9]

## Challenges of Interfaith Dialogue to Feminist Theology

Taking the issues of interfaith dialogue seriously could help feminist theology explore deeper concepts that are already central to it, such as the principles of contextuality, self-definition, and relationship mentioned above by Brewster. There is already a growing awareness of the complexity of reality, where male/female is only one strand in a web of race, class, ethnic, and other affiliations, but the issue of religious plurality could help deepen this awareness. Contact with feminists from other religious and cultural contexts could also prevent white Western feminists from falling into the colonialist trap of condemning other religious or cultural habits from a Western perspective. The ideal of letting people define themselves is put to the test here.

Is a pluralist position the only one possible for a feminist engaged in interfaith dialogue? Gross argues that it is, saying, "It is inconceivable that a femi-

6. Alan Race, *Interfaith Encounter* (London: SCM Press, 2001), p. 71.
7. I have developed these ideas in my M.Phil. dissertation, "Sophia in Interfaith Dialogue" (Irish School of Ecumenics/University of Dublin, 1997).
8. Kwok, p. 17.
9. Brewster, p. 404.

nist theologian would go through all the heartache of being excluded from her own religion and doing the theological work required to include herself back in, only to turn around and make exclusive or inclusive truth claims about the religion that excluded her!"[10]

I don't find that self-evident. It should be perfectly possible to arrive at a "feminist Barthian" standpoint and claim that "religion is patriarchal" while revelation through Jesus, Wisdom incarnate, alone is liberating. Or to be an inclusivist, claiming that Jesus is the supreme expression of Shakti, Prajna, or whatever feminine religious principles may be relevant.

However, I think Gross has a point when she says that since a major value of feminist theology is to include the voices that have not been heard, to widen the circle, to learn how to welcome diversity, it makes no sense for those values to stop when they hit the boundary of one's own religion. The necessity of "widening the canon" is an important concern of feminist theology — but other religious traditions have not been among the sources commonly used. On the other hand, Gross warns against "inappropriate appropriation," when symbols are thoughtlessly borrowed from other traditions without proper knowledge of their original settings. Parts of the feminist spirituality movement have been guilty of indiscriminate and unauthorized borrowing from Native American traditions.

## Challenges of Feminism to Interfaith Dialogue

As does feminist theology in general, feminist approaches to interfaith dialogue include a deconstructive as well as a constructive project. Unlike most other dialogue settings, the participants generally do not come with the presupposition that their own traditions are sufficient. On the contrary, they come with the deeply felt insight that all religious traditions include elements that are oppressive for women, and they seek to identify the sources of oppression, as well as the means to change the traditions, together.

Ursula King has noted that while the Chicago *Declaration toward a Global Ethic* says there are "condemnable forms of patriarchy" all over the world, "no connection [is] made with the patriarchal exploitation and subordination of women by the religions themselves."[11]

Women in interfaith dialogue have fewer "vested interests" in their religious institutions, and thus are able to articulate more freely their personal feel-

10. Gross, p. 89.
11. King, "Feminism," p. 8.

ings and opinions. Thereby they can challenge "malestream" interfaith dialogue to a critical evaluation of the oppressive aspects of religions.

There also seems to be a tendency to acknowledge conflict in dialogue carried out among women more than in that among men.[12] This is remarkable, as in general women are considered more prone to avoid conflict and seek harmony than men. Maura O'Neill suggests that the reason is that in the areas of religion and philosophy, women have been silenced for so long that they take the opportunity to express their anger and deal with it when they dialogue among themselves. I don't find this entirely convincing. I would rather suggest that it is in relation to men that women seek to avoid conflict, but can engage in conflict among themselves, but I don't know if this can be supported by scientific research.

There are also areas of conflict that are specific for a feminist interfaith dialogue. The most obvious example is Jewish-Christian dialogue, where Jewish women have accused Christian feminists of anti-Semitism when they too easily have contrasted Old Testament misogyny with the liberating message of the gospel.[13] Another is the critique from Third World women against the perceived imperialism of Western feminists when they criticize oppression of women in non-Western settings,[14] as well as differing opinions among Third World women themselves on issues regarding cultural practices.[15] When these conflicts are acknowledged and dealt with, conflict can be an asset, an opportunity to develop respect for the other, and a source of growth and insight.[16]

This tendency to acknowledge conflict could be interpreted as an outcome of the stress on relationship and personal experience in feminist theology. Kate McCarthy argues that feminist theories on "women's experience" offer "resources for a new approach to [religious pluralism] that is both exciting and timely."[17] "Women's experience" has been a key word in feminist theology from the beginning, and has developed from a naively universalist concept to an awareness of the complexity of women's experiences depending on class, race, culture, sexual-

---

12. Maura O'Neill, *Women Speaking, Women Listening: Women in Interreligious Dialogue* (Maryknoll, N.Y.: Orbis, 1990), pp. 94ff.; Diana L. Eck and Devaki Jain, *Speaking of Faith: Cross-Cultural Perspectives on Women, Religion, and Social Change* (London: Women's Press, 1986), pp. 12ff.

13. Katharina von Kellenbach, *Anti-Judaism in Feminist Religious Writings* (Atlanta: Scholars, 1994).

14. See, for example, Kwok, p. 10.

15. See, for example, Musimibi Kanyoro, "Engendered Communal Theology," *Feminist Theology*, no. 27 (May 2001): 39.

16. O'Neill, pp. 95-96.

17. Kate McCarthy, "Women's Experience as a Hermeneutical Key to a Christian Theology of Religions," *Studies in Interreligious Dialogue* 6, no. 2 (1996): 163-73.

ity, and other factors. This grappling with complexity could in itself be an important contribution to interfaith dialogue. However, in spite of differences, there are aspects of women's experience that remain constant across cultures. McCarthy highlights three of these as relevant for interfaith dialogue: the experience of otherness, a plurality of social location, and an embodied spirituality.

Otherness is a theme that has been developed in feminist theology: the experience of being other, excluded in church and theology as well as in society, of being other than the (male) norm. This otherness is made into a resource, which could be especially useful to a theology of religions, which has to account "for otherness without subsuming it or annihilating it, and without abandoning one's own distinctive religious identity."[18] One could also explore the parallelism between "woman" as other and "the pagan" as other in theology.

Feminist theologians have developed an awareness of having multiple identities. To define oneself, as Carter Heyward does, as a "white Anglo Christian lesbian priest and academic,"[19] is to belong to several different communities that interact and can be in tension with each other. This consciousness of multiple social locations could be a "foundation for a new kind of affirmation of religious difference."[20]

McCarthy further argues that the pattern of embodied spirituality in feminist theology could facilitate an "experientially grounded rather than conceptual inter-religious exchange."[21]

An experientially grounded interfaith dialogue must build upon relations between the participants. Women participating in interfaith dialogue have often insisted that the dialogue should start in a sharing of personal experiences and life stories. It is significant that Gross and Ruether's "Buddhist-Christian conversation" in their *Religious Feminism and the Future of the Planet* starts with the authors telling their "Autobiographical Routes to/Roots of Dialogue."

"Hearing into speech" has been a key phrase in feminist consciousness-raising groups, coined first by Nelle Morton. It is essential to create an atmosphere of listening, to enable people who have been silenced to speak from their own experience and not what conforms to conventional expectations. The experience of being listened to in its turn creates a willingness to listen. In interfaith dialogue this could help heighten the awareness that each participant comes with her/his own understanding that might not be identical with that of other adherents to the same religion, or for that matter, to other women.

18. McCarthy, p. 165.
19. Quoted in McCarthy, p. 165.
20. McCarthy, p. 167.
21. McCarthy, p. 169.

Relation is another important concept in feminist theology. It has been developed in the area of ethics, where Carol Gilligan has found that women develop a relation-centered ethics in contrast to the stress on rules and autonomy in male ethics. Relation is also a soteriological and ontological concept where "right relation" or "mutual relation" is a definition of salvation, and God is understood in relational terms: "Where there is no mutual relationship, there is no human experience of God."[22] Such an understanding of ultimate reality as relational should be fundamental to a theology of religions.

Likewise, Mercy Amba Oduyoye characterizes African women's theology as a theology of relations, from which follows that as it is developed in consciously multicultural and multireligious contexts, it is culture-sensitive and intentionally dialogue-oriented.[23]

The title of Gross and Ruether's book, *Religious Feminism and the Future of the Planet,* is significant. It indicates that in interfaith dialogue in a feminist key, dogmatic issues are not in focus, but it is more concerned with what contributes to the survival of the planet, peace, justice, and the well-being of women and men.

The dialogue, besides critiquing the oppressive elements of religions, is about sharing what is liberating and life-enhancing in the respective traditions.

For many feminist theologians from the Third World, interfaith dialogue is also an intrafaith dialogue. They appreciate the spiritual heritage from the indigenous religions, which were there before Christianity, and they are not afraid to pick the liberating elements from Christianity and indigenous religions in a kind of "life-affirming syncretism," as Chung Hyun Kyung puts it, while discarding oppressive and life-denying elements. Chung claims that this is what Asian women have been doing all along: "Since women were excluded from the public process of determining the meaning of their religion, they were free to carve out a religion on their own, without the constraints of orthodoxy. Their 'imposed freedom' allowed them to develop in private a religious organic whole that enabled them to survive and liberated them in the midst of their struggle for full humanity."[24]

Instead of looking down on these women, despising their "ignorance" and condemning their "syncretism," Chung elevates them to models for how theology should be done and even tries to reclaim the word "syncretism" from its negative connotations.

22. Chung Hyun Kyung, quoted in McCarthy, p. 170.

23. Mercy Amba Oduyoye, *Introducing African Women's Theology* (Sheffield: Sheffield Academic Press, 2001), p. 17.

24. Chung Hyun Kyung, "Following Naked Dancing and Long Dreaming," in *Inheriting Our Mothers' Gardens*, ed. Letty Russell et al. (Louisville: Westminster, 1989), p. 67.

One characteristic of the emerging spirituality of Asian women is a celebration of plurality, says Aruna Gnanadason. "Asian women of all faiths together are engaged in a common spiritual search for a new society. They transcend with ease narrow divisions of faith, caste, cultural identity, and ideology to reflect and act on issues of importance."[25]

Gnanadason talks of a "spiritual search for a new society." This holistic approach, which refuses to divide reality into a "spiritual" and a "material" realm, is typical for feminist theology, as for liberation theology in general. And the "issues of importance" to be reflected upon are probably not Christology or eschatology, but rather trafficking in women, environmental pollution, or the debt crisis. Dogmatic issues are considered important only insofar as they can provide tools for creating a just society and mutual relations, or contribute to the survival of the planet.

Paul Knitter, Marjorie Suchocki, and others have suggested that "justice" be the common norm to evaluate religious traditions in interfaith dialogue. For many feminist theologians it seems that "life" is the key word.

A feminist interfaith dialogue is a dialogue of life. The words "life-affirming," "life-enhancing," "survival-centered" echo through the writings of especially Third World feminist theologians like Chung Hyun Kyung, Mary John Mananzan, and Mercy Amba Oduyoye. It is a celebration of God as the life-giver, and the criterion for judging diverse expressions of religion is whether they are life-enhancing or life-denying.

## Conclusion

We have seen that feminist theology contains resources that could enhance interfaith dialogue. Among them are concepts like relationality, otherness, contextuality, the freedom to define oneself, hearing into speech, widening the canon, as well as feminist discourse on Christology and religious language. On the other hand, feminist theology also could benefit from taking interfaith issues more seriously.

Feminist theologians, especially from the Third World, also seem to suggest a norm for judging the validity of religious practices that has to do with what enhances and affirms life.

25. Aruna Gnanadason, "Women and Spirituality in Asia," in *Feminist Theology from the Third World,* ed. Ursula King (SPCK and Orbis, 1996), pp. 351-60.

# Theology in Dialogue with New Age or the Neospiritual Milieu

OLE SKJERBÆK MADSEN

How to develop a theology which is a good instrument to communicate Christian faith in the dialogue with the new spiritualities — often called New Age?

The best-articulated parts of the new spiritualities are inspired by the theosophical movements of the nineteenth and twentieth centuries or have developed into a *Geisteswissensschaft* — or a kind of religio-scientific system of thought — with roots in the esoteric currents of Western spirituality and philosophy. Wouter J. Hanegraaff defines New Age religion thus: "The New Age Religion is the cultic milieu having become conscious of itself, in the later 1970s, as constituting a more or less unified 'movement.' All manifestations of this movement are characterized by a popular western culture criticism expressed in terms of secularized esotericism."[1]

If the church should engage in a dialogue with New Age religion and the new spiritualities in a broader sense, it should take as a starting point what is common to esotericism as such, study some of its roots, and develop a theology with respect to the concerns of esotericism — whether it, in this procedure, finds a correction of its own theology, its own worldview (which is often estranged not only from its biblical roots but also from parts of its own spiritual traditions due to a secularist orientation), and its own spiritual practice, or criticizes trends in New Age thought, practice, and worldview which are in conflict with what is understood as the received truth in Jesus Christ.

Common themes in esotericism, according to Antoine Faivre and Hanegraaff:

---

1. Wouter J. Hanegraaff, *New Age Religion and Western Culture: Esotericism in the Mirror of Secular Thought* (Leiden: Brill, 1996), p. 522.

a. *Correspondences,* symbolic or actual, are believed to exist between all parts of the visible and the invisible universe. . . . Everything is a sign . . . the 'Book of Nature' contains the same truths as revealed in the Bible. . . .

b. *Living nature.* . . . In this context, nature is perceived as a living *milieu,* a dynamic network of sympathies and antipathies. . . .

c. *Imagination and Mediations.* The idea of correspondences implies the possibility of mediation between the higher and the lower world(s), by way of ritual, symbols, angels, intermediate spirits, etcetera. *Imaginatio* . . . is regarded as an 'organ of the soul' . . . (and) the main instrument for attaining *gnosis.*

d. *Experience of Transmutation.* (This is the experiential dimension of esotericism.)

The following two characteristics may be added:

e. *The praxis of Concordance.* (An example of this is the belief in a 'Secret Doctrine' which is the esoteric content of all exoteric religions.)

f. A final component concerns the *transmission* of esoteric teachings from master to disciple, by way of pre-established channels of initiation.[2]

These themes reoccur in New Age and the neospiritual milieu, but one must take into consideration that the framework in which New Age, due to a process of secularization, deals with the traditional themes of esotericism is

- a weak this-worldliness
- holism
- evolutionism
- psychologization of religion and sacralization of psychology
- expectations of a coming New Age[3]

## Spiritual Conflict

The vast majority of Christian literature on New Age and new religions stresses the differences between Christianity and the new religions — sometimes even demonizing New Age beliefs and practices and warning against them. The

2. Hanegraaff, pp. 398-400.
3. Hanegraaff, pp. 365-66.

common roots are seldom taken into consideration as an opening for mutual understanding, and the New Age criticism of dogmatic Christianity is considered enmity rather than a challenge to reconsider the expressions of our faith and spiritual practice. Of course, there are many areas of spiritual conflict, as New Age spirituality meets Christianity and vice versa, which must be addressed in the process of developing a theology in dialogue with the new spiritualities.[4] In a paper at the consultation "Deliver Us from Evil," held in Nairobi in August 2000, I pointed to some of these areas of spiritual conflict.

## Area of Conflict: Alternative Culture

Since the seekers' milieu is to be understood as an alternative culture, the first area of spiritual conflict is to be found on the cultural level, including politics, economy, and science, including the criticism of dualistic and reductionistic tendencies in "dogmatic Christianity" and materialistic scientific ways of thinking.

The danger for the church is to become hypnotized by the apparent criticism of the church and of our most precious doctrines, excluding ourselves from a constructive dialogue and cooperation on the many areas where we share common interests. Materialistic reductionism in the name of science is also our "enemy." It is a real temptation to avoid engaging in the work for world peace and justice, for the protection of nature, for animal rights, for a sound ecology in order not to be classified New Age or for fear of the church being infiltrated by New Age through these people of good will.

The second danger in this area is that culture will only be influenced by New Age paradigms and paradigm shifts and thus lose its contacts with its spiritual roots if Christians, for fear of being identified with New Age, withdraw from any contact with the new spiritual milieu and its ideologists as well as its seekers. If we as Christians are not present to modern seekers and in an open dialogue, sharing the dreams of a healed earth as a common quest, we will not be able to give a biblical perspective of holism, of how God through his creative

4. As an example of the more moderate and honest Christian critic of esotericism and occultism, I will refer to Håkan Arlebrand, *Det ukendte. Om okkultisme I en ny tidsalder* (Copenhagen, 1993). Other Christian books on New Age which are well informed though critical are: Douglas R. Groothuis, *Unmasking the New Age* (Illinois, 1987); Elliot Miller, *A Crash Course on the New Age Movement* (Grand Rapids, 1989); John Warwick Montgomery, *Principalities and Powers* (Minneapolis, 1981). More paranoid Christian books are Constance Cumbey, *The Hidden Dangers of the Rainbow* (1983), and Texe Marrs, *Dark Secrets of the New Age* (Illinois) (Danish edition, 1990).

Word, the divine Logos, ordered the universe so as to find its meaning, goal, and consummation in Christ, who thus establishes the logos of creation, and of how sin disrupted this logos of creation, and of how we are in need of the same Christ for salvation and restoration of creation.

The third danger in this area has to do with a more or less conscious identification with the paradigms of the new spirituality. The conscious identification happens if a secularized church which is in need of spirituality indiscriminately adopts any religious practice which happens to fill the spiritual void of its members and clergy. But as noted by A. Scott Moreau, it is also a danger for evangelicals, perhaps unconsciously. I quote: "The Culture, and together with it the evangelical church, has moved in a spiritual direction in the sense that personal spiritual powers, once out of sight in our worldview, have now come into prominence. In one respect we can rejoice — a spiritual approach to the world is more in tune with the biblical worldview than an agnostic (or atheistic) scientific materialism. In another respect, however, we must be aware of the danger of shifting too far into what may be termed a functional evangelical animism and a corresponding set of 'Christian magical' practices."[5]

## Area of Conflict: Anthropology, Worldview, and Ethic

In the new spiritual milieu man is understood from an evolutionary point of view. Man is understood as consciousness or as a soul learning in a long process of transformation, traveling through many lifetimes and in many incarnations to true self-consciousness, realizing his/her ultimate oneness with God, life, all that is. Man is thus his/her own savior who may or may not need the help of spiritual masters or guides. Man is often understood as a microcosm who, like a fragment of a holographic plate, contains the whole picture. This is exemplified in the use of astrology. In the New Age worldview this means that holism is not just the harmony of body, soul, and mind/spirit, but tends to be monism. The antidualistic stance of New Age means a dissolution of the opposites male-female, good-evil, true-false, etc. The Christian will see a danger in this kind of relativism in the area of morals and truth. What will be the consequences for society if it abandons absolute values? Will this relativism endanger human responsibility? We need gifts of discernment, wisdom, and love to maneuver in this area. For example, New

5. A. Scott Moreau, "Religious Borrowing as a Two-Way Street: An Introduction to Animistic Tendencies in the Euro–North American Context," in *Christianity and the Religions: A Biblical Theology of World Religions*, ed. Edward Rommen and Harold Netland (Pasadena, Calif., 1995), p. 172.

Agers will understand our concept of salvation and forgiveness as moral laziness and irresponsibility, that we will not take responsibility for our own lives, whereas they see the concepts of karma and reincarnation as an expression of learning through experience and thus taking responsibility for one's own life. How to communicate our concern? How to explain that through recognition and confession of sin we really take responsibility, and that we, through forgiveness, are reinstalled in the freedom of the children of God and are able to engage fully in loving care for our neighbor and for our fellow creatures without losing our energy in the effort of saving ourselves? This is truly an area of spiritual conflict, because human longings for wholeness and for personal and social transformation are veiled in the illusions of monism and evolution.

### Area of Conflict: Religion

In this area we are confronted with both practical and conceptual sides of New Age religion. I want to point to just a few areas of conflict.

The most important spiritual conflict with New Age and the modern Western seekers has to do with conscious or unconscious teachings which obscure, twist, or contradict the saving truths of God's self-revelation in his eternal Logos and his Spirit, in creation, in the history of salvation, and in the Bible. It is very obvious in the understanding of Christ in that part of New Age which is influenced by Theosophy. Christ, or Maitreya, as he is often called, is together with the Buddha in this context understood as the leader of the Hierarchy, master of the second ray or emanation of the Solar Logos, the god of our solar system; Jesus is a lower master who was overshadowed by the Christ; and there are many male and female masters in the Hierarchy.[6]

---

6. As an illustration of this conflict and what to discuss in an open dialogue with New Agers, I quote the conclusions of my paper "The Maitreya-Theosophy of Asger Lorentsen and the Shan-Movement," in *New Religions and New Religiosity,* ed. Eileen Barker and Margit Warburg (Aarhus, 1998), pp. 191-203:

> The Theosophy of Asger Lorentsen and the Shan-movement is a challenge to Christians because of its revivalist language, as, for example, its use of the heart metaphor brings it close to revivalism's "Jesus in the heart." The fascination with Jesus is strong within the movement, and Asger Lorentsen even wants his new work to be done under the Master Jesus.
>
> In this interest in Jesus we have a good starting point for a dialogue, in an exchange of the experiences of healing, salvation, and peace. But this does not exclude an honest talk about Jesus as the Christ/Messiah: First, there is no valid argument from the scriptures in which the word Christ originates to understand "Christ" as anything other than

What are the sources of these teachings? Often they are channeled from
the entities of the Hierarchy through the minds of human channels; sometimes

the title and the function of the promised saviour, born into the family of the great king
David.

Secondly, in the experience of the Christian and in the evidence of The new Testament Jesus and Christ cannot be separated. Thirdly, it is unhistorical to use Christ synonymously for the Maitreya. It is not true to either Jewish/Christian or Buddhist tradition. Seen from a Christian viewpoint, what is Christ if he is not the historic Jesus? It is not satisfying to the Christian that the Maitreya Theosophist states that his sources are not historic, but esoteric.

What is also challenging is the understanding of the planetary or cosmic meaning of the death of Jesus on the cross. In the revivalist Christian tradition, we have concentrated on what Jesus has done for me; but with their cosmological considerations the Maitreya Theosophists challenge us to take up the Christology of the letters of Paul to the Ephesians and the Colossians.

According to the Shan movement, the redemptive work of the Christ is the transformative energy emanating from the Solar Logos; but it is not an active saving act from outside fallen humanity. It is rather a release of what is hidden in man, since he is essentially a minor aspect of the divine. The Christ is an archetype of the human soul. The grace of god means, in an occult sense, that the individual soul will get the help he is ready to open up to and receive. Thus the energy of the crucifixion is not redemptive in a Christian sense, but is facilitating the self-redemptive work of the soul.

This is a consequence of what I shall call the impersonal understanding of the divine. I know that Asger Lorentsen will say that god is not experienced in an impersonal way, because he/she is experienced through beings who are like god to us. However, the ultimate source of life is not conceptualised by the Theosophists in personal terms, just as human beings have to abandon personality to be made whole to themselves. The Christian experience, however, is that of a personal encounter with God, a communicating with him and a resting with him in adoration.

I can of course see other areas for an honest conversation on the contents of our respective spiritualities, experiences and faiths. I could mention a talk on eschatology and the meaning of history, question what man is, and how to discern true and false channelling or overshadowing, and how cognition is possible if creation from the highest point of view is illusion.

I don't consider the members of Shan movement to be enemies. I see in them brothers or sisters who like me are on their way to God — or, at least, are searching for him. I want an honest dialogue with them in which we dare to recognise the differences in our beliefs and that our truths cannot be reconciled without violating our basic assumptions and experiences. Such an honest dialogue about religious truth will help us to avoid slander. It will also help us to be honest about where we see the dangers of getting lost in illusions and seduction. An honest dialogue will help us to learn more about ourselves from the critical viewpoint of others. What shall we do if Asger Lorentsen is right in what he wrote to me august 1992?

"The lack of sanctifying light in the churches make many people seek the inner way at other places, where the experience of an inner reality is stronger."

they are conceived through visions or other intuitive means or faculties, in sudden mystical experiences or a growing awareness of the spiritual dimensions of the world facilitated through meditation. We have every reason to be suspicious of sources of spiritual information which speak of another Christ than Jesus. In January 2000 I thus heard a lecture on the Holy Grail in which the speaker said that Jesus, in a former incarnation, was known as Melchisedek and in fact was the Babylonian god Ea, who created the first man out of clay but now had to bring into order what he disturbed when he, through a wrong warning, hindered man in receiving the bread and water of life. The speaker also said Ea was a fallen angel. Such information makes one wonder if the Jesus of this particular teacher is not an anti-Christian figure. As Christians, we have to oppose such notions and help the modern seeker in her quest for truth to set things in order in accordance with God's true self-revelation.

Such views are, of course, in harmony with the above-mentioned criticism of dogmatic Christianity and any established religion as such: "The presentation of divine truth, as given by the churches in the West and by the teachers in the East, has not kept pace with the unfolding intellect of the human spirit. . . . The Church today is the tomb of the Christ and the stone of theology has been rolled to the door of the sepulchre. . . . Christianity cannot be attacked; it is an expression . . . of the love of God, immanent in His created universe. Churchianity has, however laid itself wide open to attack."[7]

Another problem in the religion of modern seekers is the elitism, the sense of having reached a higher level of consciousness, sometimes combined with the idea that those who have attained higher consciousness in the new era, the age of Aquarius, will have the right to execute a kind of consequence pedagogy toward those who have not attained the same higher consciousness. Also, some of the religious practices are dubious from a Christian point of view. What is the source of channeled messages? What does mediality do with the medium? How do mantic practices determine the life of the client, and what are the energies or entities behind the symbols of tarot and astrology? What happens to the person as person if the techniques of healing or self-realization blur personality? In my practice as a pastor I have met several persons who mentally and spiritually were deeply hurt through such practices and left in confusion because of the above-mentioned doctrines; some had to be helped through inner healing or deliverance, many through an act of confirmation and renewed commitment to their baptismal covenant — in short, they had to receive Jesus in their heart and turn to God as God has revealed himself in Jesus Christ.

---

7. Alice A. Bailey, *The Reappearance of the Christ* (New York, 1984), pp. 139-40.

*Ole Skjerbæk Madsen*

## Disciples of Jesus Christ in the Milieu of
## Western Seekers: Conflict and Contact

As mentioned, we as Christians have a lot of opportunities for being involved in a spiritual conflict with modern seekers and the New Age as such. The conflict is a fact, no doubt, but the fear of demons and of being demonized through contact with the new spirituality and the milieu of seekers is perhaps the greatest danger for us. I think one of the strategies of the Foe is the blinding of our spiritual and mental faculties from recognizing the truths, the dedication, and the insights of the quest for meaning, wholeness, and fulfillment in our fellow men. We must not be so preoccupied by our resentment of many of their (in our eyes) wrong or strange practices, their false doctrines, that we forget that they are sincere seekers, loved by God, potential disciples of Jesus and potential worshipers of the true God — if they meet the love of God in Jesus Christ and in the power of the Holy Spirit. I have lost many chances of leading seekers into the presence of God by making right doctrines a condition for ministering to them, e.g., by demanding that they renounce their past-lives experiences and their understanding of reincarnation before I would go on praying for healing. Now I want them to meet Jesus Christ and God in him first, through love-care being present to them in a way that will help them interpret their experiences in another way.

My concern in this paper, however, is not to explore and perhaps perpetuate spiritual conflict, but to attempt to express a theology as one who is challenged by the new spiritualities on the quest for truth, or rather the quest for the healing of humankind and creation through contact with the source of life and in the longing for a new age, the kingdom of God. Part of the challenge is the recognition of common roots of New Age religion and Christian spirituality. I do not give the outline of a complete systematic theology. Thus important subjects such as the uniqueness of Christ, evil, and sin are only hinted at, since my focus is esoteric themes. I just want to share some thoughts in the relevant areas in the hope that I may receive some help from other theologians, scholars of religious studies, and practitioners of dialogue and mission to express Christian faith in a way that is relevant to the neospiritual milieu.

## Toward an "Esoteric" Theology: God, Creation, Man

We thus need a Christian theosophy, cosmology, and understanding of nature, a theology which does not limit creation to the first person of the Trinity but sees God revealing Godself in the uncreated energies of the Logos and the

Spirit, thus creating the world. Through God's uncreated energies God gives a quality of the Logos and the Spirit to every creature. This way of thinking will give us a way of understanding the sign character of the world, of honoring our cocreatures, and thus understanding creation as the basic sacrament, the restoration of which through the saving work of Christ is celebrated in the sacraments and sacramentals of the church. In this way the common themes *(a)*, *(b)*, and *(c)* in traditional esotericism are addressed — and yet we will be able to acknowledge the difference between Creator and creature. It will also help define man's role in creation. The main insight of esotericism is that every single creature, the network of creatures, the greater structures or organisms of which every creature is a part, and the process of creation are signs concealing the mystery of life. There is a coherence of meaning and purpose between the spiritual, the psychic, and the physical worlds. Macrocosm and microcosm mirror each other. What is this hidden mystery? How is it possible to read nature as a book of revelation? What are the laws governing this world with purpose, or what is the *magia* of nature? What is the role of humanity, and how may the human person be seen as a key for understanding or restoring nature? Why is the human person seen as a microcosm? Some of the key words used are "Tao," "energy," "Logos," "dharma," "transmutation/transformation."

By using words such as "creature" and "creation," Christian theology presupposes a Creator. How will this concept of a personal God Creator meet the concept of a more impersonal divine and undivided Consciousness — the cosmos with all its entities being an emanation of the divine imagination, living in its energy? How does the biblical God match a God who is described as the Monad, the Source, Love, Father-Mother-God, All-That-Is?[8]

In speaking of God I would, as indicated above, suggest to speak of God as beyond human comprehension as God is in God's essence, but at the same time visible in God's *energeiai* (manifestations or operations) — not a copy or reiteration of patristic and Eastern Orthodox ways of speaking about God, but

---

8. Cf. Lazaris, *The Sacred Journey: You and Your Higher Self* (Orlando, 1987/1999), p. 88. In "Esoteric Psychology I" Alice Bailey mentions a number of basic propositions, which summarize the divine plan for creation: "There is one Life, which expresses Itself primarily through seven basic qualities or aspects, and secondarily through the myriad diversity of forms. These seven radiant qualities are the seven Rays, the seven Lives, Who give Their life to the forms, and give the form world its meaning, its laws, and its urge to evolution. . . . The Monad is the Life, lived in unison with the seven ray Lives. One Monad, seven rays and myriads of forms, — this is the structure behind the manifested worlds. . . . Life, quality and appearance, or spirit, soul and body constitute all that exists" (quoted from *The Seven Rays of Life Compiled by a Student from the Writings of Alice A. Bailey and the Tibetan Master, Djwal Khul* [New York, 1995], pp. 1-3).

inspired by them.[9] There is a need for theology to relate the popular thoughts of energy/energies in the neospiritual milieu and its practices of healing to a Christian understanding of energies which prevents a pantheistic monism and at the same time helps Christians see the workings of God in the created world and its beings.

It might be helpful to open with some reflection on the self-designation of God to Moses in Exodus 3, "I AM THAT I AM." This will also clarify the biblical foundations in the dialogue with the "I AM" teachings and meditations of some esoteric movements, which more or less identifies the absolute "I AM" with the lesser "I am" of the human person.[10] God reveals Godself in the glory of God *(kabod* or *doxa),* and God speaks to Moses out of God's glory through the angel of God. It is a personal encounter with God, yet God is hidden in God's self-revelation and self-communication. The same tension is seen in God's self-designation and the way the name of God is to be known or used by the Israelites. God tells Moses, "I AM THAT I AM," but God's name is rendered in the third person, *Yahweh,* to the people. This prevents an idolatrous confusion of God's absolute "I AM" and our qualified and subjective "I am." God *is,* with no other reason or cause for God's being/existence than Godself, while we are created in God's creative "thou," which gives to us our existence and identity. The Logos of God called our names, and spoke us thus into being. The incomprehensible God, whose innermost being is a hidden mystery, is known in God's speaking out of God's essence in the creative Logos, and is known in God's self-designation and in the Logos made flesh (when humanity suffered from the alienation from God, our fellow creatures, and our own self). So the hidden and incomprehensible God is known to us as the God of personal relationship — the God of Abraham, the God of Isaac, the God of Israel, and today your God and mine. This could be expressed in two simple sentences: God is, and God loves.

God's essence or being is complete, whole, perfect, incomprehensible. God is holy, but God's being is never self-sufficient; it is a being for others than Godself, transcending Godself in the process of creation, sharing what God is with what is neither God nor has any existence or being by itself. This transcendence in God's essence is the Logos (the Son of God) and the Breath (the Spirit

---

9. A useful summary of the trinitarian theology in the Cappadocians by Thomas Hopko is found in Bernard McGinn, John Meyendorff, and Jean Leclercq, eds., *Christian Spirituality: Origins to the Twelfth Century* (London, 1989), pp. 260-75. A summary and discussion of the Palamite understanding of the Trinity is found in Catherine Mowry LaCugna, *God for Us: The Trinity and Christian Life* (San Francisco, 1992), pp. 181-205.

10. For example, Summit Lighthouse/Church Universal and Triumphant. See the decrees in Mark L. Prophet and Elizabeth Clare Prophet, *The Science of the Spoken Word* (1965/1991).

of God). The Logos and the Spirit are the *energeiai* of God in the process of creation. These uncreated energies of God are manifested in the energies of creation in such a way that every creature individually as well as collectively mirrors the working of God and thus proclaims the glory of God; the earth is full of the glory of the Lord. The presence of God is seen in God's creative work.

## The Logos

The uncreated energy of the Logos manifests Godself in the process of creation, thus giving the created energies of the created world their logos. When the Gospel of John used the term "Logos" to express the relationship between the Son of God and the Father as well as that between the Son and the created world and mankind, God did not of course speak into a void. The whole understanding of the order of the universe was personalized in the creative Word of God who was made flesh. The logos of the world was not an abstract law or principle, but a self-communication of God calling his creatures into a relationship of love with Godself. The Logos of God thus determines the inner order of the world as reflecting the creative love of God. The logos of the universe as well as the interrelatedness of creatures and every entity in the world is a servant love which mirrors or responds to the love of God (sharing what God is with us, calling us into existence out of nonexistence). Every energy and energetic pattern or interrelatedness must conform with this logos. The purpose and the laws of nature refer to God as being and loving. No creature is self-sufficient; mirroring God, expressing the logos implanted in creation by the Logos, every creature exists for the sake of another and the whole. The logos is also experienced in the lives of human persons as the voice of silence, their conscience, and in the revealed law such as the Torah and the commandment to love God and neighbor.

Speaking of the Logos/logos is especially relevant in communicating with Theosophy, which however operates with a much more complex understanding of logos. Theosophy thus speaks of the Solar Logos, the God of the Sun System, the planetary Logos, the God of the planet Earth, a Logos-being on each different plane of consciousness, in a hierarchy of beings. The Christian understanding has as its focus the incarnate Logos of God in Jesus Christ and recognizes through the work of Christ how God created the universe by God's Logos and how the creative love orders creation according to the Logos.

The concept of Logos as known, manifested, and revealed in the logos of the created world may be combined with a Christianized use of the concept of Tao. This is relevant to the neospiritual milieu, perhaps even more than using the logos terminology, since the concept of Tao pervades much New Age thinking and practice. Thus "The Tao of Physics" by Fritjof Capra, who compared the organic, unified, and spiritual vision of reality in Eastern philosophy to the emerging paradigm of physics — to quote the characterization of his work by Marilyn Ferguson. The latter, in her *Aquarian Conspiracy,* offers this quote: "Mystic traditions such as Taoism may offer the most thoroughly developed bodies of Unitary Operational Thought."[11]

Tao signifies the eternal order or the foundation and basic principle of life. Tao is the cause of the universe. But Tao in this sense is incomprehensible, unspeakable, and transcendent. Nevertheless, the term "Tao" is used because the unspeakable Tao is also immanent in the created world. In this second meaning, Tao is the mother of creation, power and norm of existence. In the Chinese Gospel of John, "Logos" is translated as "Tao." John 1:14 thus means that the eternal foundation and basic principle of life is not impersonal, but is met in person in a human life, thus reestablishing the order of life in the disorder of human existence. All life has its origin in Tao or is caused by Tao/Logos, but this experienced Tao is grounded in the unspeakable and transcendent Tao, which Christian tradition calls God, Father. The incomprehensible Tao, unspeakable and nameless, which is the source and cause of life, is known to us in the order, which due to the act or process of creation is found in cosmos. The unspeakable Tao expresses itself in the act of creation and is known in the order which calls cosmos out of chaos.

If the relationship between the unspeakable Tao and the immanent Tao, and the created order and man, is described in the language of music, the keynote of cosmos arises as the sound of silence out of the unspeakable Tao. The cosmos and the earthly sphere of life vibrate around this keynote. The immanent Tao is the composition, the harmony, the order, the evolving rhythm. Every single creature must find itself in harmony with this Tao, serving the whole in the interplay with the other parts of the same greater whole. The role of mankind is to be the precentor of the earthly creatures, interpreting and expressing the tune of man's fellow creatures.

In the Gospel of John, Tao is said to be incarnate in Jesus Christ; the Tao was made flesh to be manifested in an experiential way among human beings, who have lost their state as children of God and thus loved darkness more than light. The keynote from the silence of God's eternal being, which sang everything into being, sings once more — where human persons had stopped listening to God and to their fellow men — to call us once again into the cosmic and creative dance and song of praise. The human nature of Jesus Christ is the

11. Marilyn Ferguson, *The Aquarian Conspiracy: Personal and Social Transformations in the 1980s* (Los Angeles, 1980), pp. 172 and 372.

268

true human nature restored, a life lived according to the Tao of human life and in harmony with the Tao of creation, a life characterized by servant love to other people and creatures and by an unrestricted openness toward God and God's will. But the keynote from the depth of God's being is also incarnate in him. In following the master Jesus, humans find their original fellowship with God as the children of God; to find the Master is to find Tao. In meeting Jesus Christ a human person finds the divine keynote, and through this recognizes his or her own personal keynote, the fulfillment of the quest for the meaning of life.[12]

Some theosophical thinkers use the concept of dharma to balance the negative weight of the concept of karma, or the law of cause and effect. In the light of their thoughts we may ask whether the logos of the created world and of each creature may be compared to the concept of dharma?[13] The term "dharma" signifies order and purpose. The dharma of fire is to burn, and in a similar way every human being has his or her dharma, an order or pattern of life which must be followed to live in harmony with the greater whole. The dharma of the human person is a part of the dharma of the planet, the solar system, the universe, just like the dharma of every limb of the body is a part of the dharma of the human person. Dharma is law and covers a spectrum from common practice to rituals to moral and ethical standards.

What has been said above about the creative Logos and Tao suggests that the created world/the universe/nature has a quality of God, a logos quality, which is the origin of the sign-character of every creature as well as all of nature as understood in the esoteric tradition. Because of this quality, nature must be held in a much higher esteem in theology and in the spiritual praxis of Christians. Nature is a book of revelation of the glory of God since the uncreated *energeiai* of the Logos and the Holy Spirit are at work through the created energies in the universe and in our earth and its entities. This sign-character should be interpreted by humans, and through them the light of nature should find its expression *coram Deo* and in the interplay of the creatures of the earth. This role of man is explained below with the concept of the human person as a microcosmos. The world and the processes of life are thus not only understood as functions within the established physical and chemical laws, but as part of a greater semiotic dynamic. The interpretation of the processes of the living nature as sign-processes is studied in bio-semiotics. Maybe it is not so inappropri-

---

12. The paragraphs on Tao are inspired by Karl Ludvig Reichelt, *Fromhetstyper og Helligdommer I Øst-Asia. Bind I* (Copenhagen, 1947).

13. The rendering of the meaning of the term "dharma" is based on a seminar by Svend Trier at Holistisk Sommerfestival, Tisvilde, Denmark, June 2000.

ate to look for the design of the created world.[14] This sign-character means that every creature and nature as such is a sacrament: it is called into existence by the Logos of God; it is a created expression of the servant love of God and communicates an aspect of that love in its uniqueness. This is the foundation of the church sacraments; water, oil, bread and wine in their logos have a quality which through thanksgiving and prayer and the coming of the Holy Spirit is made explicit as conveying that grace of God of which they are the physical expression.

The sign-character of nature calls for the humility of man. The recognition and understanding of life is a gift of God conveyed to us through God's revealing Godself in the process of creation, through the created *energeiai* of nature, and through the logos quality of nature. Nature is a book of revelation. Nature contains a divine wisdom which humans do not possess by themselves. God is offering us Godself and life with God through nature. Man just reads the book of wisdom, and only then becomes wise. Humans are able to read the book of nature and find the sign of God in nature, because mankind is created in the image of God to imagine this light of nature, and this in turn will help the human person fulfill his or her logos in relationship to both God and fellow creature.[15]

## The Holy Spirit

The Holy Spirit manifesting itself in the life of the created world may be described with words such as *prana* or *ch'i* to those parts of the new spiritual milieu which use and are familiar with these concepts.

In an attempt to outline an ecological theology in a Taiwanese perspective, Timothy Yong-Xiang Liau has some relevant thoughts on this question.[16] He sees the honoring of nature in Taiwanese culture as a bridge between local

14. *Danmarks Nationalencyklopædi*, s.v. "Biosemiotik." On design, cf. William A. Dembski, *Intelligent Design: The Bridge between Science and Theology* (Illinois, 1999).

15. In esoteric tradition we find this recognition of the light of nature with Marsilio Ficino, to whom the natural magic was the love of God flowing through the world and the planes of the world in such a way that what is above influences what is below. We find it with Paracelcus and with Gerhard Dorn. Cf. Aksel Haaning, *Naturens Lys. Vestens naturfilosofi i højmiddelalder og renæssance 1250-1650* (Copenhagen, 1998), e.g., pp. 182-86, 188-89, 246, 249f., 315-24.

16. Timothy Yong-Xiang Liau, "Die Bioregion Taiwan und eine heutige chinesische Theologie der Erde," in *Ökologisches Weltethos im Dialog der Kulturen und Religionen*, ed. Hans Kessler (Darmstadt, 1996), pp. 164-82.

culture and a Christian ecological theology which sees God living in the world and the world living in God. There is an immanent tension in God: God created nature and at the same time entered nature, even manifests Godself through nature. This means that we may experience the presence of God's divinity in the created nature. Without sharing the pantheistic understanding of nature and God in Taiwanese folk religion, it is still possible for the Christian to share the experience of the intimate relationship between nature and God. If God has never stopped creating and caring for nature and the world, this God will always communicate with human persons by means of every creature in nature. Every creature in the universe is a symbol of the presence of God.

What is interesting and relevant in this theology of Timothy Yong-Xiang Liau to New Age spirituality is his use of the *feng-shui* concept. Nature is working according to the interaction of yang and yin in the ongoing process of change. Man has to live in harmony with this dynamic of nature. In this process the Holy Spirit may be understood as the power uniting every creature and as the principle of the whole *(Ganzheit)*. He refers to the Augustinian concept that the Holy Spirit is the uniting bond of love between the Father and the Son. In creation this is manifested as the dynamic power to unite yang (heaven) and yin (earth). The fellowship between creatures is the sign of the loving unity between yang (Father) and yin (Son).

He goes on to suggest that the concept of *ch'i* is a means of explaining the presence of the Holy Spirit. *Ch'i*, like *pneuma/ruah*, etymologically means wind and breath; spirit and *ch'i* are understood as a communication between heaven and humans and as a power of integration and synthesis. By using *ch'i* in explaining the working of the Holy Spirit, Christian ecological theology better expresses how the Spirit, like *ch'i*, is flowing through everything, giving everything its specific qualities; the Holy Spirit is the life of creation, giving life to every creature, living in every creature. Being the life-giving Spirit, the Holy Spirit unites everything: the inner life of the Trinity, Christian life, and the untold created entities of the universe, being the one life-giving breath of all that is (*t'ong t'ien-hsia i ch'i* = "das ch'i integriert die unzählige Dinge unter dem Himmel dahingehend, ein ch'i zu werden"), and in such a way that every creature interacts. In this way the Spirit is guiding history toward the final unity of heaven, the earth, and mankind. Just as Tao is the origin of everything and the creative force of nature, Tao is the end of everything; the *ch'i/pneuma/ruah* of God brings everything together toward this end, establishing the shalom of the new heaven and earth (to rephrase the conclusion of Timothy Yong-Xiang Liau a bit).

I think his thoughts are very helpful in communicating with a range of therapies which operate with the concepts of *ch'i* and yin/yang. Even if many of the practitioners do not understand their practice as religious, most of them would consider it a spiritual practice.[17] This spirituality must not be seen as an infiltration in the West of a foreign religion, but as a spiritual practice which, interpreted rightly, may be an eye-opener to the therapists as well as to their clients for the working of God through God's life-giving Spirit, and Christians might honor the working of the Holy Spirit in these therapies and see the presence of the Logos made flesh in the therapists as servants of the servant love of God-in-Jesus and his coworkers in helping their clients regain the lost logos of their physical/psychological/spiritual existence. What I find less helpful is the reference to the traditional Augustinian understanding of the Trinity which tends to reduce the Spirit to the relational bond of love between Father and Son. I would rather see the unity of the Godhead in the Father as the ultimate, transcendent, and inexplicable Tao which reveals Godself in God's uncreated energies, the Logos (the God revealing Tao) and the Spirit *(ch'i)*, who thus in the process of creation gives order and life to the universe and every being and entity in it — also maintaining the dynamics of yin and yang while holding them together in unity through the servant love (logos/tao) and one divine breath of life *(pneuma/ch'i)*.

## The Planes of Creation

The presence of God in the process of creation through the uncreated energies of the Logos and the Spirit is so rich and full that it is expressed in the myriads of creatures. The created world, nature, is a world of diversity and variety, but also an ordered world, a cosmos. This diversity finds its expression in the different planes of existence, different worlds or the different kingdoms of nature, mainly the planes of spirit, soul, and matter. In Theosophy we will find a much more complex description of the planes of nature, but it will probably be enough to distinguish between three planes of nature in order to understand nature in its relation through man to God and to understand how God works through nature and communicates Godself in the process of creation.[18]

---

17. Cf. David G. Benner, *Care of Souls: Revisioning Christian Nurture and Counsel* (Grand Rapids, 1998), pp. 89f. "The most basic form of spirituality is what I would call nonreligious spirituality. This is a quest for self-transcendence and surrender."

18. Cf. n. 8. The theosophical "map" of creation with its seven planes is depicted in A. A. Bailey, *Letters on Occult Meditation* (New York, 1922 and 1966). The classical esoteric tradition as represented by Ficino says nature has four grades or planes: physical existence, the soul of the world *(anima mundi)*, pure spirit, the good as such. The physical world is pervaded by spirit in such a way that the visible world is a living organism through the working of the *anima mundi*. Humans are a part of this organism through their body and soul. The *anima mundi* mediates between God and the corruptible world; it is divine love and the natural magic. Cf. Haaning, pp. 175f., 197-208.

The spiritual world is first of all the Holy Trinity itself; secondly those beings who live in the glory of God (i.e., the angels), in the radiance or aura of God's presence; and finally the unseen world behind physical-psychic reality. Because of the fall of some of the angels, the unseen world is not spiritually neutral, but also contains a counterspiritual realm. In the unseen world we meet light and darkness, entities living in the glory, will, and love of God and entities living in darkness, pride, vanity, and vainglory. It will be necessary to develop angelology afresh to give a sound balance to much of the angelology of the New Age and to understand the logos or dharma of the angelic world to grasp some of the ways God has ordained a mediation between heaven and earth.

If we concentrate on the earthly creation, the unseen world is at work mediating between the creatures of the earth and the spiritual plane of existence; it is the noosphere of the earth. The plane of the soul is the biosphere of the earth, containing both animal and human life, the plane of senses, emotions, consciousness, self-consciousness and planetary consciousness. The plane of matter is the physical plane of the earth which is often described in terms of the four elements.

The elements are ordered according to the logos given them by the creative Logos of God. Following their logos or dharma, the elements reveal the loving kindness of God serving us through their specific nature: The *earth* as mother of life, the material of which plants, trees, birds, animals, and humans are made. The *water* quickening plants, trees, animals, and humans. The *fire* transforming matter into energy (warmth and light). The *air*, the element in which we breathe. As long as the elements follow their logos/dharma, they mirror qualities of God's being for God's creation, e.g., sustaining or quickening or cleaning us like water or breathing the breath of life into our world as a gentle wind of Paradise. But if they do not follow their logos, they lose their orderliness and open up to chaos, e.g., like a flood destroying a city at the seashore.

The quality of the elements then points to God; the world of the elements or of matter is a physical expression of the grace of God and thus not opposed to the spiritual world. But the physical realm contains a drive toward life in such a way that the psychic world is the aim of its existence; in the same way the world of spirit is what transcends the plane of the soul, and through the spiritual plane creation strives for God. This interplay of the planes of existence is manifested in the nature of human persons.

Ole Skjerbæk Madsen

## Man as Microcosmos

Humans are physical matter as the clay of which we were formed; humans belong as it were to the mineral kingdom. But we also belong to the animal kingdom, being created on the sixth day like the animals. Humans have life like animals, are living beings like them. We belong to the realm of soul with the animals. But humans are more than emotional reactions and do not only respond to stimuli; we have individual souls that are self-conscious. Furthermore, we are spiritual beings; we have a spirit; we are spirit. We know the inner voice of conscience; we have reason and an ability to reflect. We know that we, in our individuality, have a responsibility for our lives, the lives of others, that we live in relationships to other persons and first of all to God. We become ourselves in meeting the "thou" of God and in the "I-thou" relationship with other humans. Humans are body, soul, and spirit, and our nature comprises the four elements. In this way man is a *microcosmos* of the cosmos of the earth and her entities and of the earth in her relationship to the Creator.

The microcosmic calling of mankind is to be the conscious expression of the potentials, the logos, and the end of earthly creation, which is the one who is the Creator of creation. In mankind our fellow creatures of earth recognize the image of the Logos who called nature, the earth, and all of creation into existence, and in man every plane of earthly creation, the kingdoms of matter, soul, and spirit see themselves as endowed with soul and spirit, or rather as part of a physical, psychic, and spiritual whole. Man embodies and displays the logos quality of creation.

Man as microcosmos has a double role.

1. As said above, humans are called to read the book of nature, interpreting the sign of God in nature and thus calling forward the light of nature in the earth and in every earthly creature. Humans must recognize the logos of each fellow creature, and in every organism or structure recognize the design in creation. Man is the name giver of his or her fellow creatures — like Adam calling the animals by their names and thus giving them their distinctive identity among other creatures and *coram Deo*.
2. Mankind is to embody the servant love of God toward creation. Being a composite person (body, soul, and spirit), man in his or her right relationship to God brings the planes of matter, soul, and spirit into a right relationship to God. This is the secret of the Psalms when they express the praise of God on behalf of speechless creation. Mankind is also called to channel the love of God to his or her fellow creatures.

This understanding opposes an interpretation of Genesis 1:28 which advocates an anthropocentric understanding of the man-nature relationship that establishes an ideological basis for the exploitation of nature. Rather, I would understand the utilitarian attitude toward nature as a departure from the dharma/logos of humankind — thus bringing disorder, chaos, and death instead of shalom to the earth. The dominion over nature as the right to exploit it is a misunderstanding of the role of man on earth among his or her fellow creatures. The human person is a gardener, a cultivator, a protector, a name giver, a lover — not a consumer, a pleasure seeker, an exploiter. Esoteric tradition helps Christian theology to preserve humility in the midst of earthly creation and to rediscover the logos of human life as serving fellow creatures in the servant love of God.[19]

Another way of describing the role of humankind in creation is the concept of Raimundo Panikkar of a cosmo-theandric experience and relationship to nature. We have to learn how nature is our third body, the first body being our physical body and the second body all of mankind.[20]

As already hinted at, the order of earthly creation is broken through the misinterpretation of the role of humankind in creation. Humans are not fulfilling their dharma; they have fallen out of the logos of their existence — we have sinned: humankind is not a channel of the servant love of God, is not an interpreter of the book of nature, and humankind has left God out of sight. In the spirit of the humans, another spirit than the Spirit of God is ruling and the human mind does not listen to the Logos of God and the logos of the heart or the conscience. This is the root of the disharmony of the earth and her inhabitants. This leads to a crisis in the life of the earth. Are the sufferings of creation the birth pangs of a new age or the kingdom of God, or the forerunner of a cataclysm which extinguishes all earthly life or at least the human torturer of creation? Both interpretations are found in New Age literature — most often as a choice for mankind, but with the perspective of a new golden age on earth when the consciousness of humans vis-à-vis the present situation is raised to a planetary level. Romans 8 has a key as to how the disciples of Jesus, who by his Spirit have rediscovered themselves as the children of God in the midst of a still-suffering earthly creation longing for redemption, may become the hope of their fellow creatures for deliverance of evil, suffering, and corruption.

19. Cf. Ulrich Berner, "Religion und Natur: Zur Debatte über die historischen Wurzeln der ökologischen Krise," in *Ökologisches Weltethos im Dialog der Kulturen und Religionen*, pp. 40f. See his exposition on Barnardus Silvestris and the concept of nature as goddess, pp. 47f., and his conclusion, pp. 50f. Haaning, *Naturens Lys*, is an excellent introduction of the roots of Christian esotericism.

20. Raimundo Panikkar, "Ökosophie, oder: der kosmotheandrische Umgang mit der Natur," in *Ökologisches Weltethos im Dialog der Kulturen und Religionen*, pp. 58-66.

## The Logos Incarnated

The Logos incarnated in the Son of Man is the center of the redemption of creation and the reinstatement of humans in their logos as created in the image of God to grow into the likeness of God and thus once again to become mediators between the earthly creature and the spiritual world. In the Son of Man true humanity is regained and God is again known among humans, who thus once more are a true microcosmos of the world.

The key to unfold the mystery of the incarnation of the Logos of God in Jesus Christ is the "I AM" sayings of Jesus. All of them reveal the "I AM THAT I AM" in God's making Godself known to humans; the sayings reveal aspects of God's approach to humans, how God acts; and at the same time the self-disclosure of God is linked intimately and inseparably to Jesus Christ. Human persons meet I AM in the one who utters these sayings. But Jesus is not only God revealing Godself to us in a human form; Jesus is a human person. He is true man displaying the true human nature, that humans created in the image and likeness of God are created to be transparent to the glory of God and to serve their fellow creatures and each other in servant love of God.

The Son of Man in his true human nature is not God; he is the Son of Mary, and yet the Logos of God has united himself with the embryo growing in Mary in such a way that the son of Mary is confessed as the Son of God, and Mary is blessed by all generations as the mother of God. This is unique. Through the incarnation of the Logos of God the human nature of Jesus becomes the glory of God. The embryo in Mary's womb is a creature of God's Logos; as every other creature and as any creature, this human creature is called to proclaim the glory of God; but because God and man are united in one person in Jesus Christ, the Logos and Glory/Presence of God proclaims itself in him, touches us in that human nature which the Son of God shares with humans. In this sharing of natures human nature is reopened toward communion with God, the image grows into likeness, and in Christ humans are partakers of divine nature — and this on behalf of all earthly creation as its microcosmic representation.

## Toward an "Esoteric" Theology: Knowledge (Cognition), Mediation, Transformation

It is an insight of esotericism that the semiotic character of creation and of nature as a living milieu traversed and united in the divine breath or a light/fire circulating through it implies the possibility of mediation between the different planes of existence, between the higher and the lower worlds. This mediation is worked through intermediate entities such as angels, but also mankind has a mediation role in creation, especially seen in masters and saints. For humans to fulfill their intermediate calling, they will have to get into contact with and develop their faculties of knowing, especially the *imaginatio*. But the aim of mediation is transformation, which is often described as an alchemic process or a series of initiations. Other means of transformation are rituals, symbols, and different spiritual practices and disciplines. This transformation has personal and collective aspects. Masters, adepts, gurus, or spiritual guides may or may not play a role in the process of transformation for the disciples engaging in the alchemic quest for the philosopher's stone or in the process of initiation into adepthood.

### Angels

I have already mentioned how angels live in the radiance or aura of God's presence and stressed the need to understand the logos or dharma of the angelic world to grasp some of the ways God has ordained as a mediation between heaven and earth. Because of the incomprehensible and holy character of the essence of God, every creature would perish in the unmediated vision of God. Only the glory or aura of God is perceivable. The angels are creatures of light living in the radiance of God's presence to be the means through which God is revealing Godself to humans and other creatures. God is speaking to Moses in the burning bush in the voice of the angel, and the angel of God is the glory of God leading or accompanying the Israelites out of slavery in the pillar of fire or the pillar of cloud. God speaks to Mary through the angel Gabriel. That is why these intermediate spirits are called angels. Even though they, as messengers of God, represent the personal approach of God toward creation, they also protect the depths of God's essence as life and love against a penetration which surpasses the faculties of understanding in humans and other creatures and thus endangers their wholeness and integrity. This understanding of the angels should not be seen as excluding the revelation of God through the book of nature, through conscience, through the working of the Holy Spirit in the hearts and minds of human persons and certainly not the revelation of God in the incarnation of the Logos of God in Jesus Christ.

Ole Skjerbæk Madsen

## Mediating Mankind, and Jesus the Master

The role of humans as mediators has been indicated through the concept of the microcosmic man developed above. The saints of the church and saintly people who serve as spiritual directors or counselors help other persons enter a process through which they themselves will grow into a microcosmic state of existence. But as said above, the true human nature is seen in the humanity of Jesus Christ. To be a disciple of Jesus is to acknowledge him as Master, and to follow the Master is to become like the Master.

Christology has often been more concerned with Jesus as Savior and Lord, as God-with-us, than with his human person and his role as Master. Because the Logos of God is incarnate in him, he is the world teacher, but because he is the Master who has fulfilled the logos of humanity as a human person among humans, he is the guarantor and his life the pledge of the possibility of every human person and of humanity as such for their attaining perfection in the true human nature. What the Master has achieved, his disciples will eventually achieve if they follow the path of discipleship. The end of human transformation into true humanity is fulfilled and prefigured in the Master. Without the Master there is no hope of transformation.

This concept of the Master is very important to the dialogue with those parts of the spiritual milieu that follow or are inspired by gurus or by living or ascended masters, and the uniqueness of Jesus Christ as the Master and world teacher has to be highlighted in comparison with the idea of the world teacher or world teachers appearing in the different dispensations of human history.[21] Is the Master Jesus only one among many world teachers? What is common between Jesus the Master and other masters or gurus, and in which way is he different? What was said about the I AM sayings might be helpful in this area of dialogue, because the exclusivist handling of the I AM sayings is challenged by the universal content of the sayings as inclusive, i.e., applying to all creatures since it is I AM revealing Godself. It is not because of his realized humanity as a master that Jesus is considered the world teacher; rather, he is the world teacher in a unique sense because I AM through God's eternal Logos teaches us in the Master.

Another aspect of understanding Jesus as the Master who has realized true humanity as mirroring and even channeling the servant love of God is the concept of the crucified Master or crucified guru.[22]

---

21. Examples of such realized masters and world teachers are Sai Baba, Shanti Maya, Mother Meera. The masters of the great white brotherhood are described in, e.g., Alice A. Bailey, *The Externalisation of the Hierarchy* (New York, 1957, 1982).

22. Much inspiration is found in M. Thomas Thangaraj, *The Crucified Guru: An Experiment in Cross-Cultural Christology* (Nashville, 1994). I have written on the Master and disciple-

However important the concept of the Master and the masters and gurus is in the dialogue with Theosophy and some other parts of the neospiritual milieu, it will be of lesser or no significance to the major part of New Agers, as Hanegraaff writes: "The idea of being dependent on somebody else (rather than on one's own inner self) for spiritual illumination is not congenial to New Age individualism." The value of the master-disciple terminology will to this major part be the emphasis of a learning process, that the spiritual quest goes on, and a Christianity presented in this way to New Agers will seem less dogmatic and much more process-orientated.[23]

## Faculties of Knowing, Imaginatio, and Means of Mediation

*Imaginatio* is understood as a faculty of the inner man to perceive, contact, and establish a relationship with the inner worlds of creation. Through imagination the human person knows himself/herself and the surrounding world, penetrates the appearances of the outer world in order to see the inner meaning, the logos, and the interrelation of every creature and every part of creation, reading nature as a book of revelation. Imagination is in traditional esotericism linked to words like *magia* and *imago.*

Humanity is created by the Logos of God as any other creature; humans share with all of creation an immanent logos which is a quality laid down in nature in order to help each part of creation to serve the whole and each other in love. This logos is the *magia* of nature, the bond of love in nature, and the light of nature — revealing God, proclaiming the glory of God. *Magia* is the inner life of nature — its correspondences, its "logic" or "algebra," its music — which our *imaginatio* imagines.[24] As an added grace, humanity is not only created but created in the image of God *(imago Dei);* because of the *imago Dei* character of humans, they are able to read the book of nature and to imagine the logos of creation, the *magia* of nature, and to see the presence of God in the works of creation. Through imagination humans not only perceive the inner order of creation, they receive nature as a gift according to the logos of each creature or element, and they perceive God as giving Godself to God's

---

ship inspired among others by this book and by Annie Besant's *The Masters* in *Salige er I!* (Copenhagen, 1999), pp. 71-79.

23. Hanegraaff, p. 400.

24. An example of *magia naturalis* in classical esotericism is Ficino, who describes it in terms of perceiving the positive influence of heaven for strength and healing through the natural phenomena. Ficino sees this *magia* in music. Haaning, pp. 186-97. Cf. Antoine Faivre, *Theosophy, Imagination, Tradition: Studies in Western Esotericism* (New York, 2000), pp. 99-135.

creatures in the process of creation as well as through every single element, entity, or organism of nature. Thus, to imagine is "to correspond in the light of Nature, and in an experience sui generis, to the invisible fullness of the world, of Man and of things."[25] This *imaginatio* enables humanity to make the invisible visible, to be a cocreator with God in relationship to the earth and her creatures, "a transformer of an awaiting Nature" — as A. Faivre reformulates Romans 8[26] — thus facilitating the union of creation and Creator in Christ.

This way of describing the imaginative role of humanity in creation is ideal, but in fact the faculty of imagination is hurt or bent through the fall of man. *Imaginatio* is because of sin misused imagining of vain things, phantasmata, evil. *Imaginatio* will only be set right in redeemed humanity, and that is what the incarnate Logos of God did in Christ.

How to grow in spiritual perception through the faculty of *imaginatio* in a sound way? Christian spiritual tradition recommends several disciplines of spirituality and the guidance of a spiritual director, a father/mother confessor, an older Christian brother or sister, a counselor. Dallas Willard in his classic book on the spirit of the disciplines outlines the following *disciplines of abstinence:* solitude, silence, fasting, frugality, chastity, secrecy, and sacrifice, and *disciplines of engagement:* study, worship, celebration, service, prayer, fellowship, confession, and submission.[27]

These disciplines and the spiritual growth under the guidance of a spiritual director may be unfolded in a fourfold way as described by Peter Halldorf after the inspiration of the desert fathers.[28]

1. Asceticism is to fix a limit to oneself instead of allowing one's needs to grow unrestrainedly. Asceticism is self-control and an exercise in forming one's life according to the measure of the kingdom of God, daring to pray with Jesus: "Not my will, but yours be done," or to say to God with Mary: "I am the Lord's servant. May it be to me as you have said." The disciplines of abstinence belong to the exercise of asceticism, but also service and generosity are part of the training.

2. *Apatheia,* which should not be understood as the modern "apathy," hopelessness, resignation. *Apatheia* is a dispassionate state not governed by

---

25. Faivre, p. 117.

26. Faivre, p. 125.

27. Dallas Willard, *The Spirit of Disciplines: Understanding How God Changes Lives* (London, 1988), pp. 160-99.

28. Peter Halldorf, *Sandens Söner* (Göteburg, 1996). What is written below is inspired by his book, but he is not to be blamed for my interpretations — especially concerning sexuality, eros, and agape.

passions, desires, worries, and anxiety. It is to live like the birds of the air or the lilies of the field. *Apatheia* is freedom and trust.

3. Agape is the love which flows by itself from the presence of God's love in the heart. When God speaks God's loving word into the emptiness and darkness of the heart, the *imago Dei* in the heart is reborn in an overflowing and unconditional love for God, neighbor, and fellow creature. Agape completes every love, from sexuality on the physical plane over eros on the plane of soul to servant love on the spiritual plane. Agape reveals that humans are meant to transcend themselves to others than self and finally to union with the other and with God.

4. *Theoria* is to see and experience the truth. It is not "theory" in modern understanding, but a practically experienced truth. "Blessed are the pure in heart, for they will see God." Only walking the path, we attain truth; the human person on his/her way to *theoria* cannot start with a concept, theory, or intellectual understanding of truth, not even the soundest confessional writings or the right view on the Bible, but he/she must enter and walk in the experiential reality of the Bible.

Meditation is an important tool in this process of imagining the logos and the *magia* of the world, of knowing oneself and God. Man is a contemplating being. Through meditation humans learn a focused attention and an attentive presence in the world, which goes beyond distractions, appearances, the outward forms and detects the logos and the *magia* and, behind them, God.

A church which wants to meet the need for spiritual life and the quest for meaning will have to offer spiritual guidance through the use of adequate disciplines and, among other things, make room for meditation and the practice of silence in its daily life, its liturgical life, its mission, and its ministry, and offer retreats for personal growth in Christ.

Out of a life with meditation and contemplation other gifts may flow which will be means of mediation and by which humans may help each other to grow in servant love or be set free of what hinders the stream of life in them.

Among New Agers channeling and healing are in the forefront of such mediating faculties — very similar to the charisms of prophecy and healing. Through these faculties the energies of the invisible reality are experienced — whether the energies come from the plane of soul or the plane of spirit, in a sort of impersonal contact with energies or under the guidance of the entities in the astral or spiritual sphere or even the divine plane of love unity. When they are combined with *imaginatio*, a transformation may happen in which the inherent logos is reestablished because it is recognized and visualized, e.g., in a healing.

Charisms are in a similar way the working of the Spirit of God; they are the *energeiai* of the Holy Spirit and manifestations of the grace of God. God is experienced in the charisms, and the charismatic person is the channel for the *energeiai* of the Spirit, but at the same time the Spirit is working through the person, activating his or her created energies and inviting him or her to cooperate with the Spirit, thus fulfilling his or her logos/dharma.

Without charismatic gifts operating in the fellowship of the disciples of Jesus, the church will not offer a practical demonstration of its faith relationship with God. Every sermon or theological statement concerning God is not communicating with the neospiritual milieu if it lacks an experiential dimension. Gifts of healing and revelation mediate the presence of God; the kingdom of God is at hand.

Even though esotericism has a resentment toward the outward forms of established religions, especially of dogmatic Christianity or Churchianity, new rituals, ritual practices, and even liturgies — e.g., meditation at full moon, magical practices, sacred dance, etc. — are created in the new spiritual milieu. Theology and church should thus not be discouraged by the criticism of its liturgical practice, but rather find those models of liturgy and those traditions which at best mediate between the different planes of existence and in this way would form the starting point of a process of the inculturation of Christian liturgy in the neospiritual milieu.[29]

I shall point to a few aspects of Christian liturgical spirituality and practice which might be helpful in the dialogue with New Age religion.

The liturgy is a reflection of the heavenly world. The daily prayers of the liturgy of hours are understood as a *laus perennis* in which humans partake in the heavenly and unending worship of God. The beauty of the liturgy — its music, its symbols and colors, the icons — all is a reflection of the aura of God's presence in which angels and humans are united and uplifted to communion with God. The eucharistic liturgy is the mystery in which the incarnation of the Logos of God into our history is celebrated as eternal and finished, as the High Priest Jesus Christ is offering himself to God. The angels bring him as king to the throne of God as sung in the Cherubic Hymn in the Orthodox liturgy, when the gifts of bread and wine are brought to the altar. This liturgy opens our senses to the hidden world — and men do not know if they are in heaven or if heaven is on earth.

Christian liturgy is a microcosmic event; this is the core in a sacramental

---

29. Cf. Ole Skjerbæk Madsen, "Kontekstualisering og inkulturation. Gudstjenester i et nyspirituelt miljø," in *Gudstjeneste som mission,* ed. Mogens S. Mogensen (Copenhagen, 2001). Very helpful in identifying different models is James Empereur, *Models of Liturgical Theology* (Nottingham, 1987).

understanding of the liturgy. This is, as said above, due to the sign character of creation and of every creature. The church sacraments are honoring the sacramental character of all of creation, but not the sacraments alone; also the lesser sacramentals and blessings are founded in the sign character of nature and will thus give a Christian interpretation of the reenchantment of nature which is happening in New Age. The liturgy manifests furthermore the fellowship of disciples as the body of Christ in which everyone finds his/her dharma/logos in servant love, finding his/her charisms, and as parts of the whole, shows forth what creation hopes for: the freedom of the children of God united in Christ — at once his body and his bride, prepared for the final consummation of creation in Godself.

Partaking in liturgy is partaking in a process of mediation: "Through Jesus Christ, God is persuading the church in the direction of greater union with Godself. Through the church and the liturgy, Jesus Christ is luring the world in the direction of greater humanization."[30]

In its sacramental and process-oriented aspects, Christian liturgy also has a therapeutic dimension which focuses on the immanence of God's presence; e.g., in praying for a sick or suffering person it focuses on the reestablishing of the logos of the malfunctioning organs of the body in asking the Logos of God once more to call the organs back into their logos, their natural order. In the therapeutic model there will be much more room for the body and the bodily expressions in the liturgy such as dancing, healing touch, foot washing, incense, aromatic oils and fragrances, and healing music.

### The Process of Transformation

Describing the fourth theme of classical Western esotericism, the experience of transmutation, Hanegraaff quotes Faivre saying that without this experience the concept of esotericism "would hardly exceed the limits of a form of speculative spirituality."[31] Similarly it might be said that without changed lives, conversion and sanctification, there is not much reality left in Christianity. The term "transmutation" fits well in the language of alchemy, but in New Age I think the term "transformation" is more useful. It is thus the concept of transformation which pervades the classical presentation of New Age, Marilyn Ferguson's *The Aquarian Conspiracy* with the subtitle: *Personal and Social Transformation in 1980s.*

30. Empereur, p. 33.
31. Hanegraaff, p. 399.

Ole Skjerbæk Madsen

Christian understanding of the process of transformation has to ponder that "'transmutation' was not originally an evolutionist concept; this is, however, how it has been represented almost universally since the 18th century." The transformation language of New Age thus is an evolutionist concept, and it is in this context that the doctrine of reincarnation should be seen. The traditional Christian concept of transformation and the traditional preromantic understanding of transmutation are understood in a personal way, "an inner process or mystical 'path' of regeneration and purification."[32] The Christian concept of personal transformation in a process of conversion, initiation, and sanctification may challenge the New Age evolutionist concept, guarding the precious and unique character of the actual person as a daughter or son of God. Since Christian spirituality recognizes the fact of sin and evil and understands transformation in the light of salvation from the powers of darkness, it will not see "evolution" as necessarily good and thus challenge the optimism of popular evolutionism.

In Theosophy the life of Jesus serves as a model for the initiations, but these initiations take several incarnations. Nevertheless, they challenge Christians to reconsider the imitation of Christ and look upon discipleship in terms of initiations with a content like the most significant episodes in the life of the Master: conception, birth, empowerment for service (baptism in the Jordan), transfiguration, Gethsemane and Golgotha, resurrection, return to the Father (ascension), union.[33]

Alchemy, understood as a process of transmutation, might offer an adequate language of speaking of the path of discipleship and sanctification because it is used in the psychologized spirituality of many therapies and as a science of self-transformation in some groupings. Martin Luther in his *Tischreden* appreciates the art of alchemy as the ancient philosophy of nature and sees in the alchemical process an image of the final judgment. A more current interpretation is in the light of John 12:23ff. to understand the transmutation as following the pattern of Jesus' suffering/death, resurrection, and ascension, which is reproduced in the conversion/sanctification process of the disciples. The state of *nigredo* is the grave in which all false images of self, world, and God are broken down; *albedo* is the resurrection and the state of justification and restoration; *rubedo* is the ascension and the state of sanctification and wholeness. The gold of the process is union with God. This process is mirrored in the transmu-

32. Hanegraaff, pp. 399f., 420, 462ff.

33. A theosophical classical work is Annie Besant, *The Path of Discipleship* (Adyar, Madras, 1910), with several reprints. Cf. Ole Skjerbæk Madsen, *Salige er I!* (Copenhagen, 1999), pp. 71-79.

tation of physical matter. Thus the concepts of alchemy may help us understand personal transformation not only individualized, but as a microcosmic event transforming matter. The personal transformation of humans serves the transformation of humanity and our fellow creatures into the body and bride of Christ, and finally experiencing union with God as God becomes all in all.[34]

### Partners in a New Ecological World Ethos

If this mediating role of humanity is taken seriously, Christians cannot help being partners in a new planetary ecological world ethos. The core of such a spirituality which is sensible toward nature and human society will, according to Hans Kessler, be compassion and solidarity with a suffering world, attentive presence, good will toward every creature, and simplicity in lifestyle. Christians might help New Age to remain faithful to some of its visions, that of a transformed earth, a new planetary consciousness, a holistic view on society and environment — themes that tend to diminish in a form of private spirituality concerned only with self-realization in an almost hedonist manner. Christian engagement in establishing a new ecological world ethos will be realistic (because of the recognized fact of sin and evil), but with hope (because of Jesus Christ) and in compassionate power (because of the gift of the Spirit).[35]

## Tolerance or Monism?

Theme *(e)* (see above, p. 258) of traditional esotericism will be an area of conflict if expanded in a way which will not honor actual and real differences between religions. Is it really true that a secret doctrine or an eternal philosophy exists, that the esoteric traditions and the mystics of the religious systems have a common source in the ancient wisdom? Tolerance is often understood as accepting that truth is what is true to any given person, and the conviction that finally we all have the same God. Hanegraaff says: "[R]eligious exclusivism is unacceptable to New Agers, but relativity is equally unacceptable: there must be one religious truth, and all religions must be allowed to participate in that one-

34. Saint Germain, *Studies in Alchemy: The Science of Self-Transformation*, dictated to the Messenger Mark L. Prophet (Malibu, Calif., 1962, 1985). J. Peter Södergård, "Den konungliga konsten — alkemin — som psykologi och teologi," in *Att se det dolda*, ed. Owe Wikström (Borås, 1998), pp. 182-211.

35. Cf. Hans Kessler, "Suche nach einem planetarischen Öko-Ethos," in *Ökologisches Weltethos im Dialog der Kulturen und Religionen*, pp. 267ff.

ness. The problem is what to do with religions which refuse to fit in this scheme because they do not share its premises."[36] Consequently, the traditional religions represent a "false" spirituality because they are dogmatic and exclusive, or they represent a past phase of spiritual evolution — the age of Aquarius is replacing that of Pisces. It is also unacceptable that Christianity does not share the thought of reincarnation, and therefore it is postulated that material advocating reincarnation was left out of the Gospels. "Tolerance" has its limits.

Tolerance, of course, does not mean that we agree, but that we accept differences, respect the choice of the other person, even if it hurts and we long to share the life which is true to us with him/her. Tolerance defends the dignity of the other person and his/her right to live according to his/her spirituality. However, tolerance is not abstaining from discussion, discernment, and mission. Christians cannot accept a monistic version of tolerance on the basis of the dictum "you are that" (= *tat twam assi*), proclaiming the illusionary character of every duality. Good and evil cannot be identified or viewed as different modes of the same reality. Therefore Christians have to discern sound or unsound religions and spiritual practices, and New Agers unconsciously do the same in their criticism of dogmatic religion. Some spirituality and some religious/spiritual practices do not lead to God or might even be demonic, belonging to the energies of the Black Lodge, or the dark centers of the astral or mental planes — to use theosophical terms, even though Theosophy would state that energies per se are neither bad nor good.

And yet we see the image of Christ in every human person; we recognize a longing for God and a longing for unity, for the brotherhood-sisterhood of mankind. This longing and the *imago Dei* in humans is the starting point of dialogue and forms a basis for tolerance and right human relations.

---

36. Cf. Hanegraaff, pp. 324-30; the quotation is from p. 329.

# Conversion between Islam and Christianity in a Danish Context

MOGENS S. MOGENSEN

When I left Denmark in 1981 to become a missionary in the Lutheran Church of Christ in Nigeria, Islam was about to be implanted in Denmark. Since 1967 migrant workers mainly from Turkey and Pakistan were invited to Denmark to work in our factories. They stayed on as immigrants and brought their families, thereby forming a new nucleus of a Muslim community in Denmark. Their number was still fairly small, and their presence was felt mainly in Copenhagen and other larger towns.

While I was away from Denmark, I observed (and was a participant in) the encounter between Islam and Christianity in northern Nigeria. Whereas Christianity was brought to northern Nigeria about one hundred years ago, Islam had been implanted there for more than six hundred years and was the predominant religion. Since both are missionary religions, Muslims and Christians endeavored to spread their message, and as a result of the encounter between them in daily life settings and in missionary settings some Muslims converted to Christianity and some Christians converted to Islam. In most places the encounter was peaceful, but in the 1980s increased tensions were felt, in connection with the Islamic revolution in Iran, and violent episodes took place among various Muslim groups and between Muslims and Christians.

By 1991, when I returned form Nigeria, the situation in Denmark had changed dramatically. Now Islam was high on the agenda in the political life and in the conversations between ordinary people. During the 1980s the number of Muslims had increased significantly due to the influx of refugees from Muslim countries. While I observed (and took part in) the encounter between Muslims and Christians in Denmark, I reflected on the similar encounter in northern Nigeria, and in 2000 I completed a Ph.D. on one aspect of this encounter, namely, the conversion of Muslim Fulanis to Christianity.[1] This study made me curious about the encounter between Muslims and Christians in Denmark and the conversions that had been reported.

So far nobody has carried out a study of conversion between Islam and Christianity in Denmark, and this paper does not pretend to present such a study. This paper, however, is part of my preparation to undertake such a study. Through an exploratory study of certain aspects of the Danish encounter between Muslims and Christians in general and conversions between Islam and Christianity in particular, I hope later to be able to formulate a proper research project.

After a survey of the literature on the topic in Denmark in particular and in the West in general, I will describe briefly the present Danish context for this encounter and outline how Christians face Muslims and Muslims face Christians. In the main part of the paper I will analyze a limited number of conversion accounts to identify some of the dynamics of the conversion process. Finally I will conclude with some perspectives for my future research.

## Survey of Literature

Islam in Denmark has been the topic of several research projects and books. From 1982 to 1990 Statens Humanistiske Forskningsråd published a series of nine research reports on "Islam i Nutiden," most well known of which is "Islam I Danmark. Muslimske institutioner I Danmark 1970-89," by Jørgen Bæk Simonsen. Other important studies on Islam in Denmark include those by J. Nielsen and Simonsen.[2] Muslims have also published books about their religion and culture and their situation in Denmark, seen from various perspectives.[3] A variety of Christians have published their perspective on the encounter between Islam and Christianity in Denmark.[4]

---

1. Mogens S. Mogensen, "Livshistorier," *Kritisk Forum for Praktisk Teologi 77* (1999): 19-33; Mogensen, "Contextual Communication of the Gospel to Pastoral Fulbe in Northern Nigeria" (Ph.D. diss., Fuller Theological Seminary, 2000).

2. Jørgen Nielsen, *Muslims in Western Europe* (Edinburgh: Edinburgh University Press, 1995); Jørgen Bæk Simonsen, *Det retfærdige samfund* (Viborg: Samleren, 2001).

3. E.g., Náser Khader, *Ære og skam. Det islamiske familie-og livsmønster fra undfangelse til grav* (Copenhagen: Borgen, 1996); Aminah Tønnesen Echammari, *Islam i europæisk klædedragt. Stof til eftertanke og selvransagelse* (Copenhagen: Fremad, 1998).

4. E.g., Steen Skovsgaard, *De fremmede har i altid hos jer. Om Kulturmødets udfordringer* (Copenhagen: Unitas, 1994); Skovsgaard, ed., *Kristendom og Islam. En mosaik fra Stiftsudvalget vedrørende Islam/Kristendom i Århus Stift* (Aarhus, 1999); Niels Henrik Arendt, *Gud er stor! Om islam og kristendom* (Copenhagen: Forlaget Anis, 2001); Harald Nielsen, ed., *Samtalen fremmer forståelsen* (Conversation furthers understanding) (Copenhagen: Unitas, 2000); Lissi Rasmus-

The literature concerning conversion between Islam and Christianity in Denmark, however, is extremely scarce. So far no scientific study has been carried out. We have only a number of interviews with converts or their own accounts in newspapers and magazines. Until Danish studies are carried out, we may draw on research from other Western countries.

Larry Poston set out in a 1992 study "to determine the nature of conversion to Islam within Western contexts with respect to the sociological characteristics of the converts (i.e., age, gender, religious background, etc.) and the motivational factors involved in their decisions to become Muslims,"[5] which is fairly similar to the type of research I hope to carry out. Originally he hoped to base his analysis on questionnaire interviews with North American converts to Islam. Twenty Muslim organizations were contacted and anonymity promised to the interviewees, but most of the organizations were not ready to cooperate or did not respond. The disappointing result was that only twelve questionnaires were completed and returned. Poston concludes that "The poor response was probably due to the suspicion that exists among American Muslims regarding research into their lifestyles and religious experiences. There is a lack of confidence in the ability of non-Muslims to properly understand and portray those who adhere to the Islamic faith."[6]

Poston, therefore, based his analysis on sixty written conversion testimonies from a variety of sources. A little less than half the sample were Americans, the rest Europeans, mostly from Great Britain. This of course limits the value of the research.

In Great Britain Ali Köse was much more successful in obtaining the cooperation of Muslim authorities and organizations, probably because he was a convert to Islam himself. In 1996 he published his very thorough study, *Conversion to Islam: A Study of Native British Converts*. His research is based on analysis of questionnaire interviews with seventy converts to Islam. Although the sample, established through snowball and convenience sampling methods, cannot claim to be representative of all conversions to Islam, his research gives an extremely valuable insight into the conversion process. There will probably also be some significant similarities between conversion to Islam in Great Britain and in Denmark, but the Muslim community there has a much longer history

sen, *Diapraksis og dialog mellem kristne og muslimer — i lyset af den afrikanske erfaring* (Aarhus: Aarhus Universitetsforlag, 1997); and Rasmussen, ed., *Muslimer og kristne ansigt til ansigt* (Copenhagen: Islamisk-Kristent Studiecenter, 2001). This book contains both Christian and Muslim perspectives on the encounter.

5. Larry Poston, *Islamic Da'wah in the West: Muslim Missionary Activity and the Dynamics of Conversion to Islam* (New York: Oxford University Press, 1992), p. 160.

6. Poston, p. 161.

than the few decades in Denmark. Also, the political, cultural, and religious milieu in Great Britain differs significantly from Denmark, so we should be careful in our comparisons.[7]

Based on the studies by Poston, Köse, and Gerholm and Litham,[8] Colin Chapman points to the following factors that, in various combinations, have influenced the conversion process:

1. Dissatisfaction with a previous religion or ideology
2. Disillusionment with Western society
3. Conversion through marriage
4. Personal contact with Muslims
5. The Quran
6. Islam as complete philosophy of life
7. The simplicity and rationality of Islam
8. Moral and ethical standards in Islam
9. Disgust with racism outside Islam and the universal brotherhood and sisterhood inside Islam
10. Special appeal to women: the respect shown to women by Islam
11. Sufism, e.g., the spirituality and the spiritual power that Sufism offers
12. Balance between the communal (human bonds) and the individual (direct access to God) aspects of Islam
13. Supernatural phenomena, e.g., dreams[9]

In other Nordic and Western countries, research on conversions has been carried out or is being conducted right now. Lena Larsen has a thesis, which unfortunately is not yet published, about conversion to Islam in Norway, "'Velkommen til en stor familie' Islam og konversion i norsk kontekst," and Anne Marie Roald is about to publish her research about conversion to Islam in Sweden. These reports will be very valuable for research into conversion in Denmark because the cultural, political, and religious context and the history of the Islamic presence in these countries are fairly similar to what obtains in Denmark, although there are also significant differences, among them the ethnic composition of the Muslim communities in the Nordic countries.

So far, all the literature mentioned here studies conversion to Islam.

---

7. Another British study of conversion to Islam is Harfiyah Ball, *Why British Women Embrace Islam* (Leicester: Muslim Youth Education Council, 1987).

8. Thomas Gerholm and Yngve George Litham, eds., *The New Islamic Presence in Europe* (London: Mansell, 1988).

9. Colin Chapman, *Islam and the West: Conflict, Coexistence, or Conversion* (Carlisle: Paternoster, 1998), pp. 61-73.

There are hardly any studies about conversion from Islam to Christianity in the West! The only exception is Jean-Marie Gaudeul's book from 1999, *Appelés par le Christ ils viennent de l'Islam*.[10] Gaudeul has collected the written conversion accounts of 175 Muslims who have converted to Christianity. For the purposes of this paper, however, the problem is that all the converts converted in Africa and Asia except nine, who lived in France. For the purposes of my research, it is important to heed Gaudeul's warnings: "First of all, therefore, there is a demand for direction. A certain number of the converts are in danger. Many Muslims will not tolerate a member of their community changing his or her religious affiliation, even if family and social ties are preserved. The cases of assassination or attempted assassination are not rare."[11]

Gaudeul quotes only from testimonies that the converts themselves have published or testimonies from people who have passed away.

## The Encounter between Muslims and Christians in Denmark

After a brief description of the Danish scene for the encounter between Muslims and Christians, the encounter will be analyzed from the perspective first of the Christians and then of the Muslims.

### *The Danish Context for the Encounter*

The Danish experience with this encounter is very short. In the 1950s and most of the 1960s the number of Muslims in Denmark was so insignificant that most people had never seen a Muslim, much less talked with one. The Muslim presence in Denmark today is a result of two factors.

It is primarily due to an economically determined immigration of work migrants about thirty years ago. The economic boom in the 1960s led to a shortage of workers. Since the other western European countries experienced a similar boom and also were in need of workers, and Eastern Europe, minus Yugoslavia, was closed by the Iron Curtain, the labor immigrants came to Denmark primarily from areas fairly far away such as the former Yugoslavia, Turkey, Pakistan, and Morocco. The last three countries being Muslim countries,

10. There are also collections of accounts of conversions to Christianity, such as Mark Hanna's *The True Path: Seven Muslims Make Their Greatest Discovery* (Colorado Springs: International Doorways Publishers, 1975), but they contain no academic analysis of the accounts.

11. Jean-Marie Gaudeul, *Appelés par le Christ ils viennent de l'Islam* (Paris: Les Éditions du Cerf, 1999), p. 30; my translation.

most of the so-called guest workers who arrived from 1967 onward were Muslim men. When immigration was stopped in 1973, fifteen thousand people had come to Denmark. As guest workers, the Muslims were expected to return to their Islamic home countries when their work was no longer needed. However, they remained and brought their families to Denmark.

The second reason for the presence of Muslims in Denmark is the influx of asylum seekers over the last twenty years. Many of these people fleeing wars, oppression, and natural disasters came to Denmark from the 1980s on from Muslim countries such as Iran, Iraq, Palestine, Bosnia, Somalia, and most recently Afghanistan. When they were recognized as refugees, they could, according to the international conventions, bring their relatives to Denmark too.[12]

The guest workers and the asylum seekers have now lived in Denmark with their families for so many years that a significant number of the Muslims in Denmark today were born here. As Jørgen Bæk Simonsen pointed out in his 1990 report, "Islam I Danmark. Muslimske Institutioner i Danmark 1970-1989" (Islam in Denmark: Muslim Institutions in Denmark, 1970-1989), the Muslims have already developed a network of institutions that support their Islamic (and often also their ethnic) identity as a minority group in the Danish Christian majority society. Apart from the Ahmadiyya mosque in Hvidovre, no traditional mosques have so far been built in Denmark, but Muslims gather for Friday prayers in about seventy mosques in schools, apartments, and simple mosques in all the bigger towns. Often organized along ethnic lines, a number of institutions have been established such as primary schools, Quran schools, cultural centers, burial organizations, etc.[13]

In Denmark the religious affiliation of people is not registered by the government, the only exception being members of the Folk Church, that is, the Evangelical Lutheran Church in Denmark. Based on analysis of the country of origin of the immigrants, the number of people who consider themselves Muslims in Denmark today is estimated at about 170,000, i.e., more than 3 percent of the population. Unless the number of immigrants changes significantly, by 2020 the number may be around 300,000, i.e., 6 percent of the population.[14] As a result of the integration law from 2000, the refugees granted asylum have been distributed among all local governments so that today the encounter between Muslims and Christians is no longer limited to the bigger towns but is a reality also in most villages.

12. Jørgen Bæk Simonsen, *Islam i Danmark. Muslimske institutioner I Danmark 1970-1989* (Aarhus: Aarhus Universitetsforlag, 1990), pp. 5-19; Poul Chr. Matthiessen, "Befolkningens sammensætning i Danmark og udvikling i de næste 20 år," in *Samtalen fremmer forståelsen*, pp. 104-5.

13. Simonsen, *Islam i Danmark*, passim.

14. Matthiessen, p. 108.

In the late 1960s and the 1970s the encounter between the ethnic Danes and the immigrants was fairly peaceful. When it was realized that the work migrants were not returning to their home countries, and the number of asylum seekers rose significantly in the 1980s, the attitude of many ethnic Danes slowly turned more skeptical and negative, and political parties began to advocate much harsher policies toward immigrants. In the 1990s heated debates occurred in the press, in the parliament, and among people in the workplaces. Among the issues debated were the wearing of veils by Muslim women at work, plans for building mosques in Copenhagen and Aarhus, and cemeteries for Muslims. The tragic events on September 11, 2001, added fuel to the fire, and the election campaign up to the general elections on November 20, 2001, came to focus on immigration policies and the fear of Islam.

Polls taken in various countries in Europe seem to indicate that the attitude of Danes has been more negative toward immigrants in general and Muslims in particular than in many other European countries. It has been suggested that this might be connected to the fact that Denmark has been one of the most homogenous countries in Europe, both in ethnicity and religion. We have had waves of immigration before 1967, but their impact has hardly been felt by ordinary people. The immigrants coming to Denmark within the previous one hundred years were fairly few; many returned to their country of origin again; and all came from the Christian European cultural circle. The recent immigration, however, has been quantitatively and qualitatively quite different. The immigrants and their descendants are counted in the hundreds of thousands, and most come from ethnic groups whose culture and religion are considered very foreign by most Danes.

Denmark is fast becoming a multiethnic society, and due to the nature of the new ethnic groups, our society is also turning multicultural and multireligious. Due to lack of experience with other ethnic groups, cultures, and religions, tensions have been rising, in particular between some ethnic Danes and Muslims.

## Christians Face Muslims

Denmark has been under Christian influence for more than twelve hundred years, and Christianity has been the official religion for more than a thousand years. Today the Evangelical Lutheran Church in Denmark is — according to the constitution — the Danish Folk Church, and as such is supported by the state. About 87 percent of the population are members of this church. Only since 1849 has there been freedom of religion in Denmark, allowing for other churches to be established. The membership in all the so-called Free Churches, such as the Catholic Church, the Pentecostal church, the Baptist church, and the Apostolic church, is probably less than 2 percent of the population. Even many of the 11 percent that belong neither to the Folk Church nor the Free Church probably consider themselves Christians in some sense of the word today. The presence of a very visible Islamic religion, and the growing tensions around Islam in the world and in Denmark, probably prompt more people today than twenty years ago to identify themselves as Christians or at least point to the Christian cultural inheritance which is also of great importance to them.

The Christians in Denmark may be grouped in a variety of ways, but for the purposes of this research, apart from the distinction between Folk Church and Free Churches, the distinctions made by Hans Ravn Iversen seem to be most relevant. Iversen distinguishes between three types of Christianity: culture Christianity *(kulturkristendom)*, church Christianity *(kirkekristendom)*, and charismatic Christianity *(karismatisk kristendom)*. Culture Christianity is the religion of the majority of the Christians in Denmark, who are far distant from the church and its practice but are still influenced by Christian values.[15] Church Christianity is the religion of those who not only share the Christian values of the culture Christians, but also accept the faith in Jesus as Son of God and savior of mankind, accept the Bible and our confessions as an expression of Christianity, and participate in the services and the work of the church.[16] Charismatic Christianity is the religion of those whose hearts are burning for the gospel and who therefore become the activists of the church.[17]

It is my hypothesis, which will require more research to substantiate, that the way Christians face Muslims is among other factors determined by which of these types of Christianity they represent. Ralf Pittelkow,[18] Søren Krarup,[19] and Steen Skovsgaard,[20] who all have participated in the debate about Islam in Denmark, can be seen as coming out of the culture, church, and charismatic Christianity traditions, respectively. This does not mean that others from the culture Christianity tradition will agree with how Pittelkow faces Muslims and Islam in Denmark and the world, but there will often be similarities in the way they ar-

15. Hans Ravn Iversen, "Kulturkristendom, kirkekristendom og krismatisk kristendom. Kristendomsformernes baggrund og samspil i folkekirken," in *Kulturkristendom og kirke. Ny Mission nr. 1*, ed. Jørn Henrik Olsen (Copenhagen: Unitas, 1999), p. 20.

16. Iversen, p. 25.

17. Iversen, pp. 28-29.

18. Ralf Pittelkow, *Efter den 11. september Islam og Vesten* (Copenhagen, 2002).

19. Søren Krarup, *Dansen om menneskerettighederne* (Copenhagen: Gyldendal, 2000); Krarup, *Kristendom og Danskhed* (Hovedland, 2001).

20. Skovsgaard, *De fremmede har i altid hos jer.*

gue. Whereas Pittelkow will typically take his starting point in the human rights and the history of enlightenment in the West, Krarup will take his in the Danish people as a Christian people and the history of the church and the Christian people in Denmark, and Skovsgaard will take his in an understanding of the missional obligations of the church and the experience of the worldwide mission. In this way they will reach quite different conclusions concerning the way to face Islam and Muslims in Denmark.

In the political realm we can distinguish between attitudes toward Muslims (and other non-Western immigrant and refugee groups) that reflect goals of either isolation/deportation of the Muslims, integration of the Muslims, or assimilation of the Muslims. According to the first goal, Islamic presence in Denmark should be discontinued. The leader of one rightist party has consistently called for a *Muhammedanerfrit Danmark,* i.e., a Denmark free from "Mohammedans." According to the goal of assimilation, Islam should be relegated fully to the private realm, so that in the public sphere there would still be only one Danish culture. Integration of Muslims, however, would allow for Islam also to be part of the public sphere in a way where it is recognized that Denmark is a multiethnic, multireligious, and also multicultural society.

Theological approaches to Islam differ and may be summarized under the well-known terms "exclusivist," "inclusivist," and "pluralist." An exclusivist will be hesitant to see anything divine in Islam; some would even claim it is demonic and would call for evangelism without necessarily emphasizing dialogue. A pluralist would consider Islam and Christianity more or less on the same level in relation to God and mainly call for dialogue between Muslims and Christians and see no need for evangelism. An inclusivist would look for elements of truth (as seen from a Christian perspective) in Islam and call for both dialogue and evangelism.

Traditionally those Christians who have been engaged in ministry among Muslims have engaged in one or more of the following three types of activities: (1) *diaconia* and social work, (2) dialogue and bridge building, and (3) witnessing and proclamation. These approaches are based on the traditions for mission work in Africa and Asia and the tradition for church work in Denmark. In the Danish church tradition these activities have been carried out not by the official church, i.e., the local congregation, the diocese, or the whole Folk Church and its leaders, but by private individuals organized in Free Church organizations such as mission societies and diaconal societies. Today, however, a discussion is going on also in Denmark about the concept of missional church, according to which the diaconal and missional activities should have their locus in the local congregations.

Danish mission organizations who were working among Muslims in Asia and Africa were the first in the church in Denmark to respond to the challenge of the presence of Muslims in Denmark. Already in 1978, when there were probably only around twenty thousand Muslims in Denmark, the Danish Mission Society (DMS) and Sudanmissionen published the book *En ny tærskel,* which comprised a translation of David Brown's booklet *A New Threshold* and articles about Islam in Europe and Islam in Denmark. The book, which with its inclusivist approach to Islam was strongly criticized by conservative groups in the Lutheran church, advocated both witness to and friendship with Muslims.[21]

The DMS (since 2000 united with the Danish Santalmission in Danmission) in 1984 opened Mødestedet for indvandrere og danskere (The Meeting Place for Immigrants and Danes) in cooperation with local parishes on Vesterbro in central Copenhagen primarily to establish contact between Christians and Muslims. A couple of years ago Danmission established Folkekirkens Tværkulturelle Arbejde i Odense (The Cross-cultural Ministry of the Folk Church in Odense) in cooperation with local congregations, with the goal of welcoming both Christian and Muslim immigrants to the church. In the same vein Sudanmission, in cooperation with the Folk Church congregation in Gellerup in Aarhus, established a ministry among Muslims, which has now been named KIVIK, i.e., Kristent Informations og Videnscenter om Islam og Kristendom (Christian Center for Information and Knowledge about Islam and Christianity), with the aim of entering into dialogue and sharing the gospel with Muslims and equipping local congregations to do the same.

Christian organizations, traditionally working among Christians in Denmark, such as Indre Mission (Inner Mission), Luthersk Mission (Lutheran Mission), and Kristeligt Forbund for Studerende (Christian Association for Students), have also set up ministries among Muslims in Denmark. Together with mission societies, these organizations in 1994 established Tværkulturelt Center (Intercultural Center), a networking organization that brings together most of the organizations, and many congregations, that are involved in ministry among people of other faiths and cultures in Denmark.[22]

In 1997 a center for dialogue between Christians and Muslims, called Islamisk-Kristent Studiecenter (Islamic-Christian Study Center), was opened in Copenhagen. Inspired by the Centre for the Study of Islam and Christian-Muslim Relations at Selly Oak Colleges, Birmingham, Rev. Dr. Lissi Rasmussen, who for many years has studied and practiced dialogue in Denmark and Africa, pioneered this work together with other dialogue-minded Christians and Muslims. The purpose for the center is "Through teaching, information, counsel-

---

21. David Brown, *En ny tærskel. Kirken og muslimerne* (Copenhagen: DMS-forlag, 1978).
22. H. Nielsen, *Samtalen fremmer forståelsen.*

ling, conversations and common praxis — to bring about a dialogue and a mutual respect among people with a Christian and a Muslim background."[23]

A survey conducted in 2000 indicated that only 1 percent of the local congregations in the Folk Church had initiated ministries addressed to Muslims.[24] Recently, however, the official Folk Church has taken initiatives to face the challenge of Muslims. In 1998 the bishops set up a committee to consider how the Folk Church should face the multicultural and multireligious challenge. In their report, *Samtalen fremmer forståelsen* (Conversation furthers understanding), the committee concluded that the presence of Muslims challenged the Folk Church (1) to strengthen the Christian identity of its members, (2) to build bridges between Christians and Muslims, and (3) to engage in mission among Muslims.[25] As a follow-up to this report, the bishops in seven of the ten dioceses in the Folk Church in 2001 set up a new organization called Stiftssamarbejdet "Folkekirke og Religionsmøde" (Cooperation between Dioceses "Folk Church and Religious Encounter"), whose objective it is "on the basis of the preaching of the gospel to strengthen the encounter of the Folk Church with other religions."[26]

Some of the Free Churches, however, have been more active in intercultural work and in work among Muslims than the Folk Church.[27] A small group within certain Free Churches has employed an aggressive crusadelike rhetoric toward Muslims (e.g., Moses Hansen), but the vast majority focus on peaceful evangelism.

### Muslims Face Christians

No statistics are available concerning Muslims in Denmark. The approximately 170,000 Muslims today are the second-largest religious grouping in the country, after the Folk Church. The most significant characteristic about this group is

23. Lissi Rasmussen, "Islamisk-Kristent Studiecenter," in *Samtalen fremmer forståelsen*, p. 33, translation mine.

24. Kristine Kaaber Pors and Anette Nielsen, "Fokus på sameksistens. Folkekirkemedlemmer, muslimer og andre danskere," in *Samtalen fremmer forståelsen*, p. 79.

25. Nielsen *Samtalen fremmer forståelsen*, pp. 161-82.

26. Vedtægter for samarbejdet mellem stiftsøvrigheder om "Folkekirke og Religionsmøde" (2001).

27. The minister for ecclesial affairs, Rev. Tove Fergo, commenting on the information that a Pentecostal congregation had baptized fifty Iranians with Muslim background, noted that Free Churches "by their very nature are much more active in mission than the Folk Church. I am really of the opinion that it would be good for the Folk Church to be inspired by them. If we believe in the holy gospel, then we also ought to make it known to people" (Mads Gravers Larsen, "Muslimer bliver kristne," *Fyens Stiftstidende* 16, no. 3 [2002]).

that it is a religious minority, and therefore often also feels under pressure from the majority society. How does this Muslim minority face the majority Christians? The statement by a member of a Muslim student organization is typical for the Muslim community in Denmark. "Our goal is not to convert Danes to Islam. We never engage in mission. But, in a matter of fact way we inform and answer questions about our daily life and our religion, so that people will get a more realistic idea of who we are."[28] Hardly any experts on Islam will deny that Islam in one sense or another is a missionary religion, and *da'wa* (invitation to Islam) is part of the teaching of Islam. In an article about *da'wa* in western Europe, Lars Pedersen observes, "The scepticism and hostility that Islam encounters in the West necessitates that Muslims state that *da'wa* is not directed against non-Muslims."[29] When we analyze the situation in more depth, however, we will no doubt find out that Muslims in Denmark have quite different understandings of *da'wa,* and also have quite different ideas of how to face Christianity, Christians, and the so-called Christian society.

Muslims in Denmark are, like Muslims in other parts of the world, divided along Sunni and Shia lines, but it seems that the most important divisions have to do with their ethnic origin. The largest groups are those with a Turkish and a Pakistani background. Others come from Morocco, Iran, Iraq, Palestine, Somalia, etc. Many mosques and other religious and social organizations seem to be organized primarily according to ethnic lines, and this ethnic affiliation probably influences the way they as Muslims face Christians.

Another very important parameter seems to be what kind of relation they have to their Muslim faith and practice. Similar to Hans Ravn Iversen's grouping of Christians, it seems Muslims may also be grouped in three sections: (1) secularized cultural Muslims with almost no religious practice but who are still influenced by Islamic values, (2) traditional Muslims whose religious identity is strongly tied to their ethnic identity and whose level of religious practice may vary, and (3) activist Muslims whose religious identity is not primarily tied to ethnicity but to one or the other transethnic interpretations of Islam.

The way Muslims face Christians in Denmark will probably also be related to their general approach to the Danish society. Here we may find a parallel to the approaches of various political and other groups toward Muslims: (1) isolation: some Muslims want to limit the contact with non-Muslims to an absolute minimum; (2) integration: others want to maintain their Islamic iden-

---

28. Anette Marcher, "Vi er danske, vi er muslimer," *Politiken. Islam. Særtryk,* January 16, 1997, p. 16, translation mine.

29. Lars Pedersen, "Invitation til islam. Da'wa i Vesteuropa," *Tidsskriftet Antropologi* 23 (1991): 147-59, here 147, translation mine.

tity also in the public sphere while they participate as much as possible in the Danish society; (3) assimilation: others try to become as Danish as possible, thereby avoiding Islamic appearances in public.

Traditionally, Islam has been spread in two different ways, either top-down or bottom-up. According to the top-down method, a geographical area, a country or a community, is included in the Islamic world for example following a jihad, and Islamic law, shari'ah, is introduced. When this Islamic ambience has been created, the inhabitants may over time become Muslims. In Denmark there are groups such as Hizb-ut-Tahrir that seem to favor this approach. According to the bottom-up method, individuals are converted to Islam through *da'wa,* and such conversions may in the long run affect the society from bottom to top. With few exceptions those Muslim groups who are actively concerned about spreading the Islamic faith to non-Muslims in Denmark favor this method.

The term *da'wa,* however, has different dimensions and has been interpreted differently. Some Muslim groups mainly emphasize the internal aspect of *da'wa,* according to which the efforts are directed toward Muslims in order to strengthen their Islamic faith and practice. Other Muslim groups, without neglecting the internal aspect, underline the external aspect, which aims at presenting Islam to non-Muslims in the hope that they become Muslims.

When engaging in the external form of *da'wa,* three different approaches to Christians may be identified, also in the Danish Muslim discourse. (1) The supersessionist position. Here the Quranic principle of "abrogation" *(tansikh),* according to which a later verse abrogates an earlier one, is applied to the history of religions so that the Quranic revelation of Islam abrogates the authority of the (earlier) religion of Christianity. Christianity has been fully superseded by Islam. *Da'wa,* according to this position, is often controversialist, an example of which is the writings of Ahmad Deedat, which are also distributed by certain Muslim groups in Denmark. (2) The revisionist position. According to this position, Christianity as a revealed religion being based on natural religion *(din al-fitra)* is in harmony with Islam, but the truth of the gospel has been corrupted by generations of Christians. The goal of *da'wa* is to bring Christians back to the original truth. (3) The ecumenical position. This position advocates a pluralistic approach according to which there is no need for Christians to become Muslims. The purpose of *da'wa,* then, is to invite Muslims and Christians into dialogue of mutual self-criticism.[30]

The external *da'wa* has traditionally taken two forms: (1) lifestyle *da'wa* and (2) direct *da'wa* through preaching, distribution of literature, etc. The

---

30. David Kerr, "Islamic Da'wa and Christian Mission: Towards a Comparative Analysis," *International Review of Mission* 89, no. 353 (2000): 150-71, here 160-62.

question about who in the Islamic community is supposed to be involved in *da'wa* has been answered differently by different groups. Some charge the whole *umma* with this responsibility, while others point to special individuals and groups who should be trained for this purpose.[31]

Even a cursory reading of Muslim literature distributed in Denmark and Danish Muslim websites[32] reveals that Muslim groups in Denmark are concerned about *da'wa* and are engaging in *da'wa*. On the website islam.dk a guide telling prospective converts how to become Muslims is advertised, and a number of conversion accounts from Denmark and other countries are also available. On the same website a so-called starting kit *(StartPakken)*, with the basic literature on Islam, a prayer rug, compass, calendar, prayer timetables for *salat*, etc., is advertised. This kit is addressed to converts, young Muslims, and other Muslims who need it, and is prepared by cooperation between a number of Islamic organizations and individuals.[33] It would, however, require more research to outline the most significant *da'wa* activities carried out by Muslims in Denmark.

## Conversion to Islam — Conversion to Christianity

After a short overview of the sources and the methodology employed for the analysis of conversions between Islam and Christianity, we will introduce the converts from Islam to Christianity and from Christianity to Islam and analyze their accounts.

### Sources and Methodology

Since the religious affiliation of the inhabitants of Denmark is not recorded (apart from the membership of the Folk Church), nobody knows for sure the exact number of Christians and Muslims in the country. The exact number of converts from Islam to Christianity and from Christianity to Islam is even more difficult to estimate. Christian leaders involved with ministry among Muslims estimate that between three hundred and five hundred have converted to Chris-

31. Safet Bektovic, "Mission og/eller dialog?" http://www.ikstudiecenter.dk/artikler 12-05-2002.

32. A search on www.google.com for Danish websites with *da'wa* and *da'wah* gives eighty-four hits, most of which are Muslim sources.

33. Among the participating organizations are Det Islamiske Trossamfund (Waqf), Independent Scandinavian Relief Agency (ISRA), Islam.dk, Murabitun c/o AbdAllah Tolstrup, Zahra Bookshop c/o Abdul Wahid Pedersen.

tianity.[34] The Danish convert Imam Abdul Wahid Pedersen estimates that about five thousand Danes have converted to Islam. There is no doubt, however, that the number of converts to Islam by far exceeds the number of converts to Christianity. A fairly safe estimate is that the latter is a few hundred whereas the former is a few thousand.

A number of converts to Christianity and to Islam have published their conversion story or have been interviewed by newspapers and magazines. The number of accounts of conversions to Islam, however, is much higher than of conversions to Christianity, and often converts to Christianity are referred to only by pseudonym and without specific information that might help the reader identify them. The reason seems to be that Muslims who leave their faith and community think their conversion might attract negative reactions from the Muslim community or even persecution; whereas Christians who convert to Islam do not believe their conversion will endanger their welfare. In Denmark freedom of religion is guaranteed all, including the right to convert from one religion to another, but according to Islam law, which in some respects may still inform some Muslims though they live under Danish law, there is no freedom to leave Islam, and apostasy is punishable by death.

In this initial exploratory research I have selected six accounts of Muslims converting to Christianity and seven accounts of Christians converting to Islam, from among the available published accounts. The selection does not in any sense claim to be representative; I selected the accounts so as to identify aspects of conversion processes in a Danish context within the last twenty years. The conversion accounts, whose details about the spiritual journey of the converts vary a lot, present the converts' perception of their own conversions, or at least what they want the readers to know about them.

These thirteen conversion accounts will be briefly analyzed. A variety of models, based on decision-process thinking, have been developed, but for the purposes of this study I have chosen an adaptation of the conversion model developed by Allan R. Tippet using Van Gennep's theory of rites of passage and his own study of conversion in the Pacific Islands.[35] This is a simplified model that is useful in analyzing the spiritual journey of people in Denmark converting to Christianity or Islam.

This model underscores that the communication of the gospel is not a

---

34. Lissi Rasmussen, who is a pastor in Copenhagen in the Evangelical Lutheran Church in Denmark, reports that she has over the years baptized about twenty-five former Muslims, including children. In the Pentecostal church in Odense, about fifty former Muslims, primarily from Iran, have been baptized (Larsen, "Muslimer bliver kristne").

35. Alan R. Tippet, "Conversion as a Dynamic Process in Christian Mission," *Missiology* 5, no. 2 (1977): 203-21.

single event, but a series of communicational events that form a process or a spiritual journey. The conversion process is here depicted as consisting of three phases: the awareness phase, the decision phase, and the incorporation phase, which might also be considered as three dimensions of the conversion process: the dimension of awareness, the dimension of decision, and the dimension of incorporation.

Whereas Tippet in his original model has a fourth phase, the maturation phase, I follow Seppo Syrjänen, who in his research of the conversion of Muslims in Pakistan combines this phase with the phase of incorporation.[36] The phase of incorporation in this study therefore has no definite end; rather it continues throughout the life of the converts; similarly, the awareness phase has no definite beginning.[37]

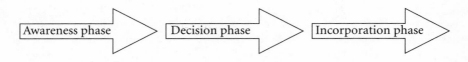

**Conversion Process Model**[38]

The movement from the awareness phase to the decision phase is not marked by any observable events; and often the two phases overlap. The awareness of the gospel, that is, the understanding of Christianity as an alternative to one's present way of life, may come to individuals or groups by

36. Seppo Syrjänen, *In Search of Meaning and Identity: Conversion to Christianity in Pakistani Muslim Culture* (Vammala, Finland: Missiologian Ja Ekumeniikan Seura R.Y., 1987), pp. 63-66.

37. In Tippet's original model, the four phases are clearly separated by observable events. The point of realization separates the awareness phase and the conversion phase, the point of decision (or encounter) separates the conversion phase and the incorporation phases, and finally the point of consummation (or confirmation) separates the incorporation phase and the maturation phase. Implicit in his model, however, is an understanding of conversion, which is based on a bounded-set theory. Tippet's model, however, does not do full justice to the theological understanding of conversion as a very dynamic process as outlined above, according to which the crucial issue is the direction of the movement. Here the centered-sets model may better help us understand and describe conversion. Whereas the bounded-sets model emphasizes the relationship of the individual or group to certain boundaries, the centered-sets model focuses on the relationship of the individual to the center, which is God/Allah. Here the critical issue is whether a person is moving toward a new center. Conversion, then, is manifested in the act of changing directions (Paul Hiebert, "Conversion, Culture and Cognitive Categories," *Gospel in Context* 1, no. 4 [1978]: 24-29, here 26-29).

38. Adapted from Tippet, p. 207.

way of discovery, through a natural development, through pressure from without, through the internal pressure of a crisis situation, or through direct advocacy. When the receptor has not only been exposed to the gospel message but has also understood it so well that he/she is ready to respond to it meaningfully, either positively or negatively, he/she has entered the decision phase. In this phase the receptor begins to consider the gospel and its implications for him/her and finally makes a conscious decision to become a follower of Jesus Christ and a member of the church. In my research I have considered the initiation rite of baptism, which confirms the convert's change of religious faith and his/her transfer to the religious community of the church, to be the point of transition between the conversion phase and the incorporation phase.

### Analysis of Stories of Conversion to Christianity

After a short description of each of the six converts to Christianity, the conversion accounts will be analyzed. First some personal data, as far as they are available in the sources, will be presented. Then each of the three phases in the conversion process will be analyzed in terms of significant factors and dynamics.

#### Short Descriptions of the Converts

SHADI

Shadi was born in Iran. In 1986, when she was nine years old, she came to Denmark to be reunited with her father, who had fled from Iran two years earlier. The family lives in a town in Jylland. When she was fourteen, she participated in the confirmation class in the Evangelical Lutheran Church in Denmark and was baptized. It was, however, only two years later that she, according to her own evaluation, really became a Christian. She is the only Christian in her family.[39]

MASSOUD

Massoud was born in Iran. In 1988, when fifteen years old, he fled from Iran to avoid military service. Sometime later his mother also came to Denmark as a refugee and became a Christian. Later in 1996 Massoud became a Christian. To-

---

39. Birthe Munck-Fairwood, "Integration — for enhver pris?" *Nyt på tværs* 1, no. 3 (1998).

day he is a Danish citizen and studies theology and is a pastor for a group of mainly Iranian Christians in the Pentecostal church in Odense.[40]

## YASSIN

Yassin was born in Iraq. After nine years in the army, including participation in the wars against Iran and Kuwait, he fled to Jordan. After a year in Jordan he was recognized as a convention refugee and was granted asylum in Denmark in 1994. In the process of his conversion he was in contact with the Meeting Place, run by the Danish Mission Society and local parishes in the Folk Church in Copenhagen. In 1998 he was employed by Emdrup Church in Copenhagen.[41]

## HABIB

Habib was born in Iran. In 1999 he came to Denmark as a political refugee. He fled to Denmark via Canada with his wife and their six-year-old son. He and his family became Christians while residing in an asylum center. At the time of his baptism he had not been granted asylum.[42]

## GHOLAM

Gholam was born in Iran. In 2000 he came to Denmark as a refugee, due to political persecution, leaving his wife and his little daughter in Iran. Within the first ten months of his stay in Denmark he came in contact with Christian Iranians in the Pentecostal church in Odense and was baptized. At the time of his baptism he had not been granted asylum.[43]

## BAHRAM

Bahram was born in Iran and was trained there in an insurance company. He fled Iran in 2000 because of political persecution. In 2001 he came into contact with Christian Iranians in the Pentecostal church in Odense and was baptized, twenty-nine years old. At the time of his baptism he had not been granted asylum.[44]

40. Kamilla Walsøe Frederiksen, "Flugten er indstillet," *Politiken* 21, no. 1 (2001); Leif Munksgaard, "Flygtet to gange!" *Kordegnenes Blad* 4, no. 3-5 (2002).

41. Jutta Weinkouff, "En Gud, man ikke behøver være bange for," *Dansk Missionsblad* 8, no. 18-19 (1998).

42. Birthe Munck-Fairwood, "En dag får vi et normalt liv," *Nyt på tværs* 4, no. 3 (2001).

43. Anders Eriksen, "Gholam mødte Jesus i en drøm," *KE (Pinsekirkens Blad Odense)*, October 2001, p. 21.

44. Poul Kirk, "Baram risikerer dødsstraf," *KE (Pinsekirkens Blad Odense)*, December 2001, p. 3; Larsen, "Muslimer bliver kristne."

*Personal Data*

Five of the six converts come from Iran, and the sixth from Iraq. Although no statistics are available, it seems that a very high percentage of all the converts in Denmark come from Iran. Further research is required to determine what the reasons may be.

Five of the six are men, but for two of them the whole family are Christians. From other studies about conversion from Islam to Christianity, it seems that it is after all easier for men to convert to Christianity than women.

Apart from the young girl who was baptized when she was only fourteen, all the others seem to have been in their twenties when they converted to Christianity. Massoud had spent eight years in Denmark before he converted, whereas the three other men converted to Christianity within a couple years. It would be interesting to find out in which phase of their integration into Denmark conversion occurred.

*The Awareness Phase*

What relationship did the converts have to Islam before they converted? Massoud seems to have continued to practice Islam after he came to Denmark and up to the time he converted to Christianity. His parents and he were orthodox Muslims who considered Islam the last and truest religion meant for all mankind. Others, like Gholam, grew up in orthodox Muslim homes but had lost their Islamic faith due to the oppression from an Islamic regime and were only nominal Muslims. Habib expresses it this way: "My previous religion was my family's religion. It was not in my heart."[45] Shadi is an example of a convert who grew up in a Muslim family that was not very religious.

How did the converts become aware of Christianity? First of all, coming to a country where the vast majority were Christians made an encounter with Christianity almost inevitable. In Yassin's opinion, "Christianity has quite visibly influenced the Danish culture."[46] Shadi met Christianity in the form of her classmates in primary school, and her attendance at confirmation class and a Christian youth fellowship. Habib is an example of a convert who was contacted by local Christians while still in the asylum center.

45. Munck-Fairwood, "En dag får vi et normalt liv," translation mine.
46. Weinkouff, "En Gud, man ikke behøver være bange for," translation mine.

A church near our asylum center invited the inhabitants for a cross-cultural dinner and evening song in the church. We went there, though we were Muslims. We even entered the church room. I did not understand the Bible text, because it was in Danish, but I understood that they sang about God and talked about Jesus. Being there in the church had a strong emotional impact on me. It was a good experience. Nobody asked what religion we had. Nobody advertised Christianity or encouraged us to convert. People were just friendly and welcoming. Nobody said that they did not trust us because we were Muslims.[47]

For him Denmark was the place of religious freedom where he could realize his dream of becoming a Christian.

For Massoud the most significant contact was with his mother, who had become a Christian before him. For other Iranian converts an Iranian Christian fellowship played a significant role.[48]

In Iran there are a few Christian churches, and some of the converts from Iran probably also met Christians there. Habib's aunt lived near a Christian church, and Habib said he often had wanted to enter the church but could not because he was a Muslim. "Later I got to know some Christians; they were quiet and kind people, and I was very interested in their faith. But I knew that it was impossible to convert to Christianity in Iran. It is quite simply forbidden."[49]

The converts got their information about Christianity from Christian friends and from participating in Christian programs, either Danish or Iranian Christian. Apart from that, the reading of the Bible played a significant role for their conversion (Massoud, Yassin). Yassin reports that "When I began to read in the New Testament, I felt that Jesus spoke directly to my emotions. Jesus talks about forgiveness, peace and love. It gave me an inner peace that I did not know before, for here was a God that I needed not be afraid of."[50]

## The Decision Phase

Why did the converts get frustrated with Islam? For some Islam was closely as-sociated with what they wanted to escape in their homeland, such as political

---

47. Munck-Fairwood, "En dag får vi et normalt liv," translation mine.

48. This applies not only to Gholam, but also to many other Iranian converts (Kirk, "Baram risikerer dødsstraf"; Eriksen, "Gholam mødte Jesus i en drøm"; Larsen, "Muslimer bliver kristne").

49. Munck-Fairwood, "En dag får vi et normalt liv," translation mine.

50. Weinkouff, "En Gud, man ikke behøver være bange for," p. 19, translation mine.

oppression and war (Yassin, Gholam, Massoud, Habib, and Bahram). For some the lack of assurance of salvation in Islam was a problem (Yassin, Massoud). Massoud said, "I could not come close enough to God (in Islam). I felt that it was difficult to have to live all your life without knowing whether you would end up in Paradise or Hell."[51]

What attracted them to Christianity to the extent that they decided to become Christians? Following what was said above, assurance of salvation by faith in Jesus Christ played a significant role for some. Others report that the warm fellowship in the congregations was very attractive (e.g., Gholam), or they point to the focus on love in the Christian religion (e.g., Bahram).

For some converts dreams also seem to have played a significant role in helping them commit themselves to Christianity (Gholam). Saida, who is from Iran and not among the six converts studied in detail here, regularly visited the Meeting Place in Copenhagen and even attended services.

> "Once when my children were small, they were very sick. One night Jesus appeared to me in a dream, and the following day they were well again. Therefore I have several times, both in Iran and here in Denmark, visited a church to pray."
>
> "But Saida," I then say, "are you not a Muslim? How come you go to a Christian church to pray?"
>
> Saida is quiet for a moment. . . . "When I pray to Allah, I do not receive answer; when I pray to Jesus I receive help."[52]

There may, however, also be other, less spiritual factors at work. Shadi's parents worked hard to become as Danish as possible, and Shadi followed suit. "When I was fourteen years old, my class were to be confirmed. My goal was to become as Danish as possible, so I also wanted to be confirmed. My family was Muslim, but were not very religious, so I was allowed to do so. Then both my sister and I were taught by the pastor's wife every Friday for a year. We did not understand much, but this was what we wanted."[53]

Later on she experienced personal faith in God, and this helped her find her identity as both Iranian, Danish, and Christian at the same time. Still, however, she pointed out that "One of the big advantages of being a Christian is that I have a Danish circle of acquaintances. When I experience something negative, such as racism, my Danish friends help me to understand how the Danes

---

51. Frederiksen, "Flugten er indstillet," translation mine.

52. Oddrun Aasebø Rønne, "Guds mærkelige veje," http://www.dbi.edu/Artikkler 16-04-2002, translation mine.

53. Munck-Fairwood, "Integration — for enhver pris?" translation mine.

think. I have a bunch of Danes around me that I trust — the confidence is mutual. It is like a family that God has blessed me with."[54]

This sociological dimension of conversion to Christianity has been highlighted in the media in connection with the application for asylum from converts from Islam to Christianity. Habib, Gholam, and Bahram all were baptized before they were granted asylum. Did the desire to be granted asylum play any role in their conversion? All of them deny it. Gholam claims that he no longer fears to have his application for asylum turned down. "Whether I am in Denmark or in Iran does not mean much to me because I can serve Jesus in both places!"[55] Though many experts agree with the Iranian converts that their life may be in danger due to the Islamic law of apostasy if they are sent back to Iran, the governmental refugee authorities say they dare not give asylum to converted Muslims, because they doubt the genuineness of the conversions.[56]

### The Incorporation Phase

Some of the converts in this sample are incorporated in ordinary congregations in the Folk Church (Yassin, Shadi), while others — from Iran — have joined an Iranian congregation that is associated with the Pentecostal church. Led by an Iranian pastor, this congregation has experienced extraordinary growth over the last four years. About fifty converts from Islam (most of them Iranians) have been baptized, and about thirty-five of them belong to this congregation. Further research is required to find out how converts feel at home in various types of congregations.

The present data does yield much information about how the converts feel accepted by Christians (i.e., the ethnic Danes) after their conversion. Shadi apparently felt well received by her closest friends, whereas she felt that other Danes treated her negatively. Yassin was accepted by a Lutheran congregation that employed him to work as a kind of deacon, and the Iranian congregation was welcomed in the Pentecostal church.

Another aspect of the incorporation of the converts in the Christian community is the establishment of families. Some of the converts were already married at the time of conversion, and their wives and children were converted together with them. In one case the converted man married a Christian woman

54. Munck-Fairwood, "Integration — for enhver pris?" translation mine.
55. Eriksen, "Gholam mødte Jesus i en drøm," translation mine.
56. Kirk, "Baram risikerer dødsstraf."

also converted from Islam, but from another ethnic group. It requires further research to find out what is the general trend concerning marriage of converts, whether they predominantly marry Danish Christian women or Christian women with a Muslim background.

The Iranian asylum seekers felt the authorities in Denmark had no compassion on them when they foresaw that their conversion to Christianity would produce serious problems if they were returned to Iran. The Iranian pastor in the Pentecostal church in Odense observes about the attitude of the Danish refugee authorities, that "First, it prevents Muslims from becoming Christians. Second, it stops the integration completely. We ought to be much more open about taking these people's wish to convert seriously."[57]

Here the Iranian pastor sees conversion from Islam to Christianity in Denmark to be a possible element in the integration of Iranians. Others, such as Muslim leaders, might consider this an element in assimilation. As Shadi experienced personally, all converts face the challenge of establishing a new identity that accommodates both their original Iranian (or another ethnic) identity with their new Christian and Danish identity.

This identity formation is often rendered difficult by the rejection from their family and ethnic community that converts often experience in connection with their conversion. One convert expresses it this way: "Before I took the decision (to convert to Christianity), I had underestimated the price. On the other hand I had also underestimated the blessing and peace I now feel."[58]

The price he had to pay was both economic and relational. When he converted to Christianity, his former Muslim customers boycotted his bakery. When his family in Iran happened to hear about his conversion, his father got very angry and said he would no longer have anything to do with him. Years later, however, he is again on talking terms with his father. In spite of the general rejection from Muslims, he is still in contact with Muslims and also has friends among Muslims.

## Analysis of Stories of Conversion to Islam

After a short description of each of the seven converts to Islam, the conversion accounts will be analyzed. First some personal data, as far as they are available in the sources, will be presented. Then each of the three phases in the conver-

---

57. Larsen, "Muslimer bliver kristne," translation mine.
58. Frederiksen, "Flugten er indstillet," translation mine.

sion process will be analyzed in terms of significant factors and dynamics. I should note here that the data yields more information about the converts to Islam than about the converts to Christianity.

## Short Descriptions of the Converts

### REINO

Reino was born in Denmark and is forty-eight years old. He studied anthropology at the university, but he spent most of the time from his twenty-first to his twenty-fifth year traveling in Africa and the East. After a couple years as a practicing Hindu, he encountered Muslims in Denmark and in 1982 converted to Islam. Presently he is the principal of an Islamic school in Copenhagen, imam, leader of an Islamic aid organization, and vice chairman of the Islamic Christian Study Centre in Copenhagen. He is married to a Muslim woman from Morocco. Today he calls himself Abdul Wahid.[59]

### ASIJA

Asija was born in Denmark. She converted to Islam sometime after she married a Muslim man. Her original name is not known.[60]

### AISHAH

Aishah was born in Denmark. After eighteen years active service in the Jehovah's Witnesses, she converted to Islam in 1991. Her original name is not known.[61]

### MARTIN

Martin was born in Denmark. He first encountered Muslims while a student residing in a student hostel in Herlev near Copenhagen, in 1997. He converted to Islam the same year. Today he is married to a Muslim woman from Pakistan and is a teacher in an Islamic primary school. His Muslim name is Musa.[62]

---

59. Abdul Wahid Pedersen, "Den lange vej hjem," http://www.islam.dk/muslimforum 16-04-2002; Bente Clausen, "Islams Jens Vejmand," *Kristeligt Dagblad* 27, no. 4 (2002).

60. Asija Kristensen, "Møde med Islam," http://www.islam.dk/muslimforum 16-04-2002.

61. Karima Fahim, "Fra Bibelen til Koranen," http://www.islam.dk/muslimforum 16-04-2002.

62. Lars Halskov and Henrik Røjgaard, "Dansker blev muslim i en Mazda," *Politiken* 24, no. 6 (2001): sec. 3, p. 5.

## PETER

Peter was born in Denmark. He grew up in a suburb to Aarhus. In 1998 he came in contact with Muslims, and half a year later he was offered a teaching position in an American school in Egypt. While there in 1999, he converted to Islam; he was twenty years old. He returned to Denmark and was married to a Muslim woman from Algeria in 2000. Today he is an office trainee in Copenhagen.[63]

## JAKOB

Jakob was born in Denmark. He first came in contact with Muslims when he traveled through the Sahara Desert in 1991. Together with his girlfriend and cohabiter, he converted to Islam in 2000. He is today a professional text writer in Copenhagen.[64]

## KARI

Kari was born in Denmark. She grew up in Roskilde and now lives with her father in Copenhagen. In 2000, at seventeen, she converted to Islam. Today she works as a sponsor contact for the Muslim aid organization ISRA, in Copenhagen. Her Muslim name is Amina.[65]

### *Personal Data*

One of the converts was only seventeen when she converted to Islam (Amina), one was probably in her early forties (Aishah), and the remaining five seem to have been in their (early) twenties.

Four of the converts are men, three women. While most of the first converts to Islam in Denmark were women who married Muslim men (like Asija), in recent years the number of men who convert every year seems to exceed the number of women.[66]

Five of the conversions took place within the last five years, one eleven years ago, one twenty years ago, and the date of one is unknown.

---

63. Signe Thomsen, "Et dansk liv med Allah," *Morgenavisen Jyllandsposten* 24, no. 11 (2001): sec. 1, p. 5.

64. Jakob Werdelin, untitled, *Kordegneforeningens Blad* (2002).

65. Mette-Line Thorup, "Aminas svære valg," *Information* 24, no. 12 (2001).

66. This hypothesis is based on observations of reports of conversion in the press and in the mailing list dfc.dk (Danmarks Forenede Cybermuslimer, the Danish United Cyber Muslims), attached to the website www.islam.dk., and from conversations with Muslims.

### The Awareness Phase

None of the converts seem to have been practicing Christians (belonging to the Folk Church or a Free Church), and most of them come from homes where Christianity played a very small role. Peter's home is fairly typical. "We never talked very much about Christianity or any other religion. We sang the Christmas hymns and visited the church once a year."[67] One of the converts, however, had been an active member of the Jehovah's Witnesses for eighteen years prior to her conversion (Aishah), and others had been involved with New Age and Eastern religions (Jakob, Reino). Reino had even resigned his membership of the Folk Church years before his conversion.

> I was brought up in a fairly ordinary Danish home and had no real relationship with God when I was a child. In my early youth my mother had given me a book about Chinese philosophy, *Earthly Happiness* by Lin Yutang, which made me begin to think along existential lines. I was confirmed like my age-mates, but began at the same time to consider whether I really belonged in the Danish Folk Church or it was only something I was culturally conditioned to feel. When I was sixteen I resigned my membership of the church in order not to be there on a false basis. Now I wanted to find out where I really belonged and I felt that this could best be done if I was free. I therefore did not resign out of protest but simply in order not to be a hypocrite until I had made my choice.[68]

It seems that before encountering Islam, a number of the converts had felt a spiritual and/or moral emptiness and were looking for answers to their existential questions.[69] As can be seen from this quote and from other conversion accounts, Christianity and the church did not really play any role and were not seen as a viable option for a spiritual life. Before Martin decided to convert to Islam he had a secure life with a girlfriend, but he was not happy. "If I had just continued like that, I would just have ended up in a bigger apartment with another girlfriend. But it was an empty life, and I missed some spiritual and moral values."[70]

67. Thomsen, "Et dansk liv med Allah," translation mine.
68. Pedersen, "Den lange vej hjem," translation mine.
69. Martin seems to have been in a spiritual crisis before he became a Muslim. He would spend much time alone, sitting in his room and staring into the air while he thought over the meaning of life. It did not make sense to him that he had been planted on the earth by accident without any purpose. He studied Christianity, Judaism, Hinduism, and Buddhism without finding any answer (Thomsen, "Et dansk liv med Allah").
70. Halskov and Røjgaard, "Dansker blev muslim i en Mazda," translation mine.

How did the converts first become aware of Islam? Five converts met Islam through Muslim friends. Martin is a typical example of the importance of Muslim acquaintances and friends. While living in a student hostel, he met two Iraqi men who — though they were not practicing Muslims — introduced him to their religion and culture. Shortly afterward, in a badminton club, he met a Pakistani man who was a strong believer in Islam. Together with another Muslim they had daily conversations with Martin about Islam and answered his questions.[71] Asija is an example of a woman who fell in love with a man who happened to be a Muslim. "My first encounter with Islam started in my marriage. Even before I became a Muslim I had submitted to many of Islam's laws such as not to eat pork and drink alcohol. At that time I was convinced that a marriage could very well function in spite of two different cultures and religions. Eating habits were not all that important, if we only could respect each other's lifestyle and 'meet in the middle.'"[72] It was in the context of her happy marriage with her Muslim husband that she, after having begun to follow some of the Islamic precepts, got to know the deeper values of Islam.

Two of the converts encountered first Muslims and then Islam through travels in Muslim countries in Africa and Asia (Reino, Jakob), but for both of them contact with Muslim friends in Denmark also played a significant role. Living in a Muslim country (Egypt) apparently contributed significantly to the conversion of Peter, who had previously been in contact with Islam in Denmark.

## The Decision Phase

The church and Christianity did not play any significant role in the life of the converts, except for Aishah, who was a Jehovah's Witness. The data from this sample, however, does not give us more insight into the converts' evaluation of Christianity than was presented in the above section. When we in this section consider what attracted the converts to Islam, we may indirectly conclude something about their evaluation of Christianity and the church.

Peter's brief description of his first impression of Islam reflects what many converts apparently feel when they consider becoming Muslims. Peter stated clearly that it was the encounter with two Turkish young men of his own age that opened his eyes to Islam.

71. Halskov and Røjgaard, "Dansker blev muslim i en Mazda."
72. Kristensen, "Møde med Islam," translation mine.

First, I thought they were crazy when they would not go out and get drunk. But then I got curious too and felt strongly attracted by the fact that together with them I could very naturally discuss the big issues in life without a lot of alcohol on the table. I was fascinated that the Quran contains answers to the big as well as the small questions in life. It shows exactly how you must live to be a good Muslim. Christianity does not have similar rules, so it easily becomes sort of a "Sunday religion." As a Muslim you are reminded of the greatness of Allah at least five times a day.[73]

First, Peter points to the moral values he sees in the lives of his Muslim friends. When Asija's Muslim husband began to practice his religion more consistently, she saw moral and spiritual changes in his life that she appreciated and that attracted her to Islam. Similarly, when his girlfriend and cohabiter decided to convert to Islam, Jakob saw a transformation in her life. She looked ten years younger.

My (then) girlfriend and I began to practice the Islamic gender roles, somehow just to try it out. Immediately our perpetual confusion, our bickering and our mutual insecurity disappeared. We were revived to the joy of being mutually complementary parts of our relationship. In the Quran Islam is described as "the natural way of life/arrangement" — we were more in love with each other than when we met for the first time. I realized that this was the sign I had waited for — a spirituality which is practicable in the world, here and now. A reflection of the fruit and wine of Paradise, in the midst of the cement town of Copenhagen in the year 2000.[74]

Second, Peter points to the importance of the Quran as a source of wisdom in life. Most of the other converts also point to the central role that the reading of the Quran played for their decision to become Muslims. Jakob encountered the Quran three years before he actually converted to Islam. When reading A. S. Madsen's Danish translation of the Quran, he rejected its message as irrelevant, based on his modern "secular" Christian and New Age background. "And still . . . there were things in the Quran that hit me, sudden drops

73. Thomsen, "Et dansk liv med Allah," translation mine. Asked about the most common conversion motives for Danes converting to Islam, Imam Abdul Wahid Pedersen (Reino) points to the family values in Islam and concrete and practical guidelines for life wanted by young people. Imam Fatih Alev points to a renewed interest in the Quran after the September 11 events, and Tim Jensen points out that for young people today Islam is a way to express opposition to society (Signe Thomsen, "Flere unge: Ja til islam," *Morgenavisen Jyllandsposten* 24, no. 11 [2001]: sec. 1).

74. Werdelin, untitled, translation mine.

that burned their way across this unhandy translation and my own complacent and proud 'enlightened understanding' about how the facts of the matter are — so I hastened to close the Book and do what any civilized man would do, that is, open the TV instead."[75]

Martin, who began to study the Quran shortly before his conversion, felt that if he could show that it was not true, he could reject the challenge from his Muslim friends, but if the Quran was true, he would have to convert to Islam.[76]

For Aishah, who as a Jehovah's Witness was very familiar with the Bible, it was a small booklet by Ahmed Deedat about Muhammad in the Bible that spurred her on to the study of the Quran and finally led her to conclude that certain passages in the Bible had been corrupted and that the Quran was the true and final message from God.[77] For Jacob the "revelation" came when he read the Bewley translation for three weeks. "I have read many splendid philosophical works, and I am myself a professional text writer, and at once I *knew* that what I had in my hands did not come from a man."[78] All of them seem to have felt that they got logical answers to their questions from the Quran.

Third, Peter points to the values of the ordered ritual life. What impressed Reino, who had been a practicing Hindu for two years, when he visited some European converts to Islam, was their disciplined ritual life. In the middle of the night the call to prayer woke him up. He concluded that if they really got out of bed at that time of the night, washed and started praying, this had to be something more powerful than his own occasional prayers. Therefore he got out of bed and joined in their prayers, knowing that somehow they were praying to their creator. It was after their prayer that he began to ask questions about their religion. After discussions about Islam for the next two or three days, he decided to become a Muslim.[79]

The case of Reino points to the critically important role of individual Muslims who guided and directed these people toward and through conversion. In almost all the conversion accounts, we can trace the role of individual or groups of Muslims who played this role. Asija, who was married to a Muslim man, sought out a Muslim sister who over a period instructed her in Islam by answering her questions and challenging her with her own questions.[80]

75. Werdelin, untitled, translation mine.
76. Halskov and Røjgaard, "Dansker blev muslim i en Mazda."
77. Fahim, "Fra Bibelen til Koranen."
78. Werdelin, untitled, translation mine.
79. Pedersen, "Den lange vej hjem."
80. Kristensen, "Møde med Islam."

## The Incorporation Phase

Apart from Peter, all the converts seem to have taken Muslim names to signify to all who meet them that they belong to the Muslim *umma*. Female converts start following an Islamic dress code, including the wearing of veils in public, and the Islamic food laws, including the prohibition of pork and alcohol.

Some of the conversion accounts contain data about the effect of the conversion on their relationship with family and friends. Family and friends reacted very negatively toward some converts when they heard of the conversion. In most cases the relationship with the family was restored after some time, but some lost all or some of their non-Muslim friends while others were able to keep the friendships.

None of the converts lives in a mixed marriage. In one case the couple converted more or less at the same time (Jakob), in another the convert was already married to a Muslim (Asija); others married a Muslim woman from a non-Danish ethnic group after their conversion (Peter, Reino, Martin). It would be interesting to find out if it is a general tendency that converts to Islam marry Muslim women from a non-Danish ethnic background and become integrated into various ethnically non-Danish subcultures. Peter pointed out that in his marriage with a Pakistani Muslim woman, they follow Muslim traditions concerning family life. Asked whether a Danish girl would accept this, he answered, "No, but now I am married to a Muslim girl. I do not mind Danish girls, but I was more attracted to the foreign culture that my wife comes from."[81]

Aishah focuses on the need for all Muslims in Denmark to unite and seek protection in groups so that their children will be well prepared to face future problems. She warns against the bad influence from non-Muslims and from bad Muslims. "Muslims should be on the guard against integration since it is impossible to be fully integrated (in the Danish society) if you follow the rules of Allah. Satan wishes to pull all (Muslims) down to the low and immoral level on which many Danes live."[82]

For her, as for other converts, the Islamic identity seems to be primary. And since integration into the Muslim *umma* sometimes involves integration into the subculture of a certain ethnic group, conversion may for some lead to a situation where they develop an affinity to another ethnic group in addition to their Danish identity.

It requires further research to detect the long-term sociological effects of conversion to Islam.

81. Halskov and Røjgaard, "Dansker blev muslim i en Mazda," translation mine.
82. Fahim, "Fra Bibelen til Koranen," translation mine.

## Conclusion

This paper does not present any conclusive research concerning mission and *da'wa* and conversions between Islam and Christianity, but as an initial exploratory research it has aimed at presenting the broad outline of this topic and certain perspectives for further research. The paper has shown that some research has been carried out or is being carried out in other Western countries, but only concerning conversion to Islam. Conversion to Christianity in the West is still a virgin field. In Denmark no research has so far been conducted concerning conversions between Islam and Christianity. Such research will be complicated due to the sensitive nature of the data, but not impossible. Some research has been carried out about the Muslim community in Denmark, but since the history of Islam in Denmark is so short and since the Muslim community as well as the Danish context of this community is undergoing many changes these days, much more research is needed. The Christian mission among Muslims and the Islamic *da'wa* among Christians in Denmark have not been researched very much. This topic is of course also quite sensitive, but handled with much care, it should be possible to research it, at least partially. This initial exploration of the whole topic of mission/*da'wa* and conversion between Islam and Christianity has further indicated that there may be very interesting parallels to analyze.[83]

---

83. Cf. David Kerr's comparative analysis of *da'wa* and mission in Kerr, pp. 162-68.

# BIBLICAL PERSPECTIVES

# Seeking God — Sought by God: New Testament Perspectives on the Gospel in a Multifaith Context

JOHANNES NISSEN

Three introductory remarks are in order. First, this paper should be seen as a contribution to the conversation between biblical scholarship and missiology. My model of interpretation is the dialogue between the biblical texts and to-day's experiences.

Second, the Mediterranean world of the first century A.D. was very much like our own time with regard to its pluralism in religions.[1] This means that the New Testament books were written in a situation which can be compared to our present situation.

Third, we should notice that the New Testament does not offer a uniform picture of how to relate to people of other faiths. Some texts seem to be quite exclusive in nature, others have a more open character.

In this paper I shall focus primarily on the last category of texts. This is not to say that I am ignoring the "exclusivistic" texts. But in the first place the focus will be on some selected "seeker" texts (the Gospel of Matthew, the book of Acts, and the Gospel of John). The question is to what extent the religious search of human beings is acknowledged by the New Testament writers or to what extent this search is corrected. Do Jesus and the first Christians fulfill all spiritual searchings? Or, in contrast, do they contradict and nullify other faiths? In other words, what is at stake is the issue of continuity and discontinuity be-tween the gospel and other religious traditions.

---

1. Cf. T. Fornberg, *The Bible in a World of Many Faiths* (Stockholm: Svenska Kyrkans Forskningsråd, 2000), p. 119.

*Johannes Nissen*

# Seeking God

## *The Gospel of Matthew*

It is widely accepted that the so-called Great Commission in Matthew 28:16-20 should be regarded as a key to the entire Gospel of Matthew. It is also beyond dispute that this text has an important role in modern mission. The strong emphasis on Matthew 28, however, has sometimes resulted in neglect of other aspects of the Gospel.[2]

Mission as invitation is an important aspect of Matthew's Gospel.[3] It is not just a question of disciples *"going out"* for preaching, but also of the *coming* of Gentiles for worship. Three texts illustrate this point.[4]

The first is *the visit of the wise men* in 2:1-12. The wise men, or *"Magi,"* are religious specialists of astrology and occult arts. They are people capable of interpreting visions and dreams. They might be members of priestly casts in the Eastern capitals. In Hellenistic literature the term "magi" is used for serious, scientific people as well as occasionally for charlatans. In Hebrew Scriptures and Jewish tradition, however, the term often describes unacceptable religious activities. It is the more relevant that Matthew here dares give to the Magi a positive role. Indeed, there is not the slightest critical remark about their journey and search.

Through their religiously based scientific observation and interpretation of the stars, the Magi are capable of finding exactly who was born and where they have to go. The text affirms that they realize the importance of the newborn person, and are able to do so exclusively through their own scientific and religious search. Matthew shows them ready to kneel down before Jesus, in an act of humble submission and adoration.

The second text is the story of *the centurion* in 8:5-13. A main point in this story is the officer's faith in contrast to the faith of the Jews; this is made clear by Jesus' statement: "Truly I tell you, in no one in Israel have I found such faith" (8:10). Jesus' description of the Gentile nations coming to the kingdom (8:11) has a direct relation to the Magi, who also come "from the East."

If in 2:1-12 the Magi were examples of a thorough, honest, and authentic

---

2. See, for instance, my article "Matthew, Mission and Method," *International Review of Mission* 91, no. 360 (January 2002): 73-86.

3. On this issue see H.-R. Weber, *The Invitation: Matthew on Mission* (New York: United Methodist Church, 1971).

4. My analysis of these texts is inspired by J. Matthey, "Pilgrims, Seekers and Disciples: Mission and Dialogue in Matthew," *International Review of Mission* 91, no. 360 (January 2002): 120-34.

religious journey and search, and then of joyful adoration of the new Lord, in this text the officer shows how profound the confidence and faith of an outsider can be. The Magi had found Jesus on the basis of their own religious astrological knowledge. The centurion had been guided by the "fame" of Jesus. "In both cases, people from outside the chosen community appear to understand more profoundly what an important person Jesus is and what changes he can bring to human life. God clearly uses other ways and means than just the church to fulfill the *missio Dei*."[5]

The third text is about *the Canaanite woman* in 15:21-28. She represents a third religious attitude of an "outsider" toward Jesus. Her approach is a much more emotional one. She imposes herself, disturbs Jesus' own journey, and fights for her right to receive something from the one she perceives to be a holy man.

It is significant that the texts which relate the encounter with the centurion and the Canaanite woman have counterpoints elsewhere in which Jesus criticizes the lack of real faith by his own disciples; compare 8:23-27 and 14:22-33. Matthew presents the "outsider's" faith in contrast not only to his own Jewish community of origin, but also to his actual community, the church.

The gospel never allows Christians to feel superior to people who come from other religious traditions, who may encounter Christ in their own way even without later joining a church.

Matthew's Gospel opens with the spiritual journey of the Magi from the East to Jerusalem and Bethlehem. The Gospel ends with the sending out of the disciples on a missionary journey, the horizon of which is the whole world. Matthew's Gospel itself can be understood as the result of the spiritual journey of Matthew and his community, which is the journey that had not ended at the time of the final editing of his book.[6]

To sum up, then: by telling these stories, the Gospel of Matthew reflects a positive attitude toward religious seekers. Yet in Matthew, as in other biblical texts, religion sometimes seems to be ambiguous in nature. Religion can have a self-asserting, or even demonic, aspect; compare the story of the temptation in the desert (4:1-11).[7] However, we should notice that this is a risk both "outsiders" and disciples have to face. The important thing is that God's mission aims

---

5. Matthey, p. 125.

6. Matthey puts forward the thesis that Matthew's own journey somehow reflects Jesus' own spiritual itinerary, which moved him from a restricted understanding of his own mission to creative encounters with those journeying with or toward him, or who crossed his way. Matthey, p. 129.

7. See J. Nissen, "Mission in Christ's Way: The Temptation in the Desert and Christian Mission," in *Identity in Conflict: Classical Christian Faith and Religio Occulta*, Festschrift J. Aagaard, ed. M. L. Pandit et al. (New Delhi: Munshiram Manoharlal Publ., 1998), pp. 41-52.

at encounters between human pilgrimages. As was the case for Jesus himself, such encounters will result in mutual respect and recognition; in contemporary terms we would speak of dialogue, as when disciples meet people like the Magi or the centurion from Capernaum.

## Acts 17:17-34

Paul's "missionary speeches" in the book of Acts are of special interest. Each speech has the form of a monologue; nevertheless, the content is dialogical. They can be characterized as "including dialogues"; that is, Paul pays regard to the questions, viewpoints, and experiences of his listeners.

The speech at the Areopagus (17:17-34) is one of the most famous missionary texts in the New Testament.[8] How are religious seekers conceived of in this text? There is a certain tension between the context and the speech itself.

When waiting for his fellow workers, Paul spent his time walking around in the city. He then "was deeply distressed to see that the city was full of idols" (17:16). There is a puzzling contrast in attitude between this strong reaction in verse 16 and the much more conciliatory one in verse 22: "I see how extremely religious you are in every way." This comparison reveals the ambiguous character of religion. The reactions attributed to Paul show a variety of possibilities. One is the emotional disgust typical of a minority as a sect — the characterization of the images of "idols" (17:16) implies a negative judgment. It reflects a Jewish judgment on Greek piety that is a minority viewpoint vis-à-vis the dominant culture of Athens. Another is the attempt to find some positive elements in discussion with members of the majority.

The second possibility is adopted by Paul in the speech, which has three parts: (1) points of contact (vv. 22-23); (2) continuity and criticism (vv. 24-29); (3) contradiction (vv. 30-31). Paul's address begins with highest praise for the Athenians: by every criterion they are very religious people (17:22). As Paul was passing through the city, observing their sacred places and objects, he saw an altar with the inscription "To an unknown god." Such an altar was built in honor of unknown gods in order to prevent them from being angry if they did not receive any adoration. This is an expression of a radical polytheism.

It is, however, interesting that Paul interprets the inscription in a different way: behind this polytheism is a hidden longing for the one, true God. Thus he makes the decision to begin where the listeners are in their own religious quest.

---

8. For a more detailed analysis see J. Nissen, *New Testament and Mission: Historical and Hermeneutical Perspectives* (Frankfurt am Main: Peter Lang, 1999), pp. 62-66.

Paul finds a point of contact in the concept of God, but for him there is a great distance between this *"neutral"* God (v. 23) and the Christian proclamation of a *personal* God (vv. 24-31). Therefore, in the end of verse 23 he can declare his intention: "What therefore you worship as unknown, this I proclaim to you" (cf. John 4:22).

In the middle part of the speech Paul emphasizes the continuity between the search of human beings and the Christian God; compare the famous words in 17:28: "For 'In him we live and move and have our being'; as even some of your own poets have said. 'For we too are his offspring.'"

A crucial shift in Paul's argument comes in the last two verses. Here a contrast is made between two times (v. 30): the times of ignorance and the time to repent. And there is a reference to the eschatological judgment and the resurrection of Jesus (v. 31).

The main focus in the Areopagus speech is on a missionary strategy based on a positive approach to the religiosity of the Greeks.[9] At this point there is a clear difference between Romans 1 and Acts 17. Comparing these two texts, L. Legrand concludes to "two great axes . . . of continuity and discontinuity." "Discontinuity places the stress on the radical newness of Christ and his resurrection and by contrast sees the ancient world as darkness and sin. That is the viewpoint of Rom 1. The continuity, on the contrary, underlines the homogeneity of salvation unfolding according to God's plan. It is the viewpoint of Acts 17, which . . . presents a Greek world waiting for the unknown God and prepared by its poet-theologians to meet him."[10]

However, it should not be overlooked that the Areopagus speech has both elements of continuity and discontinuity. Some pluralistic theologians of religion forget or say nothing about the fact that both the Areopagus speech as well as the speech in Lystra (Acts 14:5-20) end in exhortations to repentance (Acts 14:15 and Acts 17:30).[11]

## The Gospel of John

"What are you looking for?" (John 1:38). These are the first words of Jesus in the Fourth Gospel. They indicate a theme of great importance for the author.

9. Cf. J. Dupuis, *Toward a Christian Theology of Religious Pluralism* (New York: Orbis, 1998), p. 50.

10. L. Legrand, "Jésus et L'Eglise primitive: Un éclairage biblique," *Spiritus* 138, no. 36 (1995): 64-77 (75-76). Here quoted from Dupuis, p. 50.

11. Cf. Fornberg, p. 103. His criticism may apply to W. Ariarajah, *The Bible and People of Other Faiths* (Geneva: WCC, 1985), pp. 45-46.

Throughout the Gospel people are searching for something. It seems as if they are searching for fellowship with God and other persons, for the meaning of life, for a place to belong.

In 1:35-51 this search is performed by the first disciples, but in other parts of the Gospel it is performed by persons coming from various religious traditions.[12] Three passages are of particular importance.[13] In chapter 3 Jesus is approached by Nicodemus, a representative of the *Jewish* leaders. In chapter 4 he meets a representative of the *Samaritans*. And in chapter 12 some *Greeks* desire to see Jesus. All these texts are of interest. Here I shall limit myself to the first story, 3:1-21.[14]

Two things are characteristic for religious seekers. First, they are living *"at night."* The term "night" has a double meaning. It has a literal aspect denoting the fearfulness and insecurity of Nicodemus. And it has a symbolic aspect denoting his lack of understanding.

Secondly, a religious seeker will often be content with a *"teacher."* In verse 2 Nicodemus addresses Jesus as follows: "Rabbi, we know that you are a teacher who has come from God." A teacher is a person who helps us to a better understanding of our existence.

Nicodemus's opening statement looks like an ascertainment, but it is more than this — it is a quest for salvation. The following dialogue indicates that Jesus takes him seriously in his honest search for truth. Yet Nicodemus is also corrected at some decisive points.

The dialogue focuses on the meaning of a begetting from on high. First it is argued that begetting from above through the Spirit is *necessary* for the entrance into the kingdom of God — natural birth is insufficient (vv. 2-8). In the second part of this passage, the point is that the begetting is made possible *only* when the Son has ascended to the Father, and it is offered only to those who believe in Jesus (vv. 9-21). This is another way of saying that begetting through the Spirit can come about only as a result of Jesus' crucifixion and resurrection/ascension.

John 3 illustrates the longings and aspirations uttered by a representative from one of the religious traditions (Judaism). However, the concept of rebirth

12. Cf. G. Theissen, *A Theory of Primitive Christian Religion* (London: SCM Press, 1999), p. 190: "In the first part of the Gospel of John Jesus keeps encountering people's expectations of salvation which he fulfils and transcends at the same time."

13. See also the section "Christ as God's Universal Invitation," in Nissen, *New Testament and Mission*, pp. 83-92.

14. Cf. J. Nissen, "Rebirth and Community: A Spiritual and Social Reading of John 3:1-21," in *Apocryphon Severini*, Festschrift S. Giversen, ed. P. Bilde et al. (Aarhus: Aarhus University Press, 1993), pp. 121-39.

itself conveys such a longing. It is a longing for a totally new being, a longing to transcend oneself. In New Testament times many people were dreaming of such things. Indeed, this dream seems to be as old as the human race. In the hermetic literature rebirth means a process of divinization (*Corpus Hermeticum* XIII.2).

This idea of divinization is not found in John 3. By contrast, the main emphasis is on the element of discontinuity. Rebirth means a radical transformation and is not something that can be attained through human effort.

Thus there is a novelty in John's thought when compared with Judaism as well as Hellenism. The Jewish religion — represented by Nicodemus — is inadequate. It cannot move forward continuously into the kingdom of God. A moment of *discontinuity,* comparable with physical birth, is essential. Man as such is not by nature able to enter the kingdom of God. John differs also from Judaism by saying that the kingdom has already been manifested in the person and work of Jesus.

But John also differs from Hellenism by insisting on the incarnation and the historical character of Jesus Christ (vv. 14-16). He does not just take over the concept of rebirth, but he incorporates it into his proclamation of Christ without subscribing to the idea of divinization.

The Gospel of John has a rich store of symbols. These are other examples of the importance of the search of human beings. Most of these symbols are universal and related to the ordinary life situation of man.

The "I am" sayings are of special importance.[15] Here the divine name is linked to such predicates as "bread," "truth," "life," or "way." These predicates are symbols of the human quest for God.[16] The hungers and longings signify the long search for the face of God, a search depicted in Wisdom literature precisely in such forms. John implies by such declarations as "I am the bread of life" (6:35) and "I am the light of the world" (8:12) that in Jesus, God's manifest presence and gropings of humanity for God meet. The predicative "I am" sayings are to be taken as recognition formulas in Bultmann's famous classification: "What you understand by the bread of life and long for in it is fulfilled in me."

15. For a more detailed analysis see the section "Inclusive and Exclusive Aspects of Johannine Christology," in my book *New Testament and Mission*, pp. 86-87.

16. Theissen notes that the longing for true life is present in all religions. But only in Jesus is it fulfilled. Readers of the Gospel of John know from the start that he is the embodiment of life (1:4). And each of the "I am" sayings speaks of the provision of gain in life; Theissen, *A Theory*, p. 194.

Johannes Nissen

## A Trinitarian and Christological Approach —
## Some Johannine Perspectives

It has often been argued that there are three principal approaches to other religions: exclusivism, inclusivism, and pluralism, or to be more precise: (1) a christocentric exclusive approach; (2) a christocentric inclusive approach; (3) a theocentric pluralistic approach.[17]

The debate has been largely about which approach is correct, but now a growing number of scholars are suggesting that this is a most unhelpful debate and that we need to be looking for a new approach which does not deny the strengths of these three but goes beyond them. The most exciting development at the moment is the suggestion that it is in a deeper understanding of the Trinity itself that we will be led to a clearer theology of faiths.[18] A trinitarian Christology is an alternative to exclusivism, inclusivism, and pluralism.[19]

John's Gospel is one of the strongest biblical supports for the understanding of mission as *missio Dei,* that is, the movement of God to man, in creation, in incarnation and redemption, a movement involving Father, Son, and Holy Spirit.[20] Here are a few notes on the role of these three persons in the Gospel of John.

### The Father

There are four types of sending in the Fourth Gospel: John the Baptist, Jesus himself, the Paraclete, and finally the disciples. These missions are interrelated. All re-

---

17. E.g., J. van Lin, "Models for a Theology of Religions," in *Missiology: An Ecumenical Introduction,* ed. A. Camps, L. A. Hoedemaker, M. R. Spindler, and F. J. Verstraelen (Grand Rapids: Eerdmans, 1995), pp. 177-93. Instead of the categories exclusivist, inclusivist, and pluralist, Kirk prefers to speak of *particularity, generality,* and *universality;* J. Andrew Kirk, *What Is Mission? Theological Explorations* (London: Darton, Longman and Todd, 1999), pp. 139-40.

18. Cf. *A Whole New World Together: Four Spotlights on Mission,* the CMS Bicentenary, 1799-1999 (London: Church Mission Society, 1999), p. 33; S. Mark Heim, *The Depth of the Riches: A Trinitarian Theology of Religious Ends* (Grand Rapids: Eerdmans, 2001), p. 127: "The Trinity represents the Christian context for interpreting religious pluralism."

19. G. D'Costa has five concise theses for a trinitarian approach. The first is that a trinitarian Christology guards against exclusivism (Christomonism) and pluralism (theocentrism) by dialectically relating the universal and the particular; G. D'Costa, "Christ, the Trinity, and Religious Plurality," in *Christian Uniqueness Reconsidered: The Myth of a Pluralistic Theology of Religions,* ed. G. D'Costa (New York: Orbis, 1990), pp. 16-29 (p. 18); cf. Heim, p. 127.

20. Cf. W. Klaiber, *Call and Response: Biblical Foundations of a Theology of Evangelism* (Nashville: Abingdon, 1997), p. 61.

volve around Jesus. John announces his coming, the Paraclete confirms his presence, the disciples proclaim his word to the world. But the endpoint of this Gospel's missiology is not Jesus but the Father. The Father alone is *not* sent. He is the origin and the goal of all testimony of the Gospel; compare 1:1-18 and 17:20-23.

The Gospel is about Jesus, but Jesus is about God. "John was concerned to confront his readers through Jesus with God."[21] Johannine Christology is perfectly transparent in the sense that Jesus does not attract attention to himself but points to the Father whom he constantly reveals. The Father is the center of the Gospel. Jesus is "only" a medium; in other words, "the way." As revealer of God, he lets all the light pass through him to the Father.

## The Son

John's Gospel is both theocentric and christocentric. This is particularly clear in the prologue. The central affirmations are made in verses 1, 14, and 18. Jesus is the Word with God from the beginning, and so intimately bonded with God that the Word can be called "God" (vv. 1-2). This Word is so embedded in the human sphere that it becomes "flesh" and lives in the midst of the community (v. 14). The uniqueness of the incarnation is given in the closing sentence in verse 18: Jesus Christ is the unique revealer of the living God.[22]

The Christology of the Fourth Gospel is marked by a peculiar combination of inclusive and exclusive aspects. This can be illustrated by the "I am" sayings. They have often been seen as the "exclusive verses" in the Bible, because they present Christ as unique, as the only way to God and to salvation (cf. Acts 4:12). This understanding, however, is not quite accurate. Thus the famous statement, "I am the way, and the truth, and the life" (14:6), reflects a continuity with other religious traditions as well as a certain discontinuity.

It is not accidental that John uses specific notions and terminology from the religious traditions of his contemporary world.[23] The multiplicity of religious ways and paths was an issue in the New Testament period — as it is today.

---

21. C. K. Barrett, *The Gospel according to John* (London: SPCK, 1978), p. 97; cf. Nissen, *New Testament and Mission*, p. 78.

22. The important thing in the prologue is the movement from the first part (vv. 1-13) to the second part (vv. 14-18), which is a movement from the universal to the particular, from eternity to history, from the impersonal to the personal. And men and women are called to follow that movement, and thereby realize that Jesus Christ is the unique revealer of the living God (v. 18).

23. For instance, in Jewish tradition we meet the term the "Way of the Torah," and the Qumran community designated itself as the Way. A third example is the "way" of John the Baptist.

The first sura of the Quran is seen as the way (or straight path). Hinduism knows of three ways to salvation. Buddhism talks about the Eightfold Path. In Chinese tradition Tao is seen as the Way, the chief way.

These traditions from the New Testament period and from modern times indicate that such longings and aspirations of humanity are to be recognized. They reflect the universal condition of all mankind, created in and through the eternal word. Here is the element of continuity. But equally the Christian community believed then, as it must still, that the Way of God has been most clearly discerned in the way that Jesus followed — the path of rejecting and suffering, of abandonment and death. This way is clearly discontinuous with all other religious ways.[24]

The Christology of the Fourth Gospel is marked by a peculiar combination of inclusive and exclusive aspects. In certain passages Jesus not only provides a place, but also becomes the *entrance* to that place or even *the place* itself. In the Fourth Gospel we can speak of a "hospitality christology."[25] In such all-encompassing Christology Jesus is the temple for the true worship of the Father. He is the new holy place. Yet at the same time the exclusiveness and uniqueness of Christ is maintained. He is the exclusive revealer: no one has ever seen God except the one and only Son (1:18). He is the only way to the Father (14:6).

### The Holy Spirit

The Holy Spirit plays a significant role in John. Two of the most interesting passages are 3:8 and 16:12-15.

The function of the Holy Spirit is to lead the community into *all* truth (16:13). There is the prospect here of coming into a new understanding beyond what the community has already reached. A similar dynamic understanding of the Spirit is reflected in 3:8: the Spirit blows wherever it pleases.[26] The promise in 16:13 is a remarkable one. We are plainly told that there is more to be learned than can be found in the recorded teachings of Jesus to his disciples during the years of his ministry (cf. 14:12). We might tend to think of the Bible as a book

---

24. Cf. K. Cracknell, *Towards a New Relationship: Christians and People of Other Faith* (London: Epworth, 1986), pp. 84-85.

25. J. Koenig, *Jews and Christians in Dialogue: New Testament Foundations* (Philadelphia: Fortress, 1979), p. 133.

26. Thelle argues that the concept of the Spirit in John 3:8 should be linked with John's Logos Christology; N. R. Thelle, *Hvem kan stoppe vinden. Vandringer i grenseland mellom Øst og Vest* (Oslo: Universitetsforlaget, 1991), pp. 13-14.

containing timeless truths. This, however, is not how John sees the work of the Spirit. The Holy Spirit enables the community to perceive senses of the biblical text that had previously remained hidden.

The Holy Spirit makes Christ more present, more comprehensive, more transforming. In its Spirit-prompted mission to the world, the church will discover the true meaning of the Word made flesh.[27] The church must continue to grow in a more profound understanding of the words uttered by God "once for all" in the divine Word incarnate. To this end, the church is assured of the constant assistance of the Spirit that guides it "into all the truth" (16:13).[28]

## Love and Truth

To these observations regarding the three divine persons should be added a few notes on the role of love and truth in relation to a theology of religion.[29] Both concepts are of great importance in John's Gospel.

In John "truth" is not to be understood as a conception which can be acquired and owned once for all. Truth cannot be achieved through philosophical and religious speculations. "Truth" is related to a person, not a dogma: "The truth will make you free" (8:32); "The Son makes you free" (8:36). "Spirit and truth" (4:23) means that God is a living person who has revealed himself in Christ.

John's hermeneutic can be described as a "hermeneutic of the Spirit and of Love."[30] The love of the disciples among themselves and their unity let the world recognize that the Father has sent Jesus into the world as the bearer of his love (13:34; 17:23).

27. Cf. D. Senior and C. Stuhlmueller, *Biblical Foundations for Mission* (London: SCM Press, 1983), p. 288.

28. Cf. Dupuis, p. 250. Dupuis speaks of "a continuing divine self-revelation through the prophets and sages of other religious traditions, as, for example, through the prophet Muhammad. That self-revelation has occurred and continues to occur in history. No revelation, however, either before or after Christ can either surpass or equal the one vouchsafed in Jesus Christ, the divine Son incarnate" (pp. 249-50).

29. On the question of truth see, for instance, H. Ucko, "Truth or Truths," *Current Dialogue*, no. 37 (June 2001): 30-37. According to Ucko, the Bible itself portrays truth in more than one way. The Hebrew word for truth is *emeth*, which denotes a reality, which is firm, solid, valid, and binding. The emphasis is not so much on truth as being as on truth as truthfulness, trustworthiness, and dependability. God is truthful. One can rely on God. The Greek word *aletheia* says Christ is the answer to the question of true being in an absolute sense. Traditional Christian theology oscillates at best between these two understandings. It would be important to keep this in mind when seeking to come to terms with the question of truth in a religiously plural world (p. 34).

30. Cf. Klaiber, pp. 72-74.

The "new command" to love one other is mentioned in two passages, 13:34-35 and 15:12-17. There is a clear indication in the second passage that the most important thing in the Gospel of John is now being said. Previously Jesus had often proclaimed that he has to proclaim the decisive message from God, that he says what he has heard from the Father. But we never hear what he has heard there, in the heavenly world. Only once in the Gospel is it expressly emphasized that Jesus has now said *everything* he has heard from the Father, namely, the second formulation of the commandment to love.[31]

If Jesus has said everything in the commandment to love, he has indicated that agape is the only way to the Father, the only truth, and the only entrance to life.[32] In other words, what is absolute in John's Gospel is this love. It is the way, the truth, and the life. No one comes to the Father except through it. Jesus is "the way, and the truth, and the life" precisely because he himself is the manifestation of this love. The implication of this for a theology of religions is that the love must be the critical yardstick for everything, even our own religion.

It seems that the Christian criterion for discerning truth and revelation in other religions can be summed up in one word: love *(agapē);* for "God's central revelation, which is given in Jesus Christ, is *agapē.*"[33] In Christ God has united with humankind in an irrevocable bond of love. This is why saving *agapē* finds in Christ its decisive theological foundation.[34]

## Sought by God

### *Integrity and Openness*

The primary attitude of Jesus, as demonstrated to those he encountered in his lifetime, was respect and love. As Jesus is seen as respecting the faith and integrity of others, commonly meeting people on their own ground — and often at

---

31. Cf. Theissen, *A Theory*, pp. 196-97.

32. The following remarks are inspired by G. Theissen's paper "Johannes 4:5-30" ("Deutsche Kirchentag," 5-9 June 1991). See also my article, "Vejen, sandheden og kærligheden," *Præsteforeningens Blad* 85 (1995): 49-57 (esp. 56-57).

33. P. Starkey, "Agapè: A Christian Criterion for Truth in Other World Religions," *International Review of Mission* 74 (1985): 425-63 (433).

34. Cf. Dupuis, p. 325. In his fifth thesis on a trinitarian approach to other religions (cf. n. 19), D'Costa claims that the normativity of Christ implies the normativity of crucified self-giving love, and this prescribes the *mode* of relationship with those of other traditions; in addition, the pattern of self-giving love is a standard that can validate witness to Christians from other traditions. D'Costa, p. 20.

the far borders of acceptable religious behavior in his day — so are Christians called to relate in such a way to others, going to the borders of faith and unbelief.[35]

Following Kosuke Koyama, I would argue that a theology of religion must have this openness toward the faith of other people. But at the same time it must also be christocentric. That means it should be based on the crucified Christ.[36]

The question is: How can we maintain genuine Christian integrity while at the same time being open to people of other faiths? A similar question is addressed by Paul in 1 Corinthians 9:19-23. In this passage integrity and openness are held together. The text clearly implies that Paul allowed circumstances and situations to determine the statement of his kerygma to a considerable degree. How can Paul be "all things to all men"? Only by finding a point of reference outside himself. The law of Christ (9:21) is the law of love which becomes the authority of Paul's missionary adaptation.

If we want to get an accurate picture of Paul's attitude toward people of other faiths, his openness toward Jews and Greeks in 1 Corinthians 9:19-23 should be counterbalanced by his critique of Jewish and Greek culture in 1 Corinthians 1:18-25. This is another way of saying that the cross is an indispensable part of Christian integrity. Therefore, when we attempt to understand the dialectic relationship between integrity and openness, we must ask the important question: How can our witness to the particularity of the cross, which is so offensive and foolish to others, be shared without a show of arrogance?[37]

Paul's reflections in 1 Corinthians 9 indicate that he as a missionary cannot compel, he can only persuade and appeal; but as a missionary Paul is himself under compulsion, constrained by Jesus' love, the one unfailing missionary motive of all time (cf. 9:16). Paul does not think of the Christian mission either in competitive or humanitarian terms. "He is not pitting one religion against another or making claims of superiority for his own beliefs. He is presenting Christ, for the sole sufficient reason that he deserves to be presented."[38] Authentic mission must be characterized by bold humility.

---

35. This point is underlined by K. Koyama. See also M. Morse, *Kosuke Koyama: A Model for Intercultural Theology* (Frankfurt am Main: Peter Lang, 1991), pp. 196 and 222.

36. Koyama's approach recognizes the absolute reality claims of Jesus (the "absoluteness" of Christ) while respecting and affirming the integrity of people of other faiths; cf. Morse, p. 222.

37. Nissen, *New Testament and Mission*, pp. 122-23.

38. D. Webster, *Local Church and World Mission* (London: SCM Press, 1962), p. 71.

*Johannes Nissen*

## Continuity and Discontinuity

In the introduction I raised the issue of continuity and discontinuity. This issue can be related to the fact that the Bible has two major traditions or "economies":[39] On one hand is the "economy" of the covenant, that is, the covenant granted to Israel and to the Christians. On the other hand is the "sapiential economy" in which all people are embraced. The Wisdom literature describes the action of God through Wisdom. It highlights the human search for the meaning of life. While the first tradition emphasizes a *discontinuity* between Christian revelation and the whole range of non-Christian experience, the second tradition emphasizes the *continuity* between God's activity in Christ and his activity among persons everywhere.

The important thing is that both economies, that of the Mosaic covenant and that of Wisdom, are in a New Testament perspective joined and fused in Jesus. He is "the beloved of God" and the "Son" in whom Israel is resumed. But he is also the "Wisdom of God" present throughout the universe. Both traditions must be affirmed and maintained.

The implication of this is that Christian theology must have a respectful and humble approach to people of other faiths. People search for the truth or for God. We are all on a journey.[40] This search for the truth or for God is seen as something positive in the Bible (Acts 17:27; John 1:38). The decisive point, however, is that regardless of humanity's religious search for God, God is coming to us.[41] With this everything begins. This is the essence of the Bible.[42]

Again and again the synoptic Gospels tell how Jesus is searching for those who are miserable ones, the marginalized, the small. This is the crucial point in the parable of the lost son (Luke 15:11-32). In his story about Zacchaeus, Luke

---

39. Cf. P. Rossano, "Christ's Lordship and Religious Pluralism," in *Faith Meets Faith*, ed. G. H. Anderson and T. F. Stransky, Mission Trends, no. 5 (New York: Paulist; Grand Rapids: Eerdmans, 1981), pp. 20-35 (28-29).

40. K. Koyama reminds us that Jesus Christ means a continuous story, not a deus ex machina answer. One knows what Jesus means when he says, "I am the way . . . ," by walking with him. "Unless one walks on the way, one does not know the way"; K. Koyama, *No Handle on the Cross: An Asian Meditation on the Crucified Mind* (New York: Orbis, 1977), p. 71.

41. In the apostolic letter *Tertio Millennio Adveniente* (1994), the pope states that "Christianity has its starting-point in the incarnation of the Word. Here, it is not simply a case of a human search for God, but of God who comes in person to speak to human beings of himself and to show the path by which he may be reached. . . . *The Incarnate Word is thus the fulfillment of the yearning present in all the religions of humankind:* this fulfillment is brought about by God himself and transcends all human expectations. It is the mystery of grace" (*Acta Apostolicae Sedis* 87 [1995], pp. 8-9).

42. Cf. J. Aagaard, "Christian Faith and the Religions," *Areopagos* 4, no. 3 (1991): 45-46.

narrates that Zacchaeus is seeking to see Jesus (Luke 19:3). Yet it is Jesus who finds him. He is the Son of Man who "came to seek out and to save the lost" (19:10).

The Gospel of John in a similar way describes God as one who is searching for human beings. When the Samaritan woman asks for the right place to worship, Jesus answers that "the true worshipers will worship the Father in spirit and truth, for the Father *seeks* such as these to worship him" (John 4:23). The point is that he seeks such worshipers by sending his Son.

The ultimate theological foundation of mission is this movement of the triune God toward human beings. Mission is first and foremost the God who comes.[43] Moreover, God's mission is the invasion of love in history. It is of vital importance that God finds us in Jesus Christ. Jesus Christ is God in search of man. This notion of the searching God is fundamental to a Christian approach to people of other faiths.

43. Cf. L. Legrand, *Unity and Plurality: Mission in the Bible* (New York: Orbis, 1990), p. 152.

# A Biblical Critique of Jewish-Christian Exclusiveness

KLAUS NÜRNBERGER

The question addressed in this paper is whether the powerful exclusiveness found in both the Old and the New Testaments is part of an obsolete imagery or whether it belongs to the very identity of the biblical faith. After indicating the sociopsychological roots of religious exclusiveness, the essay traces the evolutionary trajectories of a number of soteriological paradigms in biblical history. This exercise shows that there is a strong current of meaning which moves below the situationally conditioned texts in the direction of God's vision of comprehensive well-being for all of humanity in the context of the well-being of God's creation as a whole. Metaphors, such as the king as mediator of divine order and blessing, may have become obsolete. However, the contents of the underlying concern, evolving from the motif of power through the motif of justice to the motif of the suffering, redeeming acceptance of the unacceptable, as well as the assumed agency of salvation, God acting through divinely empowered human action, constitute the identity of the biblical faith and cannot be compromised without abandoning its identity.

## The Problem

The biblical faith, both in the Old Testament and the New Testament, is inescapably exclusivistic. As far as the Old Testament is concerned, one only needs to refer to the Shema — the most fundamental statement of the Israelite-Jewish faith — or the Deuteronomistic introduction to the Decalogue. In the New Testament Christ is taken to be the Alpha and the Omega, and there is nothing and nobody who could compete with him.[1]

1. The biblical reflections are based on an extensive study in my book *Theology of the Biblical Witness: An Evolutionary Approach* (Münster: LIT-Verlag, 2003).

Hear, O Israel: Yahweh is our God, Yahweh alone. You shall love Yahweh your God with all your heart, and with all your soul, and with all your might. (Deut. 6:4f.)

I am Yahweh, your God, who brought you out of the land of Egypt, out of the house of slavery; you shall have no other gods before me. (Exod. 20:2f.)

I am the way, and the truth, and the life. No one comes to the Father except through me. (John 14:6)

There is salvation in no one else, for there is no other name under heaven given among mortals by which we might be saved. (Acts 4:12)

This exclusiveness seems to be based not on peripheral but on fundamental assumptions of the biblical faith. There is one God, the God of Israel. There is one Christ in whom the God of Israel has disclosed his ultimate intentions. Christ sits at the right hand of God, above all principalities and powers which determine the world. He is the long-expected Messiah, the Judge of the last judgment, the King of the coming kingdom, the Head of the church. Pluralistic indifference and postmodernist relativity are clearly out of step with the basic character of the biblical faith.

This paper attempts to probe into the motives for this exclusiveness. Is it due to obsolete, culturally conditioned sets of metaphors which can easily be abandoned? Or is it an expression of the very identity of this faith, without which it would disintegrate? Is it unforgivable religious arrogance and intolerance? Or is there an underlying rationale which, for the sake of the well-being of humanity as a whole, we dare not abandon or compromise?

We shall follow an inductive method. A propositional or positivistic reading of the Bible will not yield answers to these questions. We begin with an analysis of the sociopsychological roots of religious exclusiveness. Then we highlight the fundamentals of an evolutionary hermeneutics of the biblical Scriptures. On this basis we sketch the evolutionary trajectories of six biblical paradigms of salvation. These will reveal that the horizons of the biblical faith have become more inclusive over time, and that it was radically transformed from within. From that we draw some conclusions concerning the legitimacy of the exclusiveness of the biblical faith.

*Klaus Nürnberger*

## Sociopsychological Roots of Exclusiveness

### The In-Group/Out-Group Phenomenon

Under this heading we shall discuss three roots of exclusiveness. The first deals with two basic anthropological motivations: self-protection and self-realization. The womb is a cozy place to be — without danger or want, but also without challenge and freedom. Birth is a traumatic experience because it exposes the infant to a potentially hostile, potentially luring environment. The oscillating balance of power between the organism and its environment leads to the dialectic between withdrawal and conquest — a dialectic which continues through all phases of life. Through maturation the organism gains strength and competence, but never enough to be on top of all situations.

The coziness of the womb is replaced with the love of the mother, then the family, then an array of primary groups. Primary groups fulfill three fundamental religious needs: (a) they convey a system of meaning which defines one's individual and collective identity; (b) they develop a system of values and norms according to which the individual is either accepted or rejected; and (c) they allocate statuses and roles which grant the individual authority to act. Meaning, acceptance, and authority are the three basic spiritual needs of any human being.

Defining its identity, the social group distinguishes itself from other such groups. Whether implicit or explicit, there is a clear boundary between us (the in-group) and them (the out-group). Its function is to keep those inside in and those outside out. Insiders are required to toe the line; outsiders are kept at bay. Depending on the severity of contrasts and the power of interests to be defended, outsiders may become visitors (who are carefully surrounded with politeness, which functions like a layer of cotton wool), strangers, enemies, or outright devils, but never those who belong.

For the sake of stability, the group tends to become homogeneous. Individuals and groups that do not fit are either jettisoned or subdued. Deviant assumptions, values, norms, and behavior are not tolerated. The system of meaning is idealized, if not absolutized. The blame for predicaments and tensions is projected outward. The group sweeps its yard clean, as it were, and throws the rubbish over the fence into the yard of its neighbors.

Where challenged or threatened, the group closes ranks and develops an edifice of rationalizations to justify its stance. Where the power interests of leaders take hold of a social group, this edifice may develop into a full-blown ideology. As we use the term, ideology is a combination of selected facts and clever arguments which is designed to justify the pursuit of collective self-interest at the expense of the interests of others.

The more powerful the underlying interests, and the more persuasive their legitimating ideology, the more exclusive the group will become. The balance of power to which the group is exposed will then determine to what extent it will withdraw into isolation or embark on forays to pressurize, incorporate, or eliminate other groups. In the case of incorporation, the group will impose its rationale on the conquered and exploit their resources.

Prime biblical examples of these sociopsychological phenomena are the divine commandment to expel the Canaanites from the land in Exodus 23 and Deuteronomy 7, the divine legitimation of Davidic rule over conquered kingdoms in Psalm 2, and the prophetic vision that Jerusalem will become the capital of a world empire.

The powerful conviction that they were the chosen people of God lent resilience to the Jewish minority in the face of dispersion, humiliation, and oppression in ancient times. It is also the root of the intense hostility among many Jewish groups against any interpretation of the God of Israel which could erode this particularist self-consciousness. For better or worse, Israel has become the prototype of the religious legitimation of ethnic exclusiveness. But the basic phenomenon as such occurs all over the world, and there is no reason to assume that the idea of being the chosen people of God is unique.

### Widening Horizons

Every individual once emerged from one specific womb. This is every person's primeval point of reference. After birth the mother's love affords a new realm, less securely protected, yet allowing glimpses into a world which becomes progressively more tantalizing and challenging. The sphere of the mother is widened in concentric circles to include the primary family, the extended family, the clan, the tribe, the nation, the nations, humanity as a whole, the spiritual and social powers which rule the universe, and finally the cosmos as a whole as far as humans can perceive it.

This widening of horizons applies not only to individuals but also to cultures and religions. Though not necessarily in a clean historical sequence, it can definitely be observed in the evolution of the biblical faith. The God of Abraham is, for all intents and purposes, a clan God, then a God of different tribes, then the people of Israel, then the nations, then the gods, then the universe as a whole. Universalization in turn goes hand in hand with individualization. The God of all people is the God of each individual.

## Historical Flux and Cultural Lag

The flux of time has afflicted human beings since time immemorial because it implies a fleeting and uncertain human existence. The Egyptian attempt to reach immortality, to which the pyramids bear witness, and the Platonic attempt to abstract an ontologically based essence from the flux of empirical reality (expressed in timeless ideas) are two prominent examples.

Concepts such as eternity (the dissolution of time), universality (the dissolution of space), and perfect harmony (the dissolution of power differentials) have no demonstrable referent in empirical reality. In fact, they represent an escape from reality. The only eternity we can imagine is the past, because the past can no longer change, but the past is also no longer real. It is potent only in the form of memories and consequences, both of which are also subject to the flux of time.

Religion posits what reality ought to be, in contrast to an experienced reality which is less than desirable. Perceptions of what ought to be are, of course, also subject to the flux of time. If the projection of what ought to be is combined with the attempt to escape from time, space, and power differentials, religious perceptions are absolutized into what is perceived to be divine, perfect, eternally and universally valid. That is the root of fundamentalism. Fundamentalism can degenerate into fanaticism.

This general phenomenon is exacerbated by the fact that historical processes are subject to differential acceleration. All cultures evolve in time, but some evolve much faster than others. For reasons we cannot discuss here, the evolutionary pace of the modern civilization has reached breathtaking dimensions. In contrast, traditionalist cultures remain relatively stable through long stretches of time. The encounter and conflict between modernism and traditionalism opened up and continues to open up vast and growing discrepancies in power, productive capacity, income, and life chances.

Moreover, the inherent dynamic of modernism erodes the very foundations of traditionalism, making it vulnerable to humiliation, oppression, and exploitation. Though extremely flexible and open for emerging insights, modernity is the most exclusivistic worldview the world has ever experienced. Drawing on empirical research and logical inference, it feels entitled to assume that it represents the cutting edge of an unfolding insight into the truth of reality. By implication, traditionalist assumptions are taken to be either obsolete or superstitious. The incredible success story of science, technology, and social differentiation has pushed traditionalism onto the defensive.

Traumatized by this unequal contest, traditionalist cultures have reacted to this threat in three ways: withdrawal, dependency, or rebellion. When the fire of rebellion combines with the motive of withdrawal, it leads, again, to fundamentalist fanaticism. More promising, however, is another development: traditionalists transfer their built-in dependency instinct to the dominant culture, acquiesce in the superiority of the latter, learn its tricks and eventually learn to fight for a place in the system with its own weapons.

Deeply wounded by persistent humiliation and discrimination, these colonized yet modernized elites may then search for an identity of their own by exploring the traditions of their forebears for elements and clues which can be built into what is, essentially, a modern yet distinct mind-set. Postmodernism, whose subversive agenda in fact represents an extreme form of modernity, seems to give legitimacy and dignity to any construction of meaning which may emerge from this endeavor — as long as it remains private and does not interfere in areas of life which really matter, such as science, technology, power, and profitability.

These then are the sociopsychological roots of exclusiveness. They are found in all their variations right within the biblical witness. This brings us to the next topic.

### Evolutionary Hermeneutics

We assume in this essay that the processes of evolution and entropy are found at all levels of reality, including the contents of collective consciousness. The biblical tradition is a case in point. Evolution is a process of constructive unfolding, or a growth in complexity. Entropy is the tendency of all constructs to disintegrate. Combined, the two processes lead to the rhythm of emergence, evolution, deterioration, and decay.

The vitality and viability of a construct can however be prolonged through the import of unused energy (low-entropy energy). That is why the earth's system needs the constant inflow of solar energy. That is why organisms need food to survive and prosper. In our case, religious traditions will become obsolete and irrelevant unless they are constantly rejuvenated by the import of new insights and challenges.

As I have shown in my book, *Theology of the Biblical Witness*, this process can be observed in the history of the biblical tradition. There is a redemptive experience (such as the birth of male progeny in the case of Abraham, or the exodus) which is attributed to the benevolent intervention of God. The collective memory of such experiences leads to a tradition which reassures the community of the benevolence of God. When new calamities strike, they appeal to God, who has helped in the past, to help again.

Constellations of needs and patterns of interpretation constantly change. To retain its viability the tradition must cover the new situation. In other words, environmental challenges lure the original story into an evolutionary process. My research has shown that living traditions are extremely adaptive and flexible. Moreover, over the millennia of biblical history, they tend to turn onto their heads.

Expressed in theological terms: the Word of God enters human consciousness in its primitive and largely undesirable state and gradually transforms it from within. Christ is the "Word become flesh," but this statement is only the outcome of a long history of discernment. Single texts are only single frames of an ongoing movie. To get the true picture, one has to see them in their historical sequence and dynamic. It is possible to discern an undercurrent of meaning the thrust of which can be extrapolated into present needs and predicaments. In this way the canonical or formative function of the biblical tradition is retained without undue absolutization of its concrete contents. These insights now have to be applied to the topic at hand.

## *Evolutionary Trajectories of Some Fundamental Biblical Paradigms*

### *Patriarchal Promises*

Abraham is considered the prime ancestor of a chosen ethnic group, the Israelites. Abraham had, of course, his own ancestry. But the latter is not relevant. The beginning of this particular lineage with Abraham is marked by the promise given to the prime ancestor by Yahweh, the God of Israel, that Yahweh would be the God of his offspring. In concrete terms Yahweh would grant Abraham descendants, and these descendants Yahweh's own land. At this stage Yahweh is the God of a clan.

Note that it is the promise which marks the beginning of the lineage, not the ancestor as such. It is the promise to Abraham which defines Israel's identity. Israel's faith has turned very consistently and strictly against all forms of ancestor veneration or consultation of the deceased. Abraham is considered dead and buried. Yahweh is the "living God" and Israel's only religious partner.

This freedom of the Old Testament from the power of the lineage made it possible for the patriarchal promises to be superseded as an identity-defining paradigm by the exodus, the Sinaitic covenant, and the promise given to the Davidic dynasty. The national catastrophes of 721 and 586, however, questioned the continued validity of these paradigms. Instead of freedom there was enslavement; the covenant was proclaimed to have been broken by Israel; the dynasty was terminated. In this situation Yahweh's unconditional promise to the prime ancestor was revitalized and used to reestablish Jewish identity over against other ethnic groups.

The New Testament utilized the paradigm but reinterpreted it fundamentally. Christ takes the place of Abraham as identity-defining symbol of authentic humanity. He is prior to Abraham and superior to Abraham. Christ is without a father (like Melchizedek). At best Abraham is the father of all believers. The exclusiveness built into the notion of ancestry is demolished.

### Exodus and Conquest

Contrary to modern appropriations of the exodus motif, the Old Testament notion of the exodus does not signify a theology of liberation, but a theology of ethnic identity and privilege. It does not lead to the emancipation of slaves and women, nor to the prohibition of conquest and subjugation of other nations, nor to the idea that the incident could be repeated, e.g., during the Babylonian exile. It marked the foundational commitment of Yahweh to Israel, forever defining the identity of the latter.

The exodus-conquest paradigm is a typically Ephraimic (Northern) tradition and does not figure in the most important Judaic (Southern) documents such as Wisdom literature, the royal Psalms, the Zion Psalms, the first Isaiah, and Amos (except for some insertions). It was only a series of political power games which elevated a regional tradition to a symbol of pan-Israelite identity.

If the court ideology of the Davidic-Solomonic empire was Yahwism (a thesis doubted by many contemporary scholars), exodus and conquest were combined with Southern traditions to form a story which would unite the disparate regions under a central authority. The intense hostility of the South against the "apostasy" of the North during the divided kingdom led to the South ignoring, even attacking the exodus-conquest motif (Amos 9:7). Certainly at this stage it was again not a uniting, but a divisive tradition.

In 720 the Northern Kingdom collapsed. Deuteronomy, for which a combination of the exodus-conquest and the covenant-law motifs was pivotal, seems to have been brought to Jerusalem by fleeing Northerners. With the attempt of Josiah to reestablish the Davidic empire, Deuteronomic theology came into its own. It argued that Yahweh's most improbable and undeserved choice of Israel as his people could not be taken for granted and was conditional upon Israel's faithful obedience to the covenant.

We observe here that the covenant-law tradition superseded the exodus-conquest motif. When in 586 prophetic and Deuteronomic warnings (powerfully articulated by Jeremiah) seemed to have materialized, the Deutero-nomistic interpretation of history, which attributed all calamities to Israel's dis-obedience, became accepted orthodoxy. For the prophets of the time, Jeremiah, Ezekiel, and Deutero-Isaiah, other nations were of no consequence, except as tools of Yahweh's punishment or redemption of Israel.

Deutero-Isaiah abandoned the failed exodus-conquest and covenant tra-ditions and appealed to Yahweh as the Creator to bring about a completely new beginning through the Persian king. For the Priestly source the overpowering of chaos at creation was the paradigm which repeated itself in the Reed Sea miracle and the crossing of the Jordan and led to the establishment of the tem-ple cult on Mount Zion as the center of a sacred universe. Again Israelite iden-tity was the overriding motif. *Jubilees* was a particularly powerful stalwart of Jewish particularism. Conscious of the stupendous assumption of divine elec-tion, it often twisted history to legitimate the special status of Israel.

The powerful ethnocentricity of the paradigm may have been one of the reasons for the fact that, apart from the sporadic use of traditional motifs, the exodus-conquest paradigm was not utilized by New Testament authors. Its con-centration on the identity of Israel over against other nations simply did not fit the universalizing New Testament ethos any longer.

## King and Empire

The motif of the king being the representative and plenipotentiary of God on earth, and therefore entitled to universal and unquestioning obedience, may have originated in ancient Egypt. Psalm 2 testifies to its Israelite usage. Both God in heaven and his adopted "son" on earth are depicted as brutal tyrants. Only complete subservience can lead to a fulfilled life.

The positive side of the paradigm entailed that the king was meant to be the guardian of the cosmic order and the channel of divine blessing. Prophets such as Isaiah, who do not question the office of the king as such, fall back on this ideal. The incumbents do not live up to divine expectations, they main-tained, and Yahweh would soon send a real king, a pillar of divine justice, a prince of divine peace (shalom). This is the origin of Jewish messianism.

The national catastrophes of 720 and 586 made the paradigm unwork-able. Israel had lost its sovereignty, the Davidic dynasty had come to an end, messianic aspirations were politically dangerous, and the priesthood was not in the mood of sharing its newly acquired status. Under priestly leadership, David was replaced with Moses as the pivotal figure, though in due course the high priests formed a new royal dynasty.

The Maccabean and Roman periods saw a powerful revitalization of messianism, now combined with the radical expectations of apocalyptics. Throughout this period there was no question that the goal of history was a universal empire, centered in the cult of the Israelite God on Mount Zion, ruled by the Israelite king, through the Israelite national elite, from the Israelite capital Jerusalem, to which all nations would bring tribute. The idea of the pax Iudaica was no less powerful than the pax Romana!

It is striking that, with very few exceptions, the New Testament saw in Jesus the promised messianic king. All traditional titles of the king were applied to Jesus, whether Son of David, Son of God (Ps. 2), Son of Man (Dan. 7), or the Anointed (Messiah/Christ). He was not seen as the new Moses, the new prophet, or the new priest (except in Hebrews). Not the Sinai motif, but the imperial motif of Psalm 2 captured the imagination of early Christianity. Ephesians 1:20ff. is a representative example: Christ, the Son of God, is raised to the right hand of God, as the head of a privileged community (the church), above all powers controlling the universe.

However, following prophetic trends, the content of this paradigm underwent a complete inversion. In Mark 10:35-45 (Matt. 20:20ff.) the model of Psalm 2 is called "pagan" and the new elite is defined as a group of slaves led by the Slave of slaves. Self-giving, redeeming love, which gives priority to the weak, the marginalized, and the guilty, has taken the place of oppressive power, but also of merciless justice, as the overriding principle of leadership.

### Priesthood and Sacrifice

The sacrifice of something particularly precious was first given to the deity *pars pro toto* in recognition of utter dependence on the ultimate source of life. The ancient Canaanites sacrificed their firstborn sons, and Israel followed suit. Some of the Levitical laws still give a vivid expression of this fact. This sign of gratitude assumed a more serious character in the event of guilt when the very source of existence was in danger of being cut off. Then sacrifice is a symbol of accepting God's authority and falling back into line.

With the establishment of a state sanctuary by David on Mount Zion, the priesthood rose to status and power. The Canaanite Zadokites ousted the Yahwist elites. The Josianic reform concentrated the priesthood in Jerusalem and necessitated an elaborate and obligatory sacrificial system to provide for a hugely inflated priestly caste. The prophets launched a devastating critique against these developments, emphasizing the priority of obedience and mercy over sacrifice and fasting.

However, during the postexilic restoration the priestly elite developed the sacrificial system to bizarre proportions as a means of social control and exploitation. The original character of sacrifice as a sign of pious submission to the deity changed into an ideology of ritual purity. The plan of the temple reflected a clear-cut hierarchy of privilege and access: high priest, priestly caste, men, women, Gentiles, outcasts.

The cleansing of the temple by Jesus and his followers went further than the hopeless outrage felt by many of his contemporaries in relation to the temple cult. Drawing on the alternative Jewish tradition of messianism, it was an open declaration of war. Jesus also transgressed the priestly purity regulations quite deliberately, lending, once again, priority to the prophetic concerns for justice and mercy. The early church dispensed with sacrifices altogether, as did Judaism after the destruction of the temple. With the exception of Hebrews, which argues for the abolition of priesthood and sacrifice by maintaining that both have been fulfilled in Christ, the NT shuns the priestly paradigm.

Most important, however, is the fact that the original paradigm underwent a complete inversion: not the human father sacrifices his firstborn son to the deity *pars pro toto*, but the divine Father sacrifices his firstborn son to humanity *pars pro toto*. This sacrifice does not cater for a family, clan, or nation, but for humanity as a whole. Moreover, not the holiest and purest, but the most desecrated and impure, attract God's prime concern.

## Covenant and Law

Abraham is assured of God's favor. There are no strings attached, although a privileged relationship granted by the divine superior calls for a response of unflinching faithfulness from the privileged human partner. This is expressed most clearly in the narrative of the sacrifice of Isaac.

The monarchy and the rise of the great ancient Near Eastern empires led to syncretism, abuse of power, and economic injustices. The prophets castigated these developments and emphasized justice as an inescapable implication of the covenant between Yahweh and Israel.

With the demise of the Northern Kingdom in 721, the Deuteronomic movement developed a heartrending appeal to heed the law of Yahweh or face disaster. There are only two alternatives open: keeping the law meticulously would lead to life and blessing, while disobedience would inescapably lead to death and destruction. The "if-then" sequence is radicalized by this monumental theology of conditional divine favor.

When the prophetic and Deuteronomic threat seemed to have materialized in 586, the Deuteronomic link between calamity and disobedience became established orthodoxy. The most prominent protest against this simplistic argument is found in the book of Job. Deutero-Isaiah falls back on the sovereignty of the Creator to postulate the advent of a new beginning. However, the postexilic priestly restoration designed its own version of exclusiveness based on the distinction between pure and impure. As mentioned above, a concentric system of exclusiveness developed with the high priest (the Holy of Holies in the temple) as the pivot.

Jesus turned the order between acceptability and acceptance, so deeply ingrained in any theology of the law, into its opposite. Acceptance comes first, acceptability follows. Not the pious and self-assured Pharisee, but the agonizing tax collector, is justified. Impure women, social outcasts, lepers, notorious sinners, the simple, and the children are the beneficiaries of his ministry. The sick need the doctor, not the healthy. The Sabbath was made for humanity, not humanity for the Sabbath. The father of the prodigal son accepts the culprit into his fellowship and thus changes his life, while the law-abiding older brother excludes himself from the fellowship.

Paul cast this inversion of the covenant-law paradigm from the conditional, scrutinizing acceptance of the acceptable to the unconditional, suffering acceptance of the unacceptable into abstract theological terms. We are justified by grace, accepted in faith, not by the meticulous observance of the law. It is unmerited acceptance into God's fellowship which changes our lives. In the power of the Spirit we die with Christ to the flesh and rise with Christ into a new life. Christ died for us so that we can anticipate our own death; Christ rose from the dead so that we can anticipate our own resurrection into the new eschatological reality. In the deutero-Pauline letter to the Ephesians, the link between God's unconditional acceptance (2:1-10) and the formation of a new united humanity (2:11-22) is sketched within the confines of one chapter. The dividing wall of the law is dismantled through the body and blood of Christ.

The consequences of this inversion are immediate and far-reaching. There is no Jew or Greek, no slave or free, no male or female in the new authentic humanity (Gal. 3:23ff.). Jewish excellences and privileges are considered "rubbish" in relation to God's new dispensation in Christ (Phil. 3). This insight was so momentous that Peter could not keep pace (Gal. 2:11ff.), nor could Paul himself. In Romans he turned apologetic concerning Jewish privileges and soon fell back into conventional social structures, especially concerning gender relations. In 1 Corinthians 11:7f. he reestablishes the patriarchal order; 12:13 leaves gender out of the equation, and in 14:33ff. women are condemned to silence. The worst text in this regard, however, is 1 Timothy 2:8-15, where Genesis 3 is misinterpreted and Paul's doctrine of salvation is turned on its head.

We have come a long way since then, but I do not think Christians have digested and appropriated the momentous inversion of the Deuteronomic paradigm in the New Testament as yet. If they had, denominational and religious barriers would yield to suffering acceptance of the unacceptable; the community would be open; those who stay outside would do so by their own choice, not because of barriers of dogma and morality, let alone race, culture, class, caste, gender, and ethnicity. In Judaism the covenant-law paradigm is pivotal, and for good reasons. Without it Jewish identity would collapse. In the same vein, the inversion of the sequence between obedience and acceptance is fundamental to Christianity. Where this new sequence — acceptance first, transformation as a consequence — is abandoned, Christians have lost their birthright and the justification of their existence.

## Creation and Transformation

Here we must be brief. The trajectory reveals a development going, very roughly, from Yahwist protology to apocalyptic eschatology, from stabilizing myth to transforming vision. Authentic humanity is first projected to the beginning, eventually to the end of, history. It is significant that both projections assume that there is only one humanity. There is only one primeval couple, Adam and Eve. Christ, the authentic human being, is projected both to the end and to the beginning. Between these two poles lies the drama of Israelite privilege and obligation in the midst of the other nations as sketched above.

Protology is not very helpful because the attempt to go back to the beginning is futile. History always moves forward into the future. In fact, the motive lying behind protology is to stabilize a system. It is usually privileged elites who have conservative or restorative tendencies, while the underprivileged and the suffering, once liberated from the dependency syndrome, long for change and look forward to a better future.

Biblical eschatology formulates God's vision for humanity and the world as a whole. A vision is meant to give direction for the struggles of life. The goal is an undivided humanity flowering into diversity, mutual enrichment, and service. Paul's gospel of God's unconditional, suffering, redeeming acceptance of the unacceptable allows for an integrated variety in the body of Christ.

Tolerance is not misunderstood as indifference and self-concern, as in the liberal worldview, but is thought of as reconciled diversity.

A great variety of charismata — gifts granted by the Spirit to enable each member to serve the others better — takes the place of institutionalized divisions into social categories and hierarchies. There is one God, but he is the Father of all; there is one Lord, but he is the brother of all. As the great Servant, Christ rules and judges, but, being servants, his followers rule and judge with him. According to Ephesians, God moves toward a single integrated humanity. This is the closest the biblical faith has come to an all-embracing vision. I doubt that there is an alternative which could bring us closer without giving up on individual dignity and mutual responsibility.

## Discussion

We have applied the principles of evolutionary hermeneutics to our theme. Fortunately the biblical faith is not saddled with the assumption of an eternal truth, designed in a timeless and spaceless heaven and meant to be valid and applicable at all times and in all situations. What we observe in the Bible is the evolution of theological insight generated and driven by a fervent faith in the redemptive response of God to pressing human needs.

All kinds of needs are covered by the divine responses witnessed to in the biblical documents, even those which are problematic in terms of our modern value system. There are immanent needs such as the need of a patriarchal family for male progeny, the need of an enslaved people for freedom, the need of nomads for land, the need for a centralized power structure to fend off the raids of neighboring tribes, the need for healing in cases of disease or disability.

Inextricably linked to the immanent needs are the three basic transcendent needs, namely, (a) the need for an overarching system of meaning which defines the criteria of identity and acceptability; (b) the need for acceptance, belonging, or right of existence; and (c) the need for authority, that is, status and role. Transcendent needs include the need for national cohesion at a time of imperial subjugation, the need for the assurance that justice will prevail in the face of abhorrent abuses of power and privilege, the need for consolation in distress.

The evolutionary process covers all variations of the withdrawal-conquest dialectic described above. The "womb" ranges from the family, tribe, and nation to humanity as a whole. The biblical tradition was never immune against sociopsychological phenomena such as in-group–out-group hostility and the ideological legitimation of private or collective self-interest. There are no reasons to assume that these narratives must be particularly "holy," or "divinely inspired," or part of God's inscrutable "salvation history," just because they appear in biblical history.

However, as time moved on, horizons widened and solidarity became more inclusive. The expansion of the human life world from the womb to the cosmos is reflected in biblical history. This creates space for an overarching solidarity in times of predicaments and calamities.

Far more important for our theme, however, is the fact that a profound qualitative transformation occurred, a transformation from the normal human concern for individual and collective survival, identity, and security toward the divine concern for the comprehensive well-being of humanity as a whole and of God's entire creation. This transformation could be observed in all the trajectories mentioned above.

If one chooses to uphold the doctrine of revelation, one has to concede that the "Word of God" entered a problematic human history to transform it from within. This again is of immense theological significance. There are no quick-fix and miraculous interventions. God uses the historical processes he has set in motion in his creative activity to achieve his redemptive goals. The human partner is involved in God's action. The "incarnation of the Word" began in prehistoric times and reached its culmination in Christ. That is an inextricable characteristic of God's fundamental benevolence.

So it would seem that there is a powerful thrust toward greater inclusiveness at work within the biblical tradition. However, this evolutionary process does not go in the direction of general religious neutrality and ethical relativity. The biblical God offers himself in self-giving love and expects exclusive loyalty. There can be no compromise when it comes to faith in the one and only God in the Jewish-Christian tradition. Moreover, in the New Testament, Christ is taken to be the only way of salvation. Obviously salvation is here defined in terms of the biblical witness itself, as opposed to other concepts of salvation, such as nirvana.

Is this not a very radical form of exclusiveness? Indeed it is. The question is whether this exclusiveness is legitimate. Legitimacy presupposes criteria. The liberal, pluralist, and postmodern worldviews will not ascribe legitimacy to the claims that there is only one God and only one Savior. On the contrary, they will deride and reject such claims. Hard-core convictions, such as Islam and Marxism, will also reject such claims. For us the question is, rather, whether the biblical exclusiveness is legitimate in terms of the general trend of the biblical witness itself.

To answer this question we have to distinguish between culturally conditioned metaphors and the evolving undercurrent of meaning which expressed itself in these metaphors. Metaphors define religious traditions, and traditions define religious identity. Christianity will not be able to dispense with its biblical metaphors. However, the biblical tradition itself was, at all times, in vibrant flux. Driven by the intended meaning — God's redeeming response to human needs — it constantly assimilated, transformed, and utilized new metaphors.

There is no reason to assume that this process cannot, or did not, continue up to the present.

There are two outstanding characteristics of the undercurrent of meaning expressing itself in the various trajectories. (a) In terms of content, there is a powerful preoccupation with justice for the weak and needy in the Old Testament and the redeeming acceptance of the unacceptable in the New Testament. Both emphases belong to God's vision of comprehensive well-being for his suffering creation.

(b) In terms of agency, it is not the feeble and fallible initiative and power of the human partner that is expected to achieve divine acceptability, but God's own initiative and power, which evokes our initiative and empowers us to become involved in God's work. These two characteristics are fundamental for the biblical witness. Yahweh is God because he is the God of justice. Christ is Lord because in him God manifested his unconditional redeeming acceptance of the unacceptable.

Culturally and situationally conditioned metaphors, in contrast, do not belong to the nonnegotiable substance of the biblical faith. Examples are male progeny, escape from slavery into the desert, the conquest of land, a royal tyrant, an exclusive covenant, the notion of a last judgment, the healing of lepers, the acceptance of outcasts, the dialectic between flesh and spirit, death and resurrection, the expectation of a meltdown of the existing world and a new creation.

These images belong to ancient Near Eastern frames of reference. Most of them no longer fit contemporary experience, nor do they constitute our identity. What is fundamental is the powerful current of meaning underlying the trajectories of soteriological paradigms and narratives. Driven by faith in God's redemptive intentions, this current is heading toward the inclusive and comprehensive well-being of the whole of humanity in the context of the comprehensive well-being of reality as a whole.

Concerning content, the oppressive model of Psalm 2 changed into the model of self-giving service in Mark 10:35-45. The criterion of divine justice for the weak and needy among the gods in Psalm 82 changed into the model of a cosmic ruler whose self-sacrifice is meant to bring about a reconciled humanity in Ephesians 1:20ff. The criterion of acceptability which Christ will apply in the last judgment in Matthew 25 is active concern for the suffering. According to John, only those who love can be in fellowship with a loving God. According to Philippians 2:6ff. and 1 Corinthians 1–4, the defining characteristic of the authentic ruler is the death of Christ on the cross for the sake of others. What characterized Christ as the authentic human being is that he became poor to enrich others (2 Cor. 8:9), that he entered the sphere of human depravity so as to open up for humanity the realm of divine righteousness (2 Cor. 5:21).

In none of these cases is a metaphysical criterion of truth applied. Other gods (Ps. 82), cosmic or ideological powers (Eph. 1), and human rulers (Rom. 13) are not abolished or demoted for metaphysical reasons, but subjected to the criteria of justice for the weak in the Old Testament, and suffering, redeeming acceptance of the unacceptable in the New Testament. Truth cannot be defined in metaphysical terms, because all assumptions are part of historical flux and cultural relativity. Truth can only be defined in terms of its concrete consequences. Truth is a series of signposts on the way through the jungles of life which lead us to where we ought to be.

In terms of agency, justice and love are gifts of God, not human achievements. It is God's creative and redemptive activity which brings about a new reality. Human transformation is not the precondition of divine acceptance, but its consequence. God's action initiates, empowers, and involves our action.

So it is God's dynamic, inspiring, empowering vision of comprehensive well-being, brought about not by human frailty but by divine creativity, which Christians posit as the nonnegotiable criterion of truth. If this is what their religious conviction is all about, there is no reason to be ashamed of its exclusiveness. In fact, they are convinced, with considerable justification, that these assumptions constitute the prerequisites for any kind of fulfilled human life.

On this basis we can determine the relation of the biblical faith to other convictions in the form of a few propositions. (a) Valid insights into empirical reality, such as the theory of evolution, are appropriated as provisional human knowledge; (b) religious and ethical motives which are valid in terms of God's vision of comprehensive well-being are affirmed, appreciated, and shared; (c) the Christian faith in all its forms is subjected to these basic criteria as rigorously as all other convictions; (d) where convictions, whether Christian or not, do not conform to the criteria of God's vision of comprehensive well-being, or more concretely, to justice for the weak and vulnerable, and God's redeeming love for the guilty and enslaved, the Christian community will endeavor to participate in God's suffering acceptance of the unacceptable. However, it will do so in the expectation that suffering acceptance will lead to a redemptive process which involves both partners in constructive dialogue and cooperation.

# PART III

# THEOLOGY OF RELIGIONS

# Theology of Religions: A Challenge for the Churches

JOACHIM TRACK

In order to agree about the contemporary situation and the challenge of a theology of religions, it is necessary to be sure about the historical origin and form of a Christian theology of religions. I therefore begin not in a historical but in a systematic way, with some — I immediately admit — sketchy and biased observations and comments.

## Where We Come From: From Exclusivity to Inclusiveness and Superiority

Ever since Christianity progressed to being the imperial religion during the final phase of the Roman Empire, rejection and contempt have been the predominant characteristics of the attitude and relationship of Christianity to other religions. Christianity is seen as the true religion *(religio vera)* over against the other, false religions *(religiones falsae)*. We find this same approach whether we read Thomas Aquinas or representatives of early Protestant orthodoxy.

The correction of this view, which predominated in Christianity for more than one thousand years, came about during the development of modern times. Enlightened criticism of the practice and theory of Christianity, on the one hand, and a broader encounter with other religions, on the other, have led to critical questions about traditional definitions of the relationship. Not least in view of the terrible experiences of the effects of Christianity in the Thirty Years' War and the continuing warring disputes between Christian states, in the failure of churches in relation to the social problems of the nineteenth century, and in the German context, in the churches' share of the guilt for the rise of National Socialism and the lack of resistance to the persecution of the Jews, there has been increasing questioning of the assumptions about the Christian religion. Such criticism can lead one to turn one's back on the Christian faith and religion in general on philosophical and ethical grounds, but it can also be expressed in a new interest in other religions. A first wave of this began in the 1920s and 1930s, and it has become increasingly marked since the middle of the twentieth century.

In this situation Christian theology has developed a more positive assessment of other religions. But this positive assessment remains limited. Although in Protestantism other religions are no longer swept aside as mere distortions of the true religion and it is admitted that they provide a possibility for experiencing and knowing God, the superiority of Christianity continues to be voiced in various definitions of the relationship. The fundamental definitions of the relationship state that other religions offer an experience of God under the law, while in the Christian faith it comes from the gospel; in other religions the experience of God belongs to the framework of revelation through creation, while the Christian faith has a historical revelation of salvation; in other religions the experience of God is incomplete, whereas the Christian faith has the highest form of experience of God (Schleiermacher). The corresponding expressions on the Catholic side are the assessments undertaken by *Vatican II* against the background of defining the relation between nature and grace and taken up again by *Dominus Iesus,* that true experience and knowledge of God can be found in other religions (and also in a knowledge of God based on reason), but that these naturally remain imperfect under the power of sin and need their approach and attitude corrected in the light of the revelation of God in Jesus Christ.[1]

The truths in other religions shine and sparkle like gold particles in the light of God's revelation in Jesus Christ.[2]

1. Vatican II presents a model of inclusiveness and superiority. One can then state, as Vatican II does, that the Catholic Church does not reject anything in other religions that is true and holy. On the contrary, the Catholic Church looks with honest gravity at the ways of acting and living and the provisions and teachings which may deviate in many ways from what it considers true and teaches itself but which not infrequently exhibit a ray of the truth which enlightens all human beings. Then Vatican II proceeds to describe these rays of truth in other religions. Thus Muslims are respected because they worship one God, the living God who exists in himself and is merciful and omnipotent, the creator of heaven and earth, and because the Quran venerates Jesus and Mary and knows about the day of judgment. Therefore one can also join other religions in working for freedom and peace for all humanity. One can endeavor to have dialogue with other religions. But nevertheless, the Christian truth continues to be superior, especially in the form in which it is expressed and taught in the Catholic Church. So the declaration on religious liberty states: "God himself has given the human race knowledge of the way in which people can be redeemed and saved as they serve him in Christ."

2. In this sense the magisterium has the sieve to wash the particles of gold. I cannot understand why there was so much praise on the Protestant side for the statements about other re-

*Karl Rahner's* theology of religions, including his theory about "anonymous Christianity," goes a step further by describing being gripped by the experience of transcendence, a subject discussed both by philosophy and religions, as grace, and thus more clearly relating the experience of God in other religions to salvific revelation. But Rahner still considers the revelation of salvation in Jesus Christ, as comprised categorically within the church, to be an unquestioned and unquestionable criterion.[3]

---

ligions in the *Dominus Iesus* declaration from the Congregation for the Doctrine of the Faith, whereas so many people were disappointed about the statements on ecclesiology. After all, the same approach is found in both lines of argument.

3. Rahner adopts the premise that God in his grace has revealed himself definitively in Jesus Christ for salvation. But in his view this should and must also not lead to the assumption that all people who live or have lived without encountering Christ and all other religions in general are simply condemned to rejection and perdition. Rahner's question in this connection is not so much the theoretical problem of how it is still possible to claim the absoluteness of the revelation in Christ in view of a competing wealth of other religions, but rather the existential problem whether today, in view of the now incalculable number of those who do not confess the Christian faith, one can assume there is no salvation for all of these human beings who live beyond the realm of the Christian faith. Rahner believes human beings receive salvation only by experiencing divine grace, the full expression of which we encounter in Jesus Christ. If God's grace can be truly encountered in this full expression, one cannot be in a state of grace if one consciously rejects the person of Christ. Thus one cannot reject Christ and then follow a legitimate path to another religion. But according to Rahner, this does not mean that all non-Christians are doomed to perdition. On the contrary, we can believe that the offer of grace in a provisional, veiled form also comes to many people apart from Christianity. Rahner finds this universal approach of the divine reality of grace reflected in the fundamental dependency of human beings on transcendence, on the ultimate mystery of reality. This transcendental striving cannot be dismissed as an unfounded illusory attitude; it must finally be recognized as a person having been touched by God. Here too human beings have the possibility of listening to this call or rejecting it. Rahner considers it wrong and unhistorical to think that an encounter with the reality of God, with the mystery of transcendence, the last mystery of reality, which precedes the Christian faith can be limited only to the possibility of a rational knowledge of God, and to view what happens in other religions merely as the total perversion of this, as *religio falsa*. As a social being, a person who lives before or apart from Christ can express his/her inner life only in the form which is alive in the culture to which he/she belongs and thus also only in the concrete religion of his/her society and not apart from it. This leads Rahner to the hypothesis that a pre-Christian religion can be the legitimate form at a historical stage because it is at that point the only possible form for encountering the reality of God and the offer of his grace, while the real and final expression in Christ somehow still remains anonymous and veiled in this encounter. So other religions are expressions of God's will to preserve and save; they constitute expressions of God's creative grace and God's gracious care in history. However, other religions also always comprise elements of distortion and perversion. They are themselves ambiguous and ambivalent phenomena. Sin and the human rejection of God can be observed in other religions. Human beings can succumb to the elements of distortion but can also allow themselves to be grasped by the anonymous grace of the true God at work against and through these elements.

*Wolfhart Pannenberg* follows Schleiermacher here and argues like Rahner, starting from a general concept of religion. Religion is part of human existence.[4] In religions the dependency of human beings on transcendence becomes an issue when they speak of God, gods, or a divine reality. Hence the history of religions can be understood as a history of the appearance of the divine mystery which is presupposed in the structure of human existence. Just as surely as this story of God's appearing in history reaches its goal in the revelation of God in Jesus Christ, when God is understood as the God who raises people from the dead and thus gives ultimate meaning to history, one can equally surely assume that in other religions there is at least a provisional manifestation of God and God's truth. In a theology of religions, following on from and in contrast to this, the religions must be examined to see how God is revealed within them. Does a religion's understanding of God correspond to an idea of God which reasonably implies that God must be conceived as a reality determining everything, giving reality its foundation, its meaning and goal and its unity, and is effective in all realms of life? Does the religion take account of the fact that the understanding of God comes through God's historical revelation and thus the meaning of earlier revelation must always be understood in relation to contemporary revelation, that finally the meaning of history is decided starting from the end of history anticipated in Jesus Christ *(prolepsis)?* In the history of the religion, are the conceptions of God and revelation developed in such a way that the historicity of its own revelation becomes an issue, while at the same time openness remains for the new future and the coming of God? Only in Christianity are these requirements of an appropriate understanding of God, revelation, and reality (theoretically) fulfilled. Even if this cannot be proved conclusively, there are very good grounds in favor of such a claim. In a theology of religions the development of the history of religions can be interpreted starting from these criteria, and something can also be learned from other religions insofar as they are able to contribute to this understanding of God. Thus in Pannenberg we also find the attitude of superiority. One can raise the question whether it is better not only to claim it as a matter of faith but also supposedly to demonstrate it in a reasoned way. The self-critical idea formulated by Pannenberg to take us further is that the Christian religion will also be judged by the extent to which it shows itself to be general and capable of inte-

---

4. According to Pannenberg, human beings can recognize that their openness to the world is an openness which goes beyond the world and is thus an openness to God. In addition, human beings can recognize that they always rely on some kind of trust in their life in the world, on an affirmation of life which is not only based on the world and their own experiences but is a trust which goes beyond that, a trust in God. All human existence tends beyond inner-worldly, individual fulfillments toward the future, to a final, comprehensive fulfillment.

gration in the future as well. But is that sufficient basis for a dialogue of religions and a theology of religions which amount to more than putting each in its place?

That is the critical question raised by the pluralist theories of religion to which we shall now turn in the second stage of our reflection, because a contemporary responsible theology of religions cannot be built up apart from the debate on pluralist theories of religion.

## Pluralist Theories of Religion: A New Beginning and Already at an End?

The pluralist theories of religion are very diverse; indeed, they are themselves pluralist. So we can only identify some characteristics and refer to certain conceptions by way of example in order to understand the fascination of, but also the increasing contradiction between, these theories at the present time.

### Common Basic Assumptions

The following *analysis* can be considered the common background to the pluralist theories of religion. We are living in a world which is shrinking and in which we cannot avoid encountering other religions. Closer international relationships in politics and economics combined with new possibilities of communication promote this encounter. Initially, in this connection, there was talk about the "global village," but then, as the contours became clearer, talk turned to the ongoing process of globalization. In the local context the encounter also becomes unavoidable because of migration movements. So other religions are now no longer unknown and distant; as multicultural and multireligious societies develop, they become close religions. One could say that religion is experienced face-to-face. The challenge of other religions has to be faced on the spot both in theory and in practice. We have to find ways for the religions to live together. That appears all the more necessary because a multicultural, multireligious situation certainly does not automatically produce a climate of openness between communities of faith. On the contrary, there is a tendency to greater readiness for tolerance and coexistence on the one hand, but on the other, more barriers are also set up and there is a fundamentalist refusal to dialogue.

First and foremost, this raises the question of how the various religions can live together worldwide, but also on the spot in each particular society. In view of the debates about the role of religion in the modern world and about secularization and the dominance of the economic sphere in the process of globalization, and in view of experiences of crisis, the question is being asked anew how religions can also react jointly to these challenges. There is a new recognition that religions worldwide have a common responsibility. I refer only to Küng's hypothesis that no world peace is possible without peace between the religions. So it is important to become aware of this common responsibility in the relation between religions and also in relation to the world in the process of globalization. All religions face the questions of how to deal with pragmatic and theoretical atheism in connection with processes of secularization. At the same time, they have to face the ethical challenges, the questions of social justice, of dealing with the environment, of respect and dignity. Here it is not a matter of attitudes of superiority and putting others in their place, but of common life and jointly accepting responsibility. That is the difficult problem for pluralist theories of religion.

A common feature of these theories is their *basic philosophical assumptions,* especially in the realms of epistemology and ethics. The starting point for their reflections is the abandoning of the conception of an ultimate basis. No theory, as the epistemological debate has shown unmistakably, can claim to be generally acceptable to all (reasonable and well-intentioned people). The consequence of this is the relativity of all our interpretations of reality and claims to truth. The religions also have to face up to this, especially where they stand for "claims to absoluteness." Truth has diverse, plural forms and is dynamic in character. Although it is still possible in a formal sense to assume the unity of truth, this unity is nonetheless found in diverse forms marked by culture and context and also by individuals. Hence there are different ways of approaching and seeing truth. We do not possess the one truth; we are always on the way to this one truth. Precisely this insight into the plurality of truth demands two things, namely, tolerance and serious recognition of the equal rights of other approaches, views, and expressions of truth. Therefore the old model of truth in classical metaphysics is replaced by a new conception of truth which sees it as given in different connections, in different relationships to its object and also in the relationships between the different approaches which mutually enrich one another. Many representatives of the pluralist theories of religion understand this new definition of truth not as a threat to truth but as an enrichment leading to a more appropriate understanding of truth.

A truth of this kind must prove its worth, not least by also being communicable to our contemporaries. This also brings an *ethical element* into the view of reality and the encounter between the religions. Truth must always be examined to see if it serves life. From this point of view, the following criteria for truth can be listed: truth must serve life, justice, peace, and love (cf. Lessing's criterion for religions). Truth should come about by being found jointly by several actors in dialogue with one another (dialogue without dominance). That, too, is a challenge to the way religions understand themselves.

Corresponding to these insights concerning the new epistemological and hermeneutical situation, there are *basic theological assumptions.*

Firstly, the insight adopted from the preceding discourse is that God also reveals himself in other religions and, as a God who wills the salvation of all, has not simply condemned other religions to perdition. It must seriously be assumed that other religions are comprised within salvation and are thus given their own dignity. The prerequisite for a responsible dialogue is *mutual recognition in dignity and in each religion's understanding of revelation.*

Secondly, the pluralist theories of religion emphasize that the interpretation of the Christian truth has always been a *contextual interpretation* within Christianity itself, in the context of individual life histories and of culture marked by history and society. The Christian religion must recognize its own contextuality. The same then applies to the encounters between religions which have developed in very different cultural settings and influenced them.

Thirdly, in these theories of religion, one insight specially emphasized by Karl Barth[5] and Paul Tillich becomes increasingly important: *knowing that God is always more than all our experience and knowledge of him.* In this sense religion, including the Christian religion, must remember that God is greater than what we grasp of him in faith. Then, of course, different answers will be given to the question whether this applies only to our acceptance of revelation or also to the historical revelation itself, whether we must go beyond the historical revelations to the transcendence of God and thus abandon the ultimate validity of a revelation beyond its own context.

5. Barth's evaluation of other religions appears at first sight only a return to the previous model. God's revelation in Jesus Christ is clearly differentiated from religions in which human beings try to create their own God and their own righteousness. Religion is seen, like at the Reformation, as the concern of godless people. But the new aspect of Barth's view is the clear distinction between revelation in Jesus Christ and Christianity in practice. Every acceptance of revelation is always also a finite, limited reception of revelation marked by the sinful resistance of human beings to revelation. In this, Christianity is not only contrasted with other religions but also equated with them. It recognizes its solidarity with other religions. Only in later statements about his doctrine of lights is Barth able to say that the light of God can also be effective in other contexts, in other connections, and also in other religions.

## The Different Types of Argument

If I see it rightly, in the pluralist theologies of the religions there are three types of arguments, each of which tries in a different way to find a place for the religions' claims to truth and validity, to define their corresponding relationships, and to formulate rules for dialogue.

The first, rather simplistic type is the *"your way/my way hypothesis."* It assumes that in different contexts and cultural settings, in different historical situations and also in different life histories, there are different disclosures of transcendence, of divine reality, and different experiences of faith. For the sake of respect for others and in a spirit of tolerance, they should be seen as equally valuable truths in their specific contexts. To refrain from engaging in a conflict between interpretations corresponds to the epistemological situation and serves peaceful coexistence. However, since it proves difficult to avoid completely the conflict between interpretations and to recognize the right of all interpretations including those which claim exclusivity, there is at least a demand for mutual recognition as a basic norm for all and a minimum requirement for dialogue between religions, and theological reasons are given for a dialogue without dominance.[6]

The second type sees the common features of the differences mainly in the ethical realm. This has been spelled out programmatically in two conceptions, the one developed by Theo Sundermeier and others under the heading *Konvivenz* (living together), and the other in Hans Küng's efforts for a world ethos.

*Theo Sundermeier* adopted the concept of *Konvivenz* from liberation theology. God is a God who is especially concerned about the humble and the lost, the poor and those deprived of their rights. The striking thing about Jesus is his unconditional devotion to people in a way which sets social, moral, and also re-

---

6. Thus Leonard Swidler assumes that Jesus is the key figure for Christians. Through Jesus they come into contact with the dimensions of reality which go beyond the everyday and transcend the empirical. That is what Christologies are really concerned about. They are attempts to have contact with the transcendent and divine through the person of Jesus. Each Christology expresses this in its own cultural categories and terms. Some are more successful than others. In this christological confession, what links us with the other religions is the awareness of a deeper reality and reference to an encounter with the divine. For Christians it is important to maintain this access through Jesus Christ. At the same time, the knowledge must be kept alive that we are speaking in metaphors and symbols. What is required is not the reduction of this symbolic language but the recognition that we thus have access to the divine (second naïveté). This, like any other access to the divine, is limited by our perspective. All perceptions of the person of Jesus are limited by perspectives. Each person, including Jesus, perceives only a part of reality from his or her own perspective.

ligious barriers aside. His life is marked by *Konvivenz,* which is particularly expressed by fellowship around the table. That is where God can be experienced, and at the same time he initiates us into a practice which follows his movement in the option for the poor and those without rights.[7] In a similar way, there must be an effort for coexistence with other religions marked by mutual respect, mutual assistance, learning from one another, and celebrating together. From the Christian point of view, religions have the task of shaping their life together in mutual recognition.

*Hans Küng* starts from the hypothesis that a future for the world or survival is not possible without a common world ethos.[8] In this, Küng believes, the other religions also face the challenge of creating such a basic consensus and moral foundation. There are no philosophical arguments for the unconditional and universal nature of ethical commitments. But they are provided by religion. Religions do not only spell out the theory; they are the context for learning the practice. The world religions are best suited to mobilizing the people of this earth in favor of a world ethos. But to this end it is necessary for the religions to accept common responsibility. Küng also assumes for this purpose that all religions know the difference between true and false, good and bad. At the same time, there are fundamental ethical agreements. The major world religions share the content of the Golden

7. According to Sundermeier, an insight into the possibility of salvation in other religions corresponds to God's universal will for salvation. Religions are part of God's universal activity, and God is present within them. God is found at the origin and goal of all religions. In Jesus Christ God is encountered in his word to and for us. The dogmatic consequence of this is that saving action takes the form of words which call for dialogue, because the word of God does not wish to remain on its own; it is addressed to all people. Consequently the church in the power of the Holy Spirit must share in God's universal mission through its testimony as the body of Christ. This implies the practice of *Konvivenz.*

8. According to Küng, we are facing a paradigm shift. Instead of the Eurocentric constellation, we are living in a world community in which we are constantly coming closer together and are all involved in economic, social, sociopolitical, and finally also in cultural and religio-political encounters, with an interchange of, but also a dispute about, conceptions. Democracies are becoming increasingly widespread. This raises the question of on which basis consensus about values exists, however open one may be for individuality and one's own religion. Thus an ethos is needed which is aware of its planetary responsibility, responsibility for the world society, for the future, for the world around and beside us. It is a question of ethics in which human beings must never be reduced merely to means. That applies in particular to how we shape our scientific, technological civilization. That is a challenge for the religions. It leads the religions to face the question of their differences and of their common truth. Thus peace must be established among the religions and an effort made for understanding between them, not by forgetting truth and ethics but in a strategy in which the religions are aware of their differences and can also recognize what they have in common.

Rule and are aware of human responsibility, which also comprises human dignity.[9]

The third and, as I believe, most demanding type lays the basis by developing a *(fundamental theological) metatheory.* The basic terms taken as starting points for these metatheories vary, namely, religion, faith, revelation, God or the divine (transcendent) reality. Nevertheless, the epistemological difference applied to all these basic terms (in line with Kant) is that the terms we use for disclosure never capture the "thing as such" and are only able to see truth and reality from their own perspective. The fundamental phenomenon or reality reveals itself and is grasped in different, plural forms of expression. The second step is to interpret these many perspectives as an enrichment which sometimes causes tension. As a third step, these perspectives are seen as historically dynamic (we are on the way to truth or reality in a dynamic process). In a fourth step, an answer is then given to the question of how such a relativizing insight is related to religious certainty, to the aspect of being unconditionally grasped and addressed in religious experience, to the assurance of faith, and to the aspect of the unconditional in the conception of God and the understanding of revelation. The answers given here vary.

Thus it can be argued that the *"that" of faith* (faith as a particular form and an event) in a divine reality is decisive and not the individual forms of ex-

---

9. Küng specifies that five major commandments of humanity, which should also apply to politics, society, and economics, can be found in all the major world religions:

    1. not to kill (to harm others),

    2. not to lie (deceive, break contracts),

    3. not to steal (violate the rights of others),

    4. not to commit sexual offenses (adultery),

    5. to respect one's parents (help those in need and the weak).

These commandments sound general, but if they were practiced worldwide, it would mean a lot for our future and for just structures in the world. That is the issue on which an intensive dialogue must be conducted between the religions worldwide. Worded in a positive form, this was then formulated as the world ethos of the world religions at the World Conference on Religion and Peace. It comprises, firstly, a conviction about the fundamental unity of the human family and the equality and dignity of all people; secondly, a feeling for the inviolability of the individual and his/her conscience; thirdly, a feeling for the value of human community; fourthly, the insight that power cannot be equated with right, that human power cannot be sufficient unto itself and is not absolute; fifthly, that faith, love, compassion, and selflessness and the power of the spirit and of inner truthfulness are finally stronger than hatred, enmity, and self-interest; sixthly, a sense of duty to take the side of the poor and the oppressed against the rich and the oppressors; seventhly, the profound hope that finally good will be victorious (Hans Küng, *Projekt Weltethos* [München: Piper, 1990], p. 90; ET *Global Responsibility* [London: SCM Press, 1991).

pression or more precise definitions of the content of faith. *Wilfred Cantwell Smith* emphasizes that faith as going beyond the world toward transcendence and simultaneously being touched by transcendence — in whatever different forms this may be expressed — is constitutive for being human and becoming a person.[10]

A second attempt takes up the suggestion of *Paul Tillich* not only to pay attention in the encounter and dialogue between religions to the difference between the acceptance of revelation and God's revelation in Jesus Christ, but, starting from the universality of the understanding of God (God as the power over being and nonbeing which unconditionally concerns us) and from the universality of salvation (Jesus Christ as the ultimate revelation of the power of the new existence), to conduct the dialogue between the religions not only as a

---

10. In detail, Cantwell Smith assumes against the background of his studies of religious history and comparative religion that faith is a universal phenomenon. Faith is the most universal possibility and invitation to live in relation to a transcendental dimension. Faith is constitutive for human existence. Being human does not just mean reacting to reality encountered. Human existence includes being open to sources of inspiration, hope, vision, and commitment beyond the circumstances of one's immediate surroundings. To come of age, according to Cantwell Smith, means not growing out of the perspective of faith but living one's faith in the right way. People do not automatically find faith, but believing is part of being a human being. People normally have faith as something that is indivisibly connected with human truth, with amazement, joy, gratitude, and a feeling of numinous duty. Human existence is itself something unexpected, inconceivable, marvelous, and mysterious, and so faith offers the possibility of going beyond this human existence. This going beyond also always comprises being addressed by the transcendent reality. Faith is always the responsive participation of human beings in God's active dealings with humankind. In this sense the whole of human history is salvation history. Faith is human participation in God's dealings with humankind. But in this participation human beings become aware that they have been touched by transcendent reality but cannot grasp this transcendent reality. Faith also includes the recognition that we can only feel our way to what happens to us in faith. We get the impression that by believing we enter a stream which will lead us to our true home. It is our amazing movement toward our true self, toward our *theosis*. We recognize that we are more, that we are more than worldly and hence something irreducible, and we also recognize the greatness of the transcendent reality which goes beyond our reality. This faith can be expressed in quite different forms. The various religious systems in the world are not elaborate games which have been engrafted onto human history as curiosities; they are fundamental attempts to be human. They are impressive answers to what it means to be human. All religions have a pronounced feeling for the reality of transcendence and faith. It is important that faith exists and this faith lives in the awareness that what one assumes or believes is never the whole truth. The truth transcends not only the framework of perception of each one of us but also the sum total of all our perceptions. Thus faith exists in consenting to truth as such and in the dynamic and personal sense of the joyful and passionate struggle for truth, but faith is also conscious of its own relativity and must be examined to see to what extent faith includes not only the love of truth but also the love of all that is good and of the neighbor. We are always on the way to this truth and this love, both of which are indivisible, the one truth and the one love.

contemporary dialogue between religions (as it were, on the horizontal level) but also to let it serve as the occasion for religions to reflect on their own foundations and their own depths. Where religions raise the question of their own basis in a new and critical way and experience it, the way they are addressed by their own basis brings them closer together in the one truth and experience of salvation.[11] This idea was taken up and further developed by *Michael von Brück,*

---

11. Tillich's approach is based on a preparatory revelation which takes place not only in the Old Testament but also in the history of other religions. The religions are not just an illusory answer human beings give themselves; religions are the expression of people's being originally addressed by God and also an expression of God's action in history. Revelation becomes effective in them in a preparatory way. In the religions, on the one hand, there is a distortion of this revelation, especially when the finite and particular means through which revelation comes about are often equated with God and hence the finite becomes demonic. But in the religions there is also always a true experience of revelation and criticism of the distortion of an experience of revelation. Mystical criticism points to the infinity of the ground of existence in contrast to sacraments being seen as things; prophetic criticism points to the ethical demands in contrast to ritualistic rigidities. Rational criticism protests against distortions of religion which make it an unreasonable faith. What is new in Tillich are his ideas on dialogue. In his article published in 1962, Tillich initially pleaded generally for a dialogue and a constructive coexistence between the religions. The goal could not be the conversion of non-Christians; rather, the goal is authentic encounter, genuine dialogue, which finally also includes self-criticism in the light of the experiences of each other party. He takes these reflections further in the last lecture he gave, shortly before his death, in the significance of the history of religions for systematic theology. There Tillich begins by assuming that we do not judge one another but that the religions should primarily get to know one another. We can come to understand one another through practical encounter and relationships. According to Tillich, the ultimate revelation took place in Jesus Christ. It is absolutely universal and absolutely concrete at the same time. This statement is not being withdrawn, but a clear distinction must be made between the revelation and Jesus Christ and the historical form of Christianity. The historical form of Christianity is subject to threats, as all other religions are threatened by ambivalence. Within a religion heteronomies and false devilish attacks develop, as well as superficialities in which religion can lose its depth. The knowledge of God in the other religions is fundamentally only fragmentary and marked by alienation. If one is aware of this, in an encounter between the religions and in dialogue with others, one can become aware of one's own shortsightedness and historical conditioning. But an encounter between religions does not only have a critical function; it also enables one to perceive the wealth of experiences of God. God will be found in each religion, the power of existence which has demonstrated itself as the power of the new existence in Jesus Christ. Thus one can assume that in the history of the religions as well the power of the new existence to overcome alienation has been made manifest. On that basis Tillich then presents a double task for the encounter with other religions. On the one hand, this encounter takes place on the horizontal level. Each encounter with other religions means that we can also learn something from the other religions for our own religion. Each encounter with other religions is always also a question to a particular, historical expression of Christianity. In the encounter with other religions one can learn which possibility and which understanding of the ultimate revelation in Jesus Christ has also been overlooked in that historical expression and has not been fully realized.

who also refers to mystical experience as one which transcends concrete religious experiences and reveals the common depth of religions. In mysticism there is an experience of truth as the union of all contrasts, as the whole and as the individual being comprised within this whole. Naturally the mystic must then always also describe his/her experiences, but it is clear that the interpretations are also always open for the truth of God which transcends all concrete experience.[12]

Thus other religions help Christianity to criticize itself; they help it to become open and to incorporate other elements. So a critical dialogue with other religions is not a dialogue which runs one-sidedly from Christianity which has the absolute truth; on the contrary, the Christian faith also needs the questioning of its historical and concrete expression which must also always be transcended. Precisely because the universal logos became real in Jesus Christ, Christianity is fundamentally open to an interpretation of all specific experiences starting with Christ and leading up to Christ. Because Christianity is aware of the ambiguity of the nature of the acceptance of revelation and, in reverse, catches a glimpse in the other religions of the particularity and provisionality of its own truth, a genuine encounter can come about, an encounter with the divine Spirit. This encounter, which takes place at the level of a horizontal encounter, in a sense then leads again into another movement of the dialogue. If in the encounter between religions each religion is brought to examine its own depth and its own truth, that religion will come to the truth the more it examines its own depth. It will come closer to the truth of God, which is the truth of the new existence as revealed in Jesus Christ. Thus, by getting to know its own truth a religion can also open up to the truth in the other religions in which the power of the new existence is working in the same way. At the end of his life Tillich was expecting a new *kairos,* a breakthrough of grace, from such a double encounter between the religions. "In the depth of each living religion there is a point at which the religion as such loses its importance and that to which it points breaks through in its particularity, creates spiritual freedom and with it a mission of the divine which is present in all forms of life and culture." Thus, according to Tillich, universality does not lie in an all-embracing abstraction "that would destroy the religion itself — but it lies rather in the depth of a concrete religion, in the spiritual freedom which is freedom both from the religion and also freedom for the religion."

12. Von Brück assumes, on the one hand, that a theology of religions in the context of the Christian faith must be spelled out on the basis of how the Christian faith understands itself; it must have a christological basis and a trinitarian exposition. On the other hand, von Brück assumes that the concept of a theology of religions can be expanded on the basis of insight into the nature of revelation, the nature of all religious experience, and specifically on the basis of insight into the mystical character of religion. From the anthropological point of view, the religious dimension is present in human beings' questions about the nature of the world, moral behavior, human possibilities and their freedom, and in the question about real reality. Fundamentally, every religious experience is in danger of being distorted, of being interpreted in such a way that the interpretation itself is considered absolute and leads to the idolization of the symbol and the dogma. That cannot be overcome in a theology of the history of religions by claiming that Christianity meets the criteria for a universal religion (in contrast to Pannenberg). It is the task of Christian theology to ask what the Christian faith and Christian theology despite all their disagreement can offer to an understanding also of the other religions. Von Brück thinks the doctrine of the Trinity provides a starting point. Religions are part of created reality

A further attempt is found in the conceptions based on a *diversity to be affirmed in an (eschatological) unity which has not yet come about*. Thus John Hick in his theocentric theory of religions assumes that a distinction must be made between the real as such and the real as experienced by human beings. Ultimate

and belong to the basic determination of human beings, but they are also all subject to the reality of sin which will only be surmounted eschatologically in the work of perfection. Christian theology interprets history on the basis of Jesus Christ. A more precise but also more self-critical interpretation of history recognizes that the symbol of Jesus Christ is not meant exclusively; on the contrary, in Jesus Christ we encounter concern for the present world and for the reconciliation of creation. Thus God's saving will is revealed in a universal dimension. Christ wants to be at work in the whole world. In him God's love is expressed and the glory of creation shines out toward which all creation tends. Thus in Jesus Christ all religions are confronted with God's nature in acceptance and judgment; all religions are equally near to and far from God; ontologically they are on the same level. The Holy Spirit is encountered in Christ. He is referred to particularly in the views anticipating what will happen at the end. Therefore he is also at work beyond the church. On the basis of universal Christology, a theology of religions must show that Jesus Christ is the universal symbol for salvation in cosmic dimensions because in him all the powers which threaten creation are also overcome. This christological insight must now be combined with the recognition that the Christian perception of Jesus Christ is also imperfect. Hence no theology can adopt an absolute stand. That is also the limitation on a theology of religions. So Christian theology does not have the task of bringing the truth of Christ to the other religions; on the contrary, it must bring to light the truth in the depths of the other religions (Tillich). The criterion for this is that the truth must be in harmony with the spirit of Holy Scriptures and the concerns of the Christian tradition and must have an effect on the way believers live; the truth must also be constructive and build up the kingdom of God and the church of Jesus Christ. No specific religion can fulfill these criteria, and hence we are also liberated from claiming absoluteness for our own religion. All religions including Christianity share only in part and in a way beyond their control in the parable-like presentation of God's future. A theology of religions has the task of making clear to people how the love of God is working in them and they are surrounded by it. In mysticism there is an experience of the truth as the union of all opposites, as the whole, and also of authenticity as an experience of the individual being comprised within the whole. The mystic has and interprets concrete experiences, but it is clear that the interpretations are open and permeate into the whole. Mystagogical language does not only wish to maintain dogmas but also to encourage people to have their own experience. That also makes clear in connection with other world religions that a mystical approach transcends the plurality of theological hypotheses, and a defensive dispute is no longer necessary because it is a question of the way to an existence in truth, in knowledge of the love of God and of union with the love of God. Thus one can recognize that the truth of the religions is a relational truth; it wants to be evocative and stimulating. So in all religions mysticism directs attention to the fact that truth lies in a transcendency which cannot be named by making an experience possible beyond dogmas and norms. But that does not then mean that one can present a uniform basis of religions or that one is in favor of a freely floating mysticism, but that one clings to a particular truth in the approach to interpreting God and sets out from there. The various religions should be aware that they only form a framework by following a common path toward seeking the truth in love. Thus it can be said that in their own hermeneutical criteria the reli-

reality transcends all our approaches because of its unlimited nature. All religions offer access to this reality in a way which brings about a transformation. We are opened up to move from concentration on ourselves to being related to reality. All the different traditions are soteriological contexts in which people are liberated from their self-relatedness to a relation with reality and can find fulfillment. The different conceptions of God are points of contact between the real and the human spirit, and hence a joint product of transcendent presence and earthly imagination, of human seeking and divine revelation.[13] This

---

gions speak of a relative absolute, that the absolutely relative of their own situation is disclosed in relation to the relatively absolute, that the interrelational search for truth makes concrete commitment possible, on the one hand, but on the other, never comes to a standstill. For a dialogue between religions, in practice this means a call to conversion. All individual conceptions and statements must be subjected to the infinite power of God which judges this particularity; God corrects the religions through dialogue so that they do not idolize their symbols but rather develop the spirit of the gospel together. Dialogue is the foundation for joint action for the sake of a common eschatological future. We Christians are free to dialogue because we know the measure of the universal Christ who places us in the dialogue. But we also face the challenge to accept our own relativity and to express the symbols of our own faith anew in the context of contemporary and alien experience of the world. Here the acceptance of new symbols is possible; dialogue enriches our incomplete knowledge of Christ because Christ speaks to us from other religions. Hence our intention can only be to awaken Christ in others; what counts is not conversion but the realization of the content of Christ in a non-Christian setting. It is a matter of an appropriate realization of the reality of God.

13. In detail Hick assumes that in the history of religion we discover innumerable different godheads with different names and also different characteristics. Different views of life and ways of behaving are connected with these characteristics of the gods. It would therefore be possible in an outward comparison of religions to investigate which characteristics these gods have and to ascertain that many can exist side by side while other characteristics contradict one another. In monotheism it is assumed that there are not many such authorities but one alone is the authority. Hence it cannot be stated in a superficial way that all the gods listed exist, at least not from a monotheistic point of view. In addition, there is also a large number of conceptual and experiential approaches which point to an ultimate, nonpersonal reality, for example, the universal consciousness of the Brahma or the Tao as the principle of the cosmic order or the dharma or the eternal Buddha. Thus the question also arises whether the ultimate reality is personal or nonpersonal. Now there are two possible answers to all these questions. Either one says religious experience as a whole is deception and all of these things are projections. Or one gives a dogmatic, confessing answer relying on one's own experience and says everything else is deception. These solutions are not satisfactory. If one rejects religious reality as such, one is specifying a vast realm of human existence which has not sufficiently been grasped as an experience of reality. What we need is rather a nuanced theory of religious reality and religious experience. We must assume diversity within unity. This diversity in unity, however, needs expanding compared with the trinitarian model, because the trinitarian model also still partly excludes the other gods. Such an expansion assumes that God is encountered in various relationships as Creator, Redeemer, or the Holy One. Those are three modes, three ways in which the one divine re-

soteriological relevance of the religions with its ethical consequences is also the concern of Paul F. Knitter.[14]

---

ality acts. We find these three modes in the religions in various conceptions and traditions. That then also allows an expansion of the hypothesis to the nonpersonal absolute beings. In each of these categories, in the personal and the impersonal, a particular experience of this reality or absoluteness becomes concrete; one can say that the real becomes real in each case in human perception through *personae* and *impersonae*. All conceptions of God express the liberation of human beings from self-centeredness and also an encounter with the real. We refer to transformation and opening up, that is, to soteriological processes. The criterion here is soteriological effectiveness and the appropriateness of how it understands itself. Religions are under way. The implicit vision of each religion will only become acceptable in the eschaton, and hence until then a real dialogue between the religions is imperative and the soteriological force must be increased. Then we can understand for Christianity as well that, although the talk about the Son of God is unique, it does not imply exclusivity but is contextual. In this connection, for Hick, Jesus Christ is certainly wholly God but not the whole of God.

14. According to Knitter, the dialogue between the religions must be based on recognizing the possible truth in all religions. The ability to recognize this truth must be rooted in the hypothesis of a basis and goal common to all religions. One must therefore believe that one is talking about a common reality. This talk about a common foundation does not mean that this foundation is discussed in the same way in all religions. It is truer to say that the more I have experienced love in my own life, the more clearly I can also sense its presence in the lives of others. If I have experienced the divine mystery of my own religion, I am also prepared for the incomprehensible wealth of this mystery to reach me somewhere else as well. Interreligious dialogue must be an intrareligious dialogue; it must in a sense be conducted by people who not only look at themselves from outside but are also involved together in the same cause. A dialogue between the religions must be based on openness to the possibility of genuine change and conversion. Above all, it is a matter of conversion to the truth of God as it can be manifested in dialogue. This may then also have consequences for one's understanding of one's own religion, including the difference between the faith one has and the explicit convictions of faith as they are expressed. The dynamic relationship between faith and religious views, which is in flux, forms the starting point and goal for religious dialogue. So in this dialogue there will be a "passing over," namely, a switch to the standpoint of other cultures, other ways of living, and other religions, but also a "coming back," which is a return with one's own insights to one's own culture, way of living, and religion. It is therefore a search for truth together with other religions, indeed, a search for inexhaustible fullness.

These fundamental reflections lead Knitter, firstly, to a deeper confrontation with the question whether Jesus Christ is the ultimate revelation and in which sense this can be claimed, and how in this connection the question of salvation in Jesus Christ, soteriology, should be interpreted. Knitter believes that we find a theocentric religion even in the New Testament. Jesus himself was theocentric. He was looking for the coming of the kingdom of God. Then later in the New Testament Christocentricity develops, even to the extent of speaking of the uniqueness and exclusivity of salvation in Jesus Christ. Historically this can be explained by the minority situation, but today we should return to theocentricity. We have to start from the relational uniqueness of Jesus. Jesus is not exclusive or normative for the understanding of God, but is rather a relevant manifestation of divine revelation and redemption. That allows and even demands a bond with and devotion to him with the corresponding Christian practice. But it does not require us to claim absoluteness in

The striking feature of this third type of argument with its different variants is that, in addition to the open elements (emphasis on the perspective nature and the process character of religious experience and insight) in both form and content, there are also statements about the specificity of religious experience, the nature and significance of religions, divine reality and its intentions in its creative, reconciling, and redemptive action. Even the reference to a mystical experience which transcends all concrete expressions is linked with statements of content about God's eschatological will for salvation.

## Are Pluralist Theories of Religion at an End?

It is to the merit of pluralist theories of religion that they have very clearly directed attention to the changed situation, the new challenge in the encounter

---

dogmatic statements. Even the resurrection "in all of its authentic power and mystic fullness does not necessarily imply a one and only" (p. 147). Anyone who knows that God is always greater than our own approach becomes open for other insights. Whoever knows that his/her own approach to the divine mystery is particular can also be open to other particular approaches. Finally, the eschatological approach directs attention to the fact that we have not yet reached the end here, but rather that the uniqueness and universality of Jesus Christ demands that we recognize the uniqueness and universal significance of what has also been revealed in other people. Hence, as Knitter spells out in later essays, soteriology can also be understood in a new way. In the religions it is a question of experiencing salvation. And in this respect the Christian will certainly not adopt a neutral stand but reason in the light of experiencing salvation in Christ. But wherever this happens and people open themselves with all their energy and devotion to this experience of salvation, it then also becomes easier for the Christian to open himself/herself to salvation being present in other religions as well. Christ remains a universally normative and extremely important manifestation of what human existence can mean, but he must not be the only manifestation. So we Christians follow him with total but open devotion; our absolute is not Christ and not even God but rather *soteria*, human redemption, especially for those who need salvation particularly because of prevailing injustice (p. 217). With this kind of soteriological Christology we Christians can stand up for our confession and our traditions, but be open at least to the possibility that there may also be other ways to salvation. We can then enter into a dialogue and into practical competition related to the realization of the humane, that which serves life and love, and then have a competition precisely in that realm. If one makes this kind of effort to understand God's saving action better, one will also come to a better understanding of the other religions. That requires a fundamental theology in which the different presuppositions and the limitations of the fundamental theologies of the different religions are brought together to form a common fundamental theology for all religions. That demands a global systematic theology in which the statements by the founders of religions about salvation, etc., are seen as internally related in the religions. Finally, it demands a global practical theology, for example, in interreligious conversations on the relation between action and contemplation and in discussions about the relation between the mystical and the prophetic center.

with other religions worldwide and locally. It is to their merit that they stand for a culture of dialogue and encounter and call for a new way for the religions to relate to one another based on the question of the conditions for good coexistence and the call to an awareness of the common responsibility of all religions. And it is to their merit that they have departed from previous theories of exclusivity and understand religions — for good reasons in the Christian faith — in the context of creative, preserving, and reconciling action as places for and expressions of a historical experience of God. As a result, they have rightly made clear that an encounter between and the coexistence of religions no longer need a gesture of devaluation or judgment on one another without meeting, and that what is needed is recognition of the dignity also of one's partner in dialogue and talking to one another.

Nevertheless, at the present time there is evidence of disappointment and criticism. In the mutual interrelationship between the two guiding concepts in the present historical situation, pluralism and fundamentalism, support for fundamentalism appears to be gaining ground both theoretically and practically. That also affects the pluralist theories of religion and changes the discourse about a theology of religions and the concrete relations between the religions.

The growing disappointment about pluralism as a programmatic term of modern times[15] is not the fault of the pluralist theories of religion, even if they have uncritically adopted certain self-deceptions of the representatives of such pluralism about the conditions for its possibility. This kind of disappointment

---

15. Pluralism is a phenomenon of modernism. Naturally, diversity and difference have always existed, but it is only in modern times that a pluralism has developed which has the right to its own view of reality and to determining its own way of living as the characteristic of human life and coexistence. Not until modern times did the process develop of making a clear distinction between society as the world in which one lives or as a (functional) "system for making distinctions in society" in the form of partially autonomous subsystems, of distinguishing between communities and groups in society, of making a specific distinction and separation between the public and the private, of individualization and a diversity of possibilities for living, of the permanent presence of different options which determine our lives. The individual has to accept personal responsibility and to stand up for his/her truth, view of the world, life, and action. This development leads to an accentuation of individuality. It is a matter of each being responsible for the form of his/her life, of finding one's own particular place to live and concept of life. That precedes any common agreements. Thus in the modern world subjectivity, individuality, and plurality belong together. In terms of a program, pluralism is influenced by the intention to shed light on the epistemological benefit and wealth of a diversity of perspectives and at the same time to point to the impossibility of concluding one's grasp of the nature of a concrete, limited phenomenon. In the developing hermeneutical debate, this strengthens the awareness of difference and the conception of tolerance. Multiperspectivity and fundamental pluralism are seen as unavoidable and an epistemological benefit of modernism (and postmodernism).

and a turning to fundamentalism cannot be seen only as a backward-looking refusal of modernism (and postmodernism) — however much the fundamentalist approaches which are developing anew at present may evidence features of such a rejection with all its terrifying consequences; they are also an expression of noteworthy criticism of the open questions and inner contradictions of political, social, and economic pluralism, on the one side, and of cultural, religious, and theological pluralism on the other.[16] Pluralism always comprises two things: diversity and the unity (or commonality) which is the foundation for and limit to this diversity. The wealth of possibilities always exists only in a common field of reference, the universe, the multiverse, a society, a history, or a person. This raises the question of the concept to describe the relational context within which pluralism appears, develops, and is effective, whether it describes a real or a theoretical field. It thus raises the question of what is common in the differences and the things distinguished, of unity in diversity, of identity in

16. Fundamentalism in its detailed expression is a confrontation with this form of modernism. Modernism, as we have seen, comprises the pluralization of approaches to life, increasing differences and the questioning of ultimate arguments. This also includes processes of secularization which are concerned about liberation from religious convictions imposed in an authoritarian way and about the autonomy of culture and politics in relation to religion and the claims of religious institutions. This very diversity of possible approaches, the related criticism of tradition and threat to cultural and religious identities, the lack or sense of lack of common supporting and binding convictions and the associated necessity of self-determination produce not only liberating experiences but also fear and a sense of threat. They entail the "compulsion to heresy," namely, to one's own independent definition of fundamental convictions and ethical guidelines, and create a "metaphysical homelessness" (P. Berger) in a modern context in which everything is at one's disposal. Modernism may be able to provide a protective roof for different approaches to life, but it cannot offer them any ground beneath their feet. That results in countermovements and counterquestions. In fundamentalism we encounter a yearning for security and firm ties. We see there an awareness that human beings need meaning, vulnerable and homeless as they are, and security, a place where they can live and a foundation on which they can stand. In fundamentalism we see the knowledge that not everything is at our disposal and that life needs norms. Fundamentalism undeniably asks the question what, in the many things that we do and think, is the one thing which determines us and gives us a foundation. Fundamentalism is marked by a striving for clarity. It strives to reunite what has been divided, to overcome the separation between the private and the public, the individual and the community. We encounter a knowledge that identity cannot be found in an arbitrariness which makes everything equal and an openness which embraces everything. In fundamentalism we encounter the knowledge that individuality cannot be lived without the face-to-face and the relationship with the community, or it becomes a privacy in which human beings are isolated and also go to pieces. It is not the criticism of modernism that is questionable, of its reductions, arbitrariness, and dangerous consequences. But it is dangerous and contradictory if the underlying question about the truth and the right of other views and attitudes to life is replaced by a quick division into good and bad where everything different is condemned as bad and cut off.

change. That is precisely where the problem lies: What is this "commonness" within which one can speak of pluralism, what is the unity within which pluralism comes about? So pluralism comprises the permanent debate about the grounds which make plurality and pluralism possible, the limits which are set and must be set to all pluralism, and about the "counterterm" or counterterms to pluralism. Corresponding to the surges of pluralization is a necessity to point to the unity within pluralism and to establish provisions to limit pluralism. Since such an indication of unity is no longer possible by ultimate reasoning or unavoidable assumptions beyond the particular perspectives of which they are always aware, all that remains when it is a question of common life and action is the possibility of controlling the limits of pluralism. Where this does not happen and in fact there is reliance on a unity which already existed at the beginning or on the interplay of pluralist views and realizations, the question of the unity in the diversity and of the limits of plurality will be decided in line with the prevailing power, whether it be the prevailing power of state authority or the prevailing power of partially autonomous systems such as the dominance of the economic. To talk about a free play of opinions and convictions, of interests, powers, and forces, resulting without difficulty in a balance of interests and power, ignores the determination with which people stand up for their own interests, strive for power and want to be in charge, cling to their convictions and even to mutually exclusive claims to validity. That leads to inequalities, concentrations of power, and conflicts. Contrary to harmonizing theories (the "invisible hand") that in the interplay of interests, in competition and striving to get ahead, a balance of interests will come about and the welfare of all will improve, what we observe particularly in pluralist conceptions of the economy and the neoliberal economic orders derived from them is the need for regulation. At precisely this point there is an increasingly obvious imbalance between an openness for diversity and the provisions for limiting and dealing with this diversity. That makes one critical about the promises made by modernism with its programmatic pluralism. Is the pluralism of modernism merely an apparent freedom in a steel framework of modernism, in a system with its own dynamics which sets up its own economic workings as an unquestioned criterion? The system does two things: it subjects everything to its own power and provides leeway for everything on condition that it can still function. It privatizes and relativizes plurality and makes its own responsibility arbitrary and unimportant. Is leisure not also controlled by economic forces, opinion conditioned by the media under the guise of discourse, dialogue, and diversity? In the contemporary processes of transformation one can see a tendency to increasing assimilation and increasing differentiation at the same time. Our situation is marked, on the one hand, by a tendency to uniformity, especially in the partially enforced adaptation of economic conditions and forms with all the cultural consequences. On the other hand, our world is marked by increasingly obvious distinctions and differences, by strife and divisions. Under the dominance of the economic sphere, differences are increasing between poor and rich, periphery and center, creditors and debtors, those who have work and those who have no work. Both awaken resistance. People are led to reflect on their own individual and personal-collective possibilities of experience, including the tendencies to erect barriers. The religions themselves and the encounter between them are not unaffected by this. The religions are confronted with the unavoidability of encounter which results in increasing assimilation. This similarity can be seen in the introduction of religious views and practices into one's own religion. It may be expressed in a tolerant recognition of other religions. But there is not only assimilation but also increasing differentiation, underlining the differences between the religions, not only out of ignorance but also often out of growing familiarity. The reason for this can be both growing self-confidence and insight into the way religion has marked one's own culture, but also concern about losing one's own identity. In the present surge of globalization, where do we find justice, the real recognition of the other, and respect for differences? No wonder people are skeptical about the friendliness of a pluralist theory of religions — who is the main influence behind it?

Then there are specific questions connected with epistemology and hermeneutics. The references to the openness of these theories and their ability to be corrected, and also to the impossibility of ultimate justifications, obscure the fact that they claim what they claim with the relative absoluteness of all theoretical claims. The relation between the subjectivity and intersubjectivity of truth, contextuality, particularity, and the universality of truth has still not been clarified.

The "my way/your way" hypothesis tries to lead to respect for and equal recognition of differences, but at the same time it makes these differences indifferent. They then no longer challenge our own understanding and action. Contextuality becomes an alibi for no longer asking the questions which concern us all. What should we do if my way and your way cross, as is unavoidable in the present situation? We need dialogue and agreement at the level of convictions and rules of procedure in relation to the plurality desired and granted and the necessary and desired commonality.

The conceptions of *Konvivenz* and the search for a world ethos are inadequate and superficial not because they seek encounter in theory and practice and raise the question of the conditions for a good, peaceful coexistence and common fundamental (dogmatic and ethical) convictions. That is precisely what is needed in the transformation processes of the present time. What is inadequate and superficial is the way they go about it. Even if one assumes, and that seems questionable, that such a consensus on basic ethical convictions exists between the religions, the problem remains that it is easier to agree on such general abstract principles (which we hope are intended seriously) than to implement them in subsequent concrete steps. That is where the dispute begins. It then becomes evident that there are different cultural approaches to speaking about human dignity and different strategies for implementing such things as justice, peace, and the integrity of creation. We find not only common elements but also differences which must be seen not only as enriching but also as conflicting. Küng passes over this too quickly. Something similar also applies to the endeavors at *Konvivenz*. How will it be possible to live and give shape to *Konvivenz* while differences and contradictions remain? How will it be possible to find some minimum consensus about mutual respect and the way of relating to one another in the encounter between religions locally, regionally, and worldwide?

The criticism to be leveled against the nuances of pluralistic theories of religions is not that (fundamental theological) metatheories are being submitted for understanding religions and religious dialogue which interpret their development, significance, functions, goals, and tasks in the present situation (including theories of the human sciences about the "nature of human beings" and their "religiosity") and hence judge, reject, or incorporate previous theories. A theology of religions is not possible without a theory of religions. What must be criticized is again how this is being done. Here I shall mention three considerations without being able to develop them in the limited space available.

Firstly, it is not clear which is the starting point for the argument.[17] The lines of argument comprise a strange mixture of convictions derived from philosophy, for example, about the perspective determining all knowledge, of assumptions from comparative religion (concerning religiosity and religion), and of Christian theological convictions, without their internal links being critically clarified. That makes the pluralistic theories of religions helpless when faced with fundamentalist challenges, even within Christian discourse. Perspective,

---

17. In the newer pluralistic theories of religions, it is not clear whether they wish to transcend the concrete religions somehow from outside in a metatheory of religions or whether they are developing a universal view of religions based on the way the Christian faith sees itself. Cantwell Smith as well as Hick and Knitter give the impression that they approach the problem more from a general theory of religions and then want to fit Christianity into this theory of religions rather than starting from an understanding of the Christian faith which would then also be open for a new definition of the ultimate claim of Christianity and for a new relation to the other religions.

contextuality, theories of religions, theories of dialogue, and statements about the transcendence of God must (also) be based on the Christian understanding of faith if they are not to remain external.

Secondly, the theories put forward prove to be inadequately defined with regard to epistemology and hermeneutics from a philosophical and theological point of view. However appropriate the statements about the perspective in all of our thinking seems to be from a philosophical (and theological) point of view, this insight still does not solve the problem of conflicting interpretations. References to the relativity of all claims to truth, the relational aspect of truth, the experiential and practical element of truth, and the relationship to the truth perceived (trusting in . . .) do not change the fact that these theories, unless they declare themselves from the beginning to be poetry (and even then one would need to ask more precisely about their claim to truth), make claims to truth for their "sentences of truth." Even theories which are aware of the provisional nature and limitation of their insights and claims to truth maintain the truth of what they have grasped when they enter into a discussion and contribute to it. They participate in the intersubjective dialogue, in a dispute about the right view of reality. It is at least necessary to reflect more precisely on the claim to truth which I connect with "my truth" in dialogue. But this sort of reflection is missing. As a result, the dispute is conducted without such reflection.

Thirdly, it cannot be denied that the theories of religions at least maintain a claim to universality for the metatheories they have developed, whether this be from a general philosophical, comparative religious, or Christian theological point of view. Not enough attention is paid to the fact that, on the level of metareflection, the same critical questions arise about the impossibility of ultimate reasoning. I get the impression that what is being put forward here is a "uni-centric pluralism" which assumes a firm foundation common to all and rules for the dialogue accepted by all. That does not do justice to the tensions in the situation or to the relation between plurality and unity. It is a pluralism of its own making within which others have to find their place. Moreover, one cannot rid oneself of the suspicion that the Christian claim to universality and ultimate validity has indeed influenced the fundamental theological bases for some of these statements without this being mentioned. Again, it is hardly surprising that displeasure arises where this is noticed.

Thus the pluralist theories of religion have reached an end and must be brought to an end. But this is helpful only where the constructive insights of these theories are included in a new approach to a theology of religions.

*Joachim Track*

## Conflict and Reconciled Diversity:
## Basic Features of a Theology of Religions

### Basic Statements of Fundamental Theology

1. It is appropriate and necessary to develop both a theory of the Christian faith (of the Christian religion) and a corresponding theory of other religions starting from one's own Christian understanding. In line with the experience of God which concerns us directly, we should not undermine it but take it as a starting point and stand up for the truth we have experienced and grasped — as an offer for dialogue. That includes critical questioning of the previous understanding in the historical claim to truth of the Christian faith and critical questioning of the previous Christian theology of other religions.

2. According to the (my) understanding of the Christian faith, all reality with its unity and diversity is based on the action of the triune God. As the Christian faith understands it, reality is determined by God's creative acts, his (ultimate) revelation for salvation, and his presence in the strength of the Spirit. Thus one can claim that all plurality and pluralism are possible only because of God's creative acts. But even this basis, according to the witness of the Christian faith, is not to be understood as a fundamental principle but as a living counterpart, as God the Trinity who reveals himself as God as such and for us in the oneness and distinctions of Father, Son, and Spirit. God reveals himself as a God who makes distinctions for the sake of love and in whose love a unity is established of what we divide and play off against one another, love and life, individuality and community, differences and what is common, diversity and unity. Thus, starting from the Christian view of God, we must speak about the nuances in the understanding of the foundation of this world and of unity of this foundation. The unity of the world and the unity of our understanding of the world is not our doing but is found in God. The unity of God himself is a unity in difference and in mutual loving relationship. God's unity, God's one nature, is not a predetermined characteristic which we could observe and guarantee in advance, but a unity in which God wills to show himself time and again as God the Trinity, by enabling us to experience him and by directing and connecting our different, conflicting experiences. We have to learn repeatedly in a living process who God is for us in his diversity and unity.

3. The revelation event does not abolish the conditions of knowledge and experience laid down by creation. Revelation takes advantage of the possibilities present in human existence. The new element in the revelation event is to set human beings in a new relation to God in the midst of creation and open up a new future for them. The fundamental aspects for the development of faith

and of religious certainties are the experiences of disclosure. We could not speak of experiences of disclosure if there were no specific disclosure or being disclosed at the same time. Experience of disclosure is a specific experience interpreted as such in the framework of being known (even if it be *via negationis*). To this end we need words, sentences, as events which express what we have experienced, despite the knowledge that words also again hide and obscure what was revealed because the subject of the description is something indescribable. All talk about God is a matter of witnessing to the indescribable in the describable.[18] God's self-disclosure in Jesus Christ, which is the basis for our faith, means being unconditionally affected, being touched, and is understood as an encounter with God in Jesus Christ and thus "becoming one" with God. But at the same time this encounter leads to an experience of difference, of the other as being beyond our control but also concerned about us. God's revelation is the event of God's coming close to us, his entry into our world, his communion with us and, simultaneously, his remoteness in this proximity as the Other who is beyond our control precisely in his love. In the gospel the truth is revealed to us, in epistemological terms, God's perspective on the world where world and humankind experience their basis and aim, but this perspective can be present only in both its truth and questionableness, as the one perspective which is broken up into our many perspectives. Through the freedom and reason to which we are liberated, we are simultaneously called repeatedly to set our sights according to this one perspective and to line up our perspectives with it. The plurality and pluralism of our reception of revelation, of our perception of and talk about God, are based on God's coming to us and on his request for our consent, also in our finiteness, our historicity, our contradiction of God. These dialectics must not be ignored or abolished.

4. What is questionable is not the certainty of faith. But it becomes dangerous and contradictory if we reject critical self-examination and acceptance of responsibility for our own interpretation and cover up our own bias in interpreting the scriptures. Those who are aware of the contextuality and limited convictions also in our acceptance of revelation and view of reality will refrain from adopting a bird's-eye view which can survey everything. In line with the

18. When speaking about experiences of disclosure and about experience of God, we are making promises about reality, promises about meaning. We are not presenting "nothing" but a happening, an event. In our (linguistic) grasp of reality we present how it showed itself to us and what it showed of itself. By thus interpreting our experience and perception with its experiential nature and structure, placing it in the context of our previous experiences (forming a connection), our presentation or interpretation provides leeway for understanding, for the possible appearance of this event, for the possible keeping of the promise connected with our talk about this event.

perspective character of all knowledge of reality, including the knowledge of revelation, we must not try to take a stand beyond our perspective. That demands departing from a uni-centered pluralism in the Christian understanding of faith and in a theology of religions.[19] Although the Christian faith starts from a truth which forms its basis, this fundamental truth can only be grasped in plural perspectives in the conflict of interpretation within the Christian faith and in the dialogue between the religions. The diversity of perspectives is evidence of the wealth, and the tensions of difference are not only a benefit but also a burden, an expression not only of reconciled diversity but of unreconciled differences. That is the tension within which faith, church, and theology exist, and not just in modern times. We in the church must learn to face up to this anew time and again.

5. In my view we can learn from the contemporary debate about the basis for and the reasonableness of reason, that no ultimate arguments in that sense are possible for the faith, that the faith can be presented as something which everyone can grasp, even if it be only the formal statement that it is clear to everyone that the main thing which determines us is our passive constitution (Herms). All the attempts to make the faith evident by using ultimate arguments, or even to prove that the Christian claim to ultimacy is evident (Pannenberg), are circular arguments. Even the formal criteria for ultimate revelation are derived from the Christian faith.[20] This perspectivity cannot and should not be "overcome" by metatheories, not even by comparative religion or philosophy. The philosophical, epistemological insight into the perspectivity of our grasp of reality, including our metatheories, corresponds to the biblical insight that religious experience and certainty are experiences which come about (gifts by nature), and it is in line with the character of the gospel that it wishes to have no authority other than being an invitation to faith and a request for consent.

6. Tillich's suggestion, which von Brück and Knitter took up, that each religion should examine its own depths and will thus come closer to the universal logos who became flesh in Jesus Christ, contains an element of truth, namely, that encounter and dialogue between religions also cause each religion to ex-

---

19. Cf. the convincing debate on "uni-centered pluralism" and "pluralism on principle" (E. Herms) in F. Wagner, "Theologie zwischen normativem Einheitsanspruch und faktischem wissenschaftlich-kulturellen Pluralismus," in *Pluralismus und Identität* (Gütersloh, 1995), pp. 153-67.

20. Who tells us that it is right and better to have a theory of revelation which includes historicity and history's tending toward the end, instead of also transcending history and all the determination by world history toward the mystery of God, as in Buddhist traditions? Here one can only find reasons but no compelling arguments.

amine its own truth. This means that returning to one's own depths can certainly entail coming closer to one another. But every knowledge of God's revelation, however much it may be traced back to the depths, and its acceptance in the religions (including Christianity), is always concrete substantial knowledge. It is not only disclosed to us that God is more than all our conceptions of him. It is not a matter of a mystical step that leaves everything concrete behind in order to experience God. If the talk about God and the certainty of faith are not to vanish in the mists of the incomprehensible, we must talk concretely about this God and about the guidance for existence and action related to him. According to the Christian understanding, it is not a question of looking at the depths but in an eschatological direction. At the end of history God will reveal himself in his full truth. That makes God's history with humankind an exciting history. It also leaves space for different experiences of faith and problems of faith. The encounter with other religions is part of this exciting history.

7. The recognition of contextuality and the eschatological direction of all experience of faith direct our attention to the truth that faith is dynamic and not finished. Each interpretation of experience thus incorporates into its basis, and not only at the end, the insights we gain from dialogue with other religions. That then also determines our understanding of the revelation in Jesus Christ. Thus dialogue with other religions not only plays the role of our comparing our truth with the truth of other religions, it always also affects the definition of our own truth. Not only are we unable in practice to avoid an encounter with and facing up to other religions, they are always present also theoretically. Defining our relationship to other religions (including a theology of religions) is not something which should also be considered; it affects our faith as well. "Identity" can never be found apart from relationships.

## Dogmatic Principles

1. The same reservations apply to Knitter's demands for a uniform fundamental theology of religions, for uniform dogmatics and ethics of all religions — irrespective of the question whether this would ever be possible[21] — as to Küng's endeavors to find a world ethos. The dialogue between religions is not primarily a question of uniformity but of discovering possible common insights which could complement and enrich one another, whether these be acceptable, recon-

---

21. As soon as we ask about uniform dogmatics for the Christian faith in the different confessions, we quickly come up against our limitations, and this applies all the more to a uniform theology of religions.

cilable differences or differences which fundamentally contradict one another. Thus as a starting point for a dialogue comprising critical self-examination, the Christian faith's claim to truth and validity and the Christian understanding of religions with their claim to truth and validity, which we bring to the dialogue, must be spelled out in order to attempt to communicate, to discover common elements and differences in view of a communion in reconciled diversity.

2. General hypotheses can be risked only provided there is this reticence. In the Bible we find no clear basis for saying that God reveals himself in other religions[22] for the sake of salvation. Nevertheless, in my view we should assume a historical revelation of God in other religions as well. It would contradict our understanding of God's grace if he were to submit all the people unrelated to Christ in a place, all who know nothing of Christ, to condemnation and perdition. On the contrary, we must assume that God has his own ways with other religions as well. In this context the understanding of God's saving action for Israel can be helpful, that God opens up for Israel its own way to salvation, and precisely this can become a challenge to the Christian faith.

3. Other religions can be understood as a human response to what can be called, with all caution, God's revelation in creation. They are a human answer to the basic situation which exists in and with creation. Thus they express something of how humankind is questioned by the hidden God in his visible works. They reveal something of how human beings are addressed and called to a trusting relationship with God. At the same time, other religions reveal something of the recognition that humankind is far from God. Thus religions know what the human situation is, the greatness and freedom of humanity, but naturally also its threatening finiteness, suffering, and the contradictory nature of existence. Thus the religions reveal, for example, that human beings can seek truth, the right way of living, and justice. But they also give one a feel of how people err by contradicting the truth and not living in the right way. They give one a sense of the yearning people have for redemption and how they seek ways to redemption.

4. In the religions God acts in history to put a stop to human sin and self-destruction, as also in the special revelation in Jesus Christ. When God acts in this general way, it does not have to lead directly to Jesus Christ. God speaks to people in other religions whom he calls to be messengers, men and women who interpret and understand God and religious reality in a new way on the basis of religious experiences. One trace of his intervention, as Tillich has rightly described, also becomes visible in critical upsurges within religions, in a tendency

---

22. Religions form a complex structure with many nuances, and they can only conditionally be summarized in the term "religions." Therefore one must be cautious about all general statements and judgments.

toward mysticism and mystical criticism of any objectifying approach to the sacramental, in prophetic criticism and prophetic upsurges against all forms of ritual rigidity and all injustice; God's intervention can also be seen in rational criticism of all distortion of religion making it into reasonable superstition again.

5. Other religions are not only expressions and reflections of revelation through creation; they are also expressions and reflections of God's action in history. Thus other religions, just like the Christian faith, can be understood as a response to God's revelation. In other religions as well as in our reception of revelation, one always finds both truth and historical one-sidedness even amounting to distortion. As human answers, all religions including the Christian religion are responses to revelation in creation and to the action of God in history. They are a combination of distortion and perversion of revelation, and at the same time contain elements of insight into the divine reality. Thus they are simultaneously closed and open for an encounter with the true God.

6. To define the relation between the Christian faith and other religions, it is necessary to clarify the extent and validity of God's revelation in Jesus Christ. Two "critical points" must be considered: the claim to universality and the claim to ultimate validity for the revelation of God in Jesus Christ. As the New Testament makes clear, part of how the developing congregation (and later church) understood itself was to refer to the proclamation and practical life of Jesus, to the event of the cross and the resurrection, and to feel itself to be a universal confessing community which believed in Jesus as the Lord of the whole world who determines our future and will bring about the final future of the world. In line with this, Christianity also understood itself as transcending all cultures and situations. All people of all ages were called in their situations to become the people of God. The claim to universality is an inseparable part of the Christian faith, not as something external but as essential for the faith in Jesus Christ as then formulated in the early church dogma of true man and true God. Such a claim to universality stands in tension to the insight that God also follows his own way with Israel, not beyond the way he is revealed in Jesus Christ but not leading directly to Christ. The same applies in a different way to the other religions. It is part of the honesty of the Christian faith not to resolve this painful tension by simple "my way/your way" hypotheses, nor to use simple "two or more ways to salvation" hypotheses in a gesture of contempt for other religions, but to participate in the tensions of God's history with his world.

7. The Christian faith claims not only universality but also the ultimate validity of the revelation in Jesus Christ. Part of its confession is that in Jesus Christ the turning point to salvation took place ultimately for all humanity. Theology cannot abandon the claim that the final revelation appeared in Jesus

Christ. Such a claim belongs to the very "cause" of Jesus Christ, to the claim that he makes and to the hope that we can have.[23]

8. Thus, however much the claim to ultimate revelation in Jesus Christ belongs to the Christian faith, we must nevertheless resist false understandings of this ultimate revelation. The ultimate validity relates not to Christianity but to Jesus Christ as the ultimate word of God to us. What is ultimate is not our acceptance of revelation but the basis from which we come. That makes us critical of all our historical and contextual acceptances of revelation. They are ways of understanding ultimate validity while we are on the way; they are not complete but rather open to new interpretation. The claim to ultimate validity is also wrong when it leads to imperious behavior and thus fails to recognize that the authority of Jesus is an authority which requests and seeks consent. The claim to ultimate validity is also perverted — and this is the hypothesis I particularly want to emphasize — when it remains unclear to what this ultimate validity relates.

9. The final validity of the revelation in Jesus Christ relates to God's loving and reconciling will and to nothing else. The Christian gospel is ultimate in the sense that it shows God does not want to be God in any way except as the father who goes to meet the lost with open arms, the God who follows the path of forgiveness and love. He is the God who makes a new start possible for us, including a new start which goes beyond this world; the God who will appear at the end in his glory is the God who makes clear in Jesus Christ in the cross and resurrection that he is a God who has reconciled the world to himself and who does not respond with a no even to the extreme no of human beings to God, the crucifixion of God, but makes that into a place of forgiveness. Beyond all contexts, irrespective of the linguistic form of this interpretation, it is true that God does not want to be God except as a God who enables life and love and reconciliation to break through. In contrast to earlier theology, the new element to recognize and make clear is that, with regard to the ultimate validity of God in Jesus Christ, faith relates to God's loving and reconciling will and to nothing else.

---

23. Naturally an adequate basis for this ultimate claim — I prefer to use that word rather than "claim to absoluteness" — cannot be provided by reasoned argument. As I have shown, there are no compelling reasons because neither the question of God in a religious interpretation not the conclusiveness of the Christian answer can be expounded in a compelling way without going round in circles, as we saw in the paragraphs on revelation and reason. Similarly, all evolutionary models which present the Christian faith as the highest stage of development must have a basis; they also adopt a perspective and assume a preliminary grasp of what is the highest religion. We can certainly give reasons for the special experience, the special claim of the Christian faith, but these reasons do not exonerate us from the element of experience and consent.

## Challenge to Theology and Church

1. In the dialogue between the religions it is important to get to know and understand the other religions with their religious certainties and practical life in order to understand one's own convictions and to become more open for the disclosure of religious certainty in one's own and other religions. That is why the first step in dialogue is achieving an awareness of the other. Anyone who thinks he or she already knows everything learns nothing, does not get moving, let alone having an experience of disclosure. We need to learn a style of perception in which we first allow the others to speak and have an experience. Our encounter, our perspective of experience, is always determined by expectations and fears, by the ingrained patterns of our experience; in practice, encounter is determined by our good and bad experiences with these or those others and by the resulting judgments and prejudices. Hence face-to-face encounter in the local context is important, but encounter and dialogue include working on encounter and dialogue, preparatory and follow-up work, working on ourselves with others; it is equally a matter of theory and practice, working on our perspective of experience as something theoretical and practical in our life history. Our "prior knowledge" must be questioned and examined to see where it leads — into the freedom of new perceptions or into the narrowness of the person who knows everything and already has an opinion on everything. The basis and criterion for our self-acceptance make acceptance of the other possible. Because religion is concerned with final certainties, many things are at stake for us in this encounter. Hence talking about encounter and dialogue between religions is first and foremost a challenge to ourselves.

2. An encounter between religions understood in this way is a story of mutual acquaintance and recognition, of recognition and learning from one another. Precisely from the point of view that the final validity of the revelation in Jesus Christ is found in the questions of salvation and the reconciling and loving will of God, we can also learn from other religions, with their particular history with God and understanding of God, something new and different about the understanding of and relation to creation, with regard to the ways and means by which people come to understand themselves in the name of God. Thus we can explore which convictions of content unite us in an understanding of God, the world and humankind, salvation and well-being, our responsibility for and before the world. True encounter with others also implies opening up and being opened up to the certainties of the other. It leads us to the limit which is a fruitful place for knowledge. The disclosure of the religious certainty and convictions of the others can be a broadening and also a critical correction. That can draw our attention to the contextual limitations

and also the historicity and questionable nature of our own acceptance of revelation.

3. Always recognizing that we can learn more, we must allow the debate and also the dispute about the appropriate understanding of God, the world, and humankind to take place. If there is talk of a God of retribution, we must protest in the name of the revelation of God in Jesus Christ which we believe ultimate. Wherever the dignity of human beings based on humankind being in God's image and on God's forgiveness is disputed, where fundamental distinctions are made between people and races instead of assuming there is one race, where an exclusive understanding of salvation is presented, this must be contradicted. Here it is not possible in the name of a false understanding of tolerance to allow a conception of God and the world which makes everything indifferent to stand on an equal footing. Therefore not only mutual learning is required but also mutual questioning and contradiction, so that the protest through which new things can be expressed gets its place and its rights within such contradiction. As all religions follow the path to eschatological fulfillment, the religions (including the Christian faith) always also need to be liberated to see the truth in the midst of the truth they recognize.

4. Religions exist in a community of life and must shape their coexistence so that it serves life and reflects the will of God. They exist in a community of learning and in a community of conflict with its tensions. They must set mutual learning processes in motion and deal with their conflicts in such a way that the provisions found to deal with conflict will defend life and serve justice. They exist in a community of responsibility for life in this world (peace, creation, justice) and must seek possibilities for exercising their own and common responsibility for these goals and implement them. The aim is an ecumenism of religions seeking that which, at best, is characteristic of our congregations and churches and of the encounter between confessions: community in reconciled diversity.

# The Depth of the Riches: Trinity and Religious Ends

S. MARK HEIM

## A Problem and a Premise

The primary problem of the Christian theology of religions is what to make of the specific aims and ends of other religions (their uniqueness) in relation with Christian uniqueness. I would like to sketch a way in which ancient Christian wisdom (the doctrine of the Trinity) illuminates this contemporary problem. My contention is that the Trinity provides the framework for Christian affirmation and interpretation of the religious ends of other traditions, and that in the process of investigating this we gain a deeper insight into the nature of salvation, the Christian religious end.

My approach already involves a premise: there is more than one real religious end, final human state or fulfillment (in addition to the possibility of true and utter desolation, which I believe is also quite real but is not the focus of this paper). The most rigid and dogmatic Christian exclusivist and the most rigid and dogmatic radical pluralist share one dogma: there is but a single possible religious end. The only question is instrumental: What will get you there? One way or many ways? On this dogma I have been an active heretic for some time now because of my fixation on the question, Way to *what?* Gandhi once wrote, "Religions are different roads converging to the same point," and asked, "What does it matter if we take different roads so long as we reach the same goal? Wherein is the cause for quarreling."[1] Actually, as the history of violent conflict within individual religious traditions shows, it is all too easy to quarrel on exactly this assumption.

I ask instead, What if religions are paths to different ends that they each

---

1. Mohandas Gandhi, *Hind Swaraj or Indian Home Rule* (Ahmedabad: Navajwan Publishing House, 1939), p. 36.

value supremely? Wherein is this cause for quarreling? Salvation is the communion with God and God's creatures through Christ Jesus. It is the Christian religious end, if you like. This does not mean that there are not other religious ends, quite real ones. It only means that Christians hope to be saved from them, and that they believe God has offered greater, more inclusive gifts.

Christians believe this is objectively true, but it also has to be evaluatively true, chosen, or it is not realized as such. And as far as I can tell, this is exactly and legitimately the reciprocal view of other religious traditions toward their religious aims and Christianity.

I will not rehearse these arguments here, except to point to one implication. It appears to me to make perfectly good sense to say two kinds of things:

1. that another religion is a true and valid path to the religious fulfillment it seeks (to agree with the Dalai Lama, for instance, when he says there is no way to enlightenment, the Buddhist end, but the Buddhist way);
2. and, what the book of Acts says of Jesus Christ, that "there is salvation in no one else, for there is no other name under heaven given among mortals by which we must be saved" (Acts 4:12).

There is a relation with God and other creatures made possible in Christ that can only be realized in communion with Christ.

This hypothesis of multiple religious ends seems to respect and harmonize the following elements, each of which I think is sound and desirable in its own right. The first is recognition of the fundamental truth in religious witness that claims a "one and only" status for its own way or tradition. The second is the possibility for one religion to recognize *concrete* truth in another precisely where it differs, as opposed to recognizing only generic, shared truth. This would mean, for instance, a Christian affirmation of the legitimacy and reality of nirvana as Buddhism specifically defines it, rather than as a generic equivalent for what Christianity describes as salvation or as a representation of some third possibility that Buddhism and Christianity both image in an entirely nondescriptive way. The third element is the emphasis and value religious studies place on learning the specific detail, the "thick description" of religious traditions. Such an ideal is a commonplace of the study of religion. Yet absent the kind of hypothesis I suggest, this ideal is strangely groundless, unable to explain why there is any *religious* significance in the unique details and texture of particular traditions to which religious studies as a discipline attaches so much importance. The fourth element is the legitimacy of each religious tradition interpreting others ultimately in its own terms: a Buddhist interpretation of Christianity, a Christian interpretation of Hinduism. There are no epistemologically convincing claims to hold a perspective above all the religions or representing all of them. Nor is this necessary for peace, dialogue, and common life.

Many may be quite happy to dispense with one or more of these elements. Others may want to maintain them all but do not think there is any intellectually consistent way to do so. In the space of this paper I cannot adequately address those issues.[2] For the purposes of argument, I will ask you to grant the hypothesis of multiple religious ends. Our main task is to ask how it might make sense in Christian terms to conceive of a variety of distinct religious ends. I suggest that in the Trinity, Christian theology has already laid the foundation of the answer.

## Trinitarian Dimensions

Trinity is an afterthought in much of modern Western theology. But in thinking about these issues, the doctrine has worked its way into the center of my own theology, from two directions.

1. It worked its way "out" from the character of salvation. My hypothesis puts fresh emphasis on the question, what is salvation? And if we think very much about this, we recognize that for Christians salvation is a relation with God that hinges very much on what God is like. In short, it is a relation of communion with a God whose nature is communion. It is communion through Christ with God, other people, and other creatures. Trinity is an indelible structure in the nature of salvation.
2. The doctrine worked its way "in" from reflection on other religious ends. If we think about diverse religious fulfillments, these must involve some real relation with God (not pure illusion or pure idolatry). How could there be diverse, actual contacts with God? Only if God's character itself is complex. Trinity is the framework for understanding different religious ends.

I hasten to make one very important point. The Trinity is the framework for understanding religious ends *not* because different religious ends relate to different persons of the Trinity. The traditional axiom that the external acts of

2. For a more complete treatment of these issues, see S. Mark Heim, *Salvations: Truth and Difference in Religion* (Maryknoll, N.Y.: Orbis, 1995) and *The Depth of the Riches: A Trinitarian Theology of Religious Ends* (Grand Rapids: Eerdmans, 2001).

the Trinity are undivided is a sound one. The point is different. There are certain dimensions to God's nature because that nature is a communion of persons. It is those dimensions and their complexity that make various religious ends possible. The dimensions exist because God is triune, but the dimensions belong to all the persons together, not to any one.

The simplest way to describe these dimensions is to think of human analogies. So I will quickly sketch three aspects of human relations, and then we will consider trinitarian analogies.

1. Humans can have "impersonal" relations with each other — interactions that do not bring into play what we think of as personal qualities. For instance, one person receives blood from another he or she may have never met. The life processes of the two relate in a very fundamental, physiological way. Sometimes this exchange can be set in a profoundly personal relation, as when a close family member donates an organ to another. The actual connection, the impersonal sharing of biology, then may be only one dimension in a wider pattern of love and mutuality. But it is not necessarily so. And in either case, it is life-giving on its own.

2. Humans can have personal relations with each other as agents. We meet through the exchange of the characteristic products of personality: speech or acts that express ideas, intentions, feelings, experiences. These may be direct "face-to-face" exchanges or they may use more extensive media (like writing or art), so that it is possible for you to have a "personal" relation with someone you never met. This is interpersonal encounter that raises the full range of moral and social questions of human culture: duty, obligation, trust, understanding, love.

3. A third dimension of relation is communion. Here you not only encounter and relate to another *as* a person, but in some measure you *share* in that person's life. Empathy and familiarity with the way her or his emotions or responses are formed eventually give rise to a vicarious capacity to experience the same response, a kind of second nature. These arise in us not instead of our own reactions, but alongside them, though in some cases this line may blur. Take the example of two people sharing the experience of listening to a great musical performance. Being aware that another person has the same responses adds a new element to the experience. And there is the somewhat more complex phenomenon in which you are aware of, appreciate, someone else's appreciation for elements that do not directly speak to you in the same way. A simple example might be where you are both aware of the music in the same way, but you are aware of your friend's awareness (derived from your friend's long, in-

timate knowledge of the composer) of profound struggles and events in the musician's life, things known to you only indirectly. Relations of deep love or intimate friendship reflect this communion. Intimate contact with another's life shapes our own, consciously and unconsciously shapes the very modes by which we experience.

The life of the Trinity manifests three dimensions analogous to the three I have just described. Granted, it is not quite so simple, for it is certainly true that the Trinity is a reality in some ways inhabiting space between our concepts of individual and community. But these dimensions provide a complex map within which to locate and recognize a variety of religious ends.

## The "Impersonal" Dimension of the Trinity

The three divine "persons" have an "impersonal" dimension to their relations with each other. This is somewhat analogous to the life processes within an organism. Below the level of any consciousness or active agency, life is shared and exchanged among the persons. Where do you find the "life" within a single organism or within a community? Where can you see it, lay your hands on it? Not in any single piece but in the process of the whole. If you draw a circle, thinking to have encapsulated the life process in one portion, it escapes such boundaries.

In the Trinity the analogous process is the radical immanence and the radical emptiness by which each divine person indwells the others and makes way for others to effect a reciprocal action. Human persons who live together and have a close relationship may maintain a steady flow of exchange at a preconscious or unconscious level, where each registers what is happening to the other at a level that is almost physiological as much as psychological. There is data input and processing that does not require deliberation, as is the case with the processes of sight or sensory feedback that take place within our bodies. We might call this the "biology" or ecology of the divine life.

This is not the property of any one triune person. It is a dimension of their life together, of the one communion among them. And as a dimension of the divine nature, this is an external "face" of God also. It provides an avenue or frequency through which one can relate with God. Just as human personhood is not discernible at the level of the molecular interactions in our bodies, so God is impersonal when encountered solely in this dimension.

What does this dimension look like in connection with creation? One answer is to point to certain theophanies in the Hebrew Scriptures, which we might characterize as exposure to "raw" divinity. Moses, Job, Elijah, and others encounter this presence, which is typically described in natural or impersonal categories: wind, fire, a consuming presence in which mortal creatures threaten to disintegrate. This is God being God in this dimension, like a high-voltage field of alternating current.

But we can go beyond this. When externalized, this "impersonal" interchange and process within the divine life has two distinct sides. The first is the withdrawal or contraction in which God makes space for creation's own being and freedom. The second is the immanence with which God undergirds and sustains creation. In other words, God's entire relation with creation has an ecological exchange analogous to what goes on constantly among the divine persons themselves, a steady process both making space for creation and in-dwelling it.

Humans can "tune in" to God's manifestation in this dimension in two different ways, each with its own integrity. The first apprehends the ceaseless process of God's withdrawal or *kenosis* as most basic. Everything is changing and impermanent, all is arising. And behind that process and flux there is nothing more substantial than the flux itself. The only thing that could be more fundamental would be the cessation of such process, the stilling of all arising, what Buddhism calls nirvana. To take this aspect of the divine as ultimate is to isolate and purify that apophatic dimension of "making way" in the divine nature. To focus relationship with the divine on this frequency fosters a spirituality that clings to nothing, not even one's own identity, and so surely promises delivery from all suffering, estrangement, and relationship.

If creation is examined rigorously on this frequency — through meditation or science — we can rightly find "emptiness" at its base. A striking contemporary analogy for this fact comes out in physics. Quantum mechanics provides a consistent and highly effective account of the most basic constituents of our physical world, an account in which matter itself seems to dissolve into something else: energy, or fields of mathematical probability. But why (and how) these equations are taking the trouble to actualize themselves is as unclear to physicists as to the uninitiated. What is "there" is no fixed thing but rather a flux which, when smoothed out at higher levels, has a quite hard and regular tangibility. Trying to get to the very bottom of things leads us to a kind of dissolution. Even matter itself manifests an emptiness, in the sense of the lack of substance or the dissolving of entities with enduring distinct identities.

It appears to me that this insight is far more developed and its particular implications more intensely understood in Buddhism than in any facet of Christian tradition. This Buddhist vision of emptiness is an accurate picture of an aspect of the real world and an accurate, if limited, description of God's relation with the world. The emptiness described *is* one of God's relations to creation, a fundamental dimension of distance given in the creative act itself. Nor is emptiness an entirely economic feature of God, one that God has only by virtue of creation and in relation to creation. As a "making space for the other," we can say such emptiness has a root in the inner-trinitarian relations of the divine persons themselves.

If this avenue of relation is regarded, and actualized, as the sole ultimate, the Buddhist religious end becomes a real option. Emptiness becomes the dimension through which all must be filtered. Christians are obliged to coordinate the dimension of emptiness on a coequal basis with others in the trinitarian view of God.

There is a second mode of apprehending the impersonal dimension of the triune life. It reads this impersonality not so much in terms of emptiness as in terms of God's immanence. The constant process of the divine life is taken as the substratum of one great self without relation, a "person" of radically different definition.[3] The flux and impermanence humans perceive as a dimension of the divine presence is taken as something like the inner biological or psychic processes of that self. From this perspective, it is a category mistake to take the impermanence of the flux as the real story. To take an analogy from the human body, the cells are in constant exchange and alteration: they all pass away until none of the same ones are left, but the one self goes on. Once you realize the identity of everything with this single self, this impermanent activity falls into place as ephemeral expressions playing across one deeper reality or consciousness. That consciousness itself is perfectly complete, for there is and can be no other to which it relates.

The other side of the divine withdrawal from sensible, cognitive, or spiritual dominance of creation is the anonymous immanence (presence) by which God upholds each creature. There is a sense in which God is in us "by nature." This is not a relation of identity. It is not that creation *is* God, or that God's sustaining immanence is the *same* as our life and self. But there is an unbreakable link between them. As a result, we can look deeply into ourselves or nature — by meditation or science — and find not only an emptiness of substance (because of God's withdrawal) but also a positive matrix that sustains us. Quantum mechanics can be viewed from one perspective as the running out of matter into "no thing." From another it can be viewed as an indication that the material world is upheld by an active process, a highly ordered structure whose mathematical signature is one of startling elegance and compactness. Chris-

---

3. This is a "self" or a person much more like the Enlightenment view of the autonomous self, one that exists independent of others. Of course, in this case it is a matter not of an autonomous self among other autonomous selves, but of a *total* of one.

tians regard this as the immanent, sustaining activity of God. If the insight regarding emptiness can point toward a conclusion about the insubstantiability of all things, the view of a sustaining power at the base of all things can lead toward a more positive image of an underlying reality, present alike in all that is. Nowhere is this perception more powerfully manifest than in the Vedanta tradition of Hinduism. Brahman, the one unshakable reality, sustains all things by pervading all things.

Either of these apprehensions we have described — insight into a basic emptiness or insight into a total immanence — can lead reasonably to the conclusion "I am that." The boundaries that mark off any persons or creatures from others are only apparent. All things are empty, or all things share in divine immanence. This applies to us as humans: *my* being also is an instance of emptiness or immanence. The conviction that samsara *is* nirvana, or that atman is Brahman are two distinctive religious conclusions born of such insight, and they point to two distinct religious ends. Insofar as revelation and response are restricted to this particular vein, it is possible to realize "emptiness" or to lose all phenomenal self by identification with one source. Such ends are tuned to the dimension of the divine life we have been discussing, with its two faces: the distance established by God's withdrawal and the simple divine immanence which upholds our existence.

## The Iconic Dimension of the Trinity

Against the background we have sketched, and under its conditions, God also relates in another way with the world. In addition to the dimension of God's self-limitation or withdrawal in all creation and the dimension of God's universal immanence (the two sides of an "impersonal" dimension), God relates as an agent. In fact, the first kind of relation makes this second one possible. God's "absence" and background immanence allow for a free and historical encounter of humans with God as a single "Thou" on the stage of creation. We are talking of a dimension of personal encounter. The three divine persons have an interpersonal aspect to their relations with each other. The persons are distinct and asymmetrical, and encounter each other in freedom. So this dimension of relation with God has the quality of an encounter between persons, a relation of active agents.

The communion of the Trinity means that the three constitute one will, one purpose, one love toward creation. The indivisibility and unity of the Trinity's external acts mean that God is truly one and can encounter us as a free and consistent individual. We might call this kind of interaction a meeting with the ego or the common "I" of the Trinity. The focus of this encounter is the outward communication of the will, purpose, thoughts, and feelings of one to the other, on the analogy of interpersonal relations. Obviously this is a vision Christianity shares with most other theisms, certainly with Judaism and Islam.[4] This relationship exists *between* God and humanity. It is characterized by events and by mediating forms, like Scripture itself.

Raimundo Panikkar offers an important insight when he chooses to characterize this class of relations with the divine by the word (which he means entirely positively) "iconolatry."[5] Any definite positive image that represents the ultimate, and resists reduction to merely one limited expression among others, serves as an icon. An icon marks off the divine and relationship with it from other possibilities. Panikkar notes there are actually two sides to the dimension of iconolatry.

Under the influence of the biblical tradition, we tend to think of this dimension in terms of the outward expressions of God's personal nature. Through an icon, like the law given at Sinai, we encounter a crystallization of the will or purpose of a personal deity. God appears as one with whom persons can have personal encounter. This is the God of the biblical and Quranic traditions, the great "I am." This relationship with the divine is marked not by the silence characteristic of the emptiness or immanence we just treated, but by speech. God is an agent, who speaks and acts with humanity.

But it is possible to conceive a specific transcendent order or law without any personal being who expresses it, a divine "will" without a personality whose will it is, so to speak. The "Tao" of Taoism or the logos in Stoicism, or the Kantian moral law would be examples. Thus at one end of the range of this iconic dimension there is some transcendent, impersonal structure or rule (like the Tao) which has iconic representations, and at the other end there is the personal God of monotheism whose expressions of will and purpose take iconic form.

The key point that distinguishes this dimension as a whole from the impersonal one we discussed first is not personality in the divine, although that becomes a crucial feature of much "iconolatry." The key point is that an iconic view of the divine allows for — indeed requires — contrast and tension. The

---

4. I say "most" because if one takes Aristotle or Plotinus as theists, for instance, then there are instances where God is defined as impersonal. This is also the case on some understandings of ultimate Brahman as impersonal (if believers in such a Brahman are taken to be theists) or with some contemporaries who may define "god" as some impersonal or cybernetic force.

5. Raimundo Panikkar, *The Trinity and the Religious Experience of Man: Icon-Person-Mystery* (Maryknoll, N.Y.: Orbis, 1973), p. 10.

icon points to the fact that the divine is not empty nor is all being already in perfect identity with it. There is a distance between us and the divine, between us and our religious end, which must be traveled. Iconolatry typically manifests an ethical or moral emphasis, a drive toward transformation. Icons lie between us and the transcendent, pointing the way for change. It is not being, or the emptiness of being, that must be known. It is a change, a transformation, that must happen. The motto of iconolatry is not "thou art that" but "become what you are called/structured to be."

Islam is an excellent illustration. Here there is complete clarity about God as a free, transcendent, and personal creator over against whom humans stand as responsible individuals and communities. The great icon of this relationship is the Quran, for here the nature of that relation and the plan for it are clearly, divinely set forth. God and humanity meet each other as free individuals. We relate to God as to a unitary center of consciousness, a person who manifests purpose and decision. Above all, God communicates God's will for us. God calls us to live in certain ways. God loves righteousness, cares for the poor, condemns injustice, shows mercy to the repentant. This is a narrative and historical interaction.

A trinitarian perspective suggests that what is apprehended in these cases is the external unity of the Trinity, its cooperative unity in willing the good for creation. Human "reception" may focus specially on the *content* of what is willed by the Trinity (and this is consistent with impersonal icons of the divine), or may on the other hand closely connect what is called for with the personal character of the one who calls. In relating to God as personal in this way, as a single "I," Christians are on common ground with other monotheists.

Christianity characteristically qualifies this common faith in two ways. The first is the conviction that the icon for this personal God is believed also to be a living person: Jesus Christ. The second is the understanding of God as Trinity, which finds this single divine "I" grounded in a communion of persons.

## The Communion Dimension of the Trinity

We have just referred to encounter with God as a distinct personal being or through a particular icon. This can be a largely external personal encounter. It is a different matter when some further complexity is presumed in the divine itself. We said at the beginning that each of the three dimensions we are talking about exists in God through, constituted by, the relations of communion among the three persons.

The first, "impersonal" dimension had to do with the ecological continual feedback of making way and immanence among them. In this dimension each person is doing *formally* the same thing in relation with each other person: giving and taking. If we were to think of the circulatory, digestive, and respiratory systems in one body, we could say in a very real, if general, sense that each one lives by giving to and taking from each of the others, and life is the process of that giving and taking.

The second, "iconic" dimension we said had to do with personal encounter of "selves-as-different." The divine persons do not just share processes that are formally the same for each. They have distinctive relations, asymmetrical ones, that mark each person as unique and irreducible. They encounter each other in freedom and love, but definitely as "others." By virtue of their communion, we have just said, God encounters us also in this dimension, as *one* other, with one consistent character and purpose.

This brings us to the third dimension — communion itself. The triune persons do not only share the one and same divine life (the constant process of impersonal exchange). They do not only meet each other as distinctive others, honoring and enacting their identities toward each other. They also enter into communion with each other *as* different persons. To encounter each other as persons is not the same thing as to have personal communion with each other. The New Testament puts special stress on this, both in Jesus' unique relation with God and in the relation with God and other people possible for believers through their communion in Christ and the Holy Spirit: a *koinonia* or mutual participation. The incarnation is this window into the trinitarian communion, and the path to participate in it.

In this mutual indwelling, distinct persons and distinct dimensions of their relations are not confused or identified but are enriched by their participation in each other. This is a communion of persons in their distinctive personhood. This is the participation in the divine life the New Testament speaks of. By being in Christ we are able in some measure to be "in God." When Paul says "not I, but Christ in me," he does not mean "not me, but instead Christ who has now replaced me." Nor is he talking of a sudden insight that my self and Christ's self have always been the same, identical self.

This is a communion so real that a person can rightly say that certain aspects of her own willing, longing, or loving seem to arise more from the indwelling of the other person than from any purely isolated individuality of her own. It is a telling part of the description of this communion that its most characteristic manifestation is in relation to yet a third person. Communion between two who love each other can often lead to the metaphorical situation of not knowing where one stops and the other begins. This can also be confused with a *loss* of person or a fusion. The ecstatic forgetfulness of sexual union, for

S. Mark Heim

instance, can be taken as an image of undifferentiated oneness. But the typical feature of communion as I mean it is the discovery in ourselves of an openness or response to a third person which we can hardly credit as coming from us, except by virtue of the indwelling of a second in us. The effect of communion is openness to communion. No one can love God and hate the neighbor. It is not an accident, of course, that this reflects the classic trinitarian formula that sees in the communion of any two of the triune persons the implied communion of each with the third. The motto of this dimension is "transformation through communion."

On the one hand, this communion dimension of the triune life is its own distinct dimension. But it is also in some ways a recapitulation of the other dimensions, for it coordinates them in a coequality, so that each retains its own distinctive reality but cannot remain isolated or exclusive. Trinity is a nonreductive religious ultimate, in whom the three persons and their unique relations subsist as coequal dimensions of a single communion. This is like a musical polyphony, a "simultaneous, non-excluding difference" that constitutes one unique reality (on this analogy, the musical work itself).[6] Each voice has its own distinctive character by virtue of its relation with the others. We can equally well say that each receives its special voice by participation in the oneness of the whole.

Since Trinity is constituted by an enduring set of relations, the divine life has varied dimensions. So human interaction with the triune God necessarily may take different forms. It is impossible to believe in the Trinity entirely *instead* of the distinctive religious claims of all other religions. If Trinity is real, then many of these specific religious claims and ends must be real also. If they were all false, then Christianity could not be true. The Trinity is a map that finds room for, indeed requires, concrete truth in other religions. The universal and unique quality of Christian revelation and confession is the hope for the fullest assimilation of permanently coexisting truths. And here communion is the key. For the extraordinary Christian claim is that these disparate dimensions can actually be realized in one particular end.

One way of reading these various dimensions would be a flatly polytheistic (or perhaps today we could just as well say postmodern) way. That is, one could just recognize that there is a certain incommensurability about these different religious aims. They can't be unified. They just have to stay separate and distinct. All we can say is that there is no good case for eliminating any, and that

---

6. I take this phrase and the image from D. S. Cunningham, *These Three Are One: The Practice of Trinitarian Theology* (Malden, Mass.: Blackwell, 1998), p. 128. Cunningham provides a fine discussion of this analogy.

we are stuck with disparate views and valuations of the world. Any one makes sense on its own terms, but there is no way they all make sense together.

The religious traditions agree in rejecting this option. In fact, each great religious tradition in some measure recognizes the variety of dimensions we have described, and provides some resolution of them. Typically, as we have seen, this means grasping the set of dimensions *through* one of them, so that, for instance, if the chosen dimension is impersonal emptiness, then the other dimensions become useful, preliminary and subordinate formulations on the way to realization of that dimension. Christians are formally no different. They also grasp the entire set of dimensions through one: the dimension of personal communion, whose unique nature is that it does not require that the other dimensions dissolve into it, but in fact depends upon their permanence, their distinctive quality, in the divine life and in the religious end.

If God is Trinity, the various relations with God we have outlined are themselves irreducible. No one of these need be or can be eliminated in favor of the others. And any one who clings to the truth of one of the relations in isolation can never be forced from it by pure negation (by being proved flatly wrong), but only possibly by enhancement. All three dimensions of relation connect with the Trinity's own reality, though not to the same cumulative extent. All three are a feature of the triune God's integral reality. No one is a lower expression of the others, for all are integral to what "person" means. Christians hold that the richest human end is a communion with God that encompasses all these dimensions. They hold this in the face of objection from other religions that such communion precludes the realization of preferable, alternative, and purer religious ends.

The validity of human responses to each of these dimensions of the complex divine life provides the power of religious pluralism, grounds the worthy claims of alternative traditions. Christians can understand the distinctive religious truth of other religions as rooted in connections with real dimensions of the triune God. On the one hand this provides a rationale for the Christian inclusive hope that such truths might lead people toward salvation, since the ends sought through such relations have an intrinsic ground in the triune God. But on the other hand, this perspective also provides the basis to affirm the separate reality of those religious ends in their own terms. In particular veins of relation, the distinctive religious paths and truths of other traditions exhibit greater purity and power than are usually manifest in Christianity. Limit can lead to such intensification. I am convinced for instance that the Theravadan Buddhist end is in fact, as that tradition claims, a cessation of suffering. In that concrete respect it has similarity with salvation. But the realization of this end relinquishes (as unreal) a whole range of possible relations with God and others whose presence is essential to the end Christians seek. In that respect it is much more similar ultimately to what Christians mean by loss. The fact that it may be "the same ultimate reality" which is behind distinct religious experiences and traditions does not by any means require that they result in the same religious end.

## Salvation as Communion

This consideration of religious ends brings us to a fuller understanding of salvation. It is not complete identification with God (monism), nor merely perfect agreement of wills (obedience, faith) between a human and God as a pair in external relation. The Christian vision of salvation looks toward a condition in which relation with God is realized (in all three of the dimensions we have discussed) and in which one shares that realization with others. Salvation is a *complex* state, for in it a person is open to each of the dimensions of the divine life that we have described. That is why it requires sharing with others: it is crucially dependent on intersecting communions. No individual can or could realize the complete fullness of possible relation with God in all these dimensions in a self-contained way. But she or he *does* approach that fullness through communion with other persons and creatures each of whom, in relations with God and with others, fills out aspects that would be lacking for any one individual. Salvation is actually much more than the sum of any individual perfection.

The way we can most deeply participate in a divine fullness, which literally overflows our finite capacities, is through mutual indwelling with other persons. This is rather like a set of parallel computers or processors that together can solve a problem beyond any one alone, or that can together produce a graphic image of depth and resolution that is impossible otherwise. We might say the divine nature is so great that even God cannot encompass it except through "sharing." To take another analogy, the body of Christ is like the array of multiple sensors in sophisticated radio telescopes or sonar systems.[7] Humans' communion with each other is also an instrument of the fuller communion with God. Our finite receptions of the triune self-giving multiply each other, in a kind of spiritual calculus that deepens each one's participation in the communion of the triune life itself. The key is openness for communion through the whole range of the divine dimensions, and openness to communion with other persons and with

7. An important point for these analogies is that in the case of such sensors, each individual unit contributes its data to a central processor, and only there is the final "big picture" produced and consumed, quite without any benefit or further participation for the individuals. But in our imaginative extension of this image, we stress that each of the individuals involved participates in and is affected by the whole which it perceives.

their unique relations with God. Such a vision embodies a profound imperative for justice, since every wound in the social fabric of human relation is likewise a rupture in the raw material of salvation. Broken bonds of human solidarity violate God's commands, but they also cut the very circuits of communion which are the nervous system of the redeemed life.

This is why communion is the fundamental shape of salvation. "Saints," from this perspective, are as much those who have learned to participate by communion in others' communion with God as those who have developed to perfection their individual faculties for private unity with God. This is precisely what the "communion of the saints" is about. This is also why in Christian tradition community, the actual concrete body of the church, has been regarded as fundamental to the Christian life, even to salvation itself.[8] It is interesting that the official requirements for canonization in the Roman Catholic Church include authentication of a minimum number of miracles performed by the saint or through appeal to the saint. Characteristically these are miracles of healing, pointing to the fact that even the most contemplative or solitary of the saints must be seen to demonstrate the transfer of spiritual benefits to another. It must be demonstrated that others can participate in the effects of the saint's relation with God. Sanctity must be communicable, in at least some ways. Christian faith is clear that our communion with Christ is the key gate to wider communion with God in all the triune dimensions. *Based* on that relation, salvation is marked by webs of communion. In the West, the Roman Catholic tradition may have stressed too much that it is through communion with a saint that deeper communion with God is possible for others, leaving aside the equally important fact that it is through communion with others that the saint's relation with God is heightened and multiplied to its full extent.

I have tended to stress that this web of relations is necessary for any one to have access to the fullness of God's relations with us. The other side is also crucial: one can connect to this web, at the extreme, only at one point. A person can be drawn into this extraordinary, cosmic communion by even one fragile thread, through an attachment (of the most humble and basic sort) only to one

---

8. "Outside the church there is no salvation" is a phrase which expresses this conviction, though it has often been interpreted in terms that focus more on extrinsic than intrinsic boundaries to communion. For an excellent review of the history of both the phrase and the idea, see F. A. Sullivan, *Salvation outside the Church? Tracing the History of the Catholic Response* (New York: Paulist, 1992). In a different connection, we can also note that some contemporary liberal Christian theologies effectively claim that "salvation" can be identified without remainder with the creation of a just and participatory human society. The error in the exclusive narrowness of such a reduction should not cloud the legitimate basis from which it proceeds. Salvation does have an intrinsic communal and participatory character.

other. Loving relation even to one person, if that love has the character not of closed possession but of further openness *through* that person, can finally draw someone to the very heart of God. In C. S. Lewis's *Screwtape Letters,* the senior devil instructs his junior tempter to discourage human subjects from developing even an innocent love of hot chocolate.[9] Such a love can easily be *shared.* Who knows what will come next of that? Surely nothing bad, the wise tempter fears. Through Christ, God has established the network that makes this possible. *In* Christ, there is the personal relation that can begin when all others are absent and which lies at the root of all enduring human communion.

Finally, a brief word about the eschatological implications of this vision. By now it should be clear that this theological perspective offers good reason to credit each religious tradition's "one and only" claims . . . not least of all, Christianity's. But I would like to call attention to one point, and that is the way this vision deals with the long-standing question of God's mercy and God's wrath. Short of predestinarian decrees, the problem is that at least toward some people God's character or purpose must *change* at some point, from a saving will to a condemning one. The view we have sketched, while emphatically not a universalism of salvation, is different.

It says that every human response to the manifestation and revelation of God meets from God only affirmation, only God's yes of grace, of election of humanity in Christ for relation with God. Every response to the divine initiative has its reward. Every quest for relation with God that proceeds on the basis of some dimension of God's self-giving to us meets the fulfillment for which it aims and hopes, even if it cannot be persuaded to hope further. Insofar as realization of relation with God in one of the dimensions we have discussed resists or refuses communion with God through other dimensions, it leads to its own distinctive end. And of course, from the view of other religions, so long as Christians insist on clinging to distinct identities, relations, and/or communion, they are barred from realizing the religious ends of those traditions.

Christians can hope for all to be saved. But if in their freedom and their choice of gifts all are not saved, the consummation of creation will still be a wonder that testifies to the glory of God. The loss and "judgment" here are very real, but they flow only from the limits that humans impose on God's goodness. They too bear the marks of grace and truth. If God had offered creation only one religious end, or only all these other ones, God would have done well. And to sound Pauline, we would have nothing to complain of. The Christian gospel is not about a God who stints on goodness. It is like that first of Jesus' miracles, when the guests look up in surprise: "You have kept the good wine till last."

9. C. S. Lewis, *The Screwtape Letters* (New York: Macmillan, 1962), p. 60.

# Creative Dialogue

## AASULV LANDE

Over the last decades, the dominating "theology of religions," if I may be permitted to use that phrase, has probably been exclusivist. The exclusivist thought has in major world religions been an active and dynamic consolidation around their religious basics, including exclusive claims about the truth of one's own belief. Inside Christianity, groups of conservative evangelicals thus have maintained strong exclusivist profiles. These groups often show strong missionary zeal and transmit an exclusivist image of Christianity. Parallels in other world faiths are not difficult to discern.

However, the dominating perceptions within Roman Catholicism, Orthodoxy, as well as mainstream Protestantism have been of inclusivist character. Vatican II provided classical illustrations of the official breakthrough of inclusivist thought in Roman Catholicism. Pluralist theologies of religions have made little impact in religious bodies, but they have dominated in the academic discourse. In Protestantism, ecumenical church leaders like Wesley Ariarajah and Stanley Samartha have voiced pluralist theologies, but the concern is above all displayed by academic theologians like Wilfred Cantwell Smith and John Hick.

The question about what will follow pluralist theologies of religion should thus keep these considerations in mind. Pluralist theologies have mostly been voiced by a group of prominent, independent theologians. They have had the upper hand in an ongoing academic discourse — but not on the grassroots level. Although this is stated against the background of the Christian scene, I am convinced that it holds validity as a statement about the overall situation of world faiths.

*Aasulv Lande*

# The Threefold Paradigm of Theology of Religions

The theological discourse in the last decades has adopted a basic differentiation between inclusive, exclusive, and pluralist theologies. This paradigm, which pregnantly was presented by the Anglican priest Dr. Alan Race,[1] has undoubtedly been most successful. It has served as a meaningful way of classification about which all concerned have been in agreement. It has succeeded in spelling out representative contrasts in religious thought and behavior among adherents of world religions. From my own experience during the early 1990s in Birmingham, I vividly recall how functional this threefold division was. The classification described "camps" within Christianity — and one was asked to reveal one's identity in accordance with the paradigm. Although it was mainly a Christian system of classification, it was also used about and among Buddhists and Muslims. The threefold paradigm constituted norms of fellowship — intrareligious as well as interreligious. Adherents of pluralist theologies from different religions obviously felt a deeper religious fellowship across religious borders than with exclusivist groups within their own faith community. In a variety of ways the paradigm thus structured many levels of conduct and relationships between adherents of world religions.

However, the paradigm has its limitations, and as time passed, uncomfortable presuppositions became apparent. Some were convincingly identified by Mark Heim in his book *Salvations.*[2] The theocentric presupposition behind this paradigmatic classification is obvious to anyone and explicitly stated by pluralists such as John Hick. But Heim furthermore pointed out the uncomfortable presupposition of considering "salvation" *similar* in different religions. He asked the simple question: Do "nirvana" and "kingdom of God" really point to the same reality? Proceeding from Heim's critique, one might identify the view *God performs salvation* as a presupposition behind the threefold scheme. In a postmodern environment that view no longer appears so self-evident as it did only a decade ago. As soon as the identity of "God" or/and "salvation" in different religions is questioned, the scheme becomes difficult to handle. Apparently it even dissolves.

The paradigm displays some similarity with the ideas of Francis Fukuyama,[3] who saw a historical eschaton in the breakdown of communism.

---

1. Alan Race, *Christians and Religious Pluralism: Patterns in the Christian Theology of Religions* (London: SCM Press, 1983).

2. S. Mark Heim, *Salvations: Truth and Difference in Religion* (Maryknoll, N.Y.: Orbis, 1995).

3. Francis Fukuyama, *The End of History and the Last Man* (New York: Penguin Books, 1992).

Fukuyama interpreted the liberal market as the end, indeed a glorious end, of sociopolitical development. He asked whether we did not see the end of human ideological evolution and the universalization of Western democracy as the final form of human government. Religious pluralism has similarly been considered the liberal crown of a religious evolution. It appears as the last stage of unfolding interreligious thought. Theology of religious pluralism could actually be seen as fulfillment of a liberal dream. In the liberal dream theology has surpassed exclusive narrowness, transcended inclusive tolerance, and attained openness as the eschaton of theological thought. If pluralist openness breaks down, what is then beyond it? A return to less pluralist theologies seems a regression. Is meaninglessness the only remaining answer? How does one progress "beyond the end"? Is there after all an overlooked stage, a hidden secret of further theological surprises yet to be revealed?

## Elements of a Deepened Pluralist Theology

To this writer the case of pluralism is still relevant. Globalization is in some way or other rather a fate than a choice — it implies pluralist challenges and requires pluralist answers to theological questions. The question is not "pluralism or no pluralism" but "What kind of pluralism?" Sketching an answer to what might be found "after pluralism," my proposal is a critical deepening of pluralist thought, "a deepened pluralism." In the following I indicate elements I would look for in a "deepened" pluralist theology.

### Contextuality

A new, pluralist theology of religions should maintain a double character of being contextual and experiential. In its contextual foundation it should take history, heritage, and environment seriously. In my personal case it will mean to interpret religious insights and truth claims in a "Nordic" perspective. It also implies a recognition of the spiritual tradition where the Dane Grundtvig plays a significant role and where I can use my experience as a person from rural Scandinavia, but also later experiences in various environments. The experience of life in nature is also of vital importance in my understanding of a theology of religions. Ecology and environmental issues are vital for quality in contemporary and future life, and provide an important dimension of interreligious encounter.

People from other backgrounds will as a matter of course relate to different contexts and experiences. I would like to see a variety of narratives and sto-

405

Aasulv Lande

ries, events and experiences in the theology of religions. There is for instance a narrative Asian tradition used by Kosuke Koyama, C. S. Song, Chung Hyun Kyung, and others where experiences are subjected to central, theological reflection.

Contextuality further means that a theology of religions in all its concreteness will have something conditional and passing about itself — as personal experience and given contexts will be in continuous flux and basically related to varying conditions.

## Critical

Theology of religions is, like all theology worthy of its name, dependent on freedom of thought. Although religions express themselves by various kinds of dogmas, they nonetheless have a root in liberative processes. The combination of dogmatism and drive for liberty presents a delicate question for theology of religions. "Free research," the great theologian Karl Barth claimed, "for the sake of the free Bible!"[4] Religious dogmas differ in absoluteness and openness — and vary in importance. A theology of religions must be willing to question religious dogmas and the traditions in which they flow. In this procedure there is also a need for self-criticism. In its critical enterprise, theology of religions should maintain an awareness of its critical presuppositions, and furthermore, how they relate to the religions addressed or represented. The critical theology has to display a spirit of self-criticism and self-awareness. In a Christian context it is of vital importance to refer to Christian understanding of freedom, as in the above Barth quote. Looking at conservative and self-defensive features prevailing in sections of interreligious theologizing, I question whether ecclesiastical bodies really are capable of administering a sufficiently open and free critical theology of religions. We need an ecclesiastically humble type of criticism. Do, after all, universities generally provide a safer basis for a continuing, critical, and humble pursuit of a theology of religions?

## Awareness of Power

It is insufficient and highly unsatisfying to pursue a theology of religions unaware of power structures. The same doctrines or the same religious ideas may

4. "Freie Forschung um der freien Bibel Willen," a quotation frequently used by my teacher of dogmatics at Lutheran School of Theology in Oslo, Professor Leiv Aalen.

be suppressive for some but liberative for others. Statements or truth claims cannot be evaluated in abstraction or in disregard of their function. "Good sociology," that is, liberating religious practice, might be combined with "bad theology" — theologies found inadequate when measured with personal or standard ecclesiastic criteria. Personally I have for years been very critical of doctrines and practice in the Japanese religion Soka Gakkai. Nonetheless, I have lately listened to convincing testimonies of liberative experiences by members of this very religion. At times, liberative religious options are apparently offered by doctrinally doubtful movements! The classical list of such social power factors as gender, class, and race requires sophistication in the pursuit of religious truth. A theology of religions will have to face the sometimes uncomfortable question: In whose interest is the truth promoted?

Another aspect of the relationship between religious truth and power might be seen in the USA, where presently a substantial increase in the number of indigenous Buddhists is taking place. Are then questions of religious truth to be decided by popular vote among believers? Are Western, Buddhist laypeople going to decide about true Buddhism, or are these decisions left with the priesthood — generally of Asian origin? As wealth is a part of the total picture here, one might continue to ask: Are Buddhist ideas a question for the market?

Similar questions and problems are facing all world religions. The pluralization and privatization of Christianity and the emergence of Western Islam accepting Western secular society provide other and parallel examples. A question behind such relations of truth and power might possibly be formulated as: Can truth be bought? Can someone or some interest groups "buy" a religion as a rich person can "purchase" a football team? Zen Buddhism might after all produce greater profit than Manchester United!

## A "Logos" Concept: Garden of Freedom

If a mediating concept is not provided, theology of religions may be unable to perform its major task: to relate religions to each other. In the early period of Christian encounter with Greek-Roman civilizations, the concept "logos" played an important mediating role. It actually provided a link between the prevailing, old concept of truth and the truth now to be proclaimed. Mediating concepts are provided by different religions and different cultures in different ways. In Buddhist encounters with other religious worlds, the concept of "buddha nature" displays similar features and capacities as the Greek-Christian logos. Buddha nature is a general quality — found in all human beings.

The need for such a mediating topos is indicated already in the

407

contextuality briefly described above. The acceptance of contextuality of theology of religions might easily become a disruptive feature. It is, however, most unsatisfactory for a theology of religions to break up into fragments. To overcome a danger of relativism and fragmentation, contextuality requires a mediating topos which brings relationships together. My intuition says that the topos signaled by the Buddhist concept of "nothingness" might contain fascinating possibilities for interpreting interreligious relations. The concept could be worked out as a kind of logos where contextual thought, mysticism, and action meet. Poetically the mediating topos might be named a "garden of freedom," providing a fertile ground for the theology of religions based on relationships. The topos might be characterized as "ultimate relationality" and thus mediate basic pluralist concerns.

In the Asian context one will find mediating concepts of this kind in the Kyoto School of Philosophy, with scholars such as Nishida Kitaro and Tanabe Hajime. Kitamori Kazoh, with the dynamic program "Theology of the Pain of God," and his disciple Koyama Kosuke are both actually formed by basic ideas of the philosophical Kyoto School.

## Conclusion

My brief outline in four points of a theology of religions thus proceeds from a pluralist concept. Due to its contextual and experiential character, such a theology does not attempt at developing a systematic whole. It aims at formulating genuine experiences and questions against the background of interreligious relationships. The intention and hope is that *a garden of freedom*, a topos of mediation inspired by "nothingness," will positively promote interesting theologies of religions — even after pluralism.

# After Rescher: Pluralism as Preferentialism

RISTO SAARINEN

In current theology of religions many scholars are seeking a way out of pluralism. The alleged shortcomings of pluralism are many. Some say it does not pay serious attention to the truth claims of religion. Others claim it is based on a Western Enlightenment philosophy which is particular rather than universal. Still others conclude that it is claiming on insufficient grounds that there be the same supreme being behind the seemingly manifold specter of religious attitudes.[1]

But it has also become apparent that the so-called postpluralistic accounts are no easier to outline. And if they are outlined and properly understood, they look like variants of exclusivism or inclusivism rather than a new theoretical possibility. I will not, however, go into any more detail in this discussion, but will argue in a somewhat different direction. My claim is that we have not yet explored the different versions of so-called pluralism well enough, and that we do not understand properly how pluralistic theologies of religions might work. We may well be able to construct a "pluralistic" theory of religions which can avoid the shortcomings of today's solutions.

I will argue this claim with the help of contemporary philosophy of science, in particular with Nicholas Rescher's book *Pluralism: Against the Demand for Consensus* (1993). Rescher does not treat theology, but I think his philosophy is highly relevant for our topic. Although his ideas have to some extent permeated the contemporary theology of religions, especially through Heim's treatment of Rescher's "orientational pluralism" in the book *Salvations,* his work in *Pluralism* has been neglected. My presentation consists of two parts: first I will

---

1. Mark Heim, *Salvations: Truth and Difference in Religion* (Maryknoll, N.Y.: Orbis, 1995); Heim, *The Depth of the Riches: A Trinitarian Theology of Religious Ends* (Grand Rapids: Eerdmans, 2001).

outline Rescher's position, and second I will briefly discuss its relevance for ecumenical theology and theology of religions.

In contemporary philosophy of science we can, according to Rescher, find two methodological approaches which are both influential, although they are diametrically opposed. The first is the so-called consensus theory of truth which is often connected with the political and social philosophy of Jürgen Habermas. According to this theory, a community of researchers who can exercise an open and free debate can in the long run agree on what count as scientific results. The scientific method is self-correcting and, in an open community, can be mutually corrective. The consensus theory can also be applied to political and social decision making; Rescher counts to some extent the philosophy of John Rawls and other versions of the idealized social-contract theory as variants of consensus theory.

The second approach is that of methodological relativism, individualism, and postmodernism, exemplified in the slogan "anything goes" of Paul Feyerabend. This approach argues that our world is radically individualistic and pluralistic and that therefore also the results of science, or at least the interpretations of humanities, remain relative and cannot approach the objective truth in any meaningful sense. An approach which abandons all objectivity would not regard consensus as a sign of rationality or a way toward it, but simply as a coincidence of opinions. Such a coincidence might perhaps substitute for rationality in, e.g., political decision making, but it does not say anything of rationality or truth.

Rescher is arguing for a middle way between consensus theory of truth and postmodern relativism. He calls his own view a "pluralistic" position which is a middle way between Habermas and Feyerabend. Rescher is for the most part concerned with the inherent problems of Habermas's consensus theory.

A crucial part of Rescher's argument is to show that a working consensus theory would presuppose a potentially omniscient community of researchers. But this is an impossible requirement. Scientific inquiry is always, both individually and within a community, historical and perspective-related and thus limited and incomplete. As limited and perspectival inquiry, it cannot reach any such consensus which would transcend these limits and approach the so-called objective truth. Rescher concludes that scientific judgments are "best judgments" connected with available, although limited, evidence. This state of affairs necessarily prompts pluralism, since different best judgments can only partially be falsified or reconciled with one another. No rational consensus is available.

This criticism of Habermas does not mean for Rescher that a pluralistic position in this sense would entail relativism or skepticism. Rescher argues that within the pluralist situation the scientist can and should prefer the best explanation, granted that inerrancy is not reached. Thus he does not embrace methodological anarchism or "anything goes" postmodernism. His qualified pluralism can be adequately understood in terms of the following two questions and the table of answers.[2]

Q1: In general, how many of the alternatives with respect to a controverted matter are plausible in the sense of deserving sympathetic consideration and deliberation?

Q2: Within the range of such viable alternatives, how many are acceptable in the sense of deserving endorsement and adoption?

| Range of Answers | | Resultant Doctrinal Position |
|---|---|---|
| **Q1** | **Q2** | |
| 0 | 0 | Nihilism |
| 1 | 1 | Monism (absolutism) |
| 2 or more (= 2+) | | Pluralism |
| | | ***Variants of Pluralism*** |
| 2+ | 0 | Skepticism |
| 2+ | 1 | Preferentialism |
| 2+ | 1 | with reason: Prefer. Doctrinalism (rationalistic) |
| 2+ | 1 | with choice: Prefer. Relativism (irrationalistic) |
| 2+ | 2+ | Syncretism |

We can see that the general position labeled "pluralism" contains at least five different positions. Rescher himself embraces the variant which is preferential and doctrinalist. Note once again that he is not speaking of theology nor of any other ideology but of scientific alternatives. He has probably borrowed terms like "doctrinalism" or "syncretism" from theological language, but he is using them to describe scientific alternatives.

It would be most interesting to analyze further how Rescher argues for his opinion that we may distinguish between plausible (Q1) and acceptable (Q2) alternatives, and what are his strategies for preferring a given position. I have, however, no time for doing this, but will from now on concentrate on the use of his position and model for the purposes of this conference.

First, Rescher's table allows for a clear and well-defined distinction between pluralism, relativism, and syncretism. "Pluralism" simply stands for a position in which we observe a plurality of plausible alternatives which we can-

---

2. Nicholas Rescher, *Pluralism: Against the Demand for Consensus* (Oxford: Oxford University Press, 1993), p. 99.

not explain away through consensus-aiming discourse. Pluralism is a permanent state of affairs which for Rescher has to do with the limited nature of our knowledge and intellectual capacity. But pluralism is not an answer to the problems given in the situation. It is just a description of the real nature of the situation. Doctrinalism, relativism, and syncretism have more to do with answering these problems. They are rationales for the acceptance of a given worldview or many worldviews. Pluralism is not yet offering these answers as such. It is only ruling out some wrong answers, namely, nihilism, monism, and the absolutism inherent in consensus theory.

This observation or this use of language is one of my main reasons to stick to pluralist discourse rather than to say that we must proceed into a postpluralistic discourse. I think the theology of religions has been too quick in judging some contingent variants of pluralist discourse as necessary and invariant aspects of pluralism. If we claim, e.g., that the John Hick type of pluralism is simply a hidden Western Enlightenment doctrinalism or that the Raimundo Panikkar style of pluralism is nothing more than hidden syncretism, we are still very far from criticizing the pluralist paradigm as a whole. There are other versions of pluralism which avoid the shortcomings of these types.

Second, and related to the first, theology of religions has thus far understood the alternative of pluralism much too narrowly. We have not investigated the option of pluralism analytically but have been guided by prejudices and judgmental language. Theological doctrinalists have a priori claimed that pluralism must be wrong, since doctrinalism is right. They have not thought that there might be a doctrinalist option within pluralism. Theological pluralists have, for their part, claimed that their version of pluralism is not syncretistic or relativistic, but they have not cared to work out properly what this really means and whether their own position can or should be understood in terms of preferentialism or doctrinalism. What we need is a thorough analysis of what pluralism can be and whether we can have a more neutral and modest version of theological pluralism which can succeed in overcoming the problems noted, e.g., by Heim.[3]

My third comment is somewhat personal. I come myself from inner-Christian ecumenism, in particular Faith and Order ecumenism. In this work, theological consensus and visible unity are the methodological models. "Unity in diversity" is often considered a problematic notion; or at least a quantitative doctrinal core of consensus is needed before diversity is allowed. For these reasons I was myself extremely prejudiced against Rescher's claim that consensus is an illusion and pluralism should be embraced.

3. In *Salvations*.

Reading the book, however, dissolved this prejudice. The philosophical argument basing on and proceeding from the limited and incomplete nature of human inquiry is very persuasive for a theologian. Moreover, the observation that consensus is somehow conceptually connected with the hubris of omniscience is a very healthy note for all ecumenists. But of course, the additional reason why I could embrace Rescher's variant of pluralism is that it allows for a preferential and doctrinalist position within this pluralism. I think that precisely this feature is something theologians should look at more closely. Of course, one may also add that Rescher's version of pluralism is to a great extent an epistemic pluralism which does not claim that the reality as such is pluralistic in the strong ontological sense which many theological pluralists seem to advocate.

With or without Rescher, I think we are in any case amidst fruitful developments within the pluralist account. One sign of that is that Heim, after his convincing criticism of some variants of pluralism in *Salvations,* has published another book, *The Depth of the Riches.* This book is no less pluralistic, although it follows other paths than those criticized in *Salvations.* Heim's idea of "saving the particulars," that is, the specific doctrines of various religions in this process, points in an interesting direction and is very helpful in creating a new variant of pluralism that succeeds in avoiding syncretism or postmodern nondoctrinalism. Rescher's understanding of pluralism is based on the assumption that particulars are all we have as limited beings. Replacing them for the sake of some general theory or explanation, however elegant and rational that may be as a theory, is simply a case of concealing the pluralist, or conflicting, evidence. The evidence of a great variety of particular religions and the diverse views within one religion simply is a pluralistic fact which cannot be explained away. This evidence, connected with the limited and particular nature of our understanding of it, makes a strong case for pluralism. But in this case pluralism is not an answer to some ideological question, it is just the observation that there are many plausible religious worldviews. It is indeed much too early to opt for a postpluralistic era. We must rather sit down and investigate what a diverse thing a pluralist theology of religions can be.

# Theology of Religions: What Comes after Pluralism?

JAN-MARTIN BERENTSEN

Let me start with a short comment on my topic: "Theology of Religions: What Comes after Pluralism?" The topic might indicate that the so-called pluralistic theology of religions is out: there must now be something *post* pluralism. Yes, I for one think the pluralistic approach advocated by representatives like John Hick, Samuel Rayan, and others has received such substantial critique over the last ten to fifteen years that it is hard to see how it may survive as a viable option for a Christian theology of religions. On that point I tend to agree with J. Andrew Kirk when he says that "inter-*religious* dialogue may be much easier than inter-*Christian* dialogue."[1]

As for my own contribution to our panel, I approach our topic as a missiologist, and I do not intend to use my twenty minutes for a kind of minilecture. We have already had two substantial scholarly contributions this morning. I want to take a much more personal and practical approach. As we are gathered from different parts of the world and from very different religious and cultural contexts with a great variety of experiences, it may not be completely uninteresting to learn how a young missionary from homogenous Norway was introduced to the field of theology of religions from the late 1960s on.

With a view to the overall theme for our third day in conference ("Theology of Religions: A Challenge to the Church"), I shall organize my simple thoughts under the following three headings.

---

1. Andrew J. Kirk, *What Is Mission? Theological Explorations* (London, 1999), p. 142, emphasis mine.

414

## A Monocultural Mind in a Monocultural Church

When I graduated from seminary in 1964, a term like "theology of religions" was totally unknown to me as a young missionary *in spe*. Theology, yes. Theology of religions, no. An even greater handicap, however, was the fact that "religions" as phenomenon was for all practical purposes a black spot to me. Certainly I had studied some pages and passed my exams, but the real world of religions was unknown. When I left Norway for missionary service in Japan, I had never met a Buddhist. Neither do I recall having seen a Hindu or a Muslim, although probably a Jew.

My world was Christian, my people were Christian — some, for certain, less practicing than others. My church was an established Lutheran state church, and if it has any meaning to talk of a Christian culture, mine was certainly Christian. Christian education was an important part of my public school curriculum from first grade on, and those youngsters in my town who eventually decided not to take confirmation in the church were few.

So, there I was — a young missionary *in spe* with a monocultural mindset in a monocultural church in a monocultural nation. Yes, I had some knowledge of a small, different ethnic group far north in the country, the Sami people, but neither in theory nor in practice was that part of my world by then.

How could such a person be of service to the Lord in a world of religions? I do not know whether that question really struck me at all before I found myself among shrines and temples in Japan.

## Among Shrines and Temples

The question, however, became increasingly — and at times disturbingly — clear as I found myself in evangelism and church planting among old and famous Shinto shrines and Buddhist temples — and not-so-old sanctuaries of new religious movements — in Nara Prefecture. I was in for surprises and challenges.

The whole difficult issue of state-religion relationship, for example, got new perspectives in my mind as I visited the many holy places of old Japanese Shinto nationalism. How could I agree that a symbiosis of state and religion was intolerable in Japan when in principle such a symbiosis was part of my own religious and cultural heritage, although in Christian trappings?

Joined to our new, small church in the "new town" was a nice and very popular nursery school hosting almost a hundred kids. Other nursery schools in the city were run by Buddhist temples, and we had a lot of common interests.

So there was this young Norwegian missionary eventually involved with Buddhist priests on issues of social welfare in modern-day Japan.

And if that was not enough, the missionary used to take visitors through the wide worship halls at the headquarters of Tenrikyo and on to their library where the staff proudly showed their collection of Christian books and wanted to discuss religion.

A monocultural mind in a world of cultural and religious plurality. Did my mind-set change? Hopefully it did! But how?


## Challenges to My Church

"What comes after pluralism?" Let me by using the word "sharing" focus briefly on three concerns which I see as a challenge to my church today.


### Sharing Our Backyard

Great changes have taken place in Norway. The cultural scenery of the students I now teach is vastly different from that of the student I once was. The kind of religious people I had never met are today increasingly involved in setting the agenda for the political and cultural debate in the nation. A diversity hitherto unknown has its effects on the monocultural and mono-religious mind-set.

What I have appreciated in studying a pluralistic theology of religions is the strong emphasis on the need to come to terms with religious encounters in order to learn to live together in peaceful coexistence. From a time when Norwegians could agree theoretically on such a need because — after all — we knew history, the issue has now become practical and existential in a way and with a magnitude that is new to us. We are learning every day that this problem may be far more difficult to handle — not to say solve — than we thought as long as we were sharing the world but not yet our own backyards.

This process of necessary changes in our traditional, monocultural mind-set is an enormous challenge not least to the church. We are by no means through with that. It relates in numerous ways to ongoing debates on the state-church relationship, religious education in public schools, etc. We ask what role is our own Christian tradition to play as we try to share peacefully our backyards with people of other faiths, and what roles are for the others to play? We have a lot to learn. Much more dialogue on this issue has certainly to follow "after pluralism."

## Sharing the Gospel

To me, however, something more has to follow: an understanding of the need — and a wish — to share the gospel. At this point my personal journey has not changed my mind. I have learned something — hopefully — on the *how* of sharing the gospel with people of other faiths. But I simply do not understand that it may be possible for the church to be church in the historic, Christian meaning of the term without recognizing and acknowledging the need for such a sharing.

My own religious encounters and my academic encounter with the pluralistic theological paradigm have left a very simple question in my mind. Is the church really to invite people of all faiths and "no faith" to repentance and belief in Christ? Rather than being an oversimplification of difficult issues, this to me is a basic question. Whatever follows "after pluralism," a simple and unequivocal "Yes!" in response to that question must be heard in my church — and in all churches.

That is not to say that we are high-handedly inviting other people to share in our religious property. The apostolic witness to Jesus cannot be any religion's "property." It is the basis on which the church exists, the fountain to which she herself is continuously invited by the Spirit to find her own life in daily repentance and renewal. The church must be an evangelist to herself if she is to be an evangelist to others.

## Sharing in "Theological Modesty"

Finally, whether we come out of the exclusivist, inclusivist, or pluralist camp, or whatever labels we put on our different positions, we meet one another with hard questions for the other party to solve in order to appear theologically acceptable. As stated already, I never saw the pluralist position as really a viable option. I struggle much more to sort out my position in relation to the two others, because to a person like me who can see no other possibility than Scripture — after all — being the ultimate guide in theology of religions as in all theology, there are obviously hard questions.

I hope that "after pluralism" there may follow readiness and willingness to share in what some are talking about as "theological modesty."[2] Even though we may all be more or less intellectually inclined to seek theological systems

2. Cf. Daniel B. Clendenin, *Many Gods, Many Lords: Christianity Encounters World Religions* (Grand Rapids, 1995), pp. 31-33.

that neatly accommodate and answer all our questions, there is a long tradition in the church underlining the need at some points to "rest patiently unknowing."[3]

This obviously applies not least to theology of religions. To me Scripture contains basic statements that should serve to guide our thinking: God "wants all men to be saved and to come to a knowledge of the truth" (1 Tim. 2:4); Jesus is "the atoning sacrifice for our sins, and not only for ours but also for the sins of the whole world" (1 John 2:2). At the same time, there is the apostolic appeal, "on Christ's behalf: Be reconciled to God" (2 Cor. 5:20); the apostolic answer to the jailer's question about salvation: "Believe in the Lord Jesus, and you will be saved" (Acts 16:31); and the consistent emphasis that "man is justified by faith" (Rom. 3:28).

Now, if God's "works are perfect" and "all his ways are just" (Deut. 32:4), as we believe they are, we are faced with hard, well-known questions that elude our attempts at logical explanations. The New Testament "logic" at this point seems to me to be the *missio-logical* one: the apostolic sending. Even "after pluralism" we are invited — in my view — to abide by this sending, abide in an attitude of "theological modesty" where we have "to steer a path between saying too much . . . and saying too little,"[4] invited to an attitude of "theological modesty" that on some issues is content to "rest patiently unknowing."

---

3. Augustine, *Enchiridion* 5.16, quoted in Clendenin, p. 33.
4. Clendenin, p. 33.

# Religious Pluralism in Multireligiosity

## LENE KÜHLE

Many different notions have been used to characterize modern Western societies, which due to migration (primarily for labor and asylum) hold a diversity
of religious and ethnic communities. They have for instance been called multiethnic, multireligious, multicultural, or pluralistic. These notions are interrelated, but they are clearly not synonyms,[1] and the relations between them are
unfortunately not very clear. "Pluralism" has proved to be especially problematic, being "a tricky term"[2] with "several meanings and associations,"[3] "ambiguous and contentious,"[4] if not even "deceptively difficult."[5] The concept of pluralism thus isn't without its problems. Still, I will argue that there firstly are
some general lines in the debates on pluralism. Secondly, these different traditions of defining and theorizing pluralism have recently converged. Thirdly, I
will propose that if we understand religious pluralism as an extension of the
general phenomenon of pluralism, this would lead to a critique of the theologi-

---

1. In two surveys in Danish made by PLS Rambøll in November and December 2000,
"Denmark should be a multi-ethnic society" was favored by 34 percent of the respondents. A
somewhat larger quantity, 49 percent, agreed that "Denmark should be a multi-cultural society." A multiethnic society was defined as one with many different ethnic groups, a multicultural society as one where people are given the right to keep their culture alive (*Søndagsavisen*,
January 14, 2001).

2. Grace Davie, "Religion in Modern Britain: Changing Sociological Assumptions," *Sociology* 34, no. 1 (2000): 120.

3. Ole Riis, "Modes of Religious Pluralism under Conditions of Globalisation," *MOST
Journal on Multicultural Studies* 1, no. 1 (1999). Available on the Internet at www.unesco.org/
most/vl1n1ris.htm.

4. David Nicholls, *Three Varieties of Pluralism* (London: Macmillan, 1974), p. 1.

5. James A. Beckford, "The Management of Religious Diversity in England and Wales
with Special Reference to Prison Chaplaincy," *MOST Journal on Multicultural Societies* 1, no. 2
(1999). Available on the Internet at www.unesco.org/most/vl1n2bec.htm.

cal notion of religious pluralism for not being in line with the general usage in the social sciences. I find that this particular definition of religious pluralism might block an incorporation of the issue of religion into general debates of multiethnicity, multiculturalism, and multireligiosity.

## Pluralism

Pluralism is a good starting point for a conceptual discussion because it has such a long history as a scientific concept in philosophy, theology, anthropology, and political science. It seems that Kant was one of the first to talk of pluralism as "not to see all the world included in one's own self but as a mere world citizen's outlook and attitude."[6] The first "genuine pluralist" philosopher was, however, William James, who made pluralism a key concept in his *The Pluralistic Universe* from 1909.[7] James's philosophy was an attack on Hegel's idea of the absolute and its dialectical character. For James there might be more than one substance, and claiming a oneness of the real is a theoretical postulate at odds with the empirical reality we find ourselves in. The pluralism of James is therefore an ontology as well as a "plea for returning to plain honest logic against vicious intellectualism."[8] James's philosophy and his critique of Hegel became an inspiration for a group of early twentieth-century political scientists from England, with J. N. Figgis, Harold Laski, and D. H. Cole as its main representatives.[9] Their work was a reaction against political theories which didn't account for the effects of groups and communities but instead conceived of politics as something concerning the relationship between the state and the individual.[10] As Laski puts it, "you must place your individual at the centre of things. You must regard him as linked to a variety of associations to which his personality attracts him. You must on this view admit that the State is only one of the associations to which he happens to belong, and give it exactly that pre-eminence — and no more — to which on the particular occasion of conflict its superior moral claim will entitle it."[11] Though the term might be

---

6. "Dem Egoismus kann nur der Pluralismus entgegensetzen werden, d.i. die Denkungsart: sich nicht als die ganze Welt in seinem Selbst befassend, sondern als einen blossen Weltbürger zu betrachten und zu verhalten" (Kant, in Rupert Breitling, "The Concept of Pluralism," in *Three Faces of Pluralism*, ed. Stanislaw Ehrlich and Graham Wootton [Gower, 1980], pp. 1-19, here 2).

7. Breitling, p. 3.

8. Breitling, p. 6.

9. Nicholls, p. 5; Harry Goulbourne, "Varieties of Pluralism: The Notion of a Pluralist Post-imperial Britain," *New Community* 17, no. 2 (1991): 211-27, here 217.

10. Nicholls, p. 5.

11. Laski, in Breitling, p. 12.

foreign to these "pluralists," their interests could be put under the common heading "civil society."[12] Alongside these developments in political science we see a growing interest in the issue and concept of pluralism in anthropology. The American Horace Kallen is considered the first author to use the concept of cultural pluralism,[13] in an article from 1915.[14] For Kallen cultural pluralism signifies "multiplicity in a unity," and the conception is formed in opposition to authors who put a strong emphasis on the unity of culture. For Kallen there is no *core culture* which defines the soul of the nation, and he especially opposes the idea that American culture is basically Anglo-Saxon. Whatever is called American must include "the plurality of America's actual groups,"[15] for whatever Kallen understands by "multiplicity in a unity," this unity doesn't have a center. Though Kallen now has been rediscovered as an early multiculturalist, his influence on the anthropological discussions of pluralism until the 1990s seems to have been marginal. The Dutchman F. S. Furnivall is more often mentioned as the father of the theory and notion of social and cultural pluralism,[16] even though he does not speak of pluralism but prefers the term "plural society." Furnivall used the term to distinguish a certain kind of society which had arisen due to the impact of capitalism and colonialism upon traditional tropical societies. These societies contained different ethnic, religious, linguistic, or kinship groups who lived side by side but otherwise had very separated lives and only met at the marketplace.[17] The society was in this way held together by the colonial power and the dominance of a single economic system, i.e., capitalism.[18] Furnivall's theories were met with "limited interest" by his contemporaries,[19] and "the plural society" was only put on the academic agenda when Furnivall's work was continued in the 1960s by

12. R. D. Grillo, *Pluralism and the Politics of Difference: State, Culture, and Ethnicity in Comparative Perspective* (Oxford: Clarendon, 1998), p. 6.

13. Jonathan Sacks, *The Persistence of Faith* (London: Weidenfeld and Nicolson, 1991), p. 62.

14. Christopher Newfield and Avery F. Gordon, "Multiculturalism's Unfinished Business," in *Mapping Multiculturalism,* ed. Christopher Newfield and Avery F. Gordon (Minneapolis: University of Minnesota Press, 1996), pp. 76-115, here 83.

15. Newfield and Gordon, p. 85.

16. See, for instance, Yunus Samad, "The Plural Guises of Multiculturalism: Conceptualizing a Fragmented Paradigm," in *The Politics of Multiculturalism in the New Europe,* ed. T. Modood and P. Werbner (London: Zed Books, 1997), pp. 240-60, here 242; Goulbourne, p. 218.

17. Nicholls, p. 39.

18. Nicholls, p. 39.

19. M. G. Smith, "Some Development in the Analytical Framework of Pluralism," in *Pluralism in Africa,* ed. Leo Kuper and M. G. Smith (Berkeley: University of California Press, 1971), pp. 415-58, here 415.

a group of researchers including the Jamaican social anthropologist M. G. Smith. Smith said one of the problems with Furnivall's approach was that he had confined his theory to the colonial societies. Smith claimed he "committed a major methodological error by treating the arbitrary products of historical combinations as necessary and sufficient elements of a distinct societal type. . . . Pluralism is confined neither to the tropics, nor to the last centuries of human history."[20] Smith's reformulation of Furnivall's theory therefore included an extension of the theory to all kinds of societies. Smith's contribution to the debate on plural societies caused a lot of controversy, and he was forced to revise and strengthen it.[21] In its full blossom the theory is very complex and abstract, and according to Goulbourne it "is not only more sophisticated, it also exhibits a greater analytical awareness than earlier notions of pluralism."[22] For Smith, as for Furnivall, pluralism has to do with different groups living together in one society, or more precisely, with the different ways of incorporating different ethnic or social groups into society. The plural society paradigm thus evolved as a fruitful approach to multicultural societies. Apart from Smith's, however, the contributions were not theoretically strong. The lively debates on plural societies from the 1960s and early 1970s didn't survive the critique from radical sociologists, who considered pluralism "flabby and reformist, needing to be replaced by something more rigorous and revolutionary."[23]

The anthropological debate on pluralism has, however, been renewed recently. In the new pluralism, pluralism is connected to issues of equal rights and cultural recognition, and thus attains a strong normative flavor.[24] It has been criticized for the way it imports "ideological baggage" into the academic discussions of interethnic relations,[25] as descriptive and normative aspects shouldn't be confused,[26] and for its misreading of other theories on pluralism.[27] Still, the "new pluralism" has managed to bring pluralism on to the political agenda, and it owes its importance to that.

20. Smith, p. 429.

21. Goulbourne, p. 218; Nicholls, p. 43.

22. Goulbourne, p. 219.

23. Gregor McLennan, *Pluralism* (Buckingham: Open University Press, 1995), p. 43. However, Smith to a certain extent draws on Marxist theories of imperialism and global exploitation (p. 42).

24. Goulbourne, "Varieties of Pluralism."

25. Richard Jenkins, *Rethinking Ethnicity: Arguments and Explorations* (London: Sage, 1997), p. 28.

26. Beckford, "The Management of Religious Diversity in England and Wales with Special Reference to Prison Chaplaincy"; Riis, "Modes of Religious Pluralism under Conditions of Globalisation."

27. Goulbourne, "Varieties of Pluralism."

## Coherence and Convergence

The definitions of pluralism used in the different scholarly traditions have thus varied, and the controversies over the definition have flamed so high that one scholar has suggested that the notion of pluralism either be erased from the vocabulary of academic discussions or at least put in "inverted commas like the notion of 'race'" in order to "denote a degree of dissension or controversy."[28] Several scholars have on the other hand managed to find at least some way of systematizing the seemingly very different ways of talking of pluralism. One example is political scientist Giovanni Sartori, who proposes that "the messy but more serious part of the literature [on pluralism] is best addressed . . . by distinguishing among three *levels of analysis*."[29] He distinguishes between "the belief level" where pluralism shows itself in a respect for the multicultural society and acceptance of dissent. Pluralism at the societal level describes pluralism as a certain kind of differentiation, while Sartori's third level, the political level, is characterized by "a diversification of power."[30] Political scientist Gregor McLennan prefers to speak about *levels of pluralism*. What he calls "methodological pluralism" "posits the existence and validity of a multiplicity of appropriate research methods; a multiplicity of substantive interpretative 'paradigms'; many truths; many worlds." "Sociocultural pluralism," on the other hand, requires adherence to "many types of important social relations; many subcultures; multiple identities; multiple selves," while "political pluralism" "offers a scale of commitment to recognition of sociocultural difference; facilitation of difference; representation of difference in all basic decision-making arrangements."[31] Richard Mouw and Sander Griffioen conceptualize pluralism in terms of different *types* of pluralisms. "Directional pluralism" acknowledges the existence of a diversity of value systems. The term "associational pluralisms" points to a diversity of associational modes, where the pluralistic situation is characterized by the individual being integrated in many different associations and thereby in many different roles. Contextual pluralism finally regards "different racial, ethnic, geographic, gender, and class experiences."[32]

Some scholars have gone even further and suggested that all varieties of

28. Jenkins, p. 28.

29. Giovanni Sartori, "Understanding Pluralism," *Journal of Democracy* 8, no. 4 (1997): 58-69, here 61, emphasis mine.

30. Sartori, pp. 62-63.

31. McLennan, pp. 6-7.

32. Richard J. Mouw and Sander Griffioen, *Pluralisms and Horizons* (Grand Rapids: Eerdmans, 1994), pp. 16-18, here 17.

pluralism are concerned with diversity and unity within a state.[33] Yet Grillo builds his argument on a selective reading of Nicholls's statement *that for social and political theorists* pluralism is "concerned with a series of connected problems, namely the degree of unity and the type of unity which actually exists in particular states, or which ought to exist. They are in fact concerned with the relationship between unity and diversity in a state."[34] Therefore, it seems that as an argument about pluralism in general, it might be too simple. It would, however, be fair to say that there is a general realization of what one scholar calls "striking similarities" between the work on pluralism in anthropology and political science,[35] and that these two different traditions recently have showed a degree of convergence[36] due to their common interest in multicultural, multiethnic, multireligious societies. This is for instance clear in the recent writings of the political scientist Robert A. Dahl, who used to regard pluralism as a purely political concept but is now interested in cultural pluralism.[37] The way sociologist of religion and theologian Peter Berger recently has written about pluralism could seem to hint that this convergence does not only concern the notion of pluralism as invoked by political scientists and anthropologists. Berger, who used to regard pluralism mainly in terms of the mental reaction to the breakdown of the sacred canopy and the corresponding competition of a religious worldview (with an inspiration from the philosophical tradition of pluralism), now defines it as "the coexistence and social interaction of people with very different beliefs, values and lifestyles."[38] To summarize, it would seem that pluralism has been used in many different contexts and in many different ways. If we on the other hand focus on the contexts where pluralism has been put in connection with notions such as multiethnicity, multireligiosity, and multiculturalism, it would be fair to say that even though the notion of pluralism is not univocal, there are some general tendencies and that the different notions would appear to converge.

---

33. Grillo, pp. 5-9.

34. Nicholls, p. 1.

35. Avigail Eisenberg, *Reconstructing Political Pluralism* (Albany: State University of New York Press, 1995), p. 1.

36. McLennan, pp. 95-97.

37. Robert A. Dahl, "The Future of Democratic Theory," *Estudio/Working Paper 1996/90* (1996).

38. Peter Berger, "Protestantism and the Quest for Certainty," *Christian Century*, August 26–September 2, 1998, pp. 782-96, here 782.

## Toward a Definition of Pluralism

In the light of a seeming convergence, it might be relevant to ask what definition of pluralism we are converging against. If we take our point of departure in the above-mentioned statement that pluralism most often concerns unity and diversity within a state, there are in fact three different ways of approaching this. Some scholars — and most journalists, politicians, etc. — have used a definition of pluralism which takes it to mean nothing more than "diversity."[39] This is in my opinion problematic for purely terminological reasons. For as one scholar puts it, "'cultural pluralism' seems to mean essentially the same thing as cultural or social diversity, except that pluralism may be intended to carry a more favourable connotation, diversity a more neutral. I see no profit in this usage and prefer to use the term diversity instead."[40] Sartori is even more critical of equating pluralism and diversity, and sees it as an "impoverishment of the concept" and adds that for "the simpletons of the profession (and there is many), pluralism is derived from whatever is plural instead of a singular in grammar, or reduced to whatever is more-than-one. . . . But the mere existence of numerous groups — a pure and simple plural society — by no means constitutes evidence of pluralism."[41]

If we continue from the proposition that pluralism means something more than diversity, another approach to pluralism focuses on how the different groups are differentially incorporated into society,[42] and on how different groups enjoy different rights.[43] There is a wealth of approaches that differ in many ways, but they all perceive pluralism as more than just diversity. And they share in how they regard pluralism as a concept, which is as the existence of groups in a society, or more precisely a relationship between groups, society, and state. The special character of pluralism in a specific context is thus highly dependent on the society and state in question.[44]

Still other scholars have regarded pluralism as an ideology which celebrates diversity.[45] This is for instance favored by James Beckford, who defines

39. See, for instance, Rodney Stark and Roger Finke, "Pluralism and Piety," *Journal for the Scientific Study of Religion* 34, no. 4 (1995): 431-45.

40. Robert A. Dahl, "Pluralism Revisited," in *Three Faces of Pluralism*, pp. 20-33, here 20.

41. Sartori, p. 61.

42. Smith, p. 444.

43. Bryan Wilson, "Religious Toleration, Pluralism, and Privatization," *Kirchliche Zeitgeschichte* 8 (1995): 99-116, here 106.

44. Françoise Champion, "The Diversity of Religious Pluralism," *MOST Journal on Multicultural Societies* 1, no. 2 (1999). Available on the Internet at www.unesco.org/most/vl1n2dav.htm.

45. Jenkins, p. 29.

pluralism as "an ideological or normative belief that there *should be* mutual respect between different cultural systems and freedom for them all."[46] It is fair to say that there is a general acknowledgment that pluralism "is both a political philosophy and an analytical category."[47] This fact was also reflected in the before-mentioned typologies, where for instance Sartori distinguishes between pluralism at the belief level and pluralism at the societal level. It might also be worth noticing that though it is confusing that "pluralism" is used to denote an ideology and a state of affairs, the same goes for "communism," a term used both to denote an ideology and to describe the way societies are organized. If this solution is not satisfactory, the ambiguity of the term "pluralism" could be avoided by using the notion of multiculturalism to denote the ideology, which is the common usage in the United States at least.[48] This leaves the notion of pluralism which refers to the different ways a society deals with its diverse groups as the central aspect of pluralism.

## Religion and Pluralism

It has been argued that religion has been excluded from most discussions on multiculturalism[49] as well as from the related academic discourses on migration[50] and race.[51] This is not surprising considering the way religion has been absent from the agenda of most social scientists,[52] at least until quite recently.[53] It seems that religion has been excluded from many of the discussions on pluralism in the same way. It is thus striking that of the typologies mentioned, only Mouw and Griffioen allow for a discussion of religion, and for the very good reason that their main problem is whether pluralism and a Christian conviction can go together! Other ways to "handle" religion include the one es-

46. Beckford, "The Management of Religious Diversity in England and Wales with Special Reference to Prison Chaplaincy."

47. Grillo, p. 5.

48. Pierre Bourdieu and Loïc Wacqant, "On the Cunning of Imperialist Reason," *Theory, Culture and Society* 16, no. 1 (1999): 41-52.

49. Tariq Modood, "Anti-essentialism, Multiculturalism and the 'Recognition' of Religious Groups," *Journal of Political Philosophy* 6, no. 4 (1998): 378-99, here 390.

50. Viggo Mortensen, *Religion og Integration. Efter 11. September* (Aarhus: Center for Multireligiøse Studier, 2002), p. 21.

51. Jørgen S. Nielsen, *Towards a European Islam* (London: Macmillan, 1999), p. 11.

52. Beckford, *Religion in Advanced Industrial Society* (London: Unwin Hyman, 1989).

53. See, for instance, Manuel Castells, *The Power of Identity* (Blackwell, 1997), for a recent approach which incorporates a detailed analysis of religious phenomena into a broader sociological framework.

poused by Nicholls, who mentions that he will not consider what he calls "the philosophical pluralism of writers like William James . . . [and] the ecclesiastical pluralism practised by eighteenth-century Irish bishops,"[54] while Breitling argues that pluralism originated in philosophy, extended to other fields, but today "in most cases is an abbreviation of political or social pluralism"; but that he must add that religious pluralism can be used as a theological concept related to God as a finite being.[55]

It thus seems that most accounts of pluralism neglect it in regard to religion, as it is not considered part of the general phenomena of pluralism. And if religious pluralism is discussed, it is as an exception to the general usage. I would on the other hand suggest that if it is to have any meaning at all to speak of religious pluralism exactly as a kind of pluralism, then it must be seen as an extension or application of the principles of pluralism to religion(s), which would mean regarding religious pluralism as an aspect of cultural and ethnic pluralism.[56] That would enable religion to be incorporated into debates on multiculturalism and multiethnicity in such a way that the existence of religious groups in society is regarded as part of a general phenomenon of pluralism, while at the same time remaining a phenomenon in its own right with its special character and problems.

## Religious Pluralism in Theology

This is, however, not the way the notion of pluralism is used in theology. "Religious pluralism" became an important term in theology from the late sixties, when theologians, faced with a growing cultural diversity, looked for a global theology which could make different religions communicate.[57] What I'm referring to is the conception of religious pluralism developed and defended most prominently by John Hick.[58] Hick defines religious pluralism as "the view that the transformation of human existence from self-centredness to Reality-centredness is taken place in different ways within the contexts of all great religious traditions. There is not merely one way but a plurality of ways of salvation or liberation."[59]

54. Nicholls, p. 1.
55. Breitling, p. 16.
56. Ian Hamnett, ed., *Religious Pluralism and Unbelief: Studies Critical and Comparative* (London: Routledge, 1995), p. 3.
57. Adrian Hastings, "Pluralism: The Relationship of Theology to Religious Studies," in *Religious Pluralism and Unbelief*, pp. 226-40.
58. William Rowe, "Religious Pluralism," *Religious Studies* 35, no. 2 (1999): 139-50, here 139.
59. John Hick, *Problems of Religious Pluralism* (London: Macmillan, 1985), p. 34.

The problem with defining religious pluralism along these lines is perhaps more clear in the work of the theologian Lesslie Newbigin. Newbigin makes a great effort to distinguish between plural (by which he means the same as I did with the word "diversity") and pluralism, which he finds to be contained in the fact that people "of many ethnic origins and of many different religious commitments live together in our cities and share our public life." He, however, finds it necessary to distinguish quite sharply between religious pluralism as "the belief that the differences between the religions are not a matter of truth and falsehood, but of different perceptions of the one truth," and cultural pluralism, which is "the attitude which welcomes the variety of different cultures and life-styles within one society and believes that this is an enrichment of human life."[60] Religious pluralism is thus defined as the theological view that there is truth in every religion, while cultural pluralism is defined as an attitude toward diversity. In this way religious pluralism is seen as a phenomenon of a different character than cultural pluralism and basically unrelated to the societal level of religious diversity. Flanagan states in a fairly polemical article that "[p]luralism was a primitive term that has now been bypassed," but that it is ironic that "a term which became so devaluated in sociology was appropriated by theologians in the late sixties and has been so misused ever since."[61] As would probably be clear, I do not share Flanagan's conviction that the term "pluralism" has been bypassed (and I do not agree with him that theologians got it from sociology), but I do share his sense of irony in theologians not conforming with commonly accepted terms and norms when engaging in a discussion of issues concerning multireligiosity, multiculturalism, and multiethnicity.

## Where Does This Leave Us?

Let me first emphasize that I do not question the substance of the theories of Hick and Newbigin. What I question is the usage they make of the notion of religious pluralism. What is by social scientists regarded as an aspect of how different religious groups coexist within the same society is instead by most theologians seen as a concept which refers to the character of the divine. It is this usage which is problematic from my point of view. It is obviously always prob-

---

60. Lesslie Newbigin, *The Gospel in a Pluralist Society* (Geneva: WCC Publications, 1989), p. 14.

61. Kieran Flanagan, "Theological Pluralism: A Sociological Critique," in *Religious Pluralism and Unbelief*, pp. 81-113, here 85-86.

lematic when a concept is used in two different — and mutually exclusive — ways. In this case I suspect that the ambiguity about the notion of religious pluralism has marginalized religion somewhat as a subject in general debates on pluralism. The definition of religious pluralism as a strictly theological concept works in my opinion as an obstacle for a theological approach to the pluralistic society. I thus suspect that a dialogue on the multireligious or pluralistic society — not only between theology and social science, but also between theology and the political system as well as the general public — is in risk of becoming severely hampered or even impossible. I can therefore only encourage theologians to (re)consider how they use the notion of pluralism.[62] To conclude, it seems to me that if theology in fact wants to meet multireligiosity, then theologians must in fact attune themselves to the notion of pluralism usually connected to issues of the multireligious, multicultural, multiethnic society!

---

62. Some theologians have, however, seen the point in using a definition of pluralism closer to the one used in the social sciences; for instance, Diana Eck, foreword to *The Dawn of Religious Pluralism: Voices from the World's Parliament of Religions, 1893,* ed. Richard Hughes Seager (La Salle, Ill., 1993).

# Religious Pluralism as an Epiphenomenon of Postmodern Perspectivism

ANDREW J. KIRK

## The Argument

My major interest in this paper is to demonstrate that religious pluralism as an interpretative theory of multireligiosity is closely linked to an approach to knowledge known as "perspectivism." By religious pluralism I mean any view of religious life and belief which asserts *either* that the most fundamental aspects of all (major) religious traditions are manifestations of the same "ultimately Real" (the monistic thesis of John Hick) *or* that, though incommensurable, each religious tradition encompasses a path to salvation of equal worth and benefit (polymorphism). By perspectivism I understand the epistemological thesis that there is no conception of reality independent of human interpretation and that all interpretations are inevitably contextually conditioned and contingent. Although it does not logically entail relativism, in that it does not explicitly deny that particular views can be true, it has usually employed a highly relativizing technique toward all claims to knowledge.[1]

Perspectivism is associated with the philosophy of Nietzsche, who denied the existence of a single set of standards for determining the validity of specific truth claims. Nietzsche's perspectivism has been understood in two different ways. First, it has been seen as his putative theory of knowledge. Because no accurate representation of the world, as it is, is possible, there is nothing unequivocally factual to which our theories correspond, in order to confirm them as true or false. Moreover, no method of understanding our world — no form of rationality or empirical procedure — enjoys a privileged

1. Cf. Jonathan Dancy and Ernest Sosa, *A Companion to Epistemology* (Oxford: Blackwell, 1992), pp. 304-5.

epistemic status. Rather, our understanding is constituted by our desires and needs.[2]

This summary of Nietzsche's epistemic assumptions displays a frontal attack on most of the cherished beliefs of the Enlightenment. In the first place, it denies a correspondence theory of truth, namely, that our perceptions of the world and the language we use to interpret and communicate them are accurate representations of what is really there. Secondly, it denies a transcendent reality which exists independently of our mental construction. In this sense it borrows from Kant's antirealist distinction between things-as-they-are-in-themselves and things-as-they-appear-to-us. Thirdly, there is no particular foundation from which we may build an explanation of the world with confidence that it is correct. Finally, all our pretended knowledge is little more than an echo of our own place in the world. Knowledge is the consequence of power arrangements and is used to maintain relationships in favor of those who decide what is right to believe. According to this first interpretation of Nietzsche, it can readily be seen why he should be known as the "father of postmodernity."

However, owing to the self-referential contradiction of such a position — his own views, if taken perspectivally, are refuted — another interpretation has been argued by some commentators. According to this understanding, Nietzsche is employing the genealogical technique of demonstrating that, historically, most, if not all, so-called facts have proved to be interpretations. In this way beliefs once held to be unequivocally valid have been shown to be mere perspectives on life and the world that have had to be either severely revised or abandoned altogether. Thus knowledge is not something humans possess; such an idea continues the illusion of the philosophers that it is possible to reach the "holy grail" of seeing things from God's point of view. In Nietzsche's perspective, claims to knowledge and truth are rhetorical devices which summarize successful discourse, i.e., arguments that happen to have persuaded most people.[3] Perspectivism is a deeply suspicious reaction to any view that we can have access to self-evident, assured knowledge about a reality independent of our preferences and aspirations.

Whichever interpretation is adopted, perspectivism is a fundamental characteristic of the outlook on the world known now so commonly as postmodernity. Before seeking to show how religious pluralist theses are one kind of manifestation of this perspectivism, we should show how this links to the postmodern state.

---

2. Cf. Bernd Magnus and Kathleen Higgins, *The Cambridge Companion to Nietzsche* (Cambridge: Cambridge University Press, 1996), p. 4.

3. Magnus and Higgins, pp. 5-6.

*Andrew J. Kirk*

# The Marks of Postmodernity

## *The End of Metanarratives*

In his celebrated book *The Postmodern Condition*,[4] Francois Lyotard declares that no overarching interpretation of history and life is any longer possible. One of the many problems, in his estimation, of the modern project has been the attempt to find a rational explanation for the development of human life. The most elaborate and complete attempt has been made by the Marxist account of human social life divided into stages according to the current economic means of production. Marx believed he had unlocked the clue to the past divisions within society and opened up the way to a conflict-free future by uncovering the dialectic of history — the class struggle. Once the economic contradictions of capitalism were negated, in the final death throes of private property arrangements, history would usher in a qualitatively different society: one in which all needs would be met as everyone contributed to the common good according to his or her abilities.

Marxism is one of the clearest examples of a metanarrative. However, it is but one example of many attempts to harness the scientific method to different aspects of human life, in order to produce a complete explanation of a given set of phenomena. The Freudian analysis of psychological disorders would be another, insofar as it claims to give a comprehensive description of the mechanisms of mental and psychic trauma. Durkheim's explication (in *Elementary Forms of the Religious Life*) of the causes of religious belief and practice in their origins in social cohesion and psychological integration is yet another.[5]

The postmodern objection to metanarratives centers on their bid to be all-inclusive descriptions of experience, leading them to be exclusive of other ways of looking at life. They spring from the hubris of human reason, which believes it can discover a final explanatory theory for everything. Postmodernity is a repudiation, if you like, of all attempts to arrive at the final (Hegelian) synthesis of history by exhaustively analyzing all its component parts, with the intention of exposing fundamental social, economic, psychological, or biological laws which can then be harnessed to plan a more fruitful future for humanity.

---

4. Francois Lyotard, *The Postmodern Condition: A Report on Knowledge* (Minneapolis: University of Minnesota Press, 1984).

5. Even Richard Rorty's neo-Darwinian pragmatism looks uncommonly like a theory implicitly claiming universal validity, in spite of his intense dislike of Platonist metaphysics; cf. his "The Challenge of Relativism," in *Debating the State of Philosophy*, ed. Jozef Niznik and John T. Sanders (Westport, Conn.: Praeger, 1996), pp. 31ff.

## *The Impossibility of Foundationalism in Epistemology*

The drive toward metanarratives has its origins in the dual desire to possess clear and precise descriptions of every human activity, using the scientific methodology so successfully employed about the natural world, and to counter all forms of skepticism about the ability to arrive at true knowledge. In the Enlightenment view of things, knowledge was to have been the great emancipator, the way of liberating humanity from the darkness of ignorance, prejudice, and superstition. By the light of reason, one would be able to forge a new society, built on the self-evidently superior values of equality and respect for the freedom and rights of all (meaning, at the time, *all* those able to own property).

Skepticism could only be defeated by discovering a set of foundational beliefs that could not be doubted or refuted. From the time of René Descartes onward, many philosophers and scientists looked for a means of possessing an absolute certainty about certain convictions, of a kind that no amount of doubt could shake. Such convictions would have to be universally self-evident, beyond every kind of reasonable doubt. To disbelieve them would mean embracing irrationalism or remaining invincibly ignorant. Descartes, notoriously, sought to found such an indisputable belief on the thinking subject that simply could not deny its own existence without being self-contradictory. Other attempts were made by the conclusive demonstrations of scientific experimentation, said to lead to the conclusion that the entire workings of nature could be successfully deciphered once the individual parts of the gigantic machine had been taken apart to reveal the way they function.

However, successive attacks against foundationalism were made by those who argued that one could only attain to absolute certainty by stepping outside the human condition completely and seeing things from a "God's-eye point of view," that in reality all knowledge was dependent on prior theories and that such theories were, in turn, dependent on contingent historical factors. Even the most exact sciences, with the possible exception of mathematics, were always open to correction. From time to time, as Thomas Kuhn has argued,[6] science advances only by accepting fundamental "paradigm shifts" that amount to radical departures from previously accepted norms. There is now a strong body of opinion which proclaims that all knowledge is the result of the interpretation of data from a relative perspective. It depends on the particular intellectual tradition to which we adhere.

6. Thomas Kuhn, *The Structure of Scientific Revolutions,* 2nd ed. (Chicago: University of Chicago Press, 1970).

Andrew J. Kirk

## The Rejection of Technological Rationalism

A new interpretation of the history of the post-Enlightenment West comes to the conclusion that the potentially liberating force of reason has turned out to be oppressive and destructive. If Descartes believed that the argument which arrives logically and consistently at the cogito was an irrefutable truism, Enlightenment *man* (not so much woman) has acted as if the phrase *vinco ergo sum* (I conquer, therefore I am) was the new road to paradise. Modern man has conquered nature (in the name of utility), other people's territories and cultures (in the name of civilization), markets (in the name of economic liberalization and growth), and space (in the name of military superiority). All these have been justified rationally by the benefits they will bring to all humanity. However, the resulting exploitation, destruction, and obliteration of nontechnical values have been either rationalized or explained away.

The main objection to technological rationalism lies in the assumption that the technocrats know what is right and best for the rest of humanity.[7] Foucault, for example, has explored the history of so-called deviancy and come to the conclusion that a social or political consensus, in matters like mental illness or sexual behavior, is nothing more than the imposition by the powerful of their views upon the weak. He represents the postmodern tendency to repudiate clear and absolute distinctions, such as those between sanity and insanity, and to recognize and encourage difference, i.e., the right of all people to dissent from the current views of the majority.

## The Abandonment of All Truth Claims

The postmodern understanding of historical development ends up in a powerful repudiation of all claims to know the truth. There are several dimensions to this powerful mistrust of all assertions to possess the truth.

### The Desire to Dominate

The postmodern consciousness includes a deep methodological skepticism that sees claims to truth as covert claims to power. In the real world those who claim

---

7. One of the strongest critics of this form of rationalism, while remaining a critic of any postmodern alternative, is Jürgen Habermas; cf. his *The Philosophical Discourse of Modernity* (Cambridge: MIT Press, 1987).

to know the truth, whether in scientific, moral, or religious terms, have always wished to use their contentions as a means of controlling others. Far from "the truth" making people free, it has everywhere had the opposite effect.

## The Commitment to Pluralism and Relativism

Knowledge and understanding are always relative to a particular tradition. There is no way of being able to transcend the many traditions of interpretation that all claim a privileged perception of the meaning of life and what is right and good. Seeking to reach a definitive conclusion about correct beliefs and actions always leads to conflict and inhuman policies. Ultimately a free society is one which allows the maximum liberty to individual consciousness to decide on moral convictions and lifestyles. Tolerance and openness to changing patterns of behavior must be the supreme values of contemporary society. The language of "good," "better," "best" is discriminatory, repressive, and undemocratic.

## The New View of Language

Part of the rejection of foundationalism involves a crisis of representation in describing reality. It is said that no longer can we be sure that our language accurately depicts an external world. The claim that our mental images of reality exactly correspond with that reality is an unsafe assumption. The view that the world is a given is a myth. Human beings create their own world out of their imagination. Over against the so-called objectivity of reason (the alleged masculine principle), society must now recapture the subjectivity of desire (the alleged feminine essence). The rigid distinction between subject and object cannot be trusted.

We now can do no more than construct our own reality using language according to the particular rules and regulations of our own game. Meaning is a creature of hermeneutics: when interpreting texts (and nature and history, along with literature, are textual forms), the reader may decide the meaning; there cannot be any restriction on its significance. Reality is transformed into images. There are no right or wrong ways of believing.

*Andrew J. Kirk*

## The Death of "God"

The proclamation by the madman, in Nietzsche's *Gay Science*, that "modern civilisation" ("you and I") "have killed" God, "all of us are his murderers," is strikingly *post*modern. It is not so much a claim that theism is intellectually indefensible, because it is either an unnecessary or impossible thesis (according to the rationalist canons of modernity), as an acknowledgment that any divine being impedes the full liberty of human aspirations. The death of God is the death of morality followed by the attempt to exalt aesthetics as the most supreme good for humanity. Henceforth human beings are invited to throw off the shackles of conventions and reach out for a universe of their own creation.

Nietzsche's concept of deicide is complex and subtle. It is intimately linked to his declaration of the coming of the *Ubermensch*, the "will to power" and the "eternal recurrence." There are many interpretations. One of the most significant, perhaps, is that the death of "god" actually spells the death of man. The *Ubermensch* is the "last man" in the modern sense of one who believes he is able to discover the path of bliss through uncovering and exploiting the reality of the world. Nietzsche represents an immense break with the modern project. However, his "brave new world" is full of tragedy. As has been rightly said, Nietzsche, unlike many atheists, saw the full horror and immense sadness of this act of assassination, for it implied the "superhuman" task of re-creating all values, something Nietzsche was afraid humanity would prove incapable of doing. And even if they set about the task, the absolute relativism of perspectives would make the task never-ending.

Nietzsche and those who wittingly or unwittingly have followed him have declared all historical projects built on the belief in truth surpassed. There is no comfort to be had by a belief in a supposed progressive unfolding of a rational spirit in the achievements of human endeavor. Nietzsche's account of the death of "god" is nihilistic in that it announces the end of contemporary "renaissance" man, without any clear project as to what will follow. If the eternal recurrence is Nietzsche's final answer to the myth of progress, it is deeply pessimistic.

## Religious Pluralism as an Epiphenomenon of Postmodern Perspectivism

A pluralistic explanation of religious life has to be understood in relation to alternative explanations. Even if it is increasingly accepted today that the threefold classification of theoretical options into exclusivism, inclusivism, and pluralism is unsatisfactory, what is represented by the first two is philosophically and theologically antithetical to the presuppositions of the third position. Those who hold to an exclusive or inclusive view of salvation within the framework of Christian belief maintain that Jesus Christ is not just a unique way of salvation (corresponding to other unique ways in other religious traditions), but the one and only way. Moreover, they argue that he is the only way not just in the sense that he is the only way to the class of salvation that Christian faith proclaims, namely, from sin as rebellion against and alienation from God, but that there is no other form of salvation, having eternal consequences, which is achievable in any other religious tradition. The logic of this position is that salvation is the gift of the one and only true God and that, therefore, all other claims to salvation (or a near equivalent, such as liberation or enlightenment) are false and illusions.

Now this proposal breaks all the canons of postmodern perspectivism. In the first place, it claims an absolute position from which to give an account of the whole of reality. In the true theological sense, it holds to the possibility of knowing God's point of view on the grounds that God has made it known. It therefore rejects the hypothesis that all language about God is constructed from a merely human point of view.

Secondly, it affirms a transcendental realism,[8] namely, that "the intransitive objects of knowledge are in general invariant to our knowledge of them: they are the real things and structures, mechanisms and processes, events and possibilities of the world; and for the most part they are quite independent of us."[9] In other words, it is of vital importance to the question of knowledge and truth that a fundamental distinction is maintained between a subject and an object. The object of belief within a faith context is not merely a projection or interpretation of an inner experience or disposition to believe or the externalization of an attitude, wish, or imperative; rather it (he/she) has an independent and self-sufficient existence irrespective of whether believed in or not.

Thirdly, it maintains an absolute antithesis between two or more accounts of ultimate truth, wherever any one of them manifestly contradicts any other. Thus it upholds the "law of the excluded middle,"[10] thereby rendering incoherent all attempts to maintain that opposite truth claims (such as ultimate

8. For the meaning and use of the term, cf. Roy Bhaskar, "Philosophy and Scientific Realism," in *Critical Realism: Essential Readings*, ed. Margaret Archer et al. (London: Routledge, 1998), pp. 16-47.

9. Bhaskar, p. 17.

10. "The law of the excluded middle . . . says that every instance of 'A or not-A' is true, where 'not-A' is the negation of 'A'" (A. C. Grayling, *Philosophy: A Guide through the Subject* [Oxford: Oxford University Press, 1995], p. 81).

reality is both personal and impersonal, or that one can experience ultimate salvation only through Christ, but also through Krishna) can both be valid.

A pluralist theory of religious experience could only be credible and convincing if one accepts the premise that the notion of "justified true belief" is a euphemism for belief which I am able to convince others is as equally well grounded from my perspective as other beliefs are from the perspective of those who hold them. To put it another way, the only procedure by which any theory of religious experience can be justified, without entering into a circular argument, is by arguing from within a particular tradition of discourse. Precisely because there is no tradition-transcending point of reference from which a normative account of the ultimate truth of assertions may be judged right or wrong, there is no possibility of preferring one interpretation to another without being self-referring. In epistemological terms, all forms of foundationalism are untenable, knowledge can only be based on a coherentist or pragmatist view of truth. Such a view, however, although it appears to be congenial to a pluralist theory of religions, in fact paradoxically contradicts the pluralists' conviction that their account of religious traditions is exempt from relative cultural conditioning, in that they *know* the ultimate secret which explains different religious manifestations.

Religious pluralism, in either of the two definitions I offered at the beginning, is closely related to the "postmodern" theory that religious language (irrespective of the faith tradition in which it occurs) is a nonreferring human construction, elaborated to give meaning to human experience. It rejects the possibility that any one faith could have an all-encompassing explanation which accounts for other faiths. It also effectively proclaims the "death of God" in the sense of refusing the notion of an ontologically singular deity directly accessible to human cognition.[11] The word "God" is transmuted into a cipher which carries whatever content a religious community wishes to invest it with. The "death of God" is also the consequence of a radical cultural pluralism that holds that God is simply the geographically limited "tribal" God of Western theism, who has historically "passed away" in that he/she is no longer acceptable in a pluri-centered cultural world.

---

11. I have argued elsewhere that Hick's notion of an Ultimate Reality that transcends all categories, and every idea of a supreme being beyond all beings, being essentially unknowable in itself (the *via negativa* strategy leaves no alternatives), is simply a covert, if sophisticated, form of atheism. Cf. "John Hick's Kantian Theory of Religious Pluralism and the Challenge of Secular Thinking," in *Studies in Interreligious Dialogue* I (2002). Wittgenstein, perceptively and wittily, summed up the position in his aphorism (referring to the experience of pain), "a nothing would serve just as well as a something about which nothing could be said" (*Philosophical Investigations,* trans. G. E. M. Anscombe, 3rd ed. [Oxford: Basil Blackwell, 1972], #304).

Theories of religious pluralism are inextricably linked to the lines of argument that have come powerfully to the fore in postmodern consciousness, even though, as Hick rightly maintains, some of them precede modernity.[12] By the same token, they are as strong or weak as those arguments. Hence, if it can be shown that the postmodern outlook is essentially flawed, then, I would suggest, it can be established that religious pluralism, as the best explanation of multireligious phenomena, is also untenable. This, I hope, will become convincing once one sees the strength of the case against postmodern thought, applying each piece of reasoning to claims made by the advocates of religious pluralism.

## The Inherent Deficiencies of the Postmodern and Religiously Pluralist Outlooks

The fundamental reason for speaking about the impossibility of a postmodern culture is its self-contradictory nature. For its own critical stance it is dependent on assumptions that are, in turn, undermined by its own critique. For example, although it wishes to dismiss claims to truth and absolutes as imperialist and oppressive, the critique has to assume that which it wishes to deny. First, the critique depends on an unarticulated normative framework of its own when it condemns unjust and oppressive systems. Moreover, when it denounces universal systems in the interests of the emancipation of the local and the different, it implicitly assumes the universal right of all to be treated uniquely. Secondly, the tolerance that delights in distinctiveness cannot be tolerated for those who would suppress otherness. Like any perspective on human life, postmodernity is bound to limit tolerance in order to remain true to itself.[13] Therefore, in practice it poses no radical break with an ethic of absoluteness, whatever it may claim to the contrary. Thirdly, postmodernity, to be consistent to its own critique, requires both an (absolute) ethic of "responsibility to act" and an (absolute) ethic of "responsibility to otherness." A determined commitment to the deconstruction of values threatens to undermine, or at least enervate, this sense of responsibility.

12. Cf. Hick (personal communication to the author). However, it is surely more than a coincidence that contemporary (Western) arguments for pluralism as the most satisfying account of religious diversity coincide chronologically with the articulation of postmodern thinking, i.e., from the late 1950s onward. Pluralism is only plausible in an intellectual climate in which the still essentially Christian view of the world expressed in modernity's acceptance of an objective reality and a universal rationality is repudiated.

13. This is reflected in the abhorrence "pluralists" feel for all forms of "exclusivism" and their frequent dismissal of such views as "fundamentalist" and "naive-realist."

Postmodern thought has dismissed the possibility of encountering truly objective reality. Involved in this argument is the implicit assumption that the claim to objectivity is false. However, to use the language of error is in itself a claim to a superior grasp of reality! Likewise, postmodern consciousness attacks the kind of rationality that has come to the fore as a consequence of the scientific spirit — logical, consistent, self-critical of its own premises, susceptible to evidence and demonstration. However, the only way to pursue a negative analysis of rationality is by using the same techniques of reason as those being dismissed. If the dismissal of metanarratives is intended to cover all claims to possess true perspectives, it is itself a claim to enjoy the status of global validity.[14]

Insofar as the contemporary self is but the passive product of language, history, culture, and society, it cannot maintain a properly dissentient stance against history, culture, and society, for such a stance is, according to the theory, already a mere product of the transient, ephemeral, and mutable forces that happen to exist. It is not surprising then that, for example, few feminists are also consistent postmodernists. Feminism is a commitment to both an ideological critique which presupposes a meaningful distinction between a true and false consciousness and to an emancipating project. From the perspective of women seeking to reverse gender discrimination on the basis that the two halves of the human race are equal in dignity and respect, and this must be reflected in all social institutions and relationships, postmodern rhetoric is seen as deeply conservative politically. Postmodernity, in accordance with its own critique, is incapable of distinguishing valid from invalid claims about the right and the good or of properly using the language of prejudice, inequity, bigotry, or unfair discrimination. The most it can do is promote a conservative agenda of consensus-based attitudes, which equates "good in the way of belief" with pragmatic liberalism.[15]

In this regard Hick's pluralist thesis, which appears to arise from a

14. Likewise, inevitably, theories of religious pluralism have to become, in their endeavor to refute alternative theories, substitute metareligions, which claim to transcend all perspectives by giving a "true" account of all religious phenomena. In the case of Hick it is not clear to what extent he is propounding a mere hypothesis and to what extent a demonstrable conclusion derived from reasoning about evidence. However, a mere hypothesis, unless substantiated by valid criteria, does not advance understanding; it remains no more than a piece of interesting speculation. It is clear that Hick is propounding a theory he believes is "true." In contrast to nonrealists like Don Cupitt, he stubbornly maintains he is a critical realist with regard to the transcendent; cf. John Hick, "Religious Realism and Non-Realism: Defining the Issue," in *Is God Real?* ed. Joseph Runzo (Basingstoke: Macmillan, 1993), pp. 3-15.

15. Cf. J. Andrew Kirk and Kevin Vanhoozer, *To Stake a Claim: Mission and the Western Crisis of Knowledge* (Maryknoll, N.Y.: Orbis, 1999), pp. 45, 49.

"foundationalist," empirical conviction that the ethical teaching and practice of all the major religions are equivalent, requires a nonpluralist, unconditional, noncontextual, unequivocal account of the right and the good. This, in turn, calls for a singular vantage point from which to judge. Hence it would appear that the foundation on which he builds his pluralist case actually contradicts it.

In contrast, the task of unmasking certain consensus values as a smoke screen for oppressive sectional interests is part of keeping faith with enlightened, critical-emancipatory thought. Hence postmodernity, under the illusion of presenting itself as the debunker of power strategies in the name of truth claims, can itself hide an oppressive epistemology. Thus, for example, the marginalizing of the original meaning of a text in the name of hermeneutic freedom shows an unacceptable violence against the author.

Postmodernity as a cultural theory has shown itself to be remarkably weak as an interpretation of history. As an account of the way knowledge is acquired, it has no convincing explanation of scientific methodology nor of progress in science. The tendency to find reasons for scientific "success" in social, political, or cultural factors rather than in the experimental method which subjects data to confirmation or falsification is inadequate. It suggests that the cumulative growth of science is a lottery which, quite by chance, has from time to time been able to give sufficiently satisfactory explanations to allow for technological progress. If ever there was a case of a dogmatic theory seeking to impose itself on the careful accumulation of evidence, it occurs in the postmodern perspective.

Postmodernity is equally undiscerning when it comes to the all-pervading power of late capitalism to shape the contemporary world. David Harvey has written that because postmodernism "emphasises the fragmentary, the ephemeral, and the chaotic . . . while expressing a deep scepticism as to any particular prescriptions as to how the eternal and immutable should be conceived of, . . . it signals nothing more than a logical extension of the power of the market over the whole range of cultural production."[16] Postmodernity easily accommodates the capitalist world system, for in the last analysis its view of truth, absolutes, identity, the good, and the right is oriented to consumer choice in the realm of ideas, lifestyles, habits, perspectives, and opinions. The celebration of difference may be said to coincide exactly with the global manufacture of multiple false consciousnesses. If this interpretation is correct, it has significant consequences for some representations of multiculturalism. As Roger

16. David Harvey, *The Condition of Postmodernity: An Enquiry into the Origins of Cultural Change* (Oxford: Blackwell, 1989), p. 116. For a similar critique of postmodernism, cf. Jim McGuigan, *Modernity and Postmodern Culture* (Buckingham: Open University Press, 1999).

Trigg has cogently argued,[17] all we are left with is rhetoric as a mere exercise in the power of persuasion. However, he goes on to say that there is little point in being skilled in the art of persuasion if there is no ultimate right or wrong, truth or falsity left. Could not the same be said for all pluralist theories of religion? Why should we believe them or persuade others to share our views?[18] They are manifestly self-refuting. If they are assumed, as is often the case, as the basis for multireligious dialogue, they render the latter conceptually impossible. Is it not high time to abandon pluralist theories of religion as mere epiphenomena of a culturally transient, morally dangerous, and ultimately intellectually absurd "condition," already being left behind by real events in time and space?

17. Roger Trigg, *Rationality and Science: Can Science Explain Everything?* (Oxford: Blackwell, 1993), pp. 164-65.

18. "Too much toleration and even the welcoming of difference can lead to the view that it does not matter which religion one holds, and that can soon be taken to mean that it does not matter whether any religious belief is held at all. Toleration can lead to indifference and that can lead to contempt. If there are so many religious options on offer, and it does not matter which is adopted, then why, it may be asked, should one believe any of them at all? Truth has slipped totally out of our grasp" (Roger Trigg, *Rationality and Religion: Does Faith Need Reason?* [Oxford: Blackwell, 1998], p. 54).

# Religious Pluralism from a Japanese Perspective

HIROMASA MASE

Let me begin by presenting three statements that the term "religious pluralism" may possibly suggest to interested observers, along with three questions those statements are likely to raise:

1. Religious pluralism considers all religions in a relative way. Does this mean that the individual character of the different religious traditions therefore is lost?
2. Religious pluralism implies that all religions have the same original source. Does not this amount to declaring a new world religion stemming from that source?
3. Religious pluralism is like the words of an old Japanese poem: "The paths up the mountain are many, but the same moon can be seen from the heights." Does this mean that it does not matter what you believe as long as you believe in something?

## The End of Imperial Christianity

In 1995, when Japanese society was reeling from the double blow of the Great Hanshin Earthquake with many deaths and extensive damage and the fatal sarin nerve gas attack on the Tokyo subways that turned out to be a crime by the Aum Shinrikyo cult, I was at Selly Oak Colleges in a quiet suburb of Birmingham, England's second-largest city. My friends at the college expressed sympathy and concern to me over the sad and frightening news from Japan.

It was not my first stay in Birmingham. Twenty years earlier I had been living at Woodbrooke College, one of the Selly Oak Colleges residences, and had gone frequently to the University of Birmingham. The British religious philosopher John Hick was still a professor in the Department of Theology there, but he had yet to formulate his ideas about religious pluralism.

What I especially remember from that first time is that the church bells would peal loudly every Sunday morning. On this occasion, however, the church bells were still. Perhaps this was a gesture to local non-Christians, or perhaps the townspeople who no longer regularly attended church services were responsible, but for whatever reason, not a single church bell tolled on Sundays. In some instances what had been Christian churches were now mosques or Hindu temples. During the two decades I had been away, the phenomenon of religious pluralism had begun to make its presence felt in Christianity-centered English society. The age of Britain's Christian imperialism, with its emphasis on its own absolute correctness, had ended. Now Christianity was seeking ways to coexist with other religions.

When my six-month stay in Birmingham was over, I traveled to the University of Lund in the southern Swedish city of that name, an educational center, having received an invitation to lecture there. At a combined seminar at the Department of Theology and Religious Studies, I spoke about my experiences in England and my conviction that a final end had come to Christianity's imperialist age. The Swedish theological students, who knew only Lutheran Christianity, did not seem to find it easy to accept my point. They repeated the biblical admonition that there can be no salvation other than through Christ and held high the figurative banner of the absoluteness of Christianity. I therefore asked them, in as nonthreatening a way as possible, "Who then are your neighbors? Are not those of other faiths also your neighbors?" My purpose was to emphasize the vital necessity for Christianity at this time to be able to live in harmony with other faiths by engaging in dialogue with them.

I was quite surprised to find such deep-seated religious exclusivity there, a faith that was trying to preserve its particular identity at the same time that it asserted its absoluteness. Critical questions directed at Christianity, particularly such radical developments as feminism and liberation theology in the United States, seemed to have passed Lund by.

I also spent time in Leuven, Belgium's second-largest city. In that university town, which had clung tightly to its Roman Catholic tradition, the bells rang out from the high church steeples morning and evening, in a display of authority. It seems, however, that this had not been enough to put the brakes on the exodus of young intellectuals from the church, and their presence at mass was sparse. The professors, most of whom were priests, liked to speak of "the god of philosophers" as a way of trying to bring back "God," a dead word in the hearts of young people, and were sparing no effort whatever in their attempts to link this idea to the God of believers.

The attitude of the Catholic Church toward other religions has become more tolerant since the Second Vatican Council in the early 1960s, and dramatic changes have come about. Catholics now frankly acknowledge that a truth exists, something that is worthy of respect, even in non-Christian religions, taking the inclusive position that non-Christians also share in the grace of Jesus Christ, even if they are not aware of it. Such a stance, however, seems to me merely an extension of the old exclusivity: "There is no salvation other than in his name; there is no salvation other than in Christ." This is nothing more than a more moderate statement of the old conviction, a softer approach to exclusivity.

## A Copernican Revolution

After spending three months in Leuven, I returned to Selly Oak Colleges in order to deepen my acquaintance with John Hick. It was he who took me around to former churches that had been converted into mosques or temples. No person in the world has done more to disseminate the idea of religious pluralism among intellectual circles. He has been to Japan twice, lecturing at leading universities in Tokyo and Kyoto; several of his books have been translated into Japanese; and many Japanese scholars are engaged in studying his ideas.

Interreligious dialogue started in England in the 1960s when the supposed monolithic absoluteness of Christianity began to be questioned. The populations of large cities like Birmingham had become increasingly multiracial, with people of many races and ethnic backgrounds living side by side. The society had also become a multireligious one, in which Christianity coexisted with Islam, Sikhism, Hinduism, Judaism, and Buddhism. The matters of dialogue and coexistence became increasingly important for Christianity.

It was under such conditions that Hick, a Christian theologian, began to inquire how Christianity should attempt to understand itself, eventually bringing about a Copernican revolution in theological circles. This was to move away from a Christ-centered philosophy to an understanding of the existence of God within a diversity of religions. In *God Has Many Names: Britain's New Religious Pluralism* (1980), Hick wrote: "To realize that God is being worshipped, through different but overlapping mental images of him, not only in churches and chapels but also in synagogues and mosques, temples and gurdwaras, is to realize in a new way that he is the God of all mankind and not only of our own familiar tribe."

## From Self-Centeredness to Reality-Centeredness

Hick clearly recognizes the fact of religious pluralism from a Christian stand-point and seeks to promote a revolution in Christian conceptual methods. His theory of religious pluralism has become a paradigm for understanding religion in the modern age. He sketches the main points of his theory in another book, *Problems of Religious Pluralism* (1985):

> [Religious] pluralism is the view that the great world faiths embody different perceptions and conceptions of, and correspondingly different responses to, the Real or the Ultimate from within the major variant cultural ways of being human; and that within each of them the transformation of human existence from self-centeredness to reality-centeredness is manifestly taking place. . . . Thus the great religious traditions are to be regarded as alternative soteriological "spaces" within which, or "ways" along which, men and women can find salvation/liberation/enlightenment/fulfillment.

This seems to me a superlative model for understanding religions today. I have used it to analyze existence in which religion plays a key role and have been extremely satisfied with the results. These I would like to summarize here.

I am a Christian. When I traveled in Japan's Kansai region in the past, I sometimes took the opportunity to go to Okayama Prefecture, where I visited the headquarters of the Konkokyo faith. My late mother, who had never faltered in her belief, is well remembered there. I also went to Nara Prefecture and visited the Ojiba sacred ground of Tenrikyo, one of Japan's largest contemporary religious groups, and engaged in dialogue about faith with some fervent Tenrikyo friends. In such places, hallowed by other religions, I made a surprising discovery: people can gather and join one another to open up to a higher existence, and I was one such person.

Why do people seek an existence higher than themselves? It is because human existence is fundamentally defective and deficient, a depraved life in a depraved world, which clings to the illusion of being ego-centered and is tormented by suffering. By revolution in human existence, however, by moving from self-centeredness to Reality-centeredness, human beings can participate in the realm of God and can attain nirvana. The original nature of this world is to be filled to overflowing with love and compassion, to be abundantly blessed.

Zen Buddhism emphasizes liberating ourselves from the self-centeredness with which we are born. We become able to recognize our true self through our nonself. Christianity too teaches that we should allow our old self to die and be born anew. An old Japanese hymn goes:

> When we look to the Lord
> Our old self departs
> Along with the changing world.
> The self of non-self appears.
> See! Heaven and earth are renewed.

In other words, when human beings change from self-centeredness to divine reality–centeredness, therein lies the truth of salvation. I think this is an extremely modern perspective on religion, that knowing our true self is closely connected with salvation. Through my analysis of life imbued with faith, I have come to a modern understanding of religion.

## A Variety of Hypotheses

Religious pluralism is an excellent theoretical model for understanding religion in the modern age. Within this model are a number of hypotheses. One is the idea of the phenomenal "many" and the original "one." Ultimately divine reality is "one," but that fundamental truth is obscured by the "many" of the phenomena to which it gives rise. Another hypothesis is that the religious perception of the "many" and the "various" is connected with the actuality of the original form, the "one." The phenomenal world of religion is none other than the realm of the "one" that we can contemplate and experience. Thus both the ultimate world of the "one" and the phenomenal world seen by us can be distinguished according to Kant but not separated (according to Hick).

Based on these hypotheses, the "one" (ultimate reality) can be contemplated and experienced phenomenologically through two different religious concepts. One is the concept of a dominant God, as in theistic religious traditions (Judaism, Christianity, Islam), a concept that personifies the "one," and the other is the concept of an "ultimate" in the nontheistic religions (Hinduism, Buddhism), a concept that does not personify the "one." Why should ultimate reality have been contemplated and experienced on the one hand as personified and on the other as nonpersonified? This is a question I leave to you for further study.

## A Firm Denial

To the statement that religious pluralism is relativistic that was posed at the beginning of my presentation, I would like to express a firm denial. Whereas rela-

447

tivism is a viewpoint that does not allow for an absolute "one" or ultimate reality, religious pluralism hypothesizes a substantial "one" in relation to the phenomenological "many," and takes the position of clearly seeking a divine ultimate reality that has many names. In addition, individual religious traditions are allowed to maintain and preserve their individuality within the phenomenological "many."

And so to the second statement. Because religious pluralism recognizes the diversity of religions in all their aspects, it neither says all religions originate from one source nor is it yet another religion. Religious diversity is both the phenomenological "many" and, in the end, something like the ecumenical movement that has largely changed the face of Christianity. It obviously is to be desired that the various religious traditions not be regarded as mutually antagonistic religious communities.

Finally, the poem about "the paths up the mountain" may have been composed as a metaphor for what interreligious understanding should be. This does not mean, however, that all religions are equally fine or that it does not matter what people believe. Along with the word "multifaith," we now frequently hear such related words as "multiethnic," "multicultural," and "multilingual." Each refers to an autonomous and individually responsible way of existing within a larger pluralism.

Even if we say that any language will serve for communication or that it does not matter of which culture we are a member, in fact I am Japanese, I live in Japanese-speaking society, and I was reared in the Japanese culture in which I continue to live. In a similar fashion we cannot simply say that any religion will do or that it does not matter what we believe. Our religion should be related to the way we live. A Buddhist might be a follower of the Jodo-shin sect rather than of Zen; if the former, a follower of Shinran rather than Honen. A Christian might be a Protestant rather than a Catholic, and if the former, a Lutheran rather than a Quaker. Our relationship to religion is a conscious and specific thing. It develops from its specific characteristics before branching off into conceptual abstractions. The theory of religious pluralism has also developed as an abstraction out of specific religious phenomena. It is by no means a reckless adventure derived from concepts alone.

# On Difference and Conflict
# in Theologies of Religion

PATRIK FRIDLUND

Even though I would like to extend the dialogue and entertain a conversation about "the religious" with as many as possible — believers and nonbelievers alike — I do find it useful to respect the historical and concrete situation in which I find myself. The work I propound is not something to be done in a purely abstract or ahistorical way. My starting point is thus the Christian theology of religions,[1] a rather specific context.

Although this is my context, my tools are primarily philosophical and my working field is the philosophy of religion. This means I am not interested in the relation between dogmatics and the different possible philosophical positions, or in the dogmatic implications. Arguments taken or found in a specific religious tradition (i.e., here the Christian tradition) pro or contra certain things, do not play any role in the suggested enterprise.

## A New Typological Approach

Often Christian attitudes toward other religious traditions are classified according to the notions exclusivism, inclusivism, and pluralism. The model is based on questions such as: How does Christian theology look upon other religions? How can Christian theology understand other religions, especially re-

---

1. "Theology of religions" is defined either as (a) a theological reflection from within a particular tradition, a reflection based on the insight that there is more than one religion in the world, and the putative relationships of religions in a multireligious context, or (b) an attempt to combine elements from more than one tradition in order to arrive at a theology of religions which is acceptable to more than one's own religious tradition (K. Ahlstrand, *Fundamental Openness: An Enquiry into Raimundo Panikkar's Theological Vision and Its Presuppositions* [Uppsala, 1993], p. 182). I am here working with the first definition.

garding the salvation potential within them or the role they may have in the salvation plan, as perceived by the Christian tradition?

I see a need to develop a new model that would enable an examination of various existing theologies of religion, i.e., another typology than the well-established exclusivism-inclusivism-pluralism one.

I suggest that how "difference" and "conflict" between various religious systems are described is a decisive part of all theologies of religion. It would be helpful, I think, to develop a model that uses "difference" and "conflict" as key terms in order to understand the different forms of theology of religions. Such an approach would make it possible to give a new perspective on how they are based, and that would give us tools to understand better the problems and the difficulties in the actual multireligious setting, and that would, at least in the long run, facilitate dialogue.

The question of difference and conflict between religious systems has been implicitly debated over the years. According to Wilfred Cantwell Smith, we can — at least to a certain extent — decide to consider differences and conflict situations either as something destructive or as an invitation to learn something new. Joseph S. O'Leary writes long and well about the differences between religions as different approaches toward life and the existential questions. Raimundo Panikkar formulates a philosophy about the conditions for dialogue, talking about difference and disunity. Paul F. Knitter discusses the foundation for dialogue and what could be a common ground.² It would, however, be interesting to pursue this and bring this discussion to a typology level.

If "difference" and "conflict" are an issue, it appears that most theologies of religion want to avoid, overcome, or neglect difference and conflict between the religious systems,³ or take them as an unfortunate but necessary war situation. Thus two main classes may be identified:

- A thinking that sees difference and conflict as something destructive (e.g., Hick),⁴ or that does not see conflicts or differences at all (e.g.,

2. See W. C. Smith, "Conflicting Truth-Claims: A Rejoinder," in *Truth and Dialogue: The Relationship between the World Religions,* ed. J. Hick (London, 1974), pp. 156-62; J. S. O'Leary, *La vérité chrétienne à l'âge du pluralisme religieux* (Paris, 1994); R. Panikkar, "Philosophical Pluralism and the Plurality of Religions," in *Religious Pluralism and Truth: Essays on Cross-Cultural Philosophy of Religion,* ed. T. Dean (New York, 1995), pp. 33-43; P. F. Knitter, "Common Ground or Common Response? Seeking Foundations for Interreligious Discourse," in *Studies in Interreligious Dialogue* 2/1992/1 (1992), pp. 111-22.

3. In this text I use the notions "religion" and "religious system" without distinction, well aware of the fact that the relation between these notions and also the notions "religious tradition" and "spiritual tradition" is somewhat unclear.

4. J. Hick, *The Rainbow of Faiths: Critical Dialogues on Religious Pluralism* (London,

Toynbee).[5] As in this first group "difference" and "conflict" are presumably seen as destructive, their very existence seems to imply a threat, these two phenomena being considered destructive per se.

- A thinking that recognizes difference and (open) conflict by saying that the struggle is needed, that a "war"[6] between the religious systems is unavoidable (e.g., Wright),[7] or that the dynamics they can bring should be appreciated (e.g., Panikkar).[8]

It may be important to say a few words on "conflict," as the word has strong political (and so ethical) implications. The commitment to peace and justice in the world, a commitment which is urgent and should involve all of us, has of course to do also with peaceful relations between people of different faiths, among people belonging to various religious traditions, and ultimately between the religious systems. Hans Küng has seen this, and his attempt to formulate a *Projekt Weltethos* is more than needed.[9] There are weak points in his project, both regarding the theoretical foundations and the practical implications, but the intention is good, and he is bringing forth a number of central issues and proposing a possible path and concrete steps toward a better world.

When I talk about "conflict" in this paper, I do however have another perspective in mind. It is important to stress that my aims differ from Küng's insofar as I try to deal with the question of difference and conflict on a rather fundamental level. I am talking about a level where various religious traditions meet and may be found to be in conflict even without having followers beating each other up, without them necessarily throwing stones at each other, without them necessarily making war on each other.

This being said, a number of questions could be asked.

Does an encounter, or a simultaneous presence, of several religious systems always imply conflict and an intellectual "war"? Why in that case, and how?

---

1995); cf. P. Fridlund, "Un, seul et unique — 'The Real' chez John Hick, une étude critique de l'un-ité de la notion" (master's thesis, Lausanne, 2000).

5. P. F. Knitter, *No Other Name? A Critical Survey of Christian Attitudes toward the World Religions* (Maryknoll, N.Y., 1984), pp. 37-54.

6. "War" is written with quotation marks in order to indicate that I chiefly refer to a verbal "war" between religious systems, not necessarily a physical one between religious people.

7. C. Wright, *The Uniqueness of Jesus* (1997).

8. R. Panikkar, "The Jordan, the Tiber and the Ganges: Three Kairological Moments of Christic Self-Consciousness," in *The Myth of Christian Uniqueness: Toward a Pluralistic Theology of Religions*, ed. J. Hick and P. F. Knitter (Maryknoll, N.Y., 1987), pp. 89-116.

9. Hans Küng, *Projekt Weltethos* (Munich, 1999) (1990, 1992).

What is a conflict between two or more religious systems? How are difference and conflict between religious systems understood?

Is a conflict always, and necessarily, disastrous — for one or the other? Is there always a winner/loser, or is it possible to perceive difference and conflict as some sort of "sound competition" that may also involve a positive dynamics? Which are the reasons for seeing difference and conflict in one way or another in the various theologies of religion? Which is the ideological, philosophical, and theological framework for different positions? Why and how do they emerge? Which are the implications of these perceptions both in the past, in the present, and for the future?

Do religions always talk about the truth — the objective truth — in an exclusive way? (What is true is true is true, and nothing else could be true.)

If the notions "difference" and "conflict" were understood as something where there is always a winner/loser, thus defined in a negative and destructive way, a certain attitude would logically follow. If difference and conflict were defined as something purely destructive, it would be better to avoid them. If other perspectives take place, other attitudes become possible. It is about the relation between the phenomenon and its definition, or if one prefers so, about the power of the language. The issue is how and why thinkers present their ideas in the way they do; the philosophical, ideological, or theological context out of which the respective thinking emerges, which is the basis of a given attitude toward difference and conflict.

## A "Rigorous Pluralism"

Also among the "pluralist theologies," difference and conflict are much avoided or neglected. One form of religious pluralism I have called a "rigorous pluralism"[10] differs, however, from other forms of pluralism (e.g., the pluralism of John Hick)[11] insofar as it tries to recognize a fundamental diversity, giving a value to difference, and to conflict, in a radical way.[12] A plurality of religions cannot, according to this pluralism, form a unity in which all of them can be understood within the same framework, and no metaphysical totality can comprise them all on the level of contents. Difference and conflict as such are thus not a threat but a possibility, as different truths — or rather questions and approaches — exist without forming any ultimate unity. Rigorous pluralism does

10. Fridlund, "Un, seul et unique."
11. See, for example, Hick, passim.
12. Cf. O'Leary, pp. 38-39.

not try to form a system, to organize any totality regarding contents, but it rather wants to give a formal framework.[13]

It would be worthwhile to explore this rigorous pluralism. Difference and conflict are here not seen in themselves as threats but as possibilities, thanks to the different questions and attitudes generated in the religions that exist one beside the other, without being absorbed by a unity, nor by an ultimate totality.

Rigorous pluralism could be put forward from an ethical point of view (a belligerent attitude that wants one position to win over the other creates in itself "war"); from the point of view of logical coherence in dialogue (talking about dialogue implies different parts who are diverse and different); from an egoistic point of view (without diversity and difference, one learns nothing new in the meeting with the other); from a theological point of view (the meaning of religion, and its talk about the transcendent, may be understood as presupposing something that transcends the speaker herself/himself, and something that would thus be radically other/different).

From time to time one is confronted with the confused terminology regarding "plurality" and "pluralism," as well as with the term "pluralism" used in various contexts. Even though it is important to deal seriously with both questions, I intend only a brief word on my preliminary position.

"Religious plurality" is the fact that there are many — a multitude of — religions in the world, not only in a historical perspective but also in the present time. "Religious pluralism" is a name given to a certain approach toward this fact, thus an ideological or theological orientation.

In my opinion even the term "pluralism" has a specific character in the religious field. When for instance Michael Walzer writes about pluralism,[14] he moves within a political and sociological context, and Nicholas Rescher[15] deals with problems in the scientific domain. In both cases it is a question about plurality — and toleration — within a given system, while a religious plurality is about an encounter between different systems. My conclusion is that although the work of Walzer, Rescher, and others may be inspiring and most certainly useful in some respects, it is not very fruitful for an understanding of the religious plurality in the sense I deal with it. The interreligious dialogue and the encounter (in daily life or elsewhere) between religious systems must be aware of the fact that the questions raised are different and raised differently by the religions, raised out of similar situations but not interchangeable ones.

---

13. Cf. O'Leary, p. 33.
14. M. Walzer, *On Toleration* (New Haven, 1997).
15. N. Rescher, *Pluralism: Against the Demand for Consensus* (Oxford, 1993).

Exploring this rigorous pluralism, a pluralism without any overall system, without any given totality, raises some questions.

Is it possible to think or conceive of a model of this type (rigorous pluralism)? Is it not impossible to say what it tries to say? Wouldn't there just be another system creeping in and taking the place — even if it would be a different one — with another unity when it comes to contents?

What is the common ground for dialogue? What would be the meeting place? Would there be anything in common that makes the dialogue possible?

Is there anything at all that is true or false? Do we have to accept everything, without discrimination?

How to deal with attitudes that are in themselves destructive to dialogue, to all forms of dialogue?

## Working Tools

The multireligious situation is an issue for, among others, systematic theology, comparative religion, and ethics. When the position is a philosophical one, it means working with concepts and ideas, models and systems, their history and context and implications.

If we are to see, discern, understand, and create a structure, and propose possible ways forward as well as to discuss inconsistencies, difficulties, and weaknesses, the tools have to be many and diverse.

In this work one needs to analyze different thinkers on the level of concepts, on a systematic level, and the historical background (how certain patterns have evolved, i.e., where they come from, which is the context). Here traditional philosophical tools are appropriate when dealing with rationality and solidity of arguments, but also methods and insights in linguistics and literary studies for the parts dealing with how the reasoning is constructed.

We need to compare the one with the other, in order to find points they have in common and share, as well as differences, in order to discern what the debate actually is about. The comparison will also have to do with discussing the viability of various positions — and ultimately a discussion concerning the truth. In proposing solutions to different problems, one has to be creative.

During the latest decades — at least — we have learned that a double reading is an important instrument. It is not enough to analyze and deconstruct, but also to see what can be used further on, and how that could be done. A text does not have one given meaning but several layers, a multitude of possible readings and important silences. The art is to let the text interact with the reader and vice versa so that the reader's experiences may enrich the text and the text enrich the reader's experiences.

There are already existing works concerning the function of the discourse that would be helpful in an enterprise like this. See Michel Foucault for an analysis of how the discourse is formed and of its foundations. Sigurd Bergmann would be read for his discussion about the place of the *theologia perennis,* and Emmanuel Lévinas for an attempt to place the ethical relation — the relation between the I and the Other — before language and its definitions.[16]

*Function* is also important in relation to the notions "God" and "religion," and to the possibility of truth, the ground for dialogue, and to conflict. What role does conflict play in our thinking, and in our structures and consequently in our actions? How is conflict presented in our thought systems, and what are the consequences? Similar questions could be asked about difference and otherness; which place do these notions and their significance take in the relation between religions and in the interreligious dialogue?

## Questions Involved

A further question is how religion itself is transformed in the meeting between religions. If we are talking about concrete religion, most scholars seem to agree that mystical experiences of "god," for example, are formed within the framework at hand. One would then think that religious experiences change if several religious traditions are present to the subject. The same would apply for the religious expressions (rites, symbols, liturgies).

Every religious system is linked to other religious systems either by taking over elements or by marking a distance toward the other. What is included or excluded in the religious sphere depends on the context in which the other is manifest. In a similar way, I believe the religious institutions are conceived in relation to what is seen of the neighbor — positively or negatively.

If we are talking about the abstract notion "religion" — about the "religious" — is it something that has to do with emotions, metaphysics, laws, social behavior, etc.?

16. M. Foucault, *L'ordre du discours* (Paris, 1971); S. Bergmann, *Gud i funktion. En orientering i den kontextuella teologin* (Stockholm, 1997); E. Lévinas, *Ethique et infinité. Dialogues avec Philippe Nemo* (Paris, 1982 and 1992).

To work along these lines will give rise to new questions and a demand for more clarifications regarding some notions, and the relations between them:

religion — religious system — religious tradition — spiritual tradition;
diversity — multitude — plurality — pluralism;
conflict ( — consensus) — dialogue — difference — otherness.

# Life and Spirit: A New Approach
# to a Theology of Religions

ULRICH DEHN

Paul F. Knitter in his well-known book *No Other Name?* states: "From the clouded origins of the human species, as the spark of consciousness broadened and gave rise to the burning concern for the meaning of life, there have always been many religions, each with its own 'ultimate' answers. Today our intercommunicating planet has made us aware, more painfully than ever before, of religious pluralism and of the many different ultimate answers."[1] In his preface he implies that confessional models of approach to other religions have not really been able to render an ability "to listen to what the followers of other ways have to say."[2] Knitter uses the categories of conservative evangelical model, mainline Protestant model, Catholic model, and theocentric model, which nowadays is usually better known as the pluralistic theology of religions. He stresses the dialogical character of the latter one.

Knitter's perception of the world in its religious diversity is shared by many, and the U.S. context may be even more colorful than the one in most European countries. Yet, after waves of migration in a postcolonial age, Britain, France, Germany, the Netherlands, etc., have become multiethnic, multicultural, and multireligious societies to such a degree that the interreligious challenge to theology can no longer be denied. Germany, which is probably somewhere in the middle of the European scale, is estimated to have slightly more than 10 percent foreigners, representing more or less every religious tradition which might exist on this earth, not to count Germans who have opted for another than Christian faith. Next to around 3.2 million Muslims there should be close to 160,000 Buddhists of both German and Asian origin, and probably the same number of Hindus of different traditions. The Muslim number includes

1. P. F. Knitter, *No Other Name?* (Maryknoll, N.Y., 1985), p. 1.
2. Knitter, p. xiii.

the one-half million Alevites, who may or may not consider themselves Muslims. Sikhs, Jains, East Asian Taoists, people holding to ethnic religious rites, and many others are living in our immediate or larger neighborhood.

I am not going to discuss the variety of theological models of approaches to other religions but will focus on such proposals which have especially drawn from pneumatological insights. Then I will try to use their capacity to facilitate communication between religions and therefore go into depth considering some Asia-oriented traditions which value notions of life and spirit.

In Germany Reinhold Bernhardt, starting from a trinitarian approach, has opted for an ecumenical community of all religions and especially based his concept on a theology of glimpses of the Holy Spirit in the world of religions. Bernhardt talks of the "creative and inspiring presence of God in the whole created reality" as an aspect of trinitarian theology and interprets "the biblical tradition of the universal activity of the Spirit" as a "'hermeneutical tool' for the interpretation of religious phenomena and experiences of interreligious encounter." From this basis it becomes possible to take account of the presence of the "creative, healing and enlightening Spirit" in other religions as well.[3]

Bernhardt does not specify what might be seen as a sign of spirit presence in other faiths and how the term "hermeneutical tool" *(hermeneutischer Schlüssel)* is to be concretized. We will try to modify the "hermeneutical" aspect from a connotation of one-way traffic into a "communicative" and mutual one with however an understanding of the biblical *ruah* and *pneuma* in the center, as it is a Christian theology of religions we are dealing with, not a general theory of religions. The point I will make is that the notions in the various traditions which come close to life and spirit not only function as communicative facilitators within their respective streams but also have the capacity to play that role externally in interreligious interaction.

## Life and Spirit as Religious Concepts

*Life* has been an important concept for religiosity in new movements for the last decades. It indicates the idea to transpose meaning which was traditionally found in the transcendent, transempirical into this world's life and into the so-far-undiscovered depth dimensions of life. The Japanese neo-Buddhist organization Soka Gakkai (SG) has gone so far as to use "philosophy of life" as an-

---

3. Reinhold Bernhardt, *Trinitätstheologie als Matrix einer Theologie der Religionen*, in Ökumenischen Rundschau (Frankfurt am Main, 2000), pp. 287-301, 297f.

other name for Buddhist teaching *(buppō)* in its recent publications.[4] Previous books on the general teaching of SG[5] have one major chapter on *life (seimeiron)* each, discussing some philosophical options.

## Ki in Reiki, QiGong, and Taichi

Recently the notion comes close to what is usually indicated by the idea of *ki* in East Asian thinking. *Ki* is a notion which nowadays is part of many phrases in everyday small talk but expresses an important part of East Asian life mentality. *Ki* itself can be rendered with "life"; it at the same time points at the origin of life, as the absence or destruction of the flux of *ki* generates mental or physical illness and a deficit of relationship to other persons, the world around, the cosmos. *Ki* has been named the communicating element of the two components yin and yang in Taoistic philosophy. It is present in the therapeutic movements of *Reiki, Chigong, Taichi*[6] *chuan*, and others. Being visualized as energy, as cosmic force and life-generating and creating factor, *ki* has become a key concept in present-day esoteric movements in the West as well. By authors of the therapeutic movement *Reiki, ki* or *Reiki* has been paralleled to notions like *pneuma*, spirit, *ruah*, Hindu *prana*, *ka* of ancient Egypt, and other ideas which point to the life-creating and life-supporting element.[7] The implication of something transempirical, transcendent may be there, but most of them prefer the expression "spirituality." *Ki* originally had no divine but rather energetic connotations. When it is paralleled to the biblical notions of *pneuma* and *ruah*, which are considered "energetic tools" of God, tools which are subject to prayer need to be differentiated from an idea of *ki* which may as well function on its own dynamics.[8] *Reiki* teachers close to Christianity used to assert that the working of *Reiki* and the success of any such therapy is in the realm of prayer.

---

4. Seikyō Shinbun Kyōgaku Kaisetsubu, *Yasashii Seimeitetsugaku,* Study Department of Seikyō Newspaper, Life Philosophy for Beginners (Tokyo, 2002).

5. *Shakubuku Kyōten* (Textbook for mission, 1951-1968), *Sōka Gakkai Nyūmon* (Introduction to SG, 1980-2000), *Kyōgaku no Kiso* (Basics of the teaching, 2002), the latter one especially oriented to the SGI groups.

6. It needs to be noted that the *chi* of *Taichi* is a different Chinese character (meaning "extreme," "highest") than *chi* in *Chigong* (which is the *chi* being discussed here).

7. B. Baginski and S. Sharamon, *Reiki — Universale Lebensenergie,* 15th ed. (Essen, 1997), p. 16.

8. U. Dehn, "Reiki," in *Panorama der neuen Religiosität,* ed. R. Hempelmann et al. (Gütersloh, 2001), pp. 383-88.

Ulrich Dehn

## The Notion of Life in Soka Gakkai Thought

The presently most authoritative Soka Gakkai introduction[9] discusses life as a notion being beyond philosophical materialism and idealism. Also theistic ideas are sharply criticized as being one variety of philosophical idealism. *Life* is grasped as the focus of Buddhist thought, as it is identified with interrelatedness and is subject to various circumstances without being enslaved by them. Life originates from the cosmos and exists before living beings come into being. Life cannot be thought of apart from nature and the cosmos. Cosmos and life can be equaled.[10] It originates in itself according to internal rules; there is no creator, no external force, but an affluent lot of more life. Life is its own *maître du plaisir*. There shall no God and no soul be asserted. They are to be thought of as illusions. At the same time matter and soul shall not be taken as separate entities. Also the authentic and autonomous self and the environment are bound together as integral parts of one unity.[11] *Seimei* is being equaled to the Ten Worlds which constitute the ten stages of existence from hell to Buddha's World, one of the major components of Nichiren's teaching. As life *(seimei)* is the integral focus of interrelated existence in unity of matter (body), soul, and the spiritual dimension, it also constitutes the communicative element which can be brought into harmony with the notions of *ki* and spirit. Life is basic to the duality of presence and absence of emotion: these exist on behalf of the "flux of life" *(seimei no nagare)*.[12] This again drives the attention to the energetic as well as the communicative aspect.

*Life* in Soka Gakkai thought is obviously more than the notion of energy and spirit. It is an all-comprehensive idea which serves to integrate the whole existence under the SG Buddhist concepts, as the latest publication on *life* thought shows.[13]


## Life Force in Shinto Thought

Modern Japanese Shinto theologians have given some emphasis to the use of the idea of life which is supposed to be behind the veneration of various *kami*, godlike objects of prayer and confidence. The Shinto priest and theologian Sonoda Minoru states:

9. *Sōka Gakkai Nyūmon*, pp. 119-200.
10. *Sōka Gakkai Nyūmon*, p. 146.
11. *Sōka Gakkai Nyūmon*, p. 138.
12. *Sōka Gakkai Nyūmon*, p. 152.
13. *Yasashii Seimeitetsugaku* (Life philosophy for beginners) (1999; 4th ed., 2002).

Traditional Japanese religion has perceived the spiritual life force *(seimei no reiteki na hataraki)* behind all creation in its human and natural forms, invisible and beyond comprehension though it is; it has worshipped that vital life force, sometimes as kami and sometimes as Buddhas. . . . Life is that which is passed on through an unending process of birth and death from generation to generation, not only amongst humans but amongst plants and animals too. . . . The Japanese are in awe of the mystery of life beyond human understanding, and perceive here the workings of an invisible spirit. The concept of kami and Buddhas is none other than a religious expression of awe before life.[14]

This is what might be called a "Shinbutsu theology" in Japanese, meaning a combination of Shinto and Buddhist ideas. Sonoda himself talks of "complexity" and a "new symbiosis." But just by this kind of interreligious combination he comes close to the spirit element and the communicative function of life and "life force." This is a recent development in Shinto theology which cannot yet be observed in older concepts like, e.g., Ono Sokyo.[15]

## The *Life* Concept as Religious Paradigm

Besides the traditions we have so far talked about there are new meditation movements like the one of Sri Sri Ravi Shankar, which under the headline of "art of living" propagated a way of wholeness and wellness which is focused in the notion of life and living.

Besides its energetic and communicative aspects, life has become a metaphor for a spiritually fulfilled existence "beyond transcendence," focusing "salvation" and religious/spiritual destination into this empirical world's beautiful dimensions.

## Concluding Remarks on Life and Spirit as Communicative Interreligious Element

As to the empirical aspects, this is not far away from a biblical view of the spirit which from the very beginning in the creation narrative is a synonym for life-

14. Sonoda Minoru, "Shinto and Buddhism: The Japanese Tradition of Religious Complexity and the Possibility of a New Symbiosis" (paper presented at the symposium "Religions and Tolerance," May 8-9, 2000, Berlin [Japanese-German Centre Berlin]), p. 7.

15. *Ono Sokyo, Shinto — the Kami Way* (Rutland, Vt., and Tokyo, 1962); Ernst Lokowandt, *Shinto — Eine Einführung* (Shinto: An introduction) (Munich, 2001).

giving, creative wind and breath. It can express itself in fire, water, and other forms of energy; it gives freedom, time, and space. New energies are exposed, dynamics are created.[16] Interhuman relationships are facilitated by the spirit. Experience of the Spirit/of God usually is closely interwoven with interhuman experience. The experience of the Pentecostal event is not in the first place the birthday of the church but the great facilitation of human communication at an instance where it was supposed to be impossible. The spirit of God and of life makes people sensitive to each other and to the world, as well as to those places and traditions where it finds corresponding elements. We do not argue that the Christian notion of the spirit of God can be found in different shapes in other religions or is working as well in other religious traditions as it would be formulated by inclusivistic models of a theology of religions in a strict sense; this would usually imply that the spirit of God is being found in Christian thought in its pure form, whereas in other religions there are slightly deficient versions to be identified. We are not looking for "glimpses of pneumatological thinking" in other religions. We rather suggest that the spirit finds communicative elements in the world of different faiths which are perfectly true in their respective context and fit to the same "wavelength," the same "radio frequencies" as the spirit of God as revealed in the Hebrew Bible *(ruah)* and in the Pentecostal event *(pneuma)*. They enable us to hear the message of the other. The facilitation of communication, the common hermeneutical ground being supplied by the notion of "spirit" and "life," is the major point I want to drive home. I.e., I focus on the functional aspect such as the communicative and the life-creating one and suggest that by this way a larger communicative community of people of different faiths can be created, rather than by an academic discourse on doctrinal elements which may be either uniting or discriminating.

---

16. Cf. Jürgen Moltmann, *Der Geist des Lebens* (Spirit of life) (Munich, 1991), pp. 287-91.

**PART IV**

# EPILOGUE

# For All God's People: Being Church in Multireligious Societies

VIGGO MORTENSEN

The underlying assumption of this book is that the religious landscape today is going through a development that changes it fundamentally and that this changing landscape might take many shapes.

## Religious Change

The first indication that we are going through a period of religious change I take from a new book by the American professor of religious studies Philip Jenkins, *The Next Christendom*.[1] Here he describes — in view of the demographic changes that will be happening — how the future Christendom will probably look. By the year 2050 at least six nations, i.e., Brazil, Mexico, the Philippines, Nigeria, Congo, and the United States, will have more than 100 million Christians. Africa south of the Sahara will have long before overtaken Europe in number of Christians. Brazil will have 150 million Catholics and 40 million Protestants. And more than a billion Pentecostals will spread their version of Christianity.

In the Southern Hemisphere we will see a wave of nondemocratic states with theocratic tendencies compete for regional superiority. If these Christians can manage not to fight among themselves, they will gang up against the common enemy, Islam. Twenty of the twenty-five largest states will either be Christian or Islamic, and at least ten will be the scenes of bloody conflicts. Even though there may be a nominal majority of Christians, Islam will have the upper hand in these Third World wars, often supported by the industrialized

---

1. Philip Jenkins, *The Next Christendom: The Coming of Global Christianity* (Oxford: Oxford University Press, 2002).

states in the North which, because of the harsh economic facts, will tone down their emotional preference for Christianity. Extremists within both religions will still make sure women's rights, freedom of religion, and other wild ideas of the secularized North will not gain ground. At the same time, leading countries in Africa and Asia are developing a considerable military potential. These prospects for the future might very well make the sixteenth century's deadly religious wars look like a Sunday school excursion.

Jenkins attributes this prospect of the future to the Third World's demographic explosion, the poor slum dwellers' hope of rescue, and the Muslim-Christian competition for souls and proselytizing work. Jenkins would not hesitate to say that these predictions might *not* come true. On the other hand, like most futurologists, he extrapolates on the basis of the present tendencies.

What are these tendencies? Let me emphasize three, under the headings "Christianity Is Global," "The Candlestick Has Been Removed," and "Transformation of Christianity."

### Christianity Is Global

Whereas Christianity was the prevalent religion in Europe and America until about a hundred years ago, the nineteenth and twentieth centuries have seen the revolutionary change that Christianity has become global. The reason for this is the activities of the Christian missionary movement. The slogan was, as at the famous World Missionary Conference at Edinburgh in 1910, Christianization of the world in this generation. Looking at the figures, we must admit that this has not happened. The world is not Christian. Christianity has increased, but only more or less concurrently with the growth of the population. The Christian missionary movement, however, called forward the religions. They set out to find and convert "pagans," but they found people belonging to another faith. This religious encounter, which grew out of the missionary movement, radically transformed Christianity; it now became one of all the world's religions. It became itself a global religion.

### The Candlestick Has Been Removed

Having won the Jewish-Roman war in the year 70, the Roman emperor Titus, to prove he had conquered Jerusalem with the Jewish temple, took the seven-branched candlestick, the menorah, back to Rome in triumph. How this happened can still be seen at the Arch of Titus. We all know about the disastrous and far-reaching consequences of this for the Jewish people, who since then have constructed an identity as a people living in diaspora. But in a way it affected the first Christians just as much. As we learn in the first chapters of the Acts of the Apostles, they lived as a Jewish sect whose lives centered around the cult in the temple of Jerusalem. "Every day they continued to meet together in the temple courts" (Acts 2:46 NIV). After 70 it became clear to them that they would never again "continue to meet together in the temple." They would never again hear the psalms of David sung in Hebrew in the right way. They would soon disobey the ritual rules of clean and unclean and start eating pork as the most natural thing in the world. Yes, the candlestick had indeed been removed. And the first great Christian exodus started, instigated by Paul, who became the creator of Christianity as we know it today, in dialogue with the Greek-Hellenistic culture and the Roman law and religion.

My claim is thus that we are in a situation that can be compared with that of the first Christians in 70, when they had to find their way out of a situation which had deprived them of their natural spiritual basis. Even for us the candlestick is being removed. Where to? This is not a simple question to answer, but at least toward the south. If we look for growth, activity, and commitment within Christianity, we certainly have to look south.

## Transformation of Christianity

At its core, Christianity is not a religion; it is a "translation movement."[2] When Christianity reaches new people groups, the Bible has to be translated. People have not received the gospel before they have a copy of the Bible in their native language. With every translation of the Bible, God is given a new name, i.e., the name of God in the given culture. This process of translation is therefore a stage in the serial story of God. By the very fact that God is given many new names, there is a transformation of Christianity. It enters into a new context and cannot help being affected by this context, which results in a change. Therefore it should not come as a surprise to us to learn that the current movement of Christianity is also a transformation, which is indeed the case. Originally Christianity as we know it found its shape in a dialogue with Greek and Roman culture and religion. Christianity is now facing a dialogue with philosophical and religious tendencies in the South, which may result in just as radical changes.

---

2. Lamin Sanneh, *Translating the Message: The Missionary Impact on Culture* (Maryknoll, N.Y.: Orbis, 1989).

From this encounter shapes of Christianity will develop, which we sometimes find difficult to recognize as Christian in our interpretation. But this is a natural development of all religions, not just Christianity; all religions in the world are being transformed by the economic and cultural movement we designate "globalization."

### What Does This Mean for the Church of the North?

It means, first of all, that the ecumenical problem shows itself in a quite new and down-to-earth way. "Ecumenical" originates from the Greek *oikumene,* which means the whole inhabited globe. And it is therefore not sufficient to look at the position of religion and Christianity in Europe or in the North. To understand what is going on, we must involve the entire inhabited globe. The development in Europe has been described by various terms, of which I prefer "multireligiosity." The meaning of this term is not just that we are being inundated with new religiosity and new religions, but that all religions are changing and omnipresent.

In the following I have chosen to consider this development as religious change. What we are facing right now is nothing less than change of religion. This may sound rather dramatic. Does the Evangelical Lutheran Church in Denmark, in spite of a pronounced decline, not still have a firm hold of the population? Even though there is a decline in church attendance and most church statistics show downward tendencies, the church is still alive and kicking. True enough, so it is possible that, by postulating a religious change, I am saying too much. I am doing this, however, to make us realize certain features in the cultural development which we are going through right now.

Which precedents can be cited in support of religious change? Not the Reformation, as it stands for making reforms, changes within the existing frames, in order to go back to an earlier original stage. No, if we want to use a religious change in our latitude for comparison, we must go back about a thousand years to the only known and well-documented religious change, so far, in our culture.

### Religious Change in Scandinavia I: Year 1000

The reason I say 1000 is because of the decision made by the Althing to accept Christianity (Parliament of Iceland) in this year. According to experts on the

468

subject, however, we are talking about a period of around four hundred years, from 800 to 1200.[3]

One scholar, Kirsten Hastrup, says the decision by the Parliament of Iceland was just "a theoretical break in a serial story about transition, stretching over several hundred years." Both apprehensions of reality continue, resulting in a "kind of double standard of morality, which is also a double conception of society and an ambiguous relation to history." The religious change that takes place here is due to a pressure from above and makes itself seen in rituals and other expressions. If we consider the religious change to have taken place over around four hundred years, we see a process that has radically transformed religion as well as society. The external history about the Christian mission and the conversion of the kings and the upper echelons of the society to the new faith has been relatively well described. To mention one example: in Snorre Sturlason's Chronicle (Saga) of the Kings of Norway, it says about King Olav Trygvason's appearance in Parliament: "At the end of his address the King said that they had to choose between two alternatives: Either to accept Christianity and become baptized, or to fight him. When the peasants realized that it would not be possible to fight, they agreed to become baptized."

How it actually came about "on the ground" among ordinary people, however, we know far less about. That Christianity was adopted piecemeal in Denmark and Norway, we can take for granted. When Harald Bluetooth (Son of Gorm the Old) of Denmark, on his famous rune-stone at Jelling, tells us he "made the Danes Christian," this at best proves that, as far as the divine is concerned, the king decides which faith the people should have. It is not at all likely, however, that Christianity was considered anything but a thin veneer. Did they become Christian at all, our ancestors?

This uncertainty has brought about some emphatic attempts to describe what happened. The Danish writer Vilhelm Grønbech, for example, in his *Religious Change in the Nordic Countries* (*Religionsskiftet i Norden*, 1913), talks about the "mental change" of the people of the northern countries and compares this to contemporary missionaries' understanding of conversion. Only the clergy, as a matter of fact, represent the conversion, whereas remnants of paganism continued among ordinary people. Another Danish writer, Martin A. Hansen, in his great work *Serpent and Bull* (*Orm og Tyr*, 1952), makes hard attempts to un-

---

3. "Nogle overvejelser over begrebet "Religionsskifte" med henblik på problematisering af termens brug I forbindelse med overgangen til kristendommen I Norden), in *Medeltidens Födelse*, ed. Anders Andrén (1989". (For a handy outline of the discussion, see Jens Peter Schjødt's article "Some considerations on the term 'religious change' with special reference to the problems in connection with the use of the term about the conversion to Christianity in Scandinavia.")

derstand what is happening during the change. "They do not yet change their attitude of life, they do not really change religion. They change God and they change form of worship. They transfer to the faith in Christ the only philosophy left in their minds about the divine, faith in strength. And they get a god who is not just present on Sundays, who does not only look after the hereafter, salvation, but an almighty god who is present in space, in the weather, in the clouds, in the fields, in people, in all events in everyday life."[4]

The white Christ thus conquers the souls slowly, whereas Harald Bluetooth conquers the land and at the same time makes the Danes Christian. The official worship was changed, but what survived in the depths of people's minds? We realize that, eventually, Christianity gained root. We must, however, dissociate ourselves from the forcible christening that was ordered on people from above. After a few generations Christianity was accepted; it gains a foothold by having to do with ordinary people's ordinary lives. They get a God who is present in all events in everyday life. Not until the gospel gains a foothold *in all events in everyday life* has the religious change been accomplished.

## Religious Change in Scandinavia II: Year 2000

The thesis that I tentatively present here is that today, around a thousand years later, we face a similar situation and are about to go through another religious change. This time, however, it is not being dictated from the ruling powers, but it happens on the individual, personal level. Because it has been prepared with the modern emphasis on the individual, it happens by changes in the individual's religious conviction. As mentioned, this does not mean extermination of Christianity. On the contrary, it grows and changes. But the form of Christianity practiced in Europe is facing great problems.

### Is Europe an Exceptional Case?

The British sociologist of religion Grace Davie, in her book *Europe: The Exceptional Case,*[5] advocates the thesis that Europe is indeed something special. This

4. Martin A. Hansen, *Orm og Tyr* (Copenhagen, 1969), p. 225.

5. "The 'keystone' of the arch of European values is crumbling. . . . Europe is in the process of removing the 'keystone' in the arch of its value system, without being altogether clear about what should be put in its place." Grace Davie, *Europe: The Exceptional Case,* Sarum Theological Lectures (London, 2002), p. 147.

means that the development that Europe has gone through will probably not repeat itself anywhere else in the world, which we have usually with pride presumed. What we are talking about here is the secularization thesis.

## The Relation between Modernization and Secularization

The secularization thesis presumes that economic and social modernization leads to secularization, which in this connection is defined as the withdrawal of religion from the public space. Not necessarily from the private space; secularization may, on the contrary, lead to privatization of religion and greater influence on the personal level.

We usually draw a line from the Reformation, over the Enlightenment, to modern times. The Reformation starts the development by questioning the authority of the Catholic Church. This is done by emphasizing the individual, the *pro me* of creation and salvation. What is the meaning of the creation? It means that God created *me* and all other creatures. This leads to an individualism, which again questions our common basis for religious faith. Rationality takes its toll on the religious traditions. This is the beginning of the end of the sacred canopy, which had so far circumvented the societies. Individualism and reason are emphasized further by the Enlightenment. This leads to increased pluralism and secularization.

Secularization was the most important issue of debate among the generation of theologians preceding us. All my teachers of theology considered secularization the decisive theological problem, which they tried to solve each in their own way. It was the basic condition, though. Some went against it, like Løgstrup, who formulated his metaphysical project in the image of the fighting of the rear guard of a retreating army. "Seen through the eyes of our epoch when its glance is mildest, this book will have the appearance of a retreating army fighting a rear-guard action before it disappears into the darkness of anachronism."[6] I think that, as time goes by, it gets more and more difficult to see what is the advance guard and what is the rear guard. Løgstrup describes here how the rationalizing power of religion has been taken over by the rationalizations of politics, economics, technology, and science. We may therefore get the impression that "religion is a thing of the past." But the epoch is wrong, continues Løgstrup. There are basic phenomena, which will always require a religious interpretation. Because we believed that religion was a thing of the past,

6. Knud E. Løgstrup, *Metaphysics*, vol. 1 (Milwaukee: Marquette University Press, 1995), p. 1. Danish edition: *Skabelse og tilintetgørelse. Metafysik IV. Gyldendal* (Copenhagen, 1978), p. 9.

the awakening to the actual experiences of the power of religion to change the world became especially rude.

From the point of view of systematic theology, secularization was an interesting concept that facilitated new and exciting attempts to preach the Christian gospel. But as far as the church was concerned, it led to de-Christianization, which in the long run made it difficult for the church to survive as more than a service institution. The Protestant ideal of the relation between the gospel and society is "like sugar in water." The gospel is the herb that, when dissolved, gives flavor to the drink. On the whole, it has worked like that. Something, however, has not been taken into consideration, namely, that if we want the flavor to remain in the drink, we must store a reservoir of herbs, a supply of undiluted flavor, for when the course of society has to be adjusted. This was omitted, and therefore secularization resulted in de-Christianization. The reformers were right in saying every day is the Lord's Day, and therefore the seventh day might well be less holy. But to be able to say: This is the day that the Lord made — meaning every day — there must have been and still be an actual Lord's Day.

The de-Christianizing trend makes itself known through the numbers. Statistics show this development in a slackening of the institutional discipline. People are not actively involved with the institution, but they do not abandon their affiliation. People have not stopped believing, but they have stopped letting faith form their lives. Faith becomes a private matter, something personal, which does not exist in the public space.

As Christianity was the prevalent religion, this also meant a de-religionization or, at least, a dilution of religion to such an extent that it was not always sufficient to satisfy the religious feeling, which was the reason why people looked around to fill the empty space. Secularization and the appearance of the new religious movements thus became interrelated.

## How Do These New Conditions Affect the Role of Religion, in casu Christianity?

First of all, like everything else in a consumer society, religion becomes a choice. The peculiar thing about pluralism is that it leads to relativization. When more than one faith is recognized, all religions are being relativized, which again leads to secularization and indifference. Pluralism brings an increased supply, gives people a choice and thus stimulates "sale." Religion is no longer a matter of necessity, but is about choice and like, and is seen in connection with choice of lifestyle. Sometimes people make the choice in the dark, or they may even take over something by tradition. On the other hand, people will — as in other consumer cases — make an informed choice, by which the function of the religion in the modern society plays an important role. Scholars of sociology have brought forward the terms that religion may take care of the "collective memory," the "common discourse," or the "social capital."

### Religion as a Collective Memory, Common Discourse, or Social Capital

The French anthropologist Hervieue-Legere sees religion as a form of collective memory. When societies become less based on religion, they are not able to keep the collective memory. She refers to such societies as "amnesic societies," societies with amnesia. This is the basis for my thesis: We live in a post-Christian culture with amnesia.

Others mention that we have lost our common discourse. What might replace such a common discourse? It might be increased consumerism, but most people can only satisfy their hunger once, so they start looking around for things to fill the empty space. Especially sports is becoming to many a replacement for religion. Sport arenas around the world are today the scenes of great solidarity and a roar of atmosphere. Thus we see innovations in the rituals that have to do with sports.

This still leaves the unsolved question: What provides the coherence of societies? Religion has in many societies played exactly this role. The American social scientist R. Putman has been studying the leisure time behavior of modern people, and in his book *Bowling Alone* points to religion as a contributor to "social capital formation" in society. When, according to a survey made by sociologists of religion on the relation of the Danish church to the rapidly increasing religion of Islam, the church plays a vital role in what was called "the quiet integration," this has to do with the social capital.[7] The church thus still administers part of this social capital in today's society, but the share is declining because faith does not lead to commitment and taking responsibility. People are believing without belonging.

Modern sociology describes the different sectors and segments of the late modern society. One can distinguish between "state," "market," "civic society," and "individualized forms of life."[8] The church, whether it likes it or not, has to

7. See the final report (in Danish): "Dialogue furthers understanding" (Samtalen fremmer forståelsen) (Copenhagen: Unitas, 2000) of the Ad Hoc Committee "Islamudvalget," set up by the Danish bishops.

8. "Folkekirken i moderniseringens malstrømme), Kirken og det civile samfund, Det økumeniske Center (Aarhus, 2000)." (See Jens Erik Kristensen: "The Evangelical Lutheran Church in Denmark in the whirlpools of modernization" ).

relate to this segmentation of society. This also means that the relationship between "church and society" has to be rephrased as the relationship of the
church to the fields of state, market, civic society, and the liberated individual,
who must be taken into account as user or customer. Kristensen concludes that
"the tendency shows a slow, but consistent transformation of the Danish state-
supported Evangelical Lutheran Church into a more-and-more responsive
user-service church, in which community and churchgoers increasingly will
appear as and understand themselves as individual and personal users of or
customers to the Church's social, spiritual, ceremonial and ritual services."[9]

The problem of the church is that it feels obliged to be present in all segments of society. It would be much simpler if one could concentrate on one
segment or one group. But it is an inherent part of the ideology of the Danish
church that it must be "for everybody," just like the gospel. But this exactly
causes the problem that the message will be spread so thinly that it may be difficult to identify it as the Christian gospel. Consequently people accept a "stand-
in" or "substitute" religion. When the churchgoers fail to turn up, more members will be employed in the choir.

As far as I can see, there is no other way: we have to follow segmentation. But
we must be conscious of the uniqueness of the Christian gospel. The Christian is
thus obliged to be present in the various sectors of society with an increased voca-
tional consciousness. Such Christian presence must then appear in different
shapes in various segments. The following issues need therefore to be discussed.

## State

Is the church going to consider itself a state organization, a supplier of public
services? There are many indications for that in the present situation, one being
the electronic parish register. The resulting professionalization, however, has to
be balanced by a greater concentration and participation. We need to rediscover and reintroduce into the debate what Lesslie Newbigin called "the Gospel
as public truth."

## Market

Obviously the church is also in the market. Therefore it has to submit to the conditions of the market, and there is a lot to be done on product development and

9. Kristensen, p. 58.

quality control in order to meet the demands of the market. To apply economic categories to the services provided by the church has become popular within a movement that considers humans rational beings whose behavior is based on rational choice. This is called "the Rational Choice Theory."[10] According to this, we have a constant need of religion. Being religious is part of being human. If the need is not fulfilled, people will turn toward surrogates. An interchange is imagined between the individuals of society and the religious institutions. The religious institutions, e.g., the church, fulfill some individual needs for community, security, or comfort and get their need for participation and support fulfilled. According to this theory, it is imagined that individuals, consciously or unconsciously, weigh the pros and cons before making their choices. If we want more community, we must accept more participation. Liberal religions, which provide less security and community, also demand less participation of their members. If one wishes to join the community of David Koresh or Jim Jones, on the other hand, it may be at the risk of one's life. To participate in the Evangelical Lutheran Church in Denmark only costs a small amount of tax money. Otherwise it demands nothing of its members. To act as a reliable and trustworthy partner in the market, a community identity must be established. This is — in a technical term — referred to as "branding." The gospel as "brand," as something you identify yourself with. "I am Christian, and it appears in this and that way. . . ."

### Civic Society

"Europeans regard their churches as public utilities rather than competing firms," says Grace Davie.[11] Having lost the collective memory or the common discourse, people may be content with the church upholding the idea that it is still alive, even though the majority of people would never consider banking on this social capital except for very special occasions, like birth and death. And we all know various theological theory formations which make a virtue out of this view by mentioning that services are being held for the sake of the parish, or that Mass is celebrated also for those who are not present. But for the church to fulfill a reliable civic function, it must provide more humanity and participation and go against the trends of increasing professionalization. There are many good causes where the church could play a much greater role, being an efficacious NGO (nongovernmental organization). It has a great tradition of — and there is an increasing demand for — diaconal projects with a human face.

10. See F. W. Graf's contribution in this volume.
11. Davie, pp. 43f.

*Viggo Mortensen*

## Individualized Forms of Life and New Spirituality

It is an important function of the church and the gospel to be present in the individual human being's life and to take part in forming it. These years see a change in the spiritual climate, in spirituality experienced by modern people. The chart below shows what I mean by that.

| Classical Christian Faith | New Spirituality |
|---|---|
| The transcendent God | The God within |
| We are sinners in need of forgiveness | We are wounded and need healing |
| Duty | Self-realization |
| God as master and king | God as friend and life |
| Preaching of the Word | The mystery of the Eucharist |
| Understanding | Experience |
| Faith as truth | Faith as trust |
| The narrow gate | The wide embrace |
| Go to heaven | Live on earth |
| Philosophical truth | Psychological truth ("I feel that . . .") |
| Hierarchic authority | Empirical authority |
| Strong borders — exclusivism | Soft borders — inclusivism/pluralism |
| Command | Enable |
| Obey | Encourage/facilitate |
| Hierarchic relations | Mutual relations |

A proof of the religious change is that the vast majority of modern people feel more at home in the right column, which is here called the "New Spirituality." Not everything in this column is ungodliness and unevangelical, though. Inherent in the attitudes of the new spirituality are many insights that are also prevalent in the gospel. What we need is a new type of church that can take care of the religious needs of the people who feel more at home in the right column. What does this new spirituality look like?

## "I'm Not Religious, but I Do Have My Superstitions"

It may assume various shapes; and I will finish with two references:

1. "I'm not religious, but I do believe in superstitions." This was said by a young man in a Norwegian survey. The statement shows the confusion as regards faith among people of the coming generation. They are not petty, but believe in a little bit of everything: God, Allah, and Buddha. And Jesus was proba-

bly an alien. By all standards it is syncretistic.[12] Others characterize this new kind of spirituality as "cumulative heresies."

2. The multireligious encounter gives us a chance to learn something new about ourselves and about the other. If we can elaborate our own understanding of the divine that already exists in Christ by concentrating on "the other," then we come close to the "intrareligious dialogue" suggested by Raimundo Panikkar. "The journey" and "the encounter" are two general metaphors for the intellectual and spiritual road followed in this connection. Panikkar describes his "journey" like this: "How have I fared? . . . I left as a Christian, I 'found' myself a Hindu, and I 'return' a Buddhist, without having ceased to be a Christian."[13]

Maybe this is what an authentic spiritual human being looks like in the age of globalization. To be converted is something everybody is called to be within one's own tradition, but to change from one to the other, to change confession or religion — for instance, at a fixed time and hour — this may not be possible and thus not desirable. Is only assimilation possible?

On the assumption that there is a form of contact, that there is a religious encounter, interreligious dialogue becomes a necessity. It arouses interest in the issue of the truth claims of the various religions. This issue is usually dealt with in the discipline called theology of religions. Being a Christian theologian, one is obliged to construct a Christian theology of religions, which examines how one should evaluate Christianity's absolute claim on truth in relation to other religions' comparable truth claims.

The famous epistemological dictum "There is no view from nowhere" also applies to theology of religions. Everybody has a view, and nobody can jump their own shadow; we can attempt to enter into the spirit of another person and into his or her world; we can follow in another person's footsteps; we can place our "sandals" outside the mosque and do a thousand other things. If, however, we do not maintain some kind of point of view as a basis, the result is meaningless relativism and absolute dizziness.

I am based in the Christian tradition, and I intend to stay here the rest of my life. It does not bother me that other people choose Buddha or Muhammad to be the true communicator of the transcendent reality, and I am prepared to participate in a nonviolent competition to decide who produces the most beautiful fruits.

I have thus not gone beyond the position on which there is a consensus in

12. Trosmix hos Oslo-ungdom. Verdens Gang. Oslo 3/5 2002

13. Raimundo Panikkar, *The Intra-Religious Dialogue*, rev. ed. (New York: Paulist, 1999), p. 42.

ecumenical theology of religions, and which was phrased as follows at the missionary conference in San Antonio in 1984: "We cannot point to any other way of salvation than Jesus Christ; at the same time we cannot set limits to the saving power of God." The report then demonstrates a tension between the two statements and concludes: "We appreciate this tension. And do not attempt to resolve it."[14]

It is thus maintained that the true God may make himself known also within other religious traditions. This allows for a more relaxed relationship to traditional Christian mission. It is not a question of life or death to bring the Christian religion to another person. Or as the Danish poet and historian N. F. S. Grundtvig says: "Although he is not a Christian today, he will be tomorrow."

Grundtvig reaches this conclusion in his poem "Human First, Then Christian." This has been forgotten, he says, and continues with the following unflattering description of the Christian mission: "Beasts and demons we christened, and Moors we washed, but pagans were condemned." By doing this it was forgotten that people before Christ also belong to humankind. For they were — from Adam to John the Baptist — good people, God's friends and "of true and noble ethne." Grundtvig therefore ends his poem:

> Do your utmost on this earth
> to be a true human being,
> open your ear for the word of truth,
> and praise God;
> is Christianity a matter of truth,
> if you are not a Christian today, you will be tomorrow![15]

The human and the Christian relate to each other like the Old and the New Testaments, like preparation and fulfillment. Humanity is a necessary condition for Christianity. Grundtvig may talk about pagans, but they are also people. They live the human, ordinary life, which Christianity is not supposed to destroy but to strengthen. According to Grundtvig, all people have a memory of God and an urge to true acknowledgment. Therefore the true paganism should be awakened through the civil work, bringing forth the memory of the true image of God, which does not clash with the Mosaic-Christian view. Grundtvig's

14. *The San Antonio Report, World Council of Churches* (Geneva, 1990), pp. 32f. The recently phrased ten theses for theology of religions, published by the Swedish church, contain similar positions. See Kajsa Ahlstrand and Håkon Sandvik, eds., *Samtal om religionsteologi. Tro & Tanke 201:3. Svensa Kyrkans Forskningsråd* (Uppsala, 2001), p. 18.

15. *Grundtvigs Sangværk* (Grundtvig's collection of songs) III, 2 (Copenhagen, 1983), pp. 297f.

critique of the thoughtless and disrespectful mission is based on an understanding of what it is to be true human. It is something one becomes. To become Christian in this way is not something we can choose ourselves, it must be given to us, "it is pure bliss."

All people therefore necessarily have to endeavor to be true human beings. If this is fulfilled, then Grundtvig has complete confidence that Christianity will take over, for it is on life's side. Our tradition, as exemplified with Grundtvig, thus has some resources for us to rely on when making up our minds as regards the religio-theological question in the age of multireligiosity.

## Conclusion

From the evidence I put forward above, it seems obvious that we are going through a religious change. In comparison with that of a thousand years ago, this change is not being ordered from above, but from below, caused by a certain development of society, which affects people's minds. We have drawn a line from modernization through secularization to commercialization and new spirituality.

I did not, however, mention the most noticeable proof of the actual religious change, i.e., the fact that many people convert from Christianity to something else, at the moment mainly to Islam. It should be of great concern to the church that there are so many individual religious changes. First, in Denmark mainly women who married Muslim men converted to Islam. Now also, a high degree of young men feel attracted by the men's fellowship that exists in Islam. Obviously there are also conversions the other way round, from Islam to Christianity, but to a much smaller extent, and very seldom within the Protestant churches. The Pentecostal church and the Roman Catholic Church have been much better at taking care of these converts. The Evangelical Lutheran Church has also been very slow to accept Christian immigrants of another ethnic origin.

When the Evangelical Lutheran Church in Denmark considered what should be done in a situation with many immigrants and new groups of people, a number of proposals were made: various initiatives to build bridges, discussion groups at all levels, etc. Top priority, however, was given to Christian self-reflection. The church and its members are challenged to make up their minds about their own faith when entering into the religious encounter and to prepare the members of the church for this encounter. If this is not given top priority, how can one work with religious change? For the church has to face the fact that it is either working with or against the religious change.

# Contributors

Ahlstrand, Kajsa: Director, Church of Sweden Research Department, Sweden

Ahrens, Theodor: Professor, University of Hamburg, Germany

Berentsen, Jan-Martin: Professor, School of Mission, Stavanger, Norway

Dehn, Ulrich: Dr. Ev. Zentralstelle für Weltanshauungsfragen, Humboldt University, Berlin, Germany

Egnell, Helene: Ph.D., University of Uppsala, Sweden

Fibiger, Marianne C. Qvortrup: Ph.D., Research Coordinator, the Danish Pluralism Project, University of Aarhus, Denmark

Fridlund, Patrik: Ph.D. candidate, Teologiska Institutionen, University of Lund, Sweden

Garrard-Burnett, Virginia: Ph.D., Institute of Latin American Studies, University of Texas, USA

George, Geomon K.: Rev., Ph.D. candidate, The Centre for Christianity in the Non-Western World, University of Edinburgh, U.K.

Gerle, Elisabeth: Associate Professor, Lund University. Dean of the Pastoral Institute, Lund, Sweden

Graf, Friedrich Wilhelm: Professor, University of Munich, Germany

Hauge, Hans: Professor, University of Aarhus, Denmark

Hedetoft, Ulf: Professor, Academy for Migration Studies in Denmark, University of Aalborg, Denmark

Heim, S. Mark: Professor, Andover Newton Theological School, Boston, USA

Hewer, Chris: Dr., Adviser on Inter-Faith Relations, Birmingham, U.K.

Hock, Klaus: Prof. Dr. History of Religions — Religion and Society, University of Rostock, Germany

Ipgrave, Michael: Canon, Dr., Archbishops Council, Church of England, U.K.

Kirk, Andrew J.: Professor, Department of Theology, University of Birmingham, U.K.

Kühle, Lene: Ph.D. candidate, Sociology of Religion, University of Aarhus, Denmark

Küster, Volker: Professor, Intercultural Theology, University of Kampen, Netherlands

Lande, Aasulv: Professor, University of Lund, Sweden

Leirvik Oddbjørn: Associate Professor, University of Oslo, Norway

Madsen, Ole Skjerbæk: Rev., Areopagos Foundation, Denmark

Mase, Hiromasa: Professor, Tohoku University, Japan

Mogensen, Mogens S.: Ph.D., University of Aarhus, Denmark

Mortensen, Viggo: Professor, University of Aarhus, Denmark

Nissen, Johannes: Associate Professor, University of Aarhus, Denmark

Nürnberger, Klaus: Professor, University of Natal, South Africa

Oladipo, Caleb: Professor, Baylor University, Texas, USA

Ruparell, Tinu: Dr., University of Calgary, Canada

Saarinen, Risto: Professor, University of Helsinki, Finland

Sanneh, Lamin: Professor, Divinity School, Yale University, USA

Schumann, Olaf: Professor, University of Hamburg, Germany

Thelle, Notto: Professor, University of Oslo, Norway

Track, Joachim: Professor, Theologische Hochschule, Neuerdettelsau, Germany

Westhelle, Vítor: Professor, Lutheran School of Theology, Chicago, USA

Wilson, H. S.: Rev. Dr., Wilhelm Loehe Associate Professor of World Mission and Director of the Center for Global Theologies at Wartburg Theological Seminary, Dubuque, Iowa, USA